Via Appia
Antica

Italian Bouquet

Church of Sant' Ercolano–Perugia   Drypoint

Italian Bouquet

AN EPICUREAN TOUR
OF ITALY

by

Samuel Chamberlain

RECIPES TRANSLATED FROM THE ITALIAN
AND ADAPTED BY

Narcissa Chamberlain

PRINTS, DRAWINGS, AND PHOTOGRAPHS
BY THE AUTHOR

GOURMET

Published, 1958, by
GOURMET DISTRIBUTING CORPORATION
768 FIFTH AVENUE
NEW YORK 19, NEW YORK

Printed by
EGMONT H. PETERSEN, COPENHAGEN, DENMARK

Bound by
RAND McNALLY & COMPANY, U. S. A.

Tindari

Foreword

FOR GENERATIONS, Italy has been displaying her artistic treasures and extending her hospitality to travelers, students, and *bons vivants,* many of whom come away convinced that this is the most beautiful, the most rewarding country in the world. The incomparable relics of her antiquity do not convert Italy into a musty museum, however. Her present is as exciting as her past. The adventure of visiting this vibrant, intensely animated peninsula is heightened by the character of its people—gay, musical, creative, and openly friendly. It's easy to get about here, even without a knowledge of the language. An amazing number of Italians speak English. Nor need one consider the black market in money matters. The Italian lira is firmly pegged, and its value does not fluctuate. The weather is sunny much of the time, and there are appropriate resorts for every season of the year. Visiting Italy, in short, is a full experience, long to be cherished and relived.

Tourism plays a vital part in the Italian economy, now that the lean war years are fading from memory. Italian hotels, pensions, and restaurants have achieved a new standard of excellence, a fact which we intend to prove in the pages that follow. Italian cookery has never been better, and the wines of Italy are a revelation to the oenophile who takes the time to study them. What better theme for a book than travel, wine, and food in this charmed land?

Six years ago, when BOUQUET DE FRANCE made a favorable debut in both the United States and Great Britain, it seemed logical, even inevitable, for us to continue the epicurean quest, this time to cheerful, gregarious, beckoning Italy. Here, as a result, you have the companion volume to the French book, in which we use a similar approach to the pleasant problems of travel and gastronomy in a foreign land.

The same format, the same emphasis on illustrations as well as on food and wine, are evident. But this Italian volume aspires to go a bit further than its predecessor did and to serve also as a reliable guidebook to Italy, citing the essential things to see and do as well as the places to dine and to stay overnight. We play this dual role of guide and epicurean counselor in all but the largest Italian cities, where space just isn't available for such an ambitious undertaking. In Rome, Florence, and Venice, we hew closely to the gastronomic line and, for other information, refer you to the excellent guidebooks found in the corner bookstore. In all other regions, those who carry this volume with them will, we hope, be able to see the most significant treasures of Italian art, architecture, and landscape by following its recommendations.

ITALIAN BOUQUET is based on a series of articles that were inaugurated in GOURMET in March, 1954, under the title "A Gastronomic Tour of Italy," and that continued over a period of more than two years. We made three separate trips to Italy on this pious project, using a reliable French Peugeot 203 as our means of transportation. A heavy Linhof 5×7 view camera, sketch pads, and notebooks were vital pieces of equipment, along with a picnic hamper, a battered portable typewriter, and inquisitive taste buds.

Aided by information from many sources—readers of GOURMET, Italian friends, guidebooks, and magazine clippings—and particularly by advice offered by the officials of the admirable Italian State Tourist Office, we mapped out a tour that embraced the entire Italian peninsula and Sicily. Italy is divided into seventeen regions, containing ninety-one provinces and 7,764 municipalities. Except for the island of Sardinia, all of the regions and almost all of the provinces appear in this book. Beginning in Liguria, our eighteen chapters sweep across the broad, mountainous top of Italy to the Adriatic, then down to the tip of the peninsula, ending on the island of Sicily. A separate chapter has been dedicated to the splendors of dining in Rome.

There are, needless to say, several ways to approach Italy with appetite atingle. An ocean liner will land the inquiring gourmet within a three-minute walk of a fragrant Neapolitan *pizza* or the most subtle of Genoese ravioli. Or, stepping off a plane, he will find himself only a bus ride away from the fastidious restaurants of Rome, Milan, Florence, or Bologna. Trains or express autobuses will take him to less easily accessible cities. Then again, he may approach this fair peninsula by car, through steep Alpine passes or by way of the Riviera. Sun-seeking sybarites that we are, we chose the latter approach for our gustatory expedition.

However, it is by no means necessary to have a car in order to enjoy Italy to the full. Train service is very good, and the network of routes covered by modern, luxurious CIAT buses constitutes one of the wonders of the transportation world. These letters stand for Compagnia Italiana Autoservizi Turistici, a national organization that is the tourist's best friend. With superb drivers and pert, multilingual hostesses, these clean dependable buses have revolutionized travel in Italy. They will take you practically anywhere and pick you up again on a later trip. And the tourist finds them more economical than a private car.

For those who plan a comprehensive trip through Italy, the Michelin guide to Italy, *Guida Michelin Italia,* revised annually, is almost indispensable. Thinner than its French counterpart, it contains succinct, essential information about principal hotels, restaurants, and garages, together with town maps.

Another helpful source is a two-volume paperback publication called *Alberghi d'Italia,* an extraordinarily complete book written in four languages and containing the names of all hotels and pensions in Italy where a traveler might stay. It gives accurate information on the category of each place, on the rooms, baths, and facilities available, and on current prices.

The traveler in search of information about Italy has a staunch and generous friend in the Italian State Tourist Office, which publishes *Alberghi d'Italia* (and in whose offices it may be consulted) and many another booklet of interest. Known in Italy as E. N. I. T. (Ente Nazionale Industrie Turistiche), it maintains offices in cities abroad, including London, Paris, and New York, and bureaus in literally hundreds of Italian towns. Here the interested tourist receives a bounty of information and advice for the asking. The amount of free literature—folders in full color, booklets, guides, maps, and hotel price lists—that one carries away from a visit to a regional E. N. I. T. office is almost embarrassing. It isn't always easy to uncover the E. N. I. T. headquarters in a provincial town, and you may have to climb stairs and wander through corridors before finding it. But the goal is worth the effort, and the staff is invariably eager to be of help. E. N. I. T. does not compete with travel agencies. Its mission is to give information, as much as you can take.

Motorists can obtain excellent road maps in Italy, among them free ones from service stations. To provide more detailed road information, the Italian Touring Club publishes a fine set of road maps drawn to a scale of 1:200,000, the same scale used in those good Michelin maps in France. One centimeter on the map represents two kilometers on the earth's surface, and one inch, 3.15 miles. These maps can be found at the offices of the Italian Touring Club and in better bookstores. They introduce one interesting innovation: when a road becomes steep, its color on the map changes to red.

Hotel standards are commendably high in most parts of Italy, particularly in the north and in the large cities. But in some of the more remote parts of the peninsula, and on the islands, hotel accommodations, until recently, have been below the standard sought by most Anglo-Saxon travelers. This situation has changed in the past few years because of a remarkable chain of small, ultramodern hostelries that have sprung up in the neglected parts of Italy. Called the Jolly Hotels, they will make travel immensely more pleasant for you, just as their name implies. We mention them in the ensuing pages—so often, in fact, that you might begin to suspect that we have been lavishly subsidized by them, which is not the case.

The Jolly Hotel enterprise is the brain child of a prominent financier, Conte Gaetano Marzotto, who perceived the lack of worthy hotels in provincial towns and did something about it. The first Jolly Hotels, spotless, well run, and comfortable, were opened in 1950 and became an immediate success. There are now forty-two of them, and seven others are due to enter service in 1958. Almost all of them are located in towns otherwise lacking good hotels, rarely in holiday or beach resorts. To travelers in Apulia, Calabria, and the islands, they change the whole tourist picture immeasurably for the better.

After the Italian articles appeared in GOURMET, a copy of the magazine was sent to the owner of each hotel and restaurant mentioned in the text. Later, we wrote a letter to each of them, stating our plans for assembling an Italian companion to BOUQUET DE FRANCE and asking each owner to send us a few of his favorite recipes, if he felt so inclined. We also, at times, made this request on the spot. The response was just what it had been in France—generous in the extreme. Recipes poured in, many of them authentic secrets of celebrated Italian chefs. A few of them, of course, were purposely vague, and there were many duplications—a cascade of *cannelloni,* for example. But we reaped a rich harvest of useful recipes. Many of them are scattered throughout the text, and many others are grouped in the Treasury of Italian Recipes, which appears near the end of this volume. With some exceptions, they have been translated into basic recipe English, a crisp and unemotional language that may be a trifle startling to our Italian friends. To those who may be puzzled by the translation of their words, we offer apologies, and we assure them that the essence of their instructions has been faithfully transcribed, despite the briskness of our style. Eloquent proof that Italian cooking means far, far more than pasta, *pizza,* and *pomodori* is furnished by this versatile group of formulae from Italy's best chefs. We owe them a debt of deep gratitude.

We have selected only those recipes that can be achieved by enterprising English and American cooks using materials readily available, with the addition of a few Italian specialties found in our shops and supermarkets. Food and dairy products, together with wine and vermouth, today rank among Italy's most significant exports. The loyal *fiasco* of Chianti, the disks of Gorgonzola and Bel Paese, the tins of olive oil, anchovies, *antipasto,* and tomato paste are familiar to most Anglo-Saxon shoppers. Prepared pasta and Italian herbs have become staples in many of their market baskets. So the materials for making flavorful, original, and nourishing Italian dishes now usually lie near at hand, and we hope fondly that our readers will explore these recipes and brighten their kitchens with the aromatic Italian bouquet.

We cannot claim total coverage in this volume of *all* the good Italian hotels and restaurants. A good percentage of them receive mention, however —enough for the needs of the most avid traveler. Everyone has his own opinions on this subject, of course, and we would appreciate new recommendations from our readers and their candid reactions to the places we have listed. Those who are generous enough to share with us details of a favorite *trattoria* or a country inn that serves particularly fine food would enrich subsequent editions of this book.

May we make a discreet suggestion to travelers who carry the book to Italy? If you take it with you to the dining room and, after your meal, ask the proprietor or the chef to autograph the page on which his place is mentioned, he will, we think, consider it a friendly gesture. You will no doubt end your meal in an atmosphere of genial good will. Travelers who have sought such autographs for BOUQUET DE FRANCE have testified to the warm response produced by this request.

ITALIAN BOUQUET, as you will see, provides a photographic panorama of this beautiful country, aided by drawings and prints. But picture books of Italy are not, of course, rarities. More than 300 tested recipes, many of them regional specialties furnished by Italy's fine chefs, qualify this volume as a reliable cookbook, a worthy rival, we trust, to the Italian cookbooks in English that already exist. Detailed recommendations on what to see, where to dine, and where to stay overnight are harder to find. It is in combining these three components, in serving as a photographic record, culinary counselor, and discriminating guide at the same time, that this volume finds its justification.

We hope that it will prove a trustworthy and entertaining companion to the food-conscious traveler, whether he journeys to Italy by air, sea, or land, or merely in the comfort of a library armchair at home. The aroma of Italy awaits him in fragrant fields of wild flowers in the Valle d'Aosta, in the smart cafés on the Via Veneto, in countless *salumerie,* and in the herb-scented kitchens of noble Italian restaurants.. It is a bouquet that does not draw heavily on garlic, as is too often assumed, but on subtler things, especially such seductive herbs as rosemary, basil, and orégano. May your Italian travels be brightened by the fragrant bouquet of Italy and by the friendly charm and hospitality of the Italian people.

Buon viaggio e buon appetito!

ITALY

Valle d'Aosta

Turin
Piedmont

Lombardy

Milan

Trentino
Alto
Adige

Veneto
Euganea

Friuli
Venezia
Giulia

Venice

Liguria

Emilia-Romagna

Genoa

Florence

Tuscany

The
Marches

Umbria

Rome

Latium

Abruzzi
e
Molise

Campania

Apulia

Naples

Basilicata

Sardinia

Palermo

Sicily

Calabria

Table of Contents

Acknowledgments

The authors are grateful to scores of generous people for their help and cooperation in the preparation of ITALIAN BOUQUET. To the many hotel and restaurant owners scattered all over Italy, and to their gifted chefs, who have shared their choicest recipes with us, we wish to express warm appreciation. In particular we wish to thank Conte Dr. Sigmund Fago Golfarelli, of the Italian State Tourist Office in Rome, and Mrs. Manolita T. Doelger, director of the same admirable organization in New York, who have given us boundless encouragement and assistance. We are thankful also to Captain Armando Tosi, of the Home Lines, and to our friends at the American Express Company, for their timely aid. In preparing this large volume for publication, we have been privileged to enjoy the help of two alert and painstaking young ladies, Miss Ruth B. Krenz of Marblehead, Massachusetts, and Miss Eleanor Porter of GOURMET. To them goes our deep gratitude. Finally, to the late Donald Moffat, whose friendly editorial advice was of inestimable help, we are indebted most of all.

Liguria

Chapter 1

LIGURIA

THERE COULD be no more auspicious way to begin these epicurean rambles than by traveling along the Italian Riviera, the two-hundred-mile arc of radiant Mediterranean coast that faces the Bay of Genoa. Liguria, as this bright crescent of shore and mountain is called, stretches from the French frontier at Menton east to La Spezia, the stronghold of the Italian Navy. In area this is the smallest of the nineteen regions into which Italy is now divided. But size isn't everything. In sheer beauty, in its appeal to pleasure-seekers, and particularly in its gentle climate, Liguria's place is near the top. And while this particular approach to the pleasures and beauties of Italy can hardly be called original, we are confident that Liguria's sunny charm, her gaiety, animation, and culinary excellence will justify the choice in your eyes.

Back in the faraway chapters of history the Gauls, Romans, and Franks have possessed in turn the mountain-sheltered coast now called the Riviera. In the Middle Ages it belonged to Genoa, then its ownership seesawed back and forth until the early nineteenth century, when it became a part of Piedmont. Ever since the treaty of 1860 ceded Nice to France, however, this narrow strip of coast tumbling into the Mediterranean from the Alpine watershed has been divided equally between France and Italy.

Though France seems at first sight to have got the best of the bargain—certainly from a sophisticated point of view—the Italian Riviera has a straightforward simplicity that actually comes as somewhat of a relief. How bereft of artifice seem these first few miles of Italy after the endless succession of perfume shops, lottery booths, and purveyors of jewelry and candied fruits that sprinkle the French coastal towns!

Here in Liguria, beyond a doubt, lies the hard-working elbow of the

2

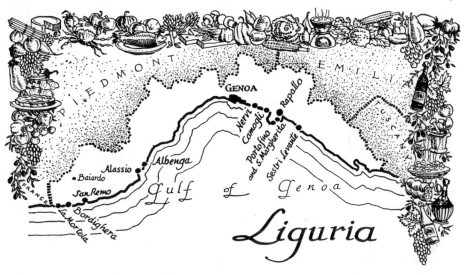

Liguria

Azure Coast; here the husky *paesano* must climb the hills all day long to wrest a living from his high, terraced farms. The impression of thrifty toil is heightened too by the sight of small donkeys, heavy laden with casks of wine or olive oil, plodding along the coastal roads. These would be a rare spectacle in Nice, Monaco, or Menton, as would the straight-backed peasant women balancing jugs of water, bags of laundry, and immense bundles of fagots on their graceful heads. How primitive and restful is seems, you may murmur to yourself as you approach Bordighera—dear sleepy Bordighera, for generations the winter refuge of fog-fleeing Londoners.

Then suddenly you're aware of two strident notes, nerve-shattering and insistent, that characterize the staccato pulse of postwar Italy: one, the blatantly repetitious roadside advertising (we shall try to go into this later, when our power of invective has had time to warm up); and the other, the locust-plague of scooters, a word now admitted to every Latin language. This fat-wheeled little monster has been developed to such a point of efficiency and mobility that to own one of them is the cherished dream of every Italian youth. The commonest of them is the Vespa, a waspish name it well deserves. Its wide-open blasting cutout may bring unbounded joy to the heart of its rider, but to the pedestrian in the narrow streets of Italy's towns the scooter causes nothing but apprehension and anguish. This feeling is slightly mitigated, perhaps, by the demon's one pleasantly debonair feature, the postilion seat for the inevitable girl friend. Here perches the unfettered *signorina* of modern Italy, sidesaddle, balancing with the aplomb of a circus bareback rider, ankles crossed, waving to her friends, and even nonchalantly knitting as the exhaust roars beneath her and the scooter scoots away!

By the time you arrive in the seaport of San Remo, glistening with luxurious hotels and an ornate casino, it is clear that first impressions may indeed be wrong. There is more play than toil along this sunny shore, especially in summer. The Italian Riviera is quite as dedicated to the business of attracting travelers to its hotels as it is to growing flowers, squeezing olive oil, or building ships. Aware of the phenomenal percentage of warm, sunny days throughout the year, a rate of foreign exchange that greatly favors the visitor, and a supremely beautiful seacoast, it is not surprising that the tourist responds readily to the siren call. He finds good hotels in all categories, from *lusso* to modest, costing less than he expects to pay, and serving ample, conventional Italian meals, with a *fiasco* of good red wine close by.

And how does the pilgrim of good living find things? It is gratifying to report at first hand that the exacting gourmet will encounter rewarding adventures in Liguria and, for that matter, in almost all other parts of Italy. Regional dishes and local wines have a charm and variety all their own here, just as they have in France.

Before we take you for a brief tour of this aromatic coast, a preview of its epicurean resources may be welcome. A mere glance at these immense mountainsides carpeted with olive trees reveals Liguria's foremost treasure— the clear, appetizing olive oil used in almost all Genoese cooking. A cow would have to be an acrobat to exist on these rocky slopes, and even goats are rare. No need, therefore, in view of the scarcity of milk, to look for local cheeses. For generations Italian farmers have built up stone terraces on the precipitous Ligurian hills. By dint of hard labor, and aided by concrete water tanks imbedded high above each terrace, they have made the land productive. Fruit trees, flowers, and vegetables are box-holders in these fertile balconies facing southward to the sea. One herb flourishes here in unrivaled abundance—basil, the aromatic key to Genoese cooking. Higher in the mountains grow orange-roofed mushrooms, pine nuts for the asking, and a rich yield of chestnuts, the biggest of which ultimately find their way into pastry-shop windows as *marrons glacés*.

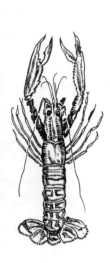

Obviously the sea must furnish part of Liguria's larder. Even the Genoese admit that the fishing isn't as good here as in some parts of the Adriatic, but to a layman watching the catch being taken from the nets, the yield is impressive. The aristocrats are blue-gray fellows called *ombrine* and *dentice,* the latter so named on account of his ostentatious teeth. Both are delectable when poached and served with hollandaise sauce. Then there are the old standbys, red mullet, mackerel, and *dorade*—and plenty of shellfish. An *aragosta* bears a close resemblance to a *langouste,* and *gamberetti* are a delicious variety of miniature shrimp. It is among the smaller fry that adventure lies, particularly the baby squids, *calamaretti,* about the size of our fried clams, and *bianchetti* (whitebait), both of which are delicious *alla genovese.* Finally there are *datteri* (mussels), some of which have almost the exact size, shape, and color of a palm date. When "date stew" appears on the menu, it indicates a local variant of *moules marinière*.

Though the wines of Liguria are few and far between, they are good and rather easy to remember. A sloping valley only a few miles beyond the French frontier produces the most agreeable red wine in Liguria: Rossesse; and the best is grown in an attractive vine-clad community musically entitled Dolceacqua. Fragrant and dry, in color a delicate rose, it has unexpected power. Say "roe-say-say" to the waiter, and look for something pleasant! Coronata is a golden white wine from the hills above Genoa. When genuine, it is an ideal companion for Genoese fish dishes. More usual is a pale, aromatic white wine from the

Mattavana

region of La Spezia, called Cinque Terre, from the five communities which produce it. The remainder of your Ligurian wine list calls heavily upon its wine-rich neighbors—Piedmont and Tuscany.

Almost all of the regional cookery along this coast stems from Genoa, and in its variety and succulence it is second to none. Most Genoese dishes are mild, subtle, and not too difficult to prepare, quite different, in fact, from the highly seasoned Neapolitan dishes best known in America and England.

The keynote is struck, not by a dish, but by a meatless sauce called *pesto,* suitable for Lent, for Friday, and, in Genoa, for almost any other day of the week. Ah, that sublime *pesto!* Its bouquet adds something indescribable to *minestrone* and green-stuffed ravioli, and, though good with any member of the spaghetti family, its aromatic green coating does something special to *trenette,* freshly made noodles about the width of an old-fashioned shoestring. Put down *trenette al pesto* as a gustatory experience not to be forgotten.

You might translate the word *pesto* as "I pestle," since it is the product first of the chopping board and then of a good stiff session with mortar and pestle. It is made up of chopped leaves of basil, garlic, grated Sardo cheese, pine nuts, and olive oil. Sardo is a dry, salty cheese made from sheep's milk. Some cooks use the more common Parmesan cheese. Chopped walnuts may be added, or may replace the pine nuts.

The food-conscious visitor with a penchant for regional dishes will find many other appetizing specialties here. It is worth scanning a menu atten-

5

tively to seek them out. Genoa claims a long roster of dishes as its own, including the world-famous ravioli, which originated in Genoese kitchens. The familiar little pillow of pasta is rich with eggs, stuffed with a subtle mixture that usually includes chicken, calf's brains, sweetbreads, spinach, and spices, and is generally served with *pesto* or the savory local meat sauce called *tocco*.

BASIL

If you have the good fortune to be here at Eastertime, a tasting of the famous *torta pasqualina* may be yours. This large, unsweetened pie is stuffed with green peas, chopped artichoke bases, and often other greens, bound with egg, milk, and a gentle suggestion of cheese, and wrapped with multiple layers of flaky pastry. When it appears hot on the table, the crackling layers of golden-brown crust rise high above the gold-and-green stuffing. A pleasant sight it is as it crunches under the knife.

Another characteristic dish found only in Liguria is called *cima di vitello,* a lightly seasoned galantine. Enclosed in a thin wrapping of veal is a mixture of eggs, green peas, artichoke hearts, cubes of meat, and a subtle yellow, custardlike binding. A slice of *cima* with a green salad makes an enticing entrée. You may see this specialty and the *torta pasqualina* by pressing your nose against the window of almost any Genoese *salumeria,* or delicatessen, and it may be made in your own kitchen by following the recipe that appears in the group of regional dishes at the end of this book. It is an admirable item for a roadside picnic. Add a little fruit, a slab of cheese, and a fine flagon of red wine, and your day is made!

Stoccafisso plays a popular role in Genoa. A local writer well describes this concoction of dried fish as "steeped in milk and drowned in oil, with anchovies and grated walnuts, and served covered with olives and more black walnuts." This is no dish for a timorous digestion, but it is a fast favorite of the Genoese.

Cappon magro, or meatless capon, is the facetious name for an astonishing salad-to-end-all-salads. This awe-inspiring pyramid of almost everything that is delectable in Liguria begins with a foundation of unsweetened wafers soaked in olive oil and garlic, and is topped by a layer of half a dozen cooked vegetables marinated in French dressing. Then comes the gaudy part. On top of the vegetables are piled poached fish, lobster, shrimp, oysters, and thin slices of octopus. Decorative flourishes are added by the artistic application of anchovy filets, slices of hard-cooked egg, olives, pimiento, capers, and baby onions. When garnished with crisp, fresh greens this dish really looks like what its inventors claim it to be—the best salad in the world!

Finally, there is a favorite pastry in Genoa called *baci di casella,* delicate "kisses" made up of two little macaroons held together with a rich chocolaty cream. They are utterly delicious.

It might be well to keep other Ligurian specialties in mind as you scan the restaurant menus. Among the soups are a particularly fragrant *minestrone*

Menton and the Franco-Italian frontier

alla genovese and a *zuppa di pesce* containing fresh anchovies. In addition to the irresistible *trenette al pesto* and ravioli, there are *gnocchi alla genovese* and *gnocchi verdi,* both provocative ways to begin a meal with pasta. Genoa is known for the subtlety of its fried fish, and a *fritto misto pesce* can be truly inspiring in the better dining places. If you yearn for snails, look for *lumache alla genovese,* which are cooked in a casserole. Tripe addicts will find solace and joy in *trippa alla genovese,* and the larger circle of those who share an enthusiasm for mushrooms will welcome *funghi al funghetto,* sliced and sautéed in oil with plenty of parsley and garlic.

With the hope that your taste buds are now sharpened in anticipation, let us return to the French border and begin a conducted tour of the Ligurian coast, showing due concern for gustatory felicity.

Perhaps it is naïve, but we invariably find excitement in crossing a frontier. This is particularly true at Garavan, the easternmost segment of the French Riviera, shown in the photograph of Menton, above. The Franco-Italian boundary is marked by an international bridge between two steep walls of stone. An immense triangle is painted on the rock to indicate the spot. After a final look at the dignified French gendarmes and leisurely customs officials with their burned-out cigarettes, you cross the bridge and are confronted by *carabinieri* and stocky little soldiers, all carefully schooled in the art of politeness. The formality of passing customs here is child's play compared to the ordeal that awaits the traveler when he returns to his native

La Mortola

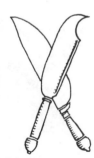

land. One thing to remember is that a frontier is never the best place to change money. Here the rate is considerably lower than that offered by inland banks. This *is* the place, however, for the automobilist to speak up and ask for fuel coupons for his car, and the Italians extend a real privilege to foreign motorists by selling them. These coupons are available once the motorist has presented his *carnet de passage en douanes* and other documents, and they allow him a thirty per cent reduction in the price of carburants during a limited stay in Italy. Of course this doesn't tell how startlingly expensive motor fuel is on the Italian peninsula. By noting the rate of exchange, the cost per litre in lire, and the relation of the litre to the British or American gallon, you can lay out a tidy equation. If you extract a slide rule and calculate just how much the fuel is costing you per gallon, the answer will explain why there are so many small cars in Italy!

Luckily a slide rule is not a customary item of luggage, so nothing should spoil your first happy moments in Italy. A glance at the road markers will show you that you are on Highway No. 1, the Via Aurelia, one of the most famous of the thoroughfares that fan out from Rome, 426 miles away. This coastal road is not precisely new—Roman legions used it at the dawn of the Christian era—but new things are being added, especially flowers. Local pride refers to the road as a "ribbon of flowers," and the name is justified. Purple bougainvillaea overflows the roadside walls, seconded by flaming red canna, assorted cacti, and bountiful pink geraniums. Young pines are being planted along the ledges, each protected from the harsh sea breeze by an individual bamboo screen.

The hungry traveler does not have to go far beyond the frontier to find a worthy restaurant in Italy—only three miles or so, in fact. Then he comes to

La Mortola

LOCATED IN a bend of the road in this village is a charming stronghold of both French and Italian cooking. The RISTORANTE LA MORTOLA perches on a precipitous landscape of pines, olive trees, and pencil-thin cypresses, plunging headlong into the Mediterranean. Its fan-shaped terrace, well sheltered by awnings, shows up clearly in our photograph. Here is a highly civilized restaurant, its staff bilingual, its menu varied, and its cooking excellent. Almost all of its guests are people who are about to motor across the frontier, or have just done so—hence a very cosmopolitan group. There is no question about the praiseworthy fare or the picturesque setting of the first restaurant on your path. The main drawback is its price scale, which is outrageously high. It seems a pity that the first dining place the eager epicure comes upon is also one of the most expensive in Italy. We recommend it nevertheless— but only to gourmets who don't count the cost. This restaurant is closed during the slack season, October and November.

Ristorante LA MORTOLA

La Mortola offers opportunities to horticulturists as well as gourmands. On a superb site near Cap Mortola are the Hanbury Gardens, open to the public for a modest fee, and probably the most beautiful on the Italian Riviera. Over six thousand different plants prosper in this lovely setting that reaches to the water's edge. Already you begin to savor the bouquet of Italy.

This, the beginning of the Riviera di Ponente, and the western segment of the coast, is marked by a succession of sunny towns of varying character. Some are tourist resorts, with good beaches and comfortable hotels, others fishing villages, or little factory towns with scant appeal to the visitor. We shall limit our comment to a few favorites that appeal strongly to the traveler.

On this basis, we should skip Ventimiglia, in whose dingy railway station millions of passengers have passed through French and Italian customs. Ventimiglia isn't much to gaze upon, it is true, unless one takes the trouble to seek out its rocky beach. Then it becomes quite dramatic, with twin fortified hills towering above its laundry-strewn shore.

Bordighera

A SHORT eight miles from the frontier, Bordighera is one of the oldest and most firmly established of Riviera resorts. A favorite with British sun-seeekers for decades, it amply repays their loyalty with a gentle winter climate. The

BORDIGHERA

sleepy little town luxuriates in flowers raised for the perfume industry, and is even more celebrated for its immense date palms. Fronds from these palms are shipped all over Italy prior to Holy Week.

There is also a close-packed old hill town of Bordighera, picturesquely dominated by the rose-tipped tower of the Church of Santa Maria Maddalena, the subject of our pencil sketch.

The hotels of Bordighera, most of them bearing the signs of dignified middle age, are not cramped for space, as is this hill village. They enjoy plenty of latitude at the foot of the slope, with ample room for gardens and terraces. There are about a dozen hotels, all solicitous of the needs of Anglo-Saxon visitors. The ROYAL and the JOLANDA are probably the best, but the ESPERIA and the BELVEDERE will also reward you well.

There is an attractive café and restaurant at the water's edge here, called PININ LA RESERVE. Passing motorists should find it a charming place for a noonday *aperitivo* and luncheon.

The Via Aurelia winds round a cape occupied by the forlorn ruins of a bombarded casino and leads presently to another relaxed resort, Ospedaletti. The vegetation is lush here also—palms, flowers in abundance, especially carnations—and the scene includes impressive villas, a small casino, cafés with dozing waiters, yawning shopkeepers. It would be hard to find a more restful place, or a hostelry more comfortable and quiet than the GRAND HOTEL REGINA. Ospedaletti now enjoys a brisk summer popularity, as its beach, once you have ducked under the railroad tracks, is very fine.

San Remo

HERE IS the teeming metropolis of the Riviera of Flowers, and the setting of its most celebrated casino. Gambling establishments are rare in Italy, and this one is among the few authorized to conduct games of roulette, *chemin de fer,* and other innocent pastimes. While no Monte Carlo, the casino attracts a large enough conservative international clientele to keep it rolling during the week. Then, on Saturday night, the big sheep come down from Genoa, Milan, and Turin for a trimming.

San Remo is both luxurious and colorful. It too has an ancient hill town, La Pigna, from whose wooded heights the intrepid climber has a dizzy view of the city. There is also the old port, whose clear waters reflect more glittering yachts than fishing boats. Market day in sun-drenched San Remo is an experience not soon forgotten. The heart of the palm-sheltered city is filled with canvas-topped stands selling everything from horse blankets to rosaries. And over all drifts the fragrance of flowers, jasmine and carnations especially—the bouquet of Italy.

Since 1861, San Remo has been a cosmopolitan resort par excellence, and in that span of time it has developed some superlative hotels. We had lunch at one of them, the ROYAL, and have rarely visited such a beautifully run establishment. Our host was the owner, Signor Bertolini, a courtly, faintly wistful man. He was born in this hotel, and it is now his turn to inherit its responsibilities. We decided that the look of disillusioned sadness in his eyes comes from a lifetime of associating with the arrogant rich. He offered us a luncheon which we shall never forget—small melons with *prosciutto, trenette al pesto,* chicken *cacciatora,* zabaglione, accompanied by a strawberry-red Rossesse and a fragrant dessert wine from Asti. It couldn't have been more Italian, or more delicious. Although few of his guests ask for regional dishes, his cooks are overjoyed to prepare them. The Royal has a sumptuous swimming pool, with an outdoor bar and soft music. The size of the white-coated staff is impressive. These sleek, black-haired young men seem to outnumber the guests two to one, and every one of them is attentive. There can't be many hotels in Europe that outrank San Remo's Royal. We'd be inclined to put it almost on a par with the Villa d'Este on Lake Como.

Royal
Hotel
SAN REMO

Signor Bertolini typed out three of his favorite recipes for us, all of them feasible in an American or English kitchen. The most tempting, and fattening, is a glorified green pasta, generously anointed with two sauces and presented in a tender crust. It is called

Tagliatelle Verdi Pasticciate
GREEN NOODLES IN PASTRY SHELL

Tagliatelle verdi are noodles made of egg pasta to which thoroughly drained puréed spinach is added for color and flavor. For 4 people, cook 3/4 pound of green noodles in salted boiling water in the usual way. Drain the noodles and mix in 1 tablespoon of butter, 4 tablespoons of grated Parmesan cheese, about 1 cup of Bolognese sauce (see index), 1 cup of rich cream sauce, and 4 or 5 large mushrooms that have been sliced and sautéed 3 minutes in butter. Pour the noodle mixture into a large puff-paste patty shell or ordinary deep-dish pie crust which has been baked but only lightly browned. Over the noodles pour a little more cream sauce and melted butter and sprinkle grated cheese. Bake the filled pastry shell in a 400° F. oven for about 8 minutes.

There are other luxurious hotels in San Remo to choose from—the nearby SAVOIA, for example, or the LIDO-MÉDITERRANÉE, which boasts a *"parco fiorito con piscina olimpionica,"* a superb setting for your preprandial dip and, among the others, the ASTORIA WEST-END, MIRAMARE, NAZIONALE, and VITTORIA E ROMA.

Au
Rendez-vous
San Remo

For those who are merely passing through San Remo, there is a good restaurant at Number 90 Via Matteotti called AU RENDEZ-VOUS. This is a clean, cheerful, well-managed place, rejoicing in many regional dishes and wines. Despite its French name, its cooking is entirely Italian. Signor Mattiuzzi, the director of this restaurant, has contributed a typical Genoese dish to our collection:

Lasagne al Pesto
LASAGNE WITH GREEN GARLIC SAUCE

Make a sheet of fresh egg pasta (see index) and cut it into rectangles about 1 1/2 by 2 1/4 inches. Cook the pasta rectangles, a few at a time, in abundant boiling water for 4 to 5 minutes. Skim them out as they are done and drop them into a bowl of cold water. Drain them and place them in layers in a capacious earthen baking dish, sprinkling each layer with *pesto alla genovese* (see index) and grated Parmesan cheese. Bake the *lasagne* in a 425° F. oven until the dish is bubbling hot.

The harbor—San Remo

San Remo also has a charming restaurant called LA LANTERNA, built on the breakwater and overlooking the harbor crammed with yachts and fishing boats. This is a summer place, specializing in sea food—and scenery. We recommend it strongly to motorists from France who are seeking their first idyllic luncheon on the Italian Riviera.

For automobilists who would like a change of pace and don't mind a dizzy succession of hairpin turns, we suggest a favorite local excursion up the mountainside above San Remo, ending at Baiardo, a frosty hill town some three thousand feet above sea level. The road winds up through an amphitheater of hills, their terraces close-packed with carnations in well-regimented rows and with blowzily beautiful chrysanthemums. As you push higher, the flowers suddenly cease and olive trees monopolize the scene. Then the olives find the going too tough and yield to chestnut trees, which, in turn, give way to pines. One learns a lot about the rigors of rural Italy in these few miles! Baiardo lies at the end of the road, crowning a terraced camel's hump of rock, a thrilling climax to the trip.

Back on the coastal highway near San Remo, the roadside flowerstands begin to flourish with tempting blandishments. Young men and old hold up

The hilltop town of Baiardo

immense bouquets of carnations almost under the nose of the passing motorist. Though these merchants could be brushed off, our sales resistance melted completely when we saw a little black-eyed girl, lifting a huge checkerboard bouquet as big as she was.

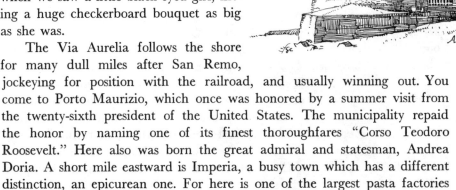

Alassio

The Via Aurelia follows the shore for many dull miles after San Remo, jockeying for position with the railroad, and usually winning out. You come to Porto Maurizio, which once was honored by a summer visit from the twenty-sixth president of the United States. The municipality repaid the honor by naming one of its finest thoroughfares "Corso Teodoro Roosevelt." Here also was born the great admiral and statesman, Andrea Doria. A short mile eastward is Imperia, a busy town which has a different distinction, an epicurean one. For here is one of the largest pasta factories in Italy, the house of Agnesi. The pleasant little resort town of Diano Marina is next, followed by the best bathing spot of all,

Alassio

HERE AND there the rocky Riviera relents and allows a stretch of sandy shore to creep in. Almost automatically, the sand means a summer resort. Though there are several other bathing places along this sunny crescent, our choice falls unhesitatingly on the shimmering two-mile half-moon of beach fronting Alassio. We have been restrained in the use of superlatives so far, but here we will let go and characterize this beach as one of the finest in Europe. Although it is crowded in summer, the sun worshiper could hardly find a cleaner, more relaxing place. The beach is kept in splendid condition by a company of bronzed custodians, who begin raking the sands at five in the morning. You can rent a beach chair, an umbrella, and a big fuzzy towel for a ridiculously small daily fee. A sailboat, paddle cruiser, or a rubber raft are yours for little more. Alassio is all vacation, all fun. Its cafés are gay, and the largest of them offers a six-piece orchestra with a girl soloist swinging her attributes before a microphone. And there is a night club featuring "I Jits-Bops," the hottest of the hot.

Alassio was not always like this. Once it was a simple fishing village, dominated by an old maritime fortress. The rounded mass of masonry still stands, but the rest of the old town has succumbed to the sun-lover. Dozens of hotels, each with its own segment of beach, have replaced the fishermen's houses. The top-ranking hotel is the MEDITERRANEO, a newcomer to Alassio

THE BRICK TOWERS OF ALBENGA

at the western extremity of the town. At the eastern extremity is the BEL SOGGIORNO, a place that owes much of its charm to its pine-shaded setting. Between the two are several pleasant hostelries bearing the names of ALASSIO, ALFIERI, FLORA, SAVOIA, GENOVA, and PALACE. After an extensive scouting expedition, we chose the HOTEL SAVOIA, the only hotel whose dining salon fronts directly on the beach, and we were not disappointed. The café tables are spread out under an immense fig tree. This is a family hotel, casual, unpretentious, informal, and gay. The food is of the best quality—standard Italian dishes, and a worthy wine list. The clientele comprised at least eight nationalities, all intent on spending the maximum amount of time on the beach. The nights are cool, and you fall asleep to the sound of lapping waves.

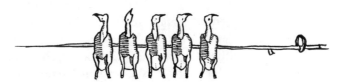

Though scant mention of architecture has appeared so far in these wanderings, the traveler who thirsts for antiquity comes finally into his own in Albenga, Alassio's eastern neighbor four miles away. This venerable walled town once bristled with tall, fortified brick towers. Four of them are still standing, grim and faintly tipsy reminders of an earlier day. Albenga's churches are also interesting, especially an ancient baptistry whose age may be guessed by the fact that it reposes ten feet below the present street level. Scholars place it as early as the fifth century. Albenga's hotel situation is modest, therefore it is best to visit it from Alassio.

Beyond Albenga the shore road loses some of its interest. Here industrial towns, rapidly recovering from their war wounds, prevail as the Via Aurelia and the electrified railroad struggle for the right of way. Wherever the highway wins, the train is obliged to tunnel through the cliffs. Once in a while, but not often, a courageous citizen manages to outwit them both by building a villa directly on the sea.

You wouldn't be tempted to stop in the town of Pegli, an industrial suburb west of Genoa, unless you had read the guidebook carefully. But unhurried travelers will find here an oasis of remarkable beauty in the poetic Villa Durazzo Pallavicini, now an archaeological museum. Its rambling nineteenth-century gardens, bizarre but beautiful, contain a curiosity shop of quaint objects—an artificial grotto, a Chinese bridge and pagoda, an Egyptian obelisk, and an idyllic circular Temple of Diana. There are medieval castles, fountains, tropical flowers, and a subterranean lake with rowboats for hire—altogether a surprising experience, which we recommend with enthusiasm.

Genoa

THE FOREMOST port in Italy, Genoa, dating back some twenty-five centuries, claims many distinctions besides that of being the home of Christopher Columbus. But for some reason it is often overlooked by travelers. Too often they consider Genoa merely a place to disembark and to escape from as quickly as possible for the blandishments of Rome, Florence, or Venice. After the quiet of an ocean voyage, Genoa seems to them crowded and noisy. Its immense cubes of modern architecture appear cold. But there is an adventurous, a picturesque, a gastronomic side of Genoa that really shouldn't be ignored. Since its rise as a seaport centuries ago, Genoa has faced a fantastic problem in urbanism, for its steep stone cliffs rise almost perpendicularly at the edge of the ancient city. The difficulty that San Francisco, California, was able to solve with cable cars calls for more drastic steps in Genoa. Streets are tunneled under hills, funiculars slide over them, and everywhere there are elevators cut in solid rock to hoist the hill dwellers quickly to their modern apartments. When the Genoese recently built two *grattacieli* between twenty and thirty stories high, these scratchy-sounding skyscrapers caused hardly a flurry. They are almost lost in the surrounding amphitheater of apartment-clad hills. Genoa's beautiful deep harbor, which allows an ocean liner to dock far closer to the railroad station here than in New York, is a result of this rocky steepness.

We urge the traveler with a sense of the good things in life to award a few days to Genoa, and be richly repaid. A prosperous city with handsome shops, particularly in the neighborhood of the Via Roma, it has also a grandiose side, best exhibited on the Via Garibaldi, a street choked with the immense palaces of the former great Genoese families, and now utilized by banks, museums, and colleges. Seekers of the unusual will find in the Municipal Palace Paganini's violin and letters written by Columbus. Lovers of music will rejoice that the famous old Carlo Felice theater is being restored after the damage it suffered in World War II. This teeming, active, maritime city bristles with interest. Its picturesque side is perhaps the most gratifying of all. The intricate web of tightly-packed streets that trickle down to the waterfront from the Piazza De Ferrari is utterly enchanting, or else we are growing naïve. Called *caruggi* in the local dialect, they are densely lined with cavernlike shops, now made bright and cheerful by the blessing of neon lights. They are clean, too, and largely free from odors, except pleasant ones emanating from pastry shops, perfumeries, and coffee roasters.

Porta Sant'Andrea and the house of Christopher Columbus—Genoa

Church of San Giovanni di Prè—Genoa

Guy de Maupassant was fascinated by "this immense labyrinth in stone" and wandered through it for days. American writers, Mark Twain and Long-fellow among them, were equally delighted. In this neighborhood stands the handsome Cathedral of San Lorenzo and the *palazzo* that belonged to Andrea Doria, the famous patriot. The remains of the house where Christopher Columbus spent his youth is only a short walk from the *palazzo*.

If there is much to be ferreted out by the sightseer, the prospect for the discriminating diner is every bit as good. Genoa has impressively good hotels, many of them clustered near the Piazza Acquaverde, which adjoins the bustling Principe railway station. Two of them are the luxurious COLOMBIA-EXCELSIOR, and the SAVOIA-MAJESTIC, recently rebuilt on its lofty perch of stone with the added comfort of air-conditioning. The best conventional meal we ate in Genoa was at the HOTEL BRISTOL E PALAZZO, a landmark on the busy, arcaded Via XX Settembre. Those who like to hark back to the Good Old Days will rejoice in this turn-of-the-century hotel clinging proudly to its dignified décor and Edwardian ideas of good service. It is well known to world travelers, especially those who are exacting about their nourishment. Our luncheon at the Bristol consisted of paper-thin slices of smoked salmon, consommé, boiled *dentice* with steamed potatoes, sautéed veal tenderloin with *haricots verts,* vanilla soufflé, fruit, coffee, all impeccably prepared and served, followed by a venerable Armagnac.

While you can hardly go wrong in Genoa's large hotels, its many restaurants, particularly the more pretentious ones, do offer a few pitfalls. The loftier their site, the higher their prices, we found. The finest view, beyond a doubt, is from the top of the skyscraper where the OLIMPO restaurant is installed. It is a popular stop on guided tours, with prices adjusted to its exalted setting.

Profiting from the advice of a few Genoese *bons vivants,* we spent many happy hours on the subject of where to eat, and here submit a half-dozen shrines of local gastronomy that merit enthusiastic study. Four are restaurants, and two are content with the modest appellation of *trattoria*. The discriminating Genoese patronizes one category quite as often, and as happily, as he does the other.

Though our favorite among Genoese dining places is not in the least pretentious or expensive, it is a true citadel of Genoese cooking. The RISTORANTE OLIVO is a lively establishment at Piazza Raibetta 15, just beyond the Sotto Ripa, that vibrant succession of arcaded waterfront buildings known to countless foreign sailors. Olivo seems small as you enter, but its white vaulted upstairs rooms are extensive enough to hold a large daily quota of local epicures, and its majestic menu lists not only the famous local specialties but a full roster of all-Italian dishes as well. Here is the obvious place to try *minestrone,* ravioli, *cima di vitello,* and the famous *trenette al pesto,*

Hotel
Bristol
e
Palazzo
Genoa

Ristorante
OLIVO
Genoa

The fishing port of Boccadasse

all in the best Genoese tradition. The service is competent, and the head-waiters have more than a smattering of English and French at their command. If you are curious to see what *pesto* looks like, ask one of them to show you a green-and-gold bowl of it, straight from the icebox. A fine wine list and very fair prices help to make a visit to Olivo's one of the pleasantest experiences in Genoa.

Another favorite of the food-conscious Genoese is VITTORIO, RISTORANTE AL MARE, on the city's southern shore. Noted for its sea food, this attractive restaurant is perched over a fishing village that has been absorbed in Genoa's growing perimeter. As you enter its awning-sheltered terrace or its glassed-in salon, the waiter assumes you have come for fish, and automatically places a cool bottle of white wine on your table. We began with *lasagne al forno*, which was scrumptious, and then plunged into a *fritto misto pesce* that included shrimp, *langoustines*, whitebait, baby octopus, and several other fish we couldn't attempt to identify—but they were all delectable. The menu, written in four languages, suggests that you may even have meat if you really want it; and there is a waiter who speaks a pungent Brooklynese. The clientele in gay and cosmopolitan, but Vittorio's greatest distinction is still its view of the powder-blue hills converging on the pale promontory of Porto-fino, the multicolored little fishing port of Boccadasse (Monkeymouth), and its gossiping fishermen. It's almost as exciting as the Bay of Naples.

One last touch brightens the ceremony of your bill: it is held down by glasses of liqueur—on the house! Vittorio's prices are somewhat above the ordinary, meaning that a meal there costs about half as much, wine included, as at the same category of restaurant in New York.

VITTORIO
Ristorante
al Mare
Genoa

Along the sea front, somewhat closer to the heart of Genoa, is AI PESCI VIVI, a first-class sea-food restaurant. It is gay and roomy, with wide bamboo-shaded terraces and dancing at night. The spiny lobsters of the Mediterranean greet you as you come in the door, and the classic Genoese dishes, *zuppa di pesce* or *fritto del mare,* await your command. There is a tempting choice of pasta also, including Genoa's own ravioli, and the pastry wagon is loaded with delicacies. We think you'll like it.

Ai
Pesci Vivi
Genoa

Near the top of the fashionable Via Roma, facing a palace guarded by costumed *carabinieri,* is a shop whose food-laden windows will cause anyone with epicurean leanings to pause with pleasure. All of the Genoese specialties—*cima di vitello,* ravioli, *torta pasqualina*—are here in abundance, framed in a delectable still life of sausage, salads, cold meats, vegetables, and fruit. The intrigued gourmet finds that this is also a restaurant, and a quite acceptable one, called SACCO. You may enjoy the Genoese specialties in attractive dining rooms, or you may buy them over the counter and repair to the nearby Piazza Corvetto and its sheltered park benches. In either case, your meal will be a pleasant one, but you'll be stared at less if you choose Sacco's cool salons.

Ristorante
SACCO
Genoa

You can't get much closer to the heart of Genoa than in the TRATTORIA MARIO, at Via dei Conservatori del Mare 32–40. Though a little hard to find, being situated on an obscure side street near the Piazza Banchi just off the waterfront, it is well worth the search. This *trattoria* is almost a trade secret among discriminating devotees of Genoese cooking. One glance at the prosperous, well-rounded businessmen who comprise almost its entire clientele, and you have no misgivings about the menu. It is top-heavy with local specialties—ravioli, *zuppa di pesce, minestrone, gamberi, stoccafisso* (dried cod), right down the line. The atmosphere is informal and the waiters are in their shirt sleeves instead of in white coats, the subtle stamp that establishes this eating place as a *trattoria,* nothing more. It is noisy, amusing, gay, and absolutely genuine.

Trattoria
Mario
Genoa

On a little side street called the Mura delle Grazie, overlooking the harbor, is the TRATTORIA RINA, an entirely different kind of place. It couldn't be farther removed from the swanky Olimpo, perched in its skyscraper, for this is a modest family affair, cheerful and ultrademocratic. Within a quarter of an hour after you are met by the host, a smiling, solicitous man named Augusto, you begin to feel like a member of the family. Ten-year-old daughter proudly shows you her art work. Older daughter and black-eyed son, in shirt sleeves and apron, wait on the table. Augusto happily produces his guestbook. In the meantime, a formidable meal is getting under way. We had been told what to expect. First came *bianchetti,* whitebait, with a savory sauce, each minuscule white fish casting a reproachful blue eye at us, then *lasagne al pesto,* the classic pasta dish, followed by *pesce ai ferri,* a trim little

Trattoria
RINA
Genoa

boned fish sautéed in an iron pan, and a salad of raw baby artichokes, thinly sliced, with French dressing. For dessert, *banana ai ferri,* oranges and bananas cooked under a flame with sugar and kirsch, followed by coffee and, as a final surprise, Augusto's *"minestrone,"* which turns out to be an exotic mélange of liqueurs. The Trattoria Rina is certainly no place for a mink coat or a lorgnette, but Augusto and his smiling family will offer you a chance to know warm-hearted Italian people for a fleeting hour or so— an unforgettable experience—and a delicious home-cooked meal as well.

Nervi

THE RIVIERA DI LEVANTE, which begins just east of Genoa, is rockier and more precipitous than the western shore we have just covered. Its vegetation is more dense, its villages far more sketchable, but good bathing beaches are fewer. Six miles from the heart of Genoa is the oldest winter resort along the entire shore, Nervi, a place that has been in favor since the days of Pliny the Younger, who came here about 100 A.D. Nervi is sheltered from cold winds by a pine-clad mountain that permits its tropical gardens to thrive even in midwinter. A favorite Sunday pastime of thousands of Genoese is to stroll along the sea walk, literally carved out of the rocks, and then to visit the magnificent botanical gardens of the Villa Groppallo. In contrast to the bustle of the city, sylvan Nervi seems serenely quiet. We recommend it particularly to homebound travelers who have a few days to while away before sailing from Genoa. It is infinitely more restful than the teeming seaport, and its hotels are most inviting.

Of the several good hotels and pensions here, we have a strong preference, the HOTEL SAVOIA-BEELER, a roomy and immaculate Swiss hostelry overlooking the sea. Its garden is a prodigal miscellany of palm, olive, fig, and orange trees, mimosa and cactus, with dozens of shaded bowers for guests. This has always been a Swiss hotel, with all the desirable things that the word implies—alert and cheerful service, a maximum of comfort, and quadrilingual courtesy. The cuisine is "international" with Italian overtones, and excellent. The wine list is filled with the best of Italian vintages, almost all marked at under a dollar a bottle. Being Swiss, and neutral, the Savoia-Beeler managed to stay open during the recent war, and naturally became a favorite of the more glittering military brass. If Field Marshal Kesselring's signature is on one page of Herr Beeler's guest book, General Clark's is on the next! It appealed to the lesser brass too, it appears: one American major came back here after the war and stayed for two years.

HOTEL
Savoia-
Beeler
Nervi

The harbor–Camogli

Pencil sketchers and water-colorists have a rewarding opportunity in the chain of highly paintable fishing villages stretching east from Nervi. Bogliasco and Sori are both worth a detour if you cherish the picturesque. Camogli, a riot of animation and color, is best of all. The little harbor is filled with boats and hemmed in by a rococo church and steep cliffs of white tenements fluttering with the family wash. We run no risk at all in calling Camogli one of the most sketchable villages in Europe. Furthermore, it rejoices in the HOTEL CENOBIO DEI DOGI, an attractive and tranquil *albergo* overlooking the Gulf of Paradise. What better place for a painter?

The Via Aurelia here deserts the coast for the first time, and cuts across the Portofino Peninsula. Your next glimpse of the sea reveals the Tigullio Gulf and a trio of famous resorts, equally popular in winter and summer.

Rapallo

So MANY glittering paragraphs have been written about Rapallo and its horseshoe bay that we hesitate to say more. It is a peaceful spot, temperate in summer and mild in winter, just the place for diplomats to meet and thrash out their differences. Here Italy and Yugoslavia signed a treaty on the thorny subject of Fiume in 1920, and, two years later, Russia and Germany inscribed the Treaty of Rapallo, the first of the Communists' diplomatic successes.

Rapallo appeals strongly to men of letters. The late Max Beerbohm lived in a quiet villa here for decades, and it was in the wooded hills of Rapallo that Nietzsche set down his ideas for his superman. Ernest Hemingway and Sinclair Lewis and Ezra Pound have wintered along this semicircle of shore. Rapallo is also the darling of the movie stars—here even Garbo once smiled at a photographer! Probably the most relaxed place on the Riviera, it is a hotel man's heaven, patronized the year round by well-to-do foreigners. The leading hotel is the EXCELSIOR PALACE E KURSAAL, enjoying a wonderful view of the sea. Three other first-rate hotels are the GRAND HOTEL BRISTOL, GRAND HOTEL E EUROPA, and the GRAND HOTEL SAVOIA E PALAZZO. For a long and economical stay in Rapallo, there are many second-category *alberghi* and at least thirty *pensioni*. Nobody seems hurried in Rapallo. Cab drivers doze in their open-air landaus. Italian honeymooners hold hands, and dear old ladies sit on café terraces reading Agatha Christie's latest. Children ride in pony carts while their parents gaze languidly at the shop windows. We found no shrine of gastronomy in Rapallo outside of its excellent hotels.

Santa Margherita Ligure

THIS PRETTY little seaport has given up fishing in favor of exploiting its balmy climate and good harbor to attract yachtsmen, newlyweds, and vacationists. Personally, we find it more attractive than its vaunted neighbor, Rapallo. Villas and "palaces" dot its wooded hillsides, but the town itself remains simple, hospitable, and inexpensive. You have a choice of fairly luxurious hotels on the hillside or simple ones in the town. Among the former, the IMPERIAL PALACE ranks first. The MIRAMARE, EDEN, and REGINA ELENA are all handsome hotels with ample gardens and a full view of the gulf. As for restaurants, we tried one in the lower town called LA TERRASSE-HELOIS, and found it most acceptable.

The shore line—Santa Margherita Ligure

Portofino

A MUSTY old Baedeker from the 1920's describes Portofino as a quaint, half-forgotten fishing port that may be reached by horse and buggy from Santa Margherita. It's far from half-forgotten now! People come in flocks, and the local population is waiting for them with homemade lace, table linen, straw hats, *espadrilles,* and postcards. When a smiling *signorina* offers to deck you with garlands of hazelnuts or walnuts or almonds, it is difficult to refuse such comestible ornaments. The little port, hemmed in by its olive-clad hills, is much as it has always been, entrancing in its brilliance, an explosion of Latin color reflected in the green water, a paradise for the amateur photographer. Local fishermen pose obligingly for him, and so do the old women making lace. The inquiring gastronome is tempted by the many seductive open-air restaurants along the *quais,* each shouting its specialties on signboards: *Frutti di Mare! Zuppa di Pesce! Ravioli! Lasagne al Pesto!* But, as so often happens, the song is sweeter than the bird. Though the food and service are only fair, the atmosphere is so engaging, and the passing throng so extraordinary, that a meal along the harbor front shouldn't be missed. We had our best *quai*-side luncheon at the NAZIONALE, situated at the head of this bizarre and beautiful port. Another good place, a bit on the expensive side, is IL PITOSFORO. It claims an aloof view of the harbor from its sheltered second-floor terrace.

High above the town you will, however, encounter another gastronomic level, and a remarkably good hotel as well, dug into the olive-clad slope. This is, of course, the HOTEL SPLENDIDO, whose most celebrated guests were the honeymooning Duke and Duchess of Windsor. Its standards of cuisine, service, and comfort are in keeping with its breath-taking view of the Tigullian Gulf. The Splendido is immensely popular with *le monde où l'on s'amuse,* and reservations should be made well in advance. It is closed in December and January.

Hotel
Splendido
Portofino

If you fall in love with Portofino, as so many people do, you'll be happy to know that many of the fishermen's houses have been converted into comfortable furnished apartments. The most exotic spot on the Italian Riviera, its cosmopolitan, unconventional cross section of the visiting human race presents a spectacle at which we pedestrian gourmands can merely gaze open-mouthed. Portofino, incidentally, is said to derive its name from *"portus delphini,"* because of the schools of dolphins that often seek refuge in its bay.

Dozing fisherman at high noon—Portofino

The quai—Portofino

Snug harbor—Portofino

The Romanesque abbey—San Fruttuoso

A favorite excursion for trippers to Portofino takes them by launch to the fascinating fishing hamlet of San Fruttuoso. Here the harbor is so narrow that a cable can be stretched from one cliff to the other, and on this cable the fishermen's nets are hoisted by pulley to dry. The effect is wonderfully colorful. In the background is a Romanesque abbey, founded in the year 409, with medieval cloisters. San Fruttuoso is worth the boat ride, even in choppy seas. A footpath leads to the village, but no road to it has ever been built. There is a little bar-restaurant here where you may obtain a satisfactory luncheon.

After Portofino almost anything would be an anticlimax, and you will probably find, as we did, that your interest will taper off along the rest of the Riviera di Ponente. But just as the coastal highway turns inland to the mountains, you will find one more charming spot along the shore,

Sestri Levante

A STEEP, wooded promontory juts out into the water at the eastern extremity of the Tigullio Gulf. The isthmus connecting it with the mainland is the heart of the old city of Sestri Levante, and very picturesque it is. Still an active fishing port, its harbor is full of life, and its long stretches of sandy beach are also most inviting. It has an epicurean specialty of its own, called *ciuppin,* an Italian version of bouillabaisse. We tried the dish at the RISTORANTE MIRA, and came away impressed with the piscatorial mélange.

Grand Hotel dei Castelli *Sestri Levante*

Sestri Levante possesses a remarkable hostelry to tempt the summer vacationist, the GRAND HOTEL DEI CASTELLI. Installed within the romantic walls of an ancient castle on the peninsula, it is different from anything on the Riviera. It has lovely gardens and terraces overlooking the sea, and rejoices in a swimming pool, tennis courts, and other accessories for an auspicious outing. To many visitors, a stop here may prove a triumphal climax to a trip along this iridescent shore.

Lake Orta

Piedmont

Chapter 2

PIEDMONT

I T WOULD be logical to assume that Piedmont, the corner of Italy closest to
France and Switzerland, must share heavily in their tourist trade, and that
it would be the first stopping point for optimistic travelers about to explore the Italian peninsula. To a limited extent, this is so. It is amazing, nevertheless, how many people skip Piedmont entirely in their headlong haste to
reach Florence, Venice, and Rome. Such hurry is unseemly, to put it stuffily,
and it is downright disgraceful in the case of anyone interested in mountains
or skiing, in good provincial food and wines, or in the idyllic prospect of a vacation on the shores of an Italian lake. The uninformed passenger who merely
crosses Piedmont on the Orient Express is missing something good. We hope
to prove this point to him in the paragraphs that follow, and to coax him
off the train at either Stresa or Turin. If he descends at Stresa, he is in the
plushiest resort of the Italian Lakes. If he chooses Turin, he will find himself
in one of the most civilized of cities—cheerful, clean, and sophisticated.

We don't pretend that all of Piedmont will fascinate the traveler. Its
factory towns, as might be expected, lack charm. Few people visit Alessandria unless they are interested in the manufacture of felt hats. Here is the
famous house of Borsolino, one of the world's greatest hatmakers. There are
wide, flat agricultural stretches in southern Piedmont which are uninspiring,
to say the least. Even the wine country around Asti and Alba seems dull
after a few miles.

But the *best* of Piedmont is something else again, and passing visitors
who concentrate on Turin, the Lakes, and Sestriere, will be richly rewarded.
Piedmont claims a fair share of the famous Italian Lakes, including the
western, and most interesting, shore of Lake Maggiore, and the exquisite
little Lake Orta and its picture-book island. Sestriere is the Sun Valley of

Italy and a mountain resort immensely popular with both skiers and "summer people."

Best of all, the strolling epicure has a wonderful time in Piedmont. Its culinary standards are high, its bread sticks and white truffles are famous, and its wines rank at the very top in quality and finesse.

Among the contributions that Piedmont has made to the felicity of hungry mankind, the divine *grissini,* or bread sticks, probably should be given top rank. Turin is the home of this farinaceous fantasy, which delights diners everywhere. Bread sticks were invented in 1679, in the ovens of a Torinese baker named Antonio Brunero. Long, thin, and crisp, *grissini* provide a constant temptation in the interval before a leisurely waiter brings your first course. Napoleon loved them and always asked for *"les petits bâtons de Turin"* during his Italian expedition. You will see *grissini* all over Italy, but the best, and the thinnest, are made in Turin.

Piedmont is also the land of the white and the lavender truffle, genuine curiosities that are found in the hills around Mondovi, and in the neighborhood of Alba, headquarters for the wine and truffle trade. Italian *tartufi* are toasty gray-buff in color as they repose in the grocer's basket. When fully ripe they may be sliced paper-thin and still retain their subtle, persistent aroma. These fragrant wafers are sprinkled over many dishes that require a final browning in the oven, and the result is little short of seraphic. They are unbelievably good in an omelette. Cut in thin slices, they are served as a wafery topping to a scrumptious green salad. The dressing consists of oil, vinegar, finely chopped hard-boiled egg, mild mustard, and anchovy filets cut in fine squares. King Umberto was fond of this salad, with a few green nasturtium seeds added. The ultimate, of course, is a salad of sliced truffles alone, bathed in this dressing, but such a salad is so expensive that it remains a seldom-realized dream.

The *tartufi* of Piedmont have never been tinned, shipped, or publicized as much as have the black truffles of Périgord or Umbria, nor are they as versatile or quite as pungent with flavor. But they are exquisite nevertheless, and somewhat daintier.

One is hard put to make a choice among the regional dishes of Piedmont. An all-star team, however, would certainly include these four: *agnolotti, bagna cauda, bollito,* and *fonduta.* You will find them in nearly all of the good restaurants of the region.

Agnolotti are northern and somewhat larger cousins of Genoa's famous ravioli. Though the most common stuffing for these flavorful little pillows is composed of rice, beef, cooked cabbage, egg, and Parmesan cheese, there are many other stuffing mixtures, including chicken, sausage, onions, brains, and so forth. *Agnolotti* are a favorite Christmas dish, and Piedmont's outstanding contribution to the great family of Italian pasta preparations.

Bagna cauda is a hot anchovy dip, heavily scented with garlic, a Piedmont specialty that might spread to your own tray of cocktail delicacies if you have stouthearted friends. In Turin they scoop it up with leaves of *cardo* and munch it on the spot. *Cardo* is hard to come by, but leaves of endive make a good substitute. Slices of green pepper, small leaves of Chinese cabbage, celery, and artichoke are other vehicles to transport this uninhibited mixture to the consumer, on whom it will make a lasting impression! The recipe for the fragrant *bagna cauda* appears near the end of this book.

Il Bollito is the classic Italian boiled dinner, the Torinese version of which has savory variations. It is, in fact, a heroic dish. Built round a king-sized morsel of beef, it often contains sausage, chicken, turkey, calf's liver, pig's head and feet, and a veal knuckle and shinbone for flavor. It is surrounded by boiled cabbage, potato, and onion, and served either with a piquant green sauce or a well-seasoned tomato sauce. This magnificent spectacle appears in many a country inn in Piedmont, and in some Turin restaurants, so scan the menu closely.

There are rice fields in Piedmont, too, and *risotto alla piemontese* is an added cause for cheering.

Cheese fondues prosper mightily in Switzerland and France, of course, but the Piedmontese *fonduta* is different, largely because of the delectable Fontina cheese of which it is made. It is produced in the Valley of Aosta. Rich yet delicate in flavor, the cheese is amalgamated with butter, yolk of egg, and a little milk. When properly molten, the mixture is covered with a sprinkling of wafered truffles. It is a privilege to join a circle of congenial friends and to dip a crust of good Italian bread into the creamy concoction, especially if there is a good flagon of old Barolo on the table.

It is in the realm of wine that Piedmont makes its most illustrious contribution to gastronomy. A large part of this region is planted in vineyards.

Its Alpine foothills are green with ribbed patches of them. Vines grow on pergolas, on step terraces, in festoons between trees, and on endless stretches of wire along the plain. The yield is impressive, the quality high. Not only is Piedmont the land of the regal reds, Barolo and Barbera, but it also produces Asti Spumante, the queen of Italian sparkling wines. Finally, it is the birthplace of vermouth. Asti and Martini—what multilingual names they have become!

Sagra di San Michele

Barolo, the prince of Piedmont red wines, comes from Alba, whose vintages were praised by Caesar, Pliny, Henry II of France, and many another *bon vivant* in his time. A robust and generous wine with an alcoholic content that varies between thirteen and fifteen per cent, it is ideally adapted to roasts and game. Its ruby red, clear to the last drop, changes to an equally fine russet as the wine ages. Bottled after three years, it matures beautifully, and its name on a wine list is always a sign of felicity and good cheer to the traveler.

Barbaresco is a slightly less stalwart younger brother of Barolo, resembling its relative in every way except that it reaches full maturity at the age of three. Both are pressed from the noble Nebbiolo grape, which also is the source of Gattinara, Carema, and Ghemme, and a few local wines that take this grape name—Nebbiolo d'Alba, Nebbiolo di Castellinaldo, and others. Gringnolino, Freisa, and Dolcetto, the last a red dessert wine, are other vintages worth tasting.

Along with Barolo, Barbera is the outstanding pride of Piedmont. It comes from an immense territory in the Alba-Asti sector, and varies somewhat in quality. At its best it is a soul-warming, sturdy red with a fresh, hearty bouquet—a cheerful companion for pasta or poultry. But a word of warning! There are two vastly different red Barberas. The one that sublimates your spaghetti is Barbera *asciutto*. The other, called Barbera *amabile*, is sweetish, highly fragrant, and somewhat fizzy. If you wish to avoid the disaster of drinking such a sweet "friendly" wine with your *bistecca alla fiorentina*, insist on the word *"asciutto"* on the label.

The statistics are surprising—red wines represent about nine-tenths of the crop in Piedmont. Yet the whites are famous. Asti Spumante is the most celebrated sparkling wine in Italy, and is known all over the world. Sometimes labeled as Moscato Spumante, or Moscato di Canelli, it is a fixture for festivities, from baptisms to wakes. Though very low in alcoholic content, its aroma alone makes your head swim. The sweeter sparkling Astis are the best known, but there are a few enchanting dry ones. Our thirsty expedition stopped at a café terrace in Asti on a hot August afternoon and polished off a cool, dry bottle of Asti as an *apéritif* with complete gusto. Cortese might be called the Chablis of Piedmont. Grown in Alessandria, it is dry, good to inhale, green-gold in color—wonderful with Piedmont's lake trout.

In addition to these viticultural accomplishments, Piedmont also claims the distinction of being the birthplace of vermouth. An ingenious citizen of Turin, Antonio Benedetto Carpano, raised the curtain back in 1786, when he first experimented in combining the fragrant wine of Piedmont with aromatic essences and herbs. The name Carpano (accent on the first syllable) is still seen all over Italy, but there are other famous names that originate in this region: for example, Cinzano, Martini and Rossi, Gancia, and Cora, household words among connoisseurs the world over. Martini-lovers owe Turin a little visit, we feel. They'll find the site of Signor Carpano's discovery right in the heart of the city. Of course, there are many other vermouths, from Tuscany and France in particular, but Torino accomplished it first!

If you aren't obliged to gallop through Italy in a fortnight, we feel that Piedmont deserves a portion of your time, and that it will reward you far beyond expectations. Though Turin and the Lakes are easily accessible by train or bus, it is the summer traveler with a car who gets the biggest break in this region, whose name, of course, means "at the foot of the mountain."

Crossing the Alps in a car from Switzerland by the Simplon Pass is a breath-taking experience. You leave the excessively quaint Swiss town of Brig and climb countless hairpin turns to the historic pass built by Napoleon at the dawn of the nineteenth century. We crossed it on a June day and encountered a snowstorm. But after another nightmare of sharp turns, we were coasting down the river valley to Domodossola, once again in bright summer sunlight. Lake Maggiore lay temptingly just ahead, its shores dotted with inviting hotels.

Motoring from France rather than Switzerland, you have two approaches to Piedmont. One leads from Nice through the scented hills of the Alpes Maritimes and crosses the frontier at the village of Tende, a small community awarded to the French after the last war. If you are motoring along this road and don't happen to have a loaf of bread, a segment of sausage, a slab of Gorgonzola, and a *fiasco* of Chianti, we suggest that a good stopover for luncheon is at Cuneo, the only town of importance along the way. Just off the large, bleak, arcaded square on the Via Pascal is the RISTORANTE SUPERGA, a country inn reminiscent of the France you've left behind. But the food couldn't be more Italian. *Grissini* greet you at the table, as do mountain trout, *trote salsa*

Ristorante
SUPERGA
Cuneo

Frowning fortress at Esille, near Susa

Superga, a dish to remember. The waiters, who are bilingual and obliging, bring roses on the plate with your bill.

The remainder of the road to Turin is flat, and rather dull. A more interesting drive awaits the automobilist who proceeds from Grenoble and crosses the frontier at either the Col de Montgenèvre or the Col du Mont-Cenis. Both are at an altitude of more than six thousand feet, but the roads are so well graded that the little European cars take them in stride. Both roads lead past frowning fortresses, slotted with gun openings overlooking the more peaceful landscape beyond. If you cross the Alpine pass at Montgenèvre and fork to the right at the village of Cesana Torinese, you soon arrive at an ultramodern paradise for winter sportsmen called Sestriere.

37

Sestriere

Sestriere

You've probably seen pictures of Sestriere, imbedded 6,560 feet up in a thrilling setting of snow-clad mountains. Here is one of the best-known skiing resorts in Europe, with a multiplicity of trails, hoists, jumps, and skating areas. Besides the four aerial trams leading to neighboring peaks, Sestriere offers some seventy different open slopes, many of them with ski tows, and there are facilities for renting all the equipment you need. Sestriere also has many fine hotels, as modern as tomorrow, including two extraordinary cylindrical skyscrapers. The leading hotel is the PRINCIPI DI PIEMONTE, ably seconded by the DUCHI D'AOSTA. A weekend with either the Princes of Piedmont or the Dukes of Aosta is a memorable experience, and you don't have to be a skier either. Sestriere is popular with summer visitors too. It is a real adventure to discover such total comfort in such remote surroundings, with a golf course and a cinema thrown in.

If you take the left fork in that village of Cesana Torinese, or if you cross from France via the Col du Mont-Cenis, your path leads to the charming frontier town of

Susa

This close-packed place, hemmed in with mountains wreathed in mist, is said to be the cradle of the House of Savoy. It well repays an hour's visit, especially if you ask for the Via degli Archi, which leads to the ancient Roman citadel. Ever susceptible to triumphal arches, we were enchanted to find two of them here for the price of a slight walk. The more elaborate of the two was erected by the Gallic King Cattius in honor of Emperor Augustus, eight years before the dawn of the Christian era. Our picture shows it framed in the fine unmortared stones of the lesser arch. From these same heights you obtain a sweeping view of the old town and the Cathedral of San Giusto,

38

The old town, with the tower of San Giusto–Susa

whose eleventh-century Lombard campanile is one of the loveliest in Piedmont. There is also an imposing castle, with a narrow entrance that makes an agreeable pen-and-ink subject.

Susa has its quota of gastronomical specialties, too, among them mountain versions of *minestrone* and ravioli, a savory *risotto,* and fine salmon trout from nearby Alpine streams.

After Susa, the road to Turin follows a picturesque valley, passing the Sagra di San Michele, a twelfth-century sanctuary crowning a dizzy mountain peak. Italy, as well as France and England, has its Saint Michael's mount! There are wide-roofed farm buildings with overhanging wooden balconies to tempt the camera, before you come to Rivoli, a hill town with grotesquely crooked thoroughfares. This, however, is not the Rivoli whose name is bestowed upon one of the most famous streets of Paris. That street is named for Rivoli Ve-

The Roman gates–Susa

39

ronese in Veneto, where Napoleon won a crushing victory over the Austrians, in 1797. Still, this Piedmont town, only nine miles from Turin and almost unknown to tourists, is well worth a visit. As you leave it the road flattens, and the towers of Turin spike the distant landscape.

Turin

YOU MAY approach this city, the capital of Piedmont and the industrial heart of northern Italy, with the same apprehension that we felt—namely, that it would be a sooty, gloomy place, with factory chimneys belching smoke and housing developments cluttering up the place. One couldn't possibly conjure up a more erroneous idea of Turin. Though its factories, including the vast Fiat plant, are numerous, they are all in the distant outskirts. The city that travelers see is the most modern in Italy, highly civilized, clean, prosperous, dynamic—and a pleasure to visit.

The founders of this metropolis on the river Po were Celtic tribesmen, who fought Hannibal's elephants as part of the day's work. Centuries later, it became the capital of the far-flung Kingdom of Sardinia, and it was in Turin's Palazzo Carignano that the Kingdom of Italy was proclaimed on March 14, 1861. Today, it is the stronghold of Italian textiles, chemicals, and motors. Every year, Turin's Automobile Show attracts visitors from all over Europe—and its hotels are jammed. Its population is approaching a million. A far more tranquil city than either Milan or Rome, Turin makes the most of its river Po, and lines it with parks. An Egyptologist finds a collection of Egyptian art here unsurpassed in Europe. Devotees of the opera will find that the Regio Theater in Turin is a worthy rival of La Scala. Shoppers encounter irresistible temptations under the broad arcades, nor are they confronted with special "tourist" prices. One has the comforting feeling that equal treatment is accorded to everyone in Turin's prosperous shops.

The city is large and cubelike and sprawling, but luckily the best of it is concentrated in such a small area that you can do it easily on foot. A stroll from the railway station north to the cathedral, a distance of about a mile, will take in the high spots. These begin with the Piazza Carlo Felice, a spick-and-span public garden with a towering fountain and the most immaculate thick green lawn we've ever encountered outside a putting green. Surrounding the park are formal ocher-colored buildings under whose arcades a continuous and animated bazaar goes on. Here are cafés and pastry shops, music counters and bookshops, a noisy miscellany of chocolate stores, tobacco stands, and newspaper kiosks, not to mention something for stamp collectors, souvenir hunters, antiquarians, and camera fans alike.

Proceeding northward, the street takes on an added dignity as it turns

The Porta Palatina—Roman gate to Turin

into the Via Roma, a creditable monument to discredited Fascist days. Probably the most luxurious street in Italy, its pavement consists of smooth, massive granite blocks, and its two-storied arcades are supported by monolithic columns, the like of which can be seen in the National Gallery in Washington, perhaps, but nowhere else. Continuing under the arcades past shop windows filled with shimmering silks and handsome leather goods, you come to the broad Piazza San Carlo, fashionable heart of the city, and the setting of its most elegant café, the Caffè Torino, and one of its finest restaurants, the Caval 'd Brôns. In the center of the square, in Roman times the site of a pagan altar, stands the dashing equestrian statue of Emanuele Filiberto.

Dedicated sightseers will find three museums of interest nearby: One is the Palazzo Carignano, a ponderous brick Baroque structure, within whose walls Victor Emmanuel II, first King of Italy, was born, and now a civic library and museum. Close at hand is the Palazzo Guarini, containing the famous Egyptian museum—the finest, from scarabs to sarcophagi, outside of Cairo itself. At the end of the Via Roma is the formal Palazzo Madama, housing a museum of antique art. Here the civic landscape opens into an immense courtyard leading to the seventeenth-century Royal Palace of the House of Savoy, where amateurs of medieval armor will find one of the finest collections in Europe exhibited in halls almost as imposing in scale as those of

41

The medieval village—Turin

Versailles. Adjoining the palace looms the vast Baroque cathedral; its unique treasure is the Holy Shroud. The faithful believe that this cloth, sealed in an urn in a special chapel, is the cerement in which Christ's body was wrapped after the Crucifixion. It is the property, not of the church, but of the House of Savoy.

Finally, at the end of the broad piazza facing the cathedral, stands the gaunt brick form of the Porta Palatina, one of the Roman gates to the city. It is preceded by two Roman bronze statues, badly pierced by bombing during the last war. Thus ends the one-mile stroll. We have purposely refrained from directing you to the Mole Antonelliana, Turin's loftiest tower and probably the most ghastly bit of architecture in Italy.

Down by the banks of the river Po one encounters a very different phase of Torinese charm, the Parco del Valentino. This handsome park is the setting for a restored medieval village, relic of an exposition held decades ago. Its shops are occupied by artisans proffering a variety of agreeable souvenirs—dolls, pottery, book bindings, and artificial flowers. We found this *Borgo Medioevale* to be fascinating and certainly the most photogenic spot in Turin. There is, moreover, a very fair restaurant, the SAN GIORGIO, incorporated in the village. The *agnolotti* were appetizing, and so was the Barbera. You dine on a wide riverside terrace overlooking the placid Po, its surface rippled by occasional scullers, or by unhurried lovers in rowboats. The place isn't quite so idyllic during the annual Automobile Show, however, for the huge modern building where new cars are viewed by admiring throngs is barely a stone's throw away.

Another reason for our thumping the tub for Turin is the profusion of its admirable hotels and restaurants. Two hotels in particular are worthy of high praise: the GRANDE ALBERGO PRINCIPI DI PIEMONTE, a modern skyscraper with perhaps more comfort than atmosphere, and the GRANDE ALBERGO LIGURE, facing the green-carpeted Piazza Carlo Felice. Though this hotel is of a certain age, it has been restored with good taste, and the service is excellent. We think that either of these will serve as a worthy base for epicurean adventure.

As a first step we suggest an *apéritif* in the CAFFÈ TORINO, smartest in the city. In the cooler months, you sit in its stately salons indoors, but when summer arrives, the tables are scattered under its arcades and far out into the Piazza San Carlo. Animated and fashionable and filled with interesting people, this café makes a memorable setting in which to enjoy a taste-sharpener and to consider the question of dinner. There are several good prospects. One lies diagonally across the square—the CAVAL 'D BRÔNS, a gay, Tyrolean type of place offering good beer served by pretty waitresses. Under a neighboring arcade is the admirable IL CUCOLO. Turin's top choice, CAMBIO, is only a five-minute stroll away. Let's go there first.

If you want to visualize how your distinguished grandfather dined in the 1890's, park your modern automobile in the spacious Piazza Carignano and turn your footsteps in the direction of this nostalgic restaurant. Cambio is definitely *vieux style,* and by far the best in Turin. The long, high-ceilinged dining salon is lighted by three immense chandeliers. Red velvet banquettes with lace toppings line the four walls. There are mirrors everywhere, divided by thin, reeded pilasters, gilded and Adamesque, and murals of capering cupids that might have been painted by Veronese himself.

Ristorante
CAMBIO
Turin

The waiters are venerable here, as is the grandmotherly hat-check girl. The headwaiter is of the ambassadorial type that really belongs in Geneva— thin, cultured, cutawayed, multilingual. He greeted us with diplomatic deference and we readily put ourselves in his hands in ordering a light dinner. The result was brilliant, beginning with just about the best *risotto al parmigiano* we've ever encountered. How many years of experience does it take to make a *risotto* like that? The ambassadorial maître d'hôtel wasn't sure. It would take time to learn how to make Cambio's veal cutlet also. *Costolette alla valdostana* are sautéed in butter (good Piedmont cooking is exclusively *au beurre*), then covered with a layer of Fontina cheese and sprinkled with thin slices of lavender truffle before they are passed momentarily under the broiler. A crisp green salad, a choice from a tempting plank of cheese, then coffee and Strega, and our felicity was complete.

Far more elaborate dinners were being consumed around us. At the next table two contented tycoons were polishing off a prodigious *bollito*—sausages, ham, chicken, beef, tongue, and vegetables in Gargantuan mounds. Near them sat two lean, vigorous men wearing dark blue shirts and monocles whose French guest was obviously enchanted with his *tournedos Rossini.* There were starry-eyed couples to whom the food meant nothing, and cranky old lawyers drinking only mineral water and insisting that the headwaiter peel their oranges. Nevertheless, the gastronomic plane remained exalted, and we entreat you to try Cambio, whether you dine in this mirrored banquet hall or on the inviting open-air summer terrace. Without question, it is one of the best restaurants in Italy. The great Cavour dined here often, and his favorite table is marked by a plaque.

Ristorante
IL
CUCOLO
Turin

At Via Roma 234, under those polished granite arcades, is a display of delicacies and a whiff of enticing odors that proclaim another citadel of good food, IL CUCOLO, "The Cuckoo"—and quite a bird it is. In the window are immense *langoustes,* stuffed mussels, galantines, stuffed peppers, *foie gras,* smoked salmon, and other tested temptations. If these aren't enough to allure the dining trade, the *lista del giorno* is. It is a menu richly truffled with regional specialties. There are fish dishes, too, but most of the marine life seems to be on exhibition only. At each table is an illuminated aquarium of guppies and their silent companions, and cages of birds chirp away spas-

modically round the cashier's desk. By such devices the owners of Il Cucolo
have transformed a long, low, upstairs room into a most attractive restaurant.
Smiling lasses in the peasant costume of the Piedmont hills brighten the
atmosphere, as do the live nasturtiums hanging from the cornices. The eye is
also attracted by rolling carts of *antipasto,* cheese, and glistening Italian
pastry. An erudite diner will surely enjoy his evening at Il Cucolo, especially
if he orders *agnolotti* or *fonduta piemontese* as a first course, and follows it
with a particularly fragrant *fritto misto italiana* or *castellane alla Cucolo,* an
inviting veal specialty of the house. Signor Cucco, the director of this epicurean stronghold, kindly gave us the recipe for the *castellane.* It calls for
Fontina cheese, which may now be found in many Italian shops in America
and Britain. If you can't find Fontina, a combination of Swiss cheese and
mozzarella will aid you in preparing this delicate dish:

Castellane alla Cucolo
VEAL CUTLETS CUCOLO

Select individual veal *scaloppine* and pound them very thin. Put in
the center of one cutlet a good tablespoonful of Fontina cheese, cut in
small dice, together with some thin slices of truffle (Italian or French),
and a pinch each of salt and pepper. Cover the filling with a similar
slice of veal and thus form a package by pressing the moistened edges
together. Dip each double cutlet in flour, beaten egg, and bread crumbs,
and cook them in butter in a moderately hot oven (375° F.) for about
half an hour, turning to brown both sides and thoroughly melt the cheese.

'L CAVAL 'D BRÔNS is the gayest, smartest, most colorful and sophisticated
restaurant in Turin, and it has the best location, too. Its complex name, which
means The Bronze Horse in local dialect, refers to the dashing equestrian
statue in the middle of the Piazza San Carlo. During the summer months,
patrons of the Bronze Horse have their dinners under the stars in the piazza,
secure behind green hedges, with never a mosquito to disturb them.

*Birreria
'l Caval
'd Brôns
Turin*

This restaurant is owned by a brewery, and we suspect that the dining
public benefits largely thereby. The menu is long and fantastically ambitious.
It is difficult to believe that one restaurant can produce the wide array of
international dishes—French, Chinese, Greek, English, Spanish, American, and
Malayan—which are indicated in the appropriate languages on the menu,
but there it is, all down in black and white, with a squad of top-flight cooks
in the kitchen to prove their international versatility. This menu, by the way,
took up eight pages, and was by far the most elaborate and artistic we encountered in our Italian travels. Beautifully printed in several colors, it is a
collector's item worth preserving.

There is a smart little bar, too, crowded with young people drinking
nothing stronger than vermouth, and except for this fact, quite reminiscent

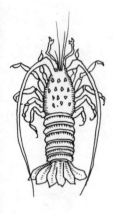

of Fifty-second Street. The interior décor is amusing, with Tyrolean wood-work to harmonize with the costumes of the waiters. The principal novelty is a set of fine color prints, beautifully framed and set securely—in the ceiling! Very effective, but tough on the engraver. A good print-maker deserves a better fate!

Accompanied by a sympathetic Italian epicure, we enjoyed a momentous dinner in the main dining room, a large, animated place buzzing with the low-pitched voices of attractive people. We began with *antipasto*—not the usual oily, heavy kind, but a series of delicate stuffed mussels, fish salads, rice and saffron, stuffed peppers, *foie gras,* sausage and paper-thin ham, fol-lowed by beautiful *scampi,* roasted on a skewer and bathed in a rich, piquant sauce. Then, to test the French cook, we chose tender *tournedos des gour-mets* that came to the table irresistibly covered with melted *foie gras* and delicately perfumed with Madeira. Everyone liked the pastry, a rich, four-story affair abounding in calories, and we ended the evening in the best of spirits with an excellent *caffè espresso* and Cognac.

Signor Erminio de Franceschi, the generous director of the Bronze Horse, has provided us with a small treasury of recipes from his kitchen. Many of them appear at the end of this volume. One of the most striking recipes is a festive *risotto,* which should enchant Anglo-Saxon gourmands once they prepare it in their own kitchens. This rice dish is light, colorful, and gay, and should never be allowed to become mushy.

Risotto 'L Caval 'd Brôns
RISOTTO OF THE BRONZE HORSE

In 3 tablespoons of hot butter place half an onion, finely sliced, half a carrot, grated, and 1 crumbled bay leaf. Add 1/4 cup of ground veal, the meat from one quarter of a small chicken, boned and ground, 3 table-spoons of ground ham, and 1/8 teaspoon of saffron, and let all brown slightly. Add 1/4 cup of white wine, 1 fresh tomato, peeled and chopped, 1 small sweet red pepper, chopped, and a pinch each of salt and pepper. Cover the pan and simmer for 45 minutes, adding from time to time a few spoonfuls of good stock and a bit of meat glaze. Cook 1 pound of rice in 3 quarts of boiling salted water, drain it, and steam it dry. Pour the sauce over the rice, mix it with two forks, and put in a hot oven for a minute or two. Serve immediately. Pass grated Parmesan cheese with this *risotto,* which will benefit by the companionship of a substantial Barolo.

The Abbey of Vezzolano, near Turin

In the heart of Turin, the stronghold of Piedmont cookery, an intruder from Tuscany appeared about thirty years ago, and has prospered mightily. Now called AL GATTO NERO, The Black Cat, it will be found at Via Santa Croce 2, about four blocks east of the Piazza San Carlo. This Tuscan restaurant, featuring the fine steaks, cutlets, and Chianti of Florence, is enormously popular with the informed gourmets of Turin. The cooking is simple but masterful, supervised by Signor Ezio Vanelli, son of the original founder. His cousin Ciro acts as host and assures his guests of a delicious repast. The Piedmont specialties aren't overlooked, of course, and you will see plenty of wafered truffles fluttering about, and a good Piedmontese Barolo to rival the Chianti. This restaurant is distinctly off the tourist track—and worth tracking down.

Al
Gatto
Nero
Turin

The subject of dining in Turin is not completed by an appraisal of these few outstanding restaurants. There are plenty of other gustatory adventures awaiting you in Turin, if you fall in love with it, as do many travelers, and decide to prolong your stay by a week or so. You will also discover some fruitful excursions in the nearby countryside. Before taking you northward to Lake Maggiore, we can recommend a pleasant morning trip through the neighboring hills, ending at a good rural spot for lunch. Your itinerary is: Turin, Superga, Chivasso, the Abbey of Vezzolano, Chieri, Pino Torinese, and back again to Turin.

The first of your stops, the Basilica of Superga, is the most dramatic. Set on a lofty hilltop some twenty-two hundred feet high and about six miles east of the heart of Turin, the basilica is a truly beautiful structure in the classic eighteenth-century tradition, with a finely designed dome and portico. It was built to fulfill a thanksgiving vow made by Victor Amadeus II during

47

The cathedral doorway—Chivasso

the siege of Turin by the French in 1706, and is the masterpiece of one of the best architects of his day, Filippo Iuvarra. This is the pantheon of the House of Savoy, and its crypt contains many illustrious tombs. The view, not only of Turin, but of the sweeping panorama of the distant Alps, is stunning. Tragedy struck at the basilica in May, 1949, when a plane carrying the championship Turin football team hit the structure during a storm and crashed in flames.

A zigzag descent leads you back to the river road paralleling the Po, and a right turn takes you to Chivasso, a flat valley town famous for its cathedral doorway, an amazing bit of brick Gothic detail with a gallery of terra-cotta saints framing an entrance-way and a rose window, the whole climaxed by a straight, pointed arch. By stretching our camera's rising front to the utmost, we have been able to give a full-length view of this Gothic rarity. Chivasso is also noted for an intriguing pastry called *nocciolini,* whose name you see emblazoned on every pastry shop, grocery store, and café in the town. A *nocciolino* is a miniature macaroon, hardly bigger than your little fingernail and flavored with browned hazelnuts, chopped small. We urge you to buy a few packages of this specialty for munching or giving to friends. We have never tasted anything quite like them.

Turning southward, your Touring Club map guides you through dry, rolling hills to the isolated Abbazia of Vezzolano, an unheralded Romanesque treasure identified with the name of Charlemagne. In the choir of the twelfth-century abbey is a picture of the conqueror invoking the Madonna. If you can rouse a resident priest, a visit to this architectural rarity, and its lovely cloister, will prove a charming experience.

For luncheon, however, we suggest turning your car in the direction of Castelnuovo and then to Chieri. The latter, a cheerful town, is famous for that garlic-scented dip, *bagna cauda*. Chieri's brick cathedral, especially its high, octagonal baptistry, is worth a visit before you resume the highway to Turin. Halfway back you pass a restaurant that we recommend to make your morning a complete success. This is the RISTORANTE PIGNA D'ORO, a delightful country inn, with laudable Piedmontese cooking and hearty local wines, in the mountain village of Pino Torinese, some seven miles east of the metropolis. The view is startling, and so is the food.

Ristorante
Pigna d'Oro

Lake Maggiore

THE ITALIAN LAKES, rare jewels that they are, have been divided up among Switzerland, Lombardy, and Piedmont. Piedmont's share of the booty is the best, or western, shore of Lake Maggiore, and placid little Lake Orta. Lake Maggiore, despite its name, is not the largest in Italy (an honor that falls to Lake Garda), but it is the longest, and many consider it the most beautiful. Over forty miles in length and averaging two miles wide, its upper reaches extend into Switzerland. The lower part of the lake is somewhat frustrating to the motorist, who feels rebuffed by the high walls of summer estates on one side of the road, and who catches only rare glimpses of the lake on the other.

A curiosity of the first magnitude, however, awaits him just north of the village of Arona, at the lake's southern end. A steep turnoff to the left leads to a promontory above the lake and the ruins of a *castello*. Crowning everything is the largest piece of sculpture we have ever seen, with the exception of the Statue of Liberty. It is, in fact, the second largest in the world, a copper colossus in the magnified likeness of San Carlo Borromeo, archbishop of Milan, who was born in the neighboring castle. The immense bronze and copper statue, seventy-five feet high, was erected in 1624 by the saint's nephew, and is still a staunch favorite with Sunday trippers. For a modest fee you, too, can climb up inside the shell and admire the landscape through San Carlo's eyes.

The copper colossus—Arona

Hotel
MILANO
Belgirate

Belgirate

THE LANDSCAPE opens invitingly as you follow the shore northward and at Belgirate you come upon a lovely lakeside village, bursting with azaleas, magnolias, and gaiety. The thing we like best about this holiday resort is the HOTEL MILANO, which claims to have "the largest and most beautiful terrace on the finest lake in Italy." It is a modern, comfortable hotel, at the water's edge, with a shaded dining esplanade extending into the lake, a most romantic spot for a sentimental luncheon, or a week's vacation. And the cooking is on a really high plane. The handsome salmon trout, carp, and perch from Lake Maggiore are shown particular deference in this resourceful kitchen, and the poultry specialties are good. We should also mention a charming local wine, Chiaretto dei Colli di Belgirate. Signòr Mugnai, the director of the Hotel Milano, has sent us a half dozen appealing recipes, among them the Piedmont version of this familiar classic:

Pollo al Cacciatore Piemontese
CHICKEN HUNTER STYLE PIEDMONTESE

Cut a frying chicken in serving pieces and marinate the pieces for 2 hours with a little salt, half an onion, sliced, the juice of half a lemon, a few sprigs of parsley, and 1/4 cup of olive oil. Drain and wipe the pieces dry and dip them in a batter made as follows: Blend until perfectly smooth 3/4 cup of flour, 3 tablespoons of olive oil, 1/2 cup of tepid water, and a pinch of salt. Let stand 2 hours. When ready to use the batter, stir in 1 egg white, beaten stiff. Grill the pieces of chicken, coated with this batter, under a moderately hot broiler, turning them to cook thoroughly. Serve them on a hot platter surrounded by fried onion rings that have been dipped in the same batter. A Madeira sauce (see index) containing a little julienne of ham is served with the chicken.

Stresa

THREE MILES to the north you come to Stresa itself, the Cannes, the Deauville, the Biarritz of the Italian Lakes, with a casino, palm-sheltered promenades, dressy people, inviting cafés and restaurants, and eager merchants who keep their shops open until ten at night. Stresa enjoys the best position on the lake, looking out on the four famous and picturesque Borromeo islands, and attracts the aristocracy of summer residents. Its handsome villas and gardens leave no doubt of its pre-eminence among fashionable resorts. Stresa is also, as you may recall, a favorite spot for international conferences, some of which have floundered rather badly. Situated on the main railway line from Paris, Stresa is a stop for the Orient and Simplon express trains, a real convenience for diplomats. This is distinctly a fair-weather place, the season running from April through October. Though the lake and its many excursions are the great attractions, there is another to remember–the cog railway that runs to Monte Mattarone. This eminence, nearly a mile above sea level, commands one of the most famous views in Italy.

The hotel situation is wonderful in Stresa, but if you come at the height of the summer season, don't neglect to telephone ahead for a room! Our first visit here was in early May, when it was easy to obtain accommodations. In fact, the competition for clients was so keen that almost every hotel had its bus boy in green apron, a trim-ankled maid, and often the frock-coated *concierge* himself standing on the curbstone to nail the sought-after passing motorist.

Two of Stresa's hotels are in the luxury class and are absolutely huge, with handsome tropical gardens and highly-cushioned comfort. The GRAND HOTEL ET DES ILES BORROMÉES was so imposing, and so reminiscent of plush, turn-of-the-century tranquility, that we couldn't resist taking a picture of its sunny, ornate façade. Though a supersensitive architect might wince a bit at these late Victorian purlieus, other travelers could hardly ask for more. This distinguished hotel has every comfort and luxurious appointment, including a superlative cuisine. Signor Valsecchi, the hotel's director, has shared ten of his appetizing recipes with us, among them this simple and delightful way of preparing rice:

GRAND HOTEL et des Iles Borromées *Stresa*

Riso all' Uovo e Limone
RICE WITH EGG AND LEMON

Cook 1 pound of rice in boiling broth or in 3 quarts of salted water, drain it, and flavor it with this sauce: Into a bowl squeeze 1 lemon and add 3 whole eggs. Beat to a froth, together with 3/4 cup of grated Parmesan cheese. Stir the sauce into the hot rice in the saucepan over a low fire. Serve at once.

Equally large and imposing is Stresa's REGINA PALACE HOTEL, its sunny façade adorned with sheltered, inset balconies overlooking the lake. A top-ranking establishment in every respect, its kitchens are presided over by gifted chefs, particularly adept with Piedmont specialties. One of their most tempting preparations is practical for Anglo-Saxon kitchens:

Regina Palace Hotel *Stresa*

Grand Hotel et des Iles Borromées—Stresa

Petti di Pollo Regina
CHICKEN BREASTS REGINA

From a raw chicken cut away two *suprêmes* (filets of breast meat). Split them lengthwise but not completely through (like opening the leaves of a book). Pound them well until you obtain maximum thinness. In the center put a thin slice of raw ham and a thin slice of *foie gras* of Strasbourg. Refold the *suprême,* moisten the edges, and press them together as they were originally. Dust the folded *suprêmes* with flour, dip them in beaten egg and bread crumbs, and fry them to a golden color in 3 tablespoons of butter. Serve with a Madeira sauce (see index).

For an overnight stop, or even a longer stay, we are also enthusiastic about the HOTEL VILLA CARLOTTA. This hotel is smaller in size and stipend than the two just mentioned, and has charming gardens, good Italian cooking, and a notable wine cellar. We would have been happy to stay there a month. Signor Grandi, the director, has contributed six recipes to our treasury of good Italian food, among them

Hotel
Villa
Carlotta
Stresa

Filetto di Bue alla Verbanese
FILETS OF BEEF VERBANESE

In 1 tablespoon of butter, brown 2 *filets mignons* on both sides. Add 1/4 cup of white wine. When the beef is cooked but still rare, remove the two slices to a hot platter, and add to the pan juices 3 tablespoons of fresh tomato purée, salt and pepper, a few drops of Worcestershire sauce, and the juice of half a lemon, and boil the sauce until it is somewhat reduced in quantity. Stir in 2 or 3 tablespoons of cream and cook over a hot fire for a minute, beating briskly with a whisk. Pour the sauce over the *filets mignons* and serve them surrounded by tiny fresh tomatoes which have been peeled, seeded, and heated in butter.

Many people make a tour of Lake Maggiore by steamer and land in Stresa at lunchtime. They will find two lovely dining terraces just opposite the boat landing, the HOTEL MILANO and the SPERANZA HOTEL DU LAC. Both have excellent Italian food, including Piedmont specialties, and both rejoice in deft, courteous service. Among the more promising dishes that greet you at the Hotel du Lac are *fettuccine alla stresiana* and *fritto misto alla verbanese,* a diversified dish consisting of calf's kidneys, liver, brains, and sweetbreads, accompanied by artichokes, fennel, tomatoes, and zucchini, all fried in plentiful butter and sprinkled with chopped parsley. This is a much better gastronomic stopover than the famed Isola Bella, even though it isn't considered as quaint.

Isola Bella

STRESA'S fair, if somewhat lifted, face looks out on four of the most beautiful islands known to Thomas Cook. The traveling public rarely misses Isola Bella, and at full tourist tide it is a unique experience! The one tiny street on the island is a shoulder-to-shoulder succession of souvenir shops and open-air restaurants with wide, overhanging balconies. They are banal, and the food is so-so, like the talent of their long-haired mandolinists. (The Ristorante Delfino is the best of the lot.) The Palazzo Borromeo is a shuddering triumph of rococo architecture, and the palace gardens are a gay, bizarre justification of baroque bad taste. Nevertheless, they have a certain charm, especially their disdainful white peacocks. At the peak of the tourist season, the guides and their platoons of sightseers follow each other in closely knotted groups. The guides are obliged to shout their story in three languages, sometimes four, and to outshout their fellow guides as well. The stillness of this would-be peaceful spot is truly troubled.

You can go to Isola Bella by rowboat, steamer, or launch. In spite of our tart words, we wouldn't have you miss it for anything! But while you are still in a boat, please consider a visit to the Isola dei Pescatori, just north of Isola Bella. Dominated by a miniature church tower, this is a real fishermen's island, immensely paintable. The nearby Isola Giovanni, which once served as a summer retreat for Maestro Toscanini, is not open to visitors.

Isola Bella

The sheltered port—Isola Bella

Millstones in the making, near Baveno

Life becomes a bit simpler north of Stresa. You come first to Baveno, a more countrified resort with good summer hotels (particularly the BELLEVUE and the LIDO PALAZZO), and then to Feriolo, a photogenic fishermen's village with no pretensions or hotels whatsoever. Along the way you see the first of the granite quarries that prosper along this bend of the lake. Here, a patient stonecutter may be fashioning flat, cylindrical millstones, and there, sheltered from the hot sun by strips of canvas, a squad of toiling men will be chiseling away at curbstones for Milan and Turin. Above them towers a discouraging mountain of granite still to be cut. A few miles beyond lies

Pallanza

THIS SUNLIT town, jutting out into Lake Maggiore, faces Stresa from the north, and rivals it for good, if less pretentious, hotels. They bear the classic names: EDEN PANORAMA, BELLEVUE, and MAJESTIC, and they are uniformly quiet, restful, and equipped with all the comforts a seasoned traveler would require. As a stopping place for total relaxation and a minimum of sightseeing, Pallanza might prove to be your favorite lakeside retreat.

Village gathering–Feriolo

ORTA

The town hall–Orta

Orta San Giulio

ORTA SAN GIULIO is a fascinating village on the shore of Lake Orta that should appeal particularly to the leisurely soul in search of a quiet atmosphere and a minimum of ostentation. It is totally unspoiled and rejoices in a town hall irresistible to the passing pencil sketcher. Above the village looms a steep hill, crowned by an ancient monastery and a scattering of little chapels. Before it lies iridescent Lake Orta, punctuated with the thickly built island of San Giulio, a neglected rival of Isola Bella. A willing oarsman will row you across in five minutes.

Albergo
ORTA
Orta

This radiant little town is made to order for the vacationing water-colorist, the seeker for a week's total tranquility, or someone who wants to catch up on his correspondence. There is a nice, unpretentious little hotel at the water's edge, the ALBERGO ORTA, with good service, adequate rooms, and acceptable cooking. After a good Piedmont dinner on its sheltered terrace, what could be pleasanter than an evening stroll on the piazza among a throng of village dignitaries, parish priests, and quartets of giggling school girls, arm in arm? The village lads are there too, a shy lot—one of them has an accordion, while others waltz together on the cobblestones with total abandon. A tardy farm cart, drawn by two cows, rumbles across the square. You sit down at a terrace for some *caffè espresso* and a small liqueur. A bashful young man arrives on a motorcycle to present the café keeper's comely daughter with a black kitten—in a shoe box. The light is too dim to allow you to read your English-language daily paper. So you have another liqueur and watch the diminishing crowd stroll back and forth. Does this sort of thing appeal to you? If so, include Orta in your travel plans!

Mont Blanc

Valle d'Aosta

Chapter 3

VALLE D'AOSTA

T HE MOST grandiose mountain scenery in Europe is found in a small, rectangular area at the extreme northwest corner of Italy. It is called the Valle d'Aosta, and it is autonomous, bilingual, and very beautiful. The Valle d'Aosta has been officially separated from Piedmont in recent years, and it now enjoys, along with Sicily and the Alto-Adige, the privilege of being a self-governing state within the framework of the Italian Republic.

This winding valley is one of the most striking in Europe, studded with medieval castles and abounding in unsuspected waterfalls and breath-taking vistas. Its hotel accommodations are good. The opportunities for skiers and mountaineers are endless. The most magnificent peaks of the Alps tower above them—Mont Blanc, the Matterhorn, Monte Rosa. The climate is ideal for summer visitors. The people are smiling and hospitable. In spite of all this, the Valle d'Aosta remains relatively unknown to Anglo-Saxon travelers. Such a situation must be corrected!

The French are contented travelers in the Valle d'Aosta because they can speak their native language and be understood everywhere. For this parcel of Alpine land is largely French by heritage, and most of its people are bilingual. The town hall here is called the *hôtel de ville* and not the *municipio*. Street names are indicated in two languages, and so are official notices on the bulletin boards. Your hotel porter or café waiter is more than likely to murmur *"merci"* for his tip. All this makes the Valle d'Aosta a point of welcome to visitors who can get along in French but still stumble in Italian.

The path of interest in the Valle d'Aosta is a simple one, consisting of one main national highway (N. 26), which follows the river Dora Baltea, and two spectacular northern offshoot roads, one to Breuil at the base of the Matterhorn, the other to Courmayeur at the foot of Mont Blanc. On a tight schedule, a traveler in a car or in one of those efficient Italian tourist buses can cover the area in two days. For those who have more time and a penchant for skiing, exploring castles, and poking through Roman remnants, a week would not be too long a stay.

One reason this region is less frequented than others is that it is accessible to motorists from the north only during the summer and early fall months, and then only over two rather formidable mountain passes. One of these is the celebrated Great Saint Bernard Pass, which connects Martigny, Switzerland, with the city of Aosta. The pass is 8,170 feet high, and is famous, of course, for the monastery founded here in the eleventh century by Saint Bernard de Menthon. It is considered to be the highest human habitation in Europe. The famous Saint Bernard dogs are still very much in evidence. They receive special training, and are able, by their extraordinary sense of smell, to detect a man in distress from a long distance. They can find their way through fog or blinding snow. Thanks to them and the devoted monks who patrol the area, many lives are saved from the dangers of the mountain each year.

The Little Saint Bernard Pass, with an altitude of 7,179 feet, is less forbidding. It is approached by a road from Chambéry, in French Savoy, which follows valley gorges most of the way, and the going is easy until the last few miles in France. Then you experience a long series of well-graded but hair-raising hairpin turns that finally elevate you to the Italo-French frontier, a forlorn spot, we must admit. We crossed the pass in mid-June and found our summit road plowed out between ten-foot walls of snow. It seemed especially forlorn when, at this precise spot, one of our tires chose to go flat, while gendarmes were inspecting our passports. The situation began to seem a bit bleak and uninviting.

But such tribulations were forgotten after we substituted a spare tire with the gendarmes' aid and began to coast, in second gear, down the tortuous Italian side of the pass. Summer returned promptly as we descended toward La Thuile, where the Italian customs officials preside. A thrilling experience it was, especially when we stopped to gaze leftward and perceive the brilliant, statuesque form of Mont Blanc looming larger with every mile. By the time

A O S T A

TOUT EST ET N'EST RIEN

we reached Pré Saint-Didier, the hills had opened up magnificently, and the full majesty of the highest mountain in Europe was ours to gaze upon. There just isn't a more dramatic way to enter Italy!

The third approach to the Valle d'Aosta is, of course, the road through Italy itself. Though less sensational than the others, it is the most logical for our purposes, and its climax is absolutely spine-tingling. Heading northward from Ivrea, above Turin, this one major road in the valley ends dramatically below Mont Blanc itself. The Romans built it well before the Christian era, and on it Hannibal crossed the Alps in 216 B. C. There are abundant reminders of the Romans—monumental arches, rutted stone pavements, bridges and open-air theaters. But the relics of the Middle Ages are even more plentiful—a chain of seventy-two medieval castles through the whole valley. You are hardly out of sight of a *castello* along the length of the valley road. They are so close together that, according to legend, signals could be passed from one to the other up the entire valley, if danger threatened. We will point out a few of the more rewarding castles along this short but exciting itinerary as we drive along.

This chapter, which should be considered as a leisurely guided tour rather than an epicurean field day, begins just over the Piedmont border in the town of Pont Saint-Martin, a picturesque place named for the Roman bridge, built in the first century B. C., that still spans the river Lys. The bridge throws a majestic single span of stone across the chasm and still handles foot passengers and donkeys. It is known, in fact, as a donkeyback bridge, from the two steep approaches to its apex. Nearby is a modern stone bridge, the object of considerable bombing in World War II, when the little town went through some agonizing days.

Here travelers with plenty of leisure may make a dramatic detour by forking off on the mountain road that follows the Lys northward and ends in the village of Gressoney-la-Trinité. This small resort is an important base for mountain climbers, and provides an electrifying view of the immense Monte Rosa. There is a very good summer hotel here called BUSCA TEDY, with better-than-average Alpine cooking. If you fancy the idea of spending a night at the foot of Monte Rosa, second only in splendor to Mont Blanc, the Busca Tedy could furnish quite an adventure.

Back on the narrow main highway once again, one soon obtains an impressive glimpse of the might of ancient Rome. On the western outskirts of the town of Donnaz, you come upon a seven-hundred-foot stretch of the original Roman road to Gaul, much of it hewn out of solid rock. Its immense paving stones show deep grooving by the cartwheels of the Caesars, and give an alarming idea of the roughness of travel over Roman ruts. One part

The fortress—Bard

of the narrow road is arched with stone, and in another place the cliffside was neatly carved in Roman times with the figure XXXVI, indicating the distance to Aosta.

Soon the valley narrows and leads to the "vestibule" of the Valle d'Aosta, the village of Bard, dominated by a massive, forbidding fortress, which sits high astride the valley. It appears to be a totally impregnable obstruction, yet the wily Napoleon slipped through the gorge with his army in the dead of night, in 1800, and later captured the stronghold. It is said that he ordered all wheels muffled with rags that night to escape detection.

About five miles farther along, you perceive across the river a bulky, square-towered château towering over the dusty village of Issogne. Though its outer walls appear somewhat forbidding, it is well worth a visit, if only for its famous courtyard, dominated by La Fontana del Melograno. From this octagonal fountain sprouts a small bronze pomegranate tree, one of the curiosities of the valley, beautifully wrought and quite Germanic in feeling. A copy of it was made for the restored medieval village in Turin, of which we have already spoken. The walls surrounding the courtyard are brightened with frescoes of flamboyant coats of arms, and inside are several fine rooms, which a custodian will unlock for interested sightseers. This château was built by the Counts of Challant, the feudal masters of the valley, in 1480. Almost within earshot is an earlier castle built by the same family in 1390, the Château de Verrès, an immense square stronghold that towers over the valley from its rocky promontory.

Saint-Vincent

SHARP-EYED TRAVELERS will observe roadside marble quarries, and highly interesting they are, before arriving at Saint-Vincent, the most comfortable resort town in the valley. Located at the precise point where the highway bends westward, its overpowering view of the valley at sunset defies description. A pleasant town with open-air cafés, a lethargic casino, and a wide choice of hotels, Saint-Vincent is a spa of some renown, and its waters are recommended for people with temperamental digestions. A true gourmet might be inclined to avoid such a place, but we urge you to tarry and try one of its hotels, among which we have a strong favorite, the HOTEL DU PARC. We enthusiastically suggest this large, comfortable, modern chalet on the edge of the town above the somnolent casino. Its interior décor is French provincial in style. There is a sympathetic little bar with low tables, chintz-covered chairs, and soft lights, the dining room has more than a little rustic beauty, and the cuisine truly justifies rapturous praise. We try not to indulge overmuch in superlatives, but the Hotel du Parc deserves them richly. Our first luncheon began with hors-d'oeuvre worthy of a fine Paris restaurant. The mountain trout and the *tournedos Rossini* that followed were impeccable, and the noble bottle of red Frecciarossa provided a perfect obbligato. An epicure's choice would certainly fall upon this trim, well-run hostelry whose host, Signor Cerutti, is a multilingual symbol of hospitality. The guest rooms, most of them equipped with baths, are charming, and all of them afford

Hotel
du
PARC
St. Vincent

Château de Fenis

dramatic views of the valley. The Hotel du Parc is open the year round and is an understandable favorite with skiers as well as with less athletic summer guests.

Among the dozen other hotels in Saint-Vincent, one of the best is the long-established GRAND HOTEL DE LA SOURCE, open in summer only. Its food is good and its view equally dramatic.

While on the subject of food, here are a few words on the gastronomic resources of the Valle d'Aosta. One product stands out above all others, the superb Fontina cheese, famous all over Italy and fast becoming known abroad. This Alpine valley is better adapted to pasturage, vineyards, and orchards than to agriculture, and the landscape is brightened by endless herds of clean cattle and hillside terraces of fruit trees. Fontina is a soft cheese in the form of a large disk and is notable for its fragrance and its gentle, almost sweet taste. It melts in your mouth and it also melts in cooking—just the thing for a savory *fonduta* or for making a *gratin* on top of a veal cutlet with paper-thin slices of Piedmont truffles. This is one version of the dish called *costolette alla valdostana*. Please pounce on it promptly if you see it on a menu. It is also sometimes made according to the following recipe:

65

Costolette alla Valdostana
VEAL CUTLETS VALLE D'AOSTA

Split open little veal chops like the leaves of a book and flatten them as thin as possible. (Or you may use very thin slices from the leg.) In the center of each cutlet place a thin slice of ham and a slice of Fontina cheese (not too much). *Mozzarella* cheese is a good substitute if you have no Fontina. Press the moistened edges of the two leaves, or slices, of veal together all around, and dip each reshaped cutlet very lightly in flour (shaking off all excess), salt and pepper, beaten egg, and then fine bread crumbs. Have plenty of butter sizzling hot in your pan (about 3 tablespoons for 4 cutlets) and brown the veal 4 to 5 minutes on each side.

The fruit of the Valle d'Aosta is also choice, particularly the Martin *sec* pear, which often ends up in candied form in pastry shops, and an apple called Renetta del Canada, an aromatic type that travels widely to the better Italian fruitstands. Local strawberries are delectable, and so are the mountain butter and honey. For the better part of its comestibles, however, the Valle d'Aosta turns to the larder of its well-stocked neighbor, Piedmont.

The wine industry prospers in the bend of the valley, and vineyards cover the gentler slopes for miles on end. The grapes are grown on trellises supported by stubby stone columns, a unique feature of the Aostan landscape.

Just west of Saint-Vincent you come to a town with an equally French name, Châtillon, and it is here that you leave the valley road and follow the river Marmore northward to Breuil. One of the two detours that we implore you to take, it leads through sloping pastures and dizzy, storybook villages to the very base of the Matterhorn. The village architecture becomes more grotesque as you go north. The houses are made partly of stone and stucco, but their overhanging second stories are of wood, capped by immense wide roofs weighted down with flat stones to secure them against mountain gales.

Valtournanche, a village famous for its Alpine guides, is a close-packed community along the way that merits a pause on the upward journey. Here you obtain a glimpse of its picturesque square, with memorial plaques dedicated to the heroic guides who have perished in their rescue attempts.

Breuil

FROM THIS point north the trip gets more and more exciting. Vegetation becomes sparse and the mountains loom higher, until finally you arrive at the end of the road and the treeless town of Breuil, also known as Cervinia.

Breuil and the Matterhorn

Here you are confronted with one of the most thrilling sights in Europe, an overpowering amphitheater of mountains dominated by the stark, toothy Matterhorn and the immense Monte Rosa, magnificent in its covering of deep, perpetual snow.

Breuil is 6,575 feet in the air, but, if you have a confident attitude toward aerial trams, you may go higher still. A suspended cable car takes you to Plan-Maison, 8,531 feet up, and from *there* you go upward to the perpetual snows of the Plan-Rosa on the Swiss frontier, 11,811 feet high, where inveterate skiers can enjoy their sport in midsummer. You don't need the fast pulse of a skier, however, to appreciate the allure of Cervinia. Its cool, stimulating air makes it very popular in summer with nonathletes also. This resort has every reason to boast of its succession of cheerful, comfortable hotels, which bestow an equal welcome on winter sportsmen and summer strollers. You can't exactly expect them to reach summits of cooking comparable to their surroundings, but their gastronomic standing is good. If you choose among the ultramodern GRAND HOTEL CERVINIA, the HOTEL LA GRAN BAITA, and the HOTEL MONTE CERVINO, you can hardly go wrong.

Back once again in Châtillon, you head westward along the valley road toward the most beautiful of the castles built by the all-powerful Challants. It is the Château de Fenis, and its glistening towers are visible for miles before you come to them. Facing the little town of Nus (which means nudes in French and seems inappropriate), the château, built in 1350 and admirably restored, is a masterpiece of medieval architecture, and absolutely irresistible as a sketch subject. A custodian will show you through its paved courtyard, surrounded by ancient, two-storied arcades, and into its baronial halls, enlivened with noble frescoes. If, by any chance, you should be rationed on castles and allowed to see only one in the Valle d'Aosta, this should be your choice.

Aosta

Now THE valley widens, and after about six miles the towers of Aosta come into view. This is the administrative center of the autonomous valley region, and its most important city. It was founded by the Romans, there is no question of that. You see evidences of their presence on every side. Its original name was Augusta Praetoria, and it was laid out in a rectangular Roman plan and surrounded by fortified walls with defensive towers at each corner. They still stand, as do two monumental gates to the city. Though the triumphal Arch of Augustus, erected in 23 B. C., has a certain nobility, it has lost its full stature. Perhaps it was used as a stone quarry during the Middle Ages and thus lost its upper elements. At all events, its squat roof, crowding the entablature, makes it less impressive than the triumphal arches of Rome. Utterly massive is the Porta Praetoria, a dust-caked Roman portal in the noisy midst of town traffic. We urge you to see them both, as well as the ruins of the Roman theater, a lofty screen of masonry etched against the background of snow-clad hills.

Aosta can be proud of one more architectural treasure, the collegiate church of Sant'Orso. Founded by Saint Anselm, Aosta's most famous citizen, who became Archbishop of Canterbury in 1093, it is a serenely graceful priory, with a cloister you will long remember.

The architectural treasures of Aosta can be visited in a few hours, and not many people linger for an overnight stop. But this Roman city with French overtones offers a very acceptable hostelry, with good food, the HÔTEL DE LA COURONNE, located on the Place Emile Chanoux, opposite the *hôtel de ville*. How strangely French it is!

HOTEL
de la
Couronne
Aosta

One more castle deserves mention along your westbound highway. At Saint-Pierre is an example of pure fairy-story building, a many-towered fantasy growing out of a needle of rock. This castle, which dates from the tenth

Highland road—Courmayeur

and eleventh centuries, adjoins a Romanesque hillside church, and causes the passing motorist to slam on his brakes and gasp with pleasure.

Now your road climbs gently and the valley narrows. Ahead of you, framed in slender roadside poplars, are glimpses of the lofty white colossus, Mont Blanc. By the time you reach Pré Saint-Didier, the mountain is over-whelming. The next few miles provide an astounding panorama. We sat under a fruit tree, surrounded by thick carpets of wild flowers, and enjoyed our modest luncheon of *mortadella,* bread, Fontina, fruit, and Chianti, with the mightiest mountain in Europe towering over us. One doesn't forget a picnic like that!

Courmayeur

THIS BRIEF travelogue ends with a fine flourish, for Courmayeur is unquestionably one of the most exciting places in Italy. It is set in a verdant saucer of wild flowers, four thousand feet above sea level, and surrounded by the most overwhelming of mountain peaks. But groping for words won't do much good. You have to see Courmayeur to appreciate it. Artists, painters, and poets love its majestic calm. Skiers have a passion for it. Together with

Chamonix and Zermatt, French and Swiss respectively, Courmayeur shares the distinction of being one of the oldest and most famous centers of Alpinism. But Courmayeur is more fortunate than its rivals. Being on the sunny side of Mont Blanc, it is much warmer. In spring, cherry trees blossom next to glaciers.

Winter sportsmen have naturally adopted Courmayeur as their own. There are trim little cable cars to hoist them to fabulous, snow-carpeted playgrounds, and there are comfortable "refuges" above the two-mile mark where they can linger for days, if they wish. Alpinists find skilled mountaineers here to guide their steps upward and back again.

Though spring and autumn are dull seasons in Courmayeur, by late June its hotels begin to bustle with anticipation of the summer months ahead. Most of them are modern, comfortable, oversized chalets. The luxurious HOTEL ROYAL BERTOLINI is the patrician of the lot, but the ANGE & GRAND HOTEL, the EXCELSIOR, the MIRAMONTI, and the MONT BLANC are all very good. Or perhaps you want "something different." You'll find it, without any question, in the GRANDE ALBERGO RIFUGIO TORINO, a bleak but commodious retreat, 11,072 feet high on an Alpine slope. No wild flowers here, but a breathtaking panorama of the Alps, with every comfort, substantial food, and an "American Bar" thrown in. Just hop in the *funivia*. Only fifteen minutes by steep cable!

Above Courmayeur is an unobtrusive stretch of country road that will take on no little animation in the years to come. It leads to Entrèves, a rustic village even closer to the majesty of Mont Blanc. This is the southern terminus of the vehicular tunnel now being pierced under the Alps. Men have been blasting and burrowing their way through since 1952. Some day Entrèves will be a frontier post, with the next stop eight miles through the mountain in French Chamonix.

At this far point of our guided tour, with the mountain setting up an impassable barrier (for the moment, at least), it seems prudent to retrace our steps—this time to the Italian Lakes.

Château de St. Pierre

Sirmione

Lombardy

Chapter 4

LOMBARDY

HE CHARMS of Lombardy, the manufacturing stronghold of northern Italy, are distinctly uneven. Along this region's flat lower stretches, punctuated by factory chimneys and beribboned by sign-infested *autostrade,* they make a somewhat pallid appeal to the eager visitor. But immediately above this industrial plain rises a series of ridgelike mountains framing one of the world's great tourist treasures, the Italian Lakes. At first sight, Lombardy is a blend of the brash and the beautiful. Few contrivances of man are as shattering as a busy traffic intersection in its capital, Milan, resounding with open cutouts and the staccato beat of Vespa scooters. By contrast, however, what could be more restful than a trip along the shores of Lake Como on a small, sleepy steamboat? But if the Italian Lakes sell themselves on sight, the less obvious fascination of the plain also comes to light, especially for those civilized souls sensitive to music, painting, Romanesque architecture, and fine cooking. For all its buoyant commercialism, Milan has time to pause and enjoy the good things of life, as any visitor to La Scala can testify. Today's prosperity is reflected in resplendent shops, the most modern hotels, and a culinary standard that is a pure joy to the visiting voluptuary. Lombardy, we think, has earned a gastronomic rating as high as any in Italy, not excepting the rich bounty of Bologna. So some plump, pleasant paragraphs lie ahead.

One reason for this opulence is the immense fertility of the Lombardian plain, whose close-packed gardens, meadows, and orchards are irrigated by an intricate network of canals. Fruit, vegetables, and cereals burst forth from this dull-looking land of abundance, which also provides a rich tapestry of green for the dairy industry. The cheeses of Lombardy (Gorgonzola, Bel Paese, and Stracchino all come from here) are known all over the world. And it goes without saying that a trout from Lake Garda or a veal cutlet *alla milanese* is invariably prepared in golden Lombardy butter.

This bustling region has earned a place in the top echelon of Italian gastronomy. A regiment of famous dishes originated here, some of them absolutely basic—*risotto, minestrone, costoletta alla milanese, osso buco,* and *panettone,* for example.

In Milan, the most opulent city in Italy, a rich repertory of regional dishes has won international acceptance. That classic, saffron-tinted favorite, *risotto alla milanese* has conquered even the most fastidious of French gourmets. The Milanese insist that their own version of *minestrone* is the first, and the best. It is *so* good that they eat it hot, cold, or lukewarm with equal gusto. Whoever coined the phrase, "Dreaded Veal Cutlet," would eat his blasphemous pun on tasting a genuine thin, Milanese cutlet of tender young veal, dipped in egg and fine sifted bread crumbs, and cooked, of course, in butter. It is as golden as an autumn leaf, and very simple to prepare. The modest foreleg of Lombardy veal provides the main ingredient for *osso buco,* one of the most original of stew dishes. The bones are sawed crosswise, with the meat and marrow clinging to them, and the pieces are cooked for long hours until the meat is tender. Served with *risotto* and a *gremolada* sauce rich with lemon, garlic, rosemary, parsley, and sage, it is magnificent in its robustness and savor. The fame of Lombardy *panettone* extends all over Italy. This large, ambrosian cake, resembling an overgrown brioche, is light and not too sweet, and is made from the simplest ingredients—flour, butter, eggs, sugar, candied fruit peel, and raisins. Though some Italian housewives make these great golden-brown mushrooms of goodness for their families, the market appears to be cornered by such huge bakeries as Motta and Alemagna, who produce it by the ton for the Christmas season, in sizes from medium to Gargantuan.

Standing out from a bevy of other Milanese dishes is the *casoëula,* a glorious mixture of the spare parts of the pig—pork ears, chops, bacon, sausages—cooked in broth with cabbage, celery, carrots, onions, garlic, and plenty of pepper. It is reminiscent of the *potées* of Burgundy, and quite as heavy. We in America have our own ideas about stuffing a turkey, but the Milanese

have a savory filling that will hold its own against the fiercest competition. Their *tacchino ripieno* is stuffed with a mixture of the giblets of the bird, ham, sausage, apples, prunes, chestnuts, small onions, truffles, grated Parmesan cheese, pepper, nutmeg, eggs, and dry white wine, and the resultant aroma defies description. It seeps through every tissue of the turkey, and truly deserves the title ambrosian. Though you rarely encounter meatballs in Italy, despite their supposed affinity for spaghetti, you do find them in Milan under the name of *polpette,* and they are very presentable. Some overseas visitors exhibit less enthusiasm for another Milanese favorite, *busecca coi borletti,* a tripe soup with onions, fresh white beans, and a savory dosage of herbs, but you really should try it just once, and make your own decision.

The majority of these Lombardian dishes are simple to prepare, and may be achieved in an Anglo-Saxon kitchen with resounding success. The treasury of regional dishes at the end of this volume is especially well stocked with recipes from this food-conscious part of Italy.

The glittering cheese tray from this region deserves some elaboration, especially for those who may encounter it some day in a Milan restaurant. Bel Paese originated in the Lombard town of Melzo, and is now manufactured in other countries as well, including our own. The famous flat cylinder of soft, yellow-cream richness has imitators of course, but retains its immense following. One worthy rival comes from the picturesque hill town of Lodi, and is called Fior d'Alpe. This flower of the Alps is fragrant indeed. Gorgonzola, first perfected in a town of the same name near Milan, is produced in many places along the plain, and has several relatives abroad. The original piquant cheese, its creamy color punctuated by green spots caused by the introduction of *Penicillium glaucum,* is incomparable at its finest. Less well known is a white Gorgonzola, somewhat sweeter and not so piquant, for less robust palates. Stracchino is a melt-in-your-mouth, soft cheese in a square format that flourishes in autumn and winter. The most famous brand comes from the little town of Taleggio, and, when properly ripened, can hold its ground with the world's best. Sprinkled on countless Lombard dishes is the local version of Parmesan called Grana, which comes in a huge, husky, hundred-pound disk. Then there are the white cream cheeses, *mascherpone,* Robiolini, and Robiole, and a delicate square one called Crescenza. We've tried them all, with entire felicity.

If the cheese tray is imposing in Lombardy, the wine list, by contrast, is meager. There are no wines grown here to compare with the superlative Valpolicella of neighboring Verona, or the sturdy Barolo of next-door Piedmont. But some creditable vintages come from the slopes above Lake Garda, in this respect reminiscent of our own Finger Lakes in New York State. The wines of the Valtellina district, from the thickly planted slopes near Sondrio, will reward the explorer who seeks them out on a wine card. They are vivacious reds, pressed from the noble Nebbiolo grape, and they go under the names of Sassella, Inferno, and Grumello. From the vine-thick slopes south of Lake Iseo comes a limpid and subtle red wine called Franciacorta. It is pleasing, light, and fragrant. And there you have the highlights of Lombard wine.

A small fishing industry flourishes in the Lombardian lakes, and the trout from Garda and Como are highly prized by epicures. The backbone of the fishing industry here, however, is little lake sardines called *agoni*. Caught with light, closely woven nets in May and June, they are then salted and dried in the sun, and are ready for an eager public in September. The lake fishing boat with its square sails is as individual as a Chinese junk, and lends a pleasing atmosphere to villages along the shore.

The epicurean traveler in Lombardy has a wide and uneven field before him. The Italian Lakes have great beauty and good hotels. Milan has sumptuous restaurants, magnificent cooking. The flat plain is uninspiring, but it is dotted with cities rich in historical interest and noble architecture—Bergamo, Brescia, Pavia, Cremona, and Mantua—all with adequate hotels and food. Cover these and you have covered the best in Lombardy. Suppose we take the areas up in that order.

The Lake District

LOMBARDY CANNOT claim exclusive right to the cerulean lakes that thread through its upper hills. It shares Lake Maggiore with Piedmont, and comes out with the less beguiling portion. Lake Garda forms an eastern boundary with Veneto, and Lombardy can claim only half of its shoreline. Lake Lugano is mostly in Switzerland. But Lake Como, the loveliest of all, and the coquettish little Lake Iseo are both entirely, gloriously Lombardian.

For centuries, Lake Como has been Milan's summer retreat, its weekend country place, its refuge from the heat and turmoil of the metropolis. An *autostrada* now permits harried men of affairs to whisk out to Como in their cars in a half hour or less. What a relief is the calm majesty of the lake after the noisiest city in Italy! It loses much of its unruffled tranquility on a Sunday, however, when its roads are crowded with scooters, motorcycles, and baby Fiats from Milan, all of them with cutouts wide open and roaring.

The cathedral façade—Como

Lake Como, the Lacus Larius of the ancient Romans, owes its peculiar form, that of an inverted Y, to glacial disturbances. There are three branches of the lake—Como, Lecco, and Colico—and Bellagio, from its incomparable promontory, looks out upon them all. The lake has always been a chosen retreat of artists, musicians, and writers. Poets since Virgil, including a rapturous Longfellow, have written ecstatic verse about it. Travelers for generations have enjoyed its matchless color, its inviting hotels, its gentle Victorianism. Spring and autumn are lovely here, and the summers are mild, with every opportunity to bathe in the limpid water. Everything seems to contrive to make a visit to Lake Como one of the pleasantest experiences in Italy.

In mapping out a little conducted tour of the lake, we are choosing only the high spots and leaving the minor explorations to those who have plenty of time on their hands. Though a motor road runs around the entire Y-shaped shore, for once a car is not essential. A neat, unhurried little steamboat (or a private launch, if you wish) will take you to the major points of interest on the lake, and will leave you and your luggage almost on the doorstep of any number of good hotels. Our path begins at Como, on the southern end of the lake, and then follows the western, sun-exposed shore to its northern extremity and the lovely town of Gravedona.

Como

THIS CHARMING city provides a hint of the relaxation that lies ahead. Its sleepy waterfront is filled with rowboats and pleasure craft. Nothing is more restful than to sit here under an awning in a lakeside café, with a cool glass of vermouth, and to observe leisurely boatmen, dozing fishermen, and yawning policemen. In this choice location is the town's best hotel, the aging ALBERGO METROPOLE-SUISSE. Without being exceptional, it is quite good enough, and its open-air dining terrace is an inviting place to taste the salmon trout for which Lake Como is famous.

Both the Plinys, the Older and the Younger, were born in Como, and their sculptured likenesses occupy two niches in the façade of the marble Gothic cathedral. When you speak of volts, you are using a word derived from the name of another native of Como, the famed physicist Count Alessandro Volta. A temple along the shore has been dedicated to him. Visitors can see the skeletons of the frogs he used in his experiments, and his first electric battery.

Cernobbio and the Villa d'Este

There are several bits of fine architecture to view in Como, if you are not straining to visit the lake at once. Its fifteenth-century Gothic cathedral is an overpowering affair, its façade richly embellished with vertical ornament. Adjoining the cathedral is a handsome loggia, built in alternate layers of dark and light stone, and an immense bell tower looms in the heart of the city. On its outskirts is a very pure example of Lombard achitecture, the eleventh-century Basilica of Sant'Abbondio, which will prove a joy to architects and other enthusiasts for pure Romanesque.

Almost every country in central Europe has claimed Como at one time or another. The French, the Austrians, and the Spaniards all possessed this treasure before it became a part of the Italian Republic. Besides churches, there are many colorful streets and inviting shops to see in Como. But the average traveler has little time for sightseeing here, once he glimpses that crystal lake and its surrounding green and mauve hills. Adventure of the most pleasant sort lies ahead of him in a string of captivating villages, particularly in Cernobbio, Tremezzo, Cadenabbia, Menaggio, and Gravedona. The high spot, as far as hotels go, is reached only a few miles away in Cernobbio.

Cernobbio

WE'LL HAVE to trot out our very best superlatives in discussing the famous Villa d'Este, a short distance from Como. Probably the most princely, the most luxurious hotel in all Italy, it is the one which epicurean visitors are most likely to enjoy to the hilt. It has absolutely everything—a matchless site on the lake front, magnificent accommodations, fabulous food and service, and a rich historic past. Its prices are understandably high. The present immense villa was built on the site of an ancient convent, in 1568, by Tolomeo Gallio, the distinguished and well-heeled Cardinal of Como. It was then known as the Villa del Garrovo. Many were its vicissitudes and titled owners in the years following the Cardinal's death, but none could rival the title, or the eccentricity, of Caroline of Brunswick, Princess of Wales, who occupied it in 1815. The estranged wife of George IV of England, she created a sensation by her extravagance and her strange companions. She had a warm heart, however, and endeared herself to the villagers of Cernobbio by building them a road to Como. Another royal occupant was the Dowager Empress Sophia Federowna of Russia, who leased it in 1868. Seven years later it was acquired by the company which still operates it as the GRAND HOTEL VILLA D'ESTE. Its urbane and gracious proprietor, Signor Willy Dombré, was born here. It is natural to confuse this villa with the original Villa d'Este surrounded by fountains, in Tivoli, near Rome, but it is this marble palace on Lake Como which, as a hotel, has thrilled generations of travelers. We can't recommend it too highly. The culinary staff can prepare any Italian dish you care to ask for, and with consummate skill. Such standbys as *pizza, tagliatelle,* trout, *scampi,* or filet of sole, arrive at your table so beautifully prepared they seem unreal.

Signor Dombré has kindly contributed recipes of some of his most famous dishes to our treasury of regional cooking. Among them are *tagliatelle alla Ferdinando, risotto alla monzese, lasagne verdi all'emiliana,* and a particularly seductive *scampi alla certosina*. This dish can be achieved with our American shrimp, and we urge you to test it.

VILLA
d'ESTE
Cernobbio

Scampi alla Certosina
SHRIMP CARTHUSIAN

Brown slowly, in a combination of 2 tablespoons of oil and 1 tablespoon of butter, 1 tablespoon each of minced onion, celery, and carrot, seasoned with 1 crumbled bay leaf. Add 1 pound of peeled raw crayfish or jumbo shrimp. Sauté the shrimp for several minutes and flame them with 1/4 cup of warm brandy. Add the diced pulp of 2 large ripe tomatoes and 1/2 cup of stock and season with salt, cayenne pepper, and the juice of half a lemon. Simmer for 10 minutes more and remove the shrimp to a hot deep dish. Reduce the sauce over a high heat until it is fairly thick, press it through a sieve, and add 1/2 cup of heavy cream and 1 tablespoon of butter creamed with 1 teaspoon of flour. Reheat the sauce, blend it, and pour it over the shrimp just before serving.

But food is only a fraction of the Villa d'Este's immense attraction. The uncounted thousands of Anglo-Saxon travelers who, in the past, have stopped here can assure the thousands who will follow that they are in for the thrill of a lifetime.

Tremezzo

Ospedalletto

TEN MILES farther along the lake drive is Tremezzo, set in a mild, sheltered segment of the shore, rich in vegetation and ablaze with azaleas. This bountiful strip is called the Tremezzina. Tremezzo is famous for its Villa Carlotta, an eighteenth-century palace that is one of the outstanding curiosities of the Lake District. Built in 1747 by the Marchesa Giorgio Clerici, it took its present name from a Prussian princess who had the good fortune to offer it to her noble husband as a dowry. Now it belongs to the Italian state, and is open to the public for a modest fee. On a sunny Sunday, in springtime, the villa is packed with visitors. Its park, fragrant with jasmine and magnolias, is one of the most memorable in Europe, and its tropical gardens, a cadenza of color, make an everlasting impression. The Villa Carlotta contains numerous sumptuous rooms and many fine portraits, including some Gainsboroughs. Its most famous work of art, or at least the one that is reproduced from more angles on more postcards, is the marble copy of the statue of Cupid and Psyche by Canova. It is very sentimental indeed. You can also follow a bas-relief by the sculptor Thorwaldsen that covers the triumphal entry of Alexander into Babylon at considerable length. In fact, it goes on for 114 feet.

Albergo
Bazzoni
TREMEZZO

Tremezzo provides a memorable overnight stop, as it has a sunny, attractive, ultramodern hotel, the ALBERGO BAZZONI. This hotel towers pleasantly above the lake, each of its front rooms equipped with a bath and with a sheltered porch offering an incomparable view. Just across the lake is the green and white form of lovely Bellagio. The Bazzoni is now gay and new, but it saw tragic days toward the end of World War II when it was bombed and partially destroyed, with a serious loss of life. Its courageous owners have rebuilt on the same site.

Tremezzo has a neighbor, Cadenabbia, just north of the Villa Carlotta, and the two towns can almost be considered as one idyllic community. A ferryboat, capable of carrying several automobiles, connects Cadenabbia with Bellagio, across the lake. There are two commodious and comfortable summer hotels in Cadenabbia, the BELLEVUE and the BRITANNIA EXCELSIOR.

Menaggio

THIS CHEERFUL resort town, with villas and hotels crowding its shore, is extremely popular with summer vacationists, particularly the Anglo-Saxons. It can claim no great antiquity, and its hotels are modern, quiet, and comfortable. You have three to choose from—ALBERGO VICTORIA, GRAND HOTEL E MENAGGIO, and ALBERGO PRINCIPE, all reasonable in price and dedicated to good service and commendable cooking. They all enjoy a superlative view of Bellagio, with the purple and white silhouette of Mount Grigna towering behind it. The lake steamer stops here, of course, and it is an excellent departure point for a day's excursion. Menaggio is all resort and sunshine, all pleasure and relaxation, but it also has a gastronomic overtone, for fine lavender truffles are found in its immediate neighborhood.

Your northward road goes through a string of photogenic villages, one of which, Dongo, has a certain place in history. It was here that Mussolini and his mistress, Claretta Petacci, were arrested on April 27, 1945, as they sought to escape into Switzerland.

Gravedona

THERE ARE some delightful country churches on your northbound road before you reach Gravedona, the principal village of the upper lake. This charming town, unlike Menaggio, is no resort at all, and for that very reason may appeal to many travelers. For them it offers a perfectly adequate little hotel, the ALBERGO ITALIA.

Gravedona has two noble architectural monuments. The more obvious of them is the handsome Palazzo del Gallio at the northern end of the village, built in 1586 for Cardinal Tolomeo Gallio. This princely villa has four sturdy square towers and a double loggia facing the lake, and it imbues the spectator with a strong acquisitive urge. What an ideal place to retire—after striking oil! But somebody else got there first with the same idea—a wealthy German industrialist—and it is no longer open to visitors.

At the other end of the village, however, is the more perfect architectural gem, the lovely Romanesque Baptistry of Santa Maria del Tiglio. Almost square, it is built of dark stone relieved with strips of white, and its severe walls are brightened by three small curved apses. The whole edifice

Santa Maria del Tiglio—Gravedona   *The cloister—Abbazia di Piona*

is dominated by a sensitive Romanesque tower beginning as a square and ending as an octagon. It is a joy to visit this remote, semideserted example of restrained architecture, and we heartily recommend the pilgrimage.

Abazzia di Piona

IF YOU find yourself in Gravedona with plenty of time and the desire to discover a serene spot for a picnic lunch, we recommend an excursion to this secluded and forgotten abbey church. You must round the upper shore of the lake, turn southward to Olgiasca, and then follow a little side road through sentinel cypresses. Here, at the end of the road, is a remote, unpretentious abbey church, the Abbazia di Piona, built in 1255. Adjoining the church is a medieval cloister of great beauty. Its forty-one columns, capped by rather florid capitals, are still in perfect condition. Its reposeful setting is disturbed only by the clucking of a few wandering hens from a neighboring farmhouse. Otherwise the solitude is complete.

The promontory of Bellagio–Lake Como

Bellagio

A WRITER once described the form of Lake Como as that of a slightly berserk ballet dancer, with the village of Bellagio occupying the place where propriety calls for a fig leaf. One hesitates to carry this precarious figure of speech any farther, but there is no question about the charm of Bellagio's location, with a view of all three branches of the lake. It has been a fast favorite with English and American travelers for decades. Its climate is mild, the water is limpid, its atmosphere infinitely restful, and its hotels are more than adequate. One of them, in fact, the VILLA SERBELLONI, ranks among the best luxury hotels. It is reputed to occupy the site of Pliny the Younger's villa, and was owned by a succession of unusual people, including lake pirates,

Villa
Serbelloni
Bellagio

before it came into the hands of the Serbelloni family in 1788. They laid out the lovely park that now surrounds it. For decades it has been known as a honeymoon retreat for royalty.

There are other inviting hotels along Bellagio's lake front that merit your particular interest, among them the HOTEL DU LAC, the GRANDE BRETAGNE, and the HOTEL EXCELSIOR-SPLENDIDO, each with a vine-covered dining terrace overlooking the lake. We chose the last of the three and found it delightful. It is directed by a charming Englishwoman, who understands Anglo-Saxon tastes while maintaining an unusually fine Italian cuisine. We stayed here almost a week, tried all the Milanese specialties, and enjoyed it thoroughly. Here is one continental hotel where, if you wish, you may obtain a good, hearty, authentic English breakfast—eggs, bacon, marmalade, toast, and all. Or you can rejoice in a dish as un-English as a Lombard *polenta*. The management of the Excelsior-Splendido gave us this formula for it:

HOTEL
Splendido
Bellagio

Polenta Toc
CORN MEAL LOMBARDY

This recipe dates from the early days when countrymen were paid off with yellow flour for work done, rather than with money. Naturally, the people, having no other means, sought to improve the diet that this era thus compelled. They employed all their ingenuity to make *polenta* into a succulent dish.

For four or five people, use 1/2 pound of the finest grind of yellow corn meal (maize). Pour it gradually into 3 cups of rapidly boiling salted water and cook it, stirring often, for about 20 minutes. Now stir in, a little at a time, 1/4 pound of butter and 1 1/2 cups of grated Parmesan cheese, or the equivalent in finely sliced Provolone. Let each bit melt completely before adding more. The *polenta* should be soft. Add a little boiling water if it becomes stiff. Serve very hot.

The shops in Bellagio are tempting, the cafés are reposeful, the view across the lake is endlessly pleasant. It may not be the most original choice for a stay on Lake Como, for generations of vacation seekers have come here. But it is beautiful, hospitable, and quiet, enjoying the most privileged site on the entire lake. Bellagio shouldn't be missed!

The fortified castle–Sirmione

Lake Garda

LOMBARDY MUST share the shoreline of Lake Garda with two neighboring Italian regions, and its own part is limited to the western shore and a portion of the southern, which, fortunately, contains the theatrical citadel of Sirmione. This remarkable peninsular fishing port and the two sun-soaked resorts of Salò and Gardone Riviera make three highlights that visitors are certain to appreciate.

Sirmione

THIS TOWN, because of the fantastic medieval castle that stands sentry by its gates, recalls the Middle Ages more vividly than any other in the Italian Lake District. A fortified fishermen's village that is really an island, it perches at the end of an extremely narrow, sandy peninsula jutting some two miles northward into the lake. Its fortified Castello Scaligero, frowning from the water's edge, provides an operatic setting if we ever saw one. Dante is said to have stayed in this castle, abode of the lordly Scaligeri family of Verona. Now it is a museum and well worth your visit, especially if you like to peer from parapets.

Once beyond the fortified drawbridge you come to a comic-opera village, complete with stone-paved streets, overhead arches, donkey carts, and Teutonic tourists. Wealthy Roman families adopted Sirmione as a summer place long ago, and the Roman poet Catullus built his villa here. Its ruins are still to be seen, fragrant with jasmine and surrounded by olive and fig trees, with blue-green water on three sides. From early times, Sirmione has been celebrated for its beneficial mineral springs. If other references are needed, Sirmione was recently chosen by the Austrian Princess Ira Furstenberg and her titled husband as the setting for their honeymoon. We don't suppose they stayed in a hotel, but in their place we would have chosen the VILLA CORTINE, hidden high on a wooded promontory and surrounded by gardens. Once an imposing private villa, its rooms are few but luxurious. Guests dine in the garden under umbrella pines, and are regaled with some very fine Italian cooking and wines. They will also find a private bathing beach available.

In the lower town of Sirmione, now entirely dedicated to fair-weather visitors, is a bevy of half a dozen attractive hotels. Among those standing on the lakeside, we found the ALBERGO CATULLO agreeable and well run, with better-than-average cooking. You dine under pergolas looking out on the lake, with pleasant country maids to carry the platters and pull the corks.

For those who come to taste Sirmione's medicinal waters, or merely to spend a vacation, the GRANDE ALBERGO TERME is excellent. Its cordial director, Signor Wurmboeck, has sent us two interesting recipes, one for a regional soup that might prove to be a happy novelty in your own household. Here it is:

Villa Cortine
SIRMIONE

Albergo Catullo
SIRMIONE

Grande Albergo Terme
SIRMIONE

Zuppa alla Veneta
PURÉE OF VEGETABLE SOUP VENETO

This soup is a healthy vegetable purée with the added distinction of small fresh pasta and raw diced tomato added at the last minute. Minced carrots, onion, celery, and potato in roughly equal quantities are sautéed in oil until slightly browned. To these are added fresh white beans (or dried ones that have been soaked 6 hours in water), about twice the quantity of the combined vegetables mentioned above. These are all simmered in meat broth for 1 1/2 hours, or until the vegetables are completely cooked, the whole then put through a sieve, and seasoned to taste. A handful of cooked fresh vermicelli (or other small pasta) and skinned, seeded, and diced fresh tomatoes are added at the last moment to this purée. Reheat the soup and serve with grated Parmesan cheese.

The lakeside town of Salò

Salò

BEAUTIFULLY SITUATED in a sheltered cove at the lower western corner of Lake Garda, Salò is an iridescent spot reflected in the turquoise blue water. Though its name has a somewhat unfortunate sound in French, to other nationalities it means a bright and beckoning town with several distinctions. For one thing, it is the birthplace of Gaspare Bertolotti, who is credited with being the first violinmaker. Appropriately enough, you will find a Via dei Violini. The massive Church of Santa Maria Annunziata, with a fine Renaissance porch and a tall primitive campanile, gives the town further prestige. Finally, Salò has the dubious honor of being the ephemeral capital of Benito Mussolini's last faltering government, which collapsed in April, 1945. The Duce then lived in the Villa Feltrinelli under the watchful eyes of the Nazis.

The hotels in Salò are somewhat secondary, but there is a very pleasant one as you approach the neighboring village of Barbarano. It is called the SPIAGGIA D'ORO, and has a fine setting at the water's edge with, as you may have guessed, a golden beach!

Gardone Riviera

THIS IS probably the most sumptuous resort on Lake Garda, cheerful, urbane, and distinguished architecturally. The center of a verdant strip with numerous beaches, it is appropriately called the Riviera. This gentle area ends abruptly a few miles farther north at Gargnano, where the cliffs become precipitous, forcing the coastal road to burrow through tunnels.

Gardone's hotels are excellent and restful, particularly the luxurious GRAND HOTEL, whose lofty, semi-Venetian façade looks out on the lake. It is a well-appointed hostelry with a smart summer clientele, alert service, and commendable cuisine. The GRAND HOTEL FASANO and the SAVOY PALACE HOTEL, both facing the lake, are charming summer hotels with good Lombardy cooking.

The great curiosity of the neighborhood lies on the hilly outskirts of Gardone—the Villa Vittoriale degli Italiani. In this large estate, which was presented to him as a symbol of his nation's homage, the great poet Gabriele d'Annunzio resided until his death in 1938. His tomb is here, and so is the airplane which he flew, emblazoned with the Lion of Saint Mark. D'Annunzio transformed the villa into a museum, and it is now open to the public, for a small fee. It provides an extraordinary experience, rich with the memorabilia of a phenomenal personality.

Milan

THE SPRAWLING, vibrant city of Milan is not one of the most restful places in Italy, nor one of the most beautiful. Urbanism and the war have claimed many of its historic old quarters, and the vivid tempo of the city is such that a casual sightseer, guidebook in hand, becomes a rather harried individual. But in spite of the noise and confusion, he is richly rewarded. Fundamentally, Milan is a city of superlatives. It is the busiest in Italy, and the most prosperous. The great banks, business firms, and publishing houses are concentrated here. Italy's greatest daily newspaper, *Corriere della Sera,* is published in Milan, and here, too, is the country's first television station.

There is nothing in Italy to compare with Milan's astonishing cathedral, the most imposing Gothic edifice south of France, and exceeded in acreage only by Saint Peter's and the cathedral in Seville. Forty thousand people are needed to fill it completely. Built of white marble, it was probably begun in 1386, and grew into a structure of unprecedented splendor and ornateness, in the flamboyant Gothic style. Critics are inclined to be severe about its façade, finished in Napoleon's time, but nobody can deny the solemn magnificence of its dimly lit interior. These grandiose vaults, disappearing in the upper darkness, provide a prodigious experience, and the most casual spectator is properly awed. The three enormous windows in the apse, largest of their kind in the world, only add to the overwhelming effect.

A trip to the marble roof of the cathedral is an adventure not to be missed. An elevator takes you up part way for a slight fee, but there are many steps to be climbed before you reach the roof and wander around in a forest of Gothic spires. The very ambitious may climb higher in the central tower, almost to the base of the Madonnina, the immense gilded copper statue of the Virgin, which is regarded as the symbol of the city. On a

The façade of the cathedral—Milan

clear day, the industrious cathedral climber is rewarded by an exciting vista of the distant Alps. He is also rewarded with a soft drink, if he wants one, for a refreshment stand has been installed on the roof, and it is possible to slake one's thirst with capitalistic, non-Communist Coca Cola.

Visitors in Milan seem to gravitate first of all to the cathedral square, and usually buy a bag of corn to feed the pigeons. The passing gourmet is confronted by a strong temptation here. Just why doesn't someone think of eating these fat, greedy, pampered, aggressive pigeons, hand-fed and over-stuffed by travelers, from cornucopias of the very best grain? A profane thought, perhaps, but a tempting one.

Unfortunately, the limited scope of this book does not permit it to become a detailed guide of the great cities of Italy. Therefore, we must be content with listing a few of the treasures in Milan which no informed visitor should miss. The cathedral comes first, of course, but the Teatro alla Scala, the greatest of the world's opera houses, offers its own unique thrill. The musical glory of Milan, "La Scala" was built in 1778. Badly damaged in World War II, it was quickly restored and again open to opera lovers in 1946. Once more the careers of operatic stars are made or broken here in an evening's performance. It is an unforgettable experience to occupy one of the boxes in the many-tiered horseshoe of La Scala, glittering with white and gold and with red plush, while overhead dangles one of the world's most famous crystal chandeliers. The topmost shrine of operatic music in Italy offers perhaps the topmost privilege for travelers to Milan.

The most famous fresco in the world is in Milan. Leonardo da Vinci finished his great painting of "The Last Supper" five years after Columbus discovered America. It is found in the refectory of the convent adjoining the church of Santa Maria delle Grazie, and seems to have an almost hypnotic effect upon those who come to view it. And this in spite of the fact that it is now in a rather pitiful state because of the dampness of the wall upon which it is painted. Constant restoration keeps it intact.

Still in the vein of superlatives, you will want to see the Castello Sforzesco, the immense stronghold of one of the most powerful of medieval families. This castle of the Sforzes, dukes of Milan, is built round an enormous court-yard and surrounded by a moat. Now it serves the peaceful purpose of a many-sided museum, with vast halls devoted to sculpture and painting, and rooms given over to the famous Bertorelli collection of prints.

Milan's finest museum, however, is the Brera Gallery, on the street of the same name. It contains one of the greatest collections of Italian paintings, comparable to the best in Florence and Venice. The Pinacoteca di Brera possesses incomparable treasures, among them the "Pietà" by Bellini, the "Christ" of Mantegna, and, above all, the "Marriage of the Virgin," the famous "Lo Spozalizio" by Raphael. For those who take particular joy in

Tower of the Sforzesco castle—Milan

Italian art, books, and sculpture, there are two other superb museums, the Biblioteca Ambrosiana and the Museo Poldi-Pezzoli.

Enthusiasts of the Lombard Romanesque will rejoice in the Basilica of Sant'Ambrogio, an illustrious example dating from the eleventh century. The church is preceded by an atrium of simple arches. Its supreme work of art is the *paliotto,* or master altar, enlivened with enamels, a pure gem of Carolingian art. There is also a noble pulpit and *baldacchino.* This is possibly the purest example of early architecture in Milan, even if it fails to rival the splendor of the Duomo.

The use of superlatives can go on and on. Milan has the largest covered arcade in the world. The Galleria Vittorio Emanuele, close to the cathedral, is the pedestrian crossroads of Milan, and the meeting place of its citizens, from dawn until far into the night. Countless visitors come to this intense metropolis of one million, two hundred thousand inhabitants for another reason—its annual spring Trade Fair, also the largest in Italy. Milan is the center of the largest railroad net in the country and the most important silk market in Europe. And finally, though it has taken a long time to lead up to this, it has some of the best hotels and restaurants. Everything considered, it would seem that the businessman, the opera enthusiast, the art lover, and, we are glad to add, the gourmet, get the best break in Milan, *provided* they make sure about obtaining reservations at one of the city's modern hotels.

This word of warning is born of sad experience. We once arrived in the city blissfully unaware of the shortage of rooms, and finally ended up in Como for the night, thirty miles away! Milan provides a big-city choice of hotels, of course. Ultramodern skyscraper hostelries with built-in garages have mushroomed in the outlying Piazza della Repubblica since the war. Notable among them are the PRINCIPE E SAVOIA and the PALACE—both in the top price range. Nearer the heart of the city, the long-established CONTINENTALE, on the Via Manzoni, has a fine reputation. Near the cathedral is the newly built and very comfortable CAVALIERI, a firm favorite with Anglo-American visitors. Our own favorite is the ALBERGO MANIN, on the street of that name. It is quiet and pleasant, partly on account of its sylvan location opposite the park and zoo. This hotel is very popular, and a reservation is necessary.

Superlatives must be applied once more to the famous restaurants of Milan. On any basis—appointments, cuisine, wine, service—they are among the finest in Europe. The great Milanese dishes can be found in all of them, for they seem to take particular pride in local specialties. Milan is choked with good restaurants, and we are doing those omitted an injustice by citing only a handful. But these few should be sufficient for the passing gourmet:

RISTORANTE SAVINI—Galleria Vittorio Emanuele

Here is the patriarch of Milanese restaurants, and the ruling aristocrat as well. We were about to call it the "Café de Paris of Italy," but alas, the real Café de Paris, after a century at the top of Parisian gastronomy, closed its doors in 1955, and so the comparison falls flat. Savini has occupied its privileged spot under the glass roof of Milan's famous *galleria* for more than half a century, and is still strongly reminiscent of the *belle époque* of the 1890's. Everything is impeccable—the setting, the service, and the food, which, pleasantly enough, features the local specialties and not "international" dishes alone. If you wish to savor *risotto, minestrone, osso buco in gremolada,* or *piccata di vitello* in the company of Milan's best-dressed women and most charming citizens, this formal, expensive, *mondain* restaurant is the answer. And you never have to fear a rainstorm on its sheltered summer terrace.

Ristorante **SAVINI** Milan

Signor Angelo Pozzi, the courteous director of the Ristorante Savini, gave us the recipes of many of his famed Milanese specialties. All of them seem practical in the kitchen of an experienced cook, including this one called

I Messicani alla Milanese
VEAL ROLLS MILAN

A pound of small, very thin slices from the leg of veal is required. The slices are flattened as thin as possible by pounding them with a wooden mallet, and then trimmed to equal size. Put the scraps through the meat grinder with a good quantity of parsley and 1 or 2 cloves of garlic, and moisten this mixture with white wine. Season with salt, pepper, and nutmeg, and spread a little of the mixture on each slice of veal. Roll up each veal slice and tie it with thread. Three at a time, the rolls are threaded onto skewers, with a leaf of sage and a piece of bacon between each roll. Dip the skewered rolls lightly in flour and cook them slowly in hot butter in a skillet until browned on all sides.

RESTAURANT BARCA D'ORO—Via Borgospesso 18

We think that discriminating travelers from across the seas will take a particular shine to the Golden Bark, a plush and pleasant place with the red-carpet treatment evident in every one of its low-ceilinged rooms. The clientele is cosmopolitan and civilized, generously reinforced with pipe-smoking industrialists in British tweeds. The Golden Bark is located on a little side street parallel to the populous Via Manzoni, and is not hard to find. It would be a perfectly wonderful place to give a small dinner party. Its quiet *ambiance,* low-pitched voices, and discreet service are reminiscent of your favorite restaurant in London or New York. The menu, written in both Italian and French, is a joy to behold. There are daily regional specialties, plus a generous selection of dishes from *la cuisine classique.* Our own choice was a pilaff with

Barca d'Oro MILAN

sole, mushrooms and curry, followed by kidneys flamed in brandy and served from a handsome silvery saucepan. For wines, we drank a modest Orvieto and a soul-warming Valpolicella. The occasion couldn't have been more agreeable, and *il conto,* for all the amplitude of our long-lingering luncheon, was eminently reasonable.

RISTORANTE GIANNINO—Via A. Sciesa 8

Ristorante
Giannino
MILAN

Giannino is probably the most famous restaurant in Milan, and certainly the one that gives the customer the most visual pleasure. It possesses more than a touch of P. T. Barnum, providing a gastronomical side show as well as a top-notch dining place. The first thing you see upon entering under bright neon lights is a plump lady seated at a table before what appears to be a large, olive-green tablecloth. On closer inspection, it becomes clear that she is making a vast sheet of *lasagne verdi* and rolling it thinner and thinner on her table. As you progress down the corridor of culinary landscapes, you pass luxuriant displays of fruit, cheese, pastry and pasta, recumbent fish on ice, and trout mulling meditatively about in their fresh-water tank. There are beautiful cuts of beef to whet your appetite before you arrive at the shining summit of Giannino's splendor, the kitchen. It is immaculate and beautiful, glass-enclosed on four sides, so that the cooks, many of whom are women, are just as exposed as the lake trout. You can gaze just as long and enviously as you like at these skillful technicians; no headwaiter will hover at your elbow.

The restaurant, which began as a very simple *trattoria* over fifty years ago, is now a large, busy establishment that rambles around two courtyards. Its smiling, deferential owner, Signor Cesare Bindi, is the son of the founder; therefore it is not surprising that the service runs like clockwork. His sharp eye keeps a discreet watch on everything. The maîtres d'hôtel are trilingual and genial, and the menu includes almost all the accepted masterpieces of Italian cooking. We decided upon a simple dinner, beginning with a *risotto* rich in baby shrimp followed by a lordly *osso buco alla milanese,* one of Giannino's particular prides. It was rich, meaty, and aromatic, and infinitely satisfying. A bit of cheese, a *macedonia di frutta,* which looked like a bouquet of flowers, a worthy bottle of Bardolino, coffee, and Strega, and complete happiness was ours.

Don't be misled by Giannino's apparent salesmanship. This restaurant is a *must* if you stop in Milan!

Signor Bindi presented us with six distinguished recipes from his sparkling kitchen. Here is one of them, a particularly delicious *risotto.*

Risotto alla Certosina
SHRIMP RISOTTO CARTHUSIAN

Melt 2 tablespoons of butter with 2 tablespoons of olive oil, and in this cook briefly 1 cut clove of garlic and 2 sage leaves. Add 1 cup of raw rice and cook, stirring, until the rice is golden. Add 1/2 cup of white wine, and when this is absorbed, add 1 cup of hot chicken stock. Cover and cook the rice slowly for 20 minutes. Remove the garlic and the sage leaves, add a pinch of marjoram, 1 cup of cooked shrimp, and 2 cups of additional hot stock. Stir once with a fork, cover, and cook until the *risotto* is tender. Just before serving, stir in some bits of butter and powdered Parmesan cheese. Garnish the *risotto* with shelled cooked mussels and shrimp.

RISTORANTE ALDO—Via della Maddalena 1

Ristorante
ALDO
Milan

Maybe it is the bellboy attired in a gold-buttoned royal-purple uniform, perhaps the headwaiter in a *café crème* dinner jacket, or the immense twenty-pronged chandelier—whatever it is, one senses a certain chic upon entering this establishment. The room is a large rectangle dominated by a huge bas-relief of frolicking and unadorned maidens, youths, and horses. It is rather difficult to concentrate on the food, if you happen to be facing this playful panorama, and that is too bad. For Aldo is supposed to have the best sea food in Milan, rushed daily from the Adriatic, and offering a glittering choice of *scampi,* sole, red mullet, and lobster, not to mention a *zuppa di pesce* and a *grande misto mare Aldo* that defy description. But before embarking on the fish, we urge you to try another specialty called *gioielli Aldo,* as subtle and delicate a dish as we encountered in all our Italian travels. *Gioielli* means jewels, and these particular gems are baby ravioli, golden yellow, light, and wonderfully tender, touched up with butter and powdered Parmesan, and mixed with green peas—a symphony of yellow and green that just can't be forgotten, especially if it is accompanied by a cool, seductive Soave.

Aldo is located near the modern Hotel Cavalieri, where so many Anglo-Saxon visitors stay, and has won the acclaim of many of them. But the French have a fondness for Aldo too, always a good sign. The last time we were there, a full third of the tables were occupied by Frenchmen. Few Parisian restaurants could have made them look more contented.

RISTORANTE BIFFI—Galleria Vittorio Emanuele

Ristorante
Biffi
MILAN

The crossroads of Milan, at least as far as foot passengers are concerned, is found in the immense glass-roofed gallery adjoining the cathedral. Businessmen, politicians, musicians from the Scala, tourists, and clerics all stroll in an endless procession. There is no better point from which to view the passing throng than the terrace of the house of Biffi, a worldly complex that includes a café terrace, interior bar, pastry shop, *pizzeria,* and restaurant. The last is very well appointed, with rose-pink napery and shimmering crystal. Less awe-inspiring than Savini, which is just across the way, Biffi has also been established for decades, and can boast some top-ranking specialties. Among them are *cannelloni, lasagne verdi,* and a delectable turkey preparation called *delizie di tacchino pastorella.* For gregarious diners who enjoy a passing show with their repast, Biffi is a byword.

RISTORANTE DA MASSIMO—Via Borgonuovo 7

Ristorante
Da Massimo
MILAN

The five restaurants listed above all belong to the aristocracy of Milan's dining places. The choice among the lesser places is enormous, but also encouraging. As in Rome, it is really difficult to find a poor meal in Milan. There are dozens of everyday restaurants where the prices are modest and the food excellent. One of the most congenial is just around the corner from the American Express Company, inevitable focus for our traveling compatriots. Massimo is a civilized place without any particular atmosphere, but you can talk in a normal tone of voice and be heard, a phenomenon not always found in this buzzing metropolis. Here the reverberation of the city subsides to a murmur, particularly in the shaded summer garden, and we happily recommend it as a cheerful place for a quiet and inexpensive luncheon. The menu is more than adequate, the cooking is good, the waiters chatter quite a lot, and the customers are well-dressed, smiling people, mostly in the junior-executive bracket.

And what of the hurried visitor who hasn't time for a long-drawn-out lunch in Milano? The answer can be found no farther than fifty yards from the cathedral. There, under the arcades, is MOTTA of Milan, one of the greatest Italian confectioners, with one of his biggest, gaudiest, most seductive food shops. Every kind of snack—pastry, *pizza,* sandwiches—is available with coffee, tea, or chocolate to accompany it and a flourish of fruit-studded ice cream to back it up. Or if you're in the mood for a toasted ham sandwich touched up with capers, or sliced artichokes in oil, or yellow peppers in a piquant sauce, all are here. There couldn't be a handier, noisier, or more exciting place for a buffet lunch, and the charges are agreeably low.

Bergamo

THE TRANSITION between mountain and plain takes place in the historic city of Bergamo, some thirty miles northeast of Milan. You can whiz there in no time on the sign-infested *autostrada*. Bergamo is really two towns, one an ancient hilltop citadel, the other a spacious, modern city in the plain, with cool arcades, inviting cafés and theaters. The medieval upper town will hold the greater fascination for visitors, while the lower town will take good care of their creature comfort.

Bergamo Alta, one of the most gratifying of Italian hill towns, must on no account be missed. It dates from Etruscan times, and its forbidding stone walls and bastions are nearly intact. You reach it either by a winding motor road or a funicular that lands you in the citadel itself, whence a warren of little streets leads to the Piazza Vecchia, the historic heart of the city. This is a most dramatic spot, dominated by a massive clock tower, and enriched by noble Palladian and Gothic buildings, not to mention an operatic covered stairway, and, in the center, a gay fountain guarded by marble lions clutching chains in their teeth.

Wandering through the Gothic loggia of the Palazzo della Ragione, you

A glimpse of the Colleoni Chapel

Piazza Vecchia—Bergamo

come upon Bergamo's most celebrated treasure, the Capella Colleoni. This ornate chapel was designed in 1475 by Amadeo and built as a final resting place for Bartolomeo Colleoni, the last of the famous *condottieri,* or mercenary generals, who served as the supreme military chieftain of the Venetian Republic. His proud statue in the Campo Santi Giovanni e Paolo in Venice is still unrivaled among works of equestrian sculpture. Colleoni, who was born near Bergamo, was determined that his bones should rest there despite the hesitation of the church. To make certain, he commissioned Amadeo, architect of the famous Certosa di Pavia, to build this Renaissance chapel for him and his daughter. Though there could hardly be a "busier" façade than this one, squirming as it is with multicolored marble detail, the interior is restful. The warrior's tomb has a certain high-flown majesty, but it lacks the tender Renaissance beauty of the sarcophagus that Amadeo designed for daughter Medea.

Adjoining the chapel is the Basilica of Santa Maria Maggiore, adorned with a fine Lombard portal and Tiepolo paintings. It, too, deserves a passing visit. The cathedral nearby is disappointing, except for the Tiepolos. The Piazza Vecchia is a good place to pause for refreshment after absorbing so much architecture. There are several pleasant little cafés and one restaurant, called BIFFI, where you can have a respectable luncheon under an awning.

Bergamo's artistic charms are not limited to architecture alone. It is also a stronghold of Italian painting. Its remarkable Carrara Academy will reward visitors with masterpieces by many of the greatest artists, Tiepolo, Bellini, Mantegna, Carpaccio, Raphael, and Perugino among them. Situated below the bastions of the citadel, the Academy is a little difficult to find. But a rich recompense comes to picture-conscious travelers who seek it out.

Bergamo also has its place in the world of music. One of its native sons was the composer dear to the hearts of all Italians, Gaetano Donizetti. In the lower town is an imposing theater dedicated to him. Architects will be interested in the spacious urban development here, mostly dating from 1924, and very pleasant to behold.

Bergamo is famous for one gastronomic specialty, *polenta e öséi,* a round, golden-orange mound of cooked corn meal crowned with skewers of tiny birds interlaced with leaves of sage. During the hunting season, the birds, which are incredibly numerous in the hills, are snared by the thousands in nets. At that moment *polenta e öséi* is a staple in every Bergamese household. It didn't take the pastry shops long to imitate this famous dish with a playful cake covered with almond paste and crowned with little chocolate birds. There is no seasonal limit on these gay little cakes, and the *pasticcerie* are filled with them.

Bergamo also possesses an exceptionally good hotel, the long-established HOTEL MODERNO. Despite its name, it has an old-fashioned Edwardian char-

The cathedral square—Brescia

acter, and is well managed. In summer, its broad terrace provides a charming place to dine under the trees, and its high-ceilinged dining hall is cheerful in colder weather. The Moderno produced some of the best hotel food we encountered in our Italian travels. The hors-d'oeuvre call for particular praise. Rarely will you find as artistic and satisfying an array of *antipasti* as that which is wheeled up to your table here. The ravioli seemed on a par with the best in Milan. The *lista del giorno* glittered with Lombardian specialties, among them those little birds on beds of corn meal. We tried them with a noble Valpolicella, and were most content, ending up the festivities with an irresistible *cassata alla siciliana,* a frozen dessert without a peer.

HOTEL
Moderno
Bergamo

We have to admit that the location of the Moderno, near a busy traffic intersection, is a trifle noisy. But its epicurean joys outweigh the murmur of passing vans.

Brescia

ANOTHER ARCHITECTURAL adventure lies in the heart of the ancient city of Brescia, a busy metropolis that rises out of the plain between Bergamo and Lake Garda, alternately quite modern and steeped in antiquity. It is here that the most famous swords in the world were once forged, and there is still something bellicose about many of its medieval buildings. But there are buoyant, lighthearted examples of the Renaissance too, especially the awe-inspiring cathedral, whose towering dome is the third highest in Italy. Adjoining it is an extraordinary little Romanesque companion, the circular Duomo Vecchio, dating from the ninth century. This is a genuine curiosity, as is the Palazzo della Loggia, which was begun in the familiar year of 1492. Its walls are decorated by Sansovino, and it is the pride of Brescia.

HOTEL
Vittoria
Brescia

Many people motor around the edge of Brescia without stopping, their sights set resolutely on Milan or Venice. This is a pity, because this active, personable city has much to offer the traveler, including a good place to partake of nourishment. A satisfying luncheon awaits you at the HOTEL VITTORIA, at Via Dieci Giornate 20, near the cathedral. Among its specialties are the popular *polenta e öséi,* or, if you like baby kid, *capretto alla bresciana.* For the tender hearted, a fragrant *bollito misto* is also available. The Vittoria is pleasant for an overnight stop as well.

Cremona

SOME THIRTY miles south of Brescia, Cremona is best known as the home of the world's greatest violinmakers. Amati (1520–1570), Stradivarius (1644–

The Cathedral of Cremona   *Cathedral porch—Cremona*

1737), and Guarnieri (born 1683), all were natives of Cremona. Their technical perfection has never been surpassed. Enthusiasts for the art of the luthier will find an engrossing exhibition in the Museo Civico in which all three masters are represented. Even today, capable artisans continue to fashion violins in the old tradition, although they can't claim to rival their illustrious predecessors. The creator of the opera, Claudio Monteverdi, also lived in Cremona.

Just at present, however, music seems to be overshadowed by architecture in Cremona. The heart of the old town, dominated by a thirteenth-century Lombard-Gothic cathedral with the highest belfry in Italy, is breathtaking. It rises 364 feet above the pavement. The façade of the cathedral, pierced with a superb rose window, may not be in the purest Lombard tradition, but it is awe-inspiring just the same. To complete the ensemble is a graceful octagonal baptistry.

Parsley

Many travelers fail to visit Cremona, and if they have no particular affinity for violins or Lombard cathedrals, this is just as well. The epicurean rewards in its modest hotels and restaurants are rather meager. The town has a specialty that you might acquire for a picnic lunch, a highly-spiced pork sausage called *cotechini alla vaniglia*.

Lombardy landscape

Pavia

ONCE THE capital of Lombardy and an ancient university town, Pavia suffered cruelly during the recent war. Its famous covered bridge, dating from 1353, was destroyed, but has now been rebuilt. Its grandiose brick cathedral, where Bramante and Leonardo da Vinci worked, has been patched up. Though there are some interesting churches to visit here, there is nothing to compare with the famous Certosa di Pavia, six miles north on the road to Milan. This is one of the two greatest Carthusian monasteries, the other being the Grande-Chartreuse near Grenoble, in France. It is an astonishing building, with a façade so richly bedecked with Renaissance detail that it becomes cloying to most architectural palates. No wedding cake could be richer. The interior is simpler and more majestic, and most travelers fully enjoy the conducted tour, which takes well over an hour. They also enjoy a flavorful liqueur called Gra-Car, distilled and sold on the premises by the venerable monks. In case you are footsore and hungry after touring the Certosa, there is a more than adequate restaurant, called the CASA DEL TURISTA, not far away.

Pavia is famous everywhere for one dish, *zuppa alla pavese,* a nourishing meal in itself and a standby in Italian households. The soup is a flavorful combination of broth, egg, and pieces of bread fried in butter, all sprinkled with grated cheese and served in a crockery bowl. Its recipe will be found among the Lombardian treasures of cookery at the end of this volume.

Other specialties to remember are *torta paradiso,* a heavenly pastry, and more earthy dishes such as *zuppa di rane* (frog soup) and *lasagne* with cod. This region is rice-growing country, so it is not surprising that a noble rice dish has been perfected in Pavia. It is called *risotto alla certosina,* the recipe for which appeared a few pages back. There are some good local wines from

102

Busy corner in Mantua   *Market day in Mantua*

the neighboring slopes south of Pavia. One of them is Barbacarlo and the other is called, a bit ominously, Sangue di Giuda, or Blood of Judas.

These wines and many of the local specialties may be encountered in Pavia at the RISTORANTE BIXIO, at Strada Nuovo 81. Among its other temptations are *ossi buchi*, frogs' legs, and *agnolotti*.

Mantua

LAST OF this list of notable towns of Lombardy, Mantua, or Mantova, rises majestically out of the plain, surrounded by three lakes formed by the river Mincio. This is the land of Virgil, most famous of Latin poets, who was born in nearby Pietole about 70 B. C. Though no sign of Virgil remains, Mantua still sparkles with the splendor of the Gonzaga family, whose court was one of the most famous of the Renaissance. A complex of enormous buildings remains as a reminder of Mantua's great day. The overwhelming Ducal Palace, with all its ramifications, contains more than four hundred and fifty rooms, twelve courtyards, and a church. The room occupied by Napoleon for a night, in 1797, is still piously preserved, but there is another room that will enrich your memory forever, the exquisite Camera degli Sposi, or bridal chamber, whose frescoes kept that master draftsman, Mantegna, at work for five years. Few rooms in Italy are as beautiful. Scattered about

103

the palace are magnificent halls with vaulted ceilings decorated by the masters of the day, among them Giulio Romano. And there are priceless canvases by Rubens, El Greco, and Clouet, among others. Finally, there is an unforgettable curiosity—the Appartamento dei Nani, an apartment that housed the court dwarfs. All of its furniture and dimensions are in miniature scale. Adjoining the Ducal Palace and standing guard over it, is the immense, somber brick fortress known as La Reggia.

At the southern extremity of the town, near the race track, is the vast summer home of the Gonzagas, the Palazzo del Te, designed by Giulio Romano and embellished by some of his more sybaritic frescoes. It is startling to escape for a moment from everyday reality and to confront his bacchanalian rendition of the amours of Psyche. You should make the detour to see this palace if you seek an insight into medieval revelry.

The heart of Mantua is the Piazza delle Erbe, particularly animated on market day. The overpowering brick church of Sant'Andrea looms over a turbulent hodgepodge of pushcarts sheltered by battered canvas umbrellas. The streets are thronged, the clatter incessant. If you want to buy a goose, a guinea fowl, or some green-bean fritters, here is the place to do it. These are among the gastronomic specialties of Mantua.

Al
Garibaldini
Mantua

Other famous Mantuan dishes are *stufato alla mantovana, risotto con le salamelle,* and *agnolotti,* and the best place to sample them is a restaurant nearby called AL GARIBALDINI, at Via S. Longino 7. Here we encountered a refreshing menu that included *agnolotti,* the local interpretation of ravioli, chicken *cacciatora,* and a fine bottle of Lambrusco. Mantua is also a good place for an overnight stop. The ever-dependable JOLLY HOTEL, one of a chain less frequently met in these northern regions than in the south, offers you most comfortable and clean accommodations with bath, and a good dinner too. It is located at Via. P.F. Calvi 30.

Near Ortisei

Trentino-Alto Adige

Chapter 5

TRENTINO-
ALTO ADIGE

I T IS difficult to avoid the skyrocketing prose of a travel pamphleteer in writing of this theatrically beautiful part of Italy. Dominated by the magnificent Dolomites, the region was once the lower Austrian Tyrol. Everything about it—the awe-inspiring scenery, the opportunities for fun and travel, the high quality of the hotels and the cooking, the picturesque architecture, and the folklore—all tempt one to employ a flowery Thomas Cook vocabulary.

What the Dolomites really need is a poet, however, not a pamphleteer. These great jagged rocks leave the average beholder breathless, bereft of adequate words. Sometimes they rise up ghostlike out of the mist, immense iridescent fangs bathed in lavender light. As the day wears on, the colors change, alternately mauve and cinnamon brown, with overtones varying from pink to ocher. Millions of years of erosion have created these grotesque denticulated shapes—spires, caravans, camels' humps—which take on an indescribable violet-red at sunset.

Totally unlike the Swiss Alps in silhouette, the Dolomites resemble them in one noteworthy respect: both offer exciting inducements to the traveler, the sportsman, and, praise be, the visiting gourmet. The hotel situation is probably the best in northern Italy, and this is no shallow praise. It would take a column or two to list all of the mountain towns in this region that have comfortable small hotels for skiers and summer people alike, and with palatable cooking, too.

The motorist, the cyclist, and the gay blade on a Vespa scooter find wonderfully fine roads to take them over the mountain passes. And if they wish to roost overnight amidst the crags, there are adequate summer hotels, even in these lofty ravines. The Dolomites, in short, offer extravagant inducements, but on an economical plane. Incidentally, they were named, oddly

enough, for a Frenchman, who spent a lifetime studying them. His name was Déodat
Guy Silvain Tancrède Gratet de Dolomieu.

It seems necessary to endure a bit of
geographical briefing in order to obtain a
clear picture of the regions discussed in this
chapter and the two that follow it. The far
northeastern corner of Italy is lumped into
one area going under the name of Venetia.
It contains strange geographical bedfellows
—the lagoons of Venice, the plains of Padua,
and the jagged Dolomites. Like Gaul, in
that first famous sentence of Caesar, it is
divided into three parts. One carries the
somewhat cumbersome title of Trentino-Alto
Adige, and extends below the Austrian border. The middle part is Veneto, dominated
by Venice, the queen of the Adriatic, and
further brightened by such famous cities
as Verona and Vicenza. The third, most

eastern, part is Friuli-Venezia Giulia, and adjoins both Austria and Yugoslavia. Trieste, undisputably Italian since 1954, is its capital.

The extent to which Italy's frontiers have changed during the past two
wars is demonstrated by two of these outer regions. The Italian flag flies
over Trentino-Alto Adige as a result of the Treaty of Versailles, which awarded
this Tyrolean strip of Austria to her southern adversary in 1919. Fruili-Venezia
Giulia, on the other hand, is cramped for elbow room on its eastern frontier
because of territorial concessions made to Yugoslavia after World War II.

You have the exhilarating feeling of visiting two countries for the price
of one when you arrive in the Trentino-Alto Adige region. The language is
usually German. The architecture is Tyrolean. So is the landscape and, to
a certain extent, the food. But you are still in Italy. The region is divided
into two provinces, Trento the capital of one, Bolzano of the other.

An autonomous government prevails in this region, as it does in the
Valle d'Aosta. It has contributed greatly to a peaceful transition and good
relations between the Italians and their newly acquired populations. There
have been flare-ups, of course, but these hard-working, cheerful people are
content and prosperous under the liberal Italian Republic.

They have reason to be content, for the climate is friendly and the land
is generous with a bounty of the good things of life. For over a thousand
years, this has been a fruit-growing country. Moist, fertile valleys and hillsides make it a land of plenty, bulging with vineyards, orchards, and vege-

Castel del Monte

table patches. We drove for miles through verdant areas where fields were planted with a kind of succotash of corn and beans in alternate rows. Strips of blossoming potato plants ran next to yellow bands of ripe grain, with apple, pear, apricot, and cherry trees between them. One field seemed to produce half a dozen crops at once. The vineyards offered another evidence of concentrated farming. The vines, blue-green with early summer spray, were trained on pergolas, but the ground beneath wasn't idle. It was tapestried with potatoes, peas, corn, and string beans. Small wonder that this land abounds with canneries and jam factories. The famous house of Zuegg, well-known exporters, puts up its celebrated candied fruit, preserves, *macedonia,* and chestnut cream in this abundant corner of Italy. Delicious mountain honey is another established specialty.

Tyrolean and Italian cookery live amicably side by side in the Upper Adige. Menus are printed in two languages, sometimes with rather cumber-some results. Baby ravioli become *Schlupfkrapfeln* and vermicelli in milk must be pronounced *Tschottnudeln.* But *Würstel con crauti* combines the best of both languages, and if you order it in Bolzano, you will have a *choucroute garnie* (to make this truly multilingual) with magnificent sausages and smoked pork and sauerkraut. It is often served with *ravioli alla trentina,* the tiny cushions stuffed with roast and salted meat, chicken, onion, and parsley. And there is plenty of wonderful beer to accompany your feast!

Wild hare scamper over these wooded hills, and often appear on local tables as *lepre alla trentina.* The liver, heart, and lungs are first marinated with red wine, pine nuts, crushed grapes, sliced lemon, cinnamon, cloves, and sugar. The hare itself is cut in six pieces and browned in butter with onion and bacon. Then the entire marinade is added and the whole aromatic concoction simmers for a few hours. The result is a rich stew, which needs only a little polenta and green salad to make a royal dish.

Polenta thrives here, as in the neighboring Veneto provinces, but here it is made from dark *saraceno* grain, which closely resembles our buckwheat. Polenta is usually served with small birds or game. Here the conventional Italian *gnocchi* has an interesting variation, called *canederli*. These turn out to be dumplings made of flour, bread crumbs, milk, eggs, sausages, bacon, ham, and parsley. The local people eat them, first boiled in a consommé, in a dish with sauerkraut. Sound good?

Finally, these mountain people are inordinately fond of pastry. If you have the same weakness, some of the local favorites worth seeking out in the shops are *Mostazzon, Zelten,* and strudel. You may also ask for *orecchie di lepre* without fear of getting a rabbit's ear. It's a delicious little cake of approximately that shape.

Bacchus has his day in this joyous land, particularly in the hills around Bolzano. The vineyards date back to Roman times and even earlier, for Virgil sang the praises of these vintages long ago, and Caesar Augustus had a particular affection for them. Through two millenia, the vineyards have prospered, thanks to the devotion of hard-working peasants, and wine lovers owe these toilers gratitude.

One of the best wines in the Bolzano area is Santa Maddalena, a delicate red wine, subtle in color and agreeable in aroma, that often appears on the tables of good hotels in Bolzano. Two other respectable reds are Guncinà and Santa Giustina, both available on wine lists, and there is a good *vin rosé* with a delicate aroma reminiscent of vanilla, called Lagrein Rosato. Kuchelberg, the local wine of Merano, comes from vineyards close to the Austrian frontier.

These fresh, palatable wines are pressed from familiar, time-tested grapes —Riesling, Sylvaner, Sauvignon, and Pinot—that conspire to make life pleasant for the visiting oenophile. From the hills around Trento comes Teroldego, a sturdy, violet-scented red wine that is a fine companion for meat dishes. Muscat grapes on these lush green slopes yield a sweet wine that goes well with the Tyrolean pastry, *moscato dolce*. It is quite obvious that "local" wines alone will suffice in Trentino-Alto Adige.

Having sketched out a few of the inducements of this beckoning land, we would like to map a little guided tour, taking in the highlights that shouldn't be missed. It should be emphasized that this is a region filled with little resort towns and hotels that make a happy hunting ground for the summer vacationist, the winter skier, the motorist, the fisherman who prefers mountain streams, and for almost anyone who likes to be comfortably fed and wined and to sit and look at the mountains.

Our tour begins at the region's southern extremity and works north to the Brenner Pass. If you are coming from Austria, you will need to thumb these pages backwards.

Riva del Garda

THE ITALIAN LAKES make an abbreviated reappearance in our account due to the fact that Riva, on the northern extremity of Lake Garda, was an Austrian lake port before it became a part of the parcel handed over to Italy by the Treaty of Versailles in 1919. Riva's arcaded architecture is distinctly Tyrolean, and a bit startling after the pure Italian feeling of the rest of Lake Garda. But it is pleasant and picturesque, particularly near the central piazza, bordering the lake. All is quiet and reposeful here, under the frowning presence of an austere clock tower called the Torre Apponale, which has been surveying the scene for seven centuries. Excited animation strikes the old piazza when a fleet of buses suddenly arrives from the north. Tourists tumble out of them, intent upon two objectives, one of them a cup of hot chocolate and a bun on the café terrace. Then dozing cabmen, postcard salesmen, and orange vendors come to life, and mariners in small sailboats converge upon the scene, looking for paying passengers.

The most exciting thing about Riva, though, is its setting at the base of immense, almost perpendicular mountains of rock. By some miracle of burrowing mankind, a roadway has been gouged out of this sheer cliff of stone on Garda's western shore on which the motorist can now nonchalantly drive through a series of long tunnels, a tribute to Italian engineering skill.

There is a certain amount of summer life in Riva, abetted by a charming boat club open to visitors—swimming pool, sailing privileges, and all. Riva's hotels, open from early spring to late autumn, and all established for decades, are more than adequate. True, they are a bit "touristy," and their food is sometimes "international," in order to be acceptable to their polyglot clientele. However, an overnight stay in any one of four *alberghi* should be pleasant:

The GRAND HOTEL RIVA is a cordial, well-run establishment, and most comfortable. Here you will find good regional dishes including the famous black polenta made from *saraceno* grain, and a tempting cold dish that pays tribute to the delectable little eel of Lake Garda. Signor Sampietro, the director, gave us recipes for both, also the formula for a spaghetti sauce that he has been kind enough to name for us. This tribute has turned our head completely, and we can't resist sharing with you the secret of

Grand
Hotel
RIVA
RIVA DEL GARDA

Spaghetti alla Chamberlain

Slowly cook 1 finely chopped small onion in 1 teaspoon of butter and 1 tablespoon of olive oil until it is barely softened. Add 2 peeled, seeded, and coarsely chopped fresh tomatoes, 1 tablespoon of tomato paste, 2 tablespoons of julienne of boiled tongue, and 1 tablespoon of finely diced ham. A little curry, to taste, and a very small pinch of salt complete the flavors. The sauce is simmered about 20 minutes and served with thin spaghetti cooked *al dente,* which means "firm to the bite." Makes enough sauce for spaghetti for 2 people.

The HOTEL EUROPA, on the Piazza Catena, offers pleasant rooms and a good cuisine. Among its specialties are *baccalà al sedano* (an ingenious dish involving dried cod and celery root), *tortino di melanzane* (eggplant with tomato, Fontina cheese, and other delicacies), and a lovely rice salad mixed up with a half dozen appetizing ingredients. Signor Maturi, the director, has brightened our lives with the recipes for all three, and we share with you

Hotel
Europa
RIVA DEL GARDA

Insalata di Riso
RICE SALAD

Cook 1 cup (about 1/2 pound) of rice in boiling salted water until it is tender but still quite firm. Drain the rice and dry it in the oven in a colander. Each grain must be separate and dry. Put it in a bowl and add a heart of celery (or celeriac, if you can get it), cut fine, 8 or 10 tiny sour cucumber pickles, sliced thin, 3/4 cup of tiny artichoke hearts in oil, 3/4 cup of small mushrooms in oil, and 1 cup of tuna in oil, all of these drained of their oil and cut up fine. Now add 1 1/2 cups green peppers, measured after they have been put under the broiler until they are slightly browned and softened, then skinned and sliced fine, 2 fresh ripe tomatoes that have been skinned, seeded, and coarsely diced, 6 anchovy filets, 1/2 teaspoon of capers, and half a dozen pitted, sliced olives. With 2 forks mix this all lightly into the rice, dress with a little oil, salt and pepper, and a dash of Worcestershire. Arrange in a pyramid and garnish with hard-boiled egg, tomato, and red Italian onion rings.

The HOTEL DU LAC, on the Viale Rovereto, enjoys a choice location above the lake, and its rooms have inspiring views. It has a charming garden through which are scattered modernistic little chalets. There are also a private beach and a large trout pool. The chefs of the Hotel du Lac are adept at preparing local dishes, among them *canederli,* those flavorful dumplings served in soups, *cannelloni, capretto, baccalà alla trentina,* and *manzo brasato,* braised beef with an extra flourish. The hotel's generous director has shared these five recipes with us, one of which follows:

Hotel
du
Lac
RIVA
DEL
GARDA

Manzo Brasato
BRAISED BEEF

Lard a 2 1/2 pound piece of beef rump with half a dozen strips of salt pork, inserting them by means of a larding needle. Put the meat in a heavy pot and pour over it 1 cup of red wine. Add 1 carrot, 2 stalks of celery, and 2 onions, all chopped, 1 clove of garlic, a sprig of fresh rosemary or 1/4 teaspoon dried rosemary, a bay leaf, salt and pepper, 1/2 teaspoon of chopped basil, a pinch each of cinnamon and clove, 2 or 3 whole tomatoes, coarsely chopped, 3 tablespoons of olive oil, and a nut of butter. Cover the pot closely and simmer the meat on a very low fire until it is tender and the liquid practically consumed. Remove the meat to a baking dish. Force the vegetables through a sieve, pour them over the meat, and place it in a hot oven to brown briefly.

Torbole

ABOUT TWO miles east of Riva, in another corner of Lake Garda, is the charming resort town of Torbole, clean, picturesque, inexpensive, and unsophisticated. Its view of the turquoise lake, hemmed in by near-vertical mountains, is most impressive. Painters and musicians appear to have a particular fondness for Torbole, and it seems to have a heavy German-speaking following. There's not much to do—wait for the morning paper, stroll over to Riva, relax in a fishing boat that has an orange sail, and enjoy good Italian meals in a vine-covered pergola with the waves lapping just below. But perhaps this leisurely program is just what you have in mind. If you've had a bit too much traveling, Torbole (accent on the first syllable) might be just the place to rest.

HOTEL
Paradiso
Torbole

We wish to report a very happy twenty-four hours spent in Torbole's HOTEL PARADISO at the water's edge, a pleasing establishment that well deserves its superlative title. We found its cooking far above the average, especially the *cannelloni Paradiso*. Signor Moser, the director, gave us this recipe, which is easily adapted to the Anglo-Saxon kitchen. We urge you to try:

Cannelloni Paradiso
HEAVENLY CHEESE CANNELLONI

The pasta for Signor Moser's *cannelloni* is particularly rich and delicious, being made with a pound, or 4 cups, of flour to 4 whole eggs and 2 egg yolks. The only other ingredients are a little salt and the skill to roll this dough, after 12 minutes of kneading, into paper-thin sheets. Cut the dough into squares about 4 inches across and cook them, a few at a time, in boiling salted water for 1 minute. Drop them into cold water as they are done.

Fill each square with equal quantities of coarsely grated Swiss cheese and *mozzarella* cheese combined with a spoonful of Parmesan and a nut of butter. Roll them up and place them side by side in a buttered baking dish. Cover with a delicate sauce of fresh tomatoes, dot with butter, and cook for 20 minutes in a slow oven (275° F.).

The northern extremity of Lake Garda–Riva del Garda

Rowboat refuge–Torbole

Piazza Cesare Battisti–Trento

Trento

FROM LAKE GARDA, a valley road beside the river Adige leads north to the provincial capital of Trento, set in a stupendous amphitheater of craggy hills. This, the Tridentum of the ancient Romans, was once an Austrian frontier town. The city had previously gained renown as the setting for the historic Council of Trent, which met here in 1545 to reorganize the Roman Catholic Church. More recently, and less attractively, it served as a rendezvous for Hitler and Mussolini to discuss, a bit prematurely, how they would divide Europe between them.

Architecturally, Trento has a great deal to offer the traveler. Although somewhat austere it has a lighthearted and amusing town square, the Piazza Cesare Battisti, named for a local patriot who was executed by the Austrians in 1916. In the center is an immense, grandiose eighteenth-century fountain of Neptune, its bronze creatures squirting water exuberantly in all directions. At one end of the square, silhouetted against the powder-blue hills, is the Romanesque cathedral, a bit austere perhaps, but solid marble, for all that, and capped with an onion-bulb tower to lessen its severity. But we would call your attention particularly to the town's leading café, installed on this square in the Casa Rella. This four-story arcaded building is completely covered with bold and vivid frescoes dating back to the sixteenth century. Though they may serve better drinks on Rome's Via Veneto, this café takes the aesthetic prize!

One other building deserves to be seen, the crenelated Castello del Buon Consiglio, a vast, frowning episcopal stronghold built in the thirteenth century as a residence for the bishop-princes. Now it serves as a museum, and a fascinating one. It has also served as a prison, and a lugubrious hoosegow it must have been.

Trento is less inspiring as a hotel center than its neighbor, Bolzano. Good accommodations, however, can be found at either the large, rambling GRANDE ALBERGO TRENTO, which looks out on a park, or at the old-fashioned but alertly managed HOTEL BRISTOL, where the cooking is in the Bolognese tradition. Among the most tempting specialties are *tagliatelle alla bolognese, tortellini in brodo, fagiani allo spiedo* (small pheasants roasted on a spit), and salmon trout from nearby mountain streams. Signor Barbieri, the director of the Bristol, gave us the recipe for his toothsome *tortellini,* which is a bit complicated, but pleasant reading nonetheless.

Veri Tortellini alla Bolognese
TORTELLINI IN TRUE BOLOGNA STYLE

Put through the finest blade of a meat grinder 1/4 pound of cooked lean pork, the cooked breast meat of 1 small chicken, 1/4 pound of pork sausage, and a small slice of ham. Work this mixture all together very well and add 3/4 cup of grated Parmesan, 1 whole egg, grated nutmeg, and salt. Mix thoroughly. At the Bristol this delicious stuffing goes into little *tortellini* or *cappellini* (little hats), but you may use it to stuff your own ravioli, which are of simpler construction. Cook them in boiling broth for 5 or 6 minutes and serve in a little of the broth, with grated Parmesan.

Ristorante Forst
Trento

As for restaurants, you are certain to fare well at the RISTORANTE FORST, on the Via Mazzurana, just a short distance from that fantastic frescoed café. Forst is a *birreria,* indicating that the beer is particularly good. So are the local specialties, all of which go very well with the amber brew. Among them are *Keiserfleisch con crauti, goulasch all'ungherese,* and *canederli in brodo.* There is a fine strudel, and if you are curious to try that wild hare, here is a good place. Signor Passerini, the generous director of the restaurant (and also of the Albergo Mayer, a pleasant hotel in the heart of the town) gave us the recipes for his strudel and *lepre alla trentina,* also this delicate formula for bread and liver dumplings:

Gnocchetti di Fegato di Vitello
BREAD AND LIVER DUMPLINGS

Moisten in a little chicken stock about 2 cups of soft bread crumbs, squeeze them out, and put them in a bowl with 1/4 pound of raw calf's liver that has been put three times through the fine blade of the meat grinder. Add 1 finely chopped clove of garlic, a pinch of marjoram, salt, pepper, and nutmeg, 1 tablespoon of grated Parmesan, 1 teaspoon of melted butter, and 2 whole eggs. Mix well and bind all together with just enough flour to make a soft dough. Drop by spoonfuls into boiling chicken stock and, when the dumplings become yellow and firm, put them in a soup tureen with the broth. Serve with grated Parmesan.

Bolzano

LYING IN the Adige river valley on the arterial road to the Brenner Pass—the shortest road between Italy and Germany—Bolzano, or Bozen, is probably the best excursion center for travelers who wish to visit the Dolomites. Three river valleys converge here—the Adige, the Isarco, and the Talvero. Roads radiate in several directions, too, each promising a thrilling day's excursion. You can choose your own form of locomotion—funicular, aerial cableway, cog railway, bus, bicycle, car, or shanks' mare. Starting with the shortest trip, we would like to recommend five in particular:

GUNCINÀ—A funicular on the outskirts of Bolzano lifts you quickly to dizzy heights and a spectacular view of the city and its rim of snow-capped mountains. There is a converted villa in Guncinà where you can have lunch while absorbing the mighty panorama.

SAN GENESIO—If you like the adventure of an aerial cableway, an exciting trip awaits you to the town of San Genesio, a charming upland village. The cableway station is on the northern edge of Bolzano.

COLLALBO—From the heart of Bolzano a little rack-and-pinion railway toils upward to this idyllic village perched above the Isarco valley. Its view is breath-taking, and you can have a pleasant lunch at the Hotel Bemelmans.

CALDARO—This is a delightful wine-growing community about five miles south of Bolzano, just a short, pleasant drive. Its houses are tall, wide-roofed, and picturesque, glistening white in the sun and ornamented with graceful wrought-iron shop signs. It is a rare privilege to sit on the terrace of the towering Albergo Gasthof, an operatic "White Horse Inn" type of place, and to taste the fresh young white wine of the region, pressed from Riesling and Sylvaner grapes.

LAKE CAREZZA—An adventurous little automobile trip will take you into the back country, with a famous lake as an objective. The road leads southeast of Bolzano through the Valle d'Ega, and after a stout climb, arrives at the incredibly blue Lago di Carezza, banked with evergreens, with the fantastic cathedral-shaped peaks of the Latemar group serving as a lavender backdrop. There couldn't be a more inspiring spot for a picnic luncheon. If you continue on your road for a mile or two, you come to the Costalunga Pass and a first glimpse of the Marmolada, giant of the Dolomites.

Of course, the most famous excursion out of Bolzano is the Great Road of the Dolomites, leading eastward to Cortina. But we'll come to that later. In the meantime, a close look at Bolzano itself will prove rewarding. This is an old Tyrolean town, alternately Baroque and Renaissance, with modern Italian fringes. The houses in its center are tall and Teutonic, topped with steep-roofed towers. Graceful ironwork protects the lower windows, and there are any number of small town squares, splashing with fountains. The curving Piazza delle Erbe, the market square, brim full of good things to eat, is particularly seductive and provides a perfect milieu in which to develop an appetite.

Piazza delle Erbe–Bolzano

The country inn–Caldaro

Town gate–Merano

That appetite, we are happy to announce, will be abundantly satisfied in many Bolzano restaurants, particularly in the tree-shaded purlieus of the HOTEL GRIFONE, a busy hotel located in the heart of the city on the Piazza Walther. We have enjoyed many meals on its animated terrace facing the lovely Gothic parish church. One luncheon, for example, consisted of boned salmon trout in aspic and a vegetable salad with an exquisite mayonnaise, followed by a superb *fritatta* (omelette) with mushrooms and onions, a good local cheese, and delectable wild strawberries with ice cream. This meal was accompanied by a palatable local white wine, a *moscato dolce* with the strawberries, *caffè espresso* and a thin flute of Strega.

HOTEL
Grifone
Bolzano

The menu at the Hotel Grifone is bilingual, the other language being German. If you want *Ungarisches Gulasch* or *Frankfurter Würstel* or *Wiener Schnitzel,* there they are. If you happen here on the right evening, there is another attraction, a band concert. All the musicians wear baggy-sleeved white shirts, waistcoats of black or red velvet, and broad green suspenders. Topping their costumes are high-crowned Alpine hats, each gaily decorated with a fresh, spicy carnation. The music is precisely the kind you would expect from musicians so attired, with a strong emphasis on Viennese waltzes.

The Grifone is an excellent hotel for an overnight stop, and so is the ALBERGO CITTÀ, located at the other end of the Piazza Walther. There are others in quieter places. The best of them is the ALBERGO LAURIN, at Via Laurin 2, situated near the railway station. It is a tranquil summer place, endowed with every comfort, and most commendable cooking.

Spring and fall are the best seasons in Bolzano. The summers are uncomfortably hot. Nevertheless, a constant stream of travelers passes through the year round, and the majority of its hotels are always open.

Merano

THIS WATERING place on the fringe of the Dolomites is rapidly making its way back as one of the leading spas in Europe. Its mineral springs and radioactive waters are prime attractions to many people with all kinds of complexities and complaints, including precocious senility. Merano's cold radioactive mineral waters do them immense good. I'm told that they even bring race horses up here to inhale the radioactive fumes, but maybe somebody is trying to pull my fetlock.

At all events, Merano teems with hotels, pensions, villas, and sanatoria, all bedecked with flowers. Orchards surround the town, which is famous for its apples, especially the Calville. Each apple is protected, while maturing on the tree, by a paper bag that preserves its delicate golden skin. It is pleasant to report that gastronomy plays a part in the "cure" at Merano. Patients indulge in fruit diets; they munch apples, pears, apricots, and particularly grapes. Among the two hundred varieties of grapes grown in the Alto Adige, there is a grape for almost every ailment that man can produce.

There is an old town of Merano, close-packed and quaint, with steep-roofed town gates and tempting shops. Though German seems to be the favored language, everybody speaks Italian in a pinch. The outer edges of the town are liberally sprinkled with good, solid hotels in the Swiss and Austrian traditions. Merano doesn't sound precisely like the rendezvous of the "fast younger set." However, there is a startling newcomer they will probably like. It is the HOTEL BRISTOL, built recently by an Italian syndicate (the same people who run the Grand and the Bauer Grünewald in Venice), and as modern as tomorrow. All rooms have outside sheltered balconies with a chaise longue, and a low table on which to enjoy your breakfast. On the roof is a stunning innovation—a swimming pool and deck chairs for sun-bathing. A dance floor and a stupendous view of the mountains are thrown in without extra charge. The food is hotel food, of course, but well prepared and gratifying, especially if you order fresh mountain trout and munch quantities of fruit.

Hotel
Bristol
Merano

Bressanone

ONE DRAMATIC way to enter the Alto Adige is through the Brenner Pass from Austria. It is one of the easiest of international mountain passes, and is open the year round. The motorist drives southward and soon comes to a point of decision at the highly attractive town of Vipiteno.

If he forks to the right, he climbs a magnificent winding steep road that eventually leads to Merano. But if he takes the left fork he not only encounters an easy valley road but a rich gastronomic reward, and the handsome valley town of Bressanone, or Brixen, as well.

There are grotesque and picturesque streets in this town, spiked with numerous church towers. It lies in a fertile river valley, and is a noted health resort. However, for our epicurean purposes, Bressanone is famous for one thing—a hotel named after an elephant. The name of the HOTEL ELEFANTE harks back to the sad story of a live elephant who was presented as a gift to Maximilian of Austria, King of Bohemia, by John the Third of Portugal. The poor creature, whose name was Solomon, was sent from Africa to Genoa by ship and then began the long trek to Austria on foot (this was back in 1551) to join his new master. At Bressanone he spent several days recuperating from the brutal march over cold mountain roads, and stayed in the stables of the leading town hotel, while his attendants put up in the best rooms. The owner of the *albergo* felt greatly honored, and soon changed the name of his establishment to Elefante and had its façade adorned with large elephantine frescoes, which remain to this day. For centuries the hotel has been famous. The kings of Bavaria, Greece, and Prussia have stayed there, as have the Emperor and Empress of Austria, Ferenc

"Piatto Elefante"

Molnár, and Max Reinhardt. So have many gourmets in recent times. They are attracted by one spectacular dish, the *piatto Elefante,* a glorified meat preparation that taxes one's power of description. It is intended for four people—a glittering mound of delicacies including roasts, smoked ribs, sausages, and tongue, surrounded by a squad of luscious vegetables and spiked with a silver skewer. It is certainly the most impressive dish in this province, and worth a wide detour. The Hotel Elefante, at Via Rio Bianco 4, is also most comfortable for an overnight stop. We have sketched its wrought-iron sign so that you can find it easily.

Hotel
Elefante
Bressanone

Signor Heiss, director of the Elefante, has an interesting way of serving grilled veal chops. This was one of the recipes he gave us:

Costolette alla Tirolese
CUTLETS TYROL STYLE

Put 2 strips of bacon, cut in small pieces, into a saucepan with 1 1/2 cups of fresh shelled peas and a few tablespoons of water. Cover the saucepan and cook slowly until the peas are tender and still moist. Parboil a calf's brain, clean it, and cut it into small pieces. Sauté a cupful of the calf's brain in butter, mix it with the peas, and season with salt and pepper and a dash of Worcestershire. Pour over grilled veal chops and serve.

After these two treks northward from Bolzano, you are ready for the most exhilarating experience in the Dolomites, the spectacular run by car or bus across the mountain passes to Cortina d'Ampezzo. For downright, overwhelming beauty, this trip has few equals anywhere. A road map will show that these most dramatic of all Dolomite peaks may be approached by two southern routes, one of them passing by the incomparable Lake Carezza. Our favorite route is the northern one, following the Val Gardena to Ortisei, an excellent stopping point, from which to consider the grandeur that lies ahead.

Ortisei

THIS IS perhaps the best of many small mountain resorts that thrive between Bolzano and the mountain passes. Perched at an altitude of 4,047 feet, it is a pronounced favorite with winter and summer sportsmen. From here funiculars and chair lifts hoist skiers to all sorts of jittery heights. During the warm months it is less exciting, perhaps, but far easier on the motorist. The favorite local industry is wood carving. Few visitors leave the place without acquiring some of the wooden statuettes, dolls, toys, and bottle stoppers shown in the shops.

Hotel
Aquila
Ortisei

There are several good hotels in this delightful valley town, the most appealing being the AQUILA. From its balconies, sparkling with geraniums, guests enjoy a thrilling view of the valley, surrounded by those strange, purple-buff mountains. The hotel is spotless and spacious, with a vast central staircase suitable for a descending duchess. There are plenty of bathrooms, too, enormous ones. The meals are hotel meals, alas, contrived to please five nationalties at the same time. It can't be helped, I suppose. One ray of sunshine amidst the barley soup, chicken, peas, and pastry was a notable bottle of Sandbichler, the dry red wine of the district.

If you make an overnight stop in Ortisei, the next day's motoring holds an unforgettable adventure. Perhaps you would like to prepare for it, as we did, by assembling a picnic lunch. You can buy one in the village *salumeria* consisting of a container of fresh vegetable salad with mayonnaise, a few slices of *mortadella,* a seductive slab of Gorgonzola, some fruit, red wine, and the bread of the country, peculiar small round loaves, rather hard and seasoned with caraway seed.

Now for the ultimate splendor of the Dolomites! The road ahead is wide and well graded. It climbs steadily through the Val Gardena, passing the gay little resort town of Santa Christina, whose castle might have been designed by Maxfield Parrish. There are many rustic farmhouses along the way, overhanging wooden structures built in log-cabin style with wide planked roofs held down by slabs of stone. Highly utilitarian they are, with winter accommodations for the animals in the basement. But they are also superbly picturesque. They cling in clusters on the hillside, an indication of the gregarious instincts of these hardy herdsmen. Now and then the thin white spire

Tesoro, a village in the Dolomites

Passo di Sella

of a Tyrolean church rises in the distance, silhouetted against the hillside evergreens. Above the whole vivid landscape tower the immense triple peaks of Sasso Lungo, iridescent and eerie in the moist morning light.

After the rather barren resort village of Selva, the road does some serious climbing, indulging in any number of well-engineered hairpin turns. At one fork you must choose between the Passo di Gardena and the Passo di Sella. If you have set out to make the circular loop of the passes and then return to Ortisei, it makes slight difference which fork you take. But if you are going on to Cortina, keep to the right toward the Passo di Sella. The immense, jagged triple campanili of Sasso Lungo loom larger than ever; vegetation thins out, but the mountain wild flowers persist. There are no more farmhouses now, only gaunt little *cantoniere,* refuges for mountaineers. At the base of an ocher crag is the Passo di Sella, where you are glad to stop and allow your motor to cool. A modernistic wooden hotel built at this lofty pass should appeal to those who seek novelty combined with comfort, and an utterly indescribable panorama thrown into the bargain. What a stupendous view it is! You are almost 7,300 feet above sea level, but beyond the chasms below lie even higher denticulations, crowned by the magnificent white silhouette of La Marmolada, greatest of all Dolomite peaks.

124

Passo di Pordoi

Canazei, in the Val di Fassa

After you have slaked your thirst at the little café and bought a few postcards, a succession of added hairpin turns will ultimately lead you to the Passo di Pordoi, highest in the Dolomites, where many lives were lost during World War I. It's a rather bleak spot, dominated by a grim war monument and a summer hotel that almost disappears from view under the winter snows. At this point the long winding descent begins. From this high place where you leave the confines of the Alto Adige and of this chapter, you pass into neighboring Veneto. Far in the distance you can glimpse a delicious valley, green and inviting, just the place for that picnic lunch beside a mountain stream. Beyond you stretches another climb across the Passo di Falzarego, before you reach the sophistication of Cortina d'Ampezzo. So relax for a moment, enjoy that cheese and sausage and wine, and ruminate upon one of the most exciting journeys that today's traveler can find in Europe.

Val Pusteria

Venice

Veneto Euganea

Chapter 6

VENETO
EUGANEA

T HE SPREADING eastern hip of the thigh-high Italian boot is a rich
and diverse land called Venetia. As we have previously pointed out,
it is far too complex to be thought of as a single territory. Carto-
graphers have simplified matters by mapping three Venetian regions, the second of which is the bright star of this chapter. Called Veneto Euganea, its
variety and fascination cannot easily be compressed into a small space. It is
as richly replete with the good things of life as the proverbial fruitcake. In
addition to the unique, incomparable Venice, the awed traveler finds four
other famous Italian cities in this small area—Treviso, the citadel of brick;
Padua, site of a venerable university; Vicenza, center of Palladian architecture; and Verona, forever famed as the city of Romeo and Juliet. But that
is not all. Veneto Euganea claims the eastern shore of Lake Garda, a charming excursion in itself, and a sizable segment of the Dolomites, with Cortina
d'Ampezzo, one of the most brilliant of mountain resorts, as its center. If
there ever was a region that had an *embarras de richesses,* this is it. The
average traveler on a tight schedule will miss a great deal of it. The more
leisurely visitor with time on his hands will find a rich and exciting experience
ahead of him in Veneto Euganea.

Since we entered from the north in the previous chapter, we will resume
our travels there, and move southward. The sequence to be followed is: the
mountain towns of Veneto; the eastern shore of Lake Garda; Verona, Vicenza,
and Padua and its surroundings; Treviso and its neighborhood; and finally
the epicurean resources of Venice itself.

Our travelogue, however, should be preceded by a little résumé on food
and wine, both of which are heartening subjects in Veneto Euganea. Such a
résumé may seem a trifle impertinent. In retrospect, Saint Mark's, the Grand
Canal, and Tintoretto's fabulous murals certainly outshine the epicurean phase

of the City of the Doges. Who has the impudence to speak of baby octopus fried in deep oil, or polenta, or *scampi* when the Piazza San Marco still dazzles the eyes with its opalescent splendor and the spell of Veronese and Tiepolo and Titian remains unfaded? But impudent or not, impressionable people find it impossible not to indulge in rhapsodic reminiscence of Venetian food and wine.

We find it difficult to don artistic blinders and hew straight to the gastronomic line in this charmed city of liquid streets, directing hardly a glance at a gondola or a Gothic *palazzo,* but that's what we've got to do. So we'll turn your artistic guardianship over to a chap named Ruskin and get down to the fundamentals of Venetian fare.

Although the keystone of Venetian cooking is the magnificent sea food of the upper Adriatic, its most celebrated dishes are founded on simple things. The lowly liver and onions, for example, is transformed into *fegato alla veneziana,* an exquisite and forthright preparation. Rice and peas are cooked together to become *risi e bisi,* a famous Venetian standby. A skilled cook transforms them into unsuspected delicacies, and you can do the same by following the recipes that are quoted in the back of the book.

But the basic treasure, Adriatic fish and shellfish, is less transportable, less easy to emulate. The impressive *scampi,* or small crayfish, and their fragrant smaller cousins, *gamberetti*, leave one groping for superlatives. *Calamaretti,* those succulent baby squids fried quickly in deep, hot olive oil, and *bisato alla veneta,* an aromatic stewed eel, are two other specialties which make immediate converts. Admittedly the Venetians partake of creatures of the sea that are rather frightening to the Anglo-Saxon palate. This is particularly true of the octopus family, and in the realm of unlisted shellfish—nothing with a shell around it is too small or too ignominious to be considered. Venetians are particularly fond of *mansanete,* or female crabs, and *folpi,* which turn out to be polyps. They love fish soups, and *broeto di pesce* is something to watch for on restaurant menus. So is *baccalà mantecato,* dried cod worked up into a fine, garlic-scented paste. A Venetian *risotto* may be studded with *scampi,* squid, cockles, and mussels, and spaghetti is often served with V-necked clams, or esconced in a gentle anchovy sauce. There are conventional fish too, of course, sole, mullet, and the toothy *dentice,* and the lobsters are more than impressive.

The covered bridge–Bassano del Grappa

The hearty and unassuming polenta thrives in Venetia even more than in other parts of Italy, and corn meal has rarely been put to better use. The familiar *polenta e öséi* of Lombardy, a mound of flavorful corn meal served with small, spit-roasted birds, is also popular in Venetia, and will delight all but the too compassionate. Though this specialty makes an occasional appearance on hotel bills of fare, we must admit that the most interesting fish dishes are not in evidence within the tourist orbit. The inquiring gourmet will have to seek them out in purely local restaurants, but his reward will be substantial.

The traveler with a penchant for local wines is going to be more than happy in the Veneto, especially in the region of Verona. The foothills above this famous city are tapestried with bountiful vineyards whose product rivals the best in the three other great wine districts of Italy. A good Valpolicella stands up to the finest reds that Tuscany or Piedmont can produce, and a fine Soave has few rivals anywhere as a companion for fish. There are several other names to remember, especially Verdiso, Prosecco, Bardolino, and Valpantena. Each will produce a pleasant adventure when selected from a good wine list.

Among the reds, Valpolicella well deserves its top rank. For uncounted centuries, it has been produced by a dozen or more wine villages on the slopes northwest of Verona. It is one of the greatest of Italian red wines, subtle and velvety, well balanced, heady in perfume but moderate in strength—in short, the perfect companion to a solid Italian dinner. Given a few years to age, it becomes a superlative wine to accompany roasts and game. Some historians maintain that Julius Caesar drank this same wine in Verona and later introduced it to his friends in Rome. Whether its fame goes back so far is questionable, but there is no doubt about its present pre-eminence all over the Italian peninsula. Valpolicella is one of the most trusted names in winedom.

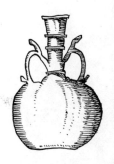

Valpantena is a close rival, almost a twin, of Valpolicella, and comes from a nearby, and parallel, valley, on the east. A noble vintage for red meat, deep ruby red in color, with a subtle and pleasing aroma, it merits high praise.

Bardolino is a sturdy red wine with, perhaps, fewer subtleties. It compares to a good sturdy Chianti. Bardolino takes its name from an attractive village on the eastern shore of Lake Garda. The vineyards rise up behind the lake and enjoy its clear breezes. A good, fragrant ruby nectar is the result. Sometimes it becomes faintly *pétillant,* but the Italians don't mind that at all. It's a very popular name all over Italy, especially in Veneto.

For those who like a sweet, sparkling, red dessert wine (even though the idea may make some fastidious gourmets shudder), the Veronese vineyards have produced a wine called Recioto. It is intensely red in color—pungently perfumed, sparkling in the bottle—just the thing for some of those voluptuous Italian pastry desserts.

Among the white wines, few in Italy can approach Soave, a limpid dry wine, the color of pale amber, with a bouquet and flavor very reminiscent of a Chablis. It is grown in the foothills due east of Verona. You can see the smiling village of Soave from the main highway to Vicenza. There couldn't be a finer choice than Soave to accompany the wonderful sea food of the Adriatic. It is subtle and suave, as its name would seem to indicate, but it has good strong shoulders too, and stands up to octopus, *scampi,* lobster, or sole with competence and authority.

Two estimable white wines come from the hills above Treviso, farther to the east. One of them, Verdiso, the pride of the wine-rich town of Conegliano, is delicate and dry, a fish wine of genuine distinction. There is also a sparkling version of Verdiso. Prosecco usually appears as a sparkling wine, and has wide acceptance for festive occasions. Golden yellow in color, fresh and aromatic in perfume, it rivals some of the *spumanti* from Asti. There are other significant vineyards in the Veneto foothills, but these half dozen or more names will give the oncoming oenophile a revealing glimpse of the good fortune that awaits him.

Now, at last, we are ready for a wide swing through Veneto Euganea.

The Mountain Towns of Veneto

An impressive segment of the Dolomites falls within this region, including the exciting Passo di Falzarego and that queen of resort towns,

Cortina d'Ampezzo

For a few weeks, early in 1956, this town high in the Dolomites was the most publicized of all mountain resorts. It was the setting of the Winter Olympic Games, and a highly successful one it turned out to be, in spite of a slight shortage of snow. The beautiful stadium, built expressly for the skating events, remains as a reminder of Cortina d'Ampezzo's most brilliant day. Gay and fashionable, Cortina lies in a sun-drenched valley, with the immense Monte Cristallo towering in the background. It was a part of Austria until 1919. Though its architecture isn't startling, except for the sturdy bell tower of the parish church, its hotel situation is enviable. There are dozens of good hotels, from palaces to simple lodges, offering every comfort to the winter sportsman. But the town also serves as a summer playground for chic people, and the winter skating rinks of many hotels are transformed into swimming pools during the warm months. The most celebrated hotel is the MIRAMONTI MAJESTIC, on the southern outskirts of the town. Two others of comparable excellence are the PALACE CRISTALLO, set above the town, in the hills, and the GRAND HOTEL SAVOIA. In such an exclusively hotel town, the restaurant outlook is rather meager. Almost everyone dines in his *albergo*. However, we shopped about and found two acceptable restaurants, one of which has the gaiety and décor of an old Tyrolean inn. This is the RISTORANTE AL FOGHÈR, Via Grohmann 12, in the heart of the old town. Many tempting things are cooked before the open fire here—roasts of beef, legs of lamb, and assorted birds. The pasta is delicious too, especially the *lasagne,* and you may wind up your meal with a magnificent strudel. Al Foghèr is a valuable name for the passing gourmet, and so is that of a simple little restaurant called DA MARIO, just across from the parish church. We found its fare surprisingly good, especially the wild hare cooked with a rich, piquant sauce.

Skiers are effusive in their praise of the varied devices that hoist them to the heights around Cortina. One trip in particular is recommended, whether you are a skier or not. This is the swing up to Tondi di Faloria by way of the *teleferica.* Adventurers who have taken it say the experience is, in every sense of the word, terrific.

Ristorante
Al Foghèr
Cortina
d'Ampezzo

Cortina d'Ampezzo and Monte Cristallo

Piazza Vittorio Emanuele—Feltre

Sappada

AMONG THE dozens of smaller mountain resorts that assert themselves close to the Austrian border, Sappada has a particular appeal. It is not a town but a series of charming hamlets, set in an enchanting valley high in the Dolomites. Well populated with cheerful white villas, inexpensive hotels, and hospitable German-speaking mountaineers, Sappada is still far from sophisticated, especially in the summertime, when it becomes a retreat of total repose. There are dozens of immaculate little hotels with good Austro-Italian food. The best of the lot is probably the CRISTALLO, in the village of Palù.

Pieve di Cadore

THIS IS one of a string of small resort towns along the Piave River, a name that carries the ring of victory to Italian ears. It was on the banks of the Piave that the Italians stopped the Austrians in 1917. Scars of that struggle have all but disappeared. Pieve di Cadore is famed, first of all, as the birthplace of one of the greatest painters that ever lived, Tiziano Vecellio, better known as Titian. Born in 1477, the master lived to be ninety-nine years old. Another town in upper Veneto claims him as a native son and casts some doubt on his legitimacy. The story is haughtily disdained in Pieve di Cadore, where Titian's own house is preserved for posterity. It is now a museum, open to visitors. An acceptable stopping place is the HOTEL BELVEDERE, in the center of the old town. The cooking is good and the view of the mountains very exciting. This small town also boasts a café in the square, reminiscent of a swank ski lodge, that proves a charming place for an *aperitivo* or a postprandial black coffee and liqueur.

Santa Croce del Lago

Ristorante Bolognese Da Beppe Sello

Santa Croce del Lago

ON THE outskirts of this mountain town stands the best restaurant we encountered in the upper Veneto, the RISTORANTE BOLOGNESE DA BEPPE SELLO. The only trouble with it is that too many people, including bus drivers, know about it and its vine-covered terraces. Located just off the highway at the southern extremity of the Lago di Santa Croce, it enjoys an inspiring view of that lake and the gallery of snow-clad mountains that encircles it. We indulged in some delightful cooked hors-d'oeuvre, thanks to Beppe Sello. They were not the monotonous oily kind, but rich, varied, and satisfying. The spe-

Titian's house—Pieve di Cadore   *Castle on Lake Garda—Malcesine*

cialty of the house is a superb trout, cooked in a paper bag, a genuine delicacy. Tourist buses stopped in relays during our repast, unloading hungry throngs of Germans, Netherlanders, and Scandinavians. Beppe Sello had fare to bring smiles to their faces, too—sausages, ham, and sauerkraut, bountiful plates of German fried potatoes, and plenty of beer.

Feltre

BELLUNO, the capital of this northern province, offers a few engaging bits of architecture, but its southern neighbor, Feltre, is far more interesting. This unheralded old hill town will come as a refreshing surprise, especially if you are an amateur of architecture. Its superb central square, surrounded by lofty houses with exterior frescoes and second-story loggias, is a joy to the lucky visitor. Palladio had a hand in designing the theater.

Furthermore, there is a very commendable restaurant close to Feltre, in the adjacent village of Pedavena. This is the modern BIRRERIA PEDAVENA, an attractive solution for the lunching problem, if you are motoring in these hills. You dine in airy rooms with wide vistas of the mountains. The food is good, following the same pattern, on a reduced scale, that can be found in the larger Birreria Pedavena in Verona, of which we'll speak shortly. Both are run by the Pedavena brewery. The beer is delicious in both establishments.

Birreria
Pedavena
Feltre

THE EASTERN SHORE OF LAKE GARDA

VENETO DOES not walk off with the lion's share of the Italian Lakes, being allotted only the least eventful shore of Lake Garda. However, there is material here to make a fruitful day's trip, and to furnish a tranquil overnight stop, in a lakeside fishing village. Furthermore, the route is of interest to oenophiles, for this is the shore where the famous Bardolino wines are grown. Vineyards blanket these gentle slopes for miles.

Our little guided tour includes five towns—Lazise, Garda, San Vigilio, Torri del Benaco, and Malcesine. They are easy to cover in a day, and suitable overnight hotels can be found in the last two named. Or, if you choose, you may push on a few miles to the beckoning hotels of Torbole and Riva, proudly situated at the top of the lake, and described in the preceding chapter.

By turning northward at Peschiera del Garda, you come to Lazise, a medieval village almost entirely enclosed within the moss-grown walls of a castle built by the powerful Scaligeri family of Verona. The crumbling castle dates from 1024, and its walls have stood up courageously against the on-slaughts of time. A custodian will receive you at the fortified gateway, whose portcullis has long since vanished, and, for a trifling fee, you can roam at will. Our photograph shows the battlements through a screen of spring foliage.

The village of Garda is a quiet little fishing community, dominated by an immense, verdant, table-top rock at the water's edge. Life is simple here, and it is just the place for a peaceful holiday. Garda has a charming summer hotel, too, the HOTEL DU PARC, inexpensive and inviting, with a sheltered garden facing the lake. Here is a favored spot to taste the famous trout of Lake Garda as well as the heartening wines of Bardolino. The market place in Garda, surrounded by old houses with Venetian Gothic windows, is a water-colorist's delight. At the northern extremity of the village is the Villa Albertini, one of the most fabulous in this lake region.

Beyond Garda the road turns westward to a point jutting out into the water, and it is here that you come upon San Vigilio, one of the most romantic spots on Lake Garda. It consists of a small church framed in immense black cypresses, and the lovely Villa Guarienti, built in 1540, with its magnificent garden. Nearby is a tiny fishing port, where a modest little restaurant prospers in summer.

Torri del Benaco is another lazy fishing village on a promontory. Lav-ender nets sway, drying between the trees, and nobody is in the slightest hurry. The Scaligeri had a crenellated castle here, too, built in 1388, that still dominates the village. The town is a strong favorite with artists and writers, partly because of the inviting hotel facing its old port. This is the ALBERGO GARDESANA, and you will rarely find a more relaxing hostelry. Its café tables are stationed under wide, sheltered arcades. From its vine-grown balconies

Albergo
Gardesana
Torri del Benaco

Lazise, a village behind medieval walls

The leisurely way of life—Torri del Benaco

guests have an inspiring view across the lake. The food is good, the prices most reasonable, and the atmosphere steeped in peaceful idleness.

Malcesine is an important village, rich in medieval atmosphere, where Goethe once got in trouble. He was suspected of being a spy and was detained in the Palazzo dei Capitani for some time, because he made pencil sketches of his artistic surroundings. Still another rugged fourteenth-century Scaligeri castle juts out into the water here, the battlements of its towers showing dark against the sky. There are a few adequate hotels, among which the ALBERGO MALCESINE is probably the best.

Verona

HURRIED TRAVELERS who shuttle nonstop between Florence and Venice are depriving themselves of one particularly rich experience—the ancient walled city of Verona. A charmingly civilized community, filled with architectural treasures ranging from an oval Roman arena to a Renaissance market place, Verona is too good to be missed. Among the cities of the Veneto it is second only to Venice, and it has something which Venice lacks—multiple reminders of its early Roman history. This city was the birthplace of Catullus. Verona served as the setting for the tragic love story of Romeo and Juliet, as everyone knows. At Number 17 Via Capello, you will see a thirteenth-century house, with a balcony, that supposedly belonged to Juliet's family. Verona was the stronghold of the Scaligeri, the famous princes Della Scala, who grew to unprecedented power from the beginning of the thirteenth century. You may still see their lofty Gothic tombs in one of the smallest but most ostentatious graveyards in the world. Quite obviously Verona is a treasure house for the  sightseer. Furthermore, it has good hotel and restaurant accommodations, and offers travelers some of Italy's finest wines. Finally, if you like horses and happen to be traveling here in March, you will find Italy's largest horse fair and agricultural exhibit.

There is so much to see in Verona that we can only sketch out the highlights here. If you want more details, ask for the fine, full-color, free folder that the town provides for its visitors. This brochure ranks with the best we have encountered.

In the heart of Verona is one of the most picturesque public squares in Italy, the Piazza delle Erbe, bordered by handsome Baroque and Renaissance buildings, many with frescoed fronts and flowered balconies. This piazza was the ancient forum in Roman times. At one end a Venetian lion perches proudly on the top of a monolithic marble column, a venerable fountain gushes forth in the middle, and a mushroom growth of umbrella-covered stands occupies the rest of this market square. Over the scene hovers

Church of San Stefano—Verona

a twelfth-century brick clock tower, 242 feet high. A fantastic bazaar booms under these disks of canvas. One dealer sells canaries, pigeons, and parakeets, another dispenses goldfish and delivers them to delighted buyers in little plastic bags filled with water. If you want herbs (for which the square was named), lingerie or flowers, artichokes or dark glasses, kitchenware or *cannelloni,* you will find them in this gay and theatrical square, as people have been doing for two thousand years.

Just a few feet away, through an arched road, is the Piazza dei Signori, sometimes called the Piazza Dante on account of the statue of the poet that stands in the middle and endures the affront of far too many pigeons. This is a restful square, bordered with the battlemented castles of the Scaligeri and an exquisite little Renaissance building with an open loggia, the Palazzo del Consiglio. Its cornice is accented with marble statues of Verona's most famous citizens. Adjoining this building is an ancient café straight out of the eighteenth century, one to recommend to all sentimentalists as a place to enjoy an *aperitivo* before dinner. Anyone who appreciates atmosphere will be charmed by the CAFFÈ DANTE. Its marble-topped tables are the ancient, immovable type. The banquettes against the wall are covered with a deep plum-maroon velvet worn thin at the edges. The crystal chandeliers and Louis XV wall mirrors are in perfect harmony. Venerable chess players spend hours in its more remote corners, and dignified gentlemen of the old school read their newspapers over a *caffè espresso* and a thimbleful of Strega.

At a far corner of the square is an archway leading to the tombs of the Scaligeri, for centuries the overlords of Verona, an astonishing mélange of ornate Gothic monuments, towering behind close-meshed iron grills. The most striking of them is embellished with the sarcophagus and equestrian statue of Can Grande, greatest of the Scaligeri and the patron of Dante. He sits high in armored splendor, his horse caparisoned in a drapery that hangs almost to the ground. There is no private burial ground like this one anywhere else in the world.

You are reminded of this powerful family wherever you turn in Verona. The city's most impressive medieval structure is the Castelvecchio, a sprawling crenellated castle on the banks of the winding river Adige, built in 1358. This, too, was a stronghold of the Scaligeri and was once used as a barracks by Napoleon, much to the humiliation of the Veronese. Now it is a museum, and well worth a visit. Adjoining the castle is the Scaligeri bridge, bristling with forked battlements. This bridge, as well as every other in Verona, suffered the indignity of being blown up by the Germans in 1945. It was restored with alacrity, and now appears as solid and formidable as ever.

The Romans, too, have left impressive monuments—town gates, a triumphal arch, a hillside theater, and a great arena in the heart of the city. Built under Diocletian in the year 290, it is the largest Roman amphitheater in

On the Scaligeri Bridge—Verona

Doorway of San Zeno Maggiore—Verona

Piazza delle Erbe—Verona

existence, after the Colosseum. Only four arches of its towering outer arcade remain, but the interior oval is well preserved, and accommodates over twenty thousand people. During July and August, it serves as a summer setting for a fine Italian opera company. An operatic evening here under the stars is one not to be forgotten. Across the river and wedged into the hillside beneath the Castel San Pietro is the Roman theater, carefully excavated and well cared for. Classic plays are given here in September, and Shakespeare, who twice favored Verona, is an understandable favorite. There is a charming little museum of Roman remains connected with the theater.

Verona's greatest church is the Basilica of San Zeno Maggiore, a dignified and exquisite example of Romanesque architecture that was finished in 1138. Its richly sculptured doorway, golden yellow with age, is one of the loveliest in Christendom. There are two superb bronze doors, dating from the eleventh and twelfth centuries, whose panels depict scenes from the Bible. The campanile, contrived in stripes of brick and stone, is in the purest Romanesque tradition, and, adjoining, there is a cloister of infinite, reposeful grace. The interior of the church is simple and majestic, embellished with many fine frescoes. The magnificent triptych of the Madonna by Mantegna overshadows the other paintings. Adding it all up, it would appear that San Zeno Maggiore is a most extraordinary church—a fitting climax to the treasures of Verona. Of course, there are many other things to see if you have the time—the Giusti gardens, the church of Sant'Anastasia, and the alleged tomb of Juliet, among others, but it is time to say a word for Veronese gastronomy.

After the formality of a dry vermouth in the Caffè Dante, you should enjoy a luncheon or dinner at a little place called the DODICI APOSTOLI, at Via Corticella San Marco 3. It takes considerable questioning and poking around through thick clusters of abandoned palaces to find this celebrated dining place, but it is worth the seeking. Half hidden in a vine-grown alley, it is very ancient, a small semivaulted hall, gay with murals and rich in uncontrived atmosphere. If you are limited to a single meal in Verona, this spot would be an excellent choice.

You will see a number of robust, conversational businessmen here, invariably a good gastronomic omen, who attack the ample fare and full-blooded Valpolicella with gusto. The food is varied, mostly cooked to order, and devoid of pretentious frills. The young proprietors speak fluent French and acceptable English, and are truly solicitous of the happiness of their guests. We found the Twelve Apostles quiet at midday, but crowded in the evening. Go early, before eight, and enjoy a blend of courtesy, atmosphere, and fine Italian cooking.

The urban life of Verona centers about the Via Mazzini, a gay, crowded thoroughfare for pedestrians only, and the broad, populous Piazza Bra (or perhaps we should say Uplift Square). Here, facing the Roman arena and

Dodici Apostoli
Verona

varied civic palaces, are sidewalk cafés with striped umbrellas and nonchalant waiters, and two restaurants worth remembering. One is the RISTORANTE DELLE TRE CORONE, a conventional place occupying a handsome, rusticated building. The Three Crowns turns out to be all that you might expect from a good, formal Italian city restaurant. The service and the cooking are well above the average. We recall, with particular affection, a handsome *fettuccine* with peas. The wide, thin, steaming noodles were quite as good as those bearing the Alfredo label in Rome. Following the pasta came delectable *costolette Tre Corone,* a veal dish of distinct delicacy and savor. The director of this urbane establishment was most obliging when we asked him for recipes, and gave us the formulae for both dishes. Here is a translation of the secret of his savory cutlet:

Ristorante
delle
Tre Corone
Verona

Costolette di Vitello Tre Corone
VEAL CUTLETS THREE CROWNS

Over a brisk fire cook 8 thin slices of veal, about 1 pound in all, in several tablespoons of butter until the slices are brown on both sides. Cover them with the following mixture:

In a double boiler heat 1/3 cup of cream with 1/4 pound of diced Fontina or *mozzarella* cheese. When the cheese is melted add a little pepper, 1 truffle, chopped or sliced, 2 ounces of ham (1/3 to 1/2 cup), cut in fine julienne strips, and 1 tablespoon of grated Parmesan. Stir in 1 beaten egg. Spoon some of this mixture over each slice of veal and brown them briefly under a hot broiler.

The other dining place on the Piazza Bra (or should we say Place Soutien-Gorge?) is the BIRRERIA RISTORANTE PEDAVENA, a large rambling restaurant run by the Pedavena brewery. It serves also as a terraced café and a tea and coffee salon. Things are a bit commercial here. A cart of glittering hors-d'oeuvre is wheeled in before the guest has had time to adjust his bifocals. Four waiters and a maître d'hôtel hover about at once, making it difficult for the diner to decipher the menu with due dignity. The place is gay and urbane, however, and the food is above the average. Pedavena specializes in its own beer, but there is a fine wine list also.

Birreria
Ristorante
Pedavena
Verona

On our visits to Pedavena we had the good fortune to try several delectable specialties, among them a rich and fragrant *pasticcio di lasagne,* containing ham and cheese, and dressed with Bolognese sauce, and *risotto alla marinara,* a flavorful rice and sea-food specialty, enriched by clams, *scampi,* and mussels. Signor Dartora, the director of Pedavena, was kind enough to send us the recipes for both. The *lasagne* appears below, and the recipe for the *risotto* will be found in the treasury of specialties at the end of this volume.

Pasticco di Lasagne
LASAGNE IN CASSEROLE

Cook 1 pound of *lasagne* in boiling salted water until tender. Drain them and cool them in cold water. In a buttered baking dish place alternate layers of *lasagne* and cream sauce combined with a little *ragù bolognese,* or meat sauce (see index), diced ham, and diced Fontina or *mozzarella* cheese. You will need about 2 cups of cream sauce and 2 1/2 cups of meat sauce. Let the top layer be the sauce combination, sprinkle it with grated Parmesan, and place the dish in a hot oven (400° F.) until the top is lightly browned.

Ristorante Fiore
Verona

For slightly pinched purses there is a good little place just round the corner at Via Dietro Distone 15, the RISTORANTE FIORE. We liked the atmosphere and the cheerful waitresses, and found no complaint at all with the *prix-fixe* meal of pasta or soup, meat or fish, and cheese or sweet, for 350 lire, service included. That's less than sixty cents, and a small carafe of honest red Valpolicella costs less than a dime.

Among the hotels of Verona we have a strong favorite, the ALBERGO COLOMBA D'ORO, on the Via C. Cattaneo, a short step from the Piazza Bra. It is comfortable and well appointed, and the service is very good. Its hotel dining room is acceptable, too. Two other good hotels are the GRAND HOTEL and the ALBERGO SAN LORENZO.

Vicenza

HERE IS the place for travelers who rejoice in utterly beautiful architecture. Located in the fertile Po valley, halfway between Venice and Lake Garda, this aristocratic city reflects everywhere the influence of its most famous son, the gifted architect Palladio. Born in Vicenza in 1518, Andrea Palladio almost rebuilt his native city in his lifetime, embellishing it with grandiose architectural conceptions and elegant, graceful façades. The last of the great architects of the Renaissance, he profited by the wealth and the refined taste of contemporary Vicenza.

As an introduction to the splendor of Palladio, we urge you to head directly for the Piazza dei Signori, to park your car in a guarded lot nearby, and to sit down in a straw-backed armchair in a café in the arcades of the Basilica Palladiana. This long, animated piazza provides one of the most thrilling architectural ensembles you'll ever encounter, besides being free of cars, and Vespas, too. It is too bad that you can't have a sumptuous luncheon under these Palladian arcades. Alas, only modest cafés are installed here.

Piazza dei Signori and the Palazzo della Ragione—Vicenza

Palazzo Chiericati–Vicenza

Above the animation of the piazza rises the twelfth-century clock tower, not a flawless bit of architecture by any means, but impressive in its soaring height. Behind you is Palladio's acknowledged masterpiece, the immense Palazzo della Ragione, another name for the Basilica Palladiana. Its brilliant façades repeat the familiar Palladian motif dozens of times in a series of double arcades. Erected in 1549, this is certainly one of the purest examples of Renaissance building. The statue of the master architect, complete with beard and classic robes, stands appropriately in front of his greatest work.

Across the way is the brick Loggia del Capitano, designed by guess who in 1571, which now serves as a Palazzo Comunale. It is heavier than Palladio's other designs, and remains incomplete. There are gay, rococo buildings, also, on the Piazza dei Signori and, at one end of the oblong, are two tall, glistening marble columns, one capped by a heroic figure of Christ, the other by the Lion of Venice, and both plentifully nicked by shell fragments. In fact, the Piazza represents an architectural banquet of marvelous savor, to be remembered for a lifetime.

We urge you to see other examples of this great architect's genius, particularly the Teatro Olimpio, his last work, and the first closed and roofed theater in Italy. You will find it by going to the northeastern extremity of the Corso Andrea Palladio. Undistinguished from the street, inside it is unique in its genre—one of the curiosities of the theatrical world. This is particularly true of its stage set, a rich architectural treatment showing a city piazza with adjoining streets, all achieved with flawlessly deceptive perspective. Palladio did not live to see his theater completed. The work was finished by his competent successor, Scamozzi.

Just across the way is one more Palladian chef-d'oeuvre, the Palazzo Chiericati, now the Civic Museum, an extraordinarily light and graceful building erected in 1551–1557, with open arcades that testify once again to the master architect's amazing originality.

Perhaps the most famous of Palladian villas may be seen on the southern outskirts of Vicenza. Known as La Rotonda, it was begun by Palladio in

146

1550, and served as the country estate of Paolo Almerigo. This work also was completed by Scamozzi, about 1606. Its walls and ceilings are adorned with skillful frescoes by Tiepolo. The design of La Rotonda is particularly pleasing, and it has been reproduced in more than one instance in England.

Vicenza went through a frightful ordeal during the bombardments of 1944 and 1945. Some of the finest buildings in the center of the city were reduced to rubble, but rebuilding has gone forward with characteristic Italian courage and energy.

This city is a pleasant place for an overnight stop, especially since it has been embellished with a new, spotless, and comfortable JOLLY HOTEL. We have already spoken in the introduction of this admirable hotel chain, and we will have more to say when we come to Ravenna. This particular Jolly Hotel faces the public gardens, not far from the railway station, and is surrounded by free parking space. Once installed in a neat room with a tiled bath and a view of the amateur soccer players in the park below your window, you can enjoy fully the peace of evening at the end of a long day's sightseeing. All this, and Palladio too! The Jolly cuisine is always satisfactory, if not inspired, and the service is far above the average.

Jolly Hotel
Vicenza

Vicenza is celebrated for one epicurean specialty, *baccalà alla vicentina,* a simple way of serving dried codfish. After a thorough desalting in water, it is stewed in milk with finely chopped onions, garlic, parsley, butter, oil, anchovy paste, and pepper—a fine dish for hearty, unprejudiced people. It might prove to be a resounding success in your own home, so we are including its recipe at the end of this book.

Motorists who wish to dine in Vicenza at midday can combine the felicity of a good luncheon with the charm of Palladio by visiting the HOTEL ROMA, on the main thoroughfare. We asked for and obtained an authentic *baccalà alla vicentina,* and found it substantial and delicious. Some native asparagus, cheese, giant cherries, black coffee, and an Aurum liqueur completed a noteworthy meal.

Hotel
Roma
Vicenza

North of the road between Verona and Vicenza the observant motorist may see two gaunt, ruined castles crowning neighboring hills. According to legend these belonged, in 1300, to the rival Montecchi and Cappelletti families. In one castle lived the dashing Romeo and in the other pined the lovely Juliet. The story is irresistible, and it is not surprising that the two castles have been dressed up a bit for the tourist trade. Now you can visit both in an American Express bus, enjoy some vivid frescoes recording the immortal love affair, and partake of a more-than-adequate meal at the RISTORANTE GIULIETTA E ROMEO, now installed in Juliet's castle. Although an obvious contraption for the tourist, it is interesting enough to merit a detour, especially for those who are romantically inclined and don't mind hobnobbing with their fellow traveler.

Il Santo—Padua

Palazzo della Ragione—Padua

Padua

SITUATED SOME twenty miles inland from Venice, this large, animated city in the plain is famous for its thirteenth-century university and a few artistic monuments of extraordinary interest. It is a great mistake to bypass Padua, or Padova, as some travelers do, in their headlong haste to arrive in Venice. The splendors of the city merit a one- or two-day stopover. In that time you can enjoy its priceless paintings, its historic shrines (including the most interesting café in Italy), and sample its rich regional cookery. Following are some of its notable curiosities. See them, and you have seen Padua's best.

In a park that contains the ruins of a Roman amphitheater is the Madonna dell'Arena, a little chapel that holds one of the most sublime treasures of Italian art, the immortal frescoes painted at the dawn of the fourteenth century by the great Giotto. This simple building with a single nave is also called the Cappella degli Scrovegni, after the family who built it. The Scrovegni family were moneylenders, and are more popular with the public now than in their own time, when they grew rich in their usurious pursuit. Giotto's divine paintings are a result of their success in the financial world. He was commissioned in 1303, at a time when he was a relatively unknown artist. The murals you now see are his most complete work, painted at the apex of his artistic career, when he was in his mid-thirties. With the aid of his pupils he painted them in three years' time. Dante visited Giotto while the work was in progress, and town historians record their friendship with due pride. The frescoes depict the life of the Virgin Mary and of Christ, and they are still in magnificent condition. You are free to view this stupendous accomplishment at your leisure, for a trifling fee, as visitors have been doing for six centuries.

If this is one of the triumphs of Italian art, the scene of one of its tragedies lies nearby. This is the Church of San Giovanni degli Eremitani, which suffered terrible damage by bombardment in 1944. Mantegna's marvelous frescoes, depicting the life of Saint James, were all but ruined by this catastrophe, and only fragments remain. The ancient church now has a new roof, but that is small consolation for the loss of Mantegna's priceless work.

The most celebrated of Padua's churches is the Basilica of Saint Anthony, known locally as Il Santo, an enormous brick structure of Romanesque tendencies, crowned by seven cupolas and numerous minarets, which give it a strong Byzantine flavor. This is the final resting place of Saint Anthony, whose inspired eloquence was known all over southern Europe. Born in Lisbon in 1195, he became a Franciscan and traveled widely, finally adopting Padua as his home. He died at the age of thirty-six, and his remains lie in a silver casket in the Cappella del Santo, designed by the gifted Sansovino. Countless pilgrims from Italy and foreign lands come to this sanctuary on June 13th, the anniversary of Saint Anthony's death. There are lovely cloisters for them to stroll in, and, if they are interested in pictures, there are two museums near at hand, well furbished with Titians and Tiepolos.

Standing before the basilica is the first great statue in bronze to be cast after the Renaissance, Donatello's superb equestrian statue of Gattamelata, the famous Venetian *condottiere*. The proud, ruthless, square-jawed despot sits astride a magnificent steed, looking every bit as impressive and scornful as his colleague Colleoni in Venice, a masterpiece of sculpture achieved forty years later by Verrocchio. Donatello finished this statue about 1447.

While you are in the neigborhood, we urge you to visit a park of exceptional beauty nearby, the Prato della Valle, a garden opulent in flowers and foliage, surrounded by a canal that follows the pattern of an oval. Bordering the canal on both sides are heroic statues of a multitude of bygone celebrities of Padua—professors, statesmen, and students who made good in the world. They stand on their cylindrical pedestals with much dignity. As a backdrop of the scene rises a huge sprawling Renaissance brick church, said to be the ninth largest in the world. It is the Church of Santa Giustina, crowned by multiple domes and minarets like its illustrious neighbor, Il Santo.

Back in the busy center of the city you will find probably the most picturesque and exciting market building in the whole of Italy. It is the Palazzo della Ragione, dating from the thirteenth century and still a beehive of food merchants, fishmongers, butchers, butter-and-egg men, fruit vendors, and florists. They thrive in its cool arcades and in the open squares on each side of it. You couldn't find a more intriguing place to acquire a picnic lunch. There is much more to the *palazzo* than the ground-floor market, of course. The immense hall above is well worth a visit. It is roofed by a huge single nave, an amazing architectural accomplishment, from which it gets its nickname of Il Salone. The building was originally designed as a Palace of Justice, but its central hall is now used for concerts.

The University of Padua, established in 1222, is one of the oldest anywhere. It is called by students and public alike Il Bo, or The Ox, a name inherited from a tavern that originally stood on its site. It has brought centuries of fame to Padua, and to countless noted men, among them Galileo, who taught physics here from 1592 to 1610. One of the most interesting spots to visit is the small anatomical theater, built in the medical school in 1594 and said to be the oldest in Europe.

But the most vital thing about the university is its student population, most of which gravitates at one time or another to the CAFFÈ PEDROCCHI. This is without doubt one of the most remarkable cafés in the world. It came into being when Antonio Pedrocchi, a modest coffee roaster, decided to transform his coffee shop into a large and beautiful café. The building was inaugurated in June, 1831, and it remains a rare, neoclassic monument to the Empire décor of the time. The café has Greek, Etruscan, Gothic, Pompeian, Egyptian, and Imperial salons, each restored to its pristine freshness. Most of the professors, the intellectuals, musicians, and better-heeled students of Padua cluster here, and we urge you to do the same. There is no restaurant, but sandwiches and snacks supplement the usual café fare. You are served on round-topped tables surrounded by chic Empire chairs upholstered in period pink, sage green, and honey brown. Everything is spotless, and there is an unobtrusive all-girl orchestra to lend further charm to your visit. On some warm evenings, the students take over one of the broad open-air terraces and have a concert of their own, with a succession of gifted amateurs clutching the microphone. They pack the terrace, and it's difficult to get a seat on such uproarious occasions.

We explored the gastronomic possibilities of Padua at some length, and have come up with a rather obvious answer—the big-city hotel at the central crossroads of everything. Though there surely must be some fine, unobtrusive restaurants in Padua, we had poor luck in ferreting them out. At the ALBERGO PALAZZO STORIONE, however, we found a genuine haven of fine cooking. Among the Venetian specialties were *calamaretti fritti, scampi,* and *uccelletti con polenta.* The *lista del giorno* was abundant with other temptations, among them sole, tuna, eel, and lobster, as well as tested favorites from other provinces—*vermicelli alla bolognese, costoletta con tartufi,* and *pollo alla diavola.* We found the food and wine to be more than commendable, and the service very good, in spite of the fact that two wedding parties were taking place. Evidently this has been the "best" hotel in Padua for decades, and the only answer to a proper wedding banquet. The large dining hall is decorated by the well-known painter Laurenti, who has given it the atmosphere of an oversized apple bower. Needless to say, the overnight accommodations here are very good.

Padua has several gastronomic specialties of note. *Risotto con fegatini* (rice with chicken livers) is one of the best. *Torresani farciti* (stuffed doves) is another. The outstanding local favorite, however, is the familiar polenta with little birds roasted on a skewer. This may be found in two restaurants called DOTTO and BI-RI. Two other sources of local pride are sausages called *salamini soppresse* and *salamini da gradela,* the latter served with the ever-present polenta. Finally, some fine liqueurs are manufactured in Padua by the house of Luxardo, among them maraschino, Double Kümmel, and Triple Sec.

Albergo
Palazzo
Storione
PADUA

The hilltop—Monselice

Città Vecchia—Treviso

Loggia dei Cavalieri—Treviso

Abano Terme

ABOUT SEVEN miles southwest of Padua is one of Italy's best known thermal stations, open from early summer through fall. The Romans knew its healing waters well, and they are still effective, after two millenia. These hot radio-active waters, which attain a temperature as high as 180° Fahrenheit, are allowed to evaporate, depositing a medicinal mud that is most effective in the treatment of gout, rheumatism, arthritis, and many other misfortunes.

We don't wish such ill luck to any of our readers, but if some of them are thus oppressed, they will find comfort and calm in Abano Terme, pleas-antly located at the foot of the Euganean hills. There are several good hotels here, many of them equipped with swimming pools, tennis courts, and other means of relaxing in addition to the mud baths. The two best are the ROYAL-OROLOGIO and the TRIESTE E VICTORIA.

If you are driving out of Padua, there is a pleasant motor trip farther south with the towns of Arqua Petrarca and Monselice as objectives. Arqua Petrarca is a dusty little medieval hill town where Petrarch lived, and where he died in 1374. His tomb is in front of the church, and his house is now a museum open to the public. We must confess that the village is a bit dull, something that cannot be said of neighboring Monselice, whose sunny hilltop is crowned by a castle and stronghold of Frederick II. We warmly recom-mend the drive to the very top of this hill, through multiple gates, past Ro-manesque churches, cemeteries, fountains, and buxom statuary.

TREVISO AND ITS NEIGHBORHOOD

USING TREVISO as a point of departure, inquiring motorists will find a re-warding trip in the heart of the Veneto. It includes one of the most extra-ordinary villas in Italy, the Villa Giacomelli, in the village of Maser, designed by Palladio and containing some of Paolo Veronese's finest murals; and three country towns of more than usual interest—Bassano del Grappa, Citta-della, and Castelfranco Veneto.

Treviso

THE TARVISIUM of the Romans is a large, sprawling city in the plain, some twenty miles north of Venice. Though it suffered cruelly from bombardment in both World Wars, its industrious citizens have already repaired most of the damage. The quaint Loggia dei Cavalieri (a good place for an *apéritif,* by the way) is now as solid as ever; so is the *duomo,* and so are the graceful,

The arcaded town square—Bassano del Grappa

arcaded houses that line many of its old streets. The fortified walls that protected this medieval stronghold are now taking their turn at being repaired. The most attractive part of the town is the Città Vecchia, laced with canals and brightened with Venetian façades. Treviso is famed as the home of three painters of the Italian School—Lotto, Rocco Marconi, and Paris Bordone. The cathedral houses a superb painting, "The Annunciation" by Titian, and five splendid frescoes by Pordenone.

Everything considered, Treviso will reward the visitor well, if not for an extended time. It also possesses two hotels that are adequate for an overnight stop, the ALBERGO BAGLIONI and the ALBERGO TREVISO.

A road map will show that our next objective, Maser, can be reached by taking a northeasterly highway through Montebelluna, and then turning off on a country road a few miles beyond. It's a rather dull detour until you reach the Villa Giacomelli, but then you are repaid tenfold for your trouble. Built from 1565 to 1580 from plans by Palladio, this serene estate is decorated with magnificent, haunting frescoes painted by Paolo Veronese between 1566 and 1568. These are joyous, sophisticated murals, executed in Veronese's sure, vigorous, superb draftsmanship. The most distinquished room is the Sala dell'Olimpo, whose ceiling is painted in multiple panels depicting the feast of the gods of Olympus. Veronese paints his own architecture, too, in steep, perfect perspective. Bright-eyed, realistic figures stare down from painted balconies to leave an indelible impression upon the beholder. Veronese's accom-

plishment is an astonishing tour de force that has captivated generations of
visitors. We hope that you will join this privileged group.

Back on the highway and about twelve miles westward is Bassano del
Grappa, a prosperous and highly picturesque town in the foothills. Its architecture is gay, its arcaded town square animated and quaint, especially on
market day, and there are cool cafés from which to watch the busy scene.
The other curiosity of the town is a covered wooden bridge over the Brenta
River, dating from the early thirteenth century and restored in 1948. It
provides an authentic picture of timbered bridges as they were built in the
Middle Ages. In the far distance looms the ominous Monte Grappa, where
thousands of Austrian and Italian soldiers were killed during World War I.
This impregnable stronghold was attacked seventy-two times by the Austrians,
the last attempt taking place a few days before the November armistice. An
immense military cemetery still serves as a grim reminder of those tragic days.

The circuit back to Treviso is begun by turning southward to Cittadella,
a walled town founded in 1220 by the Paduans to serve as a fortress against
the warriors of Treviso. Its circular medieval ramparts are still intact, still
protected by an emerald-green moat. The round town within the walls is
bisected neatly each way by a crossroad, creating four fine battlemented
gateways of brick.

On the road back to Treviso it will be worth your while to stop for half an
hour at Castelfranco Veneto, another fortified town with Venetian overtones.
Here was born the great painter Giorgione. You may see one of his masterpieces in the church, a lovely figure of the Virgin with Saint Francis and Saint
George. Another striking feature of this church is its immense brick tower,
quite reminiscent of the campanile in the Piazza San Marco in Venice, except
that it leans giddily northward. Though its pitch is not as disquieting as that
of the famous tower of Pisa, it nevertheless caused these travelers to raise
an apprehensive eyebrow.

Venice

ITALIAN BOUQUET, as we pointed out in the introduction, has certain definite
limitations. It aspires to be an epicurean adviser and, wherever possible, a
discriminating guide to the beauties of Italy. But some subjects are simply
too vast to fall within its scope. This limitation applies particularly to Rome,
Florence, and Venice, where even an abbreviated attempt at guidebookery
would lead to impossible lengths. In these three exceptional cases we restrict
ourselves to the epicurean scene alone, and refer our readers to any number
of good guidebooks, which they will find in those enchanting Italian bookstores.

And so, suddenly, we are face to face with the subject of dining in Venice, without a word about the Doge's Palace or the Accademia. It is a pleasant ritual to contemplate, and there is no more auspicious spot to discuss this delicate matter than from a table at the CAFFÈ FLORIAN on the Piazza San Marco.

A landmark among the great cafés of the world, Florian still retains under its arcades its ancient marble-topped tables that swivel as readily as a Lazy Susan, its red velvet wall benches, and its horsehair chairs. Elaborate gouache murals on its walls have been preserved under glass. On a rainy day (and there were plenty of them during our latest April visit!), it is a providential retreat. The clientele is varied. There are oblivious lovers, camera-laden tourists, lonely women, and businessmen scribbling figures on the table tops. The waiters are quadrilingual, but less attractive than the enormous brindle cat with a red ribbon around his neck who lounges about the place. Florian is essentially an open-air café, however, and when its vast acreage of tables is fully occupied on a holiday afternoon in summer, it is truly fabulous. Two outdoor orchestras vie with each other across the square. Immense banners fly from three flagpoles; Saint Mark's glistens with color and the campanile towers over thousands of citizens congregated in the piazza.

If your time is limited and you don't wish to waste it over a protracted meal, Florian serves a quick lunch of sandwiches and pastry, with good coffee to go with them. They can even make an excellent dry Martini, something which generations of American travelers have requested.

Within a short stroll of this animated terrace are several pleasant prospects for the inquiring gourmet. Directly across the square is a rival café, somewhat smaller, but distinguished by a smart little dining salon under its arcade, and with lighthearted murals and a string quartet to add a touch of gaiety. It is called QUADRI, a charming spot worth remembering, especially for its *scampi* and filets of sole. Up one flight are Quadri's two well-appointed dining salons, their walls covered with brocade and their windows giving on the ceaseless animation of the Piazza San Marco. The prices are somewhat exalted here, in keeping with the view.

Harry's
Bar
VENICE

Right behind you, occupying a choice location on the Grand Canal at the San Marco boat landing, is HARRY'S BAR, a celebrated cultural center boasting the best mixed drinks in Venice, and a patronage top-heavy with sophisticated (and other) Anglo-Saxons. If you are homesick for the dulcet tones of American voices, and in search of highly commendable food as well, Harry's Bar is a good, if somewhat expensive, solution. The food is handsomely prepared and served, and if you want curried *scampi, baccalà alla vicentina, sole Casanova,* or a superb *tournedos Rossini,* Harry's headwaiter is delighted to serve them. Signor Cipriani, the creator of Harry's Bar, has made this the smartest place in Venice. He also originated the peaceful La Locanda on the island of Torcello, a delightful place for a country luncheon.

Profile of Venice

Terrace of the Caffè Florian and the Piazza San Marco—Venice

Island of San Giorgio Maggiore—Venice

Across the piazza from your table at Florian's is the clock tower, under which is the BAR AMERICANO. It resembles hundreds of Italian bars except that it serves a varied and satisfying lunch for the visitor whose spare time is limited. There is a delicious pasta, *lasagne verdi,* and you will find small anchovy-encrusted *pizze* and baby sandwiches of ham or shrimp, squiggled with mayonnaise in the more florid Italian manner. Finally there is fruit, and pastry to go with your small cup of *caffè espresso.* Add them all together and the check is still small. Furthermore, you have a bonus of time to visit the marvels of Venice.

In the inexpensive category, you will find a whole cluster of restaurants, most of them acceptable, in the maze of narrow streets just behind the clock tower. One of the best of these is the PILSEN, at San Marco 1198. The old reliable Venetian dishes, *risotto alla marinara, zuppa di pesce, scampi alla veneziana, gambaretti, calamaretti,* and lobster, are served here with a flourish, together with more conventional dishes, including several German ones, to please the international palate. And, as you might expect from its name, Pilsen's beer is very good indeed.

If you feel in an expansive mood, it is only a short walk from the Piazza San Marco to one of the four leading hotels of Venice. Several of them have superlative cuisines, so good that their guests are seldom tempted to dine anywhere else. In addition, they throw in a view of the Grand Canal with their meals, something that very few Venetian restaurants provide. The inquiring epicure will find a particular welcome in the ROYAL DANIELI. This famous hotel has a wonderful rooftop terrace where you may dine overlooking the Grand Canal and admire San Giorgio etched on the horizon, one of the most soul-stirring panoramas in Italy. You may order conventional dishes here if you wish, but we suggest something more adventurous such as *scampi flamingo, scaloppine San Giorgio,* a chicken prepared with whisky, or a *soufflé arlequin.* Signor Zucchi, the generous manager of this hotel and the Excelsior Palace on the Lido, has given us the recipes for these and several other specialties. We have selected one to appear here, and others will be found in the recipe supplement.

Scampi Flamingo
SHRIMP FLAMINGO

In 1/4 pound of butter cook slowly 1 onion, 1 stalk of celery, and 1 carrot, all finely minced, with 1/4 teaspoon of thyme. When the vegetables have taken on a little color add 2 pounds of large raw shrimp in their shells, let them brown a little and cook until all liquid has evaporated, being careful not to let the bottom of the pan get scorched. Add a liqueur glass of cognac and flame it. Remove the shrimp and shell them. Then stir into the pan 2 cups of light cream, 1/3 cup of sherry, and 1/4 cup of very thick white sauce. Simmer for 10 minutes, replace the shrimp in the sauce, and cook 5 minutes more. Add salt and a little lemon juice to the sauce, melt in a good lump of fresh butter, and, when the sauce is of a perfect creamy consistency, remove the shrimp to a hot dish and strain the sauce over them through a fine sieve. Serve with fluffy boiled rice.

The GRAND HOTEL and the HOTEL BAUER GRÜNWALD, both bordering the Grand Canal, have inviting dining terraces at the water's edge, combined with irreproachable cuisine. Dining here on a starlit evening is a privilege that most people will recall for a lifetime. Signor Schachner, manager of the Grand hotel, has sent us a quartet of his favorite recipes, one of which is:

Involtini di Vitello alla Grand Hotel
VEAL ROLLS GRAND HOTEL

Trim and flatten 4 thin veal *scaloppine* and spread them with a mixture of 6 tablespoons of *ricotta* cheese thoroughly blended with 4 tablespoons of ground ham. Roll up the veal slices and fasten them with toothpicks or tie them with thread. Cook the veal rolls slowly on all sides in 2 tablespoons of oil and 2 tablespoons of butter combined. After 20 to 30 minutes, or when the veal is cooked, blend 1 tablespoon of Marsala into the pan juices. Serve with mashed potatoes.

Your hotel possibilities are not yet exhausted, by any means. After that second Martini at Florian's, the HOTEL LUNA is only a step away. The menu is extraordinarily good and diverse, with many French dishes in evidence. You can order a delicious *prix-fixe* luncheon or dinner here at a most reasonable price. Finally, there is the GRITTI PALACE, another of the famous hotels bordering the Grand Canal, and very good it is.

During a month's foraging in Venice, we went much farther afield than the immediate area of Saint Mark's, of course, and were richly rewarded. There is no question about it—in addition to its hotels, Venice rejoices in several restaurants capable of brightening a gourmet's existence. We propose four for your delectation, mindful of the fact that our omissions are positively sinful.

TAVERNA LA FENICE—Campiello Fenice 1938

This, to our way of thinking, is the most gratifying dining place in Venice, and deserves to be the epicure's number one choice. Finding it for the first time, however, is a rare feat of map reading and instinctive orientation. Once you discover it, you will wish you had unrolled a ball of string so that you can find your way back again. However, on the parchmentlike menu there is a map that will serve almost as well as a string trail, and will also lead you to the most celebrated theater in Venice, the Teatro la Fenice. Just behind it, facing a quiet open space, is our *ristorante*. Here an immense summer dining terrace has been installed, with only the ripple of a passing gondola to furnish added animation. During the colder months, the Taverna is not so quiet. The ceilings of its interior rooms are low, and the conversational pitch runs high. But it should be remembered that the Italians like noise, and prefer reverberation to discreet quiet. Summer or winter, calm or chatty, the Taverna la Fenice has an immense attraction for luxury-loving people. You'll be sure to meet your American and English friends here, and you may see some celebrities, too, judging by the gallery of famous patrons on the wall. Here are Clark Gable, inscrutably admiring the way Signor Zoppi tosses his noodles, Tyrone Power looking very manly and in need of a shave, the regretted Mistinguett showing all her teeth, and assorted opera singers, accordion players, violinists, and ladies with low necklines.

Though La Fenice is more expensive than the average Venetian restaurant, we believe it justifies the price, and for a variety of reasons. For one thing, the service is excellent, largely because alert and fairly comely maids serve the tables, and *not* those noisy, hissing waiters. We are getting to be more of a feminist every day in the matter of table service. Signor Zoppi is a very attentive host, and an individual one. With his fine, snowy mane he resembles a concert pianist, and you want to address him as *maestro*. You are aware of his artistry at once. A magnificent phalanx of boiled lobsters greets you at the door, and the full repertoire of Venetian delicacies is

Taverna
La
Fenice
Venice

Ca' d'Oro—Venice

listed on the menu—the flavorful *scampi,* boiled, roasted, grilled, or fried, or served with an aromatic sauce, if you prefer, Adriatic sole, red mullet, and filet of beef, among other things. The famous *risi e bisi* and polenta are superb, as are other classic temptations—*osso buco,* a worthy rival of any French ragout, *saltimbocca,* the perfect marriage of veal and ham, and that Venetian sublimation of calf's liver and onions, *fegato alla veneziana.* The wine list is impressive; the atmosphere is hospitable and friendly. A joyful evening is inevitable at the Taverna la Fenice.

ALLA COLOMBA—San Marco 1665

Alla Colomba
VENICE

Although this is essentially a place for food-loving Venetians, particularly writers, poets, and musicians, the roving voluptuary from far away will find a warm welcome and sumptuous fare, if he seeks out the Sign of the Dove. This restaurant is also near the Teatro la Fenice, and its dining terrace almost blocks the street on a warm summer night. Inside, in the string of seven dining rooms, one is struck immediately by the profusion of paintings on the walls. It turns out that Signor Arturo Deana, the owner, is an ardent patron of the arts. Many of his acquisitions do real credit to contemporary Italian painting. None of them, however, can approach the real still life of recumbent fish that greets the guest as he enters. The whole piscatorial parade is here, fresh from the Adriatic and glistening on a center table. There are schools of lobsters, deep orange *langoustes,* prickly red crabs, sleek *scampi,* and *gambaretti* in profusion. Ah, this rhapsodic Venetian fish! Here are squads of squid and sole and pinkish mullet, overflowing baskets of oysters, *datteri* (mussels), and *vongole,* those small, two-necked clams best known in Naples.

Aside from the paintings, there is nothing unusual about the décor of La Colomba. It has the white napery and bright lights common to so many Italian restaurants. But exceptional cooking comes from La Colomba's large and spotless kitchen, and the service is prompt and courteous. At one time, before Signor Deana's day, this was a small and unpretentious *trattoria,* and while it still keeps this designation on its menu, it has long since outgrown the name, and should be considered one of the top dining places in Venice. Care should be taken not to confuse it with another restaurant called Al Colombo. The names are closely similar. La Colomba proved to be a treasure to this scouting party, and we think you'll feel the same way about it.

Signor Deana was more than generous in giving us Venetian recipes that flourish at La Colomba. Among a half dozen, we have chosen this as one which can be deftly accomplished in your own kitchen.

Risotto di Scampi
SHRIMP RISOTTO

Make a fish stock as follows: Peel 1 pound of raw shrimp and put the shells to boil in 4 to 5 cups of water together with several fish heads or other fish scraps, 1 stalk of celery, 1 small onion, and 1 small carrot, all sliced, a bay leaf, and salt and pepper. After half an hour of simmering, strain off the stock.

Start the *risotto* by stirring 1 cup of rice into 2 tablespoons of butter heated in a heavy pot. When the rice is slightly golden, add 1 cup of fish stock, cover the pot, and allow the rice to cook very slowly for about 10 minutes, or until the stock is absorbed. Add 2 1/2 cups of the fish stock, cover, and continue cooking the rice.

Meanwhile, in 1 tablespoon of olive oil cook for 1 to 2 minutes 1 minced clove of garlic and 1 teaspoon of minced parsley. Add this mixture to the rice with the second quantity of stock. After 10 minutes, add the raw shrimp. When all the stock has been absorbed and the rice is done, add a dash each of cinnamon, nutmeg, and clove, 1 teaspoon of butter, and 3 tablespoons of grated Parmesan. The total cooking time is 30 to 40 minutes. The *risotto* should not be mushy.

TRATTORIA ANTICA CARBONERA—S. Luca 4648

They do things differently in Venice—numbering houses, for example. Numbers run inexplicably into the thousands, and it takes a slide rule, a compass, and a garbled conversation with the corner policeman to figure out the system. We became rapt converts of the Antica Carbonera once we had wandered through a maze of side streets, over canal bridges, and under vaulted passageways to find it. Its street, San Luca, is obscure and just about six feet wide, and you have to look hard to find Number 4648. But you encounter pure Venice when you finally get there. The place has the long-established atmosphere of Lüchow's in New York or Durgin-Park in Boston— a smooth-running place with no pretense and no particular style in its décor, but one that has been dedicated for decades to wholesome food. Inexpensive and a bit rough-and-ready, it is eminently worth your visit. In this busy, popular *trattoria* the kitchen is right in the middle of everything. It is amusing to choose a table where you can watch the venerable chefs in action behind their plate-glass window. They are experts at their trade and quick enough to have spare time to exchange witticisms with favored customers. One of them needs bifocals, for he wears his horn-rimmed glasses continually on the tip of his nose. We watched him with fascination as he whipped up a *fegato alla veneziana* in a few swift minutes.

Almost everyone was having *risotto* as a first course that day, and it was superb, nuggeted with shrimp and rings of octopus. Fragrant and fat-

Trattoria
Antica
Carbonera
Venice

Canal bordering the Scuola di San Marco—Venice

The Grand Canal—Venice

Statue of Bartolomeo Colleoni—Venice

Porta della Carta, the Doge's Palace—Venice

tening, it was precisely the dish for a disconsolately rainy day. There were three different fish soups for dissenters from the *risotto,* and a fine array of conventional meat dishes to supplement the matchless Adriatic fish. Good red Bardolino and white Soave came in flagons holding more than a quart and costing less than forty cents. For substantial nourishment and pure Venetian cuisine, Antica Carbonera is surely one of the best, and worth many times the effort you make to find it.

AL PEOCETO RISORTO—Calle della Dondella 250–251

This *ristorante* was revealed to us as a favorite among Venetian gourmets, and is not too well known to the traveling public. You approach it by crossing the Rialto Bridge and walking through the hurly-burly of umbrella-topped cheese stands, vegetable carts, pastry and fruit pushcarts which make up the Rialto market. The experience may serve as a fascinating hors-d'oeuvre all by itself, depending upon how many acres of raw meat and miles of uncooked sausage you can look upon with equanimity.

A neon sign points to the narrow side street where Al Peoceto Risorto is located—a neat little place, unpretentious and clean. On our first visit there, all the other clients were well-upholstered Italians with napkins under their chins. The atmosphere was congenial, in spite of two doleful guitarists who broke in on the scene.

Fish soups and deep fries are the specialty here. One of our fun-loving gastronomic quartet accosted *fritto misto di pesce* and found it not too heavy and totally delicious, even though he couldn't identify a single fish that came from that hot cauldron of olive oil. Another tried *calamaretti al limone,* those fabulous baby octopuses, hardly bigger than your thumbnail, also fried in deep olive oil and served with parsley and lemon. Nothing could be simpler or more satisfying. Can they rival New England's famous fried clams? Well rather! For one thing, they don't have to be shucked, and we believe they are more tender in texture and subtler in taste. A third individualist ordered *risotto espresso alla veneziana,* a *risotto* truffled with *scampi, gambaretti,* and tiny firm bits of fish, which was pronounced perfectly divine. We indulged in an old favorite, *vermicelli alla vongole* with total success. The pasta had the perfect consistency, and the tiny clams, their necks forming a Churchillian V, were the foundation for a salubrious sauce. After this, a bit of grilled beef, cheese, and coffee, accompanied by generous beakers of wine from the Verona hills, and our evening Al Peoceto Risorto was complete.

Without resorting to superlatives, we think this restaurant, whose destinies are guided by a cordial man named Pietro Polo, will meet with the approval of most gourmets, especially those who are interested in the piscatorial treasure of the Adriatic.

Fishermen's canal–Chioggia

Signor Polo has shared five of his favorite recipes with us, including this formula for preparing Adriatic sole:

Filetti di Sogliola alla Peoceto
FILETS OF SOLE PEOCETO

Dip 6 filets of sole in flour, shake off the excess, and brown them on both sides in 2 tablespoons of olive oil and 2 tablespoons of butter heated together. Season the filets with salt and pepper and place them on a hot platter with a dozen or more mussels that have been steamed open and removed from their shells. Over them pour a cream sauce made as follows: Blend 1 teaspoon of flour with 1 tablespoon of butter, add gradually 3/4 cup of cream, and season the sauce with salt and pepper. Simmer it for 1 minute, and at the last thicken it with 1 beaten egg yolk, pour it over the fish and serve at once.

Coupled with the privilege of being in Venice itself are the excursions by boat to the Lido and to the islands of Murano, Burano, and Torcello. A little steamer makes a most pleasant trip to the fishing town of Chioggia also, and there are few places with as much local color. We urge you to visit them all, even though we can't guarantee great epicurean rewards. It goes without saying that you can dine superbly by the sands at the EXCELSIOR or the GRAND HOTEL DES BAINS on the luxurious Lido. People don't go to Murano to dine, but to watch the glass blowers, and to acquire pieces of the famous Venetian glass at slightly reduced prices. In Burano, the finest of Venetian lace is offered for sale, together with table linen, scarves, and no end of things to tempt the gourmet's wife, while he explores the sea-food situation. Burano is an active fishing port, and we saw many happy couples dining in the open air on plump, wine-red octopus. This is an acquired taste, however, and we are cautious about recommending that you do the same. The lovely island of Torcello, last of the three, will provide the aesthetic thrill of the trip. It was a city of importance during the Middle Ages, as its beautiful cathedral, dating from the seventh century, and the octagonal Church of Santa Fosca will testify. The haunting beauty of this ancient island can never be forgotten. Furthermore, there is a delightful spot to have luncheon, LA LOCANDA. This

La Locanda
TORCELLO

cheerful little place faces the canal, which leads to Torcello's architectural treasures. Under its gay awnings you dine at leisure, and both the food and wine are impeccable. There couldn't be a more relaxing place to sample the beauty of Adriatic sea food, or to spend a night or a weekend. There are half a dozen guest rooms for tranquility-seekers who choose this reposeful spot. La Locanda is owned by Signor Giuseppe Cipriani, the creator of Harry's Bar in Venice, so you may be sure it's good.

Chioggia is at the southern end of the lagoon, and can be reached by boat in about two hours. This city is a miniature Venice with the added picturesqueness of a fishing fleet and enough canals and multicolored sails to make it a water-colorist's dream come true. The boat stops there long enough for you to admire the city's quaintness, inhale its atmosphere, and visit some of its fine churches. You also have time for lunch. A little restaurant called AL CAVALLO will provide more than adequate fare, particularly in the realm of sea food. Here they are again, *calamaretti, gamberetti, scampi,* and *zuppa di pesce,* followed by a rich maritime *risotto.* For the more adventurous epicures, the octopus family is here in full array. Isn't this a good place to let go and try them?

Friuli-Venezia Giulia

Chapter 7

FRIULI - VENEZIA GIULIA

THE FAR northeastern region of Italy, hemmed in on two sides by Austria and Yugoslavia, offers definite inducements to the more enterprising traveler. It can hardly claim the multiple charms of its rich neighbor Veneto, but it has enough to reward both the sightseer and the gourmet. It boasts two noble cities, Udine and Trieste, and a squad of minor attractions—mountain resorts, beaches, and a fascinating, forgotten Roman metropolis called Aquileia. Parts of it are dull, too—flat stretches of plain and heavily wooded mountain areas. But take the best of it and a pleasant trip should result.

The Italians feel badly about the eastern frontier of this region, which was moved radically inward as an aftermath of World War II. Trieste is theirs at last, but Friuli (a corruption of the Roman Forum Julii) seems cruelly maimed in Italian eyes.

The mountainous part of the region is called Carnia, a pleasant hill country without remarkable peaks. There are several resorts of interest here, particularly Tarvisio, at the extreme northern corner, almost on the frontier. This ancient town has good small hotels for summer holidays seekers and winter sportsmen. It is in the plains, however, that the foraging epicure will encounter the most encouragement. Our little guided tour concentrates upon five spots of unusual interest, all of which deserve a visit—Pordenone, Udine, Aquileia, Grado, and Trieste. But first a few words about food and wine.

Austrian, Slavic, and Hungarian overtones are evident in the versatile cuisine of this far corner of Italy. A prime favorite is *costoletta alla viennese,* which is, of course, the old standby *Wiener Schnitzel* all dressed up in a Latin name. Dipped in egg and bread crumbs, fried in fine olive oil, or butter, discreetly ornamented with a green olive and an anchovy filet, a veal cutlet can hardly appear in more becoming attire. In Trieste, the Hun-

garian national dish, *gulyás* is enthroned as a local favorite. But Trieste goulash is concocted of lean beef rather than veal or pork. The meat is cut in cubes and cooked with smoked bacon, many onions, copious seasonings of paprika and ardent Hungarian pepper, with appetizing results. Though neither of these dishes claim great originality, of course, it comes as a surprise to find them so perfected in this remote niche of Italy.

Trieste has a noble soup all its own, however. This is *iota triestina,* a sturdy *potage* contrived of beans, potatoes, and sauerkraut, boiled with pig's feet and ribs of roast pork, and flavored with leaves of laurel and cloves of garlic. There is obviously nothing timid about local Trieste cooking! Naturally enough, there is a special fish soup in this famous seaport. It is called *brodetto di pesce alla triestina* and contains a miscellany of Adriatic fish, with mullet, eel, and turbot heading the cast. Finally, there is a specialty for you to seek out in the pastry shops. It is called *presnitz alla triestina*—puff pastry with almonds, candied oranges, nuts, and honey. When sprinkled with chocolate, the *presnitz* becomes a *putizza.*

Some palatable little wines are produced on the slopes above Trieste, particularly in the neighborhood of Istria. The best of the reds, called Terrano, we sampled with pleasure in the Dante Restaurant in Trieste. Another is Del Carso. If you prefer a sparkling red wine, there is one called Refosco, dry, fizzy, and a bit heady. It also comes from Istria. To end a good dinner in Trieste, a Prosecco is very much in order. This is a limpid, golden nectar, not too sweet, and just the thing to go with that flamboyant pastry.

Pordenone

THIS ANCIENT town on the road from Venice to Udine is mentioned principally for enthusiasts of Lombard Gothic architecture. The immense brick campanile of its cathedral, bulging subtly at the top and capped by an octagonal spire, is one of the unheralded treasures of the region. Another is the ancient town hall, also of time-weathered brick. Pordenone is famous principally as the birthplace of the painter Giovanni Licinio (1483–1539), known in the museum world as Il Pordenone. If you happen to arrive late in the day, there is a suitable hotel here, the ALBERGO MODERNO. Pordenone suffered cruelly during the last war, but is rebuilding rapidly.

Piazza della Libertà–Udine

The clock tower–Udine

Campanile of the cathedral–Pordenone

Udine

THIS PLEASANT metropolis on the road between Venice and Vienna is seldom visited, and undeservedly omitted from many tours and guidebooks. Udine once bristled with brass, for it served as Italian GHQ from 1915 to 1917. The city was sacked but not badly damaged in the Italian retreat from nearby Caporetto, one of the most tragic names in Italian history.

If you like your architecture served in one concentrated dose, you will find it all lumped gloriously together in Udine's Piazza della Libertà. Monumental buildings burst out all over the place. There is the Palazzo Civico, a glittering marble structure built in the Venetian style—ornate as a wedding cake, and much more satisfying. Across the way stands the faintly Florentine Loggia of San Giovanni, dominated by a clock tower, its crowning glory a duo of bronze gentlemen who strike a large bell on each quarter hour. Scattered nearby are two imposing Venetian columns, a rotund fountain, and assorted marble statues of muscular Roman giants. Above it all, approached by a Palladian archway, towers the immense bulk of the *castello,* now converted into a museum. This is one of the spots in Italy for which we reserve the much-abused designation breath-taking. We can't say as much for the hotel accommodations, or the restaurant food, but both are adequate. One good hotel is the EUROPA, down by the railway station. We chose the quieter ITALIA, located on the pleasant Piazza XX Settembre, in the heart of the city. The rooms were all right, and dinner was served under the trees on a little terrace. The specialties here are *minestrone* made with local beans, Montasio cheese, polenta, and the famous San Daniele ham, from a village close by.

From Udine, a rewarding side trip can be made to Cividale del Friuli, about ten miles eastward. This is an ancient Roman town with a good cathedral and many sketchable houses and market places. Spanning the river Natison is the Ponte del Diavolo, a superb stone bridge that has been rebuilt in recent years, after being demolished in the retreat from Caporetto.

Aquileia

THE SLEEPY agricultural village in the flat lowlands below Udine is but a mute, somnolent shadow of its former self. Once it was a magnificent seaport, one of the four greatest cities of the Roman Empire, and a favorite residence of the Emperor Augustus. The sea has long since retreated from Aquileia, but recent excavations have brought to light its extensive stone docks, as well as a Roman forum.

Aquileia's greatest treasure, however, is its ninth-century basilica, an astounding structure recalling the fact that this later was an ecclesiastical stronghold. It has the incredible good fortune to be built over mosaic pavements dating from the fourth century and still in near-perfect condition. The mosaics depict many familiar scenes, Jonah's encounter with the whale among them. Beside the inspiring basilica stands an immense detached campanile, built partly by depleting the neighboring amphitheater—a lofty boneyard of Roman stones. There is a very touching cemetery nearby, shaded by olive trees, where repose the remains of several unknown Italian soldiers.

A pensive, haunting calm pervades the site of this forgotten seaport. Umbrella pines and cypresses provide shade for the relatively few visitors who linger awhile. The epicurean possibilities of the village are about exhausted when you buy an ice cream sandwich from a drowsing vendor nearby. Never mind! Bring a picnic lunch, or go hungry, but don't miss the richest archaeological experience in this part of Italy!

Grado

IF YOU motor seven miles south of Aquileia, across the lagoons, you come to another ancient seaport. Grado, however, conceals its venerable origin under the trappings of a modern summer resort, and a Bikini is far more in keeping with the place than an archaeologist's shovel. But, if you persist, you will find Roman and Byzantine columns in its cathedral.

Grado is an unsophisticated fishing port, filled with vacationers in search of clean sand and sunshine. The local municipality deserves a vote of thanks for closing off the center of the town to motor traffic. As a result, you stroll blissfully through its streets, secure in the knowledge that no baby Fiat can run you down, no sputtering Vespa can trouble your benign calm. It is pleasant to sit in the brightly lighted main street after dinner and to gaze at the passing throng. It is not a worldly pageant—just family groups, sailors, naval officers, and an assortment of leisurely tourists, very few of them Anglo-Saxons.

There is a picturesque fishing port, with a full complement of wooden vessels. On the prow of each are two local symbols, wood carvings that resemble enormous snails. On the hot August day we visited Grado, the seafaring men were not dedicated to piscatorial pursuits. Instead they sat barefoot on the decks under russet awnings and played cards. Obviously, this town is a perfect place to relax. There are two acceptable hotels along the beach, the ASTORIA and the ESPLANADE. The former has a night club, a jittery jazz sextet, and ample parking space, all in season.

Excavations of the Roman forum—Aquileia

The ninth-century basilica—Aquileia

Leaving Grado the next morning we saw a cheerfully ungrammatical bilingual sign that read: *Au Revoir*—Let Us See Again. We intend to accept the invitation!

Trieste

OCCUPYING A choice setting at the northern extremity of the Adriatic, and serving as its principal port, Trieste has always been a prize coveted by neighboring countries. For centuries it was the port of Austria. But the Romans had it long before that and have left the remains of an amphitheater as proof of their presence. Today, following the agreement made with Yugoslavia in 1954, the Italian colors fly from its gleaming flagpoles, and it is now a far more pleasant and relaxed place than when it was a free city under military supervision.

Many transatlantic vessels dock in the deep harbor at Trieste, so there is a chance that you may find yourself one day in this gusty, bustling city of a quarter million and more. It is well worth a visit, and the prudent traveler will not neglect to take a light coat along to protect him from the high wind that often sweeps through this top pocket of the Adriatic. Sometimes it is so gusty that ropes have to be strung along the streets of Trieste to help struggling pedestrians.

You will find that the most tranquil and beguiling spot in the teeming city is a tree-covered hilltop crowned by an ancient *castello*. From this lofty eminence you have a superb view of the close-packed city and its busy harbor, without hearing its commercial clatter. Nearby is the reposeful Basilica of San Giusto, built on the ruins of a Roman temple. Its rose window is lovely, and its doorway is curiously framed by Roman sarcophagi, turned on end. You will find ancient Roman columns inside its campanile, probably filched from the partially restored forum nearby.

Ristorante
Da Dante
TRIESTE

If this hilltop constitutes the touristic high spot of Trieste, we also have a glowing nominee for its gastronomic pinnacle, the restaurant called DA DANTE, a large, animated, ambitious establishment at Via Carducci 12. The length of the menu that confronts the eager diner is awe-inspiring—more than twenty pasta preparations, fifteen Adriatic fish dishes, and over thirty meats. We had the good fortune to be guided through the maze of dishes by a qualified expert. He recommended two specialties that were so good that we pass them on to you. Both delicacies were prepared at the table by a gifted waiter-cook. The *sontuose lasagne di Mamma Rosa* were thin, extra-wide noodles mixed in butter in a chafing dish with bits of ham and cheese, and finally thick cream. *Filetto di bue Voronoff* was a fine filet of beef browned in butter, to which were added mixed mustard, lemon juice, a

Canale Grande–Trieste

Basilica of San Giusto–Trieste

trickle of Worcestershire sauce, then sherry, and finally brandy. The sauce was blended and the whole dish ignited in another spray of brandy. With a slice of marrow on top, and a loyal bottle of Terrano, it was a dish to remember.

Trieste has two good hotels, both accustomed to coping with Anglo-Saxon needs. They should be, after catering to British and American officers for years. The imposing SAVOIA EXCELSIOR PALACE, which prides itself on its cuisine, faces the harbor near the maritime station, while another JOLLY HOTEL, a large and luxurious one this time, is near the railway station. We will have more to say of this hotel chain in the next chapter.

Signor Anfossi, the director of the Savoia Excelsior Palace, has shared three of his treasured recipes with us. We urge you to try his inspired formula for preparing *scampi,* using our good southern shrimp as a substitute.

Savoia Excelsior Palace

TRIESTE

Code di Scampi Imperiali San Giusto
SHRIMP SAN GIUSTO

Peel and devein 1 pound of large, raw shrimp. (This is easy to do by cutting the shell with scissors the length of the back, the outer, rounded side of the shrimp.) Marinate them for an hour in the juice of half a lemon with 1 bay leaf and a little salt and pepper.

With the shells make stock by simmering them for half an hour in a small saucepan with 1 1/2 to 2 cups of water, 1 bay leaf, a slice of onion, a pinch each of orégano and thyme, and salt and pepper.

Heat 1 tablespoon of butter and 2 tablespoons of olive oil in a shallow saucepan, and add 1 onion, 1 clove of garlic, and 1 teaspoon parsley, all finely chopped. When the vegetables are softened, add the shrimp, previously dipped in flour. Brown them a little on both sides, with the vegetables, on a fairly brisk fire. Add 1/3 cup of dry white wine, lower the heat, and simmer until the wine is almost evaporated. Now add 1 large tomato, peeled, seeded, and chopped, and 1/2 cup or more of the strained fish stock. Simmer all together for 15 to 20 minutes, or until the sauce is of the right consistency.

San Vitale–Ravenna

Emilia-Romagna

Chapter 8

EMILIA-
ROMAGNA

E
VEN THE most enthusiastic Emilian press agent would hesitate to designate his two sprawling regions as among the most seductive in Italy.
The upper part, which stretches almost entirely across the high calf
of the Italian boot, is as flat as Iowa, and just as fertile. The southern strip
consists mainly of Apennine foothills, and is somewhat forbidding, as any
veteran of General Mark Clark's Italian expeditionary forces will tell you.
The famous Via Emilia, built by the Romans in the year 187 A. D., which
runs in an almost straight line for one hundred and fifty miles from the
Adriatic shore to Piacenza, is not an imposing highway today. It is beset
with impacted road signs, clouds of dust, and incessant repairs, and cluttered
with the cacophony of sputtering scooters and motorcycles. Yet, by some
peculiar justice, the Via Emilia is one of the most fascinating roads in Italy,
a happy circumstance due solely to the chain of medieval cities that it connects, and the extraordinarily brilliant cuisine that distinguishes them. From
the Adriatic shore a string of significant names stretches almost to Milan—
Rimini, Cesena, Forlì, Bologna, Modena, Parma, and Piacenza, each famous
in its way, each offering something unusual to the observant—and hungry—
traveler.

For this region, to Italian epicures, is the cradle of the best food in Italy.
Their faces light up when they talk about *la cucina bolognese*. Bologna, the
Eden of gastronomes, the city of fine cooking and keen brains! This is
the land of those famous egg noodles with a savory meat sauce, of the immortal *mortadella* sausage, of Parmesan cheese, and of turkey breasts sublimated
with melted cheese and wafers of truffle!

The Bolognese are proud not only of their cooking but of their robust
appetites, and cite, as an example, a wedding feast held in 1475 when the
bride and groom and a thousand guests sat down to table for three consec-

utive days, attacking such substantial fare as pasta, assorted
roasts, sausages, hams, truffled
turkeys, cheeses, fruits, and
pastries. All this food was lubri-
cated with the good wine of
Montedonato and interlarded,
one supposes, with judicious
intervals of sleep.

In the minds of most epi-
cures, *ingrassamento,* or fattening, is the word for Bolognese dishes. The outstanding
specialty, the key to everything,
is called *sfoglia* (meaning leaf
or sheet), the basic homemade egg pasta that forms the foundation for any
number of farinaceous dishes. Their names ripple along—*tortellini, tagliatelle,
lasagne, pappardelle, cappelletti, tortelli*—what musical names they are, and
how gratifying to the gourmet! Each of them deserves a separate essay,
sprinkled with tinkling adjectives! A rapturous Bolognese gourmet hit the
proper poetic peak when he termed the *tortellino* the "umbilicus of Venus."
These incredible little "lifesavers" of *sfoglia* are rolled around a stuffing
composed of ham, *mortadella,* chopped veal, Parmesan cheese, and a suspicion of nutmeg. When this tender delicacy is cooked in a good chicken
broth and lightly sprinkled with Parmesan cheese, it is no slight tribute to
the goddess of love, I assure you. *Cappelletti,* or little caps, are somewhat
similar. *Tagliatelle* are famous throughout Italy—wide egg noodles with a
delicate meat sauce. *Lasagne* are wider, thicker, inclined to be a little heavier,
and are often tinted green from an increment of spinach, as are *pappardelle.*
But one cannot paint word pictures of these splendors. They must be tasted.

The porkers who snort about in their restricted back yards in Emilia
are among the noblest in Italy, and they end up in some sublime disguises
—the ample *mortadella* of Bologna, the hoofed *zampone* of Modena, and
a variety of succulent *salami* from Parma and Ferrara. Only one sausage
is totally missing from local shops in this region, the one we call Bologna.
Nothing vaguely resembling it can be found anywhere. Yes, we have no
Bologna in Bologna. *Mortadella* is that city's particular pride. As you know,
it is different from other sausages—larger, wider, redder, interlarded with
white cubes of fat, and more delicate in taste. Its origin dates back to the
Middle Ages, and the monks may have been mixed up in its invention. At
all events, old engravings show robed ecclesiastics happily pounding pork in
a mortar, while large sausages hang overhead.

The wines of this region are honest, hearty, and acceptable, but they lack the luster of those from neighboring Tuscany and Veneto. Though the best wine lists feature the latter, there are several local wines worth asking for. The best is Lambrusco, grown near Modena. L'Albana di Bertinoro and Il Sangiovese will reward you well if you see them on a rural wine list.

In sketching out a gastronomically guided tour of Emilia-Romagna, we are arbitrarily beginning in Romagna. This route puts Ferrara, Ravenna, and Rimini at the head of the list. The savory path of interest then leads straight up the Via Emilia, where Roman legions once marched to conquer the world, and ends in the beguiling city of Piacenza. Along the way are some memorable experiences.

Ferrara

THIS FEUDAL city in the plains of Romagna is off the beaten path, and richly deserves a detour by travelers, especially those interested in medieval mores and manners. From the thirteenth to the sixteenth century, this was the stronghold of the rich and fantastically powerful d'Este family, and the Castello Estense remains intact as a reminder of their ambition and splendor. Built of brick with four enormous battlemented towers, surrounded by moats and bridges, it is probably the best example of medieval military architecture in Italy today. It was begun in 1385, and its four towers were built to new heights in 1570. The d'Este family were generous and enthusiastic patrons of the arts, and the court life of the castle was brightened with poets, painters, and playwrights, as well as with the usual courtiers and brocaded ladies.

Dark things have also transpired behind these thick and frowning walls. Perhaps the most macabre event occured in 1425, when Parisina, the twenty-year-old wife of Nicolò III, and her lover, who happened to be Nicolò's natural son, Ugo, were beheaded to avenge the duke's wounded honor. The dank dungeons where they were confined may still be visited. Byron was so moved by this story that he wrote a poem about Parisina. A later lord of the castle was Alfonso I (1505–1534), an Este par excellence, and the reluctant, youthful fourth bridegroom of the somewhat shopworn Lucrezia Borgia. This dubious marriage, by the way, turned out happily. He adored her for the remaining eighteen years of their married life.

The dry-goods market—Ferrara

A corner of Castello Estense—Ferrara   *Central doorway of the cathedral—Ferrara*

At the present time, the castle serves as the prefecture, and many of its imposing rooms are open to the public. Several of them, including the chapel, are decorated by painters of the Ferrarese school. Ferrara was the birthplace of Savonarola (1452), the eloquent Dominican whose days came to an end on the scaffold in Florence. A monument to the martyred monk stands near the castle.

Nearby is Ferrara's twelfth-century Cathedral of San Giorgio, with a noble three-bay façade pierced with triple arcades in the best Lombard-Romanesque tradition. The central doorway dates from 1135 and is adorned with rich sculpture dedicated to a rather alarming interpretation of the Last Judgment. The south wall of the cathedral is lined with arcaded shops that bulge picturesquely into the street. This is the market area of Ferrara. Dry goods dominate one side of the square, groceries the other. The whole scene basks in the atmosphere of an Oriental bazaar. Across the way are animated, open-air cafés and indoor coffee shops. It is endlessly diverting.

For those who seek out the quieter refinements of museums, Ferrara offers a few rewarding choices. One of them is the Palazzo dei Diamanti, so-called because of the facing of some twelve thousand marble blocks, each cut in diamond facets, that adorns its exterior walls. This sumptuous palace was built for another prince of the House of Este. Badly damaged during the last war, it has been restored and once again serves as an art gallery for painters of the Ferrarese school. Among them are Benevenuto Tisi, better known as Garofalo, and an artist with the euphonious name of Dosso Dossi. There are works of Carpaccio, fine prints by Mantegna, and more recent paintings by Giovanni Boldini, a native of Ferrara who made a name for himself in Paris at the turn of this century.

Near the eastern extremity of this walled city is another building of great artistic interest, the Palazzo Schifanoia, built in 1391 by Borgo d'Este as a summer house and place of pleasure. *Schifanoia* means *sans souci,* and it must have been easy for the Estes to forget their cares in such luxurious surroundings. At present, the *palazzo* is visited principally on account of the Salone dei Mesi, a remarkable achievement in mural painting by Francesco Cossa, aided by Cosimo Tura and by their pupils. Each of the frescoes represents an allegory of one of the twelve months, and they add up to a stunning historical picture book. One obtains a most realistic impression of Italian life in those eventful times. Cossa's interpretation of the Triumph of Venus, for example, gives reassuring evidence that love has lost none of its ardor down through the centuries. The Palazzo Schifanoia also serves as a civic museum.

There are several other treasures in this articulate and energetic city, and we recommend it warmly as an overnight stop for unhurried travelers. There is an entirely adequate hotel to offer them shelter and a good breakfast. It is the ALBERGO EUROPA, at Corso Giovecca 49. The hotel is listed in the most antiquated Baedeker, but has recently been modernized after the bombardments of over a decade ago. Now the elevator works as flawlessly as the sanitary fixtures. Some of the plumbing in Italian country hotels can only be referred to as of the ventriloquist type. When you pull the plug in the bathtub, the gurgle comes not from there but from the bidet far across the room. The Europa is not in this category.

Though there are several choices for lunch or dinner in Ferrara, one stands out above the others, the RISTORANTE ITALIA DA "GIOVANNI," which occupies an unpretentious orange-and-ocher building facing the *castello* and its moat, its portcullises and its bloodthirsty legends. Perhaps they do not constitute the best *aperitivo* to an expansive repast Da Giovanni, but never mind. Here is a thoroughly professional restaurant, with the proprietor, the venerable waiters, and the plump lady at the cash desk all on their jobs. When we dined here, the headwaiter was presiding over a shimmering, ambulant tub containing the boiled dinner of the day. From this *bollito* he fished forth for his customers robust chunks of boiled beef, calf's head, *zampone,* and tongue, and very aromatic his catch was.

On another day the steaming chariot contained chicken and its fellow travelers—a much subtler *bollito*. There are other savory specialties to look for, including *lasagne verdi al forno, tortellini alla ferrarese,* and

Albergo Europa
FERRARA

Ristorante Italia da Giovanni
Ferrara

melanzane parmigiana, a particularly palatable way of presenting eggplant.

Ferrara is the home of a savory red wine, and a pork ragout called *salama da sugo.* Sturgeon from the Adriatic, and *capitone,* a large, disquieting eel, are also local specialties, but we could not find a trace of them in Ferrara's restaurants. Pastry lovers should seek out a flavorful spiced bread called *pampepato,* the pride of local pastry chefs.

Abbey of Pomposa

ONE EXCURSION out of Ferrara is especially recommended to those who have a penchant for inspiring architecture. It involves a flat and rather monotonous thirty-four mile motor trip over reclaimed marshes, but at the end of the dusty road is the noblest and highest Romanesque bell tower on the Adriatic. Rising majestically from the flat, poplar-grown plain, the beautiful campanile has an electrifying effect. It is built of brick and a certain amount of stone, in nine corbeled stages, becoming subtly more open as it rears upward. It dates from 1063 and is capped by a brown-red conical tower.

This structure is a part of the celebrated Benedictine Abbey of Pomposa, whose most famous *pensionnaire* was the gifted monk, Guido d'Arezzo (c. 995–1050), said to have invented the medieval "great scale" within these walls. For centuries the abbey lay abandoned in the marshes because of the threat of malaria. But the land has now been reclaimed, and Pomposa again beckons to visitors in this haunting and unforgettable site near the sea. Furthermore, it offers them some superb frescoes attributed to Giotto.

Ravenna

AT FIRST sight, it is hard to believe that this flat, somnolent, inland agricultural city was once a bustling Roman seaport and a naval base under the Emperor Augustus. Far more, it was the capital of western civilization from the fifth to the eight century. While the rest of the world was in blackness, Ravenna prospered, first under the Goths and later under Byzantine rule. As a reminder of its great days, Ravenna has retained the richest treasures of early Christian art in Italy. The mosaics of Ravenna have been acclaimed for fifteen centuries, and have never been surpassed, even in Monreale. It is understandable that almost every informed traveler stops to visit this foremost treasury of Byzantine art. He will see the tomb of the divine Dante, who took refuge in Ravenna and died here of the fever in 1321. Lord Byron lived in this city for two years, spending much of his time courting the lovely Contessa Teresa Guiccioli. The Italians were pleased to play host to so famous

The Abbey of Pomposa

Church of Sant' Apollinare in Classe—Ravenna

Interior, Basilica of San Vitale—Ravenna

Interior, Sant' Apollinare in Classe—Ravenna

a poet, and named a square after Byron. Mussolini's fascists did not approve,
however, and changed the name to the Piazza del Silenzio, a poor name
for a typically noisy Italian piazza.

There is so much to be seen in Ravenna that a keen student of mosaics
and early Christian architecture usually spends several days here. We will
attempt to mention only the highlights, first of which is the most prized jewel
of Byzantine art in the west, the Basilica of San Vitale. Begun in the fifth
century under Theodoric, this octagonal building is one of the most remarkable in the world, especially in regard to its interior mosaics. They portray
the Byzantine court of the Emperor Justinian and his domineering wife, the
Empress Theodora, and defy all attempts to describe them in words. The
beautiful altar is carved of pure alabaster.

There is a fine museum adjoining San Vitale, and also within its en-
closure is the extraordinary little Mausoleum of Galla Placidia, which contains the oldest and most exquisite mosaics in Ravenna. You cross a grassy
plot before coming to this small building, designed in the form of a Latin
cross. The Empress Galla Placidia had it built about 440 as her final resting
place. Her sarcophagus remains there still, together with those of two em-
perors—Constantine III, her second husband, and her son, Valentinian III.
This inspired building can be likened to a casket of jewels. Bright sunlight
seeps through alabaster windows, illuminating the incredibly intense blue
of the mosaics, certainly among the most beautiful in the world. During the
centuries, the ground level has built up five feet above the floor of the little
building.

Second among Ravenna's famous churches is Sant'Apollinare Nuovo,
with the finest circular bell tower in the city. This noble basilica dates from
the time of Theodoric, King of the Goths, and was built as an Aryan cathedral, later converted into a Catholic church. Its twenty-four marble columns
came from Constantinople. Above them are two prodigious mosaic friezes.
One shows twenty-two slim virgins in white walking against a pale gold background to offer gifts to the infant Jesus, seated on His mother's lap, between
four angels. Across the nave is a similar procession of white-clad martyrs
approaching an enthroned Christ. The dramatic effect is unsurpassed. World
War II caused serious damage to this church, and much restoration has gone
on as a consequence.

There are other superb mosaics to be seen in Ravenna, particularly in
two small baptistries. The Battistero degli Ortodossi, a fifth-century edifice
that is a converted Roman bathhouse, glories in a decorative dome of great
beauty. The Battistero degli Ariani, an octagonal building, pictures in its
dome a dramatic version of the baptism of Christ.

Of Ravenna's two famous tombs, that of Theodoric is the more impressive, even though he was by far the lesser personage. This mausoleum,

built of hewn Istrian limestone without the aid of mortar, is an austere, ten-sided structure with a pronounced Germanic feeling. Built in the year 520, it is roofed with one single circular block of stone, three feet thick and thirty-five feet in diameter. It weighs over three hundred tons, and how Theodoric's builders got it up there is still an unsolved mystery.

The tomb of Dante is found in a small domed building near the Church of San Francesco. The immortal poet sought refuge in Ravenna at the court of Guido da Polenta, and here he wrote most of his Divine Comedy. He spent the last four years of his life in Ravenna and died there of fever, at the age of fifty-six. His tomb, erected centuries later, is a much-visited shrine of Italian patriotism. Since 1908, a flame of remembrance has burned continously in this impressive sanctuary.

One more "must" lies on the sightseer's schedule, the Church of Sant' Apollinare in Classe. It rises up about three miles south of the city, the only remaining edifice of the ancient Roman seaport of Classis. This is the largest of Ravenna's basilicas, built in the first half of the sixth century. Its fine circular brick tower is freestanding. Inside is a noble, rounded apse tapestried with mosaics. The nave is supported by twenty-four large columns of Greek marble, and in the aisles are some marvelous sarcophagi.

If the churches and the mosaics of Ravenna deserve extravagant praise, the same superlatives can hardly be heaped upon its hotels and restaurants. They are adequate, but uninspired. We suspect that generations of one-night guests have made their owners unconcerned about the morrow, knowing that another shift of hungry Anglo-Saxons, French, and Germans will be on hand to accept what is offered. For decades travelers have chosen one of the old-fashioned hostelries near the Piazza del Popolo, the best of which is the Nuovo Hotel San Marco. We suggest that you sit in one of the populous cafés in this piazza, enjoy a Carpano or a Cinzano, and then become acquainted with one of a new chain of ultramodern hotels that are scattered across Italy. They will be your best friends in later chapters! We have already mentioned them in the pages devoted to Vicenza and Trieste.

Jolly
Hotel
RAVENNA

They are called the JOLLY HOTELS, a name that causes a little confusion among the populace, since neither "j" nor "y" are active ingredients of the abbreviated Italian alphabet. But if you'll ask the nearest pedestrian for the "Albergo Ee-yoly," your chances of success are good. There is one in the Piazza Mameli, near the railway station in Ravenna.

These hotels mark a new, if somewhat mechanistic, concept in Italian *alberghi*. Most noticeable is the carefully trained service, from bellboys to managers (often women, by the way), and the unfailing courtesy. The architecture is extremely simple, with rooms almost monastically small. But all the comforts are there, ensconced in miniature Italian tile. The hotels have self-operating elevators, marble floors, good baths and showers, and many assets that should please guests who are willing now and then to forego Old World atmosphere for spotlessness. Everything is immaculate, and there is always an adjoining garage.

One of the best features of the Jolly Hotels, as you will find in both Ravenna and Parma, is the food. It is genuinely good, simple, and well served, and the wine list is always adequate. Jolly Hotels spring up in places where no good hotels exist, rather than trying to compete with top-notch establishments. Thus a traveler in the more remote stretches of Italy, Apulia, and Calabria, for example, will find them to be absolute lifesavers.

Cesenatico

THE ADRIATIC shore below Ravenna is brightened by a succession of beach resorts, most of them inexpensive, all of them luxuriating in clear summer sunshine and beautiful soft sand. They are immensely popular with the Italians, and they will provide a sun-drenched vacation at a most reasonable price for visitors from overseas who must watch their budget. Their hotels and *pensioni* are clean, cheerful, and modestly priced, and are usually surrounded by palms, pines, and flower gardens. A gay vacation spirit pervades them. Their epicurean level may not be lofty, but it's good nourishment. Among several such citadels of sunshine—Bellaria and Viserba are both pleasant—we have a pronounced favorite, Cesenatico. We prefer this spot because it is not only a civilized beach town but also an immensely picturesque seaport. Its canal is filled with a constantly shifting panorama of fishing boats adorned with multicolored Adriatic sails. There couldn't be a better place for a painter with a limited expense account. Our favorite hotel in Cesenatico is the BRITANNIA MIRAMARE. On a moonlit Saturday night, we partook of *scampi* on skewers in the company of a chilled bottle of Soave, danced under the stars to soft Italian music, and felt very much at peace with the world.

Rimini

YOU ARE reminded of the fact that this is a Roman city by a triumphal arch that stands on its southern outskirts, the Arch of Augustus, built in 27 B. C. to mark the junction of two great Roman roads, the Via Flaminia and the Via Emilia. It has withstood the centuries fairly well, but its upper stonework is incomplete and has been replaced by turrets of medieval brick. Another Roman relic is the Ponte di Tiberio, a massive stone bridge begun in the time of Augustus and finished in the year 20 A. D. Despite its age, it handles the heavy strain of modern truck traffic without flinching.

Fishermen's haven—Cesenatico

Pastorale in the plain—near Rimini

The Arch of Augustus–Rimini  *Ponte di Tiberio–Rimini*

This exposed city on the Adriatic shore was the scene of intense fighting in 1944, and it suffered nearly four hundred air and sea raids. The damage was ghastly. The lovely shore resort of Marina di Rimini was almost obliterated, and the old city lost many of its finest buildings. But Rimini has been quickly and courageously rebuilt, and today stands as one more example of Italian vitality and building skill.

There is one remarkable church in Rimini that deserves a visit, the Tempio Malatestiano, one of the best Renaissance churches in Italy, despite its unfinished façade. Its architect, Leon Battista Alberti, built it in 1447 under the sponsorship of Sigismondo Malatesta to honor his mistress, Isotta. The Malatesta family of overlords ruled Rimini with an iron hand for centuries, and their tombs are scattered about the church. You will see Sigismondo's initials romantically intertwined with Isotta's in several places. You will also see a fresco by Piero della Francesca which shows Sigismondo devoutly kneeling, palms pressed in prayer. Such a pose is somewhat droll for this tyrant, who had the unsavory record of murdering three wives in succession. To compensate for his peccadillos, however, he was an avid patron of the arts.

Marina di Rimini, adjoining the old town, enjoys the reputation of being one of the most distinguished seaside resorts on the Adriatic, second only to the Lido in Venice. The beach is a beautiful, wide stretch of soft sand, fitted with cabanas and every other pleasant convenience. Desperately damaged in World War II, Marina di Rimini is now completely rebuilt, spanking clean and new, with all of today's comforts and luxuries. There is a glittering choice of summer hotels and pensions. The most impressive is the palatial GRAND

Grand Hotel
MARINA DI RIMINI

HOTEL at the north end of the beach, a beautifully appointed *lusso* establishment that ranks with the best in Italy. It has a private beach, tennis courts, and other advantages, among them a superlative Bolognese cuisine featuring *lasagne, tortellini,* and *tagliatelle alla crema.* The tempting sea food of the Adriatic couldn't be closer at hand, and the wine list contains all of the good regional vintages, among them Lambrusco, Sangiovese, and Albana.

Among a dozen other hotels along the white sands are two that should especially please fastidious visitors, the EXCELSIOR-SAVOIA, with gardens and private cabins on the beach, and the HOTEL DEL PARCO, occupying two buildings on the park. It, too, has private cabins and its cuisine abounds in Bolognese specialties and classic Adriatic dishes.

Now it is time to turn inland. The long, straight drive up the Via Emilia begins at Rimini and continues westward for long and somewhat monotonous miles. Along the way lie cities that tempt the hungry motorist—Cesena, Forlì, and Faenza—before he reaches the epicurean pinnacle of Bologna.

Cesena

Ristorante
Casali
Cesena

FOOD-CONSCIOUS friends told us of an oasis of good food in this rather dull town astride the Via Emilia. The location of the RISTORANTE CASALI next to the railway station is not inspired, but the food is, and many an Italian gourmet makes a detour to dine there. We did the same, and came away with a high regard for Adratic fish and *scampi* as served *alla Casali,* and a particular affection for *passatelli,* a delectable pasta soup, a specialty of Romagna that all but the weight conscious should enjoy hugely. Casali has good local wines too, among them Albana and Sangiovese.

Forlì has its attractions, and Faenza is worth a brief stop, especially for those who have a penchant for decorative earthenware. Faenza is the town that gave its name to faïence, and interested visitors will find a wealth of ancient and modern pieces in the international museum of ceramics here.

Bologna

THE CHIEF city of Emilia-Romagna is a vibrant, thriving metropolis of 350,000 scurrying inhabitants. It is one of the most ancient cities in Italy, and today is one of the most prosperous, go-getting, sophisticated, and—let's face it— perhaps the noisiest, if Milan doesn't win first place in this respect. Its university, founded in 425, is the most venerable and respected in Italy, and its cooking achieves one of the loftiest peaks in Italian gastronomy. What better phrase to describe it than *grassa e dotta,* fat and learned, and

The Neptune Fountain—Bologna

what better place to indulge in a serious appraisal of Italian cooking at its best?

Bologna lies in the middle of the Via Emilia, a vital crossroads in the plain. Built almost entirely of brick, it has preserved its ancient *portici,* or arcades, so that its citizens can walk almost endlessly in the shade and out of the rain. There are uncounted miles of arcades in Bologna, as well as princely palaces and a succession of brick churches with greater historic interest than downright beauty. Bologna is a city of exquisite Renaissance doorways and of two famous leaning brick towers that recall the days of the powerful Guelf and Ghibelline factions. In the dangerous Middle Ages, every wealthy Bolognese family had a tower in which to take refuge. The two that remain are rather alarming and unbeautiful curiosities. The Torre degli Asinelli is 320 feet high and leans four feet out of the perpendicular. Stout-hearted mountaineers can still climb the 447 steps to the top and obtain a remarkable view of the city. But this climb is not advisable after a typical Bolognese meal! The smaller Garisenda tower, dating from the year 1110, is unfinished and leans crazily toward its neighbor with an even more pronounced hangover. It is 156 feet high and veers ten feet from the vertical.

The city scintillates with carefree students, astute faculty members, and a buzz of businessmen. To an outsider it appears to be the most articulate, intense, swift-paced city in the peninsula, and to mingle with the gesticulating strollers on the populous Via Ugo Bassi is an invigorating experience. Another exciting place to watch the panorama of fast-moving humanity is the Piazza Maggiore, a great triple square facing the largest church in Bologna, the unfinished Church of San Petronio. Everyone in the city seems to congregate here, where a gay, bursting fountain dedicated to Neptune is the focal point for all tourists, peanut vendors, pigeons, and tintype photographers. The bronze statue of the God of the Sea, and the superimposed quartets of spouting cupids and mermaids were completed in 1566 by Giovanni da Douai, known locally as Giambologna. On either side of the fountain stand vast crenellated *palazzi,* one of which, the Palazzo del Podestà, shelters a pleasant open-air café, a good place to sit down before an *aperitivo* and map out a visit to the city.

When one visits Ravenna, one goes not for epicurean reasons, but to see the mosaics and the churches. When one comes to Bologna, a city famous for its cooking, the shrines of gastronomy come first. We suggest that the more food-conscious readers of these pages limit their sightseeing to a few important churches and indulge themselves thereafter in gastronomy. The Church of San Domenico is of interest because it contains the mortal remains of the founder of the Dominican order, who died in Bologna in 1221. His tomb is embellished by beautiful bas-reliefs by Nicolò Pisano. The Church of San Stefano is a curiosity because it is not a single edifice, but a series of seven brick churches of different dates, linked together by quiet courtyards

The leaning Garisenda tower–Bologna   *The arcaded Piazza Mercanzia–Bologna*

and cloisters. That wraps up our ecclesiastical sightseeing for the moment, and leaves us free to stroll along these arcaded streets. They are absolutely jammed with food shops!

Amble under the arcades of the Via Caprarie, for example, and you will see fruit stores with bananas, pineapples, and coconuts hanging from the ceiling together with great festoons of artichokes and grapes. A table shimmers with dates, dried prunes, apricots, raisins, and figs. There are multicolored mushrooms, asparagus, and *spugnole,* which look very much like French *morilles.* The only foreign article visible is a neat wooden box of endive from Belgium.

Next door is a *salumeria,* its ceiling hung with hundreds of huge Italian sausages—immense *mortadelle* and thinner *salami.* Cream-colored balloons of Provolone cheese are suspended in the same place, aging amicably with their neighbors. The popular smoked sausages seem to be *zamponi,* the specialty of the neighboring city of Modena, and *bresaola della valtellina,* a peculiar dark maroon number that looks like cured beef. Then there is *salame d'oca,* cured goose meat carefully sewn into its own skin. Packets of dried mushrooms in cellophane are best sellers, and the Italian housewife now accepts tomato concentrate, anchovy paste, mustard, and mayonnaise in tubes without protest. Cartwheels of Swiss cheese, gallon tins of olive oil, and hundreds of straw-clad *fiaschi* of Chianti brighten the picture. Wine is certainly one of the least expensive items in the shop. A husky *fiasco* of Lambrusco or Zoave or Frascati costs less than fifty cents.

The most typical Bolognese shop is probably the one that sells the farinaceous splendors. We stood spellbound before the window of a pasta shop, notebook in hand, trying to absorb at least a partial nomenclature of its offerings. Some were easy—the familiar *tagliatelle, vermicelli,* tubelike *maccheroni,* green *lasagne,* ravioli, and the inevitable spaghetti. They are practically English words. But others were more complex: *sfoglia al matterello* (a maidenhair *vermicelli*) and *denti di cavallo* (horse's teeth) and little pinched bow ties that were called both *farfalle* and *fiocchettini. Tortellini* is the umbilical-like specialty we've already mentioned, and *anolini, agnolotti,* and *cappelletti* are ravioli's first cousins. *Paternostri* are elbow macaroni, and *conchiglie* are small and shell-shaped. Finally there are the miniature *paste* for soups—*stellette* (star-shaped), *semi de mela* (apple seed), *grandinia,* and *pastine.* That empties the notebook, but far from exhausts the subject.

We could wander on to the *pasticceria* and the grocery store, to the shop of the butcher, the baker, and the fishmonger, but you have probably had enough. Besides, it is high time that we came to the pinnacle of this Bolognese story—the citadels of fine cooking.

Assuming that most travelers will stay no more than two days in Bologna, we take the liberty of mentioning only two hotels and three celebrated restaurants, among the countless number that exist. The HOTEL MAJESTIC-BAGLIONI, established for decades on the arcaded Via Indipendenza, is the leading hostelry in Bologna, and maintains a most commendable cuisine. Though a bit antiquated and old-fashioned, it is well managed. For those who seek something a little more modern, we suggest the new ALBERGO CRISTALLO, Via San Giuseppe 5, a thoroughly clean, comfortable, compact, well-run establishment built since the last war. It is within walking distance of all of Bologna's effervescent street life, but is located in a quiet little square, and well worth seeking out. The Cristallo has a pleasant little bar and serves a palatable breakfast, but there is no dining room. This leaves you conscience-free to search out Al Pappagallo and Sampieri without lowering your eyes as you pass the hotel doorman.

Al
Pappagallo
Bologna

And now to the feast! What better choice than AL PAPPAGALLO, on the Piazza Mercanzia, a world-famous restaurant on one of the most venerable sites imaginable. Under its dusty brick arcade, Al Pappagallo (The Parrot) looks, externally, hoary with age. Inside it is bright and worldly, illuminated by four immense crystal chandeliers. The Italians *prefer* it this way, and will suffer no Dantesque gloom with their dining. On the walls are countless pictures of celebrities who have paid The Parrot a visit and found far more than crackers. They look *very* contemporary. But a few traces of age remain. The ancient vaulted ceilings are visible, their ribs still showing despite the good cooking. And there is an imposing, though nonfunctioning, Gothic fireplace at the end of the room. What really functions is the kitchen!

Italian gourmets, by almost universal consent, rank The Parrot one of the top restaurants in the country, and the menu contains several glittering dishes to prove its supremacy. Where, after all, we thought, is a better place in the world to try *tagliatelle alla bolognese?* We tried them, and found them fascinating for their lightness. The thin, wide noodles were toothsome and tender, and the sauce was not loaded down with oil or butter. The true Bolognese "sauce" is essentially a lean-beef ragout with a judicious pointing up of tomato, herbs, and seasoning. After this we accosted half a boned chicken and a filet of turkey with paper-thin lavender truffles and a *sauce cardinale*—a lovely experience and a superlative sauce—in the discreet company of a bottle of Bardolino.

Needless to say, the service is attentive here, and the clientele most cosmopolitan (meaning that it is best to go there after nine in the evening). They still admit our particular *bête noir,* the sad-faced street vendor with the toy mechanical jackass who wiggles his ears to nobody's amusement, but that's a mere detail.

Al Pappagallo is not expensive—at least considering that you enjoy the culinary splendors of one of Italy's best restaurants. Almost all of the specialties are priced at six hundred lire, less than a dollar. There is a cover charge (this includes a fat basket of Italian bread and *grissini),* which amounts to the imposing total of twenty-four cents. At the end of the dinner you are presented with a liqueur on the house, and a pleasant gesture it is.

Al Pappagallo is owned by the Zurla brothers, who were kind enough to give us three of their favorite recipes, among them two delectable ways of serving turkey breasts. Here is one of them:

Filetti di Tacchino alla Cardinale
TURKEY BREAST CARDINAL

Cut one side of the breast meat from a raw turkey, first removing the skin. Slice this meat into 4 filets and flatten them as much as possible by pounding them lightly on a board. Dip the filets very lightly in flour and season them with salt and pepper. Melt 2 tablespoons of butter in a broad saucepan and in it cook the turkey filets over a gentle heat for about 5 minutes on each side. Stir in 1 tablespoon of Marsala and 3 or 4 tablespoons of chicken stock. Place a very thin slice of cooked ham, or smoked tongue, on each filet, then a layer of very thinly sliced white truffles that have been heated in butter. Over the truffles spread a layer of grated Swiss cheese, spoon a little of the sauce on each filet, cover the pan, and heat again until the cheese is just melted.

Ristorante Sampieri
Bologna

Only a short distance away, on a narrow side street called the Via Sampieri, is a wonderful restaurant that takes you, not back to the Middle Ages, but to the Gay Nineties. You enter the RISTORANTE SAMPIERI through a bar, pass through an immaculate kitchen whose plump feminine cooks are wreathed in smiles, and suddenly come upon the shade of Victoria. The dining salon is unbelievable, set in the spirit of *Arsenic and Old Lace*. Seven lamps, with orange-lace shades, project from the walls on gilded iron brackets. The wallpaper, of an indefinite gray-yellow-brown, is almost concealed by a cavalcade of oil paintings in tarnished gilt frames—paintings of harem ladies, watermelons, umbrella pines, lobsters on platters. A huge Baroque framed-in-gold mirror is placed catty-corner at one end of the room. On the day of our first visit, a small table was reserved for a special client, a very old gentleman with fine flowing chin whiskers and a rakish gray bowler, which he kept on his head all during his luncheon. While he dined, he read intently from a fat paper-bound book, and never looked up, to our total fascination. Everyone is well dressed, talkative, and genial, in Sampieri. There is a high quota of monocles and of French travelers, who have the instinctive faculty of choosing the right place in a foreign city. Signor Munari, the proprietor of Sampieri, is a handsome man with broad shoulders and a ready smile. He was very helpful to a table of our compatriots, who left these Victorian purlieus with enchantment written on their faces. We think that you will react the same way, for those large capable cooks up front produce some beautiful Bolognese dishes. Prices are more than fair, and the menu embraces everything that is choice in this city of fabulous fare. We had a little trouble with our red wine—it was a sparkling one, and not at all to our taste. It might be worth while, therefore, to make a note to order a *non spumante* wine in Bolognese restaurants.

Signor Munari has shared five recipes with us, one of which is:

Lasagne Verdi al Forno
BAKED GREEN LASAGNE

Make a pasta to which is added strained spinach (see index) and roll it out into a thin sheet. Cut it into rectangles about 4 inches long by 3 inches wide. Cook the pieces, a few at a time, in boiling salted water for 5 minutes, remove them with a strainer, and drop them into cold water. Drain the *lasagne* and spread them on towels. Place a layer of meat sauce, or *ragù bolognese* (see index), in a buttered baking dish, then a layer of rich cream sauce flavored with nutmeg and sprinkled with grated Parmesan, and then a layer of *lasagne*. Continue in this way until the dish is filled, finishing with cream sauce and grated Parmesan. Put the dish in a moderate oven (350° F.) for about 20 minutes. (See also *veritabile lasagne verdi al forno bolognese.*)

In addition to its long-established shrines of gastronomy, Bologna is justifiably proud of a spanking new restaurant called the TRE GALLI D'ORO, Via Santo Stefano 29. The Three Golden Roosters are making quite a sensation in the city. It is a large, ultramodern establishment, curtained, carpeted, and endowed with most of the side shows of the catering art. You enter a foyer where a plump lady is fashioning *tortellini,* tempting golden yellow in color, behind a plate-glass window. On the other flank you have an unobstructed, glassed-in view of the kitchen, and spotless it is. Cleanliness is a virtue to show to all the world—this is an Italian maxim. In addition to the kitchen and the pasta performer, you come upon a *rosticeria* turning fragrantly as you enter the dining salon. On the spit revolve chickens, baby lamb, roast beef, pheasant, woodcock and quail, according to the demand. There is a glittering display of fruit, and a metal wagon heaped high with colorful hors-d'oeuvre makes the rounds from table to table. Finally, as a *pièce de résistance,* you may gaze upon three immense glass containers filled with artichoke hearts in oil, each decorated with three red roosters artistically achieved with pimiento.

Tre Galli d'Oro Bologna

The theatrics of the Three Golden Roosters should not blind visiting gourmets to the fact that sound Bolognese cookery awaits in the background. The chef is a gifted artist, representing the very best in Italian skill and inventiveness, and we recommend his typical Bolognese dishes with enthusiasm. The prices are reasonable, too, especially if you elect the *presso fisso* menu. With pasta or *risotto,* then meat, cheese or fruit, and a little carafe of wine, this meal comes to 850 lire, service included. That's about a dollar and a quarter, and well spent it is.

Modena

SQUARELY ASTRIDE the Via Emilia, Modena is another judicious stop, both for the enthusiast for art and architecture and the passing gourmet. This is the home of *zampone,* the celebrated smoked sausage whose casing is made up of the lower skin of a pig's trotter, with a delicately sculptured hoof still showing. It's a famous sausage, partly because of the poster that is used to advertise it throughout Italy. This sign exhibits a highly congenial porker with a wooden leg and a cane, exhorting the public to sample his smoked sacrifice. They serve *zampone* hot in Modena, usually with lentils, mashed potatoes, or sauerkraut, and it is downright delectable. *Tortellini modenesi*

Piazza Grande—Modena

West portal of the cathedral—Modena   *The outdoor pulpit—Modena*

are a particularly savory version of ravioli, and they prepare a spinach soup and a veal *scaloppine* here, both of which are inviting, nourishing, and easy to prepare in your own kitchen. Recipes for both will be found in the collection at the end of this book.

Modena (pronounced Mòdena) has more enduring virtues, however. Its magnificent cathedral, the purest Romanesque in Emilia, is a thing of subtle beauty, from the slender tilted campanile to the pair of pinkish lions that guard its central portal. The tower is called La Ghirlandina, and was built by Arrigo da Campione, perhaps the greatest of the Campione master architects. It rises some 285 feet and lists a bit tipsily to the west. The marble lions at the south portal are supposed to typify the alertness and majesty of 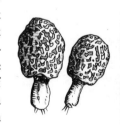 the church, but their dignity suffers at times. Untold generations of Italian gamins who have played horse on these morose crouching creatures have worn the marble down to a high polish that would do justice to a Chinese vase. There are also some naughty bits of sculpture on an upper cornice. They are mentioned in most of the guidebooks and draw many furtive glances.

It is difficult to realize that less than a century ago this populous agricultural town was the capital of a small dukedom, and not a part of Italy at all. Its vast Palazzo Ducale is a reminder of its former estate. Built in

1634 for the dukes of Este, this overpowering structure now serves as a military academy. If you can get by the sentry and peek beyond the main portal, you will see one of the most imposing courtyards in Italy.

At the eastern end of the city is a museum of more than moderate interest. The Palazzo dei Musei is really a collection of museums, one of which, the Galleria Estense, contains some noteworthy paintings by Titian, Tintoretto, Veronese, and Velasquez. Bibliophiles should not miss the Biblioteca Estense, a member of the group. It houses some 8,600 precious manuscripts and 185,000 printed volumes. Its greatest treasure is the Bible of Borgo d'Este.

A visit to the cathedral and the museums, an *aperitivo* in the crowded Piazza Grande swarming with cadets, and you are ready for one of the most rewarding lunches in this chapter—a visit to the RISTORANTE FINI. This welcoming place is far from the central hubbub, a cheerful arcaded building facing the church of San Francesco on the outer fringes of the city. The name Fini certainly doesn't have the connotation it has in French, for this restaurant is thriving, filled with discriminating diners. The cooking is excellent. Outside of Bologna, it is probably the best restaurant in Emilia. All of the celebrated Modenese dishes are listed for your pleasure, including the traditional *zampone, tortellini, scaloppine,* and spinach soup, each worth a flowery paragraph of its own. The white-haired director, Signor Telesforo Fini, is always at hand, eager to help you compose a meal. After you have finished luncheon, another temptation besets you in the adjoining Fini food shop: a square basket containing a plump smoked *zampone,* flanked by hand-sculptured *tortellini* and *amaretti,* just the thing to take home as a souvenir. But you'll never get that sausage past our customs agents!

Every two years, an Italian cheese exhibition is held in Modena. Inquiring gastronomes who visit this noble manifestation will take particular joy in the hospitable Ristorante Fini.

Ristorante FINI
Modena

Parma

THE NEXT metropolis along the Via Emilia is Reggio nell'Emilia, but this we shall bypass to head directly eastward for Parma, an ancient city that claims the interest of musicians, artists, bibliophiles, and gourmets alike.

As the birthplace of the great Toscanini and the city of Giuseppe Verdi, Parma is a natural magnet for music lovers. It is the setting of the famous neoclassic Teatro Regio, which concedes but little to La Scala. In Parma's Villetta cemetery is the tomb of Nicolò Paganini, the great genius of the violin.

Three renowned artists are closely identified with the city. Benedetto

The cathedral tower and the baptistry—Parma

Antelami, perhaps the greatest of medieval sculptors, has left masterful examples of his skill and vision. The cathedral contains his wonderful relief of the "Descent from the Cross," which was completed in 1178. It is Correggio, more than any other painter, whose name is linked with Parma. Born Antonio Allegri, two years after Columbus discovered America, in Correggio, he took his surname from his native town, but spent most of his forty years in Parma. One of the greatest painters of all time, he was influenced by Michelangelo in his audacious ability to paint foreshortened figures hovering in mid-air. This quality is dramatically demonstrated in his greatest work, the soaring fresco of the Assumption in the cupola of Parma's cathedral. But he also had a marvelous mastery of chiaroscuro, the soft play of light and shadow, evident in his Madonnas and figure painting. His painting was joyous and sometimes sensuous. His Leda was so voluptuous that some prudish museum viewer cut her head off, a damage that was later restored. Third of the artists is Parmigianino, a gifted portraitist and muralist, who throve in the early sixteenth century and first introduced etching into Italy.

Rosemary

Typographers and bibliophiles will find something of particular interest in Parma, too, for it was here that the great Giambattista Bodoni worked. One of the world's foremost type-face designers, his printed books are now rare-book-collectors' treasures. Original editions of them may be seen in quantity in Parma's Palatine Library.

This teeming city of some 130,000 inhabitants suffered severe damage during the recent war, and many of its fine buildings will never be the same. The city is still rebuilding, and is therefore not exactly a restful place. But everything is calm in the neighborhood of the cathedral, providentially spared by the bombs, and it is here that we advise you to go first. On the Piazza del Duomo is a low building housing the E.N.I.T. tourist bureau, the government agency that does so much for visitors from abroad. If you don't know E.N.I.T., here is a good place to begin. You will come away with a sheaf of handsome free illustrated folders, written in very good English, and with any practical information you may request.

The cathedral is pure Lombard-Romanesque, with an arcaded façade and a tall handsome portico, supported by crouching marble lions. Adjoining it is a noble brick-and-stone campanile. But its greatest treasures, Correggio's frescoed cupola and Antelami's sculpture, are inside.

A few feet away is the magnificent old baptistry, designed by the same versatile Antelami. Through the centuries, its pinkish Veronese marble has faded to a delicious dull rose color. The building, dating from 1196, is tall and octagonal, with superimposed arcades. Inside it is sixteen-sided, its walls liberally embellished with dimming frescoes. The superb bronze portals are also Antelami's work. This is the architectural pinnacle of Parma.

There are plenty of other things to see in Parma, as those free E.N.I.T.

folders will tell you. The National Gallery, located in the huge Palazzo della Pilotta on the banks of the Parma river, is one you cannot afford to miss. Here is Correggio's great canvas, the tender and beautiful Madonna di San Girolamo. And here, too, are notable works by Leonardo, Van Dyck, El Greco, Holbein, Tiepolo, and Canaletto, among others. In the gallery you obtain tickets to visit a final masterpiece of Correggio, known as the Camera di San Paolo. This is a domed room in an old convent, decorated by Correggio in 1517. His theme is the "Allegory of Human Life" and it is unfolded on semicircular lunettes and ovals in the master's exquisite style.

Parma has its pinnacle of pre-eminence in the realm of food also. Everyone knows that it is the source of the Parmesan cheese that is sprinkled on millions of plates of pasta and ravioli and *risotto* daily. Because of it, all sorts of delicious dishes are credited to the Parmesan cuisine, more perhaps than it deserves. Any number of *plats* that are sprinkled with cheese and then browned in the oven are called *alla parmigiana,* though the dishes may be quite unknown in Parma.

The famous hard, granular cheese is cherished throughout the world, and has been for a long time. Boccaccio mentions it lovingly in his *Decameron,* written in the fourteenth century. It is piquant but not too strong, easy to grate, and reveals a pleasant, aromatic bouquet. It generally comes in large cylindrical cartwheels weighing from fifty-five to sixty-five pounds. You will find them stacked ceiling high in many of the food shops. They are matured from two to four years, and are priced and named according to age—*vecchio, stravecchio,* and *stravecchione,* the last being the choicest. Parma has no monopoly on its cheese. The same cheese is produced in the neighboring provinces. Italians just couldn't get along without it. Neither can the French, who employ it for countless dishes that must be *gratiné au four.*

Porkers abound in this region, accounting for the fragrant *salami* for which Parma is noted. The best sausage is said to come from the village of Felino, in the southern foothills. Noble smoked hams come from the hill town of Langhirano in the same neighborhood. Three other basic items of good cooking abound in Parma—fine butter, tomato conserves, and white mushrooms. They result in some highly palatable local dishes, among them *anolini in brodo,* a toothsome pasta, *gnocchi alla parmigiana,* and *tortelli d'erbetta,* both swimming in butter. Tripe may appall you, but you might well cotton to *trippa alla parmigiana. Bomba di riso* are rice balls, and very good. Most of these names will appear on the *lista del giorno* of an average Parmesan restaurant.

A few praiseworthy wines are produced in the foothills of the Apennines just south of Parma. This is wonderfully picturesque country, particularly if you travel to Torrechiara and Casatico. Here are immense crenellated castles crowning hilltops and surrounded by endless terraces of vines. This

West porch of the cathedral–Fidenza

little detour only a few miles south of Parma should delight motorists who
have tired of the flatness of the Via Emilia. The best red wines come from
Felino and Langhirano, also noted for their hams. You can always find the
trustworthy ruby Lambrusco in restaurant carafes. To accompany those Italian
desserts, you might approve of a laudable sweet wine, Malvasia, the best of
which is grown near the hillside village of Maiatico. While these wines lack
the aristocracy of those of Piedmont or Tuscany, they are honest and
rewarding.

Though restaurants in the city are adequate, a truly first-class establishment has yet to appear in postwar Parma. When the long task of rebuilding
is complete, a shrine of fine Parmesan fare will doubtless come along. For
the moment we recommend the ever-dependable JOLLY HOTEL. There is a
newly opened one facing the river, on the Viale Arturo Toscanini, a distinguished address if we ever saw one. It is large and comfortable, and has a
swimming pool. Here you can taste those *tortelli d'erbetta* and chicken on
the spit, with Lambrusco as a drinking companion.

One last thought about Parma. It is quite possible to have one of those
cartwheels of cheese delivered to your British or American doorstep. The
cheese dealer swore to it.

Piazza Cavalli–Piacenza

The village well—Grazzano Visconti

Salsomaggiore

BY PURSUING a westerly direction on the Via Emilia, you approach Salsomaggiore, one of Italy's finest spas. You leave the highway at Fidenza, but
before doing so we urge you to make a detour to see the twelfth-century
duomo at the western end of the city. Though Fidenza suffered cruel bombardments during the last war, its cathedral was luckily spared. The façade
was never finished, but as far as it goes, this edifice is superlative. It has the
usual portal with crouching lions and numerous bas-reliefs and statues of
great beauty, all from the Antelami school of sculpture.

About six miles southwest of Fidenza, in the foothills of the Apennines,
you come to the cheerful, fashionable, much-frequented thermal resort of
Salsomaggiore, whose season runs from April to November. The saline waters
for which it is famous were known in antiquity and were once used for making
salt. Today they attract both the afflicted and the affluent. The Oriental
architecture of the Berzieri thermal establishment may cause sensitive people
to shudder, but its waters are beneficial for arthritis, rheumatism, bronchial
difficulties, and various other ailments.

We found the hotel situation excellent in Salsomaggiore. The GRAND
HOTEL PORRO is reputedly the best, but the REGINA, the MILANO and the
CENTRALE-BAGNI are all praiseworthy. Furthermore, there is a first-rate casino
restaurant called the POGGIO DIANA, with tennis courts, gardens, and a swimming pool among its attractions.

Piacenza

ALMOST AT the termination of the Via Emilia, this ancient walled Roman
city is a significant crossroads, and a good place to stop when motoring
between Milan and Florence, as many travelers do. The French and English
name for the town is Plaisance. Built on the left bank of the river Po, it
is quite as thriving and animated as its neighbors. Its architectural treasure
is a marvelous thirteenth-century civic palace, a symphony of Verona marble,
brick, and terra cotta. Some critics consider it the finest civic building in
Italy. This towering Lombard-Gothic affair was built by the Farnese dukes,
whose prancing equestrian statues stand guard in the adjoining square, aptly
named the Piazza Cavalli.

The cathedral of Piacenza is the other notable attraction for visitors.
It is Lombard-Romanesque like others in Emilia, its façade brightened with
porches, multiple arcades, and a good rose window. From its massive brick

campanile hangs the *gabbia,* the iron cage in which criminals were once exposed naked to public ridicule. Here the gentle Ludovico il Moro suspended his enemies.

Albergo Croce Bianca
Piacenza

Getting back to more appetizing subjects, we are glad to report that there is a prosperous provincial hotel in Piacenza with better than average food and service. The rooms are clean and attractive and well suited for an overnight stay. This hostelry, called the ALBERGO CROCE BIANCA, is located in the heart of the city. We have tried it on two occasions and found it more than adequate. Here is a good place to try the pasta and pork products for which Piacenza is widely known.

There is one memorable excursion to make from Piacenza, and we recommend it enthusiastically to motorists in search of variety. About eight miles due south of the city is a most remarkable village called Grazzano Visconti, conceived entirely in medieval style. It is a synthetic village, if you wish, for it was built in the last century, but it enables the visitor to carry away an indelible picture of life in the Middle Ages. Its superbly picturesque houses and *palazzi* are vine grown and colorful. There is not a single discordant note: not a wire, a telephone pole, a Vespa, or an automobile is in sight. Yet the village is fully inhabited, mainly by artisans who offer their handiwork to tourists, and very skillfully executed it is. There are aged fountains and marble columns, cool cloisters, and best of all, an attractive medieval place to dine, the ALBERGO BISCIONE. The food is good, and if you become enraptured with the village, as many do, there are seven rooms for an overnight stop.

The cathedral—Siena

Tuscany

Chapter 9

TUSCANY

I<small>T IS</small> difficult to avoid a torrent of superlatives in appraising Tuscany and her contribution to the culture and the beauty of this world. The list of her famous sons is even now astounding, centuries after they were born. How much richer is mankind for the genius of Dante, Leonardo da Vinci, and Michelangelo, to consider only the pinnacle of the region's greatness. They all belonged to Tuscany, as did Petrarch, Galileo, the mathematician, Boccaccio, the father of Italian prose and the racy yarn, and Machiavelli, the unscrupulous statesman whose name has become a synonym for sly plotting and malevolent schemes.

Tuscan painters and sculptors have no peers in the realm of art. From Cimabue, Giotto, Fra Filippo Lippi, Botticelli, the della Robbias, and Donatello to the boastful Benvenuto Cellini, the majesty of Florentine genius remains unrivaled, and puts the mere earth-bound, camera-toting, twentieth-century traveler in a mood of awe and wonder.

Tuscany, whose name is derived from its ancient Etruscan origin, is one of the larger Italian regions, containing ten smaller provinces. Its long coastline borders the Mediterranean, and it includes the Isle of Elba, made famous by Napoleon's enforced residence. Aside from the flat valley of the Arno, most of Tuscany is either hilly or mountainous. The higher stretches of the Apennines can be grim, as veterans of the Fifth Army who spent the winter on the Futa Pass can tell you. But most of this region is picture-book stuff—hills carpeted with vineyards, olive trees, and umbrella pines and crowned with regiments of solem cypresses, villas with wide roofs and formal gardens, fortified hill towns, remote monasteries. Its seacoast is seductive to the vacationist, particularly in the region of Viareggio, where the soft sands are irresistible. The world's most famous marble quarries are in Tuscany, running from the outskirts of Carrara up the slopes of Monte Sagro. It is a chore to visit them, but a rewarding one. Tuscany also has two fine thermal establishments for people seeking a cure or relaxation. Both Mon-

tecatini Terme and Chianciano Terme
offer fine hotels with every comfort.
But Tuscany's cities, in the long run,
exert the strongest appeal upon
travelers. Florence, Pisa, Siena, Lucca,
Pistoia, Arezzo—these and a dozen
smaller towns have for centuries fascinated visitors, especially the Anglo-
Saxons. Some of these visitors have been
famous—Lord Byron, Keats, and Shelley, for example. Robert and Elizabeth
Browning could not be separated from
Florence, once they came to know it.
Many another English expatriate feels
the same way, going there for a week
and remaining a lifetime. Throughout
the last war, many of them stayed
grimly on, despite hardships, indignities,
and cold. That is true loyalty, for the
winter climate is far from ideal.

The charm of Tuscan speech and
manners has much to do with the
popularity of this region. Laughter and animation and industry are here,
and if there is less singing of operatic arias in the streets than in Naples,
the people are unfailingly gay and gracious. The pure Florentine tongue
is the standard of Italian letters. This city is a stronghold of arts and crafts,
and few places in this world produce as many well-made things to buy for
your friends back home. The shops have an intoxicating effect upon the
wide-eyed tourist, and especially upon his wife. What skilled Florentine work-
men can do with leather, silver, gold, precious and semiprecious stones, colored
marble, and silk is almost beyond belief. We firmly believe that the travel
budget trickles away faster on the shop-crammed Ponte Vecchio in Florence
than anywhere else in this tempting land.

Confronted with the splendors of Tuscany's brilliant history, the mere
needs and pastimes of the present seem insignificant. How does one dare to
think of food? Why not live on ambrosia and a still life in the Pitti Palace?
Today's visitor, however, is obliged to come down to earth every few hours,
if only because his rebellious feet remind him that he can look at pictures
in the Uffizi Gallery just so long, and no longer. The normal, unethereal
desire to sit down and relax must have its turn. Only because such mundane
phenomena as thirst and hunger unfailingly assert themselves do we come
to the relatively minor art of Tuscan food. True to Tuscan supremacy, it

ranks with the best in Italy. And if this art failed to produce culinary geniuses on the lofty plane of Dante or da Vinci, it has the distinction of being the most ancient in Europe. It dates from Etruscan times, a full millennium before the Christian era.

This is admittedly a remote boast. But Florentine gastronomy can claim another honor that comes right down to the present—it was the forerunner of the French cuisine as we know it today. It was Catherine de' Medici, a Florentine name deeply etched in French history, who started a new era of French cooking. When she became the wife of Henry II and queen of France, she brought her own Italian cooks with her. Their new culinary techniques, their sauces and their sweets, revolutionized court dinners in France and launched a wonderful new trend. French ingenuity has done the rest down through the ensuing centuries.

The keynote of Tuscan gastronomy is furnished by its fertile hillsides, tapestried with the good things of life: olive trees, vineyards, green gardens, and pastures dotted with plump young cattle. The ancient culinary maxim that the best dishes are often the simplest is proved to the hilt in Tuscany. Taking advantage of the excellence of his own meats, vegetables, fruit, and oil, the good Tuscan chef presents them with simplicity and good taste—and a minimum of manipulation. There are many succulent specialties, however, particularly in the field of pastry, where the city of Siena has produced delicacies prized all over Italy. Here are a few of the treasures of the Tuscan *cucina* which you will encounter in restaurants and *trattorie:*

Bistecca alla fiorentina. The most celebrated meat dish in Tuscany is probably the most elementary. It is a youth's-size steak broiled only with olive oil, salt and pepper, and served with a quarter of lemon. Nothing could be simpler. It is good young Tuscan beef, somewhat sophomoric in comparison to the ponderous steer one encounters at American county fairs. A Florentine beefsteak (in French, *biftek,* in Italian *bistecca)* falls somewhere between a porterhouse and a veal chop, but is much closer to the latter. They are justly proud of this steak in the restaurants of Florence, and the headwaiter often has the whole cut brought forth from the icebox to be admired by carnivorous guests. We saw three American sailors remain stonily unimpressed when confronted with this pinkish spectacle. To the beaming headwaiter their spokesman said "Nah, we get plenty of steak. Haven't you got any spaghetti and meatballs?"

Fritto misto. The Florentine variant of this famous Italian dish contains sweetbreads, calf's brains, sliced artichoke, zucchini, and small cutlets of lamb, all dipped in flour and beaten egg, and deep fried in Tuscan olive oil. Fragrant and surprisingly light, it is a dish that goes well with a cool white Chianti. Some restaurants add a few sweet fritters—apple, apricot, or orange—thus obviating the need for the dessert course.

Tuscan landscape—Cortona

Trippa alla fiorentina. Enthusiasts of tripe—an excellent but unloved-by-many dish—will find that young Italian tripe needs less aromatic disguise than the French *tripe à la mode de Caen*. Thinly sliced, cooked long hours in a casserole with meat juices and tomato, it is usually served with a sprinkling of Parmesan cheese and accompanied by white Tuscan beans.

Lepre dolce-forte. Wild hare with a sweet-and-sour sauce is an autumnal allegory in Tuscany. The strong flavor of the hare is balanced by a brilliant sauce made with the pan juices and vinegar (this on the sour side) and a combination of sugar, Smyrna raisins, pine nuts, chocolate and chopped candied fruits on the sweet side. The combination must sound appalling to some ears, and it has to be tasted to be appreciated. It doesn't call for a distinguished wine, however. This specialty is best known in Grosseto, a large, rather dull city in the southern part of Tuscany.

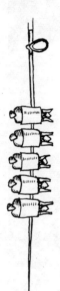

Uccelletti. This is a firm Florentine favorite that you will find in most rotisseries in the less luxurious streets of the city. *Uccelletti* are little lavender-brown birds, usually larks, well plucked. With their heads still on, a dozen or more of them are strung neatly on a skewer, with a small slice of crusty bread, cut on the bias, and a leaf of laurel between each two. Roasted on a revolving spit over charcoal and basted with butter, they are absolutely delicious to anyone who doesn't belong to the Audubon Society. Sausages and other selected fragments of the pig are harpooned between crusts and similarly served to munching Florentines. One variety is called *fegatelli di maiale all'uccelletti* (liver), and makes a good democratic noontime snack for the more adventurous gastronome.

Tortino di carciofi. Here is another delightful dish, light, original and satisfying, and a true Tuscan specialty. It is a sort of artichoke omelette, if you wish, but the cooking procedure is novel. Small tender artichokes, sometimes precooked but more often not, are cut in thin vertical slices and sautéed in oil in a small two-handled serving pan. When the slices are cooked, two beaten eggs are added and the pan is placed in the oven. The *tortino* is rushed piping hot to your table. Any good Florentine restaurant can turn out this dish with dispatch. Chefs use the same procedure with eggplant and the pale lavender truffle of Piedmont.

Cacciucco. Needless to say, plenty of fish are pulled in from Tuscany's coastal waters, and from the Adriatic, not too far away. One of the region's most individual fish dishes is *cacciucco,* a fish stew par excellence. A miscellany of Mediterranean fish is cooked in a broth based on an abundance of onions amplified with tomatoes, pimientos, garlic, salt, pepper, and a good spot of red wine. This stew is the gastronomic glory of Livorno, or Leghorn, and may someday be integrated into the folklore of American cooking. At present the American service personnel and their wives in this port of entry comprise a large community in themselves, and *cacciucco* has made its im-

Springtime in a Tuscan vineyard–Puliciano

pression upon them, to judge by a cookbook compiled by these wives, which we've just seen.

Fagioli all'uccelletto. It is fitting that the Florentines, the Bostonians of the Italian peninsula, shall we say, should be inordinately fond of beans. Let other Italians, with a hint of disdain, call the citizens of Florence *mangia-fagioli* (bean eaters). They remain faithful to their white beans, which closely resemble the French *soissons*. They serve these beans in soup, or with rice, lentils, or game. A wild boar wouldn't be countenanced without them. The best-known manner of preparing them is *all'uccelletto,* a style which involves slow stewing in salted water fortified with olive oil, pepper, a little tomato paste, and a leaf of sage.

Practical recipes for many of these specialties will be found in the Italian Treasury at the end of this volume.

Tuscany occupies an exalted niche in the oenophile's world, for it is the source of Chianti, probably the best known of all Italian wines. Endless Tuscan slopes are given over to the vine, but the best vintages come from the undulating, broken countryside south of Florence, a rugged, picturesque hill country, dotted with feudal villages and fortified castles, where the vine-grower labors hard, long, and successfully to extract a living from the soil. Of the hilltop castles that remain, two have very familiar names—Brolio and Meleto. They furnish the appellation of two of the most famous vintages of Chianti. Both belong to the celebrated Ricasoli family (pronounced Ricá-

219

soli), foremost in the production of fine Chianti. Other family names to look for on a Chianti label are Antinori and Serristori. These three and a few other exclusive producers have banded together to form a Society for the Protection of Italian Wines. The procedure is useful in distinguishing their products from certain Chiantis blended with coarser wines imported from the heel and toe of Italy. The Chianti *classico* of the elite among the winegrowers is identified by a trademark showing a strutting black rooster emblazoned on a golden dish. This bird is worthy of respect, for it signifies the best in the Chianti district, most of it from the villages of Greve, Radda in Chianti, Gaiole in Chianti, and Castellina in Chianti. There are other notably good wines of the Chianti type, of course, especially Rufina, which is produced in the Val de Sève by the house of Ruffino. Pomino is a similar wine from the same slopes. Montepulciano, a delightful hilltop town, lends its name to a noble wine of antique fame. Montalbano is another name that commands respect.

Good Chianti is a sturdy red wine, with ample bouquet and fairly intense flavor, just the thing for well-seasoned foods, cheese, and roasts. Over two and a half million gallons of it are produced annually. Bottled before its second birthday, it is a comparative juvenile when it reaches the foreign consumer in its famous *fiasco*. This familiar straw-jacketed flask is the identifying mark of Chianti throughout the world, although many other Italian wines have adopted it. The bottles are usually hand blown and therefore are round-bottomed and need the straw base to remain upright on the table. Weaving these basket bases keeps thousands of elderly Tuscan women busy the year round.

However, it is well to bear in mind that all Chianti is not presented in straw-covered *fiaschi*. In Florence, for example, restaurants usually serve it in generous carafes. The finest Chiantis, with a bit of age behind them, never appear in flask form at all, but in conventional dark bottles of the Bordeaux type. It is obvious that where considerable aging in the bottle in a humid wine cellar is required, the straw would not hold up well. So the fine years of Chianti, those of 1946, 1947, and 1949, for example, will appear at your table in straight-sided bottles. They are worth seeking out, for good Chianti ages magnificently.

Some people don't know how fine a Chianti can be. This could be due to the fact that some of the lesser and cheaper Chiantis, those from the hills around Arezzo and Siena, have captured a lion's share of the foreign market. To know Chianti in its most satisfying mood, it is therefore wise to remember those aristocratic names—Ricasoli, Antinori, Serristori, and Ruffino.

Tuscany has its white wines, too, among them a dry white Chianti that appears *en carafe* in many Florentine restaurants. Among the sweeter and heavier whites are Passiti and Vinsanti, produced on many Tuscan hillsides.

Haystacks in the Tuscan hills

For dessert wines, there are Malvasia and Moscato di Montalcino. The little island of Elba produces a Moscato too—a golden-yellow, semisweet table wine with an intense aroma—and a sparkling wine all its own. Spumante d'Elba comes in three bubbling versions—sweet, semisweet, and dry.

Our gastronomic tour of Tuscany can touch within its allotted space only the highlights, and we are conscious of a few omissions. Most of the small towns, however, offer small rewards, so that it is in the larger cities that the prospector for epicurean nuggets must plant his fork. Foremost among them, of course, is Florence.

Florence

IN THE foreword we have pointed out the impossibility, because of limitations of space, of being anything more than an epicurean guide in Rome, Venice, and Florence. We shall sketch out the beauties of other Tuscan cities therefore, but as far as the history and art of the incomparable Florence are concerned, we must reluctantly turn you over to one of the many guidebooks.

Florence is a city of over 400,000 souls, filled with well-established hotels, wonderful pensions, and a corresponding wealth of dining places. It resembles Lyon in that it would be difficult to sit down anywhere to a really poor meal. A pleasant prospect awaits the visitor after a morning in the art galleries and the leather shops. With the first pangs of hunger just asserting themselves, along with a certain foot-weariness, what a relief it is to sit down in a café before a cool *apéritif* and to select the setting of a good Florentine luncheon! Installed at a café table in the large and teeming Piazza della Repubblica, you will find the predicament an agreeable one, and not at all difficult to solve. The setting is a trifle flurried, however. Two large parking plots, four sprawling café terraces, and several newsstands take up most of the piazza. Hundreds of gesticulating male Florentines and the ceaseless staccato buzz of scooter traffic lend vibration to your *aperitivo*. A sad-faced man tries to sell you a mechanical rabbit, a wispish lass begins to coo into a microphone, accompanied by a costumed orchestra, and a black-haired waiter in a white coat comes around to take your order. At this point many a newly arrived Anglo-Saxon traveler becomes perplexed. If he says "Martini," he'll probably get a sweet vermouth. If he asks for whiskey, or brandy and soda, his luck may be more considerable, and so will the check. He may wonder about those red or brown or amber drinks that his Italian neighbors have ordered. One is Campari soda, a garishly red affair, pleasantly bitter, and not too sweet to some tastes. It comes in small iced bottles, as does Cinzano soda, sweeter and not so vivid in color. Two other established favorites of Italian café sitters are Bianco Sarti and Rabarbaro. Both are made from rhubarb and are somewhat sweet and perfumed. Another serious competitor is Cynar, dark in color, and made from artichokes, as posters scattered all over the peninsula will tell you. And you see the name Fernet Branca everywhere. This bitter one defies our adjectives assembled over the years, but it has its staunch devotees, and will not shock some of the more daring palates.

Vermouth is still the standby of Italian cafés, however, and the famous houses of Martini and Rossi, Cinzano, Carpano, Cora, and so forth, are household words here and abroad. We have a weakness for a spicy vermouth produced by the ancient house of Carpano, called Punt è Mes. Ask for

Silhouette of Florence

Loggia dei Lanzi—Florence

Detail of the duomo—Florence

"Poontaymace" and hope for the best. Cinzano and Martini both make a palatable dry white vermouth, but be sure to ask for "dry," a word the Italians use in ordering, and not *bianco*. The latter appears to be laden with myrrh, incense, and all the perfumes of Arabia. There are mixed drinks also, and in case you wish to be patriotic and order an Americano, you will find that it is composed of equal parts of Bitter Campari and Italian vermouth with lemon peel and a splash of soda. There are other facets to the *apéritif* problem in Italy. For example, if you stand up at the bar and buy a check from the cashier, you pay only about sixty per cent as much as the seated customer pays for the same thing.

Perhaps you seek something more *intime* than an open-air café for this preprandial pause. In this case we have a strong recommendation, the little bar called LELAND on the Via Tuornaboni, near the Arno. This spot has been a favorite with civilized Florentines and foreign residents for generations. The atmosphere is totally charming and the people are gay and urbane. Good sherry and port, and properly mixed cocktails, supplement the usual routine of vermouth. A memorable place in which to work up an appetite!

For those who don't care particularly for sweetish Italian *aperitivi* and also seek a quieter spot, the GRAND HOTEL offers a superb alternative. This famous hostelry on the banks of the Arno has inaugurated a perfectly charming bar and grill, very swish and handsomely decorated, where the best of international drinks may be obtained. The walls are embellished with photographic enlargements of famous engravings, and the effect is most decorative. The cocktails are inviting, especially the dry Martinis, and the service is attentive. Usually a gifted pianist is playing discreetly in the corner. Close by are two dining rooms where you can select an excellent meal from a French menu. Many visitors who stay at the Grand Hotel make no attempt to dine anywhere else, and we can hardly blame them.

Grand
Hotel
Florence

The director of the hotel presented us with recipes of four of his favorite specialties, among them the celebrated

Cacciucco alla Viareggina
FISH STEW OF VIAREGGIO

For 6 guests use about 5 pounds of assorted fish in season, such as whiting, flounder, bass, eel, and 1 lobster cut in pieces. Filet the fish or cut it in thick slices. Heat 1/2 cup of good olive oil in a large deep pot and add 2 or 3 cloves of garlic, 1/2 teaspoon of thyme, 1 tablespoon of parsley, and leaves of 1 stalk of celery, all cut coarsely, salt, and a good dash of dried red pepper flakes. When these ingredients are partly cooked but not browned, add the fish heads, scraps, and bones. Stir them over a brisk fire and add 3/4 cup of white wine, 3/4 cup of red wine, and 2 tablespoons of tomato paste. Add 2 cups of stock or water and cook slowly until you have obtained a thick and flavorful *fondo* or base. Strain this base through a sieve.

Start again with 3 tablespoons of hot oil in the pot and add garlic, thyme, parsley, and a celery stalk, about half the quantity of each as used above, all finely chopped, and salt and red pepper. Then put in the pieces of fish in layers, placing in the bottom that which takes longest to cook. Pour the prepared base liquid over the fish. There should be enough to cover all well. Cover the pot and simmer all together slowly for about 20 minutes, or until all the fish is cooked.

Serve the *cacciucco* in a hot tureen and place pieces of toasted garlic bread in each plate before ladling in the fish stew.

The chef says: "It is useless to add that the best results from the present recipe are assured by the good culinary sense of the one who executes it."

There are many other tempting choices in Florence for the hungry visitor. If you simply adore your fellow tourist and want to go just where he or she does, DONEY'S, on the Via Tournabuoni, or NATALE, facing the Arno at Lungarno Accaioli 80, will bring the sweet music of American speech to your ears, accompanied by perfectly good food and service. Both serve Anglo-Saxon dishes for those who pine for them. There is a most agreeable outdoor dining place on the Piazzale Michelangelo, high above the city, called LA LOGGIA, and there you may sit in its garden in summer and enjoy the skyline of Florence and good international food at the same time. It is the captive of the tourist also. Mind you, we don't decry the great American tourist, being precisely that ourselves. But you may share our belief that the most obvious places are not always the answer to a gourmet's prayer.

There is another category of Florentine restaurant that exerts an appeal of its own and attracts visitors in droves—the *buche,* or cellar dining places. These "holes in the ground" are vaulted cellars with somewhat contrived atmosphere and décor. The walls are thickly covered with frescoes and posters, the lights are low, and there is always music at some time during the meal.

Buca Lapi
Florence

With a bevy of schoolgirls on my hands (and it *has* happened), I would choose one of these without hesitation. The BUCA LAPI, in the cellar of the Palazzo Antinori, and the BUCA SAN RUFILLO, near the *duomo,* are the best in this category. The music may seem a bit insistent but the atmosphere is gay and the food more than adequate. The Buca Lapi is noted for several specialties, among them *cannelloni* and *bracioline de manzo alla fiorentina.* The latter is a thick meat sauce that is excellent served with spaghetti or *risotto.* Perhaps you would like to try Signor Lapi's recipe in your own kitchen:

Bracioline di Manzo alla Fiorentina
MEAT SAUCE FLORENTINE

Prepare a mixture of 1 small carrot, 1 onion, and 1 teaspoon of parsley, all finely chopped. Cook the mixture in 3 tablespoons of olive oil until it is slightly browned. Add 1 pound of chopped beef that has been dusted with flour and cook, stirring often, until the beef is lightly browned also. Moisten with 1/2 cup of red wine, and when this has almost evaporated, add 2 fresh, peeled, coarsely chopped tomatoes, or 1 cup canned Italian tomatoes, 1 cup water or stock, 1/2 cup chopped mushrooms, and salt and pepper. Simmer the sauce slowly for about 1 1/2 hours, or until it has a good thick consistency. Serve it with spaghetti or other pasta, *risotto,* or the like.

With the gentle art of gastronomy uppermost in mind, we have made a selection of a few Florentine restaurants and *trattorie* that should please most epicurean visitors. The list does not sparkle with originality. All of these *ristoranti* are familiar to local gourmets, and each has its quota of foreigners. But the names represent several weeks of poking about, and you might like to jot them down in your little black book—or do people carry those any more? These happen to be our own favorites, but there are at least a dozen other good restaurants in Florence.

SABATINI—Via Panzani 41–43r

The Via Panzani is an unexceptional street whose tranquility is troubled by a Toonerville-type tramway, but this thoroughfare happens to have a special meaning for gourmets. Here are two unassailable shrines of good food whose names are worth remembering—Sabatini and Baldini. We will stick our necks out and state flatly that there is none better than Sabatini in Tuscany. As proof, we would not submit the menu first, but the clientele, many of them single gentlemen, solitary and content at their individual tables. There are goateed professors, plum-faced industrialists, aesthetic, thin-faced men in yellow sweaters and riding boots who live in outlying villas. All of them are serene, munching their bread sticks, or *grissini,* and tipping their Chianti carafe from its silver cradle. They smile benignly over their coffee and pay slight attention to the *conto.*

Ristorante
Sabatini
Florence

Sabatini is a prime favorite with the better-upholstered Florentines and it is not always easy to get a table. The answer: get there before twelve-thirty or before eight and you're in. As for the menu—it glitters! There is a noble silver chariot loaded with *antipasti* if that is your mood, and a different pasta specialty every day—first *agnolotti* (a half-moon type of ravioli with scalloped edges), then *tortellini* (small stuffed rings of pasta with a meat and tomato sauce), then green *lasagne,* then *cannelloni,* and so on through

Michelangelo's David–Florence

Column of Justice–Florence

Church of Santa Maria Novella–Florence

the week. For the *pièce de résistance,* Sabatini offers so many good things that we are left speechless. Among them are *scampi alla marinara* and filet of sole. One of the best is *petti di pollo al burro con trifola fresca.* These are chicken breasts sautéed in butter, then spread with a mixture of rice, mushrooms, and ham. The rice is then masked with a delicate sauce and liberally sprinkled with paper-thin slices of lavender truffle. They leave a fragment of bone on each chicken breast so that the client won't think he is cutting into a veal cutlet. That gives you an idea of the tenderness of Tuscan veal! Or maybe, come to think of it, of the toughness of Tuscan chicken. At all events, it is delightful. Besides the usual cheese and fruit, you will find an extraordinary dessert here, *Saint Honoré alla panna.* If I'm ever caught using the word yummy, it will be in describing this voluptuous pastry! Though the wine list here is filled with good things, most guests seem happy with the palatable and inexpensive Chianti of the house, served in carafes. A trilingual maître d'hôtel in a pin-stripe suit handles the language problem well, the service is able, and the prices very fair. Sabatini is worth a wide detour, but if you find yourself near the *duomo* or the Church of Santa Maria Novello, the detour won't be necessary. The restaurant is between the two.

Signor Sabatini, a youngish man with a charming smile, generously gave us the recipes of five of his specialties, including

Piselli alla Fiorentina

PEAS FLORENTINE

Put 1/2 cup of olive oil in a saucepan and add 2 pounds of freshly shelled young peas, a tablespoon of parsley, finely chopped, 1 whole clove of garlic, 1/4 pound of diced cooked ham, 1 cup of water, salt, pepper, and 1/8 teaspoon of baking soda. Heat all on a good fire until the liquid boils, then lower the heat and simmer the mixture until the peas are tender. Serve immediately.

BALDINI—Via Panzani 57r

A few steps down the street, and quite unostentatious behind its narrow doorway, is another praiseworthy dining place. Baldini occupies a long, high-ceilinged room with a half-hearted tapestry as its principal decoration. Nobody wastes time admiring the décor or listening to soulful singers here. Baldini is all for fine food, and its standards are high. We like its simple dishes in particular, and jotted down a very satisfying luncheon: *fettuccine alla bolognese,* followed by *tortino di carciofi,* that light and fragrant Tuscan dish described earlier in this chapter, then a green salad, a beautiful full-ripe persimmon, and *caffè espresso.* Nothing pretentious in such a menu, but our neighbors were indulging in a *bécasse flambée* that was unmistakably the pro-

Ristorante
Baldini
Florence

Ponte Vecchio—Florence

duct of the higher realms of cooking. Baldini's waiters are cheerful fellows who muddle along fairly well in English.

Persimmons, by the way, are one of the marked compensations for coming to Tuscany in the autumn. The Italian fruitgrower allows them to cling tenaciously to the tree, getting the final bit of ripening long after the last leaf has fallen. Then they are picked at the precise moment when they are bursting with sweet juice, much in the manner of the grapes at Château d'Yquem.

OLIVIERO—Via Tosinghi 18

Ristorante
Oliviero
Florence

This establishment is far more *intime* than most Florentine restaurants, and quite reminiscent of Paris, with a faint touch of Fifty-second Street thrown in. The rooms are small, with banquettes against the wall, and if the atmosphere achieves a faint horsiness, it is due to the series of fine colored aquatints of English race horses that are the only decoration. The clientele is very discriminating and well dressed. We have counted three monocles there, at various times. We have also encountered a sad-faced and persistent little man who demonstrates mechanical animals at your table. There is a place for this, of course, but not in a good restaurant. Or am I becoming a fussy old fuddy-duddy? I don't *like* having a mechanical bear clap his silly cymbals at my table!

All this discussion has nothing to do with the quality of Oliviero's cuisine, which is very good indeed. The menu is a rich one, and the prices a little higher than usual. Our large *sogliola fritta* was the equal of a fine sole from the English Channel, and the *animelle di vitella al madera* were very tender and well-seasoned sweetbreads. The *macedonia di frutta al maraschino* tasted a bit like hair tonic, or maybe I had forgotten that this is precisely the way maraschino tastes. We asked for a good Tuscan wine for the sweetbreads and enjoyed a delicious Serristori Chianti 1949—a name and a year you'd do well to remember. Oliviero is near the center of Florence and that café table we spoke about in the Piazza della Repubblica. If you heed its siren call, you won't be disappointed.

During the warm months of the year, the owners of Oliviero operate an open-air restaurant of the same name on the Via Michelangelo, at Number 78. In this wonderful setting in a converted villa high above the city, you dine amidst semitropical flowers and look down upon the Arno and the unforgettable silhouette of Florence. The food and service are of the same high quality as in the downtown Oliviero, and there is an open terrace for dancing under the stars.

PAOLI—Via dei Tavolini 12

Here is one of the oldest restaurants in Florence, said to date from the Middle Ages, and it is certainly one of the most agreeable. Its rooms are vaulted and arched, dressed up with frescoes and escutcheons, but the colors are muted and the effect is restful. Paoli has a simple entrance on a little side street near the Piazza della Signoria. If you have emerged footsore and ravenous from the Uffizi Gallery, it is unquestionably the nearest haven of good food. We like Paoli partly on account of its proprietor, a genial white-haired man of the old school. He is alert and cordial, speaks good French and English, and is genuinely interested in the contentment of his guests. This is one of the best places to come for genuine Tuscan specialties, *cannelloni* and *scampi* among them. They cut and weigh your Florentine *bistecca* at the front counter here and charge you by weight only. Countless American and English travelers will back up the statement that Paoli is one of the most restful and satisfying places in Florence.

Ristorante
PAOLI
Florence

PONTE VECCHIO—Via dei Bardi 64

When the Germans were forced out of Florence in 1944, they blew up all the bridges across the Arno except one—the famous, shop-crammed Ponte Vecchio. To block access to this spared bridge they demolished all streets

Ristorante
Ponte
Vecchio
Florence

approaching it. Their destruction of the area was one of the more galling stupidities of the war, for the British had a Bailey bridge across the river in no time, and the old bridges and streets might just as well have been spared. It has taken the Italians years to repair this overnight folly, and the job is by no means finished.

In one of the rebuilt structures jutting out above the Arno is a new restaurant that you will probably enjoy. Named after the old bridge, it commands a view of the river from its terrace that is worth the cover charge. The restaurant, located on the ground floor, hums with activity. Coming in, you have a view of the well-scrubbed kitchen, and there is a choice of panoramic tables—for the early comers, that is. Service and wine are good here, and the cooking, which leans to the rich Bolognese tradition, is very palatable. Our carnivorous sense had been sharpened by a morning of viewing the more comestible Rubens nudes at the Pitti Palace, and our appetite was keen as we confronted *tagliatelle fresche alla bolognese,* followed by the traditional Florentine beefsteak. They were impeccable. For festive diners-out there is music and dancing at the Ponte Vecchio, and one can obtain a meal there at almost any hour.

TRATTORIA SOSTANZA—Via del Porcellana 25

Trattoria Sostanza Florence

Just as Florentine pensions are preferred to hotels by many travelers, that democratic institution, the *trattoria,* enters into the life of almost every visitor who stays in Florence for more than a few days. A fundamental difference between a *ristorante*—where the waiters are leisurely and wear white coats, the menus are typewritten, and the tables individual—and a *trattoria* is that in the latter the waiters are in shirt sleeves and often hurried to the point of hysteria, the menus are scrawled in pencil and the public rubs elbows at the same table in a spirit of *camaraderie,* or better. The prices in a *trattoria* are sure to be lower—but the food is often better. This state of affairs explains its extraordinary popularity. Believe it or not, there is a Trattoria di Bing Crosby in Florence. Our favorite, Sostanza, is on a little side street near the luxurious Excelsior and Grand Hotels. It is small, beginning with a bar—where they sell wine and bread to passing housewives as a side line—and an icebox stocked with good Tuscan meat. Beyond this you come to a longish room closely packed with tables for six or more and a small kitchen with a charcoal grill blazing away and fragrant kettles simmering in the shadows.

Two waiters handle all the customers, and they are in a frantic hurry most of the time. When Mario, the more flighty of the two, reached a truly dizzy pace, the customers called him Mercurio, and Mercury's outstretched pose is what he assumed much of the time. To judge by the gallery of postcards in the bar, Sostanza has friends all over the world, especially in

The Neptune Fountain, Piazza della Signoria—Florence

America. Departed guests send him views of skyscrapers, and nostalgic sentiments. Their nostalgia is not surprising. The pasta is tender, the sauces are rich. Steaks, chops, and chicken come sizzling forth from that grill, and they are wonderful. The waiter throws your order at you, but what of that? A perfect *bistecca alla fiorentina,* the size of a second baseman's mit, arrives at your table for just over a dollar. Everyone drinks wine from a carafe, everyone is friendly, but the conversational pitch is fortunately low. We recommend Sostanza for the lustier type of gourmet, and for friendly and gregarious people.

Here is a delicious spread that Sostanza serves its guests:

Antipasto Crostini

CHICKEN LIVER HORS-D'OEUVRE

Soften 2 tablespoons of finely minced onion in 1 tablespoon of melted butter over low heat until it is pale golden in color but not brown. Add 1/4 cup of chicken stock and simmer it for for 2 minutes, or until the liquid is almost evaporated. Add salt and 8 chicken livers that have been scraped free of fibers, chopped, and worked to a creamy consistency. Stir this over moderate heat until the chicken livers have changed color and are somewhat firm, but do not overcook them. Add 1 1/4 teaspoons of drained capers, allow the mixture to cool, and store it, covered, in the refrigerator. Serve it spread on small rounds of toasted Italian bread.

TRATTORIA CAMILLO—Borgo San Jacopo 57r

Trattoria
Camillo
Florence

We wish that some of these addresses might be in the nature of an inside tip, but that is too much to expect. Everyone seems to know about Camillo, for example. It is large for a *trattoria,* with a high vaulted ceiling and a little annex for the overflow of guests that inevitably appears. Located on a little side street close to the south bank of the Arno, it is truly a family enterprise, carefully watched by mother and father Camillo, with white-haired uncle reigning in the kitchen and an indeterminate number of younger Camillos waiting on table and tending bar. Its food and atmosphere are the pure essence of Italy, and most commendable. We liked the husky young waiters, immaculate in their white shirt sleeves and aprons, and most energetic and polite. A more friendly place would be hard to find in Florence.

Fiesole

IN THE neighborhood of Florence are several towns that call for a day's excursion: Fiesole, Impruneta, Piato, Empoli, San Miniato, and Certaldo among them. The prime favorite for generations has been Fiesole, the for-

Piazza Mino da Fiesole–Fiesole

tified Etruscan hill town crowning the slopes above the city. It is only about four miles out of Florence and is easily reached by bus or car. Ample rewards await the pilgrim, including an excellent luncheon.

This ancient city prospered when Rome was but a village, and later became the Roman Faesulae, with a fine amphitheater and vaulted baths. You can still visit them both. The theater was excavated in 1873, and many of the objects uncovered at that time may be seen in an adjoining museum. Fiesole commands a superb view of Florence and the valley of the Arno, especially for those stouthearted visitors who have the stamina to climb up to the Church of San Francesco.

The civic heart of the town is the Piazza Mino da Fiesole, named for the famous local sculptor. Here you will find the Romanesque cathedral of San Romolo, with a somewhat gawky Florentine tower. More graceful is the Palazzo Pretorio, at the eastern end of the piazza. This delightful building, with wide porches thickly embellished with carved escutcheons, now serves as the town hall. Fiesole is a fine place to acquire straw hats or baskets or handbags for your friends at home. Several gaily bedecked stands in the square compete for you attention. So do a few restaurants, among which we have a decided favorite, the ALBERGO AURORA. This hotel has a beguiling sheltered terrace overlooking the valley of the Arno, with the silhouette of the *duomo* in the distance. Sunlight filters through the leaves and you will find laughter, animation, and really good food and wine. We enjoyed one of the best *lasagne verdi al forno* in our travels on this sheltered terrace, followed by some noble *scampi* on skewers. The white Soave was delicious, as were the little orange melons and the satanic black coffee. The service was good and the damage to the portfolio slight. Small wonder that the Aurora is immensely popular with one-day trippers!

Just past the center of Fiesole, in the area called Borgunto, is another charming place to dine, the RISTORANTE RASPANTI. It is especially appealing in summer, for it is cool and airy, something that Florence often is not. From its well-appointed terrace, diners have an unsurpassed north view of the valley of the Mugnone. You can order typical Florentine dishes here.

Albergo Aurora
Fiesole

Ristorante Raspanti
Fiesole

Pratolino

FLORENTINE *bons vivants* who like to drive out into the country for a good dinner have a fast favorite in the village of Pratolino, about eight miles north of the city on the road to Bologna. The object of their pilgrimage is the RISTORANTE ZOCCHI, a cheerful country inn with a sheltered terrace overlooking the Medicean villa of Pratolino. The great specialty here is chicken cooked on the spit, but there are also delectable pasta preparations and

Ristorante Zocchi
Pratolino

satisfying steaks. This place lies far outside the tourist orbit, which might strike you as a good reason for going there.

Candeli

THIS VILLAGE on the south bank of the Arno, about four miles east of Florence, now has particular interest for travelers seeking the unusual. In recent years, the fifteenth-century VILLA LA MASSA has been restored, handsomely furnished, and converted into a very plush hotel and restaurant. Its management is British, its cuisine mainly French, and its appeal decidedly aristocratic. The Villa la Massa has been adopted by people of prominence, including ex-queens, admirals, and cinema stars, whose photographs portray them as being very well pleased indeed. All of the bedrooms have private baths. For those who seek an escape from the summer heat, there is an inviting swimming pool. Meals are served on a flowery terrace overlooking the Arno. The cooking is excellent, and the prices are understandably in the upper bracket. Many travelers will find here a refreshing variation from the usual run of Italian hotels.

Villa
La Massa
Candeli

Prato

ANOTHER REWARDING excursion from Florence leads to this prosperous textile-producing town, now recovered from its war wounds. Prato is about eleven miles northwest of Florence, just off the *autostrada*. It has two notable attractions, a cathedral and a towering brick town hall.

The cathedral is a lovely Romanesque structure with a Gothic façade, designed by the versatile Giovanni Pisano. This face of the *duomo* is built largely of alternate stripes of white and green marble, and the lunette of its Gothic doorway is brightened with a superb Madonna and Child by Andrea della Robbia. But the most remarkable thing about the cathedral is the outdoor corner pulpit of the Holy Girdle. Ornamented with dancing cupids by the great Donatello, it is unique in Italy. The stone campanile, also the work of Pisano, is tall and graceful. Inside you will see Pisano's lovely statue of the Virgin, and some inspiring frescoes by Fra Filippo Lippi, among them a very proper version of Salome's dance.

In the crowded heart of the city stands the thirteenth-century Palazzo Pretorio, a towering structure of brick and stone, richly imbedded with escutcheons. It houses a notable gallery of paintings by Florentine masters. Filippino Lippi was born in Prato, and some of his finest work can be seen in this *palazzo*.

The Pulpit of the Holy Girdle—Cathedral of Prato

Prato does not offer an epicurean experience on a level with its artistic treasures—this would be asking too much. It does have, however, an adequate country hotel, the ALBERGO STELLA D'ITALIA, just across from the cathedral, with a pleasant open-air dining terrace, sheltered by umbrellas. The cooking is acceptable, and the Chianti is fine.

Albergo
Stella
d'Italia
Prato

Pistoia

THE TRAVELER should allot this fascinating Tuscan town a day's visit and more. Its only drawback is the lack of a first-rate place to dine or to spend the night. But it is an easy drive from Florence and makes an unforgettable excursion. A medieval ironworking town, Pistoia is credited with giving its name to the pistol. It has guarded its atmosphere of the Middle Ages remarkably well, especially in the area near the cathedral. The Piazza del Duomo is lined with venerable structures from Gothic and Romanesque times, all of them impressive. We suggest that you go here first of all, and if it happens to be market day, you are in luck. Above the hubbub of canvas-covered stands looms the exquisite fourteenth-century baptistry, designed by Andrea Pisano, an octagonal building of white marble with thin stripes of deep sea-green stone. A small outdoor pulpit adjoins its doorway. One of the best Gothic edifices in Italy, it has notable rivals around the square, including the twelfth-century cathedral, whose arcaded façade is achieved in striped marble. Adjoining is a noble campanile. It begins in an austere, prisonlike style, but toward the top it bursts out with triple loggias, the work of Giovanni Pisano. Next in line is another Gothic building, the ponderous Palazzo del Comune. This is the town hall, and it houses a good civic museum. Finally, across the square, is one of our favorite buildings, the Palazzo Pretorio. We've always had a weakness for this Florentine-Gothic palace because of the bevy of armorial sculptures that animate its façade. There are at least three dozen of them.

Thus concludes the backdrop for market day in medieval Pistoia. Local citizens pay scant attention to the splendor of the setting. They are too busy shopping for shoes, kitchenware, china, and hats. The sale of food is relegated to other areas, but almost everything wearable can be bought in this piazza. The Italians are great ones for selling men's woolens by the yard. Italian housewives are obviously adept at tailoring their husbands' clothes, and lengthy family consultations take place before the right material, usually a pronounced stripe, is selected. Other merchants are not so dignified. It is quite evident that the salesman who puts on the best vaudeville act sells the most china and glassware in an Italian country market. One of our favorite vendors made such violent and extravagant giveaway offers that his wife

Porch of the Ospedale del Ceppo—Pistoia

The baptistry, Piazza del Duomo—Pistoia

ostensibly tried to restrain him. Hair and arms flying, he pushed her aside and vociferated louder than ever to the country crowds, who apparently loved it. You need to be an actor to prosper in this competitive market!

There is a lot more to be seen in wandering around the streets of Pistoia. Close at hand, for example, you will encounter the restored Church of San Giovanni Fuorcivitas, just about the most richly striped building in Italy. You should see two other superlative works of art before leaving the city. One is the Ospedale del Ceppo, a functioning hospital with a portico that can't be equaled anywhere. This typical Florentine porch is embellished with a celebrated frieze, still in magnificent condition. Achieved between 1514 and 1525 in colored enameled terra cotta, it is the work of Giovanni della Robbia and his pupils. The brilliant band of sculpture pictures the seven works of Mercy: clothe the naked, welcome strangers, care for the sick, visit prisoners, bury the dead, feed the hungry, and console the afflicted. This extraordinary masterpiece attracts countless visitors annually to what would otherwise be a routine hospital.

Pistoia's other treasure is the wonderful carved marble pulpit by Giovanni Pisano in the little Church of Sant'Andrea. Dating from about 1500, it shows the great sculptor at his best and compares favorably with his pulpit in Pisa.

For the moment, Pistoia offers only a limited recompense to the visiting gastronome. There are some passable little restaurants, LE ROSE and LE CHIAVI D'ORO among them. As for hotels, we tried the LEON BIANCO and found it clean, if elemental, with acceptable cooking. But at present, food-conscious travelers will find that Prato, Pistoia, and Lucca are best seen on expeditions from Florence. Another way to solve the problem would be to stay at Montecatini Terme, the fine thermal resort only about ten miles from Pistoia. The hotels there are numerous and excellent, and motor service is good.

Lucca

THIS ANCIENT city in the plain remains serene behind its sixteenth-century walls, a proud aristocrat among Tuscan towns. For more than four hundred years, Lucca was independent, the capital of a miniature state. When Napoleon took over the area, he made it into a principality and presented it to his sister, Elisa Baciocchi. Later it came to the Bourbons, who subsequently ceded it to Tuscany. Throughout its many vicissitudes, Lucca has retained the atmosphere of a proud, if small, capital. As every epicure knows, Lucca is famous for its olive oil, pressed from fruit grown on the surrounding hills. Its familiar ocher-printed container is known wherever fine olive oil is purveyed. Locally, Lucca's favorite delicacy is an O-shaped cake called *bucellato,* contrived of sweet pastry, vanilla, aniseed, and dried raisins. We suggest that

Broomshop–Lucca

Old house–Lucca

Kitchenware bazaar–Lucca

Arched street–Lucca

The Church of San Michele–Lucca

you drop into a Luccan *pasticceria* and buy a bag of *bucellati,* excellent companions for your tour of the city. Lucca is the birthplace of the beloved composer, Giacomo Puccini (1858-1924), and is understandably proud of the distinction. They have named a piazza for him, right next to Napoleon's.

There is much to be seen wandering through Lucca's narrow streets—fine palaces, churches and well-designed private homes from past centuries. It is even more enjoyable to take a stroll along the sixteenth-century city ramparts, flanked with ancient trees and punctuated with towers. Among Lucca's many churches, two are outstanding—the cathedral and the elaborate Church of San Michele. The former is a very ancient affair, dating back to the sixth century. What you see now is mostly from the twelfth, and that is early enough. Its façade is composed of a series of arcades in the Pisan manner. A noble, sober campanile adjoins it. The treasure of the *duomo* is a tomb, the marble sarcophagus of Ilaria del Carretto. This rare jewel of the Renaissance was carved by Jacapo della Quercia in 1406, and is considered one of the loveliest in Italy. At the foot of the beautiful reclining figure sits Ilaria's dog, symbol of fidelity.

The startlingly beautiful Church of San Michele rises in the heart of Lucca on the site of the ancient Roman forum. It positively shimmers on a sunny day. The façade scintillates with no less than four rows of loggias, above which stands a triumphant and angelic Saint Michael, flanked by two approving angels as he slays his dragon. We must admit that this elaborate façade, restored in 1866, borders on the wedding-cake style of architecture, but it is impressive nonetheless. Inside the church you will find notable works by Filippino Lippi and Luca della Robbia.

There is a pleasant hotel in Lucca, on the Piazza Puccini, in case you care to spend the night in this noble city. The HOTEL UNIVERSO has been welcoming generations of travelers. For those seeking a good Tuscan meal, Lucca offers some quite modest restaurants. You should be reasonably content at either the RISTORANTE GARFAGNANA or the BUCA DI SANT'ANTONIO, both of them near the Church of Saint Michael.

Pisa

PISA IS one of the most visited cities in Europe, and it deserves to be. It swarms with tourists in the summer season, most of them intent upon seeing its unique curiosity, the Leaning Tower. They find much more. In the same green meadow on the northern extremity of the city, which d'Annunzio called the "Field of Miracles," stands a concentration of superlative structures. The exquisite cathedral, the huge marble baptistry, and the Campo-Santo cemetery all complement the Leaning Tower.

The Leaning Tower of Pisa

The baptistry–Pisa

The southern half of Pisa suffered grave damage in 1944 when the Allies faced the Germans across the Arno for many destructive weeks. Bridges were destroyed and palaces reduced to rubble. But in Pisa's precious architectural ensemble, only the Campo-Santo was hit. A single shell shattered a part of the cloister roof, set fire to the timbers, and melted the lead roof topping. Several of the priceless frescoes on the cloister walls were damaged in the process.

Pisa is one of the most ancient cities along the Mediterranean, dating from Etruscan times, and it was once a seaport in active competition with Genoa and Venice. But the sea has retreated from it, just as it has from Ravenna, and the shore is now six miles away. The Arno remains faithful, however.

Pisa was the birthplace of the great Galileo, and of two sculptor-architects who had a profound influence on Italian art, Nicolò Pisano and his son Giovanni. It is also the setting of one of the most ancient universities in Italy. Pisa's arcaded streets and cafés are filled with hatless, talkative, well-dressed students, and its bookstores are a delight. There are some handsome palaces scattered about Pisa, notably in the Piazza dei Cavalieri, where we urge you to go. Little Pisan churches pop up at odd intervals, all of them pleasant, particularly the jewel-like little Church of Santa Maria della Spina, built in 1230 on the banks of the Arno as a chapel for seamen. It is pure Pisan Gothic, and perfectly charming.

But it is to the enchanted fields northward and the Piazza del Duomo that all steps eventually turn. There is enough here to keep you enraptured for a full day or more. The baptistry, for example, is a thing of total beauty. Begun in 1153, this lofty circular building of white marble began in the sober round-arched Romanesque style. As the work progressed through a century and more, it flowered into a lacy girdle of Gothic. The interior is impressive for several reasons. First of all, it produces a remarkable echo. Even a whisper comes back to you. The guides with the better voices are in the habit of singing four sonorous tones for visitors. These come back in the form of a rich, reverberating chord. The artistic treasure of the baptistry is the noble hexagonal pulpit by Nicolò Pisano. It is probably his masterpiece, and it stands up well in comparison with the larger pulpit in the cathedral, the work of his gifted son Giovanni. As is the custom in other large Italian cities, all baptisms in Pisa take place in the baptistry. The octagonal fonts are of chiseled marble, and large enough to permit a complete submersion.

The cathedral, a white marble Romanesque basilica begun in 1063, is the masterpiece of the so-called Pisan style of architecture. Its magnificent western façade glitters with four superimposed rows of richly sculptured loggias. Its influence upon the cathedrals of Lucca and Pistoia is obvious. Inside the basilica you will find sixty-eight monolithic marble columns, brought back from the East as plunder by Pisan warriors. The greatest work of art, how-

Piazza dei Cavalieri—Pisa

Church of Santa Maria della Spina, on the bank of the Arno—Pisa

ever, is the famous pulpit, masterpiece of Giovanni Pisano. He spent nine years on this heroic assignment (1302–1311). The pulpit was damaged in a fire in 1596, and its sculptured parts became scattered in many places. By a remarkable effort, archaeologists traced the strayed pieces, and the pulpit was reassembled in 1926. In the center of the cathedral hangs the great bronze lamp by Lorenzi that, according to legend, inspired Galileo to make his momentous experiments with the pendulum.

The most celebrated cemetery in Tuscany, the Campo-Santo is an enormous Gothic cloister paved with tombstones and embellished with ancient frescoes. As we noted above, some of these suffered greatly during the last war. The Campo-Santo has now been restored and is open to visitors.

The more leisurely citizens of Pisa love their unique architectural treasures, and spend much of their time relaxing in the shade of the Campo-Santo in summer. In colder seasons, knitting matrons, old men, and nursemaids with their charges enjoy sun-bathing on marble seats around the base of the baptistry and *duomo*. They leave the Leaning Tower entirely to the tourist. This unprecedented structure was begun in 1174 and was designed by Bonanno, who also built the bronze cathedral doors. He intended it to be a belfry with six rows of loggias. The work was well under way when the whole thing began to tip ominously, and the builders decided to give up. Many years later, when they observed that the tilting had stopped, the stoneworkers completed the structure, counterbalancing the masonry so that the center of gravity is not so perilous as it looks. At present, the top veers about fourteen feet from the vertical. From here, according to tradition, Galileo carried on his experiments with falling bodies. Stouthearted tourists who climb to the top of the Leaning Tower will never forget it. Few experiences can equal the extraordinary sensation of circling up and down these steps, alternately too steep and too easy.

A visit to the Piazza del Duomo would not be complete without a look at the souvenir shops across the way that specialize in marble and alabaster carvings at popular prices. The Leaning Tower comes in all sizes, from a pink marble giant two feet high to a peewee plastic imitation for twenty-five cents. You can have the Venus de Milo, Cupid and Psyche, or that man hurling the discus in alabaster, too. If you have a pixy friend who treasures ghoulish horrors, we recommend a pink alabaster bed lamp modeled on the famous tower.

Hotel dei
Cavalieri

Pisa

For generations, the hotels of Pisa have been accustomed to droves of hungry one-night guests, and they are geared accordingly. Near the Piazza del Duomo is a long-standing favorite, the VILLA KINZICA, and along the Arno is the well-established GRAND HOTEL NETTUNO. Both serve conventional Tuscan food. The best fare is probably found in the least interesting part of the city, at the new HOTEL DEI CAVALIERI, near the railway station in the restored southern fringe of Pisa. Thoroughly modern and endowed with considerable creature comfort, this hotel is affiliated with one of the same name in Milan. It has a sparkling clean kitchen, which is open to the public gaze through plate-glass windows. The epicurean specialties that our scouting party tried—*saltimbocca alla pisana* and a filet of beef with Madeira sauce—seemed to us excellent. Two other familiar specialties here are *tortino di carciofi* and *lasagne verdi pasticciate*.

Viareggio

IF THE epicurean picture has been rather subdued in the preceding towns, it changes abruptly for the better in this thriving, sun-soaked beach resort west of Lucca. The most elegant, popular, and successful watering place on the Tyrrhenian coast, Viareggio boasts a long string of hotels, each with its own beach and a flurry of canvas cabins. Its sand is fine, even, and clean, and its climate so gentle that about half the hotels stay open in winter. The best summer hotels are the ALBERGO PRINCIPE DI PIEMONTE, GRAND HOTEL E REALE, and the HOTEL ASTOR. Behind the city stands a noble forest of umbrella pines, extending for miles, a marvelous place for a picnic.

Percy Bysshe Shelley and his companion, Lieutenant Williams, came to a tragic end off Viareggio, in July, 1822. Their small schooner foundered in a sudden squall on a trip from Leghorn to Spezia, and their bodies were washed ashore near the mouth of the Arno. Shelley's ashes now rest in a Protestant cemetery in Rome.

Travelers in search of inspired cooking will find a beckoning choice of restaurants along this sandy shore, most of them serving Viareggio's two famous sea-food specialties—*cacciucco* and *anguilla alla livornese*. One of the best is the RISTORANTE TITO DEL MOLO, whose tempting terrace overlooks the sea. Its kitchen staff naturally concentrates on fish, and it is well qualified to prepare the famous *cacciucco,* that worthy rival of bouillabaisse. But there are also *fritto misto del mare,* lobster, *spaghetti alle vongole,* fish soup, and filet of sole for sea-food addicts. A worthy *bistecca alla fiorentina* or a *suprême* of chicken with rice awaits diners with other tastes, and there are good Tuscan and Piedmont wines to accompany these dishes. For a final flourish, diners may end their feast with *crêpes Suzette.*

The HOTEL ASTOR, facing the sea on the corner of the Via Carrara, is another admirable place to dine while watching the dancing waves. The pasta is good here, particularly the *pasticcio verde al ragù,* and so are the *gnocchi*. Lobster with rice and filet of sole are two of the piscatorial pleasures, while *petto di pollo alla crema* and filet of beef *alla cardinale* help to round out an admirable menu.

Ristorante
Tito del
Molo
Viareggio

Hotel
Astor
Viareggio

There are several other smaller places in Viareggio, all of them good, and we recommend it strongly for a gastronomic stopover.

Forte dei Marmi

AT LEAST a dozen smaller beach resorts are strung out along the shore road running northwest from Viareggio. Among them Forte dei Marmi is probably the most distinguished and fashionable. A long series of white villas dots the shore, together with dozens of bathing establishments, and there are many acceptable hotels. The best of them is the AUGUSTUS, which has a lovely shaded garden. There is also a summer hotel with exceptionally good food, the ALDO HOTEL, on the Via Carducci. This hotel has the same management as the admirable Ristorante Aldo in Milan, and the cooking reaches the same lofty plane, with sea food occupying the lion's share of the menu. If you choose to spend more time in Forte dei Marmi, the accommodations at the Aldo are very good indeed. They include a private beach with bountiful cabins and umbrellas, and a coquettish little "Aldobar" set up conveniently right on the sand.

Aldo Hotel
Forte dei Marmi

Arezzo

OUR TUSCAN tour turns far inland now to the venerable Etruscan city of Arezzo. One of the more neglected Italian hill towns, and for no good reason, it merits a day's visit, especially for enthusiasts of good architecture and of frescoes. Arezzo is the birthplace of many famous men, among them the great Petrarch, poet and scholar second only to Dante in Italian letters. The versatile Giorgio Vasari, writer, painter, and architect of the Uffizi in Florence, is another native son. Arezzo also claims as her own Guido d'Arezzo, the monk who reputedly invented the medieval "great scale."

The province has a certain gastronomic significance, too, for the great pasta house of Buitoni, widely known abroad as well as in Italy, has an important plant in nearby Sansepolcro that produces all sorts of staples and delicacies, besides countless kilometers of noodles, spaghetti and *lasagne*. Though the recent war was cruel to the city, its artistic monuments were largely spared, with the exception of Petrarch's house, which was destroyed. This building has recently been restored, however, and the Petrarch Academy installed therein.

Arezzo's greatest art treasure is the unfinished Church of San Francesco and the marvelous frescoes by Piero della Francesca that adorn its walls. The theme of this incomparable masterpiece is the Legend of the Cross, and

Church of Santa Maria della Pieve and the Piazza Grande–Arezzo

Piazza Grande on a quiet day–Arezzo

it ranks among the noblest works of art in Italy, even though it has lapsed into a rather neglected condition.

The sightseer's path usually leads up the busy Corso d'Italia to the curious twelfth-century Church of Santa Maria della Pieve. Its severe Romanesque façade is brightened by scores of columns, and its arcaded apse overlooks the market place. Visitors who are lucky enough to hit Arezzo on market day will never forget the Piazza Grande and the tumultuous, bizarre scene it presents. This wide, sloping square is surrounded by medieval buildings of the same type that are found in the incomparable San Gimignano, but there are Gothic and Renaissance buildings as well. They sell almost everything here, and the clatter, the banter, and the commotion are indescribable. It is one of the most picturesque sights we encountered in all our Italian travels. We urge you to continue up the Corso d'Italia, past escutcheon-encrusted *palazzi* and a bust of Vasari to the Museum of Medieval Art and the Art Gallery, the Pinacoteca. Beyond these stands the fine Gothic cathedral, occupying a serene grass-grown site above the city. It has a noble Gothic portal and a fine interior. If you have more time for Arezzo, there is still much to be seen, particularly the remains of a large Roman amphitheater and the adjoining Museo Archeologico. It has some fine Arezzo pottery.

Travelers with a car will find it worth while to seek out the Church of Santa Maria delle Grazie, on the southern outskirts of the city. The remarkable feature of this church is its wide, seven-bay portico designed by Benedetto da Maiano. This fragment of Renaissance architecture has great beauty.

Buca di San Francesco *Arezzo*

Arezzo has an acceptable hotel, located on the circular Piazza Guido Monaco, named for the musical monk. The ALBERGO CONTINENTAL, though situated in a rather noisy part of the city, is modern and comfortable. For visitors who have only the day to spend, the BUCA DI SAN FRANCESCO offers the best solution for lunch or dinner. Situated near the Church of San Francesco, it is a small cellar restaurant, gaily decorated in the manner of the *buche* in Florence. Sightseers have been coming here for years, and they find some good Tuscan dishes, among them *fegatelli all'arentina,* a savory liver dish, *capretto arrosto,* delicate roast kid, and good chicken and pasta preparations. When we were last there, most of the table service was achieved by a hurried but hilarious waiter who would make his fortune in musical comedy. We hope he is still around when you try this oasis of gastronomy.

Siena

THE MOST exciting and beautiful of Tuscan hill towns, Siena is so crammed with artistic treasures that we can only sketch out its highlights here and refer you to more comprehensive guidebooks for details. During the Middle Ages,

The Palazzo Pubblico–Siena

Siena   Drypoint

Siena was an independent republic, a fierce rival of Florence and of Pisa, and it has retained its medieval atmosphere astonishingly well ever since. Its steep narrow streets, lined with dusty palaces, haven't changed in centuries. The recent war was kind to Siena, also. Classified as a hospital city, it was spared bombardment. One of its town gates bears a cordial, carved motto: "Siena opens its heart to you even wider than its doors." Fretful motorists wish that there were some way of opening up its streets, too. Few medieval cities are as hopelessly corked up with traffic or as unsuited to the affront of the twentieth-century automobile.

Two imposing towers punctuate this matchless hilltop site and mark its two centers of artistic interest. One is the lofty, brick-and-stone Torre del Mangia, which rises 331 feet in the air and dominates the famous shell-shaped Piazza del Campo, one of the noblest public squares in Italy. At its base is a delicate little Renaissance chapel, built in commemoration of the pestilence of 1348. Adjoining it rises the Palazzo Pubblico, an enormous Gothic brick civic building, completed in 1310. Its façade is concave and its grandiose interior apartments contain heroic frescoes by Sienese artists. The most famous of these are the "Allegories of Good Government" by Ambrogio Lorenzetti, and they give a fascinating insight into everyday life in this well-run community during the Middle Ages.

Italy's roughest, most famous, and most colorful horse race takes place in the Piazza del Campo twice every summer. Called the Palio delle Contrade, it occurs on July 2nd and August 16th, before wildly enthusiastic crowds, packed sardine-tight into Il Campo. The many-storied houses bordering on the piazza are hung with crimson and gold banners. The display of medieval pageantry defies all description. In brief you will not encounter a more overcrowded, spectacular pageant in all of Italy. Jockeys wear period costumes and whip their competitors' horses as well as their own. A fine point—a horse can win if he comes in first, even without a jockey. During these two days, Il Campo becomes the most turbulent spot on the entire Italian peninsula. Usually, however, the huge, sloping piazza is quiet, except for a few vociferous chestnut vendors. The shadow of the immense brick tower swings slowly around the perimeter of the piazza, precisely like a sundial. The time of day can be closely gauged by noting the building on which the lengthy shadow falls.

Built on the site of an ancient Temple of Minerva, Siena's wonderful cathedral was finished in 1380, a masterpiece of ornate Gothic architecture. Its richly sculptured façade, bedecked with mosaics and colored marble, is the work of Giovanni Pisano, and immediately recalls the west front of the *duomo* in Orvieto. Its imposing bell tower, conceived in alternate layers of white and black marble, is more restful than the ornate façade. The astonishing interior, also achieved with contrasting layers of marble, dark green and white, can never be forgotten, nor can its pavement, unique in Christendom, inlaid with countless scenes from the Bible. Here, too, is another miraculous pulpit carved by Nicolò Pisano, aided this time by his son and by Arnolfo di Cambio.

Almost all visitors to the cathedral see its Piccolomini Library, a chef-d'oeuvre of the Renaissance that contains any number of priceless volumes of illuminated parchment. A series of frescoes by Pinturicchio on its walls illustrates the life of Pope Pius II, long a resident of Siena. Adjoining the cathedral, somewhat in the manner of a crypt, is the Baptistry of San Giovanni, containing a superb marble font, the work of Jacopo della Quercia.

There are any number of other things to see in Siena, enough to stretch your stay over several days. Among them are the Accademia di Belle Arti, filled with paintings by Sienese masters, and the Chigi Palace, now the Chigiana Music Academy. Siena is the city of Catherine Benincasa, the mystic patron saint of Italy. You can visit the house where Saint Catherine was born and where she spent a large part of her life. The church most closely associated with her is San Domenico, the towering brick structure that faces the cathedral across a ravine. It deserves a visit.

Going from the sublime to the material, it must be mentioned that Siena is famous in the world of gastronomy for its sweets. There are four celebrated Sienese specialties, all of them known far beyond the borders of Tuscany. *Cavallucci* are rounded little cakes about two inches across. Quite firm and crisp on the outside, they absolutely melt in your mouth. Not too sweet, they are liberally nuggeted with walnuts and raisins, and carry a faint aroma of many flavors, caraway and anis among them. You will find them appetizing with breakfast coffee or with tea. Sweeter, softer, diamond-shaped, and delicious are *ricciarelli*. These are cousins to macaroons, perhaps, but lighter in color and dusted with powdered sugar. They rest on thin rice wafers, and are packed and shipped all over Italy. *Copate* are something else again. This confection is a paste of honey and finely ground nuts. It is pressed into disks about three inches in diameter and an eighth of an inch thick, and then sandwiched between two almost tasteless, paper-thin rice wafers. The most famous of Tuscan sweets, and rightly so, is *panforte,* a rich and fragrant disk about half an inch thick, composed mostly of whole almonds held together by a spicy binding of flour, citron, lemon peel, and sugar, with the haunting perfume of oranges, cinnamon, and anonymous spices. It is sprinkled on both sides with powdered sugar and bound in successive layers of gaily printed paper. *Panforte* comes in many diameters and ships well—and it is shipped repeatedly, particularly at Christmastime—all over the gastronomic world. It provides a wonderful finishing touch to a roadside picnic. They say that this delicacy dates back to the tenth century, so it may take quite a time to master the technique of making it. The recipe, however, doesn't seem

Piazza del Campo—Siena

West porch of the cathedral—Siena

Profile of Siena

difficult. You will find it, together with the secret of *ricciarelli* and *cavallucci*, among the Tuscan recipes at the end of this volume.

Well-fed porkers grow plump in these Tuscan hills and contribute to other Sienese specialties—*mortadella, salami, arista* (chine of pork), and a rich dish called *buristo suino,* which consists of lean pork enhanced by small chunks of fat, raisins, walnuts, and pine nuts. And as for wine, Siena claims Chianti as its own, particularly the Brolio that is shipped all over the world by the house of Ricasoli.

The hotel situation in Siena is only fair, and could be improved. The best accommodations are found at the EXCELSIOR, which enjoys plenty of open space and affords good room for parking. The long-established CONTINENTAL in the heart of the city is more crowded, but still popular. Many Anglo-Saxon visitors have adopted the PALAZZO RAVIZZA on the southern edge of the city. It is comparatively quiet and attractively furnished. Those who wish to linger in Siena can find numerous good pensions. Among the restaurants, these two in particular should please the passing guest.

Ristorante
Al Mangia
Siena

AL MANGIA—Piazza del Campo

Squarely in the middle of Il Campo, facing the Palazzo Pubblico, is a restaurant with an absolutely unbeatable location. Its name is Al Mangia, and its tables are stretched out under awnings and umbrellas in a most inviting fashion. Inevitably it is "touristy," but the food is above the Sienese average. We asked for the specialties of the house and received a plate of *tortelli alla Mangia,* oversized ravioli stuffed with nutmeg-scented spinach, then a veal cutlet with a faintly sharp sauce, subtly seasoned with herbs, and a chocolate cake Sienese style, heavily soaked with kirsch and magnificently fattening. We had *caffè espresso* and called it a lunch, which it certainly was. We have fainter praise for the service, but maybe it has changed.

TRATTORIA TULLIO-TRE CRISTI—Vicolo Provenzano 1

This is probably the most satisfying dining place in Siena, outside of the large hotels. Situated on a little side street on the eastern slope of the city, it is not too hard to find if you follow the discreet signs that point the way. Since it has no view to boast of, it might be a better choice for your evening meal. The first thing you see is the kitchen, smack on the street corner and open to all gazers behind its plate-glass windows. Sure enough, it's spotless. The proprietor looks much like the vice-president of an American steel company, except that the stripes of his double-breasted suit are a bit blatant and pointed up with saffron yellow. The clientele is dignified and well-dressed, most of them jovial *bons vivants.* We began with a tempting *cannelloni* and had nothing but praise for it and for the parade of good things that followed.

Trattoria Tullio-Tre Cristi Siena

Tullio has had all sorts of celebrities in his place, and has extracted photographs from most of them. Many are cinema stars who have, for good reasons, adopted Italy temporarily—Tyrone Power, Lauren Bacall, Deborah Kerr, Myrna Loy, Danielle Darrieux, Randolph Scott. But a whole generation of Miss Italys have been here too, leaving their Bikini pictures behind them. They couldn't come here often and keep those lithe figures. Automobile racers, boxers, and ballet dancers fill out the list. You might as well join the throng. Come on in, the nourishment's fine!

Certaldo

WE URGE motorists with a little spare time on their hands to pay a brief visit to this strange and intriguing hilltop citadel. Though the modern town at the base of the hill has slight interest, by climbing the winding road leading to the gates of medieval Certaldo, you may turn back the pages of time several centuries. Everything is built of rosy brick in this upper town—the streets, the church, the fortifications, and the rather plain houses. Certaldo owes its fame to the fact that it was the home of the great Giovanni Boccaccio, author of the *Decameron.* He lived here most of his life and died here in

San Gimignano

1375. His house, carefully restored inside, is marked with a tablet. At the top of the steep brick street, naturally named the Via Boccaccio, is the Palazzo Pretorio, a delightful brick building absolutely plastered with ancient escutcheons and family crests. Certaldo can be pleasantly combined with a trip to San Gimignano, situated about seven miles southward.

San Gimignano

THERE ARE many rewarding one-day trips to be made out of Siena, the favorite for generations being a ride through olive-clad hills to San Gimignano, the most dramatic of all Italian hill towns. Of its seventy-two gaunt, medieval towers, thirteen are still standing, providing a silhouette which, on a small scale, rivals Manhattan. The streets and squares of this ancient town retain the atmosphere of the Middle Ages better than any in Italy. It is still enclosed within venerable walls and guarded by three fortified gates. A walk through these narrow alleys at dusk is enough to turn back the calendar five hundred years, quite an experience in anyone's life. The perfection of San Gimignano is due partly to the fact that the whole town is classified as an historical monument, carefully restored and supervised by the state.

The immense towers that frown down on the city are its greatest curiosities. Some of them belonged to the Salvucci family, who were Ghibellines, and others to their hated Guelf rivals, the Ardinghelli family. One of them rises forbiddingly above the Palazzo del Popolo, which had the misfortune to be hit by a stray shell during the recent war. This austere thirteenth-century building contains a good local museum with paintings by Pinturicchio and Filippino Lippi, among others. Here Dante, as an ambassador from Florence, delivered an address to the populace. On the same square is the unadorned

Market day—San Gimignano

Archway—San Gimignano

The towers of San Gimignano

A farm group in the Tuscan hills Drypoint

Romanesque cathedral whose conspicuous treasure is inside, the chapel of Santa Fina, an exquisite jewel of Renaissance art by Benedetto da Maiano. He designed the marble altar, while Ghirlandaio painted the moving frescoes showing episodes in the life of Saint Fina. Savonarola also preached in this cathedral square.

If you enjoy medieval painting, it is well worth your while to wander through the tortuous streets to the northern outskirts of the citadel. Here you will find the rather dull-looking Church of Sant'Agostino. But its interior holds a magnificent surprise in the form of frescoes painted by Benozzo Gozzoli in the years 1461-1464, depicting episodes from the life of Saint Augustine, and strikingly beautiful.

Hotel La Cisterna
San Gimignano

The hills around this walled town are liberally planted with vines, which produce a very dry wine called Vernaccia di San Gimignano. You may taste it in our favorite dining place. Most Tuscan towns of this size don't have much in the way of accommodations, but this one is an exception. Here in the Piazza della Cisterna, by the old stone well, you will find the HOTEL LA CISTERNA, a clean and comfortable hostelry ingeniously built into old town buildings. The rooms are pleasant, and they command a breath-taking view of the town ramparts and the countryside below. We thought the cooking was

unusual, particularly the specialty of the house, *pollo alla massaia,* a plump young Tuscan chicken sautéed in oil and butter, then bathed in a rich, fragrant sauce. We asked the proprietor for the recipe and found that the ingredients were onions, celery, tomatoes, parsley, carrots, and white wine. But there must have been a subtle turn of hand on the chef's part as well. The Hotel La Cisterna is a bit chilly in winter, but during the other months it promises a pleasant overnight stop.

Pienza

ANOTHER MEMORABLE excursion from Siena takes in the neighboring towns of Pienza and Montepulciano. It makes a charming day's trip, but we advise you to take along a substantial picnic lunch, to be consumed under an olive tree. The epicurean resources of the two towns are limited, although good local wine is plentiful.

Pienza is a rather remote little place, about thirty miles southeast of Siena, but it delights everyone who takes the trouble to seek it out. In the heart of this small community is an extraordinary concentration of beautiful Renaissance buildings. Pienza owes its Florentine splendor to the fact that it was the birthplace of Aeneas Silvius Piccolomini, who later became Pope

The Renaissance well–Pienza   *Cypresses on a Tuscan road*

Pius II. Popes apparently were not bereft of spending money in those days, for this loyal native son decided to rebuild his whole village of Corsignano, and to rename it Pienza, after himself. He engaged the architect Bernardo Rossellino to do the work, and the whole ensemble of handsome structures is attributed to him. They are clustered around the Piazza Pio II, three noble palaces and a cathedral. You may visit the Palazzo Piccolomini, named for the Pope. It rejoices in a fine cloistered courtyard and a roof garden with an inspiring view over the valley. The fairest bit of architectural detail in Pienza is an exquisite Renaissance well that stands before this palace.

Montepulciano

EVERYONE WHO visits this hilltop wine town with the lilting name seems to remember it. About eight miles west of Pienza, it occupies a magnificent site, surrounded by thickly planted vineyards. It is a joy to drive up its wide main thoroughfare, lined with noble houses. Some of them are rich with Renaissance detail and at least one of them, the Palazzo Nobili-Tarugi, is attributed to Vignola, that master of classicism whose name is a byword to every architectural student. At the top of the long hill road is the Piazza Grande, not as impressive as the one in Pienza, but far from banal. Above it rises the severe Palazzo Communale, reminiscent, with its bleak towers, of the Palazzo Vecchio in Florence. Inside is a small museum with some fine della Robbias. On the outskirts of the town is the Church of San Biagio, a delightful study in pure Renaissance form, standing alone among the vineyards and olive trees.

To many Italians the name Montepulciano implies wine above everything else. These lofty slopes produce a flavorful red wine, dry and sturdy and reminiscent of the better Chiantis. During the harvest the little town bustles with activity. There couldn't be a better time to visit the town with the rippling name—Montepulciano.

Ascoli Piceno

The Marches

Chapter 10

THE
MARCHES

W E SHALL not thrash around with superlatives in describing the region that the Italians call Le Marche. It is not a spectacular part of Italy, although its rolling Apennine hills are a joy to behold. Most of its cities are of only moderate interest, and its coastal resorts offer no threat to those of Liguria or Tuscany. As a consequence, it is neglected by most visitors and snubbed by guided tours. Despite this fact, and perhaps partly because of it, the Marches will bring surprising recompenses to enterprising travelers, particularly those free to motor where they choose. Three beguiling cities—Urbino, Loreto, and Ascoli Piceno—and the mountaintop Republic of San Marino alone justify a detour.

This is mountain country, one verdant Apennine after another, rugged, invigorating, and none too fertile. The friendly, hard-working *paesani* labor overtime to wrest a living from the land. Slow-moving white oxen pull their plows. Herds of sheep and goats populate their hillsides. The women walk erectly along the road carrying copper and earthen water jugs on their heads. They are adept at balancing any burden in this manner—baskets of laundry, bundles of hay. We even observed one economical housewife walking barefoot and carrying her slippers on her head, thus saving her footgear and leaving her hands free for conversation. Good roads weave in hairpin turns through this hilly country. They are usually well paved and graded.

Beaches along the region's Adriatic shore are inclined to be narrow, but bathing resorts—Fano, Senigallia, Pesaro, and San Benedetto del Tronto—prosper, if on a smaller scale than in the Rimini area. The most beautiful handmade papers in Italy come from the Marches. The town of Fabriano is famous for them. Finally there is something to interest the epicure. Delectable white truffles may be unearthed in these hills, and the Adriatic yields superlative treasures in the form of lobsters, fish, and varied members of the octopus clan.

The Marches have their full quota of gastronomic specialties, if not of tourists, and very appetizing they are. A superlative fish stew results from the piscatorial plenty from the sea. It is called *brodetto marchigiano,* an Adriatic cousin that holds its head proudly in the company of the bouillabaisse of Marseilles and the *zuppa di pesce* of Genoa. The *brodetto* has two distinct versions, but both are based upon the same fish—sole, red mullet, cuttlefish, baby octopus *(polipetto), palumbo,* a lean critter who looks like a baby shark, and squids, which, unlike fountain pens, are of no practical use until their ink reservoirs are removed. Garlic, parsley, onion, and oil complete the cast of characters. In one version the fish are sprinkled lightly with flour, and the sauce, saffron seasoned, is allowed to thicken. In the other recipe, the sauce is thin, vinegar replaces the saffron, and garlic is more in evidence. Either type turns out to be interesting, if you go in for this sort of thing, and you really should, just once. For your convenience, the recipe, with directions for both versions, will be found in the supplement in the back of the book.

Porchetta is a renowned delicacy here. It is a suckling pig, cleaned and rubbed inside and out with chopped fennel, garlic, rosemary, nutmeg, salt and pepper, and then spit-roasted on the hearth, a most delectable dish for all. A particularly rich pasta dish flourishes in Macerata, and may be found in Ancona. Called *vincisgrassi,* it consists of wide ribbons of *lasagne* alternating with layers of a thick rich sauce made of giblets, sweetbreads, veal, ham, mushrooms, truffles, breast of fowl, tomato sauce, chicken broth, and cream. This epicurean monument is baked in the oven and served hot—a meal in itself. Finally, the region boasts a hot aromatic sauce, its origins going back for centuries. Called *potacchio anconitano,* it adapts especially well to stockfish preparations, based on dried salted fish.

One particularly good white wine is produced in this region, whose vineyards date back to ancient Rome. It is called Verdicchio di Jesi, and comes in long bulging green bottles. It has a tempting, clean taste, a good aroma, and appears in many of the dining places in the Marches and Umbria. Vernaccia is another palatable white, and the hillsides to the south produce a well-rounded red wine called Piceno Rosso.

Our guided tour of an overlooked region of Italy begins at the northern extremity and works down. The unique little Republic of San Marino comes first, followed by four pleasant seaside resorts and four towns of exceptional

Colli, a village in the Marchian hills

interest—Urbino, Ancona, Loreto, and Ascoli Piceno. Visit these and you have seen the best of the Marches.

San Marino

MOTORISTS DRIVING out of Rimini will see the dim, craggy silhouette of Mount Titano, towering up a few miles inland. This eminence marks the site of the most diminutive and the oldest republic in the world, and if you are tempted to make a detour on Route No. 72 to visit it, don't hesitate! A refreshing experience lies ahead.

This remarkable community was founded about 300 A.D., by Saint Marinus, a pious stonemason from Dalmatia. It has retained its sovereignty as a state for over fourteen centuries, and history is replete with attempts to conquer it. These were resisted, largely because of its impregnable site on forbidding vertical rocks, a natural fortress rising over 2,700 feet above sea level. During a time when all other states in Italy changed rulers and governments over and over again, this little republic held fast, and still maintains

270

The fortified castle—San Marino

its independence. Its crenellated fortifications are intact today, and from them, on a clear day, you can catch a glimpse of the Dalmatian coast.

The republic has an area of about forty square miles, and consists of well-cultivated foothills leading to the immense fortified crag. Its population is about thirteen thousand, a tenth of whom live on the heights. During World War II, thousands of refugees crowded its borders.

San Marino suffered cruelly from an Allied air raid in 1944, and attempted to escape from the resultant economic straits by establishing a high-stake gambling casino, such as the one at Monte Carlo. The venture proved a sad flop, and the little country is now largely dependent for its revenues upon the sale of postage stamps to the philatelist world, and upon the patronage of tourists.

The republic, you may recall, was prominent in the newspaper headlines when a struggle for power between the Communist government and the non-Communist dissenters finally resulted in a victory for the latter. A democratic regime is now installed, and all is quiet and peaceful once again.

Now that the scars of war have disappeared, travelers will find the lofty hill town clean and tidy, with good hotels and restaurants. The climate is pleasant in summer, for there is always a cooling breeze. Visitors who come for the day wander happily through medieval streets and visit the Basilico del Santo, where relics of the founder-saint are enshrined. Many one-day visitors like San Marino so well that they lengthen their stay. They find comfortable accommodations in the long-established TITANO, EXCELSIOR, and BELLEVUE hotels, and a few quite luxurious ones in the newly opened HOTEL-RISTORANTE DIAMOND. The latter, located near the basilica, has two gay modernistic dining rooms carved out of the solid rock. The restaurant with the most startling view is well named—NIDO DEL FALCO, the Falcon's Nest.

Sad to relate, we don't know of any gastronomic specialty of San Marino, unless perhaps it's mountain goat. But Signor Gozi, the amiable director of the Titano, gave us three of his favorite recipes. We'd like to share this one:

Coppa Titano
TITANO FRUIT CUP

These are Signor Gozi's own words: "Prepare some fresh fruit— wild strawberries or peaches, according to the season. Marinate them for half an hour with powdered sugar and abundant . . . ? This remains one of our secrets. Pour the fruit into sherbet glasses and fill them to the brim with pure homemade ice cream. Decorate the top with fruit or with chocolate cookies. Serve it, and assuredly the American client will ask for a second, especially if the Signor Joe realizes that there is no extra charge."

Personally, we believe the "secret" to be maraschino, or perhaps a local liqueur.

The shipyards—Pesaro

The Adriatic shore between Rimini and Ancona is punctuated with inexpensive resort towns that offer the summer traveler a good deal more than a sandy beach. Some of them are fishing towns. Others have rich historical backgrounds and interesting old buildings. Their summer clientele is overwhelmingly Italian. Two of the most interesting towns are Pesaro and Fano.

Pesaro

PESARO IS a rather large coastal place with an intriguing port and picturesque shipyards. Visitors will also find a Renaissance ducal palace, a cathedral, an art gallery, and a good civic museum to vary the monotony of the usual beach town. Pesaro is very proud of its most famous son, Gioacchino Antonio Rossini, composer of *The Barber of Seville, William Tell,* and other operatic classics. He was born here in 1792, and left funds that were used to found a musical academy. The best hotel in Pesaro is also named after him, so remember the ALBERGO ROSSINI.

273

Fano

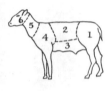

THIS TOWN, a few miles to the south of Pesaro, has a most unusual remnant from the days of Rome, the solid Arch of Augustus, built in the year 2 A. D. Only the lower part of this massive town gate remains. The upper part, above the entablature, once contained a gallery of seven arches. We know about the gallery because somebody was thoughtful enough to carve a miniature bas-relief of its silhouette on a neighboring building. In the center of Fano is an imposing piazza, which took a fearful beating during the war. Here you will find a handsome sixteenth-century fountain and several rebuilt *palazzi*, among them the Palazzo Malatestino, whose museum contains some commendable works of art. The best paintings in Fano, however, are certainly the Perugino canvases in the nearby Church of Santa Maria Nuova. Down by the beach, at the northern end of the town, stands a cluster of little summer hotels, the most satisfactory of which is the ALBERGO EXCELSIOR.

For holiday seekers who are content with a good beach resort without historic frills, both Senigallia and San Benedetto del Tronto deserve a word of favorable mention. The former is near Ancona, and popular with discriminating Italians. San Benedetto is at the southern extremity of the Marches, and had to be rebuilt after the last war. So it is new and bright, comfortable and gay. There is an excellent JOLLY HOTEL here, too, facing the sea.

The Arch of Augustus—Fano

Urbino

IF THERE is a "must" in the Marches, it is the austere and magnificent Urbino, sitting majestically on two Marchian hills, between the Apennines and the Adriatic. Beyond a doubt, this community is the artistic stronghold of the entire region, and the intellectual heart as well. Urbino is the birthplace of Raphael (1483–1520), and you may visit the modest house, at Via Raffaello 57, where this distinguished son was born to the Santi family. You can see there a fresco painted by his father, Giovanni Santi.

There is an atmosphere of youth and animation in the city, contributed largely by students of its venerable university, founded in 1506. Urbino is buoyant and unspoiled, enlivened with open-air markets, and it delights most travelers, particularly those interested in the arts of the Renaissance.

The city is dominated by the imposing hulk of its ducal palace, one of the largest in Italy, built between 1460 and 1480 of handsome Dalmatian limestone. The architect was Dalmatian too, Luciano Laurana. But the most interesting personage involved was the brilliant nobleman who ordered its construction. He was Federigo da Montefeltro, a generous man with an unforgettable, hook-nosed profile and an unquenchable passion for the arts. He was a bibliophile, a perfect gentleman, and a ferocious warrior as well. During his reign as the duke of Montefeltro, Frederick befriended poets, painters, sculptors, and writers, all of whom left their mark on his immense *palazzo*. This building heralds the beginning of Renaissance architecture, and holds great interest for architects, especially the detail of its interior doorways, fireplaces, windows, and cloisters. It is a rare experience to visit the palace and to visualize the splendor of Frederick's court, a model of its time. Most of the building is now utilized by the Galleria Nazionale delle Marche, one of the finest collections of Italian art to be found anywhere. Works by Raphael, Titian, Piero della Francesca, and Paolo Uccello lend it distinction. It takes a good half day to see the ducal palace properly, and a full day can be spent with profit, if your feet hold out.

Adjoining the palace is the cathedral, its striking feature an unusually fine classic façade. Across the piazza stands the medieval Church of San Domenico, whose central doorway is enriched by an exquisite lunette, the work of Luca della Robbia. The best of Urbino is concentrated in this area.

Though Urbino is somewhat isolated, the ALBERGO ITALIA makes it a good overnight stop. Located on a crowded, arcaded street, the Corso Garibaldi, the hotel doesn't promise much from the outside. But it merits closer attention, for here is one of the diminishing number of hotels where the landlord considers himself a host in the old tradition. He truly concerns him-

Albergo
Italia
Urbino

Cattle market and the ducal palace—Urbino

Urbino, on its hilltop

The cathedral–Urbino

Old mill in the valley below Urbino

self about the welfare of his guests. We've rarely seen such cheerful service —maids, waiters, bus boy, garageman, all doing their best to make us happy. Our dinner was genuinely good, served with a clean, appetizing wine from the surrounding hills. This is a simple hotel, mind you, and there are no frills, but many guests have reacted to its charm and hospitality just as we did. The guestbook, which runs into several volumes, is filled with the names of statesmen, ambassadors, and mere ambulant citizens who have gone out of their way to visit Urbino and have been won by the Italia's friendliness.

Ancona

THE PRINCIPAL city of the Marches and the main seaport on the middle Adriatic coast, Ancona was an ancient Greek settlement. It cannot be called a tourist city at all, but it has a few things worth seeing, and one excellent restaurant, worthy of an epicure's respect. There is a little Italian verse that sums it up:

> *Se Ancona non è bella*
> *ed ha sudicio il mar,*
> *ha buoni i calamar*
> *fritti in padella.*

Arco di Traiano—Ancona   *Cathedral of San Ciriaco—Ancona*

The cathedral porch—Ancona

In other words, if Ancona is not beautiful and has dirty sea water, it does have good squids fried in a skillet!

The harassed seaport suffered from Austrian shells in the First World War and from a hail of Allied bombs in the second, and is only now returning to normal. The yacht of the former king of Italy was moored here during the late unpleasantness. The Ancona fish market is an inspiring spectacle for gourmets with a weakness for Adriatic fish. For other visitors we suggest a trip to the harbor and then a pilgrimage to the opposite end of the city, where the best restaurant in the Marches awaits him.

In the midst of waterfront hubbub, surrounded by cranes and locomotives, you will find a Roman triumphal arch in a wonderful state of preservation. The Arco di Traiano was erected in the year 115 A. D. to honor Trajan, who established the port. In a lofty panel on the arch is a lengthy Latin inscription, now somewhat mutilated: the letters were originally pointed up with gold, too valuable a metal to escape being gouged out in succeeding centuries.

On a high promontory overlooking the hook-shaped harbor is the Cathedral of San Ciriaco, a noble Romanesque building with Byzantine overtones, whose interior is built in the shape of a Greek cross. Much of the stone used for its facing appears to have been salvaged from Roman buildings. There are two Gothic touches, also, noble pointed porticos that glisten in the intense Adriatic sunshine and make superb subjects for the camera.

There are two acceptable big-city hotels in the heart of Ancona, called the ALBERGO MODERNO and ALBERGO ROMA E PACE. By far the most exciting thing about the city, from an epicure's biased point of view, is the fine open-air restaurant that faces a park on the far extremity of the city. Don't try to walk to the RISTORANTE PASSETTO AL MARE, as we did, unless you are an avid pedestrian with hours to waste. Drive, or take a cab, to the Piazza IV Novembre and you will find a large, welcoming establishment, its circular terraces looking over the park to the sea. A cosmopolitan, well-run restaurant, it specializes in the local dishes for which Ancona is famous, above all the divine *brodetto all'anconetana*. Other notable dishes are spaghetti with mussels, *cannelloni passetto,* and the rich, fattening *vincisgrassi,* a *lasagne* preparation with symphonic sauces. If you would taste the famous roast baby pig, *porchetta,* it frequently appears on the *lista del giorno*. There is a special Ancona bean soup and a particular way of preparing tripe, both of which can be sampled at Passetto. The wine list contains a fine Verdicchio from the nearby hills in addition to good Chiantis. Even though the service is slow, it would be unthinkable for a gourmet to come to Ancona and miss Passetto!

Ristorante Passetto al Mare
Ancona

Loreto

A VENERABLE walled town about twenty miles south of Ancona, Loreto is a religious center of great importance. Pilgrims from all over the world come to see its celebrated relic, the Santa Casa. According to popular tradition, the house where the Holy Virgin was born was carried away from Nazareth in 1291, when the Arabs invaded the Holy Land. The record relates that the angels transported the house intact to Tersatto, a village near Fiume. Three years later, in the same miraculous manner, the Holy House was transferred across the Adriatic to a laurel wood high in the Marchian hills. Loreto derives its name from these woods.

A sanctuary was built round the crude little stone house in the fifteenth century. It is an imposing domed structure, the work of many architects, Bramante and Sansovino among them. Under the immense dome stands the little house of Mary, encased in a marble crust of rich Baroque architecture and visited annually by countless thousands of the faithful. At one end of the single room is an arched altar, framing the figures of the Virgin and Child carved in blackened cedar. It is said to be the first work of Saint Luke.

Italy is full of Renaissance church façades, and some of them are pretty ghastly. A shining exception is the lovely marble front of this sanctuary. The façade was built between 1570 and 1587, during the reign of Sixtus V, whose colossal statue stands before it. This is a model of classic form, and not easily forgotten.

Loreto is a town for the faithful pilgrim rather than for the inquiring epicure. The former will find several acceptable small hotels.

Ascoli Piceno

ENTIRELY OFF the beaten track of the tourist, this charming hill town at the lower extremity of the Marches will prove an exciting adventure to motorists who seek it out. A valley road climbs easily some twenty miles from the shore to the walled town, which is almost encircled by two converging rivers and surrounded by wooded hills. Ascoli Piceno is an ancient city, and has a graceful Roman bridge, the Ponte di Solestà, to prove its antiquity. Two Roman bridges once spanned the river Tronto, but the second one was a victim of World War II.

This city of close to 50,000 souls teems with activity, especially on market day, and is adorned with several fine churches. The most interesting is the Church of San Francesco, an early Gothic masterpiece with an arcaded court-

Santuario della Santa Casa–Loreto

Loggia dei Mercanti–Ascoli Piceno

The sixth-century baptistry–Ascoli Piceno

Church façade–Ascoli Piceno

yard that now serves as an immensely picturesque food market. It is called the Loggia dei Mercanti, and a perceptive water-colorist could spend a month there without exhausting the animated subjects that abound on every side.

One has the refreshing sensation of being a pioneer while wandering through the streets of Ascoli Piceno. The place has a completely undiscovered air, and is quite unmindful of visitors. The cathedral is an immense unfinished affair, not so interesting as its nearby baptistry, a severe little octagonal building with a square base. It is very ancient, said to date from the sixth century, and it stands squarely and courageously in the path of twentieth-century motor traffic, which has to detour around it.

For those who seek pure, unadulterated Italy, we suggest this admirable town as an overnight stop. Just round the corner from the cathedral is our old friend, a reliable JOLLY HOTEL, with clean, modern accommodations and dependable cooking.

Spoleto

Umbria

Chapter 11

UMBRIA

THIS APENNINE region is better known to voyagers than its neighbor, the Marches, since it serves as a verdant passageway for those who travel by motor between Rome and Venice, an itinerary that has been a classic with travel agencies for decades. It does indeed provide their clients with at least a glimpse of Assisi and Perugia, with an overnight stop in the latter hilltop city. But those who travel in the custody of a guided tour see little enough of Umbria and have hardly more than a flickering acquaintance with the seductive wine of Orvieto and the black truffles of Norcia. And that's too bad.

The more leisurely visitor, especially if he has a motorcar to putter about in, soon learns how much his hurried compatriot has missed. He finds that a wealth of hill towns beckon him closer. By the time he has seen such miniature Carcassonnes as Spello, Spoleto, Cascia, and Gubbio, he realizes that this Umbrian region is one of the neglected treasures of Italy. Though he may have found a dearth of fashionable spots for the skier, the casino hound, and the sun worshiper, he has encountered good food and wine, and comfortable places to stop overnight—almost everything, in fact, except his fellow tourist. This travelogue, therefore, is definitely for those who are happiest off the beaten path.

Umbria is one of Italy's smaller regions, and the only one on the peninsula that does not touch the sea. As a recompense, it contains the cerulean Lake Trasimeno, largest of the peninsular lakes, with its bounty of carp, eel, and pike. This region lies in hilly Apennine country, ribbed with fertile river valleys that occasionally flatten out into plains.

Umbrian civilization is ancient indeed. The Etruscans thrived here long before the Romans and have left impressive reminders of their culture, particularly in Perugia. The Umbrian school of painting is one of the greatest in the world, since it claims, among others, such illustrious masters as Piero della Francesca, Luca Signorelli, Perugino, Pinturicchio, and Raphael. Their paintings have been scattered to museums and galleries throughout the world, but enough remain in Umbria to provide a rich and rewarding field of exploration for students and connoisseurs of Italian art.

Finally, Umbria is the birthplace of the immortal Saint Francis, and the cradle of the order that he founded in the early years of the thirteenth century. Pilgrims have been coming to his native town of Assisi ever since.

There are rewards aplenty for the food-conscious pilgrim too, although he must do a bit of scouting to avoid the dullness of hotel fare. Umbrian cooking has no strong regional tradition, but a few local dishes, revolving around truffles, suckling pig, and wild pigeons, are

quite exciting. A rustling tapestry of olive trees covers these Apennine slopes, which means that Umbrian cooking basks in olive oil, of a quality only surpassed in Tuscany. In short, there is nothing sparse or Franciscan about the cooking in Umbria, in spite of the chaste example set by its greatest citizen.

A fine breed of cattle thrives in the hills around Perugia, assuring the tender steaks and savory ragouts to be found on local menus. It is more difficult to come upon an Umbrian specialty called *palombacci,* but if you are here in March or October, take the trouble to seek it out. During these months the wild pigeons fly over the local hills, and a good many of them are waylaid, to end up on the roasting spit as *palombacci.* They are served with an aromatic sauce called *la ghiotta,* based on a learned and savory combination of olives, lemon peel, sage, anchovy, vinegar, wine, oil, salt and pepper, quite enough to disguise the indiscriminate eating habits of *any* vagrant pigeon.

A favorite family dish in Umbria, as in the Marches, is *la porchetta,* a young, unfattened suckling pig, spiced with garlic, rosemary, and other aromatic herbs and roasted in the oven. His edible spare parts are cooked in a separate dish in the same oven. Whether he arrives at table with an appetizing black truffle in his mouth we don't know, but is sounds logical, for Umbria is the Italian home of the black truffle.

An Umbrian gateway

In the late autumn, the Umbrian farmer, accompanied by his truffle hound or his sow, is a familiar sight in the southern extremity of this region. Norcia, Scheggino, Spoleto, and Cascia, picturesque hill towns all, are centers for the fragrant ebony tuber that now plays such an important part in the orchestra of any fine chef. The Italian soil harbors many other varieties of truffle, of course—delicious white and lavender ones, best known in Piedmont, and some that aren't delicacies at all. There is a strong, handsome but malodorous one called *tubero bituminato,* for example, a too-coalish nugget that even pigs won't touch. The big city markets wisely follow the pig's example. But luckily the choicest black varieties, *tubero melanosporo* and *tubero brumale,* flourish in these hills, as they do under the oak trees in Périgord. In years when the truffle crop is sparse in France, it seems sensible to import from Italy. After all, *écrevisses* are flown into France from Poland to garnish many a Burgundian dish. Just how many Umbrian tubers have been shipped to Périgord to become naturalized French truffles, and to appear imbedded in the divine *foie gras* of Périgord geese, is a matter of total conjecture. It *has* happened, however, and Italian black truffles have found a warm reception in New York and London restaurants as well. They found an even warmer reception two millennia ago, when the Romans, ascribing aphrodisiac powers to them *(Philtrum quo vincere mulierem),* dedicated the tempting tuber to Venus herself. An ancient saying tells us that "those who wish to lead virtuous lives should abstain from truffles," but proof of such propensities is dismally absent.

With such a wealth of black nuggets at hand, the gourmets of Umbria have indulged themselves in a spaghetti sauce containing a substantial quantity of pounded truffles. This dish has long been a fast favorite, especially in the Christmas season.

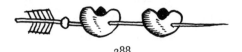

The Umbrian hills

Spaghetti alla Spoletina
SPAGHETTI WITH TRUFFLE SAUCE

In a mortar pound 4 or 5 ounces of peeled and chopped black truffles with a little parsley, 2 anchovy filets, and a clove of garlic. In a shallow saucepan heat 3/8 cup of olive oil and stir in 1/4 cup of tomato paste and enough hot water to make a sauce the consistency of thin cream. Add salt to taste and the paste of truffles, then heat the sauce but do not boil it. Use this sauce on 1 pound of spaghetti, cooked. Serves 4.

Umbrians also have a sweet tooth, to judge by the carloads of chocolate that emerge from the Perugina factory in Perugia, and by the tempting cakes that brighten its pastry shops. One of these, a lozenge-shaped concentration of goodness called *pinoccata,* is practically compulsory at Christmas and New Year festivities. It contains pine nuts, lemon peel, sometimes a touch of candied orange peel, and sugar. Some are left a golden brown, others are colored with chocolate. In either case the result is a happy one.

The shop windows also reveal abundant mounds of a sweet bun called *il torcolo,* a delicacy imbedded with raisins, candied fruits, pine nuts, and aniseed.

Though Umbria has few native wines, one of them is a bright star indeed. This is Orvieto, one of the best known of Italian wines, and one of the most accomplished travelers. Its squat, straw-covered *fiasco* goes to far corners of the epicurean world. In color it is a pale straw yellow, its bouquet is seductive, and its power (twelve degrees) well concealed. There are a sweet and a dry Orvieto, for different tastes and dishes. The dry one, which has just a suspicion of flinty aftertaste, is reminiscent of a Chablis, and a worthy companion to the superlative sea food from the nearby Adriatic. The sweet Orvieto is more than adequate as a dessert wine. The fame of Orvieto's wine goes back for centuries. Pinturicchio, the famous Umbrian painter, loved it so much that he wanted a rider put into his contract for painting murals in the Orvieto cathedral that would allow him all the wine he wanted while working. Actually most of the grapes for this wine grow on slopes far from the ancient citadel. Visitors may be puzzled, as we were, at seeing so few vineyards when approaching the town. The surrounding countryside borrows the Orvieto name and preserves its standards, but the heart of the wine business remains in the citadel itself. The inquiring oenophile also has plenty of opportunities to indulge in a private wine tasting, since the house of Bigi and several others are most hospitable in this respect. Three other wines of Umbria are secondary but worth looking for: Vino Santo d'Umbria, Sacrantino, a friendly, powerful wine grown near Montefalco, and Greco di Todi.

The larger cities in Umbria are well equipped to take care of the traveler. The smaller hill towns call for the hardier type of hotel dweller. At a minimum there are five excellent stops in this region—Perugia, Assisi, Orvieto, Gubbio, and Spoleto. Let's take them up in that order.

Perugia

The capital of Umbria is a queen among hill towns, a gay, populous, intellectual citadel built high on an Apennine ridge. Originally an Etruscan stronghold, its time-stained Arch of Augustus antedates by centuries the Roman emperor for whom it was named. Studded with Gothic palaces, fountains, Renaissance doorways, and markedly individual churches (our frontispiece drypoint shows the tall, octagonal Church of Sant'Ercolano), Perugia is a joy to the traveler, and a long-established stopping place for him. In this civilized city the scooter, motorcycle, baby Fiat, even the bicycle must bow to the pedestrian during the promenade hour. Late every afternoon the main thoroughfare is roped off to all but strollers, and most of Perugia takes a walk: town dignitaries, college professors, giggling *signorine* arm in arm, young

Fontana Maggiore and the Palazzo dei Priori—Perugia

Doorway of the Cathedral of San Lorenzo—Perugia

married couples with their perambulators, and a profusion of gesticulating college students. You see many beautiful, oval faces, just as Perugino used to paint them, but there are also many non-Italian types among these chattering pedestrians. For Perugia is the site of the Italian University for Foreigners, and many a lad or lass from Caen, Copenhagen, Canterbury, or Kansas City has learned the lilt of the Italian language here. But they study more complex subjects too, among them Etruscology.

This broad promenade is called the Corso Vannucci, by the way, and is named for Pietro Vannucci, better known as Perugino, one of the greatest of Italian painters. Born in Citta della Pieve, in 1446, he adopted Perugia as his home and has left his imprint in many places here, especially in the Collegio del Cambio, considered to be his masterpiece.

Few provincial cities reward the wandering sightseer as bountifully as Perugia. He can spend from two days to a week in this hilltop town in the heart of Umbria without exhausting its treasures. First in artistry is probably the Palazzo dei Priori, at the top of the Corso Vannucci. This rather grim structure, begun in 1281, is one of the noblest Gothic palaces in Italy. It has an exquisite Renaissance doorway framing the three patron saints of the city. Through this portal you enter to find the National Gallery of Umbria, an incomparable temple of Umbrian art. All the masters of this school are here in force, together with many others, Giovanni Pisano and Fra Angelico among them. Perugino's great "Pietà" occupies the favored position due the founder of the Umbrian school.

In an adjoining building is the Collegio del Cambio—the hall and chapel of the bankers' guild—adorned with frescoes by Perugino and his pupils. Rarely have bankers, made a wiser investment. Perugino accepted the commission to paint the premises and accomplished his greatest work in the Sala di Udienza del Cambio. His pupils worked on the ceiling decoration. The master brought his pupil, the boy Raphael, with him when he undertook this assignment. Perugino's self-portrait hangs in the same building. Visitors may also visit the elaborate Sala del Collegio della Mercanzia, a Renaissance room of elaborate beauty, richly paneled with inlaid woodwork.

A magnificent circular fountain stands at the upper end of the Corso Vannucci, the Fontana Maggiore, a worthy rival of any fountain in Rome. Designed by Fra Bevignate, it was created in 1278. The Pisanos, father and son, worked on the white marble bas-reliefs, and the three bronze nymphs, veiled by a perpetual spray of water, are by Arnolfo di Cambio.

The Gothic Cathedral of San Lorenzo rises gauntly behind the fountain. Its façade is unfinished, only partially embellished with a pattern of red and white marble, but one can imagine the superb effect had it been completed. A fine outdoor pulpit adjoins one side of the doorway and on the other side stands a handsome, benign statue of Julius III. Put them all together and

Perugia, late afternoon

Doorway of the Palazzo dei Priori—Perugia

Oratorio di San Bernardino—Perugia

you have probably the most picturesque spot in Perugia. The interior of the cathedral is lofty and inspiring. Here you find the chapel of the Sacred Ring, whose priceless relic is an agate ring said to be the wedding band of the Virgin Mary.

By wandering down little side streets behind the cathedral, you will come to the Arch of Augustus, the most interesting of Perugia's many town gates. Its base is massive and Etruscan, dating as far back as the third century B. C. The more sophisticated stonework of the Romans is set on top of this, and the whole massive gate is crowned, rather incongruously, by a graceful loggia from the Renaissance. If you wish to see a more delicate manifestation of Etruscan art, pottery and sculpture from that period are on view at the neighboring University Museum.

There are a dozen other buildings of interest to be seen in Perugia if you have the time. One is the noble Palazzo del Capitano del Popolo, with a rare Renaissance façade and doorway. Another treasure from this period is the little Oratorio di San Bernardino, an exquisite chapel with a richly carved front. Another is the extraordinary oval Temple of San Angelo at the northern extremity of the city.

There are also modern manifestations to charm you in Perugia, including bookstores, fine wool sweaters, and chocolate. Tourists flock to buy the soft, stylish Angora sweaters made by the house of Spagnoli. By changing a single letter, one may shift from the sublime to the delicious, from Perugino to Perugina, for it is here that Perugina chocolates, known the world over, are made. Behind an impassive factory façade the most extraordinary miracles in chocolate are achieved. We visited Perugia a few weeks before Easter, and the chocolate works were going all out for hollow chocolate eggs. An Easter egg with a surprise inside is a part of Italian home life, and the bigger the egg the better. Perugina vies with its rivals, Talmone, Nestlé, Motta, and others, in producing the fanciest gilt wrappings and the giddiest cellophane ribbons. What treasures they contained we never did find out, but they must be considerable. The largest egg was priced at sixty thousand lire, a sum that cuts the heart out of a hundred-dollar bill. Not all of these chocolate eggs are intended for the kiddies, by the way. Our favorite model reveals a squat bottle of old brandy, when the oval chocolate portals are thrown open.

In some Italian cities the most obvious hotel is not always the most satisfactory, but in Perugia there is no question about the predominance of the BRUFANI PALACE HOTEL, a large and long-established hostelry on the southern brink of Perugia's breath-taking promontory. Built many years ago, supposedly on the site of a vanished temple of Minerva, it gives the impression of never having suffered an instant of neglect from that moment to this. Everything is immaculate, and the large, attractive lounges are about the most comfortable places in all these Umbrian hills. Though the bar has

Brufani
Palace
Hotel
Perugia

a somewhat funereal air, the large cheerful dining salon buzzes with activity. This hotel is the crossroads for travelers of every nationality. There are menus in Italian, English, and French, and the food is the best in Perugia, a considered statement based on a ten-day stay and many foraging expeditions.

Signor Nando Curti, the cordial and charming manager of the Brufani Palace, has given us two of his best recipes, one dedicated to *risotto,* the other to *scaloppine.* The former is translated below, and the latter appears among the Umbrian recipes at the end of this book. Signor Curti explained that his *risotto* is named for the little town of Montefalco, a bird's nest of a place some twelve miles from Perugia that enjoys an inspiring view of the Tiber Valley and is known as "the balcony of Umbria." The village is celebrated for three things—the frescoes of Benozzo Gozzoli, a red wine called Sagrantino, "dark and full of pleasant thoughts," and *porcini,* mushrooms that grow in the surrounding forests. The last specialty inspired this recipe. We assure you that it comes out beautifully, even with mushrooms of another nationality.

Risotto alla Montefalchese
RISOTTO MONTEFALCO

Melt 3 tablespoons of butter in a large heavy pot and add 1 minced onion, allowing it to cook until slightly browned. Stir in 1 1/4 pounds (2 1/2 cups) of rice and cook it until each grain is pale gold in color. Add 1/4 cup of Marsala and cook slowly until it is absorbed into the rice. Now add, 2 cups at a time, about 8 cups of hot chicken stock, each time covering the pot and allowing the *risotto* to cook very slowly until the rice has absorbed all the liquid. When done, it should be fairly dry, cooked but not too soft.

Meanwhile, make the following sauce: In 3 tablespoons of melted butter cook slowly 1 finely sliced onion, a slice of ham (raw *prosciutto,* if possible) cut in julienne strips, 2 sage leaves, and a bay leaf. When all has taken on a little color add 4 diced raw chicken livers, 1/2 pound of sliced mushrooms, and 1 sweetbread that has been parboiled, skinned, and diced. Cook these together over a very low fire until all the ingredients are amalgamated and reduced. Add salt and pepper, 1 tablespoon of Marsala and about 1 cup of stock. Simmer for about 10 minutes. Stir half the sauce into the *risotto.* Place the *risotto* in a hot bowl, leaving a hollow in the center. Pour the remaining sauce into this well and serve.

Though the assured calm of the Brufani is rarely upset, it was thoroughly shattered on the third day of our sojourn, when the hotel served as overnight headquarters for the annual motorcycle tour of Italy. The place swarmed with lizardlike little men in one-piece, zippered, black leather suits, and the attendant throng of journalists, managers, massagers, and broadcasters. The man-

Mount Subasio and the hill town of Assisi

agement was quietly wringing its hands. This is the only day of the year we advise you to avoid the Brufani—in fact, may we suggest that you avoid *all* contact with motorcycle races, and the horrendous bottlenecks they create.

There is another good hotel in Perugia, facing the populous Corso Vannucci, called LA ROSETTA, with a gay little courtyard and good dining rooms. We had better than average dinners here, and the prices are somewhat lower than at the Brufani. Farther up the Corso is the RISTORANTE TRASIMENO, an attractive place for those who seek a quiet luncheon or dinner. They specialize in trout from Lake Trasimeno as well as in *cannelloni*.

Assisi

ONE EXTRAORDINARY man still dominates this beautiful hillside town, more than seven centuries after his brief lifetime of forty-four years. Saint Francis of Assisi leaves his mark on every visitor to this mystic city, and a refreshing experience it is. We don't feel qualified to make weighty observations about Saint Francis and the example that he has set the world, but we do feel strongly about one thing—a few hours in Assisi are not enough for the assimilative visitor. The average motor tour almost whisks him through. This wonderful town on the cypress-clad slopes of Mount Subasio merits a visit of at least two or three days. In addition to the Basilica of Saint Francis, and the famous buttressed Church of Santa Chiara, there are a fine cathedral, a medieval town square boasting the remains of a Roman temple, and a tower-

Basilica of San Francesco—Assisi

Buttresses of the Church of Santa Chiara—Assisi

Assisi

ing fortress from which you may obtain an inspiring view of the Umbrian hills, with Perugia looming in the distance. Some of the greatest frescoes of Cimabue and Giotto are here. In Assisi the shops are filled with tempting things —lacework, pottery, and sculpture—and the hotels are entirely adequate, pleasant, and cosmopolitan. Definitely Assisi is a place to *stay* for a few days.

The story of Saint Francis has been told many times, and memory of him is still vivid. His was a lifetime of tremendous import to the world. Born in Assisi in 1182, the son of a wealthy silk and wool merchant, he was baptized Giovanni but came to be called Francesco, from his travels in France and his ability to speak French. As a youth he led a gay life. Then a sudden and miraculous conversion took place, and the young man impulsively gave everything he had to the poor and dedicated the rest of his life to poverty, chastity, and obedience. In 1210 he established the Franciscan order based on poverty and self-denial, and since that time Franciscan convents have been established in most of the large cities of Italy, and all over the world. He traveled widely, preaching in Spain, Morocco, Egypt, and the Holy Land. His love of beasts and birds is especially appealing. The privations and hard labor that accompanied his later years cost him his eyesight, and he died on the fourth of October, 1226. He was canonized in 1228, and work was begun on the great Basilica of San Francesco.

The foundation stone of the basilica was laid by Pope Gregory, and the building was completed toward the end of the thirteenth century. It is a complex structure, consisting of two churches, one over the other, and is in the pointed-arch Gothic style, a novelty in Italy at that time. The lower church is austere, dark, and mysterious, but enlivened by fabulous frescoes by Giotto, Simone Martini, and their pupils. The tomb of Saint Francis is now in the crypt. Relics of the saint, including his simple raiment, may be seen in the sacristy. The upper church is bright and airy by contrast, brilliantly decorated with frescoes by Cimabue, Giotto, and Lorenzetti, and their followers. The life of Saint Francis, portrayed in twenty-eight celebrated frescoes by Giotto, ranks as one of the noblest masterpieces of Italian art. The famous head of the saint by Simone Martini is in the right transept. Visitors see the basilica under the best conditions, accompanied by genial Franciscan friars, who act as multilingual guides.

The heart of Assisi is the Piazza del Comune, a lively town square where most of the buildings are thirteenth-century *palazzi*. There is a gay little

Sculptor's shop—Assisi

Hilltop street—Assisi

Portico of the Temple of Minerva—Assisi

café near the fountain, a good place to sit down and admire the scene, which
is endlessly diverting. Near the end of the piazza are six unmistakably Roman
columns, the remains of the Temple of Minerva. At present they lead to a
sixteenth-century church. Adjoining them is a sturdy battlemented tower.

By continuing southward through the ancient town, you come to the
other architectural treasure in Assisi, the thirteenth-century Church of Santa
Chiara. It bears a certain resemblance to the upper portion of the Basilica
of Saint Francis, the façade being adorned with a superb rose window. But it
also has three huge lateral buttresses rising from the ground, and wonderfully photogenic they are. Inside are the baptismal fonts of both Saint Francis
and Saint Clare. The walls are filled with frescoes of the school of Giotto.

Saint Clare, a noble lady of Assisi and daughter of a wealthy family,
was one of the earliest disciples of Saint Francis. She followed his example
and founded an order for the poor, devoting her life to good works. It was
she who took care of Saint Francis, blind and ill from his privations, during
his last days. She died at the age of sixty, and her body lies in an ancient
tomb in the church that bears her name.

There is a great deal more to be seen in Assisi, and stouthearted travelers
are urged to climb to the Rocca Maggiore, a lofty fortress that commands
a magnificent view of the town and the Umbrian plain below. In the
distance they will perceive a vast domed structure, the immense Church of
Santa Maria degli Angeli, rising out of a village some two miles away. This
Renaissance temple was designed by Vignola in 1569, and is one of his finest
works. It was built to shelter a small primitive oratory, erected by the first
members of the Franciscan order. Under the same echoing roof are the
remains of the cell where Saint Francis died. These two shrines attract pilgrims from all over the world.

There are three hotels in Assisi where you may be comfortable, the SUBASIO,
the GIOTTO, and the WINDSOR SAVOIA. All of them have inspiring views of the
valley below, and all are geared to take good care of the overnight guest.
Mind you, they are all "touristy," but that is inevitable. Their cooking is
good, without being remarkable. Though Assisi does not perhaps represent
the gastronomic pinnacle of Italy, its culinary standards are far removed from
the pious poverty prescribed by its patron saint.

When we last stayed at the Hotel Subasio, we asked Signor Andrea Rossi,
the director, for some of his favorite recipes. He responded with this savory
formula for serving roast veal, a true specialty of Assisi:

Vitello all'Assisiana
ROAST VEAL ASSISI

Take a 3-pound lean piece of loin or leg of veal for roasting, pierce
it in 8 or 10 places with a sharp knife or larding needle, and insert in

each slit a small strip of ham. Place the veal in a roasting pan, surrounded by 1 or 2 onions, a stalk of celery, and 1 carrot, all finely chopped, several sprigs of parsley, 1 teaspoon of fresh marjoram, and a pinch of thyme. Salt and pepper the roast and spread it well with butter and lard combined. Put the roast in a moderately hot oven (375° F.) and, when the meat has browned somewhat, add 1/2 cup of white wine and 1/4 cup of milk. Stir this liquid into the juices in the bottom of the pan and baste the roast.

Lower the heat to 300° F. and, when the roast has begun to cook again, skim out the vegetables with a straining spoon. Mash them through a sieve into a small saucepan, blend in 1 teaspoon of flour, and add 3/4 cup of stock, 6 or 8 minced mushrooms, and salt and pepper. Simmer this sauce for 10 minutes. When the roast is done, place it on a hot serving dish, combine the sauce with the juices in the roasting pan, and pour all over the roast. The total roasting time will be about 2 hours.

Orvieto

LOOMING OUT of the surrounding plain almost like a mirage, Orvieto is built on another dramatic site chosen by the discriminating Etruscans. One of the twelve Etruscan cities that fell to the Romans in 280 B. C., the rocky plateau of tufa rock on which it stands rises more than six hundred feet from the

valley. Protected on every side by steep cliffs, it served as a refuge for many
a pope during the revolts in Rome. The motorist must negotiate several
hairpin turns before he reaches the town. Once inside the gates, he finds its
medieval atmosphere almost intact. The streets are grotesque and seem ridiculously narrow, especially toward evening when the soldiers begin to stroll.
(This is a garrison town.)

Though Orvieto is famous for its wine, its greatest glory by far is the
cathedral, one of the most beautiful Gothic buildings in Italy. Its facade,
dating from 1285, is a polychromatic symphony of sun-baked sculpture, colored
marble, and mosaic, above which glows a superlative rose window. The whole
façade has the appearance of a colossal, colorful Gothic triptych, and sometimes it seems to float in the air. The Sienese architect, Lorenzo Maitani,
designed it and its rich embellishment of bas-reliefs representing scenes from
the Bible. It is reminiscent of Siena, and so is the interior, conceived in the
same alternate stripes of gray and white stone.

It is in the Orvieto cathedral that the enthusiast of medieval art has
the best chance to perceive the genius of Luca Signorelli, one of the few
masters who influenced Michelangelo. He was also one of the rare painters
of the time who possessed and gratified the whims of a gourmet. His finest
work is in the Chapel of San Brizio, the greatest treasure of this art-rich
citadel. The frescoes in this chapel were begun by Fra Angelico, but soon the
great Signorelli had taken command, painting heroic scenes and demon-
strating that few artists can rival his magnificent draftsmanship. Critics contend that Michelangelo felt the power of Signorelli's technique when he
worked in the Sistine Chapel three decades later. At all events, the Chapel
of San Brizio is the one thing *not* to miss in Orvieto.

Adjoining the cathedral is the Palazzo Papale, now a museum. It contains many Greek, Etruscan, and Roman antiquities, together with paintings
and sculpture by such masters as Simone Martini, Luca Signorelli, and Pisano.

At the eastern extremity of Orvieto, close to a park where the funicular
lands its passengers from the railway station below, is a genuine curiosity,
the Pozzo di San Patrizio. This is a wide well, over two hundred feet deep,
which was begun in 1527 on the orders of Clement VII, so that the citadel
should have water in case of siege. It is partly carved in tufa rock and
partly built of masonry, and has two flights of intertwining spiral steps so contrived that a continuous file of water-laden donkeys could descend and climb
without ever meeting. This rare feat of stereotomy is ascribed to Antonio di
Sangallo. Robust visitors may visit the well and climb down the 248 steps
and back again, if their wind is good.

The heart of Orvieto is the Piazza del Popolo, an active town square
surrounded by crenellated palaces, one of them a papal residence in bygone
days. It is here that you will find the most acceptable hotel in Orvieto, the

Façade of the cathedral—Orvieto

GRAND HOTEL REALE, itself an old palace, dating from the seventeenth century and rejoicing in many imposing interiors.

Many visitors come to Orvieto for the day only, and this brings up the problem of a good place for luncheon. There are several solutions, none of them on a lofty gastronomic plane. However, we think you will be reasonably happy at the RISTORANTE MAURIZIO, at Via del Duomo 55. Some energetic publicist on a Vespa scooter chased our car through the streets of Orvieto and, as soon as we parked, swamped us with postcards and broadsides about the Maurizio. Though we're inclined to be testy in the face of such tactics, we decided to calm our ruffled feelings and give him a fair test. The verdict: "A" for publicity, effort, courtesy, and wine, and "B" for food and service. Our major disappointment was that they could not provide an outstanding local specialty, an alarming liver sausage prepared with sugar called *mazzafegati*. But perhaps it was just as well.

If you happen to be at the other end of Orvieto at lunchtime, there is a pleasant little place called the RISTORANTE MORINO, situated between the town gate and the Porta Romana, at Via Garibaldi 37. We found good country cooking here, in generous quantities—and the wine was delicious.

Ristorante Maurizio
Orvieto

Gubbio

THIS ANCIENT Umbrian hill town can be the climax of a memorable motor trip from Perugia. It is about twenty miles north of the Umbrian capital, over an indifferent but highly scenic road. Gubbio, where Saint Francis tamed the marauding wolf, remains medieval to this day. Built on the side of a steep hill, it recalls the Middle Ages at every step, especially along the narrow Via Baldassini, which is worth seeking out. The city is famous for its ceramics, and there are numerous shops where you can acquire a handsome bit of pottery to remind you of the day. Gubbio is also known for its fifteenth-century school of painting, led by Ottaviano Nelli. During the month of May there are two colorful festivals here. On the fifteenth occurs the Feast of the Candles, and three days later comes the Tournament of the Crossbowmen.

One building dominates the whole city, the imposing Palazzo dei Consoli, an immense soaring structure on the hill, crowned with corbels and battlements and dating from the early fifteenth century. It contains a notable museum whose prize exhibits are the Eugubine tablets, seven bronze plaques engraved in both Latin and Umbrian characters, highly prized by scholars. The town hall faces it across the piazza. Farther up the hill is the Renaissance ducal palace, built for Frederick, Duke of Montefeltro, when Gubbio was a part of the Duchy of Urbino. Adjoining this *palazzo* is an interesting cathedral. Altogether Gubbio constitutes a happy side trip.

A side street in Gubbio

Cascia

There are two simple country hotels in the lower town of Gubbio, the ALBERGO SAN MARCO and the ALBERGO ODERISI, both capable, we are told, of serving an honest, unpretentious Italian luncheon. We can't make any firsthand promises about them, however, for we had our lunch on an ancient stone sarcophagus under a tree, looking out on the ruins of the Roman amphitheater. There couldn't be a finer place to enjoy a segment of Bel Paese, a loaf of bread, a *fiasco* of Chianti, a few slices of *mortadella,* and a fragrant ripe Italian melon.

Spoleto

ANOTHER EVENTFUL and rewarding motor trip may be made in Umbria by driving southward from Assisi toward the unheralded hill town of Spoleto, with two interesting stops along the way. One of them is Spello, a village with imposing Augustan gates that date from the first century. At first glance you wouldn't suspect that this dusty little place contains much of interest, but if you are an enthusiast of Pinturicchio's frescoes, it will prove a treasure. Some of this master's best work is found in the Baglioni Chapel in the little Church of Santa Maria Maggiore.

Foligno is a larger town, a few miles farther south, and has a twelfth-century cathedral of startling beauty. The shimmering citadel of Spoleto is your next stop, and a perfectly delightful place it is. An unsung attraction, it appears unaccustomed to visitors, a fact that adds to its charm. An immense frowning fortress called La Rocca Papale dominates the town. Once the stronghold of the popes, it was here that Lucrezia Borgia lived for a few unhappy months. At presents it serves as a prison. Just below La Rocca is one of the most impressive bridges in Italy, the immense Ponte delle Torri,

La Rocca and the Ponte delle Torri–Spoleto

Cathedral façade–Foligno

Church of San Pietro–Spoleto

spanning the wide valley of the Tessino with ten sturdy arches, a gigantic piece of masonry. Still in the hilly part of Spoleto, you will find the artistic treasure of the town, its cathedral. This unusual structure is a curious combination of two styles. Its façade, adorned by eight rose windows and a colorful mosaic, is Romanesque. Its portico and the culmination of its bell tower, date from the Renaissance. Curiously enough, they get along very well together. Inside the cathedral you become conscious of one of the greatest of Italian painters, Fra Filippo Lippi. He died in Spoleto, in 1469, and his tomb has a place of honor under this roof, and here, too, are the last frescoes this master painted. They depict the life of Mary, the finest, perhaps, being the "Crowning of the Virgin." Here, also, are frescoes by the prolific Pinturicchio.

On the southern outskirts of Spoleto stands a Romanesque church called San Pietro, which appears to be ignored by the guidebooks. We urge you to seek it out, if only to see the gallery of wild and domestic animals that adorn its façade. The church sits in lonely isolation, with only a humble farmhouse as a companion. The carving of its portal and adjacent panels is very beautiful, and from this vantage point you have a thrilling view of Spoleto, its mammoth bridge and fortress.

On the gastronomic front, Spoleto offers a busy little hotel in the lower town called the ALBERGO FERROVIA. We found ourselves there on a raw March day and were entirely happy with the pasta, the grilled beef with truffles, the cheese, and the wine. As its name suggests, it is a railway hotel, and its clean rooms are handy to the station, in case you come to Spoleto by train.

There are many other hill towns in Umbria for the intrepid explorer. Narni and Todi are especially rewarding. Or perhaps you would like to visit the black truffle country in late autumn. Such old towns as Cascia, Norcia, and Scheggino beckon during the harvest season. Together with the larger cities of Umbria, they should demonstrate that this is one of the least exploited and most gratifying of the Italian regions.

Trajan's Column

Rome

Chapter 12

ROME

ROME

THE MIGRATORY scribe whose primary interest is gastronomy will find that he has ample time for truant tangents in most of the Italian provinces. Beguiling as the theme of regional wine and cooking may be, he can still wander into the green pastures of history, art, and bicycle races without neglecting his epicurean duty. But not so in Rome. The subject of wining and dining in the Eternal City is so rich and so rewarding, that vagrant deviations into the companion beauties of the capital are out of the question.

Unless the writer is to indulge in a full-length novelette, he must have the fortitude to forego the antique shops on the Via Sistina and the twinkling ankles on the Via Flaminia for the solid facts of life on the Via Gastronomia.

So, with nary a sidelong, time-consuming glance at Saint Peter's or the Forum, we plunge headlong into the theme of Roman food—and come up bubbling with encouraging facts. The much-quoted assertion that it is impossible to dine poorly in Rome turns out to be a gratifying truth. As do the Parisians and the Lyonnais, the Romans refuse to patronize a poor restaurant. You see one now and then, tables deserted, waiters balancing forlornly on their heels, cash registers silent. A few doors away is another place absolutely choked with chattering, gregarious guests. The Roman public knows the difference, and so will the timid traveler—if he follows the crowd.

The excellence of Roman cooking runs through all categories of dining places, from the humble *trattoria* to the chic casino in the park. It applies to discreet carpeted haunts of the aristocracy and to noisy night-club cellars ringing with song. Price seems to make little difference. You will find de-

Isola Tiberina–Rome

lectable Roman food in sidewalk cafés across the Tiber and in inexpensive country inns along the ancient Appian Way. Only the drab and unimaginative diner who sticks close to his hotel and submits to "international" cuisine could find Roman cooking dull. Beyond any doubt, Rome's gastronomic stature is in keeping with its historic eminence as a world capital—and that's good news.

The *carta del giorno* of any good Roman restaurant contains a tempting cross section of Italian cookery—Adriatic fish, Florentine beef, Bolognese pasta, Neapolitan sweets—but Rome's own specialties stand up well by comparison. Baby lamb, egg noodles, peas, and artichokes take on vivid originality when prepared in the Roman manner, and no visiting gourmet worthy of the name would leave the city without making the acquaintance of seductive *fettuccine, abbacchio,* and *carciofi alla romana.* Among many Roman dishes, we shall dwell only upon a spectacular few:

Fettuccine alla romana. These are thin, fresh egg noodles, served very hot with butter and finely grated Parmesan cheese. Though this definition may sound banal for a sublime dish, this preparation is nonetheless a crowning achievement in pasta, and so perfected that few outsiders can hope to duplicate it. Yet its essentials are simplicity itself. The mannered flush and flourish that accompany the serving of this famous dish in Alfredo's and elsewhere happen to be essential, even if the traditional gold fork and spoon are not. The beautiful ribbons of golden noodles arrive at your table quite dry, and as hot as live steam. Within a half minute or so, your maître d'hôtel must melt an imposing block of butter in them, together with just the right amount of Parmesan or Romano cheese, ground almost to the fineness of talcum powder. It takes a lot of lightning tossing, twirling, and mixing to melt both butter and cheese and to transfer the *fettuccine* still steaming to your plate. Apart from *crêpes Suzette,* few dishes offer such a dazzling opportunity to a headwaiter with exhibitionist tendencies.

Roman *fettuccine* are about three-eighths of an inch wide and much

Arch of Titus—Rome

thinner than other egg-enriched Italian noodles, but the secret of their beauty seems to lie in their freshness. Made in the morning, and cooked only on order, the *maestose fettuccine al triplo burro* are a thing of rich, buttery, fattening splendor. Yet the price on a Roman menu is less than fifty cents.

An *abbacchio* is a very young milk-fed lamb that looks not much bigger than a full-grown hare when it is suspended by its feet in an Italian butcher shop. It can be roasted in the oven or on a spit, and emerges exquisitely tender and delicate. Cooked *alla cacciatora* in a casserole with peppers, garlic, rosemary, vinegar, spices, and a suspicion of anchovy, it takes on a character all its own. As a delicacy, *abbacchio* is totally satisfying except to the sentimental diner. Of course, if you conjure up a picture of baby lambs frolicking among the bluebells and buttercups, you're not going to enjoy the dish as much. It is a shame to end their days even before their baas have changed, but as long as there is an insistent demand for thin, washable lambskin gloves, there will be *abbacchi*. And the Romans are winners on both counts!

314

The Roman Forum

Carciofi alla romana. An unassuming member of the thistle family, the artichoke, reaches an undreamed of pinnacle of goodness in Rome. How little the rest of the world seems to know about artichokes, compared to the Italians! The French, with their penchant for picking vegetables young—baby carrots, infant turnips, puerile potatoes, minuscule peas, string beans of maiden slimnes—have apparently overlooked the fact that very young artichokes are equally rewarding. Other countries, our own included, seem to consider that the bigger an artichoke, the better. Nibble away at the one fragment of tenderness that lurks at the bottom of each leaf, enjoy the reward of the artichoke's base, and you've had it.

How different is the Italian approach. Early in the season the producers snip off the smallest artichoke buds and put them up in herb-rich olive oil. When the unsnipped survivors become tender striplings, somewhat bigger than ducks' eggs, they are cut, with about two inches of the stalk. The sharp tips of the leaves are cut back a bit, and the rest becomes a *mange-tout,*

Lunchtime at the Arch of Constantine—Rome

totally edible down through the supposedly wiry stem. There is no need to remove the "choke" in the species of the plant the Italians serve—all of it may be eaten.

Carciofi turn into golden-green flowers when cooked, *alla romana,* in olive oil and white wine. Sometimes they are faintly perfumed with garlic, or again they are pointed up with vinegar and herbs only, but always their taste and texture are exquisite. They taste equally good hot, lukewarm, or cold. Nobody prepares this dish quite so well as the Romans, who love their artichokes as an hors-d'oeuvre, a garnish, or a vegetable course, and never seem to tire of them. If you can snare a dozen adolescent artichokes, here is the recipe:

Carciofi alla Romana
ARTICHOKES ROMAN STYLE

Remove the hard outer leaves of 8 to 10 small artichokes, trim the points of the others, and remove the choke (necessary in the non-Roman species), substituting for it a mixture of 1 part minced garlic and 1 part mint to 3 parts parsley, seasoned with salt and pepper. Make a bouquet of the artichokes in a terra-cotta casserole, moistening them with 4 or 5 tablespoons of olive oil, add a little garlic, and cook them on a moderate fire for 10 minutes. Then add 1 cup of dry white wine and 1/2 cup of stock. Cover the casserole and let the artichokes cook until the sauce is almost cooked away.

Gnocchi alla romana. There are two variations of this celebrated dish. The more familiar one consists of semolina (which resembles cream of wheat) cooked in milk, with cheese, butter, and eggs added. It is sliced, when cold, into rounds or squares, browned in the oven, bathed in abundant butter, and topped with grated Parmesan cheese. This type is the one best known in foreign lands.

The other variant is made of a paste of flour and potato that is formed into cocoon-shaped lozenges and then poached. It is sometimes served with a meat sauce, and liberally sprinkled with Parmesan or Roman Pecorino cheese.

Fritto alla romana. Roman cooks have an enviable reputation for deep frying. A good mixed fry *alla romana* is light and delicate, containing as it does the tender spare parts of very young animals—calves' brains, or the same delicacy from baby goats, sweetbreads, calves' livers, artichokes, and croutons, all dipped in milk, flour, and beaten egg, and fried in deep lard, not oil. In many a Roman snack bar you will see *suppli,* another product of the deep-fry. These are golden-brown rice croquettes enclosing a pungent meat-and-sauce center, almost as exciting as a tamale.

Saltimbocca alla romana. This preparation, of course, is a favorite device

Antiquities of the Roman Forum, around the Arch of Septimius Severus

for adding savor to an Italian *escalope* of veal, often a rather flat commodity. A leaf of sage and a thin slice of ham make all the difference when the veal is sautéed, and a thin topping of *mozzarella* cheese adds even more flavor. Some of the subtler surgeons manage to make a pocket out of the thin slice of veal and to stuff it with the ham, cheese, and herbs, a refinement that deserves, and receives, quite an accolade from the dining public. *Saltimbocca* literally means "jumps into the mouth," an apt phrase when applied to this delicious dish.

The Romans have their own ways of serving spaghetti. One is *spaghetti alla matriciana,* featuring a savory sauce concealing onions, cheek of pork, tomatoes, and peppers. Another is *spaghetti alla carattiera,* based on a sophisticated combination of tuna fish, tomatoes, herbs, and fried mushrooms. They also have their own little tricks with *suprêmes* of turkey and chicken. Peas and ham cooked in a casserole are perennial favorites. They love tripe served in the Roman manner accompanied by a sauce rich with onions, celery, carrots, cloves, parsley, ham, garlic, mint, and butter–enough to mask completely the honeycombed delicacy. Rome does not specialize in sea food, although the better restaurants import liberally from the Adriatic. But there are three noble Roman cheeses. Pecorino Romano comes in large corded cylinders

Temple of Antoninus and Faustina—Rome   *A glimpse of the Colosseum—Rome*

weighing as much as twenty-five pounds, and ages a year or more in the upper reaches of Roman food shops. Made from ewe's milk and always a little sharp, it is used as a flavorful topping for pasta and soups. Provatura Romana is a cousin of *mozzarella,* the cheese so famous in Naples. It comes from the milk of the pensive water buffalo and appears in the shops in the form and the color of an oversized egg. The highly popular *ricotta alla romana,* an important ingredient in many Roman dishes, is made from whey and resembles cottage cheese.

The wines of Latium are not the best in Italy, but they have their virtues, particularly Frascati. This fresh, palatable white wine is a deplorable traveler and rarely penetrates beyond its own province, a fact that doesn't distress the Romans in the least. They would be quite willing to drink it all. Frascati is one of several wines of the Castelli Romani, a name given to the foothills of the Apennines south of Rome where togaed patricians once built their summer castles. You may find others from these slopes on the wine list— Albano, Castelgondolfo, or Genzano, all fair enough. A pleasant and much-quoted legend has evolved around a golden wine grown on the slopes of Montefiascone, north of Rome. The German Cardinal Fugger was enough of an oenophile to take the precaution of sending his valet ahead when he

The Campidoglio–Rome   *Detail of Trajan's Column–Rome*

traveled, so that he would be sure to stop at an inn with a good wine cellar. On the door of the inn the valet would chalk *Est (è buono)* if the wine was satisfactory and *Est, Est* in case it was exceptional. When the valet and his taste buds reached Montefiascone, he found himself so enraptured that he scrawled a vigorous *Est! Est!! Est!!!* on the tavern door. The Cardinal apparently agreed with the valet's judgment, for he stayed at the inn and drank such vast flagons of the wine that he died from it. No better publicity could befall a wine in those days, and it still clings to the legendary name of *Est! Est!! Est!!!* This wine travels better than those grown south of Rome, and anyone wishing to verify the Cardinal's judgment, if not emulate his example, may find it on the British and American market.

After several weeks of foraging in Rome, we are willing to climb out on a limb and mention a group of restaurants—the product of considerable research—that should please the traveler who carries this book to Italy. We fondly picture this composite personality, by the way, as urbane, attractive, and civilized, responsive to the good things in life (among them fine cooking, worthy wines, and charming companions), but skeptical of tourist traps, contrived atmosphere, and pompous maîtres d'hôtel.

With him in mind, this cross section of Roman dining embraces many types

Fountain of Trevi—Rome

The Quirinal Palace and the obelisk—Rome

and several charming settings, some with music (it's a part of Rome) and some devoted only to pious concentration on epicurean pursuits. May we lay emphasis on the fact that the omissions are colossal. They have to be, when a choice is made from thousands. We do not mention hotels, many of which have splendid cuisines, or any of a myriad of snack bars, tea shops, *birrerie,* and *rosticcerie* where lighter fare may be found at odd hours. Among hundreds of worthy little *trattorie,* we have named only a few favorites. Everyone who stays in Rome for some time makes his own choice among them. It is genuinely difficult to go gastronomically astray in the capital.

There are a few luxurious dining places in Rome that seem better suited to the well-heeled visitor who wants to see all the sights, than to the reposeful gourmet we have mentioned above. Some lucky, carefree people head straight for the most fashionable restaurant as a matter of course. In Rome they will be rewarded by very good food as well as chic atmosphere. Just at the moment, the smart thing to do is to motor or take a taxi to the outskirts of the city where the modernistic villa of Mussolini and Clara Petacci, his mistress, has been transformed into a gay and cosmopolitan restaurant named PALAZZI. It is quite a palatial establishment with a swimming pool, tennis court, a place to dance, and two covered sun decks. The food is excellent, of "international" character, and expensive. Palazzi is located in the Monte Mario district, at Via della Camilluccia 355, and enjoys a superb view of the whole of Rome.

322

In Rome itself, the place that comes most often to mind as the smartest is the HOSTERIA DELL'ORSO, the Inn of the Bear, located at Via Monte Brianzo 93, near the Umberto Bridge, in an ancient building dating, they say, from the thirteenth century. It is furnished with magnificent antiques and has a decidedly plush atmosphere. Dante supposedly lived in this house at one time, and Leonardo da Vinci, Montaigne, and Rabelais are said to have dined in the ancient restaurant. At present, the Hosteria dell'Orso is one of the sights of Rome, visited nightly by a guided tour. It also boasts a very elegant night club. None of these factors detract from the excellence of the cuisine, which is rewarding indeed. It is not open in the middle of the day. Another favored spot for the visiting free-spender is the CASINA DELLE ROSE, a charming place in the Borghese Gardens that also offers a theater and a night club.

Finally, there is the great Alfredo, showman par excellence, who draws an endless file of amazed and hungry tourists to watch his calisthenics over a dish of hot noodles. The King of Noodles has come out of retirement, and now wields his golden fork and spoon at ALFREDO ALL'AUGUSTEO, at Number 31 on the Piazza Augusteo Imperatore. His *maestosissime fettuccine all'Alfredo* are most majestic, without a doubt. So are his filets of turkey accompanied by artichokes and the flaming omelette that he unveils at your table with a burst of cognac and song. You have to visit this place at least once, we suppose, just to say you have seen this elderly, melodramatic good-hearted clown in action. There are three Alfredo's in Rome, and this one deserves to be called the original. But we prefer the quieter, less touristy atmosphere of the Alfredo on the Via Scrofa, which we'll discuss shortly.

In contrast to the luxury establishments in Rome, you can find any number of dependable little *trattorie,* without pretense but with trustworthy, appetizing food. There will certainly be a good one in your quarter of Rome. Among scores of them, it seems almost too partial to cite two of our favorites, but here they are: SALVAGGI, Via Quintino Sella 1, and ANDREA, Via Sardegna 26–28, just off the Via Veneto.

Our intention is to leave most of the luxury establishments and the *trattorie* to your own judgment and dwell in detail upon fifteen of our favorite Roman restaurants, a list long enough for the average epicurean visitor to the Eternal City. Among these fifteen recommendations you will find every mood for dining, from chaste conservatism to bawdy murals and wild outbursts of song with your dinner.

The Romans dine late, and Mr. and Mrs. Anglo-Saxon Gourmet will have ample time to reflect upon their choice of a restaurant while sitting in one of the smart sidewalk cafés on the Via Vittorio Veneto. Almost everyone of importance in the world of the cinema, the stage, or fashion seems to drift into DONEY'S, CARPANO, STREGA, or ROSATI at least once during the

Fountains in the gardens of the Villa Borghese—Rome

day, and there is no better place to watch the sophisticated, well-dressed Roman on parade. Less obvious and far more steeped in tradition is the CAFÉ GRECO, at Via Condotti 86, a historic spot established in 1780 and long patronized by artists and writers, among them John Keats and Mark Twain. In such charming and quiet surroundings you are confronted with a cool Italian *aperitivo,* but no dining problem whatever, for only a short stroll away is:

RANIERI—Via Mario dei Fiori 26

This venerable haunt of Roman epicures stands on a side street not far from the fashionable Via Condotti and the Piazza di Spagna, address of the American Express, known to every American who seeks a letter from Back Home. Though Ranieri is positively steeped in history, it rests neither upon its laurels nor on the commendation of a century of famous visitors. Today's exacting diners will find it gratifying and reposeful. The atmosphere is definitely *vieux monde.* The faded velvet banquettes against the wall, the aged, courteous waiters, the polished gentleman of the old school who owns it, all preserve the spirit of the late nineties. The restaurant is small but uncrowded. Private salons upstairs take care of any overflow. Dignified, benign gentlemen sit alone with their quail or woodcock and their Burgundy. A gay little party of four orders *cannelloni, scampi all'orientale,* and a sweet, and needs an extra bottle of Orvieto to carry them through. A suave couple from England tries hard to select hors-d'oeuvre without pointing. There is *no* music. The wine list is short but excellent. The chef is one of the best in Rome.

Ristorante
Ranieri
Rome

Founded in 1843 by a Frenchman, the restaurant was acquired in 1861 by a Neapolitan, Guiseppe Ranieri, who had been Queen Victoria's chef and who later tried to bring culinary comfort to the unhappy Emperor Maximilian in Mexico. From the day Ranieri took the restaurant over, its success as a rendezvous for epicures and celebrities, crowned and otherwise, was assured. His direct descendant now maintains the same scrupulous standard.

Royal visitors to Ranieri have been many. The monarchs of Italy, Spain, Austria, Germany, Sweden, Greece, and Russia have signed the guestbook with due appreciation. The late George VI of England dined here twice, once as Duke of York, and later when he came to Italy in 1944 to inspect the Eighth Army.

There are many savory ways to begin a meal at Ranieri—*cannelloni alla casalinga,* for example, or *lasagne verdi al forno,* or *crêpes suisses,* little pancakes rolled around a luscious cheese paste and heated in the oven. A favorite chicken dish is flamed in brandy and named after the ill-fated Maximilian —*pollo alla Massimiliano.* For dessert you may order a tempting *zabaione.*

Ranieri's generous owner gave us five of his favorite recipes, one of which should turn out particularly well in your own kitchen:

The top of the Spanish Steps—Rome

Pollo alla Massimiliano
CHICKEN MAXIMILIAN

Take a tender young chicken split as for broiling, brush it well with oil on both sides, and season it with salt and pepper and a crumbled bay leaf. Broil the chicken about 15 minutes on each side, or until it is uniformly cooked and browned. Place it in a hot greased baking dish, pour over it a liqueur glassful of good warmed brandy and flame it at the table, shaking the dish until all the alcohol has burned away.

PASSETTO—Via Zanardelli 14

Ristorante
Passetto
Rome

One of the more recent and fashionable of Roman restaurants, Passetto is set on a broad avenue leading across the Tiber, within walking distance of Saint Peter's. Popular with discriminating Latins and Anglo-Saxons alike, its star is rising rapidly. Behind its revolving doors are two long, high-ceilinged rooms, with a simple but sweeping décor and soft lights. The banquettes are as comfortable as armchairs, the service most attentive. An imposing panorama of food greets the guest as he enters, so beautiful and so prodigal that it requires a full five minutes to view it with proper respect.

326

In the Pincio Gardens–Rome   *Church of the Trinità dei Monti–Rome*

The *lista del giorno*, which is also available in an English edition, is truly imposing, especially in the realm of fowl and game. Our exploratory trio hesitated a bit until the hors-d'oeuvre cart came by—then we knew we had no choice. They are about the best in Rome, richly varied but not too heavy, nor too weighted down with oil. After these, and a cool Frascati, we split into divergent camps: *cinghiale all'agro dolce*—wild boar with a superlative sour-sweet sauce—a regal roast pheasant with an orange-flavored sauce, and a tender half chicken *alla diavolo*. A sturdy red Valpolicella, served as a companion piece, left us bathed in contentment. We were faintly alarmed at a theatrical orange dessert in which Passetto takes particular pride, and settled for ebony cups of *caffè espresso* and a spot of Strega, feeling that this was the safest course.

During the summer months, a broad sheltered terrace appears in front of Passetto, and is instantly adopted by discriminating diners. Winter or summer, Passetto stands high on the list of Roman dining places that should never be missed by visiting connoisseurs. The prices are a little above normal, perhaps, but quite justified.

Signor Guerini, director of Passetto, has given us his recipe for a Roman classic, the famous *gnocchi di semolino*. You can easily achieve them at home.

327

Gnocchi di Semolino alla Romana
GNOCCHI OF WHEAT MEAL

Heat 1 quart of milk with a good pinch of salt and a grating of nutmeg, and, when it begins to boil, pour in gradually 1/2 pound (about 1 cup) of semolina wheat meal. (Cream of wheat is practically the same thing.) Stir the semolina well to prevent lumps and cook it for about 10 minutes. It must be very thick. Remove it from the fire, stir in 2 tablespoons of butter, 4 well-beaten eggs, and 1/2 cup of grated Parmesan cheese. Pour the batter onto a marble slab or greased tin sheet and spread it out into a layer about 1/2 inch thick. When it is cold and firm, cut it into rounds with a small glass or with a biscuit cutter. Place the disks, or squares, if you prefer, in slightly overlapping rows in a buttered shallow baking dish. Sprinkle the *gnocchi* with Parmesan, dot generously with butter, and place them in a hot oven (400° F.) until the surface is browned.

FAGIANO—Piazza Colonna 363

Ristorante Fagiano
Rome

The clamorous heart of Rome is brightened by a carved marble column built in 175 A. D. to honor Emperor Marcus Aurelius. More important, in view of present-day problems, a large square surrounds the column, providing parking spaces, at one hundred lire each, for the automobiles that choke the city, including those of its most exacting gastronomes. Fagiano (The Pheasant), a conventional Roman restaurant in the top tradition, glitters at one corner of this square, the Piazza Colonna. Its lights shine brightly in high ceilings, its linen is white as snow. Thoroughly "professional," Fagiano has been for decades an outstandingly respectable citadel of fine Roman food, and is one of the oldest restaurants in the capital. Chances for disappointment are almost nil at Fagiano, and no better place exists to savor the classic *abbacchio* or a *suprême* of turkey with artichokes or a partridge *en cocotte* with mushrooms. The chef tosses truffles around quite recklessly, and caviar, *foie gras,* and lobster await the more worldly diplomats and the fast, older hunting set who frequent Fagiano. Needless to say, the bird for which this restaurant was named turns crisply on the spit during the shooting season. Pheasant *en casserole,* flaming woodcock, and wild hare are other specialties of the chase.

The prices are entirely reasonable at Fagiano, and the service, from the bowing maître d'hotel to the bus boy, is deft and deferential. A fitting motto, *"Vita, vinum est!"* adorns the wall, and the wines are appropriately good. There is a gay little tavern with music and wall frescoes downstairs, in case Fagiano creates a mood too good to put to bed early, which will probably be the case.

Bernini fountain on the Piazza Navona–Rome

TRE SCALINI—Piazza Navona 30

On a warm summer evening few places have the setting and the romance of the restaurant of the Three Steps, situated in the middle of one of Rome's most beautiful squares. Bernini's three buoyantly Baroque fountains spout and spatter in the long Piazza Navona, but everything else is quiet, except for a few children playing and the staccato sputter of a stray scooter. This is a sidewalk restaurant with superlative dishes to match its privileged stage set. On our first visit we were urged to try its three outstanding specialties, *cannelloni* (wonderful ones with a monumental sauce), *bauletto con funghi* (a savory veal bird), and *gelato tartufo,* a chocolate dessert that seemed a trifle heavy. But we were content, since a noble Barolo kept us company. On a subsequent visit we fared even better, sticking to Roman artichokes, *saltimbocca alla romana* with sylphlike string beans, iced strawberries, coffee, and a generous tulip glass of that joyous Italian liqueur, Aurum. In the winter months the Tre Scalini must abandon its terrace for a series of cheerful modern salons, but it abandons none of its high culinary standards in the process, and provides one of the most pleasant dining experiences in the city.

Ristorante
Tre Scalini
Rome

Replying to our request for a favorite recipe, Signor Giuseppe Ciampini, director of the Tre Scalini, furnished us with three, among them this delectable preparation:

Spaghetti alla Carbonara
SPAGHETTI CARBONARA

Signor Ciampini's recipe was nothing but a brief description. We hope the following more explicit directions do not stray too far from his original.

Boil 1 pound of spaghetti in salted water for 9 to 10 minutes, or until it is cooked but still firm. In 2 tablespoons of butter and 4 tablespoons of olive oil combined, sauté on a low fire 1/2 cup each of julienne of ham and lean bacon and 1/2 cup of thinly sliced mushrooms, without allowing them to brown. The sauce must remain "blond." Remove the pan from the fire and stir in 3 tablespoons of grated Pecorino cheese and 2 large well-beaten eggs. Mix this combination quickly into the drained hot spaghetti. (If you cannot get Pecorino, use Parmesan.)

CAPRICCIO—Via Liguria 38

Capriccio
Rome

Strangely enough, the winding Via Veneto, most fashionable of Roman boulevards, has no outstanding restaurant, although it is studded with the top hotels and cafés. If you are sitting in Doney's or Rosati's, contemplating two empty vermouth glasses and wondering where to dine nearby, the perfect answer, as hundreds have found, lies close at hand on the Via Liguria. Capriccio is an established favorite with hotel dwellers in the Via Veneto belt, including a generous sprinkling of theatrical and movie people. Its atmosphere is restrained and sophisticated, its lights are keyed mercifully low, and one gets the general impression of a top-notch New York establishment. It isn't all illusion, for more than a snatch of the American idiom filters through the air, and the menu is bilingual. The cuisine couldn't be more Italian, however, and the prices are surprisingly reasonable. Don't miss their *cannelloni*. "Divine" is the word for them, but I refuse to use it. Noble steaks, chops, and cutlets emerge from the charcoal grill, and we tasted a *scampi all'americana* which pays a distinct compliment to Uncle Samuele. Capriccio is *very* popular, thus it is prudent to make a reservation, or to arrive early. The restaurant, formerly located on the nearby Via Lombardia, has found a new and delightful contemporary setting on the Via Liguria. You will find a discreet little bar and a generous, tree-sheltered terrace for summer dining. If you are blessed with a starry-eyed bride or daughter, this is the place to take her!

GEORGE'S BAR—Via Marche 7

George's Bar
Rome

Just off the Via Veneto on a side street behind the Hotel Excelsior is a most gratifying reminder of the good old days before the wars—George's Bar. It has high ceilings, paneled walls, discreet lights, and the comfortable

The Tiber and the Castel Sant' Angelo–Rome

atmosphere of the well-fed era of 1900. The bar is very much in evidence, and the barman is a genius at mixing the best of international drinks. But the food's the thing, and it is splendid. You need not limit yourself to Italian dishes here by any means. You have "international" cooking at its best, with a multilingual menu and a few gratifying specialties from England, such as flummery and syllabub. It turns out that George's Bar (also called Giorgio's) is now directed by an epicurean Englishman who was once with the British Embassy in Rome. An exacting gourmet will be gratified by the cooking and the service in this place, especially if he orders *scampi* on a skewer or game in season. The last time we paid a visit to George's Bar, a famous guitarist, Alfredo del Pello, entertained the guests with soft music, and a great addition he was. One of your most pleasant Roman evenings might be spent here.

The fountains, Piazza San Pietro–Rome

ALFREDO ALLA SCROFA—Via della Scrofa 104

Many years ago, when our own Doug and Mary, enraptured by the cere- mony and the taste of Roman egg noodles, presented a gold mixing fork and spoon to Alfredo—*the* Alfredo mind you, the real king of *fettuccine*— they quite unwittingly started a barrage of culinary hocus-pocus that can be rivaled only by the numbered ducks at the Tour d'Argent. The pompous theatrics of mixing these innocent, delectable *fettuccine* turned the dish into a vaudeville headliner and packed in the customers. Now, as we noted earlier in the chapter, there are *three* Alfredo's, two of them deadly rivals. Each displays a wall packed with autographed pictures of the stars, crested testimonials from the nobility, and a veritable five-foot shelf of autographed guestbooks. Vaudeville isn't dead, and the *fettuccine* ceremony is definitely a sight to see. But we certainly won't send you to all *three* Alfredo's! Faced with a choice, we prefer Alfredo alla Scrofa, whose proprietor is an ex-waiter from the exalted original. The place is unpretentious, pleasant, and reasonably quiet, and the service is good. The majestic *fettuccine* are superb, and the gold fork and spoon, a duplicate set, we assume, are much in evidence. Turkey breast with truffles and *petti di pollo alla cardinale,* two other classic specialties, are flawless. This is an excellent spot to savor *abbacchio* or *saltim- bocca alla romana* or those superlative artichokes in season. We have a genuine fondness for this place, in spite of the overhead lights, bright enough for an operating room, and the sallow, lugubrious string trio that wanders about strumming Italian airs.

Ristorante Alfredo alla Scrofa Roma

CASINA VALADIER—Pincio Gardens

Paris may have its chic restaurants set in the Bois de Boulogne or framed in the verdure of the Champs-Elysées, but Rome has the same thing plus a magnificent view, crowned by the dome of Saint Peter's. For decades the classic old Casina Valadier has been a favorite with smart Romans, for luncheon, tea, or dinner. Perched at the edge of the lofty Pincio Gardens, it was designed by Joseph Valadier, the talented architect of the gardens and of the Piazza del Popolo beneath them. It was intended as a residence for Napoleon's son, but he never lived in it. Instead it was transformed into a fashionable restaurant and for decades it has provided discriminating guests (among them Nathaniel Hawthorne) with a charming setting, commendable food, and a thrilling panorama of the city. Newcomers to Rome owe it to themselves to sit in the salons or under the awnings of this long-established casino-in-the-park at least once. They will enjoy a gay atmosphere, attractive people, and cooking on a lofty level, with prices only a little above the average. All of the aristocratic dishes of the Roman kitchen assemble here, together with some "international" favorites.

Casina Valadier Rome

Façade of Saint Peter's—Rome

The colonnade, Piazza San Pietro–Rome

BIBLIOTECA DEL VALLE—Largo Teatro Valle 7

Most present-day Romans prefer a gay evening to a solemn gastronomic ritual. Music of some sort, from a lone guitar to a six-piece orchestra, awaits you in many Roman restaurants, sometimes so deafening that it kills the appetite and makes a shambles of conversation. At other times it remains discreet and pleasant. The musical aspect of the Biblioteca del Valle falls in between these extremes, and you'll probably enjoy it. It is a Bohemian sort of place, with a preponderance of non-Bohemian clients, located in a basement in the heart of the theater district. The name, of course, means library, and the "books" consist of bottles of wine standing behind none too robust iron bars. The *sommelier* is not in the least concerned about the fact that they *should* be lying on their sides in less tumultuous surroundings. It's a gag, and a pleasant one, and the Roman cosmopolites have been sampling volumes from these walls for decades. They arrive late, sing later, and dance after that. A glistening cocktail and *apéritif* wagon starts them off, and a very special limpid white wine, Acqua di Trevi, takes over when a thin-faced mariner comes by with a tray of sea food—lobster, oysters, and clams. By the time

Biblioteca
del Valle
Rome

335

Piazza del Popolo—Rome

the *cannelloni* appear in the company of a *fiasco* of Chianti, the air is thick with smoke and song, and everybody's happy. For a festive evening and a not too disconcerting check, the Biblioteca has much to offer. The food? Oh yes, it's remarkably good. Four of the specialties of the house call for particular mention: *cannelloni deliziosi alla valle, filetti di sogliola alla casentina, agnello d'abruzzo alla romana,* and *rollatini di vitello Biblioteca.* Among the wines that repose, not behind bars, but peacefully in a subcellar lying on their sides, is a delicious Antinori Chianti 1945, just the thing for that Abruzzo lamb.

NINO—Via Borgognona 11

Trattoria Toscana NINO Rome

Carnivorous man has his innings in this shrine of Tuscan beef, not far from the Piazza di Spagna. Nino is famous for its steaks, and those who crave a monumental *bistecca alla fiorentina,* beautifully grilled over charcoal, could find no better place in Rome. The size of the larger steaks depends strictly on the customer—the management charges by the kilo. Those who order the largest one would do well to bring Primo Carnera along as a guest. Needless to say, he has often been here. There are daily specials *chez* Nino, from *osso buco* on Monday to chicken croquettes on Sunday, and the Chianti is superb, as might be expected in a Tuscan establishment owned by

336

a native of Florence. The "atmosphere" in Nino's is nearly nonexistent—high vaulted ceilings, no décor, no music, nothing to detract from the solitary splendor of that gorgeous steak. This so-called *trattoria toscana* is a he-man's place, but for the feminine taste the chef provides many dishes subtler than *bistecca*.

ROMA—Piazza Poli 38

This place is very much in the tradition of an old continental restaurant —conventional, quiet, spotless, and patronized almost exclusively by discriminating Romans. To judge by the décor, it dates from the late nineties. You will encounter not the slightest hint of music, and particularly attentive service. Two skilled restaurateurs in pin-stripe suits took wonderful care of us and of everybody else. We tried a *risotto alla fregoli,* a soul-warming prelude, followed by a handsome *sole meunière* and a *filetto alla rossini,* both beyond reproach.

Ristorante
Roma
Rome

The Ristorante Roma provides a comfortable shaded sidewalk terrace during the summer months. For a highly civilized dinner at reasonable prices and in a central location (just off the busy Via Tritone), bear this restaurant in mind as one of the best. It ranks among the top ten in Rome, we believe, and it makes a charming place for a quiet dinner party.

The rendezvous, Piazza del Campidoglio–Rome

AL RE DEGLI AMICI—Via della Croce 33B

The King of Friends offers a striking contrast to the conventional Roman restaurant. Atmosphere abounds in the succession of small, low-ceilinged, intimate rooms that make up this establishment, although it is hardly more than skin deep. Widely known as a Bohemian rendezvous, its colorful interior is a bit too contrived to be convincing. Artists of varied merit have contributed canvases in exchange for meals, and luminaries from the literary and theatrical world have been invited to paint their names on wall panels. A quartet of strolling musicians add to the animation. The *antipasto* wagon here is inspiring, but even more impressive are the *pizze*. The famous Neapolitan specialty appears in several delicious guises, and you should try one of them. The menu is trilingual here, as are several of the waiters. On two occasions, however, we found the latter to be abrupt, uninterested, and discourteous. But Al Re degli Amici deserves a visit in spite of them.

Al Re
degli
Amici
Rome

338

Arch of Giano—Rome

TRATTORIA GALEASSI—Piazza Santa Maria in Trastevere 3

Paris has its Left Bank, filled with beckoning restaurants, and Rome has its Trastevere, every bit as appealing to the strolling epicure. Across the Tiber are any number of charming small restaurants, and it is with great difficulty that we have limited our favorites to three. Galeassi spreads its broad awning on one of the loveliest of Roman squares. A fountain bubbles in the middle, and the polychromatic Church of Santa Maria in Trastevere looms majestically in one corner. This restaurant is simple and unpretentious—but an artist performs in the kitchen, as our *pollo toscano alla diavolo* proved. We have tried *gnocchi, fettuccine, abbacchio,* golden-brown filet of turkey, and a simple steak at Galeassi, and found them unfailingly good. In fact, we've gone back there four times or more. It is inexpensive, unhurried, and hospitable. The Frascati is cool, the *grissini* (bread sticks) crisp, and the clamor of the city seems far, far away.

Trattoria
Galeassi
Rome

339

Trajan's Forum—Rome

ROMOLO—Porta Settimiana 8

Finding this restaurant presents a little difficulty, but the goal justifies the effort. Situated just inside the ancient Roman walls, it is a venerable *trattoria* with low-beamed ceilings and dim lights. An atmosphere of genuine antiquity permeates the place, and one is not surprised to learn that Margherita Luti, Raphael's beautiful mistress, once lived there. We were only surprised

Ristorante
Romolo
Rome

to find that Raphael *had* a mistress. Instead of capitalizing on the fact and calling his restaurant the Trattoria Margherita Luti, the owner has shown restraint and named it after the first king of Rome.

Romolo is quiet, discreet, and inviting—just the place to go after the impact of too much Italian traffic. It has long been a favorite with titled Romans and celebrities in the world of art, letters, and science, who seek a quiet spot with fine food rather than a place in the limelight. The restaurant specializes in pure Roman dishes, and we've never tasted better *gnocchi alla romana, carciofi,* or *saltimbocca* than in these time-tinted surroundings. The wine list is on an exalted plane also. On the walls hang any number of good contemporary paintings.

LA CISTERNA—Via della Cisterna 10–14

You must be a dedicated devotee of song and festivity to get the most out of La Cisterna. Half hidden in a side street near Santa Maria in Trastevere, it is an ancient inn dating back three centuries and more. Its walls are gay with frisky frescoes, spoofing Roman history, and its waiters wear the costumes of another age—short breeches, white cotton stockings, colored sashes, and jackets. The food is good, especially the *fettuccine,* the wine hearty and copious, and the menu multilingual, but these hardly count. People come here primarily, we have decided, to burst into joyous song in company with a tenor, a guitarist, and a violinist. We are not quite sure, but we *think* we counted three different string orchestras in the several reverberating rooms that make up La Cisterna. Once we had shed our preposterous pretentions about gastronomy, we had a wonderful time. The tenor even taught us a song. It almost sings itself:

La
Cisterna
Rome

> *Le ragazze*
> *Di Varazze*
> *Vanno pazze*
> *Per il mar;*
> *Ma lo scemo*
> *Di San Remo,*
> *Dice temo*
> *D'affogar!*
> *Gli avvocati*
> *Di Frascati*
> *Son burlati*
> *Dall'amor,*
> *Per la salita*
> *Di Magnanapoli*
> *Van gli scapoli*
> *A far l'amor!*

The tenor told us that this silly ditty has been sung in Roman *trattorie* for decades. The words hardly broaden one's knowledge of Italian folklore. In brief, they reveal that the girls of Varazze are crazy about the sea but the monkey of San Remo is afraid of drowning. Lawyers of Frascati are inept at the art of love while bachelors climb the slopes of Magnanapoli for the purpose of perfecting that art. It's better in Italian!

Getting back to La Cisterna, it has an illustrious background, dating back as far as 1632, according to some accounts. At the turn of our century it was owned by two deformed brothers, Giuseppe and Angelo Guglielmotti, whose food was so good and whose white wine so copious that the gourmets of Rome beat a path to their door. *"Andiamo dai gobbi* (hunchbacks) *della Cisterna"* was their glad cry. In later years the brothers sold out, and La Cisterna's fortunes waned. Now it is back at the peak of popularity, and two clubs of food-and-song enthusiasts meet here regularly.

There you have it—fifteen Roman dining establishments ranging from the austere to the hilarious, all of them insistent upon a fine cuisine. We are sure that you will find some fast favorites among them. But Rome offers many other fine restaurants for the inquiring gastronome. From now on, you're on your own. *Buon appetito!*

Hadrian's Villa–Tivoli

Latium

Chapter 13

LATIUM

HE CITY of the Seven Hills is so overwhelming that it quite over-shadows its surrounding region, Lazio, which is translated as Latium in English. Visitors are so stunned by the impact of Rome that they tend to overlook the blandishments of the outlying regions, with the exception of Tivoli. Latium, as a consequence, may be considered one of the more neglected of the Italian regions, in spite of its multiple charms. We would like to do our bit to correct this situation by resuming the role of travel guide. If Rome is too immense a subject for our limited space, we can still suggest some rewarding trips that may be made in its neglected environs.

Latium can keep the avid sightseer busy for a week or more, especially if he has a penchant for Etruscan tombs, Romanesque churches, Renaissance villas, and Roman remnants. We shall begin in the northern stretches of the region, where Viterbo, Tuscania, and Tarquinia form a trio of highly artistic towns, and work southward. Closer to Rome are three separate one-day excursions—to Tivoli, Frascati, and Ostia. Southward lies Anzio, a peaceful beach resort once again, and Cassino, risen on the rubble of World War II.

Viterbo

THIS ANCIENT walled city of Etruscan origin is particularly worthy of a visit from the not-too-hurried traveler. Located some fifty miles northwest of Rome, it suffered cruelly during the recent war, and many of its fine houses and sturdy ramparts are gone. But a great deal remains, including a wealth of fountains and several medieval streets that rival those of Assisi. Water flows abundantly from the neighboring hills, and makes Viterbo a city of fountains. They are scattered everywhere, some of them imposing, others

modestly hidden on side streets. All
have architectural charm, if not the
dramatic flamboyance of those in
Tivoli.

During the twelfth century, Viterbo was the residence of the popes,
and there are moving reminders of
those days of splendor. Most striking
is the Papal Palace, dating from 1266,
whose lovely roofless loggia surrounds
a fountain, the whole edifice being
supported by a wide arch. Adjoining
stands a ceremonial hall, wherein lies
a story. The pontifical court became
disgusted with Viterbo because of the
rough treatment given it by the populace, and finally left the city. When
the cardinals procrastinated too long
about the election of a new pope, they
found their rations cut very low, and the roof torn off this meeting hall,
where they deliberated. They managed to put up tents against the weather,
but after electing Gregory X, they decided to move to a more hospitable
city, and Viterbo was very much the loser.

Adjoining the palace on the Piazza San Lorenzo is the cathedral, which
also saw dark doings. In 1271, at the altar of this church, Guy de Montfort
murdered Prince Henry of Cornwall as an act of vengeance. Henry's heart
was deposited in a golden cup and dispatched to Westminster Abbey. Those
were violent days!

A walk through Viterbo's medieval streets is highly recommended, especially one along the Via San Pellegrino, which leads to a superb thirteenth-
century piazza of the same name. We also have a particular fondness for
the Piazza del Gesù, the little market square with a shimmering fountain
playing in the midst of an animated open-air vegetable market. A gay little
church serves as a backdrop, making the whole setting a tempting water-
color subject.

Viterbo's accommodations for travelers, alas, do not live up to its other
attractions. There is only one acceptable hotel, an old-timer with rather
hesitant plumbing, but rich in the atmosphere of the past century. Called
the ALBERGO NUOVO ANGELO, it is found on the street of the old clock, at Via
dell'Orologio Vecchio 14. It has no restaurant, but, of course, serves breakfast.
Luckily, a simple good place to dine is not far away, the ANTICO ANGELO.
We found the fare well cooked and plentiful, beginning with a hearty *zuppa*

Loggia of the Papal Palace–Viterbo

Piazza del Gesù–Viterbo

Courtyard, Palazzo del Comune—Viterbo   *Newsstand—Viterbo*

Fontana della Rocca—Viterbo

Church of San Pietro–Tuscania

di verdura, followed by a juicy roast chicken, salad, cheese, and pastry, accompanied by a bottle of the famous Est! Est!! Est!!! wine from Montefiascone. The vineyards that produce this much-publicized nectar are planted on the nearby slopes above Lake Bolseno. This lake is bountiful with fish, by the way, especially with eels, of which Dante spoke with praise. We did not come across them in our epicurean search, however, nor did we find the *mortadella* of pure pork, the dried white chestnuts, or the *tortelli,* an aromatic pasta for which Viterbo is famous. This research calls for a return visit.

Tuscania

A REMOTE settlement in the midst of wide, hilly fields some fifteen miles west of Viterbo, Tuscania would be a trifle dull were it not for its two magnificent Romanesque churches, considered by critics to be among the finest in Italy. Approaching from the hills, you perceive from a distance an old fortified castle and the noble form of the Church of San Pietro, set dramatically on the brink of a cliff, the buttresses of its apse reaching far down the hillside. Begun in the eighth century and finished in the twelfth, the church has a façade of great beauty dominated by a rich marble rose window, surrounded by sculptural details representing winged animals and

Façade of the Church of Santa Maria Maggiore—Tuscania

devils, and flanked by miniature arcades framed in low relief. Beneath them is set a chaste portal, partially inlaid with patterned mosaic. It is an infinitely restful experience to browse in this lovely spot on the hilltop. Visitors are few, and you can enjoy the beauty of San Pietro and its inspiring interior undisturbed except by a few wandering chickens.

Farther down the hill, on the outskirts of the town, stands the Church of Santa Maria Maggiore. Its façade is brightened by three superb doorways, a little gallery, and a bold rose window. But the interior of this church, an authentically ninth-century specimen, makes the deepest impression, from its capitals to its graceful little *baldacchino*. Color is everywhere. Faded murals and time-stained stone blend in a symphony of subtle tone. Both of these churches were once parts of monasteries, and they still enjoy a remote, monastic quiet.

Tuscania offers very little to the traveler in the way of food and lodging, but that should not deter an enthusiast of the beauties of the Romanesque. For him Tuscania is a *must*.

Tarquinia

AN ARCHAEOLOGIST's pulse beats a little faster if you mention this ancient town in the hills above the sea, for Tarquinia occupies an eminent place in Etruscan art and history. Especially is it famous for the Necropoli di Tarquinia, a lengthy avenue of subterranean Etruscan tombs, perhaps the finest in Italy, that stretches across the treeless countryside east of the town. In the company of a competent guide, who will unlock the tombs and illuminate them, you can see superb frescoes, still in fine condition, that give a graphic picture of life as it was lived twenty-five hundred years before our time, and very pleasant it seems. Guides will be found in the National Museum, located in the handsome Gothic Palazzo Vitelleschi in the heart of the town. This museum is filled with treasures from the nearby tombs, exquisite Etruscan vases among them.

Though the student of ancient art may enjoy a field day in Tarquinia, the inquiring gourmet has a rather forlorn time. This trip would be a good time for a roadside picnic.

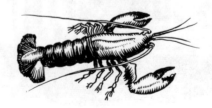

The hillside–Tarquinia

Palazzo Vitelleschi–Tarquinia

Market day—Bracciano, in Latium

The Cascade, Villa d'Este–Tivoli

Tivoli

OF ALL the trips out of Rome, the day-long pilgrimage to Tivoli and Hadrian's Villa is probably the most worthwhile. Almost all informed visitors go by bus or car to this ancient town in the foothills twenty-one miles east of the Eternal City, and return enchanted. Tivoli is truly ancient, preceding the founding of Rome by about four centuries. Later it became famous as a holiday resort for illustrious patricians, among them Cassius, Catullus, and Horace. The town occupies a distinctly barren site, but the miracle of water, supplied by the river Anio, has transformed at least a part of it into one of the world's most celebrated gardens. Although the town and its churches are attractive, despite a bad bombing experience in World War II, the

Sweet Bay

353

Fountains in the Villa d'Este–Tivoli

visiting public clamors to see two specific things—the great cascades at the northern extremity and the famous Villa d'Este.

The river Anio bursts out through a double tunnel to create these startling cascades, and there are many miniature waterfalls as well. A good place to view the spectacle is from the gardens of the Villa Gregoriana, a most dramatic spot. Here also you will find two small Roman temples, the more striking of which is the circular Temple of Vesta, which still retains ten of its Corinthian columns.

The best-known vista in picture-postcard Italy must certainly be the one of the Villa d'Este and its fountains, framed in towering cypresses. The fame of this Renaissance palace owes more to its surroundings than to its festive, exuberant mural painters, who ran riot through its expansive rooms. The building was once a Benedictine convent, but was remodeled in 1549 for Cardinal Ippolito d'Este, son of the youthful Alfonso I and Lucrezia Borgia. Although large, the building is not remarkable. But the terraced gardens, alive with gushing fountains, waterfalls, and fish ponds are something you will never forget. They are in fine running condition now, although in the past they have frequently suffered from neglect. Every conceivable type of fountain is here, some architectural, some sculptural, others consisting of vertical jets. The tourists roam delighted through the many levels of the garden, squandering as many feet of camera film as they do in the Forum.

Considerable climbing is required of the fountain-seeker in the Villa d'Este, endowing him with a vigorous appetite at the end of the visit. Luckily, Tivoli affords places where it can be assuaged. The best, we think, is the TAVERNA DELLA ROCCA, Viale Trieste 11, a better-than-average restaurant built into the walls of the old castle. The atmosphere is pleasant and, most important, it is cool inside on a hot day. The prices are very fair, and the cooking good, especially the *cannelloni*. They were so good that we asked to visit the great vaulted kitchen, where we watched plump Italian women rolling the *cannelloni* around a mixture of ground veal, chicken, and *prosciutto,* seasoned with Parmesan cheese and a dash of nutmeg. The fresh tomato sauce that accompanied them contained chopped chicken livers, and a layer of Parmesan mixed with béchamel sauce topped this memorable dish.

There isn't, however, much of a view from the Taverna della Rocca within its castle walls. Those who wish to dine with a panorama will find felicity and a superb view of the great cascades at the RISTORANTE SIBILLA, located just above the Temple of Vesta. Though the food can't quite equal the scenery from its open terrace, which would really be asking too much, it is more than creditable.

Hadrian's Villa

THE SPLENDOR that was Rome is dramatically illustrated in the ruins of the Villa Adriana, the astounding country residence of the Emperor Hadrian. You reach it by a little side road in the plain, just below Tivoli. This largest and most sumptuous of ancient Roman villas was built as the imperial palace by the much-traveled Hadrian, who had original architectural ideas of his own. Treating his estate as an enormous plaything, he reproduced around his palace a collection of famous buildings that had pleased him, particularly those he had seen in Greece and Egypt. There is a Greek open-air theater as you enter the estate. After walking up an avenue of tall, solemn cypresses, you come to an immense brick wall, the Stoa Poikile, taken from the celebrated portico in Athens that captured Hadrian's fancy. He built a copy of the Academy near Athens where Plato taught, and a replica of the Tower of Timon, which he admired. But this is only the beginning. There were once a stadium and a natatorium, a huge library, a maritime theater with a circular moat (now restored and charming still), and more minor temples than you can count in a day's exploring. All of these were furnished with treasures that Hadrian brought from his immense empire. Fortunately many of them have now found their way into museums. Hadrian's Villa remains an eloquent museum in itself, a quiet spot, never overcrowded, and strangely restful. Here is something that couldn't be achieved today, not even in Texas!

Taverna
della
Rocca
Tivoli

The large and small baths, Hadrian's Villa–Tivoli

Stoa Poikile, Hadrian's Villa–Tivoli

Though most excursionists solve their noonday lunch problem in Tivoli, those who remain overtime at Hadrian's Villa will find a perfectly acceptable little restaurant under the trees, directly opposite the entrance to the estate. We've forgotten its name (we think is was called the Adriano), but we have had a good repast there on two occasions. In the warm weather, you dine in the garden under colored umbrellas. The wine from Frascati is tempting, and so are the *antipasti,* the starchy essentials such as *risotto* and *tagliatelle,* and the inevitable veal. The place is simple and the food honest.

Frascati

IF YOU weary of metropolitan Rome and seek a breath of country air, a one-day trip to the Castelli Romani will be most rewarding. These "castles" southeast of Rome are not castles at all, but a series of towns on the slopes of the volcanic Alban hills. Among the places to see are Albano, Grottaferrata, Genzano, and Castel Gandolfo, site of the Pope's summer palace. Two pleasant volcanic lakes are thrown into the bargain. One town in the Castelli Romani stands out above all the others, in our estimation, and that is Frascati. It occupies a magnificent woodland site, just below the ancient city of Tusculum, birthplace of Cato. During the Renaissance, Frascati

Marjoram

bloomed as the most prosperous and aristocratic of the Castelli Romani. Noble Roman families built fabulous villas here during the sixteenth century, many of which have survived the wars.

Prominent among them is the imposing Villa Aldobrandini, built in 1603 for Cardinal Pietro Aldobrandini, nephew of Pope Clement VIII. Our photograph shows the villa as seen from its entrance way, but it gives not a glimpse of its beautiful fountains framed against rich Renaissance walls. The gardens range over the hillside, and are a joy to visit. A custodian is usually at hand to show you about the palace (a more accurate word than villa) and its gardens. During the last war, the Villa Aldobrandini served as the headquarters of Field Marshal Kesselring, and while it was the target of considerable bombing, escaped most of it. The town of Frascati, however, suffered a great deal of damage. The noble Villa Torlonia nearby, for example, was completely destroyed, although its formal gardens *à la française* and fountains and grottoes still remain. Could it be that the Allied fliers were instructed to bomb the wrong villa?

Another estate of importance is the Villa Falconieri, built in 1565. In its gardens lies a miniature lake surrounded by ancient cypresses and a loggia designed by Vignola. The Villa Mondragone is now a Jesuit college and the Villa Lancellotti has a noble park. Between them they will give the intrepid villa enthusiast quite a workout.

Frascati's principal contribution to gastronomy is, of course, its white wine, the noblest of the vintages of the Castelli Romani. Though poor travelers, they boast a fresh and fruity aroma. If they cannot aspire to greatness, they are nevertheless palatable when served cool with a Roman luncheon. Other good wines from these hills are called Marino and Colli Albani.

To make your visit to Frascati a complete success, you may dine at a commendable restaurant right on the Piazza Roma, near the famous hillside villas. It is called the SPARTACO, a large and bustling establishment well equipped to care for hungry out-of-towners. We have enjoyed some delicious *cannelloni* here, followed by a *pollo alla diavola* that also deserves praise. The cheese and pastry were on a high plane, and the wine was what you would expect in Frascati—cool, clear, and palatable.

Ristorante
Spartaco
Frascati

The Appian Way

THERE COULDN'T be a more pleasant way to spend a sunny day in the Roman countryside than by dedicating it to a leisurely visit to the first few miles of the Via Appia Antica, the most important of the consular roads that fanned out from ancient Rome. Beginning at the towering Porta San Sebastiano at the southern edge of the city walls, the Via Appia runs in a straight path

The Appian Way

Via Appia
Antica

through peaceful lands dotted with umbrella pines and towering thin cypresses. The road is just wide enough for two vehicles to pass, and most of it is now covered with modern asphalt. But here and there the ancient Roman blocks of basalt lava still appear, rounded with age, bringing your car abruptly to a pedestrian pace. This is surely one of the most historic stretches of road in the world, vivid with mementos of the past, especially Roman monuments, tombs, and early Christian catacombs. The Romans of today have an enormous affection for their narrow Via Appia, especially on a Sunday, when it is thronged with visitors. They bring their picnic lunches and *fiaschi* of wine, wander around the old churchyards and sculptured tombstones, and enjoy a rustic holiday without cluttering the place with papers. The first building they encounter is probably the best known to the world—the little church of "Domine, Quo Vadis." This is said to be constructed on the exact spot where Peter saw the vision of his crucified Lord, and then returned shamefaced to Rome to face his own fate. Close by are the most celebrated of all the Christian catacombs, named for Saint Callisto. You can wander through vast caverns, accompanied by friars who illuminate points of interest along the way. If subterranean labyrinths intrigue you, here is a place to satisfy your curiosity once and for all! Farther along the road stands the immense round tomb of

Assembled fragments on the Appian Way   *Tomb of Cecilia Metella on the Appian Way*

Cecilia Metella, opposite which you will find the churchyard of San Nicola, sheltered by a heavy concentration of umbrella pines, an ideal place for an open-air collation.

A picnic is not the only solution for your epicurean problems, however. Nearby you will find a most commendable country inn, named SAN CALLISTO, enjoying a fine view of Cecilia Metella's tomb, with the Alban hills serving as a backdrop. It is necessarily a "tourist" restaurant, but a good one, with several praiseworthy specialties, among them some admirable *cannelloni*. We can recommend a *pollo alla Nerone* and a *gratinata Appia* without hesitation, and the wine from the neighboring hills is, as usual, cool and refreshing.

Ristorante San Callisto
Via Appia

After a good lunch, many more sights lie in store as you progress south-ward on the Appian Way—tombs of famous Romans, Seneca among them, ruins of temples, circuses, and pyramids, all rescued after centuries of neglect. Finally, you reach the point where the road joins the new Appian Way and continues on to the far-off port of Brindisi. Now is the time to turn back to Rome. Given the right kind of weather, this excursion should be a highlight in your Roman holiday.

The Italian State Tourist Office has prepared a charming illustrated brochure on the Via Appia, enlivened with water-colors and a map in per-spective. Written in good English, it costs nothing, and will prove to be a most informative companion.

Fortress in Ostia   *Ruins of the aqueduct of Claudius*

Ostia

ENTHUSIASTS OF Roman antiquities will find something different in the excavations made during recent years in Ostia Antica, the first Roman seaport colony, located about eighteen miles southeast of the capital. Once a thriving city of perhaps a hundred thousand inhabitants, it suffered a total eclipse in the fifth century, when, deserted by its inhabitants, it became a ghost town, a wilderness of shapeless ruins of brick and stone, covered with the dust and silt of time.

Archaeologists began to take an interest in Ostia Antica during the nineteenth century, and now the excavations are almost complete. They reveal every detail of a Roman city that, in some ways, is almost as vivid as Pompeii. You can wander through its stone streets, visit its forum, baths, amphitheaters, and temples, and see hardly another human being in the process. It's still a ghost town, an enormous one, and deserves more visitors than it now enjoys.

If you would like to combine a dip in the sea with your archaeological wanderings, the seaside resort of Ostia, or Lido di Roma, is only a little farther. It is large, gay, modernistic, and rather garish. The best bathing is found at the southern end of the settlement, near the pine woods of Castelfusano.

Other attractive beach resorts adorn Latium, many of them enjoying a more discriminating clientele than one finds in the Lido di Roma. One of these is Santa Marinella, a gay little place with good hostelries and clean, white sands, about forty miles northwest of Rome. There is a congenial summer hotel here, called LA SCOGLIERA, which you will doubtless like—not expensive, and well situated on the shore.

Southward from Rome, the seeker for summer beach resorts will come upon Anzio and Nettuno, two reconstructed pleasure resorts that were anything but pleasurable during the early months of 1944, when the Anzio salient was invaded by Allied troops from the Fifth Army. A permanent American cemetery and two British military burial grounds remain as grim reminders of the heavy toll in human lives which that invasion exacted. The hotels of these twin resorts have been entirely rebuilt and the scars of war have all but disappeared. The CORSARO is the best hotel in Anzio, while the ASTURA in Nettuno is very good indeed. Travelers passing through will find that the RISTORANTE TURCOTTO in Anzio provides a praiseworthy seafood luncheon. It is an enchanting spot at the water's edge, said to be built on the foundations of Nero's villa.

Rome to Naples

MOTORISTS DRIVING between Rome and Naples find that it is an easy day's run, allowing ample time for a satisfying luncheon along the way. Your road, the new Appian Way, leads through the Alban hills and then across the Pontine marshes, those malaria-infested swamps that were reclaimed for agriculture during the heyday of Mussolini, surely one of his more civilized accomplishments, along with getting the trains to run on time. The road touches the shore at Terracina, a natural stopping place for hungry travelers. The competition among the rival restaurants was keen when we last stopped there. We were buttonholed by two aggressive headwaiters, each imploring us to try his *zuppa di pesce*. Luckily, we happened to choose the right place, the RISTORANTE AGOSTINO A MARE, with an outdoor terrace overlooking the sea. The fruit of the sea dominates the menu, with *antipasti* made of fish, and a *frittura* of a dozen unusual denizens of the deep. But there were bountiful platters of *tagliatelle* and *gnocchi alla romana* in the offing too, as well as the ubiquitous veal cutlet.

Ristorante Agostino a Mare
Terracina

Another good spot for luncheon is in the coastal town of Formia, a bit farther along the road to Naples. As you drive, keep your eye open for a tall, vine-grown Roman monument by the roadside. It is the tomb of Cicero, and well worth a passing snapshot. In Formia, the GRAND HOTEL MIRAMARE has been greeting passing gastronomes for decades. It has attractive gardens where you may dine with a view of the sea, and the food and service are good. So is the wine, the Vino Formiano, which comes from the neighboring hills.

There is a good alternate road between Rome and Naples, the inland highway Number 6. Motorists who choose this route will pass through an epic battlefield of World War II, the completely devastated city of Cassino. The bombing of the Benedictine Abbey of Montecassino, towering on a peak above the doomed city, was one of the most regrettable tragedies of the Italian campaign. When it was all over, the task of restoring the immense ruin appeared hopeless. The tireless Italians don't quail before hard work, however, especially if it involves stone, a material they have long since mastered. Without hesitation, the work of rehabilitation was begun. Though still far from finished, before long the greatest abbey in Italy, founded by Saint Benedict in the year 529, will stand triumphantly restored. It may be visited now, and numerous cars and buses negotiate the hairpin turns daily. The reminiscent soldier and the casual tourist can join in admiring the work in progress, and the incomparable view.

The city of Cassino has been leveled with bulldozers and partially rebuilt with new, modern buildings. Travelers in search of a midday meal will be well accommodated in a tidy little restaurant called DA MARIO, on the Corso Repubblica, at number 104.

Thus, you have the highlights of Latium, with a few conspicuous exceptions. If we had unlimited space we would delve into the beauties of the huge Palazzo Farnese at Caprarola and the hillside convent in Subiaco, also founded by Saint Benedict, as well as several villas in the Castelli Romani. But these will have to wait for another day.

Lake of Campotosto

Abruzzi e Molise

Chapter 14

ABRUZZI
E MOLISE

THERE IS a startling difference between Latium, rich in reminders of the Roman Empire, and its eastern neighbor, a stern, grandiose, and rather backward region, made up of the two provinces of Abruzzi and Molise. Gone is the gentleness of the Roman countryside and its architectural splendor. Instead there are mountains, endless magnificent Apennines, dotted with lakes and laced with winding rivers. Scenically, this region represents one of the most imposing parts of Italy. Economically, it has less to offer. The Abruzzi region is a rather austere country cousin of Latium, plagued by a rugged climate and menaced by earthquakes. Its villages are primitive, its industries few. Farmers work on such a small scale that they harvest the ripened wheat with sickles, as our photograph shows. Sheep grazing is another mainstay of life in Abruzzi. The flocks that roam the hills provide wool for the homespun garments of the peasants and meat for their hearty mutton stews. As it happens, the native costumes found in these forbidding hills are among the most picturesque in Italy. The mutton stews, however, do not occupy a prominent place in Italian gastronomy.

It is not difficult to see why Abruzzi is one of the least-visited regions in Italy. And yet, the comparatively rare travelers who take the trouble to explore it come away well recompensed. It appeals, first of all, to people who like mountains, inspiring scenery, and skiing. The great Apennine range, those mountains which, unlike the Alps, Italy shares with no other country, reaches its climax in Abruzzi. Here is the imposing Majella series of hills, culminating in the rocky, forbidding Gran Sasso d'Italia, whose snow-capped Corno Grande rises 9,500 feet and more. Pleasant resort towns nestle in these remote hills, cool in summer, and equipped with the tows and refuges that the winter ski enthusiasts demand.

The mountains crowd close to the Adriatic shore, but they at least concede a narrow and fertile coastline, populated by pine groves, white sandy beaches, and cheerful little watering places that enjoy a brisk summer popularity. Pescara is the only significant seaport in Abruzzi, and its importance has shrunk greatly since the Roman days, when it was the great port of trade with the Orient. Today it has become a completely modern city, apparently forgetful of its past, but very proud to be the birthplace of Gabriele d'Annunzio. Attractive resort hotels stand along the two-mile beach promenade in Pescara, among them an ever-reliable JOLLY HOTEL and the GRAND HOTEL. It is a cheerful, clean city, colorful in places, especially along its docks, crowded

with multicolored fishing vessels. You will find Pescara a perfectly good place for an overnight stop.

Since you probably won't be stopping long in Abruzzi, we won't delve too deeply into the subject of regional wines and food. The wines, in fact, can be dismissed as inconsequential but quite drinkable red *ordinaires,* and a few *moscato* dessert wines. There is, however, one outstanding dish that

Wheat fields in Abruzzi

Civitaterengo, a hillside village in Abruzzi

Assembling the grain–Poggio Picenze, in Abruzzi

merits your attention, *maccheroni alla chitarra,* an egg-rich, homemade pasta. A thin layer of it is laid on a wooden frame strung, in one direction only, with closely packed steel wires and a rolling pin is passed over the pasta, cutting it into thin strips. The apparatus bears only the smallest resemblance to a guitar, or *chitarra,* but this fact makes little difference. *Maccheroni alla chitarra* is what you must order if you are to taste the outstanding dish of Abruzzi. It is served like spaghetti, with a savory sauce made of tomatoes, mushrooms, chicken livers, and chopped meat. Not an extraordinary dish, it is nevertheless appetizing, filling, and fragrant. You may also encounter in your travels through the hills a delicate *capretto al forno* (roast kid) or *porchetta,* a suckling pig with all the bones removed, roasted toast-brown, and served with aromatic herbs. In Pescara you will come upon a commendable *brodetto,* a fish stew made from the fine catch of the Adriatic and, in L'Aquila, you may have the good fortune to find *salsiccia di fegato,* a well-spiced liver sausage dressed up with pine nuts. These are some of the minor highlights in a rather low-key gastronomical picture.

For those who have an interest in old Italian towns and architecture, however, there are a few treats ahead. One of them is L'Aquila, capital of

Dozing at the flour mill

Abruzzi. Another is Sulmona, birthplace of Ovid and the setting of several architectural gems. Finally, two exquisite medieval structures sit in solitary splendor in the Abruzzi countryside: the beautiful Abbey of San Clemente near Torre dei Passeri and the lonely Basilica of San Giovanni in Venere, overlooking the Adriatic on a ridge high above the town of Fossacesia. See these and you have seen four of the best man-made curiosities in the province.

L'Aquila

THE PRINCIPAL city of Abruzzi occupies a dramatic site, surrounded by snow-capped mountains. Its name, of course, means The Eagle. Founded by Frederick II in 1240, it is not ancient as Italian cities go. This city of some sixty thousand inhabitants has a comfortable hotel and a good restaurant, in addition to a number of worthwhile places to visit. But tourists are very rare. A day spent here can be well invested, especially if you shop around for Aquila lace and hand-hammered copper.

The architectural highlight of the city is the extraordinary fourteenth-century Basilica of Santa Maria di Collemaggio on the southern outskirts. The façade is the thing. Unique in all Christendom, it is simply a huge patterned rectangle of stone, punctuated with three Romanesque-Gothic doorways and three rose windows. The rest of the façade is an immense

Basilica of San Bernardino–L'Aquila   *Fountain of the 99 Spouts–L'Aquila*

checkerboard of crosses achieved in pink and white marble, and it must have been a humdinger when the stone was bright red and unfaded. Even now, when it has turned a quiet pink, the effect is alarming.

A towering Renaissance façade graces the Basilica of San Bernardino, set at the top of a ramp of steps in the heart of the city. Built in 1527, it seems rather coarse and disjointed. The church contains a tomb of great beauty, however. It serves as the final resting place for San Bernardino of Siena and was carved by the greatest of local sculptors, Silvestro dell'Aquila. If you look carefully, you will also find a terra cotta by Andrea della Robbia.

In another corner of the city stands an enormous pentagon fortress, buttressed with diamond-shaped outposts. It was built by the Spaniards in 1535. Severe and forbidding behind its moat, the *castello* now serves the docile role of the National Museum of Abruzzi. From this point you have an inspiring view of the Gran Sasso.

Another curiosity is the Fountain of the Ninety-Nine Spouts, located near the railway station. A high checkerboard wall forms three sides of a courtyard. Around the base of the wall are spaced ninety-nine sculptured heads, each different and each spouting cold clear mountain water. Even the Villa d'Este doesn't have a fountain like this.

Not far from here, on a narrow dirt road branching off from the Via XX Settembre, we found a deserted little chapel that has far more photogenic

371

Church of the Madonna degli Angeli–L'Aquila

Grande
Albergo
l'Aquila

L'Aquila

appeal than the larger churches. We have chosen it as our favorite picture of L'Aquila—the sun-baked façade of the Church of the Madonna degli Angeli. Its flawless doorway and rose window, set against the flat, golden stone, are details we'll never forget.

The GRANDE ALBERGO in L'Aquila is an adequate hostelry for an overnight stop, although we thought it failed to live up to its imposing appearance. There is, however, an English-speaking porter here who makes up for everything. He speaks the pure tongue of Detroit, where he spent many years. Was he happier in America, we asked. "I'll say! I sure do miss my good old U.S.A."

The best place to try the famous *maccheroni alla chitarra,* we think, is the RISTORANTE TRE MARIE, on the street of the same name. It is a cheerful, well-furnished little place in the heart of the city. We recall a very acceptable *costoletta alla milanese,* salad, and cheese, in addition to the much-publicized *maccheroni.*

Ristorante
TreMarie

L'Aquila

Winter-sports enthusiasts often use L'Aquila as a base to visit the skiing slopes of the Gran Sasso. First by car and then by cableway, they are hoisted to Campo Imperatore, a winter resort that has a certain place in recent history. It was in the Hotel Campo Imperatore that Benito Mussolini was held prisoner by the Badoglio government only to be suddenly liberated by a daring kidnapping raid engineered by the Germans.

372

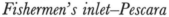

Fishermen's inlet—Pescara   *Farmlands on the Adriatic shore*

Sulmona

OCCUPYING AN important crossroads on the highway from Rome to the Adriatic, Sulmona is a town of real architectural interest. It also takes pride in being the native city of Ovid, who was born here in 43 B.C. The ruins of the great poet's villa may still be visited on the outskirts of the city. But they are much less impressive than the legacy that the Renaissance has left, particularly the Palazzo dell'Annunziata, adjoining the town's Baroque cathedral. This Gothic-Renaissance palace would seem rather severe were it not for a grouping of three exquisite Renaissance doorways, and three ornamental windows that are just as fine. There are sculptured figures on pedestals, too, making the façade sparkle with stone carving. Inside you will find a small museum with antiquities from the region. About the town are other Renaissance doorways, windows, fountains, and gateways, enough to fill handily an hour's stroll.

Coriander

In case you wish to make Sulmona an overnight stop, you will find here a reliable JOLLY HOTEL, and it's located on the Via Roosevelt!

373

The bronze door–Abbey of San Clemente   *The porch–Abbey of San Clemente*

The Abbey of San Clemente

IF YOU have a fondness for forgotten abbeys, you will want to search out a lovely one in the heart of Abruzzi, near the town of Torre dei Passeri. Inquire of the local policeman and he will send you to the outlying village of Casauria where you find an iron grill, behind which looms the graceful profile of the abbey. Pull the bell and a custodian will appear and, for a very modest fee, give you the guided tour in flowing Italian.

The abbey is very ancient, having been founded in the ninth century and rebuilt by the Cistercians in 1176. Its superb triple-arched entrance porch shelters a bronze door framed in richly carved stone. The interior is sober, simple, and absolutely beautiful. The altar, sheltered by a noble *baldacchino*, is a shining example of medieval stone carving. So is the pulpit, supported by four squat columns, and the huge paschal candlestick from the thirteenth century that stands opposite.

After the guide has finished his speech, it is an inspiring experience to wander at will through this silent edifice and its gardens, studded with mossy Roman stones. We found this abbey to be the high peak of our travels in Abruzzi, the only spectacle that can rival its mountain scenery.

374

Interior of the Abbey of San Clemente

The apse–Basilica of San Giovanni   *Basilica of San Giovanni*

The Basilica of San Giovanni

THE GREAT Basilica of San Giovanni in Venere occupies a very different site, not behind cypresses and iron grills at all, but on the edge of a windswept, barren promontory near the Adriatic shore. Motorists driving along the coastal road near Fossacesia will see its gaunt form on the horizon. We advise them to make the detour by climbing a short winding side road for about a mile and a half to the promontory's summit. They will come upon a solid Romanesque structure with a fine rounded apse. This eighth-century basilica was built on the ruins of an ancient Temple of Venus. The main doorway is flanked by twelfth-century sculpture in rather bedraggled condition, but the interior is in splendid shape, especially the crypt. It is solemn and primitive, adorned with a few well-restored frescoes. There is an ancient cloister, overgrown with grass, and the view of the vine-clad lowlands is superb. This off-the-beaten-track excursion is a brief and rewarding one, especially to vacationing architects.

Abruzzi, one must admit, has less to offer the traveler than most of the Italian regions. It is not surprising that the guided tours skip it. But the visitor who has seen the obvious things in Italy and has a penchant for exploring the more obscure will find it fertile territory.

Alberobello

Apulia

Chapter 15

APULIA

T HE HEEL of the Italian boot, and a part of the ankle as well, is a strip of often barren land that extends southeastward between the Adriatic and Ionian seas. Called Apulia (*Puglie* by the Italians and *les Pouilles* by the French), it is one of the most contradictory of all the Italian regions, alternately desolate and inviting, squalid and scrubbed, dull and highly picturesque. Apulia is one of the least visited regions of Italy. Transportation isn't up to the usual standard, as a consequence, but prices are lower. Tourists are a curiosity, and they must accept the fate of being stared at and surrounded by clusters of gaping children much of the time. This region is one of the poorer parts of the peninsula, a fact that is apparent in the crowded seaports and bleak, dusty inland villages.

Some parts of Apulia are especially familiar to the Allied fliers of World War II. The flat wheatlands around Foggia were then converted into a huge complex of satellite airfields. Bari and Foggia acted as hosts to a heavy population of young airmen throughout the Italian campaign. The author came to know Apulia rather well at that time, spending close to a year there, much of it in San Severo, an unlovely city, alas, to which I wouldn't dream of sending you. But I traveled a lot also, by jeep, and was able to observe that a great deal of beauty was strewn through this severe countryside. It will take the form of a hilltop castle or a fortified village or a Romanesque church with exquisite bronze doors. The shore is beguiling in spots, though the bathing doesn't amount to much. The seaports and fishing villages have a haunting Eastern atmosphere, clusters of rectangular white houses sparkling in the intense sunlight.

This chapter is designed for the more venturesome, for those who like to go to the very end of the road, to discover what lies really far off the beaten track. We think that the single village of Alberobello, a phenomenal cluster of cone-roofed *trulli,* will recompense the bolder visitor completely, but he will find a wealth of other things as well. A few years ago, the problem of hotel accommodations would have been a thorny one. Today, however, a chain of ever-faithful Jolly Hotels spreads through Apulia, assuring you of clean, comfortable accommodations and reliable meals at the end of every day's travel. They are located in Barletta, Trani, Gioia del Colle, Brindisi, Lecce, and Gallipoli.

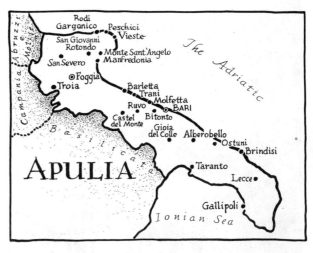

The exacting epicure will not find total felicity in Apulia, although the Jolly establishments will take adequate care of him. This is not one of the great gastronomic regions of Italy, despite its plenitude of sea food and prolific agricultural output. It is wheat country first of all, but an abundance of fruit, olives, nuts, melons, figs, and grapes also flourishes in this unpromising soil. The Adriatic is generous with piscatorial treasure, including fine black mussels, which the Apulians like to dip in batter and fry in olive oil. Some of the finest oyster beds in Italy lie in this region, near the naval base of Taranto.

Certain Apulian culinary specialties sound intriguing indeed, even though your chances of tasting them in a restaurant are a trifle slim. One of the best is *melanzane ripiene,* an eggplant stuffed with its own flesh, mixed with olives, onions, capers, tomatoes, anchovies, and bread crumbs. It is served with a meat sauce and makes a meal in itself. *Panzarotti* are little ravioli-like squares of fried pasta filled with *mozzarella* cheese, egg, diced ham, and onion. The Apulians love to stuff pasta with good things. Take *calzone,* for example: pasta turnovers containing lightly fried onions, olives, *mozzarella* cheese, capers, anchovies, baby mackerel, raisins, and beaten yolk of egg. *Focaccia piena* is a homemade tart consisting of two layers of pastry between which repose black olives, onions, capers, chicory, and anchovies, a favored dish for Good Friday.

Concentrated tomato paste is a basic ingredient of Apulian cooking, just as it is in neighboring Campania. The housewife prepares her own simply by making a fine pulp of her tomatoes and then spreading it out in flat tins, which she places in the sun. Evaporation does the rest.

Though Apulian wines are not well known outside their native habitat, you will be able to taste them if you decide to make a trip to this easternmost corner of Italy. The best known is the wine of San Severo, produced on the gentle slopes north of Foggia. It is a pale, limpid white wine, with

Willing models—Mattinata   *Graveyard gate—Foggia*

enough character to make it a fit companion for Adriatic fish and oysters. A commendable muscat is produced near the seaport of Trani. Moscato di Trani is sweet, golden, and rather heavy, running between seventeen and twenty degrees alcoholic content. The picturesque hills near Alberobello, the town we are so determined to show you, yield a wine called Verdeca, greatly in demand for the production of vermouth. You will also find a dry red wine known as Apuliano, a sweet white known as Orvino, and a sweet red called Aleatico. Finally, there is a wine in Lecce called Five Roses, which would seem to go the American distillers one better.

Apulia is not an obvious choice for people who are on a first trip to Italy, or even a second. But there is enough beauty and adventure here, admittedly interspersed with drabness, to make it fascinating to the seasoned traveler. Such a trip requires careful planning, with a good deal of weeding out. We have several suggestions about what to see and what to pass through rapidly. The big cities, with the exception of Lecce, have little to offer except good hotel accommodations. Bari, Brindisi, Foggia, and Taranto receive only brief mention in the paragraphs that follow, but near each of them is something of extraordinary interest.

We shall begin our recommendations near Foggia, and work toward the southeast. They sift down to four specific suggestions: (1) a motor trip to the Gargano promontory, (2) a guided tour of the notable Romanesque cathedrals of Apulia, (3) an expedition to the *trulli* country punctuated with cone-shaped roofs, and to its center, Alberobello, one of the most picturesque villages in Italy, and (4) a trip down the Adriatic coast to Lecce and across to Gallipoli, the jumping-off place. See these and you have seen the best of Apulia. It might take three or four days, but they will be well spent.

Foggia

THIS LARGE, modern city is an important grain and cattle center in the heart of Apulia's vast Capitanata wheat fields. An earthquake laid much of the city low in 1731, and only a few interesting bits of architecture remain, among them a fine Renaissance archway leading to—the graveyard. Thousands of wartime fliers know Foggia well, if not affectionately. We recommend it principally as a starting point for a trip to Gargano. There is a comfortable hostelry in Foggia, the HOTEL SARTI, Via Monfalcone 1. We recall a good dinner here with *prosciutto* and figs, *tortino con carciofi,* salad, cheese, and coffee, and a worthy bottle of San Severo white wine. The management of the Hotel Sarti is quite accustomed to Anglo-Saxon guests—the place had practically nothing else during the war years.

Hotel
Sarti
Foggia

THE GARGANO PROMONTORY

IF YOU make this highly recommended one-day motor trip, you will cover what very few people see in Italy, the mountainous "spur" of the Italian boot. It is an adventurous trip, over rugged hills, and requires plenty of time. The going is slow, so make an early start from Foggia. Your road passes through flat grain country, by squatty whitewashed farmhouses dwarfed by enormous stacks of wheat. On your right, if you look closely, you will see the little Romanesque chapel dedicated to San Leonardo. Twenty-three miles beyond Foggia is the town of Manfredonia, named for its founder, Manfred, son of Frederick II. There is a bathing beach of sorts beckoning here, but it would be wise to resist all temptation and follow the road that branches steeply to the left and climbs to the ancient city of Monte San Angelo, occupying a dramatic site half a mile above the sea. Here you may visit the subterranean sanctuary of San Michele, built into a troglodytic cavern and marked by an octagonal belfry. San Michele is said to have consecrated it himself in 490 A.D. and it was long a stopping place for crusaders on their way to Palestine.

Your road next climbs through the Foresta d'Umbra, a dark, cool, and mysterious forest of great beauty–beech trees, oaks, pines, firs, hemlocks, and yews, all very ancient, stretching for miles. In the middle of this arboreal splendor stands a summer hotel, the RIFUGIO FORESTA D'UMBRA, which should

Gargano Peninsula—the southern shore

Chapel of San Leonardo, near Foggia

appeal to seekers of solitude and shade. Ancient gnarled olive trees begin to line the road as you continue northward, until finally you glimpse the sea again, brilliant blue-green through the foliage. Now you come to a trio of remote and primitive fishing villages—Rodi Garganico, Peschici, and Vieste. Each is a thick cluster of interlocking, whitewashed cubes clinging to a cliff at the water's edge. Fishing boats are pulled up on each sandy beach. The odor of highly spiced cooking wafts through the air. The atmosphere is totally Eastern. You might be on a Dodecanese island. On the far outskirts of Vieste's harbor rises a weird contraption of wired wooden poles extending over the water and giving the deep-sea fisherman a favored perch.

Vieste marks the eastern extremity of the Monte Gargano circuit. The return road leads through more hills back to Manfredonia, where the thirsty traveler may stop at a beach café and enjoy a cool drink while reflecting upon the amount of beauty he has crowded into a single day.

The tour we have sketched out might include an interesting detour to the western part of the promontory and the town of San Giovanni Rotondo, where the celebrated monk, Padre Pio, is established. To this hill town near  the forest of Umbra come countless Catholic pilgrims to confess to the man they consider a living saint. Padre Pio carries the marks of the stigmata, received shortly after becoming a monk more than forty years ago. Since that time he has been credited with many miracles and cures. A new hospital has been built in San Giovanni Rotondo with funds contributed by faithful believers, and there is a good hotel, the ALBERGO SANTA MARIA DELLE GRAZIE, for those who choose to linger.

Peschici

Vieste

The bronze colossus–Barletta   *The seaside cathedral–Trani*

Barletta

THE SUN-BAKED coastal city of Barletta might serve as an overnight stop after you have made the Gargano circuit. A reliable JOLLY HOTEL will be found near the cathedral, a golden-yellow structure with a fine tower. Barletta has slight fascination as a city but it does boast a startling curiosity, a unique bronze colossus, sixteen feet high. The monument stands in front of the Church of San Sepulcro, and represents a skirted statue of a Roman emperor. It was cast in the fourth century. The identity of this proud personage is uncertain, though some students think he is Valentinian. At all events, the stern Roman has now been converted to Christianity. Into his upraised hand a thin metal cross has been carefully inserted.

THE ROMANESQUE CHURCHES OF APULIA

Trani

WITH THIS ancient seaport southeast of Barletta, we introduce the tour of the notable Romanesque churches of Apulia, with the famous Castel del Monte thrown in. With the exeption of the one at Troia, some fifteen miles

The inner harbor–Trani

southwest of Foggia, all of the churches are fairly close to Trani (which also has a JOLLY HOTEL).

Trani's cathedral rises on a dramatic spot directly at the entrance of the harbor. We had seen pictures of it, dominated by an immense campanile, and were startled by our first glimpse. The tower has disappeared, and its emplacement is now surrounded by a high construction fence. We hope that this arrangement means it will soon be rebuilt. The rest of the cathedral, begun in 1094, appears to be fairly intact, as are the famous bronze doors designed by Barisano in 1160. They are richly decorated, and rank among the finest in Italy.

Troia

SUPERB BRONZE portals also distinguish the cathedral in Troia, a small town in the hills overlooking the flat plains of the Tavoliere. These doors, designed in 1127 by Oderisio da Benevento, have a strong Byzantine flavor, and are covered with sculptured panels in high relief. A squirming bronze dragon holds the knocker in his mouth. The facade of the cathedral is rather ornate, particularly the rose window. The interior, however, is sober and fine, and is embellished by an exquisite marble pulpit.

Ruvo di Puglia

In this small inland town, about twelve miles south of Trani, you will find a thirteenth-century cathedral with a most unusual façade. On the street level is a trio of graceful Romanesque doorways, above which towers a lofty expanse of unadorned, time-stained stone, surmounted by a rose window of excellent design. Ruvo di Puglia was celebrated long ago for its antique vases, manufactured centuries before the time of Christ. A memorable collection of them, said to contain over seventeen hundred items, may be seen here in the Palazzo Iatta, a private museum. There are some splendid vases from ancient Greece as well.

Bitonto

This agricultural town on the road to Bari boasts a very pure Romanesque church. It is the most complete of the religious buildings in Apulia. The proportions of its façade are subtle, and its richly detailed doorway is a thing of great beauty. The interior is harmonious, pervaded by an austere mysticism.

Castel del Monte

As a relief from so many churches, this Apulian neighborhood offers one of the best examples of civil architecture from the Middle Ages, the extraordinary Castel del Monte, a fortified castle set on a rather desolate hilltop. It can be seen for miles around, rising out of the Murge di Minervino, some

CASTEL DEL MONTE

The waterfront—Molfetta

eight miles west of the little town of Ruvo di Puglia. It was built in 1240 by Frederick II, King of Sicily, who lived in it frequently, apparently liking its lofty isolation. The castle is octagonal, built round an eight-sided courtyard. Each of its eight corners is accented by a sturdy smaller tower, giving it a most bellicose appearance. Its walls are eight feet thick and some ninety feet high. Visitors may climb to the rooftop and admire the surrounding countryside. They may also visit the interior—baronial stairways, halls, and furnished living quarters, illuminated by Gothic windows. Most of the architectural detail, including the main doorway of rose marble, is in the fine Gothic tradition. The Castel del Monte is a most impressive museum.

Bari

THE CAPITAL of Apulia is a mushroom city grown to a population of some 300,000 souls. Bari is built along the sea, where it presents a façade of glistening white modern buildings. Among them is the GRAND HOTEL DELLE NAZIONI, Lungomare Sauro 7, a superior hostelry where the traveler will find large attractive rooms and a good cuisine. In the heart of the city he will find another commendable place, the PALACE HOTEL, at Via Lombardi 13.

Typical house in the "trulli" country

There isn't a great deal to interest you in Bari. The fortress, the closely packed old town, and the Basilica of San Nicola possess only moderate significance. But you might use Bari as a hotel base for your travels, since some forty miles southwest is the outstanding curiosity of Apulia, the famous *trulli* country.

THE TRULLI COUNTRY

Alberobello

IF YOU have a penchant for the picturesque, this one incredible village will make your Apulian detour a success. Alberobello, meaning "beautiful tree," is the heart of a region that sprouts strange conical-roofed buildings called *trulli,* a form of construction that dates back centuries before the Christian era, traces of which are evident throughout the Middle East. By some miracle, they have persisted in this one section of Apulia. Moreover, when a good citizen of Alberobello builds himself a new house, he builds a *trullo,* regardless of modern architectural ideas. The house begins as a square of stone, with windows and a simple door. Then it is roofed with a conical cupola of white sandstone blocks. These are protected by a layer of smaller flat roof

New "trulli" arising in Alberobello

stones, all set without mortar. The tip of the conical roof is painted with whitewash, a few mystical signs or crosses are added to keep off the evil spirits, and there you have a *trullo*. Walk through the hillside streets of Alberobello and you come upon hundreds of these unique dwellings. Sometimes they are solitary little fellows, elsewhere they stand in clusters of a dozen or more. They sprout as tool houses in the surrounding vineyards and they even influenced the design of the local Church of Sant'Antonio. In the neighboring city of Locorotondo, celebrated for its wines, the *trulli* have grown into impressive two-story affairs.

The little beehive houses lend white accents to the reddish earth for miles around Alberobello. Their artistic value has been recognized by the Italian government, and the old quarters of the town are classified as historical monuments. In spite of its extraordinary charm, the *trulli* country receives few visitors because of its comparative isolation. Alberobello has only scanty facilities for them, and we can't even recommend a simple *trattoria* for your luncheon. But that makes no difference. Pack up a good picnic lunch, sit under a fig tree amidst the *trulli*, and enjoy one of the most radiant landscapes that Italy has to offer.

Hilltop street in Alberobello

Whitewashed passage–Ostuni   *Cathedral façade–Ostuni*

Ostuni

A SHORT trip through the far heel of Italy will prove a pleasant way to end your Apulian travels. Following the *trulli* episode, you rejoin the coastal road at Fasano and, after a few miles, see a lovely old whitewashed town called Ostuni, just off the highway. It has an almost completely Eastern feeling, except for a remarkable fifteenth-century Gothic cathedral, which has a scalloped roofline made lacy by denticulated corbels, and a richly ornate rose window. Ostuni stands on a height overlooking the Adriatic. From here you can see the Albanian shore on a clear day. We think you will feel that this very slight detour is well justified.

Brindisi

ITALY'S LAST port on the Adriatic is still very active, particularly since traffic has been resumed through the Suez Canal. It has a fine natural harbor, pro-

Side portal of the cathedral—Lecce

Town gate—Lecce

tected by a group of islands. This point was the eastern terminus of the ancient Appian Way. The Romans marked it by two ornamental Corinthian columns, one of which remains. It was here that Virgil died in 19 B. C., after a trip to Greece. Many travelers go through Brindisi, en route to Eastern ports, but few of them are impressed with its charm. Actually, it offers little, from their point of view. The thing we recall most clearly in

Brindisi was the spectacle of a little boy having his bath in the public square, by the fountain. The water was transferred to a basin about the size of a small dishpan, and his two sisters had evidently been delegated to scrub him from head to toe with plenty of laundry soap. The large crowd in the square paid no more attention than if he had been invisible. His sisters were going at his curly head with four hands, while he stood patiently, naked except for a tiny pair of trunks. Unfortunately, we left before they got below this level, and we never knew how they completed their assignment.

Lecce

THIS ARISTOCRATIC southern outpost is the most interesting of the Apulian cities, largely because of its rich heritage of Baroque architecture. In this respect it is unique in Italy. No city of comparable size is so heavily endowed with Baroque churches, colleges, gateways, and houses—good, dignified Baroque, too, not the flamboyant, squirmy kind. You see the best of it by going to the Piazza del Duomo, around which are grouped three buildings, a richly detailed cathedral, the Bishop's Palace, dating from 1632, and an imposing seminary. Some young seminarians in their black robes were kind enough to take us into the collegiate courtyard to see the central fountain, of which they are very proud, about the juiciest assemblage of rococo detail that we've ever encountered. The side portal of the cathedral, shown in our photograph, is far more restful, especially in the late afternoon's golden light. The other Baroque church to see in Lecce is the Basilica of Santa Croce, after which you might like to wander at will through the city. You'll find a fortress, a Roman amphitheater in ruins, a museum, and several elaborate chapels and house façades. If you happen to be here in May or June, don't overlook the annual wine fair, held every year at this time.

Jolly
Hotel
Lecce

There is a fine JOLLY HOTEL in Lecce, which boasts an ultramodern swimming pool. We enjoyed a cooling dip before dinner, after a sweltering July day in this hot city.

Gallipoli

WE AREN'T speaking here, of course, of the Gallipoli on the Dardanelles, which spelt disaster to the Allies in the early years of World War I. It is far more insignificant in history, an obscure little pink and white town on an island by the Ionian Sea. Its atmosphere is thoroughly Eastern. These flat white habitations on the sea wall could be in Greece instead of Italy. In fact, it was a Greek colony more than three thousand years ago. Gallipoli's sun-

The sun-soaked streets of Gallipoli

baked houses stare out at the deep cerulean water, their windows shuttered, their doorways framed in rich, rococo detail. There is a busy little harbor dominated by a round-towered fortress built by Charles of Anjou. Nearby stands a sun-parched chapel and the architectural curiosity of the town, a fountain of Grecian origin, chewed up by time and salt air. There isn't the remotest trace of a tree in the whole community. But it's a curiosity, and should appeal to those who would like to savor the Middle East without quite leaving the heel of the Italian boot. It really seems like the jumping-off place!

Farther up the Ionian shore is Taranto, an important naval base with a well-protected harbor. Despite the fact that it has a closely packed old town, it is not particularly attractive. The new town has been rebuilt since the war, and bustles with white-clad navy personnel. The best things the gourmet traveler will find in Taranto, we believe, are its oysters and its National Museum, famous for ceramics. These are well worth a stopover. And, come to think of it, there is *another* JOLLY HOTEL here, beautifully set beside the sea.

Positano

Campania

Chapter 16

CAMPANIA

I N CONTRAST to its neglected neighbors, Apulia and Calabria, smiling, sun-soaked Campania has for generations played host to the whole world of free-spending travelers. One of the most beautiful regions of Italy, riotous with flowers and fruit trees, ringing with laughter and folk songs, it is also one of the poorest and most overpopulated. The opalescent splendor of the Bay of Naples is a subject that has tempted painters, poets, and mere pamphleteers for centuries. Guarded by two steep, romantic islands, Capri and Ischia, and dominated by the brown and lavender majesty of Vesuvius, this vivid azure-green crescent of water gives an impression of utter enchantment from the decks of an incoming steamer. This is the first glimpse of Italy for many travelers, and lucky they are. The soul of Italy and the Mediterranean seems to be condensed in this ancient, poetic, color-drenched strip of shore.

The region of Campania, set between Rome and the Calabrian toe of Italy, is agricultural. Its rich volcanic soil is kind to farmers, especially those who produce wine, fruit, or vegetables. The average country town is of scant concern to the visitor, unless he is partial, as we are, to sketchable farmhouses. The really overpowering interest of Campania is concentrated in a small area around the Bay of Naples. The secret of Naples' long popularity with travelers lies not so much in the city itself, but in this circle of treasures that surrounds it. The jewels of the Bay of Naples are imbedded in the hills and along the rocky coast, and they are unique in the world today. There is nothing anywhere to approach Pompeii and Herculaneum. Few islands have the fascination of Capri and Ischia. The Amalfi Drive remains an experience of total beauty, uncluttered by billboards. Paestum, the setting of three imposing Greek temples, can be surpassed only by Athens. Taken not by its teeming self, but with its surrounding splendors, Naples is irresistible.

There are inland attractions, of course, and we shall visit two of them

—Caserta, "the Italian Versailles," and Benevento, setting of a remarkable sculptured Roman arch and the home of that golden-yellow liqueur, Strega. But the rest of our Campania travels will be close to the shore. It is a shore well known to thousands of Anglo-Saxon soldiers, of course, for it includes the Salerno landing beach. The early stages of the Italian campaign were fought in Campania, causing cruel damage which has, for the most part, been cleared away. The traveler now sees a radiant countryside, healed of its wounds and eager to welcome tourists to its restaurants and hotels and, if possible, to sell them corals and cameos.

The epicurean aspect of Campania is today encouraging. During World War II, when we spent more than a year in this area, subsisting on army rations highlighted by peanut butter, powdered eggs, and chipped beef, the gentle art of gastronomy was in total eclipse, especially among the luckless ranks of the civilians. With memories of a pathetic population living on a diet of greens and a little fruit, of flour and olive oil that could only be bought at outrageous prices on the black market, we find it heartening to observe this fertile countryside now producing the good things of life in abundance—melons, figs, oranges, lemons, wine, cheese, sausage, and above all, a riotous plenty of vegetables. Hard work and abundant sunshine have replenished the larder and filled out the Neapolitan waistline. The shops are now crammed with food, their ceilings dangling with tight-laced sausages and Provolone cheeses, their shelves laden with the things the local populace loves best: black olives, anchovies, tomato paste, artichokes, and the famous pasta that is the backbone of Neapolitan nourishment. The sea is generous, too, and the wide marble slabs in fish shops are bedecked with a glittering miscellany of recumbent squid, octopus, eels, mussels, and lobsters. The zealous gastronome in Naples who ventures out to the phantasmagorian fish market, staked out under immense umbrellas at the Porta Capuana, will be richly repaid. Finally there is a morose, long-horned bovine, munching away in neighboring flats and marshes, who contributes a vital element to Neapolitan well-being. She is the *bufala,* and her milk makes possible *mozzarella* cheese, the vital ingredient in *pizza* and many another local specialty. A water

An archway in Campania

buffalo sounds like a dubious source of epicurean felicity, but don't be deceived. The best ice cream in the world, in the opinion of many travelers, is found in Groppi's in Cairo, and all this richness is derived from the same solemn critter.

To the average Englishman or American in his native heath, "Italian" cooking means Neapolitan cooking, for this is what has been exported to every corner of his country by Pietro, Luigi, Giuseppe, and Enrico. The *minestrone,* the *pizza,* and the spaghetti that we are accustomed to find at Tony's on High Street and North Main Street have their original models at D'Angelo and Zi Teresa in Naples. It is rewarding to compare the two. We found that the Naples originals had, in their way, the same hard-to-define aristocracy that distinguishes Dior and Balmain from their Fourteenth Street imitators. There is a subtle quality to Neapolitan pasta, be it a lacy *vermicelli* or a slab of *lasagne,* that can't quite be duplicated elsewhere. We feel it's a pity that more Neapolitan dishes haven't been imported by Giovanni and Pasquale, particularly *mozzarella in carrozza.* This famous specialty is a sort of sand-

Presenzano

wich of bread and *mozzarella* cheese that has been dipped in beaten egg and bread crumbs and fried in deep olive oil, much in the manner of a French *croque-monsieur.*

Spaghetti, of course, is the cornerstone of Neapolitan cooking, and a favorite version is *spaghetti alle vongole.* Here the tomato sauce is enriched with herbs and a wealth of tiny two-necked clams called *vongole.* You must go to Naples to taste the original! *Sartù di riso* is a tempting rice dish, rich with tomato, spices, ground meat, and *mozzarella,* covered with this sauce and with bread crumbs and browned in the oven. A favorite dish at carnival time is *lasagne imbottita,* composed of wide strips of pasta alternating with layers of meat sauce made up of minced sausage, hard-boiled eggs, and *ricotta* and *mozzarella* cheese.

Neapolitans cook *melanzane* (eggplant) with a rich mushroom and tomato sauce, which they sprinkle very generously with cheese. They prepare their veal cutlets in a highly aromatic sauce, calling them *costate alla pizzaiuola.* They have their own version of *fritto misto,* which you will find light and satisfying, that is, if you like small mullets and baby cuttlefish. Finally, they are famous for their fish soups. *Zuppa di pesce* is a prima donna on every Italian menu.

These and several other local dishes deserve equal acclaim but, in the eyes

Farmyard at Licignano di Napoli

of the outside world, the famous *pizza* has stolen the march on them all. Long ago it conquered southern France, where the *pissaladiera* is an established favorite. Its conquest of America is complete also, from the boardwalks of Atlantic City to the supermarkets of San Diego.

Just *what* is a perfect Neapolitan *pizza,* and how good can it be? A lot of controversy has raged over this subject. Our own President Eisenhower supposedly made the patriotic, off-the-record remark that we can make a better *pizza* on Mulberry Street in New York than they can make in Naples. This was one for idle newsmen, who extracted an admission from Admiral Carney, at that time commander of our naval forces in the Mediterranean, that it just couldn't be so. The Neapolitans were supreme in the art, he retorted. There ensued a typical publicity gag. A *pizza* contest was held, and a committee of international judges was selected to confront a panorama of varied *pizze* by the best chefs in the city. Subsequently a shapely brunette was elected Miss Pizza and everyone was happy with the judges' decision except the Communist press, which accused the Americans of trying to belittle and degrade a great Neapolitan institution!

We asked several qualified persons where we could find the best rendition of this famous dish, and following their recommendation, had lunch at the HOTEL VESUVIO, the newly rebuilt hostelry on the Via Partenope, facing the

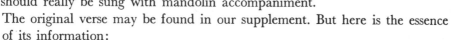

Castel dell'Ovo. Our *pizza* came as the first course in a *prix-fixe* luncheon and it proved to be a superlative pie about eight inches across, generously thick, magnificently fattening, and quite enough for an entire meal. The thin crust was firm but tender, the filling of molten *mozzarella* delectable beyond words. No other cheese was added except a sprinkling of Parmesan, no anchovies, no olives, no mussels, onions, or other distracting influences. It was topped by a purée of fresh tomatoes and a sprinkling of herbs, principally orégano and basil, although I suspect some other secret flavoring, not casually revealed to inquiring guests. The key to its sublimity, according to the chef, lies in the high quality of the *mozzarella* cheese, a most discouraging verdict for the Mulberry Street experts. Unhappily, the supply of water buffalo is rather low in America. And so the judges in this somewhat trumped-up contest were probably right. The genuine Neapolitan *pizza* still has no rival.

Signor Gino Fiorentino, the director of the Hotel Vesuvio, has given us the secret of his famous specialty, and of several other Neapolitan dishes as well. The original *pizza* recipe came to us in the form of a poem, which has the lilt of a Neapolitan street song and should really be sung with mandolin accompaniment. The original verse may be found in our supplement. But here is the essence of its information:

Pizza Napoletana alla Vesuvio
NEAPOLITAN PIZZA VESUVIO

To make *pizza* dough, use 4 cups of flour, 1 envelope of dry yeast, 7/8 to 1 cup of milk, 6 tablespoons of lard, and a pinch of salt. Dissolve the yeast in 1/4 cup of tepid water, add 1/4 cup of the milk, and 1 cup of the flour. Knead this mixture into a dough and let it rise until it doubles in bulk. Now add the rest of the flour, the salt, the lard, and the remaining milk. Rework the dough and let it again rise to double its bulk. Work it down and shape and roll it gently into a disk about 1/4 inch thick. Place the disk on a large circular tin sheet. Place pieces of peeled and seeded tomatoes and slices of *mozzarella* in lines radiating from the center. Sprinkle with orégano, Parmesan cheese, and a fairly lavish amount of olive oil. Bake in a hot oven (400° F.) for about 20 minutes, or until the crust is brown and crisp.

Campania produces its full quota of wine, most of it a lusty, full-bodied ordinary red destined to keep company with Neapolitan spaghetti and *pizza*. Time and again in Campania you will observe long garlands of vines stretched between pine trees. These bring forth the reliable *rosso* essential to every country household. But there are distinguished wines as well, Lacrima Christi, for example. Named without great piety (Tears of Christ), this faintly sweet white wine comes from the southern slopes of Vesuvius, whose powdery volcanic soil is peculiarly suited to vineyards. Excellent wines also are grown on the volcanic islands. Capri produces a fresh white of quality and Ischia produces three, one of them poetically called Sorriso (smile) d'Ischia. Ravello raises a commendable red wine on the terraced slopes above Amalfi, while, north of Naples, ancient vineyards yield the red and white wines of Falerno, descended from the Falernum wine of the Romans, which brought forth such enthusiastic praise from Horace. Most of these names appear on local wine lists, and we urge you to try them.

With this epicurean data filed away, the visiting gourmet is now confronted with the pleasant prospect of Naples itself and the historic half-circle of attractions that surround it. All of them may be visited by car or bus in a single day. Even Paestum, farthest removed, is only fifty-nine miles away. This means that you may, if you choose, use one of Naples' fine hotels as a base while making daily excursions. However, if you prefer a smaller and quieter sleeping place, there are long-established hotels in Salerno, Amalfi, Ravello, Positano, and Sorrento. The islands of Capri and Ischia have resort hotels with every comfort, including swimming pools and night clubs, while even Caserta and Benevento are endowed with the ever-reliable Jolly Hotels. Let us begin with the obvious place:

Naples

THE THIRD largest city in Italy (the first two are Rome and Milan), Naples is most beautiful when approached from the sea. It glistens in polychrome brightness beneath the frowning fortress of Sant'Elmo, its new apartment houses climbing audaciously up the cliffs. After a glimpse of the seaside Via Partenope, its smart many-storied hotels and palm-shaded parks, the impatient ship passenger can hardly wait to disembark. But when he finally sets foot in this throbbing metropolis, the scene loses a little of its perfection. Immediately he becomes a choice plum for a cluster of cabbies, porters, vultures, and multilingual smoothies whose thoughts are concentrated solely on his pocketbook. The noise, the congestion, the confusion, are intense. This is no place to arrive without a hotel reservation! Let us hope that you have made arrangements with one of the gleaming establishments on the Via Partenope,

Castel dell'Ovo—Naples

Porto San Nazzaro–Naples

facing the sea and the historic Castel dell'Ovo. There are five reliable hotels here—the two de luxe ones being the EXCELSIOR and the VESUVIO, both rebuilt since the war. Along with them are the CONTINENTAL, the SANTA LUCIA, and an ultramodern newcomer, the HOTEL ROYAL. Their prices vary, but you should be perfectly comfortable in any one of the five. If you like the idea of a room with a view of the Bay of Naples and Vesuvius, you might try the old standby, PARKER'S HOTEL, located on the hillside Corso Vittorio Emanuele.

Though we can't aspire, within our limited space, to be your constant guide in Naples, any more than in Rome, Florence, or Venice, we can list briefly a few things not to miss before setting out for Amalfi and Capri. Above all, allow plenty of time for the Museo Nazionale, one of the great museums of the world. It is here that the priceless treasures from Pompeii and Herculaneum have been assembled. It takes a morning to see them all—Greek bronzes, portrait heads of poets, philosophers, and statesmen, several *Veneri,* callipygian and otherwise, pictorial mosaics, and gay, sometimes faintly indecent Pompeiian drawings and frescoes. It is strangely exciting to come face to face with authentic busts of Aristotle, Homer, Demosthenes, Seneca, Euripides, and Julius Caesar, looking as though they had been alive only yesterday. There is a fine picture gallery too, containing masterpieces by Titian,

Piazza del Gesù Nuovo—Naples

Bellini, Raphael, and Mantegna. The museum is installed in an inappropriate, sixteenth-century barracks, and is poorly lighted. But this makes no difference, it simply mustn't be overlooked.

Neither will you want to miss the San Carlo Theater, one of the largest opera houses in Europe and the scene of Caruso's early triumphs. The great tenor was born in Naples in 1873. The huge structure was built by Charles III of Bourbon in 1747. Many of the works of Rossini, Bellini, and Donizetti made their debut here, and you can undoubtedly hear some of them still if you consult the billboards. Across from the San Carlo Theater stands the huge glassed-over *galleria,* the meeting place of all Naples. It is a liberal education to sit here at a café table and watch the whirlpool of Neapolitans hurry by.

Another landmark of Naples is the immense Castel Nuovo, a crenelated fortress which for years served as the stronghold of the kings of Naples. Composed of sturdy round towers grouped round a courtyard, it was finished in 1282 under Charles I of Anjou. Between the two entrance towers is its artistic treasure, a glorious Renaissance triumphal arch built in the middle of the fifteenth century in honor of Alfonso I of Aragon, the work of the sculptor Laurana.

Almost everyone pays a visit to the famous aquarium, located in a shaded park facing the sea. It probably isn't as remarkable as it used to be before the war, but its prima donna is still phenomenal—a diaphanous fish with its own pink parasol. You will also want to visit some of the Neapolitan churches, particularly Santa Chiara and its cloister, and, if you enjoy startling panoramas, you shouldn't miss the National Museum of San Martino, installed in the towering Castel Sant'Elmo. This eerie height dominates the whole city, presenting a truly electrifying sight. You can reach it directly by bus.

The heart of Naples, of course, no longer beats in these lofty relics of other centuries. It throbs on the commercial Via Roma and in the incredibly narrow streets that climb the slopes of Vomero. You haven't seen Naples unless you've penetrated some of its mysterious side streets, either on foot or in a horse-drawn carriage. Here, perhaps, is a good place to offer a bit of unsolicited advice to the first-time visitor, whether he's a gourmet or not, whether he knows a *pizza* from a piazza, or a *tarantella* from a *tortino*. It is simply this: keep your pocketbook tightly closed on the street at *all* times. The tourist path is cluttered with slick young men who have learned to live by their wits—and the naïveté of the trusting traveler. The police in other Italian cities would pick them up in short order, but here in Naples, where poverty and unemployment are so intense, officials are more tolerant, and the bright youths with innocent faces, curly black hair, and striped suits work at their little games with alarming success. They speak fair English and French, and are consummate actors. In a piece of tissue paper they show you a "genuine" Parker 51 fountain pen that they have just "bought from a broke American sailor," or a glittering gold wristwatch that "came from the American PX." Both are total junk, but at the least flicker of interest these lads are on your heels like nipping terriers. The ambulant money-changers offer you extravagantly good rates for dollars, francs, or traveler's checks. If you bite, they invite you into a side street where the transaction can't be observed, count the money out carefully before your eyes, and then do a sleight of hand, leaving their victim with a wad of cut newspaper enclosed in a one-thousand lire note. It's an ancient game, and it works far too often, as the weary officials of foreign consulates know.

After a fortnight's foraging in Naples, we shall risk the melancholy statement that there are no superlative haunts for the gastronome here, as there are in Rome, Florence, Milan, and Bologna. One might as well be philosophical about it and seek the next best, which is commendable indeed. There are several places where the discerning diner should be reasonably happy. One of the best is the RISTORANTE D'ANGELO, on the Via Aniello Falcone (Falcon's Lair), high on the Vomero hill above the hubbub of the lower city. It is the most publicized place in Naples, and you may have received a postcard showing its beaming proprietor, Signor Attolini, sprinkling herbs on a *pizza*

Ristorante D'Angelo

Naples

Castel Nuovo—Naples

The Bay of Naples

or dangling his magic golden horn. They flutter across the ocean in flocks daily. We were more interested in Signor Attolini's kitchen than in his publicity, and found it to be an immaculate, roomy, efficient place whose large plate-glass window competes in interest with the breath-taking view of the Bay of Naples. The latter won out, however. The lights of the city stretch out beneath you, the silhouette of Vesuvius, a thin wisp of smoke rising from its cone, looms behind, and beyond that the steep Amalfi peninsula and the dim, rocky silhouette of Capri. Of course, it's romantic and heady. And, of course, you must have soft music and a moon, light wine and dancing on a tiled terrace. D'Angelo provides it all (not guaranteeing the moon), and a sound menu for the unromantic few who are interested in good groceries alone. For them he proposes, in addition to his *pizza al segreto,* a rich *filet de sole d'oltremare* or a truly sumptuous *zuppa di pesce.* The steaks are good and so are the *agnolotti alla d'Angelo,* a savory oversized ravioli. The dining hall is large, airy, and uninspired, but on the lower floor is a more artistic salon, decorated with unusual frescoes and leading to a terrace that can be lovely on a summer's night.

In the summertime, you will find another place within a stone's throw of d'Angelo called LE ARCATE, with even more tiled space for dancing and an even closer view of the teeming city below. The cooking is commendable here also, and we were particularly struck with the hors-d'oeuvre. These often tend to be too heavily charged with oil in Italian restaurants. But the *antipasti* at Le Arcate had more of the suavity of the French—a succession of rectangular dishes containing onions *à la grecque,* peppers, pickles, mushrooms, mussels, shrimp, artichokes, tuna fish, sardines, anchovies, olives, stuffed eggs, sausage, ham, and many others.

Le Arcate

Naples

If you prefer to start your meal farinaceously, the menu provides *maccheroni ai quattro formaggi,* a steaming platter of pasta flavored with Bel Paese, *mozzarella,* Gruyère, and Parmesan cheese. There is also a handsome *buffet freddo* served from a silvery cart—cold meats, galantines, turkey, chicken in aspic, accompanied by a savory green salad. The proprietor of Le Arcate is a genial, white-haired, multilingual gentleman called Signor Izzo, who has spent half a century in the restaurant business in Naples and Capri. With his advice, you should achieve a memorable Neapolitan dinner on this lofty terrace. Signor Izzo has given us three of his favorite recipes, among them this simple way of preparing beef:

Carne alla Pizzaiuola
STEAK IN TOMATO SAUCE

Take a good slice of meat, if possible an *entrecôte* cut, and brown it briefly on both sides in the frying pan with a few drops of oil and a bit of garlic. Then add a little butter, orégano (wild marjoram), chopped parsley, and fresh tomatoes that have been peeled, seeded, and chopped. Cook the meat over a low fire for 10 minutes.

Enthusiasts for mountainside dining may reach even dizzier heights by trying the RISTORANTE RENZO E LUCIA, Via Angelina 33, an exalted spot that adjoins the Castel Sant'Elmo, and a good place to lunch after visiting the neighboring National Museum of San Martino. The restaurant seems to hang in mid-air over the city, as though you were in a plane about to land at the Capodichino airport. The panorama from its terrace is overwhelming. We think you'll like the cooking, too. Three trusted Neapolitan specialties grace the menu—*vermicelli alle vongole, calamaretti fritti* (deep-fried baby squids), and *mozzarella in carrozza.*

Ristorante
Renzo e Lucia

NAPLES

Directly opposite the quintet of celebrated hostelries on the bay shore is the fortified Castel dell'Ovo, so named because of its egg-shaped form. This small, vertical-sided island of rock, now a military barracks, extends into the bay and encloses a little fishing port called the Borgo Marinaro, now the gastronomic heart of Naples, and an irresistible magnet for visitors, even if the feasts aren't as Lucullan as one might expect. This reference is used advisedly, for the fabulous Roman gourmand, Lucullus, had a villa that crowned the site of the Castle of the Egg. Here is where the ship-borne gourmet eventually migrates, and quite an adventure awaits him.

Hotel Vesuvio
Naples

The best food in the neighborhood, we believe, is found nearby in the HOTEL VESUVIO, whose impeccable *pizza* caused us to indulge in a rapturous paragraph a few pages back. It is a mezzanine hotel dining room, if you wish, but the atmosphere is charming, and the view of the harbor animated and diverting. The Vesuvio has other temptations besides *pizza,* enough to qualify it as one of the very best restaurants in Naples. We have tried a savory *bollito* there, a miscellany of boiled tongue, veal, sausage, and chicken, all served from the same silver perambulator. This specialty was followed by green salad and cheese, a *coupe* of fresh fruit perfumed with Aurum, a worthy Italian version of orange curaçao, and a satanic black *caffè espresso.* There is no soulful music here, but you will find attentive service, masterminded by a plump, trilingual gentleman in a cream-colored tuxedo who looks to be straight from the mid-Fifties in New York. We recommend the Vesuvio warmly, especially to those who prefer to dine quietly and enjoy Neapolitan specialties.

Zi Jeresa
Naples

In the simpler days, at the turn of the century, the miniature port of Borgo Marinaro was monopolized by fishermen alone. They brought their catch to port in rowboats and sold their fish to housewives at the landing. Around that time, a young woman whose first name was Teresa decided to make a few nourishing dishes for the hungry fishermen when they landed. She sold plates of hot beans to the mariners for two *soldi*. Then she graduated to fish soups and *fritto misto,* and in time established a modest restaurant, calling it ZI TERESA. Its growth since then has been phenomenal. Now the fishermen don't go there any more; they can't afford it. But everyone else who has visited Naples knows Aunt Teresa's, including Hollywood luminaries, Somerset Maugham, the Prince of Piedmont, and the most defunct of sons-in-law, Signor Ciano. Primo Carnera had his picture taken with Teresa and a formidable panorama of pasta and *zuppa di pesce*. Lucky Luciano added further luster to her guestbook.

Teresa Fusco had more than her share of tragedy—she lost her husband and all her sons, the last of them in World War II. When she died in May, 1953, her funeral was almost a national event. Flowers and telegrams poured in from all over the world. American soldiers came especially from Rome for the last rites. Top-hatted dignitaries joined with blue-clad fishermen in a final tribute to this simple, kindly woman who knew the secret of Neapolitan cooking, and shared it with the world.

For historical reasons, therefore, Zi Teresa may be the most interesting of the four restaurants that now cluster round the Borgo Marinaro. Adjoining

Piazza Plebiscito and the Royal Palace–Naples

her is the BERSAGLIERA, which some critics contend has better cooking. I'm not sure about this, but it certainly has more original décor. Nymphs and bronzed, busty ladies disport themselves in total abandon on the ceiling, and the lighting fixtures are deftly arranged so that they extend downward from the navel of each recumbent Venus. Across the way, on the far side of the port, are two other rivals—the TRANSATLANTICO, most expensive of the four and a little dressier than the others, and DA CIRO, a smaller place with a cheerful atmosphere and good cooking. Signor Ciro has generously supplied us with the recipe for the *lasagne* dish that is such a Neapolitan favorite at carnival time. Here is a translation:

Ristorante
Bersagliera

Naples

Lasagne di Carnevale
BAKED LASAGNE CARNIVAL

Boil 1 pound of *lasagne,* a few at a time, in plentiful boiling, salted water, leaving them slightly firm. Drain them out as done and remove to a bowl of cold water. Drain again and spread them on damp towels. Butter a 15-inch, shallow baking dish and cover the bottom with a single layer of *lasagne,* allowing the ends to turn up to line the sides of the dish. Mix 1 pound of *ricotta* cheese with 1 large beaten egg and 1/2 cup grated Parmesan. Spread half the *ricotta* mixture over the *lasagne* and cover with 1/2 to 3/4 pound of thinly sliced *mozzarella*

Da Ciro
Naples

413

cheese and 1 cup of diced ham. Add another layer of *lasagne,* spread on the remaining *ricotta* mixture, and over this spread about 1/2 pound of tiny meatballs that have been cooked briefly in a little butter. (See recipe for *polpette* in the index or use finely ground lean beef seasoned with salt and pepper and grated onion. Form balls the size of hazelnuts.) Over this pour 1 1/2 to 2 cups meat juices or sauce. (See stewed beef Florentine or meat sauce Florentine, or *ragù bolognese* II in the index.) Add your last layer of *lasagne,* another 1 1/2 to 2 cups meat juices or sauce, and sprinkle the surface lavishly with Parmesan. Bake in a 350° F. oven for 20 to 30 minutes.

To be frank, the epicurean standard on the Borgo Marinaro is not extraordinary. All four restaurants offer good versions of the Neapolitan classics —pasta, *pizza, mozzarella in carrozza,* and *zuppa di pesce*—and good island wines from Capri and Ischia. They are gay, animated, and fast favorites with the Neapolitans themselves. The experience of dining here, whether under an awning in summer or behind plate-glass windows in the rainy season, is well worth your while, especially if you don't mind music with your meals. For an almost invariable ingredient in Neapolitan restaurants is music. If you squirm at the presence of a string sextet, a soulful soloist with his eyes closed, or an accordion player with a flashing gold tooth, you're going to be unhapoli in Napoli. Each restaurant has its own group of musicians, and you can no more escape the throbbing violin and the subsequent plate-passing than you can the service tax. The music isn't primarily for the tourists either. A Neapolitan couple really enjoys having a sentimental tenor sit down at their table and give tongue while their *minestrone* turns cold. They smile radiantly and sing with him, tipping him handsomely. It is a part of Naples, and we have made a brave attempt to enthuse about it. Luckily there are no rumbas and no hostesses cavorting before microphones. Neapolitan voices need no such mechanical aid, as Caruso demonstrated long ago.

Da
Giacomino
Naples

Travelers who find themselves at lunchtime in the heart of Naples, in the neighborhood of the famous glassed-in *galleria,* the San Carlo Opera House, and the Royal Palace, for example, have another problem. Prospects for gastronomic felicity are rather forlorn here. We feel that the best bet is DA GIACOMINO, Via San Carlo 29. This conventional Naples sidewalk restaurant has high standards, and a better-than-average meal lurks behind its cryptic menu. Its vaulted ceilings are lofty and light, the atmosphere is friendly, and there are a few English-speaking waiters. The accordion and guitar team is discreet, and there is a wonderful police dog dozing around the place, the handsomest and most ingratiating beggar in Naples. One of the best-known Neapolitan specialties, *spaghetti alle vongole,* appears in full splendor here. These miniature clams, hardly more than half an inch long,

Piazza Dante–Naples   *The yacht basin–Naples*

are genuine curiosities, with their necks stretching out in a Churchillian V. Other specialties are *carne ragù napoletana, vermicelli alla "come succede,"* and *insalata capricciosa,* a particularly good salad. Various fresh young salad greens are mixed with sliced tomatoes, sliced celery, black and green olives, and bits of tuna fish. These are dressed with lemon juice, olive oil, and salt and pepper. The service is good at Da Giacomino, and the prices are very fair.

Your guidebook will point out that there is a great deal more to be seen in Naples, but perhaps you are impatient to visit some of the extraordinary curiosities which await you nearby. We are eager to show them to you. Mount Vesuvius, still an active volcano, and the two cities that it destroyed yet preserved by a terrible eruption in 79 A. D., are what the newly arrived visitor wants to see most of all. To climb the slopes of Vesuvius, to visit Pompeii, emerged after centuries from its blanket of cinders and gravel, and  Herculaneum, still partly buried under volcanic mud and lava, is a natural desire. The Italian government has made it easy, installing capable multi-lingual guides in each place, and linking the two with a good, if narrow, toll road. Roomy buses will take you to all three, with compulsory stops at cameo factories along the way. The epicurean phase of these three attractions is not encouraging. A light box lunch, prepared at your hotel, may prove to be a blessing!

415

Vesuvius in eruption—March, 1944

Vesuvius

THOUGH MOST people are content to view the graceful slopes of Vesuvius from a distance, others aren't satisfied until they have climbed to its rim and gazed down on the cone of the live volcano, a weird and desolate scene. It can be reached by taking the Circumvesuvian railway or a motor vehicle up to a funicular which, in turn, hoists you within walking distance of the rim of the crater. The trip is made with authorized guides only. From this eminence you have a sobering view of arid, lava-strewn wilderness and, if you turn the other way, you find spread out before you a radiant panorama of Naples.

Vesuvius is meek most of the time, emitting only a peaceful wisp of smoke, but it bursts into fury on occasion. An active eruption occurred in 1906, destroying many villages. Another occurred in 1944, at a time when the author had plenty of time to study and photograph the event. A picture taken at that time is shown here.

Herculaneum

THE ROMAN town of Ercolano, named for Hercules, was a fashionable resort favored by wealthy people before its sudden extinction following Vesuvius' terrible eruption. While Pompeii was being smothered in ashes, Herculaneum was buried in a stream of volcanic mud and lava from forty to one hundred feet deep. Forgotten for centuries, the town was accidentally revealed in 1719 when well diggers came upon its antique theater. Excavations have been going on since the eighteenth century. Due to the hard consistency of the volcanic mud, it has been a laborious task. Many beautiful bronzes have been recovered, and may be seen in the Naples Museum. The remains of several patrician houses are worth visiting, especially the Casa dei Cervi (House of the Cerfs) and the Casa del Bicentano (House of the Bicentenary), which has beautiful frescoes. It was here that a Christian cross was discovered, the earliest ever found in a private house. The ancient baths, built in the first century B. C., also deserve a visit.

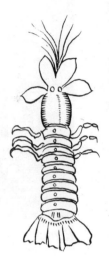

Much of the ancient town remains unexcavated, since the city of Resina was later built on top of it. Visitors to the excavations, the *scavi di Ercolano*, are comparatively few. It appeals mainly to scholars and dedicated enthusiasts of antiquity.

House of the Faun, the first peristyle—Pompeii

Remains of the Basilica and the Roman Forum—Pompeii

Pompeii

THE CITIZENS of the prosperous city of Pompeii should have been suspicious about the slumbering giant of Vesuvius that loomed above them. In 63 A. D. it had caused a disastrous earthquake, destroying much of the town. But the wealthy Romans had rebuilt their houses promptly, employing the most advanced architectural styles of the time. They were totally unprepared on August 24th, 79 A. D., for the mighty outburst of smoke, gas, cinders, and gravel that burst with frightful suddenness from the crater of Vesuvius, burying the whole city under a twenty-foot hail of hot cinders and pumice stones. More than two thousand citizens were killed in the tragedy, but nearly ten times that number escaped.

Pliny the Younger was an eyewitness of the catastrophe, as it happens, and he wrote two letters about it, recounting the death of his uncle, Pliny the Elder, who was suffocated by fumes. But the world soon forgot the eruption and Pompeii itself, which slept for centuries under its cinders. Not until 1594, when a subterranean canal was begun, did anyone suspect the secret of Pompeii. Thus, an unspeakable tragedy had the compensation of preserving for posterity, intact and in intimate detail, an entire Roman city.

A street in Pompeii

Columns of the Forum portico–Pompeii   *Marble portal–Pompeii*

Excavations begun in 1748 aroused new interest in antiquity, and they are still going on today. This Greek and Roman city is the most extraordinary phenomenon in Campania, and becomes more so with the removal of every spadeful of cinders. Today, in the company of a competent, English-speaking guide, you may visit this revealed Roman city at will, its forum, temples, theaters, baths, and brothels. You wander along rough, rutted stone roads, under memorial arches, into the bakeries, the oil shops, and fruit stores, their shop signs still painted in flowing red Roman letters. Most beautiful of all are the villas of the luxury-loving Romans. The House of the Vettii is a museum in itself, adorned with superb frescoes of cupids and children. Its flower-grown peristyle is enclosed by Doric columns, and thickly populated with fountain statues. The House of the Faun is a thing of utter beauty, one of the noblest dwellings of antiquity, and there are dozens of others. The Pompeians loved their entertainment. There is an amphitheater for twenty thousand spectators and an outdoor theater that seated five thousand. Clearly enough, one never forgets seeing Pompeii!

The excavated city may be reached easily from Naples by an electric train or by a miniature motor toll highway. Parking space is good, the guides are polite and intelligent, and their fees reasonable. The one draw-back to Pompeii is the pack of parasites and buttonholers who leap at the helpless tourist, offering him picture albums of naughty frescoes and phony

Vietri, first town on the Amalfi Drive

antique jewelry. It takes fortitude to elbow your way through these pests to a reliable guide. The gastronomic pitch is a low one. Waiters flag your car down with napkins, run after you with shouts of *"Pas cher!"* Once hooked on the restaurant terrace, you must engage in a battle of wits with a head-waiter whose overwhelming desire is to unload on his prey the most expensive *prix-fixe* menu and the rarest bottle of Lacrima Christi. It is possible to obtain a sane and simple luncheon in Pompeii, but you have to get in there and slug for it. A less complicated solution would be to equip yourself with a discreet box lunch of bread, cheese, sausage, fruit, and a *fiasco* of Chianti, and enjoy it in a remote corner of some forgotten Pompeian villa. As the best alternative, try the RISTORANTE VITTORIA.

The Amalfi Drive

AN INLAND trip of about twenty miles will take you to the charming town of Vietri, which marks the beginning of another incomparable experience, the Amalfi Drive. Many people would state without hesitation that it is the most beautiful drive in Italy. The extraordinary serpentine road, carved in the precipitous hillside, deserves all the ecstatic acclaim that it has received since its completion in 1852. Starting at Vietri, it winds westward tortuously,

Cetara

clinging to the rocky hillside, now descending to multicolored fishing villages, now climbing back through terraced slopes and over viaducts to new heights. The Italian farmer installed on this rocky balcony above the sea has accomplished miracles in raising citrus fruits, grapes, and vegetables. He hoards his precious loam in finely built terraces and diverts waterfalls to keep them irrigated. So ardent is the sun that he must build bamboo awnings over his lemon trees. One is torn between admiration for his industry and awe at the varying splendor of the view as the car whines around the sharp asphalt turns. The driver is the only one who isn't thrilled by the first trip over the Amalfi Drive. He has to watch the bends and not the beauty. Approaching Amalfi, there is a crescendo of fishing villages—Cetara, Maiori, Minori (where a remarkable Roman villa has been exhumed), Atrani (in our opinion the most paintable of all), and, finally, iridescent Amalfi itself.

422

Fishermen at Maiori

Minori

Atrani

Amalfi

Amalfi

Amalfi

THE SOARING seaport that lends its name to the Amalfi Drive (and to restaurants and apartment houses across the U. S. A.) is but a charming shadow of its former self. Once a sea power rivaling Venice, it has now shrunk to a quiet town creeping up the cliffs in picturesque abandon. Amalfi is the oldest Italian maritime republic, and once possessed colonies in Asia and Africa. But she was defeated by the rival Pisans in 1137, and then invaded by the Normans. Earthquakes and a frightful sea storm in 1343 dealt the final blows. The republic collapsed. Hardly a trace of the ancient docks remains. The population of fifty thousand dwindled away, and today's inhabitants number about eight thousand. Its mighty fleet has shrunk to a few dozen fishing vessels that venture forth at night, equipped with blinding lights to dazzle and attract their catch.

Amalfi's favorite local son was Flavio Gioia, inventor of the maritime compass. The elaborate eleventh-century Lombard-Norman Cathedral of Sant' Andrea is an eloquent reminder of Amalfi's greater days. Achieved in patterns of black and white marble, it is approached by a wide, steep set of sixty-two steps. Somehow the setting has always reminded us of a busy Oriental bazaar. Far more restful is the ancient Chiostro del Paradiso, the Norman cloister that adjoins the cathedral.

426

Waterfront skyscraper–Amalfi   *Cathedral of Sant' Andrea–Amalfi*

Amalfi has never become a tourist trap. It treats its guests with deference and good cheer, and its hotels are not cut in the usual pattern. One of them, the HOTEL CAPPUCCINI, celebrated for decades, is a converted Capuchin convent, perched on a ledge 230 feet above the sea. One of the most familiar photographs in tourist Italy shows an aged bearded monk under the flowery pergola of the *Cappuccini,* with the rocky shore in the distance. Luncheon, tea, or dinner on this long terrace is an experience to be remembered, and a prolonged stay in one of its modernized monastic cells is even better. An unlovely but breath-saving outdoor elevator now solves the problem of climbing to this unique hostelry.

The LUNA is a smaller hotel that was once a convent also. It occupies a favored promontory jutting into the sea at the eastern extremity of the town. Here you will find an attractive bar with a sheltered terrace, an admirable place for a contemplative glass of vermouth, with an unforgettable landscape thrown into the bargain.

Our own favorite in Amalfi is the HOTEL SANTA CATERINA, a well-run, spotless place with pleasant gardens and a panoramic dining terrace high above the sea. It is situated on the western fringe of the town. Its culinary standards are commendably high, the best in Amalfi, we think. Motorists will find ample garage space, something difficult to come upon in this crowded

Hotel
Cappuccini
AMALFI

Hotel
Luna
AMALFI

Hotel
Santa
Caterina
Amalfi

427

Terrace of the Villa Cimbrone—Ravello

site. Signor Gambardella, the cordial director of this hotel, gave us the recipe for *cannelloni alla Santa Caterina,* which appears among the Neapolitan dishes at the end of this volume.

Ravello

ONE OF THE MOST exquisitely romantic villages in Italy, Ravello drowses on a promontory a thousand feet above Amalfi. Once it was a part of the Amalfi Republic, occupied by its patrician families, a city of turrets and fortified walls, fine Norman churches and noble villas. Much of the city has disappeared, but the Romanesque Cathedral of San Pantaleon remains, together with a mosaic-rich pulpit and bronze doors by Barisano da Trani that acknowledge few, if any, equals.

Poets, musicians, and famous lovers have found Ravello irresistible, if local legend can be credited, and only George Sand and Chopin seem to have passed it up. Richard Wagner found its sylvan calm conducive to composing, and brought forth *Parsifal* in Ravello. A Wagner Festival is now a frequent event in the village. The lovely Arab-Norman Rufolo Palace, where he lived, is open to visitors, and a stroll through its Saracenic cloisters and cypress gardens, perfumed with jasmine and mimosa, is a serene experi-

ence. They make one think of the Alhambra. Boccaccio found inspiration in these same gardens six
centuries ago, and made ardent love to Fiammetta
there.

Later in date, but even more dramatically
perched on the heights, the Villa Cimbrone leads
one through formal gardens pointed up with bronze
figures, little domed temples, and majestic hedges
to a breath-taking terrace, populated with antique
white marble busts. From this inspiring eminence
the Amalfi coast is indescribably lovely.

S. AGOSTINO
RAVELLO

Furthermore, the gastronomic outlook in Ra-
vello is heartening. We tried two places and found both of them good. The
CARUSO BELVEDERE is a long-established house whose walls are crammed with
paintings, and whose guestbook is studded with famous names. The Caruso
family is every bit as interested in wine as in food, for they own extensive
vineyards on the neighboring hillsides and produce red, white, and rosé
Ravello vintages, all fresh and palatable. Their fame is spreading to America.

Hotel
Caruso
Belvedere
Ravello

You will find very good cooking in this dependable hotel, particularly
if you order its two outstanding specialties, *cannelloni alla Caruso* and chocolate soufflé. Generations of guests have gone into ecstasy over this soufflé,
which is pointed up with black cherries. So frequent were the requests for
the recipe that Signor Caruso had it printed in English, ready for distribution. He assumes the recipients have some slight acquaintance with the
art of the soufflé. Here it is:

CARUSO'S CHOCOLATE SOUFFLÉ

Per portion: 2 eggs
   1 tablespoon of confectioners' sugar
   1 2/3 tablespoons of unsweetened cocoa

Separate the eggs.

Beat the whites until stiff. Beat the yolks thoroughly and add, little
by little, the sugar and cocoa. Fold in the whites.

Place the mixture in a buttered baking dish on the bottom of which
has been spread a thin layer of whole preserved black cherries.

Bake near the top of a 425° F. oven, where the heat rises and
cooks the top surface, until the soufflé rises. When it has risen, remove
it from the oven and serve at once. A small soufflé takes 9 to 10 minutes, one made of 4 eggs not more than 12 minutes. The center should
be creamy.

Hotel
Rufolo
Ravello

Less expensive, but quite as happy a choice, is the HOTEL RUFOLO, a
pleasant place overlooking the celebrated Rufolo gardens. This is the most

Detail of cathedral doors by Barisano da Trani—Ravello

The Rufolo Palace–Ravello

immaculate hotel we have seen in years, glistening with marble, tile, and white linen. Our luncheon consisted of the conventional *cannelloni, scaloppini,* salad, cheese, and fruit, with a cool bottle of local wine. It was not only inexpensive, but well prepared, and served with skill and courtesy.

Positano

A TOURIST rival to Amalfi has sprung up in recent years, and its charms are beguiling indeed. Its name is Positano, a fishing village with strong Oriental overtones. Its cubelike houses have rounded Moorish roofs, and they clamber to giddy perches around this precipitous wedge of rock. If you count its many terraces, interspersed with dark green citrus groves and rows of houses, Positano is a twenty-five-story village, as our photograph proves. Artists have adopted Positano with gusto, and canvases of its exotic tapestry of houses have spread throughout the world's art galleries. But you don't have to own an easel and a broad-brimmed hat to enjoy it. There are two good hotels that welcome mere seekers of sunshine and repose to its unusually mild climate. We lunched at the better known of these, LE SIRENUSE, a gay

La Sirenuse Positano

The rocky shore–Praiano   *Positano*

pinkish structure that tumbles down the hillside, and came away in a pleasant
mist of contentment. Our meal consisted of *cannelloni*, a luscious grilled
sole, a plump juicy pear, Capri wine, and jet-black coffee—simple enough,
but served to perfection. This hotel is in the upper expense bracket, but
worth it.

Nearby is the commendable ALBERGO MIRAMARE, a smaller hotel with
a superb view of the water and coast. Its clients speak of it with unstinted
praise. We think you'll enjoy either hotel, and especially Positano itself. Here
is a good place to take up water-color painting.

Sorrento

AMONG THE diadem of attractions surrounding Naples, Sorrento offers perhaps
the most inspiring view of the bay, and certainly the maximum of creature
comfort. The ancient Surrentum, it was an established summer playground
for the rich Romans of antiquity. Since then, generations of famous people
have found inspiration in Sorrento—Lord Byron, Sir Walter Scott, and Oscar
Wilde, among them. Longfellow, James Fenimore Cooper, and Harriet
Beecher Stowe were American visitors. Goethe and Nietzsche, Stendhal and

Sorrento

de Musset, Caruso and Giuseppe Verdi, all yielded to its reposeful charm.

This town was the birthplace of the great Italian poet, Torquato Tasso (1544–1595), author of *Jerusalem Delivered,* and his statue graces the principal square of the town. Tasso had his tough moments—including the fate of being locked up as a madman for seven years in Ferrara.

Sorrento is still the most inviting place in Campania for a prolonged stay, and its shops are by far the most tempting, especially if you are partial to lace and linens. We must admit it is touristy. The open horse-drawn carriage confronts you everywhere, its driver shouting "Wanta drive? Bella panorama! Verra cheepa prize!" In the evening, after dinner, the *tarantella* is an invariable attraction in your hotel courtyard. The costumed dancers are of all ages, but they are always cheerful and agile, and the traveling public loves them. This interlude of dancing has been a fixture for decades, and we hope it never stops.

Sorrento's luxurious hotels stretch along a plateau of tufa rock that comes to a sudden stop at the edge of an awe-inspiring vertical cliff. Most of them have gardens, shaded by umbrella pines and fragrant with orange blossoms, oleander, and mimosa. At the base of the cliff are bathing beaches, and many of the hotels have sunk elevators through the stone to bring their guests quickly to the welcoming sands. The two best establishments in Sorrento are equipped with rather showy names: The EXCELSIOR GRAND HOTEL VITTORIA, which is run by the same management as the Vesuvio in Naples, and the GRAND HOTEL EUROPA PALACE, occupying a choice site overlooking the little port. Generations of overnight visitors have stayed at the COCUMELLA, established in an old convent at the eastern end of the town, and the IMPERIAL HOTEL TRAMONTANO, built at the cliff's edge. The great Tasso was born in what is now the west wing of this hotel, and its guests have included Shelley, Keats, and Lamartine. There are half a dozen other good hotels along the cliffs.

Ristorante Minervetta
Sorrento

As for restaurants, a comparatively new one, on the western outskirts of Sorrento, merits your attention. It is called the MINERVETTA. You park your car on the street-level roof of this welcoming place, and walk down marble steps to a gay, airy salon, decorated in gold and white, with picture windows opening out on a terrace. The old fishing village lies below. Ischia, Naples, and Vesuvius are silhouetted in the distance. There couldn't be a more inspiring view. Even if the food doesn't measure up to the vista, it is acceptable. The menu is simple, the wines are good, the prices reasonable. You pay nothing extra for one of the most striking settings in Italy.

Marina Grande and the town of Capri

Capri

THIS BRILLIANT, overpublicized, volcanic island, on the threshold of the Bay
of Naples, is a world in itself, and a favored retreat for honeymooners,
cinema stars, writers, and a miscellany of leisurely mankind best left unde-
fined. Its natural beauties, especially the Blue Grotto, defy shopworn adjectives. Regardless of the famous song, by the way, Capri is pronounced with
the accent on the first syllable. The island is always coupled with the name
of the Emperor Tiberius, stepson of Augustus, who was fascinated by its
isolation, and spent the last ten years of his life here. He also built a series of
twelve villas on the island and amused himself at odd moments by forcing
his prisoners to jump off the cliffs to their doom. In spite of this peccadillo,
the islanders have named a fine hotel for him.

The steamer from Naples takes an hour and a half to bring the eager
sightseer to the Marina Grande, Capri's well-protected harbor village. It
usually stops at Sorrento on the way. A majority of visitors take to smaller
boats at once, intent upon the adventure of the Blue Grotto and its incredible
sapphire waters. The foot passenger bent upon seeing the island lands immediately in a gesticulating throng of hack, cab, and bus drivers offering him
a guided tour. ("Bargaining necessary," as Baedeker used to say!) Hotel

435

Marina Grande–Capri

porters with gold letters on their caps plead with him, as do barkers from
nearby sea-food restaurants. If he chooses to ignore them, he will find a
funicular along the *quais* that will hoist him to the middle town of Capri
for a very modest fee. This settlement rests in a saddle astride the island.
Here you are in the midst of a tourist bazaar—coral, tortoise shell, mother-
of-pearl, straw hats, silk scarves, handbags, baskets, ballet slippers. In short,
it's the Capri of fiction, and quite an enticing one if you are in a shopping
mood. Though commercialism has laid a heavy hand on this charmed spot,
the contemplative soul has only to take a short stroll from the beaten path
to find himself in a different world. The island abounds in fascinating walks,
far from the tourist orbit.

Some people come to Capri for a quick look and spend a lifetime. Others
spend a winter here, but the majority come just for the day. There is some-
thing for each of them—a villa overlooking the sea, a charming hotel, or a
good noonday restaurant. The island settlements are four—the port of Marina
Grande, Capri itself, lofty Anacapri, at the western extremity of the island,
and the tiny Piccola Marina, facing a beach on the south shore.

The picturesque port-side cafés of the Marina Grande offer *zuppa di
pesce* and *fritto misto* to the public, but the wiser diners find sustenance on
a loftier plane, in the village of Capri. Prospects for a pleasant luncheon
are fair enough in these close-packed streets, even though the restaurants are
geared to the one-time tourist couple due to depart by the afternoon boat.
The GATTO BIANCO, Via Vittorio Emanuele 32, is one of the best. It has a
secluded terrace where you may enjoy the classic spaghetti, *risotto alla
provinciale,* and *pollo alla Leone,* accompanied by good Capri wine. LA PIGNA,
at Via Lo Palazzo 30, is another good restaurant, enjoying a fine view of the
port and the Bay of Naples beyond. The most luxurious place in Capri
is the HOTEL QUISISANA, the one de luxe establishment on the island. If you
dine on this wide tree-sheltered terrace, you are assured of a regal repast,
and if, as well you may, you fall in love with the island, here is a wonderful
place to stay.

By following a steep, winding road for a little less than three miles, you
come to Anacapri, a town that has the most dramatic location of all. Innumerable people have heard of Anacapri, for this is the setting of *The
Story of San Michele,* the best-seller written by the romantic Swedish doctor,
Axel Munthe. The villa of San Michele is open to visitors, and some of the
guides are characters from the original story. From this lofty western extremity of the island you behold one of the most inspiring panoramas in
the Mediterranean, and three good hotels have made the most of it. The
CAESAR AUGUSTUS, the SAN MICHELE, and the EDEN PARADISO are all excellent hostelries, and their setting defies description. We can't think of a more
restful place to spend a vacation. On our last trip to Anacapri we had

luncheon on the terrace of a relative newcomer, the little HOTEL BELLA VISTA, a trite name but an accurate one. Here we indulged in *crêpe Bella Vista,* an egg-enriched *cannelloni* filled with a mixture of *mozzarella,* Swiss, and Bel Paese cheeses, browned in the oven and served with a savory meat and tomato sauce. This specialty was followed by a *fritto misto* of *dorade,* baby shrimp, and octopus rings, light and delectable. Then fruit from the island, coffee, and a tiny Aurum and we called it quite a luncheon.

Finally, at the foot of a serpentine road, is Piccola Marina, the most exotic spot on the island—for the moment, at least. Here you will find a sandy bathing beach and chic summer villas with terraces, the most famous of which is LA CANZONE DEL MARE (The Song of the Sea), a fragment of paradise dreamed up by Gracie Fields, the famous English comedienne and singer. What was once Miss Fields' villa has been transformed into a very plush place of entertainment. You may loll on the café terrace and imbibe *aperitivi* between dips in the sea. Here also you may dine, and dance, in conspicuous luxury. The serving tables are heavy with delicacies—copious hors-d'oeuvre, cold meats and shellfish, beautiful salads. To cap it all there is a glittering pastry wagon. We've rarely seen such abundance. You pay a certain stipend for all this atmosphere and good food, of course, but you are well recompensed.

Ischia

THIS ISLAND, the largest of the group guarding the Bay of Naples, is developing rapidly as a resort, much to the despair of painters and writers who have long claimed it as exclusively their own. Attractive new hotels are cropping up round its shore, and someday it may become as popular as Capri. Surely it has almost as much to offer, including hot springs and thermal baths. Dominated by the crater of a long-extinct volcano called Epomeo, the island of Ischia is well planted with vineyards. They prosper in its volcanic soil and produce three palatable wines called Epomeo, Castello, and just plain Ischia.

Steamers from the Molo Beverello in Naples take about two hours to

The Castello—Ischia

land you in the circular port of Ischia, which is something of a curiosity. It once was a round lake filling the crater of an extinct volcano. Later a passage was cut through to the sea, making it a perfectly sheltered harbor. White buildings line its perimeter, many of them summer hotels. You will also see the Castello, a nearly deserted hump of rock crowned with ruined buildings. A road about nineteen miles long runs round the island, and offers a very exciting trip by motor. Along the way, you come to the village of Casamicciola, newly rebuilt after an earthquake in 1883. It is celebrated for its radioactive hot springs, and has a fine sandy beach. It was in this village that Henrik Ibsen died. They say he wrote a part of his poetic play *Peer Gynt* here.

You will find good hotels in Porto d'Ischia near the steamer landing: the EXCELSIOR, the MORESCO (summer only), and the GRAND HOTEL E DEI PINI. A vacation in one of them would be off the beaten path and, we think, filled with repose.

Salerno

JUST BELOW the Amalfi peninsula lies the bustling city of Salerno, on whose southern extremity is the long beachhead that will always be recorded in Anglo-Saxon naval and military annals. About fifteen years ago, at dawn on September 9, 1943, the epic Salerno landings began. After three weeks of bitter fighting, Naples was freed, and the Allies had a firm footing in

439

Italy. Contrary to the prevalent opinion, Salerno is not a shambles, although its outskirts took a beating. Several military cemeteries, however, serve as poignant reminders of the heavy sacrifice which the Salerno landings imposed.

While not as seductive as the smaller towns along the Amalfi Drive, Salerno has a superb location facing its bay, with a sandy beach lining its shore. Most of the city is modern, but there is one building worth seeking out, the Cathedral of San Matteo. Pope Gregory VII is buried here, and the bones of Saint Matthew, the evangelist, are said to repose in the crypt. Here again you will find marvelous bronze doors, made in Constantinople in 1099 and once inlaid with silver. Inside is a superb marble pulpit from the twelfth century, and around the atrium will be found twenty-eight antique columns filched from Paestum.

There are two good hotels in Salerno. One is a JOLLY HOTEL, larger and more expensive than usual, which occupies a choice site at the head of the beach promenade, the other a skyscraper affair called the GRAND HOTEL DIANA SPLENDID, on the busy Via Roma.

Paestum

THE INVASION of the Salerno coast spared a priceless relic from the days of early Greece, the flat, forlorn site of Paestum, established in the seventh century B. C. This will prove to be the ultimate treasure of Campania for many a visitor. There is a majesty, a melancholy grandeur, and a wealth of sun-baked color about these three Greek temples that is good for the soul.

Rising unexpectedly out of the plain, it is the ancient Poseidonia, the city of Neptune, founded by the Sybarites over twenty-five centuries ago. It later prospered under the Romans, but, during the Middle Ages, malaria infested its lowlands, causing the site to be totally abandoned. Though the city all but disappeared, its magnificent Greek Doric temples, apparently built for eternity, have endured. Archaeologists have been digging on this site for decades, uncovering its forum and rectangular streets. But Paestum's three majestic temples are the main witnesses of its grandeur in the days of Magna Graecia.

The Temple of Neptune, last built of the three, is Greek Doric in its purest form, and the best existing example outside the Parthenon. Dating from the fifth century B. C., it was built of travertine stone, and intended for a coat of stucco, to give it the whiteness of Grecian marble. It still retains thirty-six columns, most of the entablature, and ruins of the sacrificial altar. Adjoining it is an older temple, more extended and less beautiful, known as the Basilica. This one goes back to the sixth century B. C. and once had a central row of columns. About a quarter of a mile to the north stands

Temple of Neptune, the central nave–Paestum

The Temple of Ceres—Paestum

Interior of the Basilica—Paestum

The fountains–Caserta

the beautiful Temple of Ceres, presenting a classic silhouette against the southern Apennines.

The memory of a few hours spent wandering over these silent ghosts of Greek greatness will never leave you. There are no guides to pester you here, no slick salesmen, no gaping children. Paestum is all yours to enjoy in solitude, and to do so is a memorable experience. The custodians don't mind if you bring in a picnic lunch, and there couldn't be a more romantic place to enjoy it. However, there is a worthy little restaurant near the Porta della Giustizia, in case you didn't bring a hamper. It is called the NETTUNO, and the specialties include *cannelloni alla Nettuno, crespolini, carciofi alla Poseidonia,* and *frittura di pesce misto del golfo.* Upstairs, a few bedrooms accommodate overnight visitors who find that a few hours are insufficient time to explore this extinct city, as serene and beautiful as anything in Italy.

Caserta

SOME EIGHTEEN miles north of Naples is one of the most enormous of European palaces, surrounded by parks and avenues that are miles in length. The Royal Palace in Caserta, often referred to as the Italian Versailles, was erected

443

Marble maidens—Caserta

for Charles III of Bourbon shortly after 1750. Designed by the Vanvitellis, father and son, it was constructed with the aid of slave labor supplied by Moorish and African captives. A square building of huge dimensions, it rises around four courtyards so vast that it easily served as a square Pentagon for the combined Allied top brass in Italy during World War II. This palace was the GHQ of the Allied Command from 1943 on. The defeated Nazis came here to sign the surrender of the German Armies in Italy on April 29, 1945. Its main façade is about 785 feet wide, and the entire structure is six stories high. I recall these dimensions vividly, having climbed five flights of stairs in the palace for months on end. There *was* an elevator, but it was marked "For General Officers only," which made the rest of us pedestrians.

You may visit the palace now—its chapel, theater, and royal apartments. But the most interesting thing to see is the formal garden, stretching for two miles up the hillside. Down its axis runs a series of fountains, pools, cascades, and waterfalls, adorned with classic statues that look dated now. Nude marble maidens frolic under the fountain spray and seem far, far removed from Jacob Epstein.

Motorists who like to wind their way up hills will be rewarded by a detour to Caserta Vecchia, a hilltop village overlooking the new town. Here is an ancient Romanesque cathedral, consecrated in 1153, that has decided Moorish overtones. Overnight travelers can stop at a trustworthy JOLLY HOTEL down near Caserta's railway station.

The Arch of Trajan—Benevento

Benevento

INLAND AND some forty miles northeast of Naples, is a bustling city of fifty thousand inhabitants with a remarkable Roman triumphal arch. We have a weakness for this form of monumental architecture, and consider that the Arch of Trajan in Benevento is just about the world's finest outside of Rome itself. Built in 114 A. D., it is richly adorned with bas-reliefs depicting scenes from the Emperor Trajan's life. Its proportions are noble and its state of preservation superb. Benevento took a severe beating during the last war, but this arch was protected by a thick barricade of sandbags and escaped serious damage. The cathedral in this city is embellished with two fine thirteenth-century bronze doors illustrating the life of Christ. The local museum of Samnium deserves a visit also, particularly for its lovely Romanesque cloister.

Gourmets will take an interest in Benevento because it is heré that Strega, one of the world's most famous liqueurs, is distilled. A small, comfortable JOLLY HOTEL awaits pilgrims who wish to spend the night in the city.

This tour about sums up the highlights of Campania. There are other points of interest, of course—the Flegrean Fields, Baia, and Pozzuoli, for example. All of them are near the shore west of Naples, and would make a memorable day's excursion. But enough has been unfolded in this chapter, we hope, to demonstrate that Campania is one of the most rewarding of all the Italian regions.

A Calabrian farmhouse

Calabria and Basilicata

Chapter 17

CALABRIA
AND
BASILICATA

Aﬀter visiting the rich Neapolitan countryside, we are approaching the
end of our Italian travels. Only one shining attraction lies ahead,
the island of Sicily. In between stretches Calabria, the giant toe
of Italy, a dramatic strip of mountainous country surrounded by two seas,
the Ionian and the Tyrrhenian. If you take a ship or plane from Naples to
Palermo, Calabria need not enter into your plans. But if you go to Sicily by
train, bus, or car, you cover almost the entire length of the region before
reaching the ferryboats that carry you across to Sicily. An avid explorer can
find many fascinating things in Calabria, but the more casual traveler, for
whom this book is written, will probably be content with a two-day trip
through the mountainous roads or along the shore.

Calabria is one of the least-visited regions in Italy, for a variety of
reasons. First of all, its historical treasures are meager. Earthquakes have
harassed it for centuries, and few of its architectural masterpieces have withstood the tremors. Second, its hotel resources are not alluring, and they were
even less so before the Jolly Hotel chain established itself in several key cities,
among them Cosenza, Catanzaro, Nicastro, and Gioia Tauro. Third, it is
rather forbidding country, in spite of its impressive mountains and extensive
coastline, the longest (485 miles) of any Italian region. Most of Calabria is
a somewhat savage land, seamed with mountains, gorges, and ravines, capped
with lonely hill towns, still-used relics of medieval days. Though there are
occasional lakes, the water resources are poor. Immense forests cap the peninsula, but the impoverished farmer often must keep himself warm with fagots.

Earthquakes, the dreaded *terremoti,* have long plagued Calabria. Reggio
di Calabria was completely destroyed in 1908, along with Messina across
the channel. Earthquakes still continue, and villages disappear even now,
but the courageous inhabitants refuse to give up and they build anew.

The natives of Calabria do not appear to be a happy lot. None of the gaiety of the Neapolitans lights up their faces, which is understandable enough. The poverty of the people is all too apparent. Their lands are not fertile, their water supply is inadequate, their pleasures are few. Threatened by earthquakes, economic distress, and a rude winter climate, it is not surprising that they have grave, troubled faces. It is evident that unemployment is a major problem here, particularly among the young men, though the women all seem to have plenty to do. In spite of these somber facts, Calabria merits a visit for its romantic beauty alone. Travelers who are sensitive to its unworldly charm may remember it more vividly than they do the classic Italian areas.

Regardless of his unpromising situation, the native Calabrian is a good farmer, and carries on with tenacity. He manages to grow grapes, oranges, lemons, figs, and almonds on his more productive slopes and in river valleys. Gnarled olive trees have survived for decades on his meager soil, and he has a genius for growing vegetables, particularly his favorite *melanzana,* or eggplant. Skilled artisans populate Calabrian towns—metalworkers, weavers, tanners, and lacemakers.

The population of Calabria is a mixed one. This area was once the pride of the Byzantines, who were in turn driven out by the Normans. Traces of them have long since vanished, but the present population shows the ancestry of Albanians and Greeks who fled the Turkish invasion. The Albanians centered around Catanzaro while the Greeks favored Reggio di Calabria, where you may still observe many classic Grecian profiles.

Native costumes once provided bright spots of color in the Calabrian landscape, but most of them have now disappeared. However, in winter you will still observe groups of country women wearing warm red flannel skirts. If the costumes are few, the animals are as engaging as ever. Mules, donkeys, and a few horses furnish most of the transportation, laden down with baskets and bundles. These patient beasts usually carry a child or two for good measure.

The frugal Calabrian farmer finds a few things in his favor besides his orchards and vegetable gardens. In his back yard are pigs, meaning smoked ham and sausage, and his herds of sheep assure him of further sustenance. If he is a good hunter, the forests will provide him with partridge, quail,

Farm scene in the Calabrian hills

Stamping out the grain—Rivello

venison, and wild boar, and the mountain streams yield handsome trout to a good fisherman. Best of all, his wife is likely to be an excellent cook. She sticks to simple, sturdy, country cooking with few frills, but the experts contend that it ranks with the best in Italy. Unfortunately, the traveler passing through Calabria has only a dim chance of tasting it, unless he is adept at making friends with farmers' wives, a rather perilous pursuit in this neighborhood.

The eggplant is the most popular vegetable in Calabria, and the housewife prepares it in several different ways. She stuffs it with bread crumbs, parsley, garlic, tomato paste, and cubes of bacon; she cooks it with cheese, and preserves it in jars with mint, garlic, and chopped peppers. *Melanzana al funghetto* is sliced eggplant sprinkled with chopped garlic, pepper, orégano, and olive oil, and baked in the oven. Most formidable of all is *melanzana in agrodolce:* the eggplant is sliced, scalded in boiling oil and then cooked in a mixture of sour wine, chocolate, sugar, cinnamon, pine nuts, raisins, walnuts, and cedar bark. That's exotic enough for anybody!

Certain interesting local recipes involve fruit. *Panicelli d'uva passula* are fresh grapes wrapped in leaves from the lime tree and baked in the oven. *Crocette* are made of dried figs, cut in two and stuffed with walnuts and almonds, then baked until they turn a reddish brown color. Pasta is a tower of strength in these households and takes on many forms, from *canneroni,*

451

which are large tubes, to the thinnest *vermicelli*. The best cheeses are Cacio-cavallo, made from mare's milk, and the familiar *ricotta* and Provole.

Calabrians who live close to the sea find a plentiful supply of fish in the local shops—tuna, swordfish, pike, sardines, and eels. In the marshes near Nicastro hunters bag woodcock, wild duck, and moor hen. It would appear that nature is kind to the Calabrians in one way at least—if they invest sufficient labor, their larders are well stocked.

The Calabrian hillsides are hospitable to vineyards, and several creditable wines come from the region. They tend to be dark and heavy, and many of them are shipped to fortify the more fragile wines of northern Italy. However, plenty of good vintages remain to be tasted by the passing oenophile. The best red table wine here is called Cirò di Calabria, a sturdy fellow running between thirteen and fifteen degrees in alcohol. Two good white wines are Rogliano and the familiar Malvasia, grown in the Catanzaro region. For a dessert wine you have Greco di Gerace, an amber nectar pressed from the Moscato-Fior d'Arancio grape, said to impart a faint bouquet of orange blossoms.

The trip to Sicily through Calabria may turn out to be something of a chore, but it can be exciting as well. The motorist proceeding southward reaches a point of vital decision about twelve miles east of Salerno, at the crossroads town of Battapaglia. Here he must choose one or the other, the low road or the high road. We have done both, in summer and in winter, and will try to tell you the pleasures and pitfalls of each.

At Battapaglia, if you ignore the left fork and continue straight on, you are headed for the low coastal road, N. 18, that leads through Paestum and its temples and then climbs over winding hills, finally meeting the shore at the little beach town of Sapri. We have vivid memories of this place, for our car broke down there in a driving rain, and we spent twenty-four hours waiting for the repairs to be finished. Luckily there was an acceptable hotel called the VITTORIA, and a gay local cinema. Some twenty miles farther along the barren shore is Praia a Mare, an inconsequential little place with a good beach. But it has something far more important for travelers, a welcoming little oasis—yes, another JOLLY HOTEL.

The Naples-Reggio di Calabria railway follows this coastline faithfully but the motor road, although it appears straight on the map, is full of inland detours. The mouths of rivers and ravines are not bridged. You have to follow them inland until they narrow, then cross and come all the way back to the shore which, incidentally, is beautiful. The color of the sea can hardly be described—purple and deep indigo blue, with streaks of jade near the sand. You find immense sweeping beaches without a soul in sight, interrupted by steep rocky cliffs that plunge directly into deep water.

With improving weather we were able to take good pictures of the

The chapel–Paola

The village pump–Avetrana

The mirror–Diamante

Scilla, ancient fishing village

coastal village of Diamante reflected in the water, and Paola, a pleasantly baroque place whose town gate frames a fountain and an ornate Renaissance chapel. In Paola, the home of San Francesco di Paola, you will find, in case you arrive late in the afternoon—the acceptable little ALBERGO MODERNO. The next day, if you expect to reach Sicily, you have a fairly long run along the coast, coming first to Pizzo, a seaside town with a certain place in history. It was here that Joachim Murat, Marshal of France, King of Naples, and Napoleon's brother-in-law, was arrested in 1815 as he attempted to regain Naples. He was speedily tried and condemned, and faced a firing squad in the old Spanish castle on the village square. His grave is in the Pizzo cemetery.

Vibo and Palmi are next on the road, and many miles elapse before you come to Scilla, the most picturesque town of all, where you catch your first sight of Sicily and sense the proximity of a ferryboat. Scilla has some of the charm of a Ligurian fishing village, and is famed in antiquity. Homer wrote of the monster of Scylla as a terrifying creature with seven heads that devoured passing sailors.

The coastal route, taken as a whole, is quite slow, and we experienced a good deal of tire trouble, picking up hobnails at frequent intervals. It was a pleasure to draw into the ferry slip at Villa San Giovanni and see the blue silhouette of Sicily less than four miles away.

454

Calabrian roadside

The main or high road to Sicily begins back in Battapaglia when you take a left fork, N. 19, toward Potenza. Everything considered, this road is the better of the two, despite its interminable turns and slopes. You are called upon to make a good stiff day's run from Naples in order to reach Cosenza by dusk, the best place for an overnight stop. If you are very zealous and rise early, you can get even farther, to either Catanzaro or Nicastro, where Jolly Hotels are installed. In either case, beautiful scenery and plenty of mild adventure await you along the way. You will also learn something about the hardships of life in Italy today, after having seen so much of its rosy side.

Most of the villages you pass along this well-paved mountain highway are fortified towns, each crowning a steep hill. They were built to permit the villagers to beat off the invaders, usually Saracens, and at the same time to keep them free of the malaria that infested the lowlands. The Calabrians still cling to their native hilltops, regardless of the fact that water is lacking in most of them. This situation means a long trek down to the nearest fountain, a ceremony that populates the roads with a procession of housewives, children, and donkeys, all laden with copper or earthen jugs. There seems to be but one way for a woman to carry anything in Calabria—on her head. The balance and poise of these straight-backed figures are quite beautiful. Anything from a water jug to an immense bundle of hay goes on the head. We recall a fine looking young woman walking down a mountain path in her bare feet, carrying nothing but her shoes on her head. A splendid round figure of an older woman walked through a village street transporting four immense circular baskets, topped by a large suitcase. They added at least

455

Homeward bound from the stock fair—Calabria

five feet to her height. The women's sense of balance must be perfect. When we smiled and nodded at one woman with a heavy copper jug of water on her head, she responded with an equally friendly smile and a forward movement of her neck, something in the manner of the horizontal head movements of a Balinese dancer—a nod being obviously impossible. Little girls in Calabria begin early to learn to place a twist of cloth in precisely the right place on their heads and to rest the earthen jar at the correct angle. A lifetime of jug-toting awaits them.

The serpentine highway winds high and low through the endless torment of the hills, passing many isolated farmhouses along the way. These are humble, tile-roofed buildings with stuccoed walls, surrounded by ancient olive trees and impressive wheatstacks. Almost all of them are marked by a small open circular area that is sometimes paved with concrete. Here the Calabrian farmer extracts the wheat. He spreads the stalks under the feet of oxen who go around in a circle, blindfolded, stamping out the grain. A primitive method dating from centuries ago, it is still effective. You will see hand-hewn haystacks about these farms. They are built around poles, and the farmer whittles off fodder with a broad knife as his animals need it.

We had the good fortune to encounter a stock fair taking place in a large farm along this highway. For miles we had seen farmers leading their prize oxen, cattle, mules, pigs, and sheep to the fair. There were a glossy,

Cosenza

blond, long-haired goat, a washed and brushed black ram, and many dark purple hogs, including a baby tied by its hind leg, kicking in squealing rage. There was a she-ass with her colt, a fuzzy donkey of great charm. A circus parade could hardly have been better. Beyond the farmyard the procession was reversed. Here, purchasers led their newly acquired animals away. One was a young mule, sleek and shiny brown as a young faun, with a pale under-belly and full brushed tail, the most beautiful mule we had ever seen. We asked his proud owner to let us take his picture, which is reproduced nearby.

As you can see, a good deal of roadside animation occurs before one finally arrives at Cosenza, capital of the province, a city of some 57,000 inhabitants. The new Cosenza lacks interest, but the close-packed old town, climbing up a hillside crowned by a venerable fortress, has its attractive points, as our photograph shows. Halfway up the hill stands a twelfth-century cathedral of a certain charm. There are two good hotels awaiting the weary traveler here. One is the ever-present JOLLY HOTEL, an especially boxlike one with very little atmosphere, on the Rotonda Lungo Crati. We still prefer it to its competitor, the HOTEL IMPERIALE, that faces a park in the center of the new town. The rooms at the Imperiale are very comfortable, with modern baths. However, we would face a libel suit if we expressed our true opinion of the restaurant, and particularly the service.

Those who wish to visit the famous forests of La Sila will find Cosenza a convenient base. Sicily-bound travelers face a comparatively easy drive the next morning, whether they stay in Cosenza, Catanzaro, or Nicastro. Their road soon leads to Pizzo and the shore, and the ferryboat to Messina is wait-ing for them either at Villa San Giovanni or Reggio di Calabria.

Basilicata

THE INSTEP of the Italian boot rewards the traveler no better than the Calabrian toe. Basilicata (also currently called Lucania) is probably the poorest and least inviting of all the Italian regions. It is a rather wild, desert country, majestic but mournful in character. Its population is scanty, its agriculture and industry limited. Nature has not been kind to Basilicata. Water is scarce, and a most familiar sight is a group of patient villagers with jugs awaiting their turn at the crossroads pump. It has struck us time and again that poverty and ignorance go hand in hand with lack of water. What a different place Basilicata would be if only the engineers and the money were available to bring water to these people, irrigate their land, install public laundries in the town squares and running water in, or even near, their houses!

The people of Basilicata, however, have plenty of vitality. Dark-haired,

Matera, the lower town

black-eyed, and energetic, they are the product of a melting pot that includes Lombards, Arabs, Normans, Byzantines, Greeks, and Albanians. There are also villages occupied almost entirely by Jews, as their names—Sinagoga and Giudecca—would indicate. The courageous farmers work endlessly on their parched plains, and manage to wrest a subnormal living from the parsimonious soil.

There are two cities of importance in the region, Potenza and Matera. Potenza experienced a bad earthquake in 1857 and is newly built—and dull architecturally—and may be skipped. It lacks good overnight accommodations and needs a new hotel badly. Sightseers should remember Matera, however, for this city is one of the most extraordinary in Italy. Built grotesquely on the steep slopes of two ravines, it is an incredible conglomeration of houses and caves cut into the soft rock. A good part of the population lives in these primitive caverns, which are more photogenic than comfortable, we imagine. There are some interesting churches in the upper town of Matera and a good JOLLY HOTEL for your night's lodging. For the rare travelers who pass through Basilicata, Matera is a highly recommended stop. On the eastern outskirts of the town will be found monuments of accidental splendor—immense quarries of white stone that is soft enough to be cut with a saw. Cutting has been going on for centuries, leaving grotesque pylons and arches, superbly suited to the camera.

Venturesome archaeologists will find shades of Grecian grandeur along the Ionian shore of Basilicata. In the forlorn flatlands near Taranto stands Metaponto, the ghost of the ancient Hellenic city that was once the capital of Magna Graecia. A few Doric columns from early temples are all that remain of the city where Pythagoras founded a school of philosophy. Though the setting is desolate now, it still fires the imagination.

The gastronomic distinctions of Basilicata are few, but one is worth noting. It was here, according to legend, that the largest omelette in the world was produced. It appears that when the Carthusian monastery of San Lorenzo received a visit from the Emperor Charles V in 1535, the abbot of the order decided to put on a show for him and had his cooks produce an omelette made with a thousand eggs!

The Roman amphitheater—Syracuse

Sicily

Chapter 18

SICILY

THE LARGEST, most beautiful and inspiring of Mediterranean islands does not compress readily into a single chapter. With a history that reaches back into the dim pages of antiquity and a three-sided coastline filled with some of the world's most sublime architecture and landscape, it is a subject of infinite variety, not to be painted with rapid strokes of the brush.

Sicily signifies much more to the traveler than just a region of Italy or an autonomous island with a disquieting emblem made up of a face surrounded by wings, serpents, and three legs. It is a museum, an astonishing one, of diverse and unrelated civilizations—ancient Greek, Roman, Byzantine, Saracen, and Norman, with smatterings of Spain thrown in. When the intrepid Garibaldi stormed the island, less than a century ago, and brought it into the newly founded Kingdom of Italy, he annexed for his country an immense vineyard, an even larger orchard, a volatile, raven-haired, sun-browned population, and an absolute treasure of dramatic countryside and architecture. Carthaginian ruins, Greek temples and theaters, Roman bridges and aqueducts, Byzantine cloisters, Norman churches, and Saracen mosques all are here as reminders of the rich tapestry of Sicilian history.

In spite of these intrusions throughout the centuries, Sicily retains a mysterious atmosphere all its own—strangely African, faintly Oriental. The Sicilians sing with a melancholy Moorish wail, and their villages are pervaded with the perfume of pungent, Oriental spices. They love bright colors. What could be more African than a typical Sicilian donkey cart, painted in brilliant tones of orange, blue, and yellow! Their fishing vessels are rigged in a slightly berserk fashion, with russet-orange sails, just as they are in Tunis or Cairo. Their swarthy complexions, luxurious black hair, and fine features suggest more than a few Moorish ancestors. Though not as gay as the Neapolitans, they possess plenty of Italian virtues. The Sicilian farmers are hard workers, and have made valiant attempts to salvage every bit of arable soil on the island. The most uncompromising hills are terraced in the hope that they will provide a shelf where olive trees or a few artichokes may take root.

Sicily suffers from overpopulation, and the poverty that goes with it. The prodigious Italian faculty for producing progeny is never better illustrated than here. What Sicily needs are more fertile fields and fewer fertile women. *Bambini* positively swarm. In other fields of activity, however, unemployment among the men runs high. The streets of most Sicilian villages are crowded with idle men, all highly articulate, all gifted with flamboyant gestures. But here, as in Calabria, the

women all seem to have something to do! Their life is a ceaseless round of strenuous tasks.

Sicily is a strange, romantic land, steeped in a mythology that stirs the imagination. It is hardly a Latin country at all, and the influence of Rome in its history has been slight. The Greeks, whose colonists arrived about 800 B. C., have left the most indelible impression. Pythagoras, Archimedes, and Plato all lived in Sicily. The Greek influence is one of the reasons that the island for decades has been popular with foreign visitors. Most of the pioneer visitors, in the early nineteenth century, were Englishmen—archaeologists and historians who reveled in the remote temples of Segesta, Selinunte, and Agrigento. England also sent wine dealers who developed the sweet wines of Marsala into a formidable rival of Port in the British market. Sicily's inviting climate, mild from early autumn through spring, and its abundant, almost tropical vegetation, also attracted an increasing number of tourists to this fascinating isle. By the turn of the present century, it had become established as a major objective for sun-seeking travelers, and so it remains today.

Hotels were built at about that time to accommodate the visitors, and *they* remain the same also. Until recently, when the Jolly Hotel chain moved in en masse, there was a static charm to the hotel situation in Sicily. My venerable Baedeker dates from 1912, but its information about acceptable hostelries is quite accurate today, except that full *pensione* no longer costs twenty lire per day. At the present rate of exchange, it costs more than that to buy an Italian newspaper. The same few comfortable hotels in Messina, Siracusa, Palermo, and Taormina mentioned over forty years ago are still the ones to recommend today. Taormina has blossomed out with a few new names, and there is a startling, ultramodern newcomer at Mondello,

The cypresses—Syracuse

Palermo's beach resort, that deserves your attention. We have a firm conviction that today's traveler, unless he has had basic training in youth hostels or as an itinerant peddler, will *not* be happy in the lower category of Sicilian hotels. For this reason there is cause for rejoicing in the arrival of nine new JOLLY HOTELS, placed at convenient intervals around the island. Going counterclockwise from Palermo (where a fine new one faces the water), they now welcome motorists and bus riders at Trapani, Castelvetrano, Agrigento, Piazza Armerina, Caltagirone, Ragusa, and Messina. The housing problem is thus resolved, and very comfortably, for those who wish to explore Sicily fully and at leisure.

The dilemma of finding a truly warm climate in midwinter is rarely solved, but Sicily offers as good an answer as any of its competitors. You may have seen travel posters in symphonic yellows, comparable only to van Gogh's sunflowers, shouting Sicily's promise of sunshine, of trees heavily laden with oranges and lemons, of pink and white almond blossoms carpeting the hillsides. The travel folders tell you that there is surf bathing in January and, only a short distance away, skiing on the broad slopes of Mount Etna. Tarantella dancers brighten night clubs and hotel patios, and there are puppet shows to amuse your children. Faced with the proposition (and the privilege) of escaping the rigors of midwinter, travelers from Europe and America have heeded these extravagantly worded blandishments with high hopes, and perhaps a touch of skepticism. After all, there are other tempting places—the French and Italian Rivieras, the Spanish islands, Egypt, Greece . . . Of course, one can't guarantee Mediterranean weather.

We recall a snowstorm in Taormina on Christmas Day. But Sicily does benefit from a highly favorable climate and the thermometer rarely reaches freezing. As Cicero observed some time ago (he had a government job in Sicily), there is seldom a day in the Sicilian year when the sun fails to peek through. Moreover, oranges and lemons *do* cover the trees in midwinter, and almond blossoms *do* appear in February, just as promised. The travel folders are right! But spring and fall are still the best seasons.

Before we guide you on a tour of the perimeter of Sicily, a short briefing on epicurean matters seems in order. Gastronomy plays second fiddle for the visitor here, and we might as well be candid about it. Conventional hotel food will be the lot of all but the most zealous seekers of local dishes. Good restaurants are few and far between. Sicilian specialties exist, and they are so numerous that we can't begin to list them all. But they are home cooked, not found in hotels. However, a few of them may be obtained in Palermo's animated restaurants, notably *pasta alle sarde,* probably the most celebrated Sicilian dish. It consists of boiled macaroni, in long strands, mixed with alternate layers of baby fennel and young fresh sardines, both cooked in oil. A few anchovies, a pinch of saffron, and a handful of raisins and pine nuts are added. The dish is well anointed with olive oil before it goes into the oven. Served cold in pie-shaped portions, it tastes better than it sounds.

Risotto alla siciliana is a tasty version of this famous rice dish, built around eggplant, tomato, parsley, and basil, topped off with a golden crust of grated cheese. *La caponata* is a truly exquisite Sicilian lobster preparation including octopus, eggplant, onions, and celery, all fried in fragrant olive oil. Another version of *la caponata* concentrates on vegetables alone, without the sea food. All of these specialties are obtainable in Palermo restaurants, and we urge you to make their acquaintance.

You will find Sicilian fruit, of course, everywhere you turn. Oranges, lemons, and tangerines are irrepressibly abundant. Roadside fruitstands will display large oranges and baby ones, round and oval ones, red and pinkish ones, and a flashing brunette called *sanguigna doppia,* whose flesh verges on the purple-russet of Sicilian sunsets. A *pompelmo* is a grapefruit, smaller than those we know in America. Table grapes ripen in the summer, and some are delectable, particularly the Chasselas Dorato and the Zibibbo, a long yellow grape with a muscat aroma. Then there are medlars, which Sicilians insist are exquisite. My own ardor lags at the taste of this forlorn fruit. The Sicilian fig, however, is easily appreciated. It is a local passion, whether fresh or dried. In this land of olives, cypresses, cactus, and assorted evergreens, the fig tree in winter, blue-gray and bare, is one of the nudest objects imaginable.

The faithful olive tree lays a gray-green tapestry over the less fertile areas of Sicily, and forms the keystone of its cooking. Butter is a rarity. And the more deftly we side-step the subject of Sicilian meat, particularly beef, the better. By a twist of gastronomic justice, it doesn't make much difference to the average Sicilian family. They can't afford the stringy stuff anyway. Bread, pasta, greens, and sweets keep them going. They devour purple-faced cauliflower and *finocchio* by the cartload. They also have a country *pizza* of their own, a luxurious affair based on fresh ewe's-milk cheese, seasoned with sausage, anchovy, tomato, olives and herbs, and calling for a fine robust digestion.

The sea is moderately kind to the Sicilians, bringing them plenty of sardines, octopus, shrimp, and eel, but rarely the bountiful netfuls common to the Adriatic. The upper reaches of any Sicilian food shop are hung with twine-wrapped cylinders of cheese in multiple sizes. There are two principal types, both of which need a year of aging up there in the rafters. One is Canestrato, made from ewe's milk. The other is called Caciocavallo which, in this case, is not made from mare's milk, as the name implies, but from that of the furry and forlorn Sicilian cow.

As you have already been promised, blossoming almond trees brighten the southern Sicilian slopes in earliest spring and later provide the foundation for many baroque sweets. Coated with sugar, Jordan almonds are tossed to children at every wedding—and subsequent christening. Pistachio nuts, some of the world's best, come from orchards near Catania, and lend their perfume to ices and galantines everywhere.

It is in the realm of sweets that this country really lets itself go. Even in the rural towns, a pastry shop is a riotous panorama of the gaudiest, coziest, most flamboyant cakes extant. *La cassata,* for which we give the recipe in the back of the book, is a lush ringleader and a strong favorite at Eastertime. It is a soft, rococo, multicolored cake, filled with a chocolate stuffing and crowned with candied fruit. Incalculable calories! Perelman said it first: *"Chacun à son goo!" Cannoli* are sweet *cannelloni,* if you wish, cylinders of crust-wrapped chocolate, with a vanilla custard filling. A *torrone* is the sweetest of all, a pink and green almond candy loaf with cherries, nuts, citron, orange peel, and pistachios imbedded in it.

The soil of Sicily is friendly to the grape, and many commendable vintages, particularly dessert wines, are produced here. Marsala, of course, is the star of the lot, and known all over the world. The English were among the first to appreciate this sweet fortified wine of dark amber-brown color. It was Lord Nelson's favorite. It is produced in vineyards at the western extremity of the island, and you may visit the cellars in Marsala by ringing a few doorbells. A blended wine, it has a lingering aftertaste and is faintly and pleasantly acid, because volcanic soil produces it. Marsala is served in any Sicilian café, often from miniature casks, and appears on restaurant menus in a sauce for *scaloppine alla marsala,* or in a *zabaglione,* two of its many classic roles. Sometimes you will encounter a refreshing novelty, strawberries served with a chilled sauce of Marsala and orange juice.

Other palatable dessert wines are made from the muscat grape. Moscato di Siracusa and Moscato di Noto, both known abroad, are golden in color, with a heavy bouquet—ideal as companions to fruit and sweets. Moscato Passito di Pantelleria comes from the small island between Tunis and Sicily and has the rich taste of partially dried grapes. Malvasia di Lipari is produced on the islands of Lipari, Salina, and Stromboli, and has a full malmsey flavor. Zibibbo will prove cloying to many palates, but don't you like its name?

Among the table wines, Corvo is the significant one to remember. It comes from beautifully kept vineyards at Casteldaccia and has the hot blood of Sicily in its veins. Either red or white, Corvo is a very superior dry wine, and will be found on every respectable wine list. Other sturdy vintages originate on the slopes of Mount Etna, whose volcanic soil gives them an aggressive character, good for blending purposes. The whites are dry and straw colored, excellent with fish, while the reds need a little aging. Finally, from the eastern slopes near Messina comes Faro, a full-bodied red wine, of rich ruby color, a worthy comrade to Sicilian pasta.

Along the quais–Palermo

Today's traveler is offered a multitude of choices in Sicily. A week, a month, or a year can be spent in exploring this mountainous, ever-changing island. Within the limits of our rapidly dwindling space, we would like to sketch out a month-long visit that can be, if necessary, compressed into an extremely eventful week. Many omissions occur in such planning, of course, but the best of Sicily is along its shore, which our path follows. They call this coastal road *Il Nastro d'Oro,* the Ribbon of Gold, and it richly deserves the title. It isn't necessary to have your own car or to rent one, in order to make this perimetrical pilgrimage, by the way. Excellent guided tours will take you over the route in CIAT buses in less than a week's time and attend to all details, including meals and hotel accommodations. Stopovers can be arranged for archaeologically-minded passengers who just can't tear them-selves away quickly from Greek temples and mosaic-laden cathedrals. Our counterclockwise cavalcade begins and ends in Sicily's most important seaport.

Palermo

MANY TRAVELERS commence their Sicilian adventure in this island capital, arriving on a transatlantic liner or by the overnight steamer from Naples. Daily plane service from Rome, Milan, and Naples brings other visitors,

The cathedral—Palermo

Fountain in the Piazza Pretoria–Palermo   *The "cala" and the fishing fleet–Palermo*

sometimes in unexpected droves. Palermo's hotel facilities being limited, it is highly important, at the outset, to make reservations well in advance. Then you will feel free to enjoy the city, the sixth largest in Italy. Its history abounds with invasions. Beginning as a Phoenician foundation, it has belonged to almost every civilization. Carthage, Rome, the Goths, the Arabs, and the Normans all claimed it as their own. In the early thirteenth century, Frederick II made Palermo the setting of his court. Then it was taken over by the Spaniards, who held it for almost five centuries, until the Bourbons of Naples entered the scene in 1718. The architecture of Palermo reflects each of these periods, making it a city of many moods, all of them fascinating.

This effervescent, noisy metropolis of over half a million inhabitants offers unexpected rewards to the prowling sightseer, especially near the waterfront and the market squares. Pin-point the Piazza Caracciolo on your map and look for the ultimate in Sicilian animation. The place reverberates with the shouts of black marketeers, fish peddlers, pastry vendors, and medicine men. Street singers, hand organs, quite gruesome meat markets, and damsels of doubtful virtue enrich the atmosphere. The sheltered *cala,* where the fishing fleet clusters in colorful disorder, is another spot dear to the heart of local artists. After a rainstorm, a hundred sails in varied tints are hoisted to dry, an unforgettable sight calling for quick use of the color camera. Nor will

Porto Nuova–Palermo *San Giovanni degli Eremiti–Palermo*

you ever forget the catacombs of Palermo, dank places whose walls are decorated with the robed skeletons of long-suspended monks. A more cheerful apparition is found in the gay and pagan fountain dominating the Piazza Pretoria, as playful and irreverent a display of multiple marble nymphs as you'll see in many a day, and certain to be banned in Boston.

The sightseer in Palermo has a few exciting days ahead of him. Some of the world's most beautiful mosaics are close at hand. Among the more interesting buildings, the vast Royal Palace probably comes first. To miss it would be like missing Notre Dame when you visit Paris. Its eighteenth-century façade gives scant hint of the treasure it contains—La Cappella Palatina. Built in 1130 by the Norman King Roger II, the Palatine Chapel possesses the most richly decorated interior in all Christian art, a masterpiece of Norman-Arab style. It is floored in multicolored marble and its walls are choked with delicate mosaics representing scenes from the Old Testament and from the lives of Christ, Saint Peter, and Saint Paul. Its nave is lined with rare marble columns and roofed with a rich, gilded stalactite ceiling. Because of the dim light, it takes some time for your eyes to assimilate the subtlety of the mosaics. Your guide will have a flashlight to illuminate the darker corners.

Palermo's immense cathedral dates from 1169 and bears the distinction of having an English builder, Archbishop Gualterius Offamilius, known also as Walter of the Mill. He came to Sicily at the request of the king, Henry II, to serve as tutor for the king's son, young Duke William II, and later undertook the building of this sprawling edifice, which is richly ornate in its towers and porches. The interior has been modernized, and lacks architectural charm, but it contains one of the most interesting cemeteries to be found anywhere. For here are collected six magnificent royal tombs, those of Sicily's greatest kings, among them Frederick II, Henry VI, and Roger II.

Visitors should not miss the curious little Church of San Giovanni degli Eremiti, whose five tomato-pink domes proclaim its original function as a mosque. This ancient Norman structure was begun in 1132 by King Roger II, who doubtless hired an Arab architect. The most captivating views may be obtained from the cloister, a beautiful fragment of architecture with pointed arches half hidden by vegetation.

Equally interesting is La Martorana, a Norman church embellished with exquisite Byzantine mosaics. One of them shows a proud and perhaps presumptuous King Roger I being crowned by Christ. This church, which has a four-storied Norman campanile, the finest in Palermo, belongs to the city's Albanian colony, and the Greek rites are observed. Close at hand stands the Norman Church of San Cataldo, rejoicing in three Saracen domes.

Four religious subjects in a row may prove heavy going for some sightseers. If so, they will find pleasant variety in the National Museum, installed in an ancient convent. Here are shown the famous metopes that were rescued from the ruined temples of Selinunte. The early primitive examples from the sixth century B.C. temples show a certain heaviness, but the later ones exhibit Grecian sculpture in all its Attic grace. There are many other things in the museum, including an unforgettable Etruscan sarcophagus.

Grand Hotel
Villa Igea

Palermo

The hotel situation in Palermo is adequate, with three large hotels available. The best of them, and the most famous for generations, is the GRAND HOTEL VILLA IGEA. Facing the Golden Shell bay at the Piazza Acquasanta, on the western extremity of the city, this luxurious, Victorian establishment is definitely *vieux style*. But its old-fashioned plumbing works to perfection, and its comfortable rooms will prove a joy to those who don't mind paying top prices. The Villa Igea provides beautiful sea-front gardens for its guests, and a commendable cuisine. Its location is close to the promontory of Monte Pellegrino.

The GRANDE ALBERGO E DELLE PALME, Via Roma 398, is a busy, big-city hotel in the heart of Palermo. Until recently, it was the second alternative of the traveling public. Now, however, the JOLLY HOTEL has been installed in a fine waterside setting on the Foro Italico, giving the traveler a wider choice.

Palermo has its lighter side—a fine opera, a university whose students swarm through the busy streets between classes and, we are glad to say, a few restaurants to provide at least a glimpse of Sicilian cooking. The most satisfactory of these is the OLIMPIA, at Number 109 on the populous Via Ruggera Settimo. Recommended to us by a rotund native businessman, the place proved to be full of silver-thatched Sicilian executives, an unfailing index of excellence. On the ground floor is the CAFÉ DAGNINO, a student-choked wonderland of drinks, cakes, confections, and ices that merits exploration. The exuberant Sicilian sweets are fully bared to your gaze, and they present a startling spectacle. Can pastry *be* more baroque, can ice cream possibly glitter with gaudier colors? In the far corner is a sort of hot shop where they sell exotic unsweet things, and here is your best chance to savor Palermo's local specialties. You take your pick, prop yourself on a high stool facing a marble shelf on the wall, and you can almost imagine yourself in an American beanery—except for the food, which shatters the illusion at once. Here you may buy, for little more than a song, a segment of that famous *pasta alle sarde,* or aromatic rice fritters, assorted *pizze,* fish fries, and sandwiches that defy all precedent. It's a marvelous place to stock up on provisions for a picnic, and you don't have to know the names of things—just point. The comely brunette at this counter will wrap up a treasury of strange delicacies that taste less alarming than they look.

Up one flight is the Olimpia restaurant, a reposeful and well-lighted salon whose windows overlook the teeming thoroughfare. A conventional but varied menu contains such standbys as *ravioli piemontese, capretta alla romana,* and *fegato alla veneziana.* But it mentions Sicilian specialties too. We indulged in two of them—*pasta alle sarde* to begin with, and then *melanzane alla siciliana,* eggplant sliced and cooked in oil with a bevy of other things: tomatoes, onions, celery, pine nuts, sugar, vinegar and capers. The service in the Olimpia, performed by waiters dressed as bellboys with gold buttons, is all one could ask. The wine list is good, and the coffee hot and strong. There is a pleasant air of well-being about the place. My plump business friend was right: Some of the best food in Sicily can be found here.

We tried several other restaurants in Palermo, and think you will also like the RISTORANTE CASTELNUOVO, situated on the south side of the piazza of the same name. It is another of those high-ceilinged, all-white places, devoid of atmosphere, but dedicated to an honest standard of cooking. Here you will find good pasta, including a copious spaghetti dish adorned with tomatoes and eggplant. Anglo-Saxons are obviously happy at Castelnuovo, and don't seem to mind the ambulant salesmen who flow by the their tables without pause. Everybody but the shivering little match girl takes a try at it—the newspaper boy, the fat lady with flowers, the lottery-ticket man, the bangle vendor, and, of course, the violin and guitar duo with the silver tenor. During the warmer months, you are served on a sheltered terrace, and beset by the same distractions.

Ristorante Olimpia
Palermo

Ristorante Castelnuovo
Palermo

The cloister–Cathedral of Monreale

Monreale

VISITORS TO Palermo are privileged to be within a short drive of the most beautiful of all the structures built by the Normans in Sicily. About four miles south of the gates of the city, and set high above it, they will find the magnificent Cathedral of Monreale, built between 1174 and 1189 on orders of William II, the Good. The most significant medieval building in Sicily, it has infinite beauty. The grandiose interior is completely covered with mosaics showing scenes from the Old Testament and from the life of Christ and the Apostles, illuminated with Greek and Latin texts. The mosaics show a strong Byzantine influence, since many Greek artists worked on them. The interior is dominated by the huge figure of Christ set in mosaic in the semi-dome of the apse. Eighteen massive granite columns support the nave, entered through two sets of exquisite bronze doors. One was executed by Bonanno da Pisa in 1186 and the other, quite different in character, is the work of Barisano da Trani, dated 1190.

A superb twelfth-century cloister that belonged to a Benedictine monastery adjoins the cathedral. This quadrangle is surrounded by pointed arches sup-

Detail of the cathedral cloister—Monreale

ported by 216 twin columns. Most of the columns are encrusted with colored mosaics or carving, and their capitals are all different. In the south angle is a quiet fountain, reminiscent of the Alhambra. This is, without a doubt, one of the noblest cloisters in Italy. From the nearby terraces of the convent a priest will show you the thrilling view of Palermo and its Conca d'Oro—Golden Shell Bay.

Monreale, in short, provides a tremendous experience.

Mondello

OUR TRIP around the perimeter of Sicily leads first to this seaside village wedged between two immense granite promontories, Monte Pellegrino and Monte Gallo. Mondello, some nine miles west of the metropolis, is Palermo's Lido. Its beach is broad, inviting, and well equipped, and enjoys great popularity at the height of the summer season. Its hotel facilities, however, were neglibible until 1953, when a startling, ultramodern newcomer opened its doors. The MONDELLO PALACE HOTEL ranks as one of the most luxurious places in Sicily, judged by contemporary standards. It is something out of Rio, Hollywood, and Le Corbusier all thrown together. The architect, the decorators, and especially the unfettered artist who conceived the super-Picasso tilework were given a free hand, it would seem. The plumbers, however, held strictly to reality. Each room has its own beautiful bath and a wide private balcony overlooking the sea. The array of lights, fans, gadgets, and buttons to push bewilders the uninitiated guest, and care must be taken in turning out the light. Chances are two to one that on your first try you'll land the headwaiter at your door with an order pad in his hand!

This hotel is quiet and restful, and should be a joy to those who arrive in Sicily in the late spring and summer months. Everything is spanking new and spotless, and the service alert and polite. The place is expensive, perhaps, but far less so than the same category of resort hotel in America. The transportation problem for those without cars is not complex, since electric buses from the heart of Palermo, twenty minutes away, stop at the front door. The hotel is closed during January and February.

Segesta

To PROVE that Sicily is an island of contrasts, the next westerly move is from modern Mondello to a deserted site in the hills, once occupied by an ancient Greek city. The coastal road leads through lemon groves and fishing villages, and then turns inland to Alcamo. Then, just before Catalafimi, a country road branches off to the right, leading to the mysterious mountain site of Segesta, a city established more than twenty-five centuries ago. Here, in total solitude, is an unfinished Greek temple dating from the second half of the fifth century B. C., its columns all standing but unfluted, its entablature ready to receive carved metopes that were never achieved. Here it remains today in forlorn majesty, just as it stood when a frightful war with the Carthaginians interrupted its construction. Nearby is a semicircular Greek theater cut in the stony hillside, overlooking the barren countryside. It, too, is in excellent condition, having been completed by the Romans.

Trapani

The setting is one of utter tranquility. Crows hover, and a few goats rustle through the surrounding cactus. Otherwise all is silence. It is one of the most moving sights in Sicily.

Trapani

A SHORT run from Segesta takes you to the seaport town of Trapani (accent the first syllable), a busy, baroque place where you will find suitable hotel accommodations either at the JOLLY HOTEL or at the NUOVO HOTEL RUSSO, at Via Tintori 8. We had seen Trapani from the air during a wartime flight and had always wanted to take a close look at the picturesque windmills that dominate its salt beds. The town has been in the business of extracting salt from sea water for centuries and once carried on a thriving commerce with the Scandinavian countries. In its fine sheltered port lie boats that engage in tuna fishing. Architecturally, Trapani has little to offer except the Gothic Sanctuary of the Annunciation, but adventurous souls will relish a side trip to the nearby village of Erice, crowning the mountain of the same name. Here is a remarkable medieval hill town, protected by a battlemented castle with huge square towers. Wander through its narrow, winding streets and you will come upon the ruins of the temple of Venus Ericine, an esteemed Mediterranean goddess, and a fifteenth-century *duomo* with a fine doorway. There is a little museum and a flowery public garden from which, it is said, you can see the coast of Africa on a clear day.

Selinunte

MARSALA, a large seaport town, ships bottles and barrels of its famous wine far and wide, but it holds little interest for the southbound sightseer intent upon reaching another extraordinary glimpse of ancient Greece, Selinunte. Some thirty miles from Marsala, he comes upon the remains of this city, founded seven centuries before Christ and now in a state of incredible chaos. This settlement has none of the solemn majesty of Segesta, but rather the violence of an earthquake which, in Byzantine times, caused most of the grotesque damage. Man, in all his fury, could not have done a job so devastating. A colossal, cataclysmic stone pile is the result. In one place the massive drums of Doric columns have been thrown to the earth in even rows, and lie like fallen stacks of dominos. It is an archaeologist's heaven, if a turbulent one. Selinunte was destroyed in 409 B.C. by Hannibal's Carthaginians, and the earthquake did the rest. There were seven temples in all, but you will be most interested in the ruins of three of them on a lonely slope above the sea. They inhabit a serene, mysterious land, strangely harmonious and immensely moving. Selinunte is one of the great attractions of Sicily. Don't miss it!

Agrigento

A DRIVE of something over sixty miles along the southern coastal road brings you to the summit of Grecian beauty in Sicily, the ancient city of Akragas, called Girgenti until about twenty-five years ago, and now known as Agrigento. Occupying an easily defended site nine hundred feet above the level of the sea, it was called the "most beautiful city of mortals" by Pindar, a native son. True to the promises of the travel posters, its fabulous Greek temples were silhouetted against almond blossoms when we arrived in late February. However, the five astonishing temples aligned along the walls of the ancient city need no flowery embellishment. They are superlative in themselves. How well the Greeks understood the art of picking a site. Along a dramatic ridge they stand, overlooking the sea. The little blue guidebook to the surviving temples and the flattened ruins identifies each with a letter. Temple A refers to the remains of the Temple of Hercules, eight of whose fallen columns have been restacked. Temple E, attributed to Juno, stands imposingly on its hilltop, with many of its columns and some of its architraves still in place. Temple F is the best preserved of all Greek structures in Italy—the lovely Temple of Concord. Only Paestum can rival it in this respect. Dating from

The Temple of Concord–Agrigento

The Temple of Castor and Pollux–Agrigento

Temple of Juno Lacinia—Agrigento

the fifth century before Christ, it owes its fine condition to the fact that it was converted into a Christian church in the sixth century A.D. Temple I turns out to be only a corner fragment of the Temple of Castor and Pollux. This lovely architectural set, framed in olive trees and spring blossoms, is the best known to artists and postcard senders. The colossal Temple of Jupiter is now a shambles, having been leveled by an earthquake and then used as a stone quarry for centuries. Put them all together and you have a truly Homeric experience, and enough Doric architecture to last a lifetime. Not that the Agrigento temples could ever out-do the Parthenon. They are carved from rough, porous local stone, in contrast to the Parthenon's gleaming white marble, and were once covered with stucco, many traces of which remain.

High above the temple ridge is the modern city of Agrigento, occupying the ancient acropolis and well worth a visit. Here is a fine archaeological museum, installed in the town hall. In the cathedral you will find a Grecian marble sarcophagus of extraordinary beauty, with richly carved bas-reliefs telling the amorous myth of Hippolytus and his stepmother, Phaedra.

The hotel situation is better in Agrigento now than in the past, when Goethe, for example, searched in vain for even a simple *locanda*. The author of *Faust* finally found refuge in a spaghetti factory! Since the traditional Hotel dei Templi has been turned to other uses, today's traveler has a choice of two reputable *alberghi,* the HOTEL GRAN BRETAGNA E GALLIA, on the Piazza Gallo, and the JOLLY HOTEL, near the railway station.

A crowded day of travel lies along the southern shore of Sicily before the sightseer reaches Syracuse, our next port of call. The Golden Ribbon of road becomes sun-baked and remote. A strange loneliness pervades the beaches of Gela and Licata. The dwarf date palms are motionless and the village streets empty. It wasn't always thus, for this was the invasion beach where the American Seventh Army landed at dawn on July 10, 1943. A few shattered German pillboxes still stand forlornly by, the only visible monument to that memorable assault.

Herds of sheep and goats form a traffic hazard here. The goats, intriguing creatures with flat spiral horns, come straight from their grazing hills to the villages, where they are milked in front of the housewife's door. No middleman here, except the goat. Those yellow and orange Sicilian donkey carts that have escaped the antique dealers rattle along this southern road, every inch covered with decorative painting. The donkey wears a plumed dunce cap, and another feather duster bounces from his harness. If the day is festive, he is further bedecked with velvet and lace, and his harness is hung with colored ribbon streamers. You can't dress up a donkey much more gaudily. The burro, the donkey, the mule, the jackass (or is this list getting redundant?) still serve as the elemental means of transport in Sicily. Except, of course, for the women, who continue to carry loads of fagots and jugs of water on their heads. The Sicilian youth may slouch, but not the maiden; she has a fine erect bearing, and for good reason!

The coastal road turns inland after Gela, passing through the dramatic hill town of Ragusa, and then through Noto, noteworthy for its fine Baroque architecture. Both cities merit a pause in your travels. By now you are on the third side of the triangular island, and driving northward. The land becomes flat and fertile as the island silhouette of Syracuse comes into view.

Syracuse

As ONE wanders about this rather barren, windswept site, it is hard to believe that here stood one of the most powerful of Hellenic cities, and a formidable rival of Carthage. Founded in 733 B. C., it was for centuries the largest city of antiquity, and perhaps the most beautiful. Syracuse boasted half a million inhabitants and had city walls fourteen miles around at a time when Rome was little more than a village. It was the birthplace of both Archimedes and Theocritus, and long the residence of Plato. Here it was that Archimedes, in his bath, solved the problem of displacement and rushed naked into the street, shouting, "Eureka!"

Baroque buildings in Noto　　　　　*The hill town of Ragusa*

Syracuse fell upon sad days after the Romans sacked it, in 272 B. C., and dropped into insignificance during the Middle Ages. Today its population has dwindled to about seventy thousand, and most of the ancient city has disappeared completely. What remains, however, is impressive. First of all, there is a magnificent Greek theater, cut in solid rock at the time of Dionysius in the fourth century B. C. The Romans enlarged it and it is one of the most spacious such theaters in existence. Classic Greek plays are still given here in April and May, and constitute a major tourist attraction. There is also a grandiose Roman amphitheater built during the reign of Emperor Augustus. Now overgrown with grass and umbrella pines, and very paintable, it was once the scene of combat between gladiators and wild animals.

Distinct curiosities, although rather eerie ones, are the *latomie* of Syracuse, huge cavities carved out of the limestone in ancient times. In these quarries the people buried the dead and here, too, they incarcerated prisoners of war. It is said that seven thousand captured Athenians were left here to die of starvation. You may visit these extraordinary caves with capable guides, and see the Grotta dei Cordei where the ropemakers worked, also the Ear of Dionysius, a grotto tapering to a point where, it is said, the tyrant could listen undetected to the conversation of the prisoners below. One thing is

The Greek theater—Syracuse

certain, even now—the acoustical effects are extraordinary. A sheet of paper torn in two produces an echo like a gunshot.

A much later curiosity worth visiting is the little Romanesque Church of San Giovanni and its ancient crypt, where Saint Paul is reported to have preached. Close by are enormous catacombs, second in importance only to those of Rome, presumably built by third-century Christians. Guides are on hand to show you through them.

Syracuse is still a busy seaport, dealing mostly with African cities. French and British forces landed at the neighboring town of La Maddalena when the island was invaded on July 10, 1943, and Syracuse was occupied the same evening. The present city is concentrated on the ancient hook-shaped island of Ortygia. Many Baroque buildings of Spanish character were built here following the earthquake of 1693, one of them a rather squirming cathedral façade. Behind it, you will be surprised to find the remains of a Greek temple of Athena, that serves very effectively as the nave. Opposite the cathedral, installed in the Palazzo Bellomo, is a museum of immense interest to numismatists and historians. But the sublime marble statue of Venus Anadyomene, discovered just over one hundred and fifty years ago, is its most obvious treasure. It is headless, alas, and one forearm is missing, but

The Church of San Giovanni—Syracuse

the attributes that remain arouse considerable enthusiasm with the public. In the case of Guy de Maupassant, they inspired something stronger. His critique: *"C'est la femme telle qu'elle est, telle qu'on l'aime, telle qu'on la désire, telle qu'on la veut étreindre. Elle est grasse, avec la poitrine forte et la jambe un peu lourde; c'est une Vénus charnelle, qu'on rêve couchée en la voyant debout."* Could any Anglo-Saxon express it as well?

Though an archaeologist may well want to stay in Syracuse for a month, most travelers will settle for a day or so. Visitors who put up at the leading hotel, the GRAND HOTEL VILLA POLITI, will be within walking distance of the *latomie*, the theater, and other antique treasures. This venerable hostelry is surrounded by handsome gardens, once part of a Capuchin monastery. The site is a rather lonely one, but buses bring guests back and forth to the city. Generations of visitors have stopped at the Villa Politi, and its guest-book is replete with illustrious names. In the new town, the HOTEL DES ETRANGERS will prove a satisfactory place for an overnight stop. It looks out upon the famous Fountain of Arethusa, a legendary spring of fresh water at the very edge of the sea, and is thickly grown with Egyptian papyrus, a plant that grows nowhere else in Italy.

There is another rarity in Syracuse, a genuinely good restaurant located

Grand Hotel
Villa Politi
Syracuse

Porta Garibaldi–Catania

near the bridge that connects the old island town with the mainland. Called the RISTORANTE DELL'OROLOGIO, on the Piazza Archimede, it will prove a treasure to hungry sightseers in search of a good lunch. Local sea food is a feature, and you will find a fragrant *zuppa di pesce* and a memorable *fritto misto del mare*. An appetizing *frittura mista alla italiana* omits sea food, and substitutes a deep fry of brains, sweetbreads, kidneys, and artichokes. You will also find a good Neapolitan *mozzarella in carrozza* and a fair approximation of a Florentine steak. The wine is good, and so is the service.

Ristorante
dell'Orologio
Syracuse

The trip northward from Syracuse begins auspiciously with the overpowering, snow-crested silhouette of Mount Etna etched against the blue sky. It looms 10,784 feet high and is nearly a hundred miles in circumference. Etna's immense majesty is mixed with a faint aura of foreboding, for the volcano is still active, still capable of periodic hell-fire and destruction. Approaching Catania, the motor road cuts through a blackish chaos of porous stone, a reminder of a molten stream of lava that centuries ago pushed its way into the sea. More than one village and farm on this gently sloping giant have disappeared under the advancing clinkers, but the Sicilian farmers who cultivate these hills are tenacious. They always come back, for Etna's dusty

485

perimeter is extraordinarily fertile. Fruit trees prosper, as do chestnuts, almonds, and hazelnuts. Vineyards thrive on its lower slopes and produce a heady, acceptable table wine. Higher up stand the evergreen forests where local huntsmen go gunning for hare and wild boar, to be prepared in the piquant Sicilian fashion. Forbidding as it has been for the past millennium and more, Etna also has its bountiful side. It provides a memorable adventure to both mountain climbers and skiers, for whom some comfortable lodges are now being built.

The volcano rises up in splendor just north of the teeming metropolis of Catania, a city of over three hundred thousand inhabitants, the second largest in Sicily. Earthquakes have plagued Catania, and it has been rebuilt several times. The Baroque style of architecture now dominates its churches, public buildings, and even triumphal arches. We submit the Porta Garibaldi, complete with trumpeting angels, torsos of gladiators, and a watchful spread eagle, as the ultimate in flamboyant town gates. Those who relish the Baroque will find interest in Catania, but it is hardly a tourist attraction. Despite its size, it must bow to Taormina, some thirty miles northward, as a magnet for foreign travelers.

Taormina

THIS ANCIENT town, ensconced on a shelf 672 feet above the Ionian Sea, is more popular with travelers than any other place in Sicily, and it deserves to be. For decades Taormina has made the greatest effort to provide comfortable accommodations for its guests. Its hotels and *pensioni* are a joy—clean, well heated, and cheerful, offering excellent value, hospitality, and service, and usually a palm-sheltered garden with a view. Taormina's main thoroughfare, the Corso Umberto, is the cleanest street in Sicily, and the only one where the temptation to shop is irresistible. Recent statistics show that 226 stores crowd into this town of less than seven thousand people. The competition to sell lingerie and embroidered blouses, sweaters and scarves, jewelry and dolls, bamboo flutes and panels from Sicilian donkey carts is intense. Brightly lighted shops stay open well into the evening, Sunday included. Pastry shops, cafés and de luxe grocery stores are more than plentiful. All the shopkeepers seem to have learned at least a smattering of English, and many of them are quadrilingual, including the man who sells stamps in the post office. Taormina is the only place in Sicily where news-hungry foreigners can buy their native papers with ease, where the cinema is a commonplace, and where nobody stares at visitors.

In spite of being a traveler's resort par excellence, Taormina has not been spoiled by worldly people. By some miracle it has retained the poetic charm of antiquity. It was once an important city of Magna Graecia, founded

Taormina and Mount Etna

Ruins of the ancient theater—Taormina

The cathedral square—Taormina

Sicilian donkey cart–Taormina

on the slopes of Monte Tauro almost four centuries before Christ. The most dramatic monument of those far-off days is the semicircular Greek theater, cut in the rocky hillside and later restored by the Romans. It could hold four thousand spectators, and the acoustics are still perfect. From this exalted site, one of the most thrilling panoramas in Italy unfolds—the sunlit town in the foreground, the sea below, and the snow-covered grandeur of Etna as a backdrop. Words are futile—you must see this panorama for yourself, preferably on a sunny morning.

Relics of the Middle Ages are numerous in Taormina. There are Gothic palaces with Moorish overtones, several fine churches, including a cathedral with a grotesque marble fountain playing in front of it, and a perfectly beautiful public garden, occupying a lower level of the town. All of these attributes make it a perpetual favorite with painters and aquarellists. A sunny day in Taormina is inconceivable without a plump lady water-colorist about.

Portrait painters have their fun too, as models are readily available. Usually they are young men with dark eyes and flashing smiles, exulting in the Sicilian's crowning glory, a shock of curly black hair, glossed and highlighted with brilliantine. He considers it his ultimate badge of distinction, and it is difficult for a balding Anglo-Saxon to disagree with him.

Taormina provides the habitual stroller with any number of charming walks, including a climb to Castel Mola, a bird's nest of a village hovering high above the town. For those seeking a dip in the sea, there is an attractive beach called Mazzarò easily accessible by bus. The innocent-looking town of Taormina suffered considerable damage from bombing during the recent war, for it served as a German command center in the summer of 1943. Most of the scars have been removed, but a few ruined palaces testify to those tragic days. A part of the ancient San Domenico monastery was destroyed at this time.

The public garden–Taormina

Capo Sant' Alessio, near Taormina

**Grand Hotel
San Domenico**
Taormina

Hotel Timeo
Taormina

**Hotel Bel
Soggiorno**
Taormina

The hotel situation, as we have said, is excellent. Everything considered, Taormina's eleven principal hotels and its sprightly little *pensioni* deserve a blanket endorsement. However, we shall mention only four of our favorites.

The GRAND HOTEL SAN DOMENICO has for generations been the obvious first choice of travelers who can afford its luxury. It is established in the venerable San Domenico monastery, with beautiful cloisters and gardens, and an enchanting view of Mount Etna and the sea. Its monastic cells have been changed into handsome bedrooms with every comfort. The entire hotel is beautifully furnished, and you dine in impressive refectories. It has received countless illustrious guests, including bridegroom King Farouk, who took some sixty rooms here on the occasion of his honeymoon with Narriman.

Our own choice in Taormina is the HOTEL TIMEO, a quiet and distinguished establishment located at the far end of the town near the Greek theater. This hotel, a perennial favorite with English visitors, is furnished with restrained good taste. Its gardens are charming and its view of Etna and the gulf is something you'll never forget.

In a bend of the hill road below the town, on the Via Luigi Pirandello, is the HOTEL BEL SOGGIORNO, which has its ardent advocates among British and American visitors. This hotel is run by hospitable directors who take a personal interest in each guest.

Giardini, a village on the Sicilian shore

Finally, in the heart of Taormina, next to the old bell tower, at Corso Umberto 210, is the HOTEL METROPOLE, a long-established hostelry that has been run by the same family for generations. The cooking is good here, and the view even better.

Of course, there is a slight extra charge for Taormina's many privileges. Prices are upped on everything from a bar of chocolate to a bottle of Scotch. Your morning *aperitivo* usually costs about fifty per cent more than else-where, and you must drive a hard bargain with the taxi driver. The food situation in Taormina can be called satisfactory, but the town is no paradise for the exacting gourmet. The few restaurants are routine, and there is small temptation to desert one's hotel dining room, where good, middle-of-the-road cooking, designed to be acceptable to polyglot pilgrims from a dozen different countries, is the rule. Even if they are no Lucullan shrines, the hotels of Taormina deserve prolonged applause. They have done quite as much as the shops, the sunshine, and the scenery to make this the most charming spot in Sicily.

Hotel
Metropole
Taormina

491

Messina

YOUR ROAD clings to the shore for almost thirty miles before coming to the long-suffering city of Messina. This approach doesn't do justice to the place. It should be seen from the water. They have been talking for decades about a vehicular tunnel to connect Sicily with the Italian mainland, but the modern ferries that ply between Villa San Giovanni and Messina will no doubt always prove far more pleasant to sightseers. The ferries absorb entire trains, along with incidental passengers and automobiles, and they take only half an hour to bring you from the mainland to the sheltered port of Messina, which, as you've surely guessed, is called the gateway to Sicily. As such, it has had its troubles, particularly in August, 1943, when Italo-German forces held it against Allied bombardment to permit remnants of their troops to escape to Calabria. Parts of the city are still tattered as a result—all of this in the wake of the earthquake that made a shambles of most of Messina in 1908. Eighty thousand people perished in that frightful tragedy.

Messina has been rebuilt once again, but its buildings are not lofty. For seismic reasons they are limited to low structures. A few fine fragments of architecture have survived the turbulence, including the remains of a twelfth-century Norman church and a cathedral whose Gothic doorway is a masterpiece of finely carved marble.

Messina has two long-established hotels, the HOTEL ROYAL and the GRAND HOTEL, now augumented by a shining new JOLLY HOTEL on the Corso Garibaldi, with an inspiring view of the old port and the straits.

Ristorante
Da Borgia

Messina

There is a better-than-average restaurant, too, the RISTORANTE DA BORGIA at Via dei Mille 64. It is one of those high-ceilinged, neon-lit places with all the atmosphere of a telephone booth, but the cooking and service are good, the menu comprehensive. We indulged happily in a *tagliatelle alla bolognese,* unexpectedly tender *scaloppine,* cheese, salad, and a bottle of red Corvo.

At this extreme corner of the Sicilian triangle we begin the last lap of our circumferential trip, climbing hills laced with hairpin turns to the northeastern shore and a first glimpse of the Lipari Islands. They appear mysterious and infinitely peaceful in the soft, iridescent morning light. Beyond them is Stromboli, its volcano smoking in solitary contentment.

This northern shore of the island is precipitous. The cactus-clad mountains tumble into the sea, and the coastal road winds semihysterically at times. It takes almost two hours to get to the dramatic and sketchable citadel of Tindari, crowning a pinnacle above the water. Tindari was a Greek settlement four centuries before the Christian era, but most of it has slid into the sea. What remains is a medieval sanctuary that amply justifies a slight detour.

The Golden Shell Bay of Palermo

Cefalù

THE DRAMA of these hills begins to taper off as you approach Cefalù, one of the most memorable of Sicilian towns, crouching at the base of a Gibraltar-like limestone promontory. The square towers of its massive Norman cathedral, begun a little over eight centuries ago, emerge from a welter of close-packed waterfront buildings. This cathedral, established by King Roger II in 1131, is one of the most remarkable in Sicily. The mosaics in the choir show a strong Oriental influence, reminiscent of Monreale, especially in the over-powering likeness of Christ in the half-dome of the apse. However, they precede Monreale by a few decades, dating from 1148. It was in this cathedral that the Norman King Roger wished to be buried with his queen. He built two imposing sarcophagi of porphyry for the purpose, but his wishes were ignored. The couple have long since joined the royal family in the tombs of the cathedral in Palermo.

Adjoining Cefalù's cathedral is a Romanesque cloister of great beauty, and there are several fine buildings in the old town. It all adds up to quite a temptation for enthusiasts of Norman art. If they choose to spend the night in Cefalù, they will find a newly installed JOLLY HOTEL eager to welcome them.

The last miles of this Sicilian circuit consist of a pleasant, uneventful drive along the shore. Just beyond Capo Zafferano, Palermo's incomparable Golden Shell bay again comes into view. The sandy shore is dotted with boulders, affording perches for amateur anglers. In the background rises the majestic shape of Monte Pellegrino, which Goethe called the most beautiful headland in the world. The glistening white buildings of Palermo line the shore, and several ships lie waiting in the harbor, among them an overnight steamer for Naples and a towering transatlantic liner. This is where we came in, and where a memorable Italian adventure draws to a close.

The Domes of
San Giovanni
degli Ermiti
Palermo

A Treasury of Italian Recipes

The Castle Entrance, Susa

IN THE HOPE that this collection of recipes may truly live up to its name, we have mined the treasure of Italian cookery with care, sorted the yield with discrimination, and polished the nuggets to the best of our ability, to create a choice selection of tempting dishes. Their variety and feasibility will, we hope, throw new light on Italian cuisine, which does not consist solely of the rather heavy garlic-scented dishes best known outside of Italy. The simplicity and delicacy of much of Italian cooking may come as a pleasant surprise to many readers.

We have attempted in the recipes included in the various chapters to keep the spirit and style of the wording in the Italian versions sent to us by the chefs of various restaurants. For this reason, some of these recipes are not so explicit nor so detailed as those in the Treasury. The recipes have been gathered from many sources and are culled from a collection numbered in the thousands. Those contributed by our generous restaurant and hotel

495

friends are identified by the name of the restaurant or hotel. Our hope is that our final choices represent the cream of the crop. Although many famous classics are included, there are also a number of less well-known dishes. Complex or simple, familiar or unusual, all the dishes described can be made in the English-speaking kitchen. The true gourmet can ask for nothing finer than the intricacy of, for instance, *lasagne verdi al forno* as made in Bologna, whereas the lightness of chicken or turkey breasts sautéed in butter or the quick cooking of veal bits prepared *all'uccelletto* or the crisp frying of a *fritto misto* requires skillful handling but little time.

There is much originality in Italian cuisine, and we might do well to emulate some of its methods and economical techniques. Though modern equipment and conveniences are now fairly widespread in Italy, the average housewife has long been accustomed to working with one little charcoal brazier and miraculously manages to produce fine meals—from soups, or *minestre,* to broiled meats or savory stews—with this limited resource, a performance which might make the pampered American housewife blush. Meat has always been expensive and none too plentiful in Italy, and Italians have therefore learned to stretch the supply in many tempting ways. They make meat sauces for pasta and *risotto* and a variety of delicious fillings for rolled pasta based on the chopped meat of a *stracotta,* or beef stew. Its rich juices are used to moisten and flavor an infinite number of dishes. In fact, we have concluded that the Italian cook must keep on hand a supply of the ingredients necessary for these meat combinations a large part of the time.

The terms *zuppe* and *minestroni* designate soups that fit the Anglo-Saxon conception of soup, although these categories sometimes include main dishes or stews also, as, for instance, the fish soups and the tremendous *minestroni* that contain practically everything required in the so-called balanced meal. *Minestre* is, however, a confusing designation to the Anglo-Saxon, who will find, when consulting an Italian restaurant menu, that the dishes listed under this term include not only soups but many pastas as well, notably those *in brodo,* or broth, and sometimes heaping plates of greens. In fact, the word seems to be a catchall, meaning practically anything that may be served as a first course, with the notable exception of the *antipasti*—just to make the situation more complex.

The *antipasti* correspond, of course, to the French hors-d'oeuvre. The *antipasto* course may be an assortment of piquant little dishes from all branches of the animal and vegetable kingdom or it may be a single appetizing cold dish. The Italians have an eye for color and are fond of creating attractive designs with the reds and greens of tomatoes and peppers accented with dots of black olives, lattices of anchovy, or white strips of fennel. When it comes to desserts and pastries, they go quite mad and indulge in magenta tints combined with a green of a slightly poisonous hue and carry out elaborate flowerlike designs in candied fruits. Such tricks, of course, can be fun, and they add to the pleasure of eating when they are used with due restraint.

In presenting the vegetables and salads, we have tried not to bore you with the ordinary preparations, already familiar to you, that may be found in any standard cookbook. Our vegetables do not belong to the "meat and two veg" school. We have tried to discover original combinations of the kind usually served in Europe as a separate course.

Fish is, of course, an item of enormous importance in the diet of the sea-bordered boot of Italy. While Mediterranean and Adriatic fish differ from ours, the methods used to cook them can be applied anywhere. One could, conceivably, serve fish in Italian style every day of the year without repeating oneself, but we have spared you some of the more startling specimens, which come as a slight shock to the eye—though not to the palate, we assure you. The large and small members of the famous squid family are delicious when well prepared. But we shall leave it to the traveler in Italy, rather than to the cook who reads this book at home, to enjoy such treats as crisp fried tiny *calamaretti,* as delicate as our own famous, but rare, oyster crabs, or sections of the tubelike tentacles of the large monsters, which taste not unlike lobster meat.

We have included the famous *pizze* under the heading Breads, for want of a better home for them. After all, they are formed of a raised bread dough and baked in the oven. *Pizza* is a rather heavy and strong-flavored dish and the staggering amounts of it that the average Neapolitan seems able to absorb at one sitting are astonishing. But the present popularity of *pizza* in America indicates that it pleases the Anglo-Saxon palate, too. We have endeavored to include several versions of this satisfying dish. If you will study the recipes, you will discover that there are lighter doughs, and more exquisite ones, than the usual *pizzeria* variety. *Grissini,* or bread sticks, are too famous to need introduction. But we feel that if you will try just once to make your own according to our recipe, you will never again be quite satisfied with the ordinary packaged variety.

It should be understood that any recipe for chicken breasts applies to turkey as well. The Italians slice meat very thin and manage to flatten the slices to a remarkable degree. They are sometimes as little as one-eighth to one-sixteenth of an inch thick. This thinness contributes a great deal to the delicacy of the finished dish. As for *prosciutto* and truffles, the Italians have special tools that peel off true tissue-thin layers.

Costolette of veal are, literally, chops on the bone, cut thin, cleaned of all fat and sinew, and usually pounded to an even greater thinness before they are cooked. *Scaloppine* are thin slices from the leg or other lean part without bone. They, also, are pounded very thin. Since in many recipes Italians use chops and slices interchangeably and since young veal chops are difficult to obtain from most butchers, we often advise the use of slices —sometimes called cutlets, sometimes called *scaloppine*—from the leg or filet rather than chops. We have retained the classic Italian names for the veal recipes, however, even when, as in *costolette milanese,* for instance, the recipe calls not for chops but for thin slices.

When you come to sauces, you will find that some are included in the recipes for the dishes they accompany. Those that may be used with more than one dish are in the sauce section: classic meat, tomato, and "green" sauces, the famous and curious *pesto,* and others that are not only called for in recipes in this book, but are versatile additions to your general repertory.

You will find that all ingredients are obtainable in this country in either imported or domestic form. *Prosciutto* is raw smoked ham with a special character, but in many cases the common baked variety of ham may be substituted. The hard Italian grating cheeses, such as Parmesan and Romano, used on so many dishes, may be bought almost anywhere. So may the soft melting cheeses such as *mozzarella,* Bel Paese, and Fontina. Anchovies, so widely used in Italy where the seas supply them in quantity, are usually salted, then soaked and cleaned of bones and skin before the Italian cook uses them. If you cannot find anchovies treated in this way, canned filets will do as well.

In the north and northeastern sections of Italy, a dried hot red pepper, resembling our chili pepper, is widely used. This pepper is not the same as the more familiar seasoning, powdered cayenne. But many shops now carry small jars of crushed red pepper among their other herbs and seasonings, and these dried flakes seem identical with the Italian variety.

While olive oil is commonly used in Italian cooking, this preference does not absolutely rule out the use of other oils of good quality.

Where there is no number specified, the recipes are designed to serve six persons. However, there are so many exceptions to this rule that we hesitate to direct the reader too literally. For instance, how many people will a roast chicken serve? The number depends on the skill of the carver and on the appetites of the guests. The same uncertainty pertains to the serving of such dishes as *minestrone.* The soup may be apportioned in ample quantities as the main dish of a family supper or it may be served in smaller quantities as a first course.

The quantities of salt and of pepper in the recipes have also been left to the judgment and taste of the cook. We work on the principle that each creator has his or her own tastes and that excessively detailed instructions may sometimes serve as a limitation rather than as a guide.

Whenever you are directed in a recipe to the index, the recipe index, and not the general index, is meant.

When eggs are used to thicken sauces or soups, it is wise first to add to the eggs gradually a little of the hot liquid and then to return eggs and liquid to the saucepan, reheating the sauce or soup without letting it boil, to avoid curdling the eggs. Except in those instances in which curdling is desired, if eggs are dropped directly into hot liquid, the result may be disastrous.

The subject of pasta, which we save for the last because of its all-importance in Italian meals, would fill a book in itself. In fact, this egg dough is ever-present in Italian life. But until one has explored the subject, it is impossible to conceive of the variety and scope of this branch of their cooking. In fact, an Italian friend once remarked to us that it is astonishing but true that the same paste in different shapes, sizes, and thicknesses has different flavors. Many of the pasta types have been described in the text, particularly in the chapter on Emilia-Romagna. In this Treasury of Italian Recipes, we are, of course, limiting ourselves to the pasta varieties that can be made at home. We are not denying that excellent dried pasta of all sorts may be purchased in stores throughout the country. But we admit to a fervent hope that you will try to make your own, and we would be willing to wager that after eating fresh homemade pasta you will never again be entirely satisfied with the commercial variety. For this reason, we give recipes only for the types possible to create in one's own kitchen. The process is exceedingly simple. Difficulties arise mostly in the rolling out of the paste to get it thin enough and perfectly even and in finding space in which to dry it. Fortunately, small machines for rolling and cutting pasta at home are now beginning to appear on the American market.

Spaghetti and macaroni, of course, cannot be made at home as they must be shaped by a commercial machine. Spaghetti should not be overcooked, but should remain *al dente,* which means firm to the bite. A helpful tip about its preparation was given us years ago by an Italian cook. If you add two or three tablespoons of oil to the water a few minutes before the spaghetti is done, it will coat the strands and prevent them from sticking together.

A part of the huge series of pasta shaped and stuffed in various ways —*tortellini* and *cappelletti,* for instance, which involve technical tricks of filling and rolling—we leave to the professional restaurateur. But *cannelloni* and ravioli are of simpler construction and well worth the trouble of making them yourself. *Cannelloni* are pasta rectangles rolled up with stuffing in the center and briefly baked with any one of a number of sauces. Ravioli are cut from two sheets of dough enclosing mounds of filling. The various noodles, such as *trenette* and *tagliatelle,* are made of the same dough rolled very thin and cut in various widths. *Lasagne* are the widest strips of all, really long wide sheets. They are baked in layers, with various sauces and fillings. This is just a bare glimpse, a simple initiation into the subject of Italian pasta, which can have infinite ramifications, depending on the part of Italy you are investigating. She (or he) who achieves the *veritabile lasagne verdi al forno alla bolognese,* with its many layers of fine, tender, green, spinach-flavored sheets delicately coated with thick meat sauce and rich cream sauce flavored with nutmeg and amply dusted with powdered Parmesan cheese, has accomplished one of the really great Italian dishes. A recipe for this dish supplied by a famous local restaurant can be found in the chapter on Emilia-Romagna. But amplification can be found in the enlarged recipe given in this Treasury. We discovered that almost every restaurant in Italy has its own version of *cannelloni,* and we give some of our favorites herewith.

Some stress has been laid on regional dishes in this Treasury. But we have included many recipes of a more general character, so that you may find, we fondly hope, that the collection represents, even though necessarily only to a limited degree, the best of all Italian cooking.   N. C.

Antipasti

Antipasto Italiano
ITALIAN HORS-D'OEUVRE

Use a large round platter to present your Italian *antipasti* as a first course. Drain the oil from a can of tuna fish and remove the tuna fish in one round piece. Put the fish in the center of the platter, coat it with mayonnaise, and sprinkle it with capers. Around this arrange, in alternating rows radiating from the center, thinly sliced fennel or celery hearts, sliced tomatoes, artichoke hearts in oil, canned sweet pimientos cut in strips, small peppers in vinegar, and green and black Italian olives. You may also add, if desired, hard-cooked eggs cut in quarters lengthwise, with an anchovy filet on each quarter of egg. artichokes, and anything else your ingenuity may devise. When serving, keep the sauce hot over a spirit lamp. Serves 10.

Bagna Cauda
HOT ANCHOVY DIP
(Ristorante Il Cucolo, Turin–Piedmont)

Bagna cauda is an individual little dish, difficult to place in a meal. Italians eat it at any time of day they feel inclined to do so. In America it makes an excellent cocktail-party dip.

In a small saucepan heat together 1/2 cup butter, 5 tablespoons olive oil, and 6 or 8 cloves of garlic, peeled and sliced very thin. Let them steep for 15 minutes without letting the fat boil. Add a 2-ounce can of anchovy filets (about 1/2 cup), chopped. Stir and blend the anchovies until they are dissolved, without allowing the fat to boil or brown.

Prepare a dish of fresh vegetable strips to dip in the sauce. These may include leaves of endive, sticks of celery, green pepper or cucumber, small sliced

Caponata alla Siciliana
SICILIAN VEGETABLE HORS-D'OEUVRE
(Sicily)

Caponata is an indescribable mixture of vegetables with sweet and sour overtones that makes a delicious cold hors-d'oeuvre.

Peel 1 large eggplant, or 2 small ones, and dice it into 1-inch cubes. Heat 1/2 cup olive oil in a frying pan and fry the eggplant until it is softened and browned on all sides. Remove the pieces to a saucepan. Add 2 thinly sliced onions to the frying pan, adding a little more oil if necessary, and sauté the slices until they are soft and golden, taking care not to burn them. Add 1 cup diced celery and 2 cups Italian canned tomatoes (one 16-ounce can) that have been forced through a strainer. Simmer the onions, celery, and tomatoes together for 15 minutes and add 2 tablespoons drained capers, 1 tablespoon pine nuts, and 8 or 10 pitted, coarsely chopped black Italian olives. In a small saucepan, over low heat, dissolve 2 tablespoons sugar in 1/4 cup wine vinegar and add 1/2 teaspoon salt and a good dash of pepper. Combine all the above ingredients with the eggplant. Cover the pan and allow the mixture barely to simmer over very low heat for 20 minutes, to blend the flavors.

Let the *caponata* cool and chill it in the refrigerator before serving. Serve with crusty Italian bread.

Crostini con Salsa di Alici
CHEESE CRUSTS WITH ANCHOVY SAUCE
(Rome)

Cut 3/8-inch-thick slices of bread into 1 1/2-inch squares and thread the squares on a skewer, alternating each slice with a slice of Provaturo cheese of the same thickness as the bread but a little smaller in diameter. Place the skewer in a buttered baking dish and brush melted butter over the bread. Place the baking dish in a hot oven (400° F.) until the *crostini* are browned. Serve from the skewer and pass separately anchovy sauce made as follows: Dissolve 8 chopped anchovy filets in 2 tablespoons hot olive oil with 1 small clove of garlic, chopped and mashed. Add 2 tablespoons minced parsley, 3 tablespoons wine vinegar, and pepper to taste. Heat and blend well.

Antipasto di Pomodori e Funghi
TOMATO AND MUSHROOM SALAD

Serve the following as an appetizing first course for lunch: Slice 4 large ripe tomatoes and arrange them in overlapping rows on a serving dish. Sprinkle them with a little salt and pepper, chopped fresh marjoram, a few drops of lemon juice, and 1 tablespoon olive oil. Slice 6 or 8 large fresh white mushrooms in very thin slices, arrange them on the tomatoes, and sprinkle them in turn with a few drops of lemon juice and olive oil.

Antipasto di Melone e Prosciutto
MELON AND PROSCIUTTO HORS-D'OEUVRE

Cut a chilled small melon into crescent-shaped slices 1 1/2 inches wide at the center and remove the seeds and pulp. Run a knife from one end to the other of each slice, separating the ripe, juicy flesh from the rind, but leaving it intact in the rind. Cut the flesh vertically into 1-inch sections. Arrange the melon slices on a round serving dish, radiating from the center. Between each melon slice place slices of *prosciutto,* cut transparently thin and folded into loose rolls. Serve as a first course.

Vitello Tonnato
TUNNIED VEAL

Tie a 2-pound piece of leg of veal, without bones or fat, into an evenly shaped roll. Pierce the meat here and there with a sharp knife and insert in the openings small pieces of anchovy filets or of salted anchovies that have been cleaned of skin and bones. Place the roll in a deep saucepan with 2 slices of onion, 1 small carrot, a small piece of celery, a sprig of parsley, 2 cloves, and 1/2 teaspoon salt. Add water to cover, bring it slowly to the boiling point, and simmer the veal, covered, for 1 1/2 hours.

Drain the veal, pat it dry, and allow it to cool. Place it in a bowl and cover it with the following dressing: Mash together 4 ounces tuna fish, 4 anchovy filets or 2 cleaned, salted anchovies, chopped, 1/2 teaspoon capers, 2 tablespoons lemon juice, and a good pinch of freshly ground pepper. When the mixture is well blended add a little at a time about 1/3 to 1/2 cup olive oil, working the sauce continually until it is smooth and the consistency of cream. Cover the bowl and let the meat marinate in the dressing in the refrigerator for 2 days.

Serve thin slices of the tunnied veal with the dressing as a first-course *antipasto.*

Crostini di Pomodori
TOMATO CHEESE CRUSTS

Sauté half a small onion, finely minced, in 2 tablespoons butter until it is soft and pale gold. Add 2 ripe tomatoes that have been peeled, seeded, and diced and a little salt and pepper.

Cook over low heat until the tomatoes are thick and no liquid remains. Cool the mixture completely and stir in 1 beaten egg yolk, 1 1/2 tablespoons grated Parmesan, and a few drops Worcestershire sauce. Spread the mixture on slices of toast and place them in a hot oven (400° F.) until the topping is lightly browned. Serve the *crostini* very hot.

Uova Ripiene
STUFFED EGGS

Shell and cut in half, lengthwise, 6 hard-cooked eggs. Put the yolks in a bowl and with a small wooden spatula work them thoroughly with 1 tablespoon softened butter, 1/2 teaspoon powdered mustard, a pinch each of salt and pepper, and 1/2 teaspoon chopped capers. Add a few drops of olive oil, or just enough to give the yolks the proper consistency. When all is well blended, fill the whites with the mixture and place on each half egg a piece of anchovy filet and 1 or 2 capers. If a more bland flavor is preferred, substitute a thin slice of cucumber and a bit of mayonnaise for the anchovy.

Stuffed eggs may also be served on slices of tomato that have been sprinkled with a small amount of olive oil and vinegar, salt and pepper.

Cestini di Uova Sode
EGGS IN TOMATO BASKETS

Make mayonnaise in the usual way with 1 egg yolk, 3/4 cup olive oil, 2 tablespoons lemon juice, and salt. Cut 6 ripe tomatoes in half, remove the seeds but not the pulp, and drain out all the extra juices. Put a few drops of olive oil and of lemon juice, and a pinch of salt and pepper in all the hollow sections of each tomato. Cut the whites of 6 hard-cooked eggs in half in such a way as to remove them from the yolks leaving the yolks whole. Dice the

whites finely and mix them with mayonnaise. Cut the yolks carefully in half, place one piece on each tomato half, and cover with the mayonnaise mixture. Decorate the top of each with a cooked, peeled shrimp cut in half lengthwise.

Antipasto di Scampi
SHRIMP HORS-D'OEUVRE

Make a stiff mayonnaise with 1 egg yolk, the juice of half a lemon, a pinch of salt, and 1/2 cup olive oil. Combine it with 1/2 cup heavy cream (or the thick soured cream called "chef style"), 2 teaspoons brandy, and 1 tablespoon tomato ketchup. Boil, cool, peel, and devein 1 pound shrimp. Combine them with the mayonnaise.

Line the bottoms of individual small serving dishes with a layer of finely shredded chicory, using the tender leaves from the heart. Divide the shrimp among the dishes. Chill in the refrigerator before serving.

Peperoni alla Piemontese
GREEN PEPPERS PIEDMONT
(Piedmont)

This is a very nice addition to your hors-d'oeuvre tray. Arrange the peppers prettily in the baking dish as they will be served from the same dish.

Cut sweet green peppers into quarters, making 4 little boat-shaped pieces, and clean out the centers. If you include some sweet red ones with the green, the dish will be all the prettier. In each piece place 2 or 3 thin slices of garlic, 3 bits of peeled and seeded tomato, and over the top a filet of anchovy. Place a small piece of butter on each and pour a generous teaspoon of olive oil over each little boat. Add salt and pepper if desired. Cook in a moderate oven (350° F.) for 30 minutes. They should not become too soft.

Serve cold, as a first-course *antipasto*.

Soups

Brodo di Pollo
CHICKEN BROTH

Put a 4- to 5-pound fowl in a soup kettle with 2 quarts water and heat it gradually. Just before the water comes to the boiling point, remove all the scum from the surface. Add 1 teaspoon salt, 4 crushed peppercorns, 1 stalk of celery with the leaves, 1 onion, and 1 carrot, all coarsely sliced, and a sprig of parsley. Some Italian cooks like to include also 1 ripe sliced tomato. Cover the pot and keep the liquid at the lowest possible simmer for about 2 1/2 hours, or until the chicken is quite tender, skimming the surface occasionally. Fast boiling will make the broth cloudy. Remove the chicken and reserve it for other uses. Strain the broth, allow it to cool, and remove all the fat from the surface. Makes about 1 1/2 quarts.

Brodo di Manzo
BEEF BROTH

Make beef broth in exactly the same way as chicken broth, substituting for the fowl a 1 1/2-pound piece of lean beef and a piece of shinbone. One leek and a small white turnip may be added with the other vegetables, if desired. Cover the pot and keep the liquid at an almost imperceptible simmer for about 2 hours, or until the meat is quite tender. Strain the broth and cool it. Remove all the fat from the surface. Makes about 1 1/2 quarts.

Brodo Misto
CHICKEN AND BEEF BROTH

Some consider the finest broth of all is obtained from chicken and beef, or veal, combined. Veal gives a lighter, very delicate stock. Put a 4-pound fowl and a piece of beef shinbone with some meat attached in a soup pot with 2 to 2 1/2 quarts water. A piece of foreleg of veal, both bone and meat, or a veal knuckle, may be substituted for the beef. Continue as for chicken broth, bringing the water gradually to the boiling point, skimming, and adding the vegetables and seasonings. Cover the pot and simmer very, very slowly for 2 to 2 1/2 hours, or until the fowl is quite tender. Put aside the fowl. Strain the stock, cool it, and remove all the fat from the surface. Makes 1 1/2 to 2 quarts stock.

Minestrina di Cubetti
CHICKEN SOUP WITH CHEESE CUBES

Put 10 ounces *ricotta* cheese in a bowl and work it thoroughly with a wooden spatula, beating it until it is quite smooth. Add 1 whole egg and 1 egg yolk, blend thoroughly, then add salt, a good grating of nutmeg, and 2/3 cup grated Parmesan. When the paste is well blended, put it in a buttered earthen or glass baking dish, place the dish in a pan of hot water, and cook the paste in a slow oven (300° F.) until it is firm. Allow the paste to cool. When ready to serve your soup, cut the cheese paste into small cubes, place them in a soup tureen, and pour over them boiling chicken broth.

Straciatella alla Romana
ROMAN CONSOMMÉ

Beat 3 eggs thoroughly and stir in 2 tablespoons grated Romano cheese and 2 tablespoons minced parsley. Bring 6 cups good clear, flavorful chicken consommé to a boil. Stir in the egg mixture and continue cooking for a few seconds, or until the eggs harden. Ladle the soup at once into individual soup plates.

Zuppa alla Pavese
EGGS IN CONSOMMÉ PAVIA
(Lombardy)

This soup should be made of Italian *brodo* (see index), light in color but full of flavor and quite distinct in character from a beef consommé. Or you may use chicken consommé.

Heat the stock to the boiling point and poach in it, one at a time, 1 egg per person. First break the egg into a teacup and then slip it gently into the hot liquid. As each egg is done, skim it out and place it in a large hot soup plate. Let the stock then come to an active boil and pour some, through a strainer, over the egg in each plate. Around each egg float several small slices of bread which have been sautéed on both sides in butter and sprinkled with grated Parmesan cheese. Pass more grated cheese with the soup.

Minestrone alla Milanese
VEGETABLE SOUP MILANESE
(Lombardy)

Soak 1 cup white Italian beans 6 hours or more in water. Drain the beans and put them in a soup kettle with 2 1/2 quarts salted water and a small piece of salt pork rind. Simmer over low heat for 1 1/2 hours.

Meanwhile, put 2 strips of bacon, diced, and 1 tablespoon olive oil in a saucepan, add 1 sliced onion and cook until the onion is softened. Add 1 carrot, 1 stalk of celery, 1 potato, and 1 small zucchini, if available, all diced. After 2 or 3 minutes add 1 large tomato, peeled, seeded, and diced, 1 teaspoon chopped parsley, salt, and pepper. Stir all together and add the mixture to the soup, with half a medium-sized

cabbage, thinly sliced, 1 chopped clove of garlic, and a few leaves of basil. Simmer for 1 1/2 hours, or until the vegetables are tender and the soup is quite thick. For the last 15 minutes, add 4 tablespoons uncooked rice or a handful of vermicelli, spaghetti, or macaroni broken in pieces. Stir in 1/2 cup grated Parmesan just before serving. Pass grated cheese with the soup. Other vegetables, such as fresh peas, green beans, turnips, and leeks may be used instead of, or in any combination with, the carrot, celery, and zucchini, depending on the season. Serves 10.

The Ligurian version *alla genovese* has 2 tablespoons of *pesto* (see index) stirred in, which adds a distinctive and delicious flavor. Eggplant and mushrooms are sometimes used in *minestrone genovese*.

Minestrone alla Toscana
MINESTRONE TUSCAN
(Tuscany)

Cook 2 cups freshly shelled beans in stock to cover for about 20 minutes, or until they are just tender. Light veal or chicken stock is best but bouillon cubes dissolved in water may be used. Clean 1 small cabbage, removing the hard stem, and cut it into thin strips. Wash and cut up coarsely a handful each of beet greens and spinach. Do not dry these vegetables but put them in a tightly covered saucepan with a little salt and let them steep over low heat for 5 minutes.

Heat 3 tablespoons olive oil in a saucepan, add 2 tablespoons diced bacon, 1 clove of garlic, chopped, 2 tablespoons chopped parsley, 2 stalks celery, and 2 carrots, both sliced, 2 small zucchini, diced, and 1 small chopped onion. Brown these vegetables lightly, then add 1 generous tablespoon tomato purée and simmer all together for 5 minutes.

In an earthen soup pot put a few

pieces of fresh pork rind and add all the vegetables and their juices, 1 quart hot stock, and 1/2 cup washed rice. Cook the soup for about 20 minutes and serve it with plenty of grated Parmesan to sprinkle on each plate. Serves 8.

Pasta e Fagioli alla Giordano
BEAN AND PASTA SOUP GIORDANO
(Grand Hotel, Florence–Tuscany)

The innumerable uses to which the people of Tuscany put their local beans include this hearty and perfectly delicious soup.

Soak 1 pound white Borlotti beans overnight. These white beans may be found in Italian markets. In a soup pot make what may be translated as a "frying"—a combination of chopped ingredients sautéed in oil. Chop 1 stalk of celery, 1 clove of garlic, and 1 onion. Sauté these in 2 tablespoons olive oil until they have taken on a little color. Add a ham bone with a little meat left on it and the drained beans, and pour in 2 quarts boiling salted water. Simmer the soup for about 3 hours and take out the ham bone and about 1 1/2 cups of the beans, choosing those that remain whole. Save the meat from the ham bone. Pass the rest of the soup through a sieve and return it to the pot. Add the whole beans and 1 cup of the ham meat, diced. Bring the soup to a boil, add 1/2 cup small pasta (broken spaghetti or other) and 3 tablespoons olive oil, and boil the soup gently until the pasta is cooked. Pour the soup into a hot tureen containing 2 tablespoons of *pesto* (see index). If the soup is too thick, add a little boiling water or broth. Pass grated Parmesan with this soup. Serves 6 as a main dish, 10 or 12 as a first course.

Zuppa di Fagioli alla Toscana
BEAN SOUP TUSCAN
(Tuscany)

Soak 1/2 pound white beans over-night in water to cover. Drain them and put them in a kettle with 1 1/2 to 2 quarts water. Simmer them as slowly as possible until they are tender, which will take 2 to 3 hours. Remove about half of the beans, put them through a food mill or force them through a strainer, and stir this purée back into the soup. Season now with salt. Heat 1/4 cup olive oil in a small saucepan and in it brown gently 2 chopped cloves of garlic. Add 2 tablespoons chopped parsley, salt, and pepper, stir all together, and pour this combination at once into the soup. Taste for seasoning and serve very hot. Serves 6 to 8.

Minestrina di Riso al Limone
RICE SOUP WITH LEMON

Wash 1 cup rice and pour it into 5 to 6 cups rapidly boiling chicken or beef stock. Boil it for 15 to 20 minutes, or until the rice is cooked to your taste. Beat together 2 egg yolks, the juice of half a lemon, 3/8 cup grated Parmesan, and 2 tablespoons water. Pour this mixture into a warm soup tureen and gradually pour over it the boiling rice soup, stirring continuously. This makes a thick *minestrina* agreeable to Italian taste. You may vary the consistency by adjusting the amount of stock used.

Riso e Fagioli all' Abruzzese
RICE AND BEANS ABRUZZI
(Abruzzi e Molise)

In 6 cups salted water simmer 2 cups fresh shell beans until they are tender and keep them warm in their cooking water. Or use dried white beans, first soaked overnight. In a heavy pot heat 2 tablespoons olive oil and add 1 onion and 1 stalk of celery, both chopped. When the vegetables are slightly brown add 2 large ripe tomatoes, peeled and chopped, salt, and a pinch of crushed red pepper flakes. Simmer together for 5 minutes. Now add the beans with their water and 1/2 cup uncooked rice. Continue cooking for 20 minutes. The result should be a thick soup. Serve with grated Romano cheese.

Minestra alla Siciliana
ALMOND AND RICE SOUP SICILIAN
(Sicily)

Simmer 1/4 cup blanched ground almonds in 1 cup milk for 15 minutes. Cook 5 ounces rice (1/2 cup plus 2 tablespoons) in 3 cups boiling salted water for about 15 minutes, or until it is soft. Drain the rice and add 4 cups hot milk, and the milk containing the almonds. Bring to a boil and simmer for 5 minutes. Put the soup through a sieve, pressing the rice through, add salt to taste, reheat the soup, and melt in 2 tablespoons butter. Stir a small amount of the soup into 2 well-beaten egg yolks and return them to the pot. Beat the soup with a whisk over moderate heat, but do not allow it to boil. Serve immediately.

Minestra Perugina
LENTIL SOUP PERUGIAN
(Umbria)

Soak 1 1/2 cups lentils overnight in 2 quarts water. Put them over low heat and bring them slowly to a boil in the same water. Meanwhile, try out 1/2 cup diced salt pork in a frying pan and, when it is lightly browned, remove the pork scraps and in the fat slowly cook 1 minced onion until it is golden. Add the browned pork, the onions, and some of the fat to the soup. Simmer the lentils slowly for 1 1/2 hours and stir into the soup 3 tablespoons rice flour or corn starch blended with 1 cup cold stock. Simmer the soup about 1 hour more and, when the lentils are thoroughly cooked, strain it through a fine sieve, forcing through as much of the lentil pulp as possible. If the soup is too thick add a little water or stock. Taste for seasoning, stir in 1 tablespoon

butter, and serve very hot with slices of Italian bread, sautéed in butter, floating on top.

Zuppa di Verdure
VEGETABLE AND POTATO SOUP

Melt 3 tablespoons butter in a soup kettle and add 1 small onion, chopped, 2 carrots, sliced, 2 stalks of celery, sliced, 1 tablespoon parsley, minced, and 1 small clove of garlic. Sauté the vegetables for several minutes, or until they have taken on a little color. Remove the garlic clove. Add salt and pepper, 1 cup prepared tomato sauce, 4 cups hot stock or water, and 4 large potatoes previously boiled, peeled, and forced through a potato ricer or sieve. Stir and simmer all together for 20 minutes. Pass grated Parmesan with this soup.

Zuppa alla Modenese
SPINACH SOUP MODENESE
(Emilia–Romagna)

Wash 1 pound spinach and cook it in a very small amount of water until it is barely soft. The water remaining on the leaves after washing is usually enough. Drain the cooked spinach thoroughly, pressing out all the water, and chop it finely or force it through a sieve. Heat it in 2 tablespoons melted butter and allow it to cook for 2 or 3 minutes. Mix in salt and pepper, a good grating of nutmeg, the beaten yolks of 2 eggs, and 2 tablespoons grated Parmesan. Pour in 3 cups boiling beef or chicken stock, stir well, allow the soup to reheat to the boiling point, and serve it with sautéed bread croutons. The eggs will curdle and are intended to. Serves 4.

Paparot
SPINACH SOUP

This is a *minestra*, a classic Italian family dish served as a first course, or even as the main dish of a simple meal. It might be considered either a thick soup or a thin vegetable, falling somewhere between the two. In any case, it is served in generous quantities in large soup plates.

Wash and cook briefly 1 1/2 pounds spinach, allowing it to soften slowly in a covered pan with no more water than what remains on the leaves. When it is barely softened, drain it and chop it medium fine. In 4 tablespoons butter cook 1 minced clove of garlic for 1 minute. Blend in 2 tablespoons flour and cook about a minute more. Now combine this with the spinach, cover, and cook over low heat for 5 minutes. Add 7 cups (1 3/4 quarts) boiling water, cover the pot, and boil the *minestra* gently for a half an hour. Stir in gradually 3 tablespoons yellow corn meal, cook 10 minutes longer, taste for seasoning, and serve the *minestra* in hot soup plates.

Zuppa di Pomodoro
TOMATO SOUP LIGURIAN

(Liguria)

This is an unusual and delicious variant of cream of tomato soup.

Heat 3 tablespoons olive oil in a saucepan and in it sauté 2 medium-sized onions, chopped, until they are soft and browned. Add 4 large ripe tomatoes, peeled and cut in pieces, 2 teaspoons sugar, 1/2 teaspoon salt, and 1/4 teaspoon freshly ground pepper. Simmer the mixture for about 20 minutes, or until it is reduced to a soft purée. Force it through a fine sieve and allow to cool. This should give you about 1 1/2 cups of purée. Stir in 1 cup sour cream. Add the mixture to 1 1/2 cups hot chicken stock, heat to the boiling point only, and serve at once. Serves 4.

Zuppa di Sparagi
CREAM OF ASPARAGUS SOUP

Wash and peel 2 pounds asparagus, 2 potatoes, and 1 leek. Cut 2-inch green tips from the asparagus and tie them together in 2 or 3 bunches with kitchen string. Cut up the rest of the asparagus, slice the potatoes and the white part of the leek, and put all the vegetables in a soup kettle with enough water to cover them completely. Simmer them for 15 minutes, remove the bunches of asparagus tips, and put them aside. Continue cooking the rest of the vegetables until they are quite soft and put the soup through a sieve, pressing the vegetables through. Return the resulting purée to the fire, season with salt and pepper, and add the asparagus tips and 1 tablespoon butter. Reheat all together and stir in 1 egg yolk beaten with 1/2 cup cream. Allow the soup to thicken slightly, stirring continually, but do not let it boil. Serve at once with fried bread croutons.

Zuppa di Pesce alla Veneziana
FISH SOUP VENETIAN

(Hotel Royal Danieli, Venice–Veneto)

Cut 2 pounds of assorted fish into 1-inch slices. Prepare stock by boiling the heads and trimmings of the fish in 3 cups salted water with a few slices of onion, a bay leaf, a sprig of parsley, and a pinch of thyme. After half an hour of boiling, strain the stock.

Heat 1/2 cup olive oil in a saucepan with 2 cloves of garlic, 1 bay leaf, and a pinch of thyme. When the oil is hot put in the pieces of fish and 1 teaspoon each of parsley and basil, both minced. When the fish is lightly browned on both sides add 1/2 cup white wine, 1 cup canned Italian tomatoes, and the strained fish stock. Add a pinch of saffron, salt, and pepper and allow the mixture to simmer for 10 to 12 minutes. Serve with the soup, in the soup plates, bread croutons sautéed in butter or olive oil.

Pasta and Rice

EGG PASTA

This recipe should make enough noodles—*tagliatelle, fettuccine,* or *trenette*—or *lasagne, cannelloni,* or ravioli for 6 people.

Sift 4 cups flour into a wide bowl, make a well in the center, and into it pour 3 lightly beaten eggs. Add 2 teaspoons salt and combine the flour with the eggs by sprinkling it over them a little at a time and mixing with the fingers of one hand. Add, a few drops at a time, 1/4 to 1/2 cup water, or just barely enough to make the pasta soft enough to knead. When the ingredients are thoroughly mixed, put the dough on a floured board and knead it with the heel of the hand for a good 10 to 12 minutes, or until it is perfectly smooth and elastic. Divide the kneaded dough into 4 sections and roll these out on a large board, one at a time, into very thin, even sheets. (If you try to roll the whole quantity in one piece, you will need a large tabletop!) Flour these sheets lightly.

Noodles. Roll up the sheets of dough loosely and cut the rolls into strips about 1/4 inch wide for *tagliatelle* or *fettuccine. Trenette* are rolled about 1/16 inch thick and cut 1/16 inch wide, to make long strips of about the dimensions of a matchstick. Spread the strips on towels to dry, separating them to keep them from sticking together.

If you are fortunate enough to own a machine for rolling and cutting pasta, divide the dough into 4 to 8 sections, shape the sections into long narrow rolls, flatten these with a rolling pin into strips almost the width of the machine, and put each strip through the rolling side three times, each time

moving the rollers to a closer adjustment. Then put the rolled sheets of pasta through the cutting side, adjusted to cut the width desired, and spread the strips on towels or on a large cloth to dry.

In half an hour, more or less, the pasta will be dry enough to handle and may be cooked. Boil it in a generous amount of salted water for 5 minutes. Or the pasta may be kept and used another day. Store it at room temperature. Serve with any one of the sauces suggested for *tagliatelle,* spaghetti, and the like.

Cannelloni are rectangles 3 by 3 1/2 inches and *lasagne* are bands at least 2 inches wide and 6 to 15 inches long. The dough is rolled about 1/8 inch thick, not so thin as for other pasta, to reduce the danger of the strips tearing when they are cooked. Dry them for about an hour before cooking. Cook them 5 or 6 at a time in a large pot of boiling water, skim them out, put them in a bowl of cold water, drain them, and spread them on damp towels. Then proceed with any of the recipes for stuffed *cannelloni* or baked *lasagne.*

Ravioli are stuffed before the pasta is cooked. Roll the dough into thin sheets. On one sheet place a teaspoonful of filling every 2 inches. Cover the filling with a second sheet of dough and, with the fingertips, press gently around each mound of filling. Cut the dough into 2-inch squares with a wooden pastry wheel, making sure that it is firmly sealed around the filling. Let the ravioli stand for about an hour to dry. Cook them in a large quantity of rapidly boiling salted water or stock for 6 to 7 minutes, drain them, and serve with any appropriate sauce, such as tomato or meat sauce (see index), or with melted butter. Accompany the pasta with grated Italian cheese.

Ravioli may be made with any of the suggested fillings for pasta (see index).

Lasagne Verdi
GREEN LASAGNE OR GREEN NOODLE PASTA

Wash 1/2 pound spinach and cook it with only the water remaining on the leaves until it is just soft. Or cook it 1 1/2 minutes in a pressure cooker. Drain the spinach, press out the water, chop it, and force it through a sieve. Or blend it in an electric blender. It should retain its fresh green color and be reduced to a smooth purée. If the spinach is very wet, heat it 1 minute in a saucepan over high heat to evaporate some of the moisture. Allow it to cool.

Sift 4 cups flour and 1 teaspoon salt into a wide bowl. Make a well in the center and in it put 2 large beaten eggs and the puréed spinach. Mix gradually with the fingers of one hand, or with a fork, until the paste is well blended. If all the flour is not incorporated, add a few drops of water. If the paste is too soft, add more flour. Knead the paste thoroughly for at least 12 minutes, or until it is elastic and smooth. Divide it into 4 pieces and roll them out 1/16 inch thick with a rolling pin or with a pasta-rolling machine. Cut the sheets into rectangles 2 by 4 inches, or longer. Sometimes the sheets are cut in 4-inch squares. Let them dry on towels for an hour. Proceed with any recipe for baked *lasagne*.

Also, you may roll the paste very thin, roll up the sheets, and cut the rolls into 1/4-inch strips, to make green noodles. Dry the strips for half an hour, boil them 5 minutes, and serve them with butter and grated cheese or with any sauce of your choice. This recipe makes about 1 1/4 pounds of pasta.

Veritabile Lasagne Verdi al Forno Bolognese
TRUE BAKED GREEN LASAGNE BOLOGNESE

This splendid dish is one of the glories of the Italian cuisine and the particular pride of its native Bologna. Though time and care are required for its preparation, the combination of tender green fresh pasta, satisfying and creamy sauces with flavorful cheese results in an utterly delicious dish, which will be an everlasting honor to the cook.

Make green *lasagne* pasta (see above) and cut the thin sheets into strips about 2 inches wide and 4 or more inches long. Dry the strips on towels for 1 hour. Boil them a few at a time for 3 minutes in a large kettle of salted water, remove them with a strainer, and drop them into cold water. Drain them again and spread them on damp towels. Use 3/4 pound *lasagne*, 2 1/2 cups meat sauce (see meat sauce Bolognese I or II), 3/4 cup grated Parmesan, and 2 cups cream sauce for the completed dish. To make the cream sauce, blend 2 tablespoons melted butter with 2 tablespoons flour, stir in gradually 1 cup milk and 1 cup cream, and season the sauce with salt and pepper and a good dash of grated nutmeg.

Butter a rectangular baking dish and coat the bottom with a small amount of meat sauce, a small amount of cream sauce, and a sprinkling of grated Parmesan. Place on this a layer of green *lasagne* with the ends turning part way up the sides of the dish. Now repeat the thin layers of meat sauce, cream sauce, and grated cheese. Continue in this way, forming 6 layers, more or less, and coat the top with meat sauce, cream sauce, and a generous amount of grated Parmesan. The trick is to make as many layers as possible and have the ingredients come out even. This distribution of textures and flavors constitutes the charm of the dish. Bake the *lasagne* in a moderately hot oven (375° F.) for 20 to 25 minutes, or until it is bubbling hot and shrinks a little away from the sides of the dish. Serves 6.

Lasagne alla Calabrese
LASAGNE CALABRIA
(Calabria)

First make a tomato sauce as follows: Heat 4 tablespoons olive oil in a saucepan and add 1/4 pound each of fresh Italian pork sausage and fresh Italian hot sausage, both peeled and chopped, 2 teaspoons fresh chopped basil, 2 chopped cloves of garlic, and a pinch each of salt and pepper. Sauté the mixture for 3 or 4 minutes and then add 1 small can of tomato paste and 4 cups (1 large can) of Italian tomatoes, well mashed or forced through a colander. Simmer the sauce until it is fairly thick.

Boil 1 pound *lasagne* in a large kettle of salted water. To prevent their sticking together, cook a few at a time, removing them to a bowl of cold water as done. Drain them on damp towels. In an oiled baking dish place a layer of *lasagne,* then a layer of crumbled *ricotta* cheese mixed with finely sliced *mozzarella.* (About 2 cups of *ricotta* and 1 1/2 cups *mozzarella* are needed for the completed dish.) On the cheese, spread a layer of sliced mushrooms previously cooked for 3 or 4 minutes in a small amount of water with a little lemon juice and olive oil. (About 3/4 pound mushrooms are needed for the completed dish.) Over the mushrooms pour a layer of the tomato sauce and continue adding the ingredients in

layers, ending with tomato sauce and a layer of grated Romano or Parmesan.

Bake the dish in a hot oven (425° F.) for 15 minutes and serve it piping hot.

Tagliatelle Ferdinando
CREAMED NOODLES FERDINAND
(Hotel Villa Carlotta, Stresa–Piedmont)

Boil 1/2 to 3/4 pound *tagliatelle,* or egg noodles, in salted water. Drain half of them and place them in the bottom of a buttered baking dish. Over them scatter 2 tablespoons diced *foie gras,* 1/2 cup cooked, diced sweetbreads, and 3/4 cup cooked, diced chicken. Make 2 cups cream sauce with 2 tablespoons butter, 1 1/2 tablespoons flour, and 2 cups light cream and flavor it with 1/2 teaspoon curry powder. Pour half the sauce over the mixture in the baking dish, add the rest of the *tagliatelle,* and pour over these the remaining cream sauce. Sprinkle with grated Parmesan, a little melted butter, and paprika, and brown lightly in a hot oven (400° F.).

Maccheroni alla Chitarra
EGG NOODLES ABRUZZI
(Abruzzi e Molise)

The *chitarra,* or guitar, in this dish refers to the wired rack on which the pasta is cut into narrow strips. Otherwise, these noodles do not differ from similar pasta in other parts of Italy. The meat sauce made with lamb is, however, a local specialty.

Boil 1 pound noodles made with egg pasta (see index) in salted water for 5 minutes and drain them. If dried "store" noodles are used, cook them for 9 minutes. Serve them with the following sauce:

Heat 1 tablespoon butter with 1/4 cup olive oil in a frying pan and add 1 pound ground lean lamb and 2 chopped green peppers. Season with salt and brown the meat slightly, stirring it from time to time. Add 1/2 cup white wine and simmer the liquid until the wine is almost evaporated. Add 2 large ripe, peeled, and coarsely chopped tomatoes and simmer the mixture for half an hour, or until it is reduced and has a thick consistency.

Tagliatelle della Casa alla Triestina
HOMEMADE NOODLES TRIESTE
(Savoy-Excelsior Palace, Trieste–Friuli-Venezia Giulia)

Make egg pasta (see index), cut it into 1/4-inch strips, and boil them in a large quantity of salted water for about 5 minutes. Or use egg noodles of a good commercial brand. Drain the *tagliatelle* and serve with the following: For about 1 pound *tagliatelle,* melt 3 tablespoons butter in a deep saucepan, add 3/4 cup *prosciutto* cut in fine julienne strips, heat them together for about 1 minute, add 1/2 cup meat juices from stewed beef Florentine or other meat sauce (see index), 1/2 cup cream, and blend well together. Add the hot *tagliatelle* to the pan and stir and heat all together, adding 3 tablespoons grated Parmesan as you toss them. Serve piping hot.

Spaghetti alle Vongole
SPAGHETTI WITH CLAM SAUCE
(Campania)

Vongole are a species of very small double-necked clams that are found off Italian shores, but not in America. Any of our own clams—whole, if small, chopped, if large—may be used in this recipe.

Boil 1 pound thin spaghetti until it is tender but still firm, drain it, and serve with the following sauce:

Heat 3 tablespoons olive oil in a saucepan, add 1 clove of garlic, minced, 2 teaspoons minced parsley, and 2 cups Italian tomatoes (one 16-ounce can) or fresh peeled and chopped tomatoes. Add the strained juices from about 2 dozen small steamed clams. Simmer the sauce until it has a good consistency and then add the clams removed from their shells. Cheese is not served with this sauce.

Spaghetti alla Siciliana
SICILIAN SPAGHETTI
(Sicily)

Boil 1 pound spaghetti in abundant water for about 9 minutes, or until it is tender but still firm, and serve it with the following sauce:

In a frying pan heat 1/2 cup olive oil and add 2 cloves of garlic cut in quarters. Allow them to brown and then remove them from the oil. Add half a medium-sized eggplant, peeled and diced, and 6 large ripe tomatoes, peeled and cut in pieces. Simmer the vegetables for 30 minutes. Partially cook 2 green peppers on all sides under the broiler, peel off the loosened skin, cut out the pith and seeds, and slice the peppers. Add to the pan the peppers, 1 tablespoon fresh basil, chopped, 1 tablespoon capers, 4 anchovy filets cut in small bits, a dozen halved and pitted small black Italian olives, and salt and pepper. Cover the pan and simmer the sauce for about 10 minutes, or until it is well blended and has a good consistency.

Sformato di Maccheroni alla Partenopea
MACARONI TIMBALE
(Hotel Vesuvio, Naples–Campania)

Sift 1 3/4 cups flour with 1/2 teaspoon salt, cut in 4 tablespoons butter, broken in bits, and, when these are well blended, add 1 large lightly beaten egg. (Save 1 teaspoon of the egg for the little meatballs.) Add about 1 or 2 tablespoons milk, or just enough to make a dough. Roll two-thirds of the dough out 1/8 inch thick. With this paste, line a buttered round mold 3 inches deep or a deep pie dish. Roll out the rest of the dough for the cover.

Boil a little more than 1/2 pound small macaroni in salted water and drain it. Mix 1/4 pound finely ground beef with a pinch each of salt and pepper, 1/2 teaspoon minced parsley, a little grated nutmeg, 1 tablespoon bread crumbs, and the reserved teaspoonful of egg. Form the mixture into small balls no larger than hazelnuts. and sauté them 2 to 3 minutes in 2 teaspoons hot butter. Remove them from the pan and, in the remaining fat, sauté briefly 2 tablespoons julienne of ham. Add 2 large ripe peeled and seeded tomatoes, cut in pieces, 1 tablespoon olive oil, salt and pepper, and 1/2 teaspoon chopped fresh basil. Simmer the sauce until it is moderately thick. Combine the macaroni, meatballs, and sauce and add 1/2 cup *mozzarella* cheese cut in small dice and 2 tablespoons grated Parmesan. Fill the mold with this mixture and pour in 3 or 4 tablespoons of meat juice from stewed beef Florentine or another meat sauce (see index) to keep it moist. Cover with a round of dough. Press the edges of the dough together, prick the top with a fork, and bake the pie in a very hot oven (450° F.) for 20 to 25 minutes. Serve it turned out on a hot dish or from the mold. Pass meat sauce with this dish, if desired.

Cannelloni Villa Carlotta
CANNELLONI WITH MEAT FILLING
VILLA CARLOTTA
(Hotel Villa Carlotta, Stresa–Piedmont)

Make homemade egg pasta for *cannelloni* according to the recipe (see index). For the filling for a dozen *cannelloni* use 2 1/2 cups of the chopped meat of a *stracotta,* or Florentine meat sauce (see index), mixed with a good pinch of grated nutmeg, 1/2 cup grated Parmesan, and 2 large egg yolks. Place a little of the filling on each pasta rectangle, roll up the *cannelloni,* and

place them side by side in a shallow baking dish. Pour over them 3/4 cup of the juices of the meat sauce, then 1/2 cup cream. Sprinkle with grated Parmesan, dot with butter, and cook the *cannelloni* in a moderate oven (350° F.) for about 15 minutes.

Cannelloni alla Santa Caterina
CANNELLONI WITH MEAT FILLING
SANTA CATERINA
(Hotel Santa Caterina, Amalfi–Campania)

Make a meat *ragù* such as stewed beef Florentine (see index).

Remove the meat and put it through a grinder. Strain the juices and combine part of them with a scant cup of bread crumbs. The crumbs should be moist but not too soft. Mix meat and crumbs and add a grating of nutmeg, 1/2 cup grated Parmesan, and 2 beaten eggs. This makes enough filling for about 2 dozen *cannelloni.*

Cut rectangles for *cannelloni* from fresh egg pasta (see index). Cook a few of them at a time in boiling salted water for 3 minutes and drain them on damp towels. Put a little of the filling on each one, roll them up, and place them side by side in a baking dish containing the rest of the meat *ragù* juices combined with 3/4 to 1 cup tomato sauce. Sprinkle them lavishly with grated Parmesan and cook the *cannelloni* in a hot oven (400° F.) for 10 to 15 minutes.

Cannelloni alla Caruso
CANNELLONI CARUSO
(Hotel Caruso Belvedere, Ravello–Campania)

Cut rectangles for *cannelloni* from fresh egg pasta (see index). Boil these a few at a time in boiling salted water for about 3 minutes, being careful to remove them while they are still firm. Drain them on damp towels.

For the filling, make a thick cream sauce with 3 tablespoons butter and

3 tablespoons flour blended over gentle heat. Add gradually 2 cups hot milk. Add salt and pepper and a little nutmeg and stir the sauce until it is smooth and somewhat thickened. Allow it to cool. Add 2 tablespoons grated Parmesan, 2 egg yolks, 3/4 cup thick meat sauce (see index), 1/2 pound *ricotta* cheese, 1/4 cup finely diced *salami*, 1/4 cup finely diced ham, and 1/2 cup finely diced *mozzarella*. Mix all well together and fill the pasta rectangles with this delectable combination. This is enough filling for about 2 dozen *cannelloni*. Roll them up and place them side by side in a buttered baking dish containing a thin layer of juicy meat sauce or tomato sauce (see index). Dot them with butter, spread a few spoonfuls of sauce over them, sprinkle lavishly with grated Parmesan, and cook the *cannelloni* in a hot oven (400° F.) for about 10 minutes, or until they are very hot and the ingredients are well blended.

Ravioli alla Genovese
RAVIOLI GENOA
(Liguria)

Sift 3 cups flour into a bowl with a dash of salt. Stir in 2 eggs, lightly beaten, and enough water to make a rather stiff dough. Knead the dough for 12 minutes, or until it is smooth and elastic, cover it with a warm bowl, and let it stand for about 10 minutes.

In a skillet sauté half a chicken breast, 1 parboiled sheep's brain, 1 parboiled sweetbread, and 1 chicken liver in 2 tablespoons butter until the meat is lightly browned. Cover the skillet and cook the meat gently for 12 minutes. Run it twice through the fine blade of a meat chopper and add 3/4 cup bread crumbs moistened with 1/4 cup beef or chicken stock. Add 2 tablespoons slivered ham, 1 cup cooked, sieved spinach, salt, pepper and nutmeg to taste, and 2 egg yolks and mix well.

Cut the dough in half and roll out each half on a lightly floured board into a thin sheet. Fill and cut the dough according to the recipe for egg pasta (see index). Cook the ravioli in a large quantity of rapidly boiling salted water or stock for 6 or 7 minutes, drain, and serve with *pesto* (see index).

SIMPLE MEAT OR POULTRY FILLING

Combine 2 cups ground leftover meat or poultry (beef, veal, pork, chicken, or a combination of any of these), 1/2 cup finely chopped parsley, salt, pepper, nutmeg, and 2 beaten eggs. This filling may be used to stuff 2 dozen ravioli or 1 dozen *cannelloni*. Serve the pasta with tomato sauce.

MEAT OR POULTRY FILLING FOR RAVIOLI

Combine 1 cup ground, cooked chicken, turkey, or veal with 1 teaspoon melted butter, 1 tablespoon grated Parmesan, 1 teaspoon minced parsley, 1/2 teaspoon finely grated or minced lemon rind, half a small clove of garlic, minced, and salt and pepper. Add 1 small beaten egg or enough of it to bind the mixture together.

MEAT AND SPINACH FILLING FOR RAVIOLI

Combine 1/2 cup ground, cooked veal, pork, or chicken (1 chicken liver may be included with any one of these), 3 tablespoons ground, cooked ham, 1/2 cup cooked spinach that has been squeezed as dry as possible and finely chopped, 2 tablespoons grated Parmesan, 1 teaspoon parsley, finely minced, a dash of nutmeg, and salt and pepper. Add 1 beaten egg or enough of it to bind the mixture.

SPINACH FILLING FOR RAVIOLI

Wash 1 pound spinach and remove

the heavy stalks. Plunge it in boiling salted water and cook it for 3 to 5 minutes. Drain the spinach thoroughly, squeezing out all the water, and chop it very fine. Add 4 tablespoons ground cooked ham, a good dash of nutmeg, salt and pepper, 2 tablespoons grated Parmesan, and 2 tablespoons melted butter. Add 1 beaten egg or enough of it to bind the mixture together. If you prefer, you may add 1 to 2 chopped hard-boiled eggs and just enough cream to moisten the mixture.

RICOTTA SPINACH FILLING

Mix lightly but thoroughly with a fork the following: 1 pound *ricotta* cheese, 2 or 3 tablespoons tepid water, 1/2 pound spinach that has been cooked, drained, pressed just as dry as possible, and finely chopped, salt, pepper, a good dash of nutmeg, 3 beaten eggs, and 1/2 cup grated Parmesan. Fill *cannelloni* lightly with this mixture, do not pack, roll them up, and place them side by side in a shallow baking dish. Pour over them fresh tomato sauce (see index), sprinkle with Parmesan, dot with butter, and heat in a moderate oven (350° F.) about 15 minutes.

This filling may also be made without spinach. It is enough for 2 dozen *cannelloni*. It may also be used to stuff ravioli and in baked *lasagne*.

Crochetti di Riso Palermitana
RICE CROQUETTES PALERMO
(Sicily)

In 2 cups light stock or salted milk, cook slowly 1 cup rice until all the liquid is absorbed. Remove the pan from the heat and stir in 2 tablespoons finely chopped parsley, 1 cup finely chopped cooked meat or poultry, a pinch of cayenne pepper, and 1/2 cup grated Parmesan and add finally 1 well-beaten egg. Cool the mixture and form it into balls or croquette rolls. Dip them in flour and let them dry for 1 hour. Dip them in 1 egg beaten with 1 tablespoon water, then in fine bread crumbs. Fry them in deep hot fat (390° F.), a few at a time, until they are golden brown. Drain them on absorbent paper. Serve them just as they are or accompanied by a tomato sauce.

Arancini alla Siciliana
STUFFED RICE CROQUETTES SICILIAN
(Sicily)

These *arancini,* or little oranges, may be served as a first course, with a little sprig of parsley stuck in each to give the effect of a green stem.

Heat 4 tablespoons olive oil and 2 tablespoons butter in a saucepan and add 1 small sliced onion. Allow it to soften and take on a little color and then add 3/4 pound chopped veal. Stir and cook it until it changes color. Add 1 pound peeled, seeded, and coarsely chopped tomatoes, 3 or 4 leaves of fresh basil, and salt and pepper. Cover the pan and cook the mixture slowly for about an hour, or until it is very thick. Pour off any juices remaining in the pan and reserve them. Let the veal mixture cool. Heat the reserved juices in a saucepan and stir in 1 1/2 cups rice. Let the rice color a little and add, a cup at a time, 5 cups stock or water with bouillon cubes. Cover the pan and cook the *risotto* slowly, allowing the rice each time to absorb all the liquid before adding more. When all the stock is absorbed, stir in 3 tablespoons butter, 4 tablespoons grated Parmesan, and 2 egg yolks, one at a time.

Spread the *risotto* on a platter and chill it and the veal stuffing in the refrigerator.

When you are ready to cook the "little oranges," take spoonfuls of the *risotto* and form it between your hands into round balls 1 1/2 inches in diameter. With one finger make a hole in the center of each, fill it with the veal mixture, and cover the hole with more rice. Roll the balls in bread crumbs and fry them to a golden color in deep hot oil or shortening (390° F.). Drain them and heap them on a hot platter with a sprig of parsley stuck in each one. Pass tomato sauce separately, if desired.

Risotto alla Marinara
SEA FOOD RISOTTO
(Birreria Ristorante Pedavena, Verona–Veneto)

In 2 tablespoons melted butter and 2 tablespoons hot olive oil combined cook slowly 1 onion, 1 clove of garlic, and 1 small stalk of celery, all chopped, until they have taken on a little color. Add 12 small clams and 12 mussels that have been steamed open and removed from their shells and 8 or 10 peeled raw shrimp. Reserve the juices from the clams and mussels. Cook the mixture for about 2 minutes and add 1/2 cup white wine and 1 teaspoon brandy. Stir in 1 cup rice and add 1 cup hot fish stock that includes the juices from the clams and mussels. Cover the pan and cook the *risotto* very slowly for 10 to 15 minutes, or until the liquid is absorbed. Add about 2 cups more hot fish stock or water and cook very slowly until the liquid is absorbed. Stir in a lump of butter, 1/4 cup grated Parmesan, and 2 tablespoons finely chopped parsley. Serve at once.

Risotto alla Milanese
RISOTTO MILANESE
(Lombardy)

In a heavy saucepan melt 2 tablespoons butter with 2 tablespoons olive oil. When it is hot stir in 1 cup rice that has been wiped in a clean cloth, but not washed. Let the rice become pale gold in color, stirring it with a fork over moderate heat. Add 1 onion,

chopped, and 1 clove of garlic, chopped and mashed. Cook another brief moment and add 1 cup hot chicken stock. Cover the pan closely and cook slowly over low heat for 10 to 20 minutes, or until the liquid is absorbed. Add 1/2 teaspoon saffron, or more, according to taste, that has been dissolved in 3 tablespoons white wine or Madeira. Now add 2 1/2 cups more hot chicken stock, stir the rice once with a fork, cover closely, and continue cooking until all the liquid is absorbed and the rice is fluffy. Add a lump of butter and 1/2 cup grated Parmesan, stir very lightly, and serve at once.

If desired, 1/2 cup sliced mushrooms or dried Italian mushrooms that have been soaked in a little water may be added with the second quantity of stock.

Risi e Bisi
VENETIAN RICE AND PEAS
(Veneto)

Heat 1 tablespoon olive oil and 1/4 cup butter in a heavy kettle and in it brown 1 small onion, chopped, and 1/2 slice of bacon, cut in dice—about 1 tablespoon. Add 2 cups freshly shelled green peas and cook for 5 minutes, stirring frequently. Add 3/4 cup rice and cook for 3 minutes longer, stirring often, until the grains are well coated with oil and butter. Add 1 3/4 cups chicken stock and salt and pepper to taste, cover the kettle, and cook the mixture over low heat for 15 to 20 minutes. The rice should absorb all the liquid and it should be tender but not mushy. Toss with 1 tablespoon grated Parmesan. More cheese may be sprinkled on the individual servings, if desired.

Eggs

Uova al Piatto alla Parmigiana
SHIRRED EGGS WITH CHEESE

Grease with butter or bacon fat as many individual shirred-egg dishes as desired. Break 1 egg carefully into each dish. Sprinkle each egg with salt, pepper, and 2 teaspoons bacon that has been diced and lightly browned. Cover each egg with 1 tablespoon grated Parmesan, sprinkle with melted butter, and bake the eggs in a moderate oven (350° F.) for about 10 minutes, or until they are set and the cheese is melted.

In place of the bacon you may use julienne of cooked ham.

Uova al Piatto con Acciughe
SHIRRED EGGS WITH ANCHOVIES

Butter a shallow baking dish and break into it carefully the desired number of eggs. Or you may use individual shirred-egg dishes. Sprinkle a pinch of salt and pepper on each egg, place 2 anchovy filets in a cross on each, and then a thin slice of *mozzarella*. Bake the eggs in a moderate oven (350° F.) for about 10 minutes, or until they are set and the cheese melted. For 4 eggs, melt 2 tablespoons of butter with 1 chopped anchovy filet. Pour a little of this sauce over each egg and serve at once. Serves 4.

Uova al Piatto all' Emiliana
SHIRRED EGGS WITH CHICKEN LIVERS

Dice 4 chicken livers and sauté them in 2 tablespoons hot butter for 2 minutes. Add salt and pepper, 1 tablespoon Marsala, and 2 to 3 tablespoons warm water and continue to cook for 3 minutes. Meanwhile break 4 eggs carefully into a buttered shallow baking dish, add salt and pepper to taste, and bake the eggs in a moderate oven (350° F.) for 10 minutes. Pour the diced chicken livers and their juices over the eggs and return the dish to the oven for 2 or 3 minutes. If desired, a dozen cooked asparagus tips may be added to garnish the dish before adding the chicken livers. Serves 4.

Uova Affogate in Pomodoro
EGGS POACHED IN TOMATO SAUCE

Heat 4 tablespoons olive oil in a broad, shallow pan and add half an onion, chopped fine. When the onion is soft and golden add 1 small clove of garlic, chopped and mashed, 2 cups Italian canned tomatoes, 2 teaspoons finely chopped parsley, salt, and a pinch of crushed red pepper flakes. Simmer the sauce for about 20 minutes. Break 6 eggs, one at a time, into a teacup and slip each one with care into the sauce. Cover the pan and cook the eggs over low heat for 3 to 5 minutes, or until the whites are set. Serve at once.

Uova alla Cacciatora
EGGS HUNTER STYLE

Heat 3 tablespoons olive oil in a broad shallow pan and in it sauté 1 tablespoon onion, finely chopped, until it begins to soften. Add 4 chicken livers, each cut in 3 or 4 pieces, and sauté them slowly for about 3 minutes, stirring occasionally. Add salt and pepper, a pinch each of chopped basil and thyme, and 1/4 cup dry white wine. Blend 1 tablespoon tomato paste with 1/4 cup warm water (or use a generous 1/4 cup prepared tomato sauce), add this to the pan, and simmer the mixture for 3 to 4 minutes. Break 4 eggs, one at a time, into the sauce, cover the pan, and let the eggs poach over very low heat 3 to 4 minutes, or until the whites are well set. Remove each egg carefully to a piece of toast, spoon chicken livers and sauce over each one, and serve at once. Serves 4.

Uova Fritte con Panini di Mozzarella e Prosciutto
FRIED EGGS ON CHEESE AND HAM FRITTERS

Cut 1/2 pound *mozzarella* into 3/8-inch slices. Between each 2 slices of cheese place a slice of cooked ham. Make 6 of these "sandwiches," shape them evenly, and dip them in flour, then in beaten egg, then in fine bread crumbs. Brown them on both sides in 4 tablespoons hot butter over a fairly hot fire. Remove them to a hot platter. Meanwhile fry 6 eggs slowly in 4 tablespoons hot olive oil until they are set, cut the uneven edges neatly, and place a fried egg on each fried cheese "sandwich." Serve at once.

Tortino d'Uova nella Neve
BAKED EGGS IN SNOW

Boil about 1 pound potatoes in salted water. Peel them and mash and beat them to make a purée, adding, a little at a time, about 1/2 cup hot milk, 3 tablespoons melted butter, and salt and pepper. Spread the mashed potatoes in a buttered baking dish and on them lay about 1/4 pound *mozzarella,* thinly sliced. Make 6 slight indentations on the surface with the back of a large spoon, leaving a little space between them, and break an egg into each. Season the eggs with salt and pepper, sprinkle with 4 to 5 tablespoons grated Parmesan, dot the surface generously with butter, and bake them in a very hot oven (450° F.) for 5 to 8 minutes, or until they are just set and the cheese well melted.

Uova in Tegame con Prosciutto e Mozzarella
BAKED EGGS WITH HAM AND MOZZARELLA
(Campania)

Butter a baking dish with 1 tablespoon butter and place in it 6 equal-sized slices of *prosciutto.* Cooked ham will do. Cover the ham with thin slices of *mozzarella* cheese and carefully break an egg over each ham slice. Dot the eggs with bits of butter, add salt and pepper, and bake them in a hot oven (400° F.) until the cheese is melted and the eggs are just set.

Uova Fiorentina
EGGS FLORENTINE
(Tuscany)

Wash thoroughly and remove the larger stems from 1 pound spinach. Put 2 tablespoons olive oil in a saucepan and add the spinach and a little salt and pepper. Cover the pan and cook the spinach until it is softened, which will take about 5 minutes. Drain the spinach if necessary, chop it, and place it in 4 individual baking dishes (or one large one, if desired.) With the back of a large spoon make 4 indentations in the spinach bed and carefully break an egg into each one. Sprinkle a teaspoon grated Parmesan or Pecorino cheese over each egg and bake them in a moderate oven (350° F.) for 5 to 8 minutes, or until the whites are set but the yolks are still soft. Serves 4.

If you choose, you may put a little anchovy paste on top of each egg as well as the cheese.

Tortino di Carciofi alla Fiorentina
TORTINO OF ARTICHOKES FLORENTINE
(Tuscany)

The variety of tender small artichoke used in this and other Italian dishes has been more readily available in Italian markets than in our own. But by a happy chance little fresh artichoke hearts have recently appeared in American markets in quick-frozen form. A *tortino* resembles an omelette cooked in the oven.

For a Florentine *tortino* for four, slice thinly and vertically 4 artichoke hearts and allow them to thaw. Pat them dry in paper towels and sprinkle them with a little lemon juice. In a skillet or *gratin* dish heat 1 generous tablespoon butter and 2 tablespoons olive oil. Dredge the artichoke slices with flour and cook them slowly in the hot fat until they are golden brown, which will take 4 to 5 minutes on each side. With a fork beat 4 eggs for about 30 seconds with salt and pepper and 2 tablespoons milk or water. Pour the eggs over the artichokes and place the pan in a moderate oven (350° F.) for about 5 to 10 minutes, or until the eggs are set but not dry. Serve in the dish.

(Some people prefer to sauté the artichokes without dredging them with flour, though they do not brown quite so well this way.)

Scrippelle Imbusse
STUFFED PANCAKES ABRUZZI
(Abruzzi e Molise)

Beat 4 eggs well in a bowl and add gradually 1 cup flour and 1/2 teaspoon salt. When the mixture is smooth and creamy add just enough water to make a thin flowing batter. Heat a 5-inch frying pan, grease it with oil, and pour in a spoonful of batter just large enough to spread and coat the pan, forming a thin pancake. As soon as it bubbles, turn it with a spatula and cook the other side. Make the pancakes one by one, greasing the pan each time, and lay them on a board or aluminum sheet. Sprinkle them well with grated Parmesan or Pecorino cheese mixed with a little minced *prosciutto*. Roll them up rather tightly and place them side by side in a shallow baking dish. Pour over

the pancakes enough boiling chicken broth to cover them to about one-third of their depth. Cover the dish and let it stand in a hot place (for instance, a heated oven with the heat turned off) for a few minutes so the broth will be partially absorbed.

Frittata con Peperoni
GREEN PEPPER OMELETTE

Wash 3 green peppers, cut them in half, and remove the seeds. Cut the peppers into 1/2-inch strips. Heat 4 tablespoons olive oil in an omelette pan and add the slices of pepper and 1 clove of garlic, cut in two. Sauté the peppers gently until they are soft and slightly browned, remove the garlic, and add 5 slightly beaten eggs seasoned with salt. Stir the mixture only once, distributing the pepper slices evenly. Cook the eggs over low heat, without stirring, until they are set and turn the omelette out on a small platter. Serves 4.

Frittata alla Trentina
OMELETTE TRENTINA
(Trento–Alto Adige)

Beat well 3 egg yolks and add 3 tablespoons flour, stirring until smooth. Add a little salt and stir in gradually 3/4 cup milk. Beat the 3 egg whites stiff and fold them in carefully but thoroughly. Heat an omelette pan and melt in it 2 tablespoons butter. When the butter is hot, but not brown, pour in the egg mixture and cook it over low heat without stirring for 1 or 2 minutes. Then cover the pan to cook the top of the eggs a little. Turn the omelette out on a platter, folded. It may be served with a *ragù bolognese* (see index) or thick tomato sauce, or it may be served as a dessert with jam folded into the center and sugar sprinkled on top. Serves 2.

Fish and Shellfish

Ostriche alla Napoletana
OYSTERS NEAPOLITAN
(Campania)

Open fresh oysters, clean the deep sides of the shells, and rub these with a cut clove of garlic. Replace the oysters in the prepared shells and cover each one with about 1 teaspoon fine bread crumbs mixed with finely minced parsley, a pinch of thyme, and freshly ground pepper. A few chopped anchovy filets may be included, if desired. Spoon a few drops of olive oil over each oyster and place them under a hot, preheated broiler just long enough to gild the surface. Add a few drops of lemon juice just before serving or at the table.

Vongole Siciliana
SICILIAN STEAMED CLAMS
(Sicily)

In a kettle put 3 tablespoons olive oil, 2 cloves of garlic, and 2 tablespoons parsley, both finely minced, and a pinch of pepper. Heat these together for 2 minutes and add 3 dozen well-cleaned, soft-shell steaming clams. Cover the pot and steam the clams over moderate heat until the shells open. Serve the clams in their shells in soup plates, with their broth poured over them. Serves 3.

Scampi alla Griglia
GRILLED SHRIMP

Scampi are salt-water crayfish resembling what the French call *langoustines.* Our jumbo shrimp are a close approximation.

For 4 persons use 2 pounds jumbo shrimp and cut them lengthwise without removing the shells, leaving one point on the convex side joined. Flatten them out, skewer each one with a wooden toothpick, if desired, to hold them flat, baste them with olive oil, and season them with salt and pepper. Grill them under a hot broiler, first the cut side and then the shell side. This will take 6 to 8 minutes, depending on their size. Serve them on a hot dish, sprinkled with minced parsley, olive oil, and lemon juice.

Scampi alla Peoceta
SHRIMP PEOCETA
(Ristorante al Peoceta Risorto, Venice–Veneto)

Shell and devein 1 pound shrimp and cook them in 4 tablespoons hot butter for 3 minutes. Add 1/2 teaspoon capers and pour on 1 tablespoon flaming brandy. Add pepper and salt and 3/4 cup cream. Peel, seed, and cut coarsely 1 large fresh tomato and add this to the pan. Cook for 5 minutes and add 1 cup steamed shelled mussels and 2 teaspoons tomato paste. Blend, taste for seasoning, and reheat for several minutes. Serves 4.

Spiedini di Scampi alla Moda del Chef
SKEWERED SHRIMP CHEF'S STYLE
(Grand Hotel Villa d'Este, Cernobbio–Lombardy)

Peel 2 dozen raw jumbo shrimp and wrap each one in a small thin slice of Canadian bacon. Thread 6 shrimp on each of 4 small individual serving skewers and brown them a little on each side in a broad pan in 3 tablespoons olive oil. Sprinkle over the skewers 1 tablespoon brandy and add 1/2 cup cream, a drop of Worcestershire sauce, the juice of a quarter lemon, 2 tablespoons meat juice or strong stock, salt, pepper, a pinch of cayenne, and 2 teaspoons parsley, finely chopped. Cook the shrimp in this sauce for 10 minutes and then remove the skewers to a hot serving dish. Whisk 1 teaspoon fresh butter into the sauce and pour it over the shrimp. Serve them with fluffy boiled rice. Serves 4.

Baccalà al Sedano
SALT CODFISH WITH CELERY
*(Hotel Europa, Riva del Garda–
Trentino-Alto Adige)*

Cover 2 pounds filets of salt codfish with boiling water and let the fish soak for 2 hours. Drain it and repeat the process. Pour 4 tablespoons olive oil into a deep baking dish and on it place a layer of the salt codfish. On this place a few very thin slices peeled celery root, or celeriac, a few slices peeled raw potato, a little chopped garlic, a pinch of crumbled bay leaf, pepper, a few drops of oil, and bits of butter. Repeat the layers, using for 2 pounds of codfish, 1 celery root, 1 large or 2 medium potatoes, 1 clove of garlic, and 1 bay leaf. Add 3/4 cup milk and bake the fish in a very slow oven (275° F.) for 1 hour, adding, a little at a time, another 1/2 to 3/4 cup of hot milk. Sprinkle the surface with grated Parmesan and melted butter and continue cooking until a brown crust forms on top.

Baccalà Mantecato alla Triestina
SALT CODFISH "POUF"
(Fruili–Venezia Giulia)

Soak 1/2 pound salt codfish filet for 6 hours, changing the water twice. Put it on to heat in fresh water, bring the water slowly to the boiling point, and drain the fish. Put it twice through the finest blade of the meat grinder and then work it in a mortar, adding alternately and a little at a time 1/2 cup

olive oil and a scant 1/2 cup milk. When these ingredients are well mixed, add 2 small cloves of garlic and 2 teaspoons parsley, both finely chopped, freshly ground pepper, and 2 teaspoons lemon juice. Beat the mixture until it is fluffy. Shape it into a mound and chill it in the refrigerator. Serve with crusty Italian bread as *antipasto* or with salad. Serves 2 to 4.

Baccalà alla Vicentina
SALT CODFISH VICENZA
(Ristorante alla Colomba, Venice–Veneto)

Soak 1 pound salt codfish in water for 6 or 8 hours, changing the water several times. Put the fish on to heat in cold water and let the water come just to a boil. Drain it off and place the fish in a baking dish. Cook 2 chopped onions in 1/2 cup olive oil and when the onion is pale gold and soft add 1 tablespoon minced parsley and blend in 1 1/2 tablespoons flour. Pour this mixture over the fish, add 3 or 4 anchovy filets cut in small pieces, pepper, and 1 cup milk. Stir the liquid together and bake the fish in a very slow oven (275° F.) for 1 hour or more, or until the milk is absorbed. Serves 4.

Acciughe all'Abruzzese
ANCHOVIES ABRUZZI
(Abruzzi e Molise)

Ideally, small fresh anchovies should be used for this dish, but whitebait or small smelts will do nicely. If the fish are too large to be eaten in their entirety, remove the backbone before stuffing them.

Clean, wash, and dry the desired amount of small fresh fish. Place a filet of salted anchovy inside each fish and close them up again. Dip them in flour, then in beaten egg seasoned with salt and pepper, and then in fine bread crumbs. Fry them in deep hot oil (375° F.) for 3 to 5 minutes, until they are browned on both sides, and drain them on absorbent paper. Serve them on a hot platter with sprigs of parsley and lemon sections.

Trance di Pesce alla Siciliana
FISH SLICES SICILIAN
(Sicily)

Shell 2 pounds fresh peas. In a broad, shallow pan heat 1/2 cup olive oil and in this brown on both sides 4 slices of fish weighing about 1 3/4 pounds in all. (Halibut or swordfish steak is good in this recipe.) Add 1 tablespoon parsley and 2 cloves of garlic, both chopped, and 1/2 cup white vinegar. Allow the vinegar to cook until it has practically all evaporated. Add 2 pounds peeled, seeded, coarsely chopped tomatoes and salt and pepper to taste, and simmer for 5 minutes. Add the peas and a little water, if needed, cover the pan, and cook slowly until fish and peas are both tender. This will take half an hour, more or less, depending on the type of fish. Remove the fish carefully to a hot platter, pour the tomato and peas mixture over it, and serve with bread croutons browned in oil.

Nasello alla Ligure
HAKE LIGURIA
(Liguria)

Nasello is hake, but any good fileted fish such as haddock, cusk, whitefish, or small cod steaks may be used. The fish is cut into serving pieces, dipped in seasoned flour and fried in hot oil, a good 1/4 inch deep in the pan. When the fish is cooked and well browned on each side, drain it and place it on a hot platter. For 1 pound fish add 1 chopped clove of garlic and 1 tablespoon chopped parsley to the oil and brown these slightly, being careful not to burn them. Stir in 1 teaspoon flour, and when it is well blended add gradually 1/2 cup water and 1 teaspoon vinegar. Season the sauce with salt and pepper and simmer it on low heat for

5 minutes. Beat 1 egg yolk with a few drops of oil and stir it in over very low heat. When the sauce is thick and creamy pour it at once over the fish. Serves 2.

Cernia alla Luciana
SAUTÉED PERCH LUCIANA
(Hotel Vesuvio, Naples–Campania)

The original recipe calls for Mediterranean perch, but any fish of good quality and firm texture—such as halibut—may be used.

Heat 2 tablespoons olive oil and 1 tablespoon butter in a frying pan. Put in a 1 1/2-pound slice of perch, or other fish, which has been dusted with flour and seasoned with salt and pepper. Brown it on both sides and then add 1 small minced clove of garlic, 1 teaspoon minced parsley, and 1 cup (one 8-ounce can) Italian tomatoes. Cover the pan and simmer the fish for 10 minutes. If you have 4 mussels and 4 small clams to add the last few minutes of cooking, so much the better, though this dish is very good without them. Serves 4.

Triglia alla Livornese
RED MULLET LEGHORN
(Grand Hotel, Florence–Tuscany)

The fine little red mullet that live on the sandy, rocky bottom of the Mediterranean have been appreciated since Roman times as a delicacy, and the local style of preparing them brings out their character.

When the mullet, which should be about 8 inches long, are cleaned and ready, coat them well with seasoned flour. Dip each fish separately for a split fraction of a second in cold water and put it instantly into hot oil 1/2 inch deep in a frying pan. Brown them well on all sides, drain off any excess oil, and put the pan on the side of the stove. In another saucepan heat 1 tablespoon oil, add 1 clove of garlic, minced, 1 teaspoon each of parsley and basil, chopped, and a pinch of crushed red pepper flakes. Sauté the mixture briefly and add 1/4 cup dry white wine. Simmer the wine until it is reduced by one-third. Add 2 ripe, peeled and chopped tomatoes, salt and pepper and simmer the sauce for about 20 minutes, or until it is somewhat reduced but not too thick. This is enough sauce for 4 small fish.

Pour the sauce over the fish and reheat them together. Serve the fish with their sauce on a hot dish, sprinkled with a little chopped basil and parsley. Serves 4.

Orate Fresse all'Anconetana
COLD RED SNAPPER ANCONA
(The Marches)

Clean 2 small red snappers and marinate them in 1/4 cup olive oil and 1/4 cup white wine with half an onion, 1 shallot, chopped, 1 bay leaf, a pinch of thyme, and salt and pepper for several hours. Split them open and broil them on both sides, sprinkling them with a little of the marinade. Arrange them on a platter and serve them cold, covered with the following sauce: Work in a mortar 8 anchovy filets, 4 yolks of hard-cooked eggs, and a clove of garlic, all chopped. Add pepper, 2 tablespoons bread crumbs soaked in a little vinegar, 3 tablespoons olive oil, and 1/4 cup white wine and blend all well together. Strain the sauce and pour it over the fish.

Sogliole al Piatto
STEAMED SOLE PUGLIA
(Apulia)

This simple method of preparing sole results in a surprising delicacy of flavor not obtained in any other way.

Arrange 1 pound filets of sole in a shallow heatproof dish and sprinkle them with 1 tablespoon finely minced parsley, 1 minced clove of garlic, salt, and 3 to 4 tablespoons olive oil. Place the dish carefully on a rack over boiling water in a steamer or casserole. Cover the dish and steam the fish on top of the stove until the flesh is white and firm. Serve in the same dish, with segments of lemon. Serves 2 or 3.

Filetti di Sogliola Richard
FRIED FILET OF SOLE WITH
VEGETABLES
(Birreria 'L Caval 'D Brôns, Turin–Piedmont)

Dust 8 filets of sole lightly with flour and cook them in a frying pan in 1/2 cup hot olive oil, together with 4 halved peeled jumbo shrimp and 2 thinly sliced artichoke hearts, for 3 to 4 minutes. Add salt and pepper, 2 boiled potatoes cut in sticks, and 1/2 cup cooked peas. Brown the ingredients on both sides, turning them with care and shaking the pan to keep them from sticking. Sprinkle on 1/4 teaspoon orégano and 1 teaspoon finely chopped parsley and add 1 peeled, seeded, and chopped tomato. Place the pan in a moderate oven (350° F.) for about 5 minutes to complete the cooking. Serve very hot. Serves 4.

Sogliole alla Veneziana
SOLE VENETIAN
(Veneto)

Choose fresh sole or flounder, 1 per person, and remove the skin from both sides. Make 2 or 3 light diagonal slashes on each side of the fish and in these spread the following mixture: For 2 sole, cream 2 tablespoons butter with 1 tablespoon chopped fresh mint, 1 chopped clove of garlic, 2 tablespoons finely minced parsley, salt, and pepper. Broil the fish 5 to 7 minutes on each side under moderately high heat. Add the following sauce to the broiler juices and pour over the fish just before serving: In 1 tablespoon butter sauté 1 thinly sliced onion over moderate heat until it is soft but not brown. Add 1/2 cup white wine, salt, and pepper and simmer for 5 minutes. Add 1/4 cup water and continue to simmer the sauce for about 10 minutes longer. Serves 2.

Brodetto alla Triestina
FISH STEW TRIESTE STYLE
(Friuli–Venezia Giulia)

In Trieste this dish, more a stew than a soup, would contain perhaps sole, mullet, eel, mackerel, and cuttlefish. But you may design your own combination.

Clean 2 pounds of assorted fish and cut it into fairly large pieces. Wash the pieces, dry them well, and brown them slightly on all sides in 1/4 inch of olive oil heated in an earthen casserole or heavy enamel pot. Lower the heat, add a good pinch each of salt and pepper, and continue to cook the fish slowly until it is well browned and almost done. Remove the pieces of fish to a warm place and in the same oil cook 1 onion, minced, until it is softened. Add 1 clove of garlic, 1 tablespoon tomato paste, and 1 tablespoon vinegar. Add 2 cups boiling water, cover the casserole, and simmer the mixture slowly for 30 minutes. Now replace the fish in the sauce and simmer for 5 minutes. Serve very hot with garlic croutons —bread browned in butter with a little crushed garlic.

Cacciucco Livornese
FISH STEW LEGHORN
(Tuscany)

This characteristic fish stew contains lobster, scallops, and squid, the latter obtainable in many Italian markets. For the other Mediterranean fish used in Italy, you may substitute our own Atlantic types, such as halibut and haddock. Cut 1 small uncooked lobster into sections and remove the intestinal vein. Discard the head. Skin and clean enough squid to make 1 cup, and slice it into small pieces. Slice or dice 1 cup scallops. Cut 1 pound haddock filet and 1/2 pound halibut into 1 1/2-inch sections.

Heat 1/2 cup olive oil in your soup kettle and in it cook 1 minced clove of garlic, 2 teaspoons minced parsley, and 2 or 3 leaves of sage until they are slightly browned. Add the lobster sections, shells and all, the squid and salt and pepper, and a few flakes of dried red pepper. Cover the pot and simmer the stew for 15 minutes, stirring occasionally. Now add 1/2 cup dry white wine and cook until the wine is almost evaporated. Stir in 2 tablespoons tomato paste, add 3 cups hot water, the scallops and the rest of the fish. Simmer the stew for 20 minutes, adding more salt if needed. Ladle it into individual hot soup plates containing slices of toasted Italian bread that have been rubbed with garlic.

Brodetto Anconetana
ANCONA FISH STEW
(The Marches)

In Ancona the famous local fish stew may contain as many as thirteen types of Adriatic fish, including cuttlefish, dogfish, squid, sole, mullet, and others impossible to translate.

We suggest an assortment of 4 pounds of any good salt-water fish available, including squid. Have the ink bag removed from the latter. Clean and skin the squid and cut it in thin slices, enough to make 1 cup. Clean the rest of the fish, making about 1 3/4 pounds of filets, which you cut in pieces. In 1/2 cup olive oil simmer 1 large sliced onion until it is golden, add the squid, salt, and pepper, and cook for 2 or 3 minutes. Add a good pinch of saffron so the mixture takes on a fine yellow tone, and enough water to cover well. Simmer the squid for about 1/2 hour. In the meantime place the rest of the fish in layers in a large earthen or enamel pot and, when the squid is tender, add it with its juices. Add enough water and white wine, combined, to cover the stew, more salt, if necessary, and boil the fish over high heat for 10 or 15 minutes. Serve very hot with crusts of fried bread.

Another form of the same stew is made by adding, in place of saffron, 3 or 4 peeled, diced tomatoes, 2 whole garlic cloves, chopped parsley, and 1 or 2 tablespoons vinegar. Continue the cooking in the same way.

Luccio de Trasimeno
PIKE OF THE LAKE OF TRASIMENO
(Umbria)

Cut a few diagonal slashes across a fresh cleaned pike, or other freshwater fish, and rub into it some salt and pepper, rosemary leaves, and a little chopped garlic. Brush the fish plentifully with oil and grill it under moderate heat. In a small saucepan heat 1/2 cup oil and add salt and pepper, 1 clove chopped garlic, 1/2 teaspoon rosemary, 1/2 teaspoon capers, and 6 chopped anchovy filets. Steep the mixture over the lowest possible heat while the fish is cooking. Force this sauce through a fine sieve and serve it very hot, with the fish. Serves 4.

Luccio alla Romana
FRESH PIKE ROMAN STYLE
(Rome)

Melt 3 tablespoons butter in a fish kettle with 2 tablespoons oil. When it bubbles add 8 or 10 chopped anchovy filets, 1 tablespoon finely minced parsley, and 1 minced clove of garlic. Let these simmer together for a few seconds and then blend in 1 tablespoon flour. Add 1 1/2 cups dry white wine and 1 cup water. Let the liquid come to a boil and simmer it for 5 minutes. Put in a 2-pound pike, first cleaned, scaled, and washed. Add salt and pepper and simmer the fish over the lowest possible heat for 1/2 hour.

Meanwhile melt 1 1/2 tablespoons butter with 2 tablespoons oil and add 2 teaspoons minced parsley. Stir in 3/4 pound sliced mushrooms, salt and pepper and allow them to cook for 3 minutes. Add 1/2 cup white wine and cook the mushrooms over low heat for 5 minutes, stirring from time to time. When the fish is done, transfer it with care to a hot platter. Reduce the juices in which it was cooked to 1 cup, add them to the mushrooms, let all steep together for a few minutes, and pour the sauce over the fish. Serves 4.

Anguilla Napoletana
EEL ROLLS NEAPOLITAN
(Campania)

Have a skinned eel split lengthwise, remove the backbone, and flatten the halves. Cut these into 3-inch pieces, evenly shaped. For 8 pieces, grind enough of the extra meat to make 1/2 to 3/4 cup, and work this together well with the yolks of 2 hard-cooked eggs, 1 generous tablespoon butter, 2 teaspoons minced parsley, 2 minced fresh scallions, and salt and pepper to taste. Add the yolk of 1 large egg. Spread about 1 tablespoon of this mixture on each filet of eel, roll the filets up, and tie them with kitchen thread. Melt 3 tablespoons butter in a saucepan, add the eel rolls and the juice of 1 lemon, cover and simmer for 1/2 hour, turning them now and then. Let the rolls cool, remove the thread, dip them in batter for frying (see index) and fry them in deep hot oil (390° F.) until they are a good golden color. Serves 8.

Anguilla Rivana
MARINATED EEL RIVA
(Grand Hotel Riva, Riva del Garda– Trentino-Alto Adige)

Use about 2 1/2 pounds cleaned, but not skinned, large fresh-water eel.

Cut it into round slices about 2 1/2 inches thick. Cook the pieces on a grill or under a broiler, without any seasoning, until they are cooked through and place them in a layer in a deep dish. Meanwhile boil together 1 cup vinegar, 1 cup water, 1 clove of garlic, chopped and crushed, 1 onion, finely sliced, salt, a bay leaf, and a good pinch each of marjoram and thyme. After gently boiling the marinade for 20 minutes, pour it over the eel. Allow it to cool and let the eel stand 24 hours. Serve cold.

Trote in Bianco
TROUT POACHED IN WHITE WINE

Make a court bouillon by simmering together for 15 minutes 2 cups water, 2 cups white wine, salt, 3 peppercorns, 1 bay leaf, 1 small sliced onion, 3 or 4 slices of carrot, a sprig of celery leaf, a sprig of parsley, 2 slices of lemon, and 3 tablespoons olive oil. Place 4 half-pound trout, or 2 larger ones, in the simmering liquid. Cover the pan and poach the fish, without letting the court bouillon boil, for about 10 minutes, or until it is firm. Remove the fish to a hot platter and serve with green sauce (see index). Serves 4.

Trote in Salsa Acciughe
TROUT WITH ANCHOVY SAUCE

Clean, wash, and dry 6 small fresh trout and roll them in seasoned flour. Heat 6 tablespoons olive oil in a frying pan and in it cook the fish 3 to 5 minutes on each side, or until they are nicely browned. Keep them hot on a serving dish. In a small saucepan heat 3 tablespoons butter with 4 chopped anchovy filets and stir until the anchovy is dissolved. Add freshly ground pepper, salt if desired, 1/4 cup Marsala, and 1/4 cup dry white wine and simmer the sauce for 3 to 4 minutes. Add 1 teaspoon each of fresh chopped mint and parsley and 1 teaspoon lemon juice.

Bring the sauce just to the boiling point again and serve it with the trout.

Trote al Burro
POACHED TROUT WITH BROWNED BUTTER

Slice 1 small onion and sauté it in 1 tablespoon butter until it is softened. Add salt and pepper, 1 bay leaf, a sprig of parsley, 1 1/2 cups white wine, and 1 1/2 cups water. Simmer this stock for 5 minutes. Place in the liquid 4 half-pound trout, cover the pan, and let the fish poach without boiling for 10 or more minutes, or until they are firm to the touch. Drain the fish with care and place them on a hot serving dish. Spoon over them 2 tablespoons of their cooking stock, 1/2 cup butter cooked until it is brown, and 1/4 cup small sautéed bread croutons. Serve with quarters of lemon. Serves 4.

Trote coi Funghi
BAKED TROUT WITH MUSHROOMS

Melt 1 tablespoon butter in a baking dish and spread 1/2 pound thinly sliced mushrooms in the dish. Season with salt and pepper. On the mushrooms place 4 half-pound trout seasoned with salt and pepper. Pour over them 2 tablespoons melted butter, coat them well with bread crumbs, and sprinkle them with 2 more tablespoons melted butter. Bake them in a moderately hot oven (375° F.) for 15 minutes, or until the crumbs are browned. At the last minute heat 3 tablespoons butter with 2 finely minced scallions and when the butter foams pour it over the fish. Serve the trout in the baking dish, with quarters of lemon. Serves 4.

Poultry

Petti di Pollo o Tacchino Milanese
CHICKEN OR TURKEY BREASTS
MILANESE
(Lombardy)

Remove the breasts, or *suprêmes,* from young frying chickens. One whole breast makes two *suprêmes.* Allow one or two per person. These should be skinned, trimmed, and flattened as thin as possible. Season with salt and pepper, dip in flour and shake off the excess, then dip in beaten egg and fine bread crumbs. For 3 chicken breasts (6 slices), heat 3 tablespoons butter and 2 tablespoons oil in a frying pan and when the bubbles have subsided, but before the fat browns, put in the chicken breasts. Keep the heat moderately high and cook the chicken breasts several minutes on each side, or until they are golden brown. Place them on a hot platter, pour over the remaining butter, sprinkle with chopped parsley, and serve with lemon quarters.

Turkey breasts, each cut into several slices, can be prepared in the same way.

Petti di Pollo alla Valdostana
CHICKEN BREASTS VALDOSTANA
(Lombardy)

Remove the two breasts, or *suprêmes,* of a chicken, take off the skin, and flatten the chicken breasts with a blow or two with the side of a cleaver. Allow one or two *suprêmes* of chicken per person. Dredge them lightly with flour and cook them slowly in hot butter (2 tablespoons for 4 pieces) for 5 to 6 minutes on each side. Remove them to a shallow broiler pan, season with salt and pepper, and arrange on each breast half a dozen small dice or thin

slices of white Italian truffles and a slice of Fontina or *mozzarella* cheese. Now into the brown juices left in the frying pan stir 1/2 cup white wine, 1/2 cup chicken stock, and 1 tablespoon brandy. Simmer for 10 minutes, or until the liquid is reduced and has thickened slightly. Add salt and pepper if necessary. Stir in a lump of butter at the end. Place the chicken breasts under a hot broiler just long enough to melt the cheese and serve them at once. Pass the sauce separately.

Black truffles may be used in place of white ones, or, lacking these, use for each chicken breast 1 mushroom, sliced and simmered in butter for 2 minutes.

Turkey breasts, sliced horizontally, can also be prepared *alla valdostana.*

Petti di Pollo alla Cavour
CHICKEN BREASTS CAVOUR
(Lombardy)

These are prepared as are chicken breasts Valdostana except that on each breast a very thin slice of ham is placed and then a slice of cheese. Truffles are heated in the sauce, which is served separately.

Petti di Pollo alla Sabatini
CHICKEN BREASTS SABATINI
(Ristorante Gino Sabatini, Florence–Tuscany)

Slice the uncooked breast meat of a chicken, free from all skin and bone, into thin cutlets, and flatten the slices as much as possible with a rolling pin. The thinner the slices the more delicate will be this dish. Coat the slices lightly with flour and brown them delicately on each side in 1 tablespoon olive oil and 2 tablespoons butter heated together in a skillet. Season the slices with salt and pepper and coat each one carefully with a light layer of grated Swiss cheese and finely diced or shredded boiled tongue. Add to the pan juices 3 tablespoons fresh tomato sauce or meat juice, as from stewed meat Florentine (see index) or other beef gravy, and 3 tablespoons chicken stock. Put the pan in a slow oven (325° F.) until the cheese has melted and the sauce is slightly thickened.

Serve the slices of chicken breast on a hot serving dish with their sauce poured over them and with green peas, mushrooms, asparagus tips, and mounds of mashed potatoes arranged in a border around them. Serves 2 to 4.

Turkey breast meat may be prepared in the same way.

Pollo alla Crema
CHICKEN IN CREAM WITH WHISKEY
(Hotel Royal Danieli, Venice–Veneto)

Truss a 3-pound chicken and brown it on all sides in 1 tablespoon butter and 1 tablespoon olive oil combined. Add 1 small onion, 1 small carrot, and 1 stalk of celery, all chopped, 1 teaspoon fresh rosemary, a pinch of thyme, and salt and pepper. Let the vegetables take on a little color, add 2 tablespoons Marsala, and simmer the mixture until the liquid evaporates. Blend 1 1/2 teaspoons potato starch with 1 cup cream and pour the cream over the chicken. Stir in 2 generous tablespoons *ragù bolognese* (see index). Cover the pot closely and bake the chicken in a slow oven (300° F.) for about 1 hour, or until it is tender. Strain the sauce through a fine strainer, add 1 tablespoon whiskey, reheat it, and pour it over the chicken.

(In place of the *ragù bolognese,* you may use the following: Sauté a slice of onion, chopped, in a little butter, add 2 tablespoons raw chopped beef, 1/4 teaspoon meat glaze, 2 or 3 tablespoons stock, and salt and pepper, and cook the mixture until it is thick.) Serves 3 or 4.

Pollo alla Cacciatora
CHICKEN HUNTER STYLE

Cut a small roasting chicken into serving pieces and brown the pieces on all sides in 4 tablespoons olive oil heated in a heavy pan. After about 10 minutes add 1 small onion, chopped, 1 green pepper, cleaned of pith and seeds and thinly sliced, 1 tablespoon minced celery, 1 clove of garlic, chopped, salt and pepper, and a pinch of rosemary. When the vegetables are slightly browned add 3 peeled and seeded tomatoes, coarsely chopped, 1 tablespoon parsley, finely chopped, and 1/2 to 3/4 cup red wine. Cover the pan and simmer the chicken slowly for 25 to 35 minutes, or until it is almost tender, adding a small amount of hot water should this be necessary. Add 1 cup sliced mushrooms and cook for 15 minutes more. Serves 4.

Pollo Grillettato alla Siciliana
SICILIAN SAUTÉED CHICKEN
(Sicily)

Peel 1/2 pound very small onions and parboil them for 5 minutes in salted water. Drain them. Have a 3-pound chicken cut in pieces as for frying. Heat 3 tablespoons butter and 1/4 cup olive oil in a broad sauté pan and add the pieces of chicken and the onions. Brown them slightly on all sides. Season them with salt and pepper and add 1/2 cup Marsala. Simmer until the wine is reduced by half. Add 2 peeled, seeded, and diced tomatoes, 2 sprigs of parsley, and 1/2 cup chicken stock. Cover the pan and continue to cook the chicken for 30 to 45 minutes, or until it is tender, adding a little more stock if necessary. Arrange the pieces of chicken on a

hot dish and pour the sauce over them.
Serves 4.

Pollo alla Maceratese
SMOTHERED CHICKEN
(The Marches)

Chop very finely the liver and giblets of a small roasting chicken and
cook them briefly in a heavy pot or
Dutch oven in 1 tablespoon each of
butter and olive oil combined. Put in
the chicken, trussed as for roasting, having rubbed the surface with oil, salt,
and pepper. Pour in combined water
and stock to a depth of about 1 inch.
Cover the pot closely and cook over
low heat until the chicken is done and
the liquid simmered almost entirely
away. Carve the chicken into serving
pieces and arrange them on a platter.
Into the rich juices remaining in the
pan, stir 2 egg yolks that have been
beaten with the juice of 1 small lemon.
Heat the sauce without allowing it to
boil and pour it over the chicken.
Serves 4.

Pollo alla Mantuana
CHICKEN MANTUA
(Lombardy)

Heat 2 tablespoons butter in a heavy
casserole or iron pot, and in this, brown
on all sides a 4-pound chicken that has
been cleaned, dried, and trussed. Add
1 onion, 1 stalk of celery, 1 tablespoon
parsley, and 2 tablespoons carrot, all
finely minced. Brown the vegetables a
little, season them with salt and pepper,
and add 1/2 cup consommé and 1/2 cup
tomato juice. Cover the pot and cook
the chicken slowly over low heat for
about 1 hour. Add 4 whole green olives,
4 minced green olives, and 4 whole black
olives. Cook for another 5 minutes.
Serves 4.

Pollo alla Romana
CHICKEN ROMAN STYLE
(Rome)

Cut a young chicken into pieces as
for frying, rub the pieces with olive oil
and salt and pepper. In a heavy frying
pan heat 1/4 cup olive oil, add 1 slice
of bacon, diced, and 1 clove of garlic,
cut in two. Sauté these for a few seconds
and then put in the pieces of chicken.
Cook them until they are golden brown
on all sides. Sprinkle the chicken with
1 teaspoon minced fresh rosemary, add
1/2 cup dry white wine, and continue
cooking until the liquid is reduced by
half. Remove the pieces of garlic. Stir
in 2 teaspoons tomato paste and 1/4
cup or more hot chicken stock. Cook
just until the chicken is tender and the
sauce reduced to a moderate amount.
Serves 4.

Pollo al Forno
OVEN-BAKED CHICKEN

Cut a small roasting chicken into
serving pieces and brown the pieces on
all sides in a heavy skillet in 2 tablespoons olive oil and 2 tablespoons butter heated together. Arrange the pieces
of chicken in a single layer in a shallow
roasting pan or leave them in the skillet
if it is broad enough to hold them. On
each piece lay a slice of bacon and a
thick slice of fresh tomato. Sprinkle
with 1 teaspoon fresh basil, 1 teaspoon
parsley, and 1 clove of garlic, all chopped, and salt and pepper. Baste the
pieces with the fat in which they were
browned, add 1/2 cup white wine to
the pan, and bake the chicken in a
moderate oven (350° F.) for about 30
minutes, or until it is tender.

Pollo alla Diavola I
DEVILED BROILED CHICKEN I
(Tuscany)

Chop together finely 1 small onion
and 1 tablespoon parsley. Have a 2 1/2-
pound chicken split for broiling, brush

both sides generously with olive oil, and season it with salt and a good dash of dried red pepper flakes.

Broil the chicken slowly for about 15 to 20 minutes on each side. When each side is half cooked, add some of the onion and parsley mixture. Serves 2.

Pollo alla Diavola II
DEVILED BROILED CHICKEN II
(Ristorante Tre Scalini, Rome–Latium)

This recipe is simplicity itself, but results in a surprisingly delicious dish that has more character than the usual broiled chicken. Split a 2 1/2-pound broiling chicken in half, brush both sides lavishly with olive oil, and sprinkle with a good pinch each of crushed red pepper flakes and salt. Cook the pieces 15 to 18 minutes on each side under a preheated broiler, not too close to the heat. They should cook through, but do not let the surface burn. Transfer the chicken to a hot dish and cut it in sections as desired. Put the broiling pan, which has caught the juices, over moderate heat and stir in 3 tablespoons dry white wine. Reheat the liquid and allow it to boil for 5 or 6 seconds. Pour this sauce over the chicken. Serves 2.

Pollo alla California
CHICKEN CALIFORNIA

This recipe came from a Californian whose parents brought it with them from the old country.

Warm 4 tablespoons olive oil in a roasting pan and add 1 frying chicken cut in serving pieces. Turn the pieces to coat all the surfaces completely with oil. Place the pan in a moderate oven (350° F.) for 15 minutes, or until the chicken barely begins to take on a little color, turning the pieces once. Roll the pieces of chicken in 1/2 cup fine bread crumbs combined with 3 tablespoons grated Parmesan, 1 tablespoon parsley and 1 clove of garlic, both finely

minced, and salt and pepper. Return the pieces to the roasting pan and bake the chicken in a moderate oven (350° F.) about 30 minutes, or until the pieces are browned and somewhat crisp. Sprinkle the chicken with a little of the remaining bread-crumb coating from time to time as it cooks and baste carefully once or twice with the pan juices. Serves 3.

Pollo Fiorentina
FRIED CHICKEN FLORENTINE
(Tuscany)

Have a frying chicken cut into serving pieces and marinate the pieces for several hours with 3 tablespoons olive oil, the juice of half a lemon, 2 teaspoons parsley, chopped, and salt and pepper. Turn the pieces occasionally. Pat them dry with absorbent paper and coat the entire surface with flour. Dip the pieces in 1 egg beaten with 1 teaspoon milk. Brown them quickly on both sides in a frying pan in hot olive oil deep enough almost to cover them. Lower the heat slightly, cover the pan, leaving a space for steam to escape, and cook the chicken until it is tender, about 15 minutes in all. Serves 4.

Pollo Ripieno
STUFFED ROAST CHICKEN OR TURKEY

The following stuffing is enough for a 5- to 6-pound roasting chicken. Double the amounts to stuff a small turkey.

Heat 2 tablespoons butter in a saucepan and add 2 fresh sweet Italian sausages and the giblets of the bird. Sauté the meats for about 5 minutes, or until they are partly cooked, and add 1/2 cup stock and salt and pepper to taste. Simmer the meats for 10 minutes, drain them, peel the sausages, and chop them and the giblets. To the pan juices add 1/2 cup stale bread crumbs or enough to make a thick but not dry paste. Add the chopped meats, 1 small sliced truffle or 2 or 3 sliced mushrooms, and a dash of nutmeg. Add 8 or 10 crumbled chestnuts that have been roasted, peeled, and simmered until they are just tender, and mix in 1 beaten egg. Stuff the bird and roast it in the usual way.

Pollo alla Giudecchina
STUFFED CHICKEN GIUDECCHINA
(Grand Hotel, Venice–Veneto)

Roast a 3- to 4-pound chicken with the following stuffing: Heat 3 tablespoons butter and 2 tablespoons olive oil in a saucepan and in it cook slowly 1 chopped onion until it is softened. Add 1 1/2 cups bread crumbs, the liver and heart of the chicken, chopped, 1/2 cup minced ham, 1/4 cup grated Parmesan, and a little salt and pepper. Stir and cook all together until the crumbs are slightly browned. Add 1/2 cup stock or water. Cool the mixture completely before stuffing the bird and roasting it. Serves 4.

Tacchino Ripieno alla Lombardia
STUFFED TURKEY LOMBARDIAN
(Lombardy)

With a sharp knife, slash a cross in the flat sides of the shells of 2 pounds chestnuts. Heat a small amount of any cooking oil (barely enough to coat the chestnuts) in a broad frying pan, add the chestnuts, and stir and roast them slightly until the shells begin to dry and curl where they have been cut. Peel the chestnuts when they are cool enough to handle and boil them in salted water or stock until they are soft but not mushy. Remove all the inner skin and crumble the chestnuts coarsely.

Put through a meat grinder 1/4 pound beef, 1/8 pound veal, 1/4 pound Italian sausage, peeled, and 2 slices of bacon. Mix together with 1 chopped onion and 1 chopped clove of garlic and sauté the mixture briefly in a little butter and olive oil combined in a fry-ing pan. Remove the pan from the heat and add about 8 or 10 prunes that have been stoned and chopped (soak them first to soften, if necessary), 3/4 cup grated Italian cheese, 2 beaten eggs, 1/2 cup white wine, a pinch each of nutmeg and rosemary, salt and pepper, and the chestnuts.

When the stuffing is cold fill the cavity of a 15-pound turkey, sew up the opening, coat the bird with butter, and roast it about 4 hours in a moderately slow oven (325° F.), basting often with the pan juices. Simmer the neck and giblets in a saucepan with water, salt and pepper, 1 onion, a bay leaf, parsley, and a pinch of thyme. Add some of this stock to the roasting pan from time to time to blend with the fats in the pan for basting. Stir more of this stock into the brown pan juices at the end, strain the juices, and serve with the turkey.

Fegatini di Pollo alla Salvia
CHICKEN LIVERS WITH SAGE

Cut 1/2 pound chicken livers into 3 or 4 pieces each, season them with salt and pepper and 4 or 5 fresh leaves of sage, chopped, and cook them for 3 to 4 minutes in 2 tablespoons butter heated with 2 slices diced bacon. Remove the livers and keep them hot. Add 1/4 cup Marsala or white wine to the pan and simmer the sauce for 2 to 3 minutes. Arrange the chicken livers on triangles of bread that have been browned on both sides in butter and pour the hot sauce over them. Serves 2.

Gallina di Faraone
GUINEA FOWL PIEDMONTESE
(Piedmont)

Stuff a 2 1/2- to 3-pound guinea fowl with 2 or 3 slices of stale crumbled bread mixed with 2 tablespoons finely chopped ham, the chopped liver of the bird, 8 juniper berries, pepper, and a pinch each of sage and orégano, and moistened with a little stock and 1 tablespoon melted butter or chicken fat.

Truss the fowl and brown it a little on all sides in an iron pot or casserole on top of the stove in 1 tablespoon butter combined with 1 tablespoon olive oil. Remove the guinea fowl and tie a piece of bacon across its breast. In the casserole place 1 small sliced carrot and 1 or 2 small onions and return to it the guinea fowl. Add 1/4 cup stock and 1/4 cup white wine and roast the bird, uncovered, in a slow oven (300° F.) for about 1 hour. For the last 10 minutes remove the bacon and turn the heat up to 400° F., to brown the surface. Add more liquid to the casserole as the bird browns. Strain the liquid and pour it over the bird on the serving dish. Serves 3 or 4.

This is good served with polenta (see index).

Quaglie alla Piemontese
QUAIL PIEDMONTESE
(Piedmont)

Place 2 quail in a small baking dish with a band of bacon tied over each. Add 3/4 cup concentrated stock of fowl or game and 1 tablespoon Marsala and roast the birds for 20 minutes in a moderate oven (350° F.), basting several times.

Make a *velouté* sauce of 1 tablespoon butter blended with 1 teaspoon flour combined with 1/2 cup chicken stock. Remove the quail from the baking dish and keep them hot. Stir the *velouté* into the juices in the baking dish and strain the sauce into a small saucepan. Add 1 thinly sliced truffle that has been heated in a little butter and reheat the sauce.

On a small serving dish make a ring of cooked rice that has been mixed with a little melted butter, 2 or 3 tablespoons chicken stock, and 1 or 2 truffles, sliced and heated in butter. Remove the bacon from the quail, arrange them in the center of the rice ring, pour the sauce over them, and serve at once. Serves 2.

Pernici Arrosto
ROAST PARTRIDGES
(Lombardy)

Stuff 4 partridges with the following: Chop the livers of the birds and add 2 slices bacon, 1/4 cup ham, and 1/4 pound mushrooms, all chopped, 12 juniper berries, and freshly ground pepper.

Spread the birds with plenty of butter and roast 50 minutes in a moderate oven (350° F.), basting several times with the fat in the pan.

Sauté 4 slices of bread on both sides in butter. Arrange them on a hot platter and lay a partridge on each.

To the juices in the roasting dish add about 1/2 teaspoon potato starch blended with 3 to 4 tablespoons strong stock. Simmer the juices 1 or 2 minutes and pour a little over each bird. Serves 4.

Palombacci alla Perugina
WILD PIGEONS PERUGIAN
(Umbria)

Roast 3 wild pigeons on a spit before an open fire until they are half cooked. Now place them in a heavy casserole with 1 cup red wine, 2 tablespoons olive oil, 8 or 10 olives, 4 leaves of fresh sage, 1/2 teaspoon juniper berries, and salt and pepper. Continue cooking them in a slow oven (300° F.) for about 1/2 hour, or until the pigeons are tender. Serves 3.

The pigeons may also be first browned on all sides in olive oil in the casserole on top of the stove and then cooked in the oven 50 minutes to 1 hour.

Beef

Arrosto di Manzo alla Livornese
ROAST BEEF LEGHORN STYLE
(Tuscany)

This method is particularly good for preparing the less expensive cuts of beef that do not quite stand on their own merits with simple roasting, as do the choicer pieces.

With a sharp pointed knife or larding needle, pierce the top of a 4-pound roast of beef in 8 or 10 places and insert strips of smoked bacon. Press 8 or 10 cloves into the meat here and there. Place it in a bowl with 1 cup red wine, a little chopped parsley, 1 clove of garlic, and salt and pepper and let it marinate for 8 hours or overnight. Turn the meat once.

Remove it from the marinade, pat it dry, and place it in a roasting pan with 6 small onions, or 2 large ones, quartered, which have been parboiled and drained. Spread a little butter on the meat and roast it 15 minutes per pound (for rare) in a moderate oven (350° F.), adding some of the marinade to the pan juices from time to time and basting the roast often.

Strain all the remaining marinade and add it to the pan juices a few minutes before serving. Slice the roast and serve the pan juices with it.

Manzo Lesso colla Salsa alla Genovese
BOILED BEEF WITH GENOA SAUCE
(Liguria)

Place a 2-pound piece of lean beef (rump, round, or other piece suitable for boiling) in a kettle. Add salt and pepper, 1 stalk of celery, 1 small carrot, and 1 onion, all cut in pieces, a clove of garlic, a sprig of parsley, and a pinch of orégano. Cover the meat with water, put the lid on the pot, and simmer for 2 hours, or until the beef is tender. Drain it, place it on a hot platter, garnish with parsley, and pass the following sauce separately: In a saucepan melt 2 teaspoons butter, blend in 1 teaspoon flour, and add gradually 3/4 cup hot salted water. Heat 2 tablespoons oil in a small frying pan and in it sauté 1 small chopped onion until it is soft and golden. Add 3 anchovy filets cut in small pieces, 10 ground bitter almonds, 2 teaspoons capers, 1 tablespoon sugar, 2 chopped mushrooms, and 1 1/2 tablespoons chopped sour pickle. Mix well and simmer for a minute. Add this mixture to the first liquid and stir and simmer the sauce over low heat until it is quite thick. This thick flavorful sweet-sour sauce should be used sparingly with the sliced boiled beef.

Bue Stufato al Vino Rosso
BRAISED BEEF IN RED WINE

Rub a 2-pound piece of bottom round of beef with salt and pepper and grated nutmeg. Marinate it for 4 or 5 hours in a cup of red wine with 2 bay leaves and a clove of garlic cut in pieces. Strain the marinade and wipe the beef as dry as possible. Heat 1 tablespoon olive oil in a heavy iron pot, add 2 or 3 small pieces of bacon rind or rind of salt pork, and remove them when they are crisp. Rub the meat lightly with flour and brown it on all sides in this fat over moderate heat. Add 1 chopped onion and, when it has taken on a little color, add the strained marinade. Cover the pot closely and simmer the meat over low heat for about 3 hours, or until it is tender. Add a small amount of hot water or stock from time to time, if needed.

Carne al Sugo all'Anconetano
BRAISED BEEF WITH ANCONA SAUCE
(Marche)

Brown on all sides a 2-pound piece of round of beef in 1 tablespoon butter. Add hot water to half cover the meat and simmer it until it is tender. Remove the meat from the pan and keep it hot. Reduce the remaining juices to 3/4 cup, should this be necessary, and add 6 or 8 anchovy filets, 2 teaspoons capers, 2 teaspoons parsley, all finely chopped, and salt and pepper. Let this sauce steep a few minutes over very low heat without letting it boil. Slice the meat on a hot platter and pour the sauce over it.

Carne all'Ungherese
HUNGARIAN GOULASH ITALIAN STYLE
(Trentino–Alto Adige)

The influence from Italy's neighbor to the east is evident in this dish.

Cut 1 1/2 pounds good stewing beef into 3/4-inch cubes and brown them lightly in 3 tablespoons hot olive oil together with 2 chopped medium-sized onions. Blend in 1 tablespoon flour and add 3 chopped cloves of garlic, 1/3 teaspoon marjoram, 1/2 teaspoon paprika, 2 tablespoons tomato paste, the rind of 1 lemon, grated, and salt. Simmer 1 or 2 minutes and then stir in 3 cups hot water, blending well. Cover the saucepan closely and simmer the goulash over low heat for 2 hours, or until the meat is tender. Serves 4.

Il Garafolato
BEEF STEW WITH CLOVES
(Rome)

Heat 2 tablespoons olive oil in a heavy pot and in it brown 2 pounds lean stewing beef cut in cubes. Add 3 cloves of garlic, each cut in 2 pieces, salt and pepper, a 1/2-inch piece of cinnamon stick, a good grating of nutmeg, 6 cloves, and a sprig of parsley. Add 1/2 cup red wine and 2 large ripe, peeled tomatoes cut in pieces. Cover the pot closely and simmer the beef over very low heat for 3 hours, or until it is tender. A half hour before serving time remove 1/2 cup of the liquid to a saucepan, add 1/4 cup hot water, and in this broth cook 2 cups sliced celery, covered, until it is tender. Add the celery to the stew.

Stufato di Manzo Genovese
STEWED BEEF GENOESE
(Liguria)

In a heavy pot or casserole heat 2 tablespoons good fat and in it brown on all sides a 2 1/2-pound piece of eye of the round or other good lean beef of comparable quality. Add 4 sliced onions and cook them until they are pale golden and soft. Add 2 tomatoes, cut in pieces, 1 carrot and 2 stalks of celery, both sliced, salt and pepper, a branch of fresh basil or a small teaspoon of dried basil, and 3/4 cup dry white wine. Cover the pot and simmer the beef over very low heat for 3 hours.

It is best that the pot or casserole fit the piece of meat closely, so that it will bathe in the juices and not dry out. Turn the piece once during the cooking.

Fetta di Manzo al Forno
BEEF OVEN STEW

For this dish use a 1 1/2-pound slice of chuck beef or bottom of the round. In an iron skillet on top of the stove heat 1 teaspoon butter with 1 teaspoon olive oil, add 1 clove of garlic cut in 2 or 3 pieces, and brown the meat five minutes on each side over moderate heat. Add salt and pepper, 1 teaspoon minced fresh rosemary, 3/4 cup tomato sauce, and 1/4 cup meat stock. Put the skillet in a moderate oven (350° F.), cover it, and cook the meat for 1 hour to 1 1/4 hours, or until it is tender.

Instead of tomato sauce, you may use 1 cup tomato juice with half a small onion, minced, a pinch of orégano, and a sprig of parsley.

Stracotta alla Fiorentina
STEWED BEEF OR
MEAT SAUCE FLORENTINE
(Trattoria Sostanza, Florence–Tuscany)

This *stracotta*, or "extra-cooked" stew, may be eaten as is or the meat may be used for fillings for ravioli and *cannelloni* and its juices used as sauce for these dishes. The juices may be used in any recipe in which meat juice is called for, as, for example, in tripe Florentine or in *lasagne*.

In a heavy pot or casserole heat 2 tablespoons butter and add 1 onion, 1 small carrot, and 1 small stalk of celery, all finely chopped. Sauté the vegetables until they are lightly browned and add a 1- to 2-pound piece of lean beef and a scant 1/4 pound lean pork or pork sausage. Brown the meat lightly on all sides and then add 1/2 cup white wine and 1 tablespoon tomato paste blended with 1 cup meat stock. Or you may use instead 2 peeled and coarsely chopped ripe tomatoes with 1/4 cup stock. Season with salt and pepper, cover the pot closely, and cook the stew in a very slow oven (250° F.) for 3 hours or more. Add more liquid, if necessary, during the cooking period. The meat should be quite soft and the juices thick.

Stufatino alla Romana
BEEF STEW ROMAN STYLE
(Rome)

Cut 2 pounds lean stewing beef into slices about 3/8 inch thick. Heat 1 tablespoon butter with 1 tablespoon olive oil and add 1 small sliced onion, and 1 clove of garlic, chopped. When these are slightly browned add 2 tablespoons diced bacon and cook it for 1 minute. Put in the pieces of beef and brown them on both sides. Add salt and pepper, a good pinch of orégano or marjoram, and 1 cup dry red wine. Simmer until the wine is reduced by half, stir in 1 tablespoon tomato paste, and add enough hot water just to cover the meat. Cover the pot and simmer the stew very slowly until the beef is tender and the sauce of a good rich consistency. This will take 2 or more hours, depending on the cut of beef.

Bue alla Moda del Lago di Como
BEEF À LA MODE LAKE COMO
(Grand Hotel Villa d'Este, Cernobbio–Lombardy)

Take a 3-pound piece of rump of beef and lard it here and there with strips of salt pork and of carrot that have been rubbed with a cut clove of garlic and dusted with powdered clove. Heat 2 tablespoons butter in a heavy pot and place the meat in it together with 1 small stalk of celery, 1 small carrot, and 1 onion, all sliced, and 2 bay leaves. Brown the meat on all sides with the vegetables. Add 1/4 cup wine vinegar, 1 1/2 cups white wine, 2 pounds tomatoes, peeled and cut in pieces, and salt and pepper. Cover the pot and cook the beef over very low heat for at least 3 hours. Remove the meat to a hot serving dish. Strain through a sieve the juices remaining in the pot. Reduce this sauce quickly over high heat, if it is too liquid. Stir in 1/4 cup cream, more or less, a pinch of sugar, and the juice of half a lemon. Slice the beef and pour the sauce around it.

Bistecca alla Fiorentina
STEAK FLORENTINE
(Tuscany)

Prepare a mixture of 2 or 3 tablespoons olive oil, 1 tablespoon minced parsley, 1 minced and crushed garlic clove, salt and pepper, and 1 teaspoon lemon juice. Dip a thick steak in this, covering both sides, and let it marinate in the mixture in the refrigerator for 2 hours. Drain off the surplus marinade and broil the steak under a very hot broiler for 3 to 5 minutes on each side. Serve the steak on a hot platter, with a lump of sweet butter on it.

Filetto Conti
BEEF TENDERLOIN CONTI
(Birreria 'L Caval 'D Brôns, Turin–Piedmont)

Heat 1 tablespoon bacon fat or butter in a frying pan and drop in a dozen small green Italian olives that have been pitted and sliced. Sauté the olives for 5 or 6 seconds and then put in 4 slices of beef tenderloin, each 3/4 inch thick. Brown them quickly on each side over high heat. Add 1/4 cup dry Italian vermouth mixed with 1/2 cup heavy cream, a pinch of salt, and a good pinch of paprika. Lower the heat and simmer the meat for about 2 minutes, or until it is cooked but still rare. Remove the meat to a hot platter, reduce the sauce quickly over high heat, and pour it over the meat.

Tournedos Forlanini
BEEF TENDERLOIN FORLANINI
(Hotel Vesuvio, Naples–Campania)

In 2 teaspoons hot butter brown 2 slices of beef tenderloin, each an inch thick, for 2 minutes on each side over high heat. In another pan in 2 teaspoons melted butter sauté 6 tablespoons minced mushrooms and 2 tablespoons julienne of ham until the liquid from the mushrooms has entirely evaporated. Season the mixture with salt and pepper. Cut a double thickness of wax paper into 2 squares and place a beef filet in one corner of each. Spread half the mushroom and ham mixture on

each filet and pour over each 1 tablespoon Bordelaise sauce (see index). Fold the paper to form triangular envelopes, seal it as securely as possible by bending the edges, place the envelopes in a shallow baking dish, and cook the filets in a very hot oven (450° F.) for 5 minutes. Serve them with a border of fried artichoke hearts and with the remaining Bordelaise sauce. Serves 2.

Filetto Siciliana
BEEF TENDERLOIN SICILIAN STYLE
(Sicily)

Use 4 slices of beef tenderloin cut 1 inch thick. In a frying pan heat 2 teaspoons butter with 2 tablespoons diced bacon until the bacon begins to brown. Add 1 small sliced onion and allow it to brown slightly. With a slotted spoon remove the onion and bacon. Put the slices of tenderloin in the hot fat and broil them over high heat for 2 minutes on each side, or until they are browned. Add salt and pepper, 1 1/2 tablespoons melted butter, 3/8 cup Marsala wine, and 1/4 cup hot water or stock. Lower the heat and continue to cook the meat for 2 minutes on each side, turning the slices once. If you prefer a less sweet sauce, use dry sherry in place of Marsala. Serves 4.

Filetto Sorpresa
TENDERLOIN SURPRISE

Slit horizontally 4 half-inch slices of tenderloin of beef, leaving one edge intact so that they open like leaves of a book. Season with a little salt and pepper, and, in the center of each, place a thin slice of *prosciutto* or ordinary baked ham, a thin slice of *mozzarella* cheese and several thin slices of truffle. Now close the two halves of the pieces of tenderloin like sandwiches, press the meat together around the edges, dredge the slices lightly in flour, and dip in beaten egg and then in fine bread crumbs. Heat 3 tablespoons butter in a small frying pan and when it is bubbling hot put in the tenderloins and cook them gently until they are nicely browned on each side.

Asticciole alla Calabrese
STUFFED BEEF ROLLS CALABRIA
(Calabria)

Cut small thin slices from a filet of beef and flatten them with a rolling pin. In the center of each, place a slice of *mozzarella* cheese and over it several thin slices of Italian pork sausage. Roll the slices up and skewer them, about 3 on each skewer, with a small slice of stale bread and a bay leaf between the rolls of meat. Dip the skewers in olive oil and cook them under a hot broiler for about 8 minutes, turning them once to brown each side.

Polpette alla Napoletana
NEAPOLITAN MEATBALLS
(Campania)

The term *polpette* describes various combinations of chopped meat formed into meatballs or cakes. The following combination is typical of Naples.

Grind together 3/4 pound lean beef, 1/4 pound lean pork, and 1/4 pound veal. Add 1 tablespoon minced parsley, 1/2 cup bread crumbs, salt and pepper, and 2 tablespoons seedless raisins that have been soaked in warm water until they are soft, then drained and coarsely chopped. Stir in 2 lightly beaten small eggs, form the mixture into small balls or flattened cakes, and sauté them in hot butter about 2 minutes on each side. The meatballs may be coated with fine bread crumbs before they are cooked, if desired. Serves 4 to 6.

Polpette
MEATBALLS
(Lombardy)

These *polpette* are glorified meatballs that have that typically Italian flavor given by a mixture of lemon peel, garlic, and parsley that is known as *gremolada*.

Mince very finely together the zest of 1 small lemon, 2 teaspoons parsley, and 2 cloves of garlic. Add this to 1 pound ground beef, together with salt, pepper, and a good pinch of grated nutmeg. Stir in 1 slice crumbled white bread that has been soaked in a little milk and squeezed dry. Finally, stir in 1 beaten egg. On a floured board, form the mixture lightly into small flattened cakes about 1/2 inch thick and 1 1/2 inches wide. Do not work the mixture or press it too much. Brown the cakes in 1/4 cup hot olive oil for about 2 minutes on each side. Drain them and serve at once. Serves 4 to 6.

Veal

Vitello coi Piselli all' Uso di Romagna
VEAL ROAST WITH PEAS ROMAGNA STYLE
(Emilia–Romagna)

Use a 3- to 4-pound piece of veal leg or loin for roasting. Pierce it in six or eight places with the point of a knife. In half of the slits insert slivers of garlic and in the rest put sprigs of rosemary. In a heavy pot put 2 table-spoons olive oil and 1 strip of bacon, diced. When the fat is hot, brown the meat in it on all sides. Add salt and pepper, 1 tablespoon butter, and 1 table-spoon tomato paste blended with 3/4 cup dry white wine. Cover the pot and roast the meat in a slow oven (300° F.) for about 1 1/2 to 2 hours, or 30 min-utes to the pound. Baste it now and then, remove the cover for the last half hour of cooking, and add a small amount of stock should the juices be-come too reduced.

Remove the meat to a hot dish, add about 2 cups half-cooked peas to the juices in the pot, cover it, and sim-mer the peas on top of the stove until they are tender. Pour them around the piece of veal on the platter before serving.

A small leg of lamb may be cooked in the same way.

Osso Buco
BRAISED VEAL MARROWBONE
(Lombardy)

Have the meaty part of foreleg shin-bones of young veal sawn into six 3-inch pieces with their surrounding layer of meat, each piece forming a sort of indi-vidual circular steak with marrowbone in the center. Brown them in a heavy pot with 2 tablespoons butter and 2 tablespoons olive oil, turning them to brown on all sides. Then turn the pieces upright with the bones vertical, to hold in the marrow. Add salt and pepper, 1 small grated carrot, 1/4 cup chopped celery, 1 medium-sized onion, chopped, and a pinch each of rosemary and sage. Cover the pot and simmer for about 10 minutes.

Blend 2 tablespoons tomato paste with 1 cup dry white wine and stir this into the juices. Add 1/2 cup water or stock, cover and simmer over low heat, adding small amounts of liquid from time to time should this be neces-sary. In about 2 hours, or when the meat is tender, sprinkle in a mixture known as *gremolada,* made as follows: Combine the grated rind of a small lemon, 2 tablespoons finely chopped parsley, and 1 chopped clove of garlic. Serves 6.

Serve with boiled rice or *risotto.*

Vitello alla Perla
BRAISED VEAL PERLA
(Emilia–Romagna)

Choose a 2- to 3-pound piece of veal for roasting and brown it on all sides in a deep heavy pot in 2 table-spoons olive oil and 1 tablespoon butter heated together. Add 4 tablespoons diced ham and 2 medium-sized onions, coarsely chopped. When all have taken on a little color, add 1/2 cup white wine and let it simmer down until it has almost evaporated. Add salt and pep-per, 3 cloves, a good pinch each of nutmeg, cinnamon, and orégano, and enough hot water to cover the meat to three-quarters of its depth. Cover the pot and simmer the veal for 2 hours, turning it once or twice. Reduce the sauce, if necessary. It should be thick. Slice the veal on a hot platter and pour the sauce over it.

Stufatino
VEAL STEW
(Tuscany)

Heat 4 tablespoons olive oil in a heavy pan, add 2 cloves of garlic, chopped, and 1 1/2 to 2 pounds young leg of veal cut in 2-inch cubes. Brown the meat a little on all sides, season it with salt and pepper, and add 1 to 1 1/2 cups of the pulp of Italian canned tomatoes, reserving the juice to add later if it is needed. Add 1/2 cup dry white wine and 2 sprigs of rosemary, cover the pan, and simmer the meat over low heat for 1 1/2 to 2 hours, or until it is tender. Add a small amount of the tomato juice, if needed. Remove the meat to a hot platter and strain the sauce over the meat through a sieve.

Tenerumi di Vitello alla Paesana
BREAST OF VEAL PEASANT STYLE
(The Marches)

In a Dutch oven on top of the stove heat 2 tablespoons butter with 1 tablespoon olive oil and add 1 onion and 1 small stalk of celery, finely chopped. Sauté the vegetables for 3 or 4 minutes and add 1 1/2 to 2 pounds breast of veal cut in pieces. Brown these slightly on all sides and add salt and pepper, 4 peeled and coarsely chopped tomatoes, and several leaves of basil. Cover the pot, place it in a very slow oven (275° F.), and cook the meat for about 1 1/2 hours. Dissolve 1/2 teaspoon meat glaze in 3/4 cup water and add a little of this liquid to the pot from time to time. In the meantime shell 1 pound peas and cut 3 carrots into dice. Melt 2 tablespoons butter in a saucepan, add the vegetables, salt them lightly, and add 3/4 cup hot water in which is dis-

solved a bit of meat glaze. Cover the pan and cook the vegetables slowly until they are barely tender. Ten minutes before the meat is done, skim the fat from the surface of the sauce and stir in the vegetables and 1 tablespoon minced parsley.

To serve, place the meat in the center of a hot platter, spoon the vegetables around it, and pour the sauce over all. Small sautéed potatoes may be added, if desired.

Vitello all' Uccelletto
SAUTÉED VEAL SCALLOPS
(Hotel Royal, San Remo–Liguria)

Signor Bertolini's little veal *scaloppine* are an unusual preparation of a very usual Italian dish. The distinction is in the herbs and the quick, delicate handling throughout.

Cut tender veal into small, very thin slices. Flatten them with the side of a cleaver. Dust very lightly with flour and shake off the excess. For 4 people use 8 or more little slices, season them with salt and pepper, and brown them quickly 2 to 3 minutes on each side in 2 tablespoons butter and 1 tablespoon olive oil, melted and sizzling hot in your frying pan. Add 1 bay leaf, broken in bits, and 1/4 teaspoon dried sage or 2 leaves of fresh. Stir in 1/4 teaspoon meat glaze blended with 1/4 cup white wine. When all is well blended and the sauce reduced to just enough for a good spoonful for each slice of veal, add at the last minute 1 teaspoon unsalted butter that has been creamed with 1 teaspoon finely chopped parsley. The whole should be rapidly done and served at once.

Scaloppine di Vitello coi Tartufi alla Modenese
VEAL CUTLETS WITH TRUFFLES
MODENA
(Emilia–Romagna)

The not uncommon breaded veal

cutlet is here treated with a slight difference that adds immeasurably to its flavor.

Marinate 6 thin, neatly trimmed veal *scaloppine* for 1 to 2 hours with the juice of half a lemon, salt, freshly ground pepper, and a light sprinkling of grated Parmesan.

Heat a broad, heavy skillet, melt in it 3 tablespoons butter, and place in it, side by side, the veal slices, which have been dipped lightly in flour, then in beaten egg, and then in fine bread crumbs. Over moderate heat cook them for 3 to 5 minutes, or until they are browned on one side, turn them, and place on each a layer of thinly sliced truffles or, lacking this, sliced raw mushrooms. As a variation of this recipe, place a thin slice of *prosciutto* or cooked ham on each veal cutlet in place of the truffles. Spread a good spoonful of grated Parmesan on each cutlet and let the undersides brown. Sprinkle the cutlets with a tablespoon of good stock per slice. Place the skillet in a moderate oven (350° F.) for 3 to 4 minutes. Serves 3.

This dish is succulent, flavorful, crisp without being dry, and quite worthy of the tradition of this region.

Scaloppine Brufani
VEAL CUTLETS BRUFANI
(Brufani Palace Hotel, Perugia–Umbria)

Signor Nando Curti has no doubt encountered difficulties persuading his English-speaking clientele to face one more veal cutlet. He says, "This is a recipe that we have invented to persuade Americans to eat the milk-fed calf."

Use 4 or 6 thin slices of veal weighing 2 ounces or less apiece. Coat them with a mixture of flour, grated Parmesan, and salt. Break 2 large eggs into a bowl and whip them up, adding a little minced parsley and more Parmesan. Dip the slices in this preparation

and let them stand a few minutes to take on flavor. In a sauté pan heat 3 tablespoons butter with 1 tablespoon olive oil and when it is barely hot cook the veal slices in it on a rather low fire for 5 minutes on each side. Cut 3 1/2 ounces of white truffles in paper-thin slices, heat them in melted butter, and sprinkle them over the veal. With this dish serve as a border small molded spinach timbales, potato croquettes, tomatoes stuffed with rice, and creamed asparagus tips. Serves 2 or 3.

"In general," he adds, "this recipe has had much success among the 'beef eaters.'" And well it might!

Costolette Bolognese
VEAL CUTLETS BOLOGNESE
(Emilia–Romagna)

Cut 4 thin cutlets from a veal filet or leg. Pound them as thin as possible, dust with flour and salt and pepper, and brown them on both sides in 2 tablespoons butter over high heat. Add 2 tablespoons Marsala and 1 tablespoon water and blend them with the pan juices. Lower the heat and spread grated Parmesan on each piece. Add 2 tablespoons good stock to the pan, sprinkle a little of the juices over each piece, cover the pan, and cook the veal gently for 5 minutes. There should remain a spoonful of reduced sauce to pour over each slice. Serves 2.

Scaloppine Zia Teresa
VEAL CUTLETS AUNT TERESA
(Campania)

Flatten 6 evenly and thinly cut veal cutlets to 1/8-inch thickness and dust them lightly with flour seasoned with salt and pepper. Melt 2 tablespoons butter in a large skillet with 1 tablespoon oil. When the fat is sizzling hot, put in the slices of veal and cook them until they are nicely browned, about 5 minutes on each side. Remove them to a hot shallow heatproof dish and stir into the pan juices 1 tablespoon Marsala, 2 tablespoons white wine, and salt and pepper. Spoon this over the cutlets, lay on each a thin slice of *prosciutto*, or other good ham, previously heated in butter, then a smaller slice of *mozzarella*, and place in the center of each a spoonful of fresh peeled, chopped tomatoes that have been cooked until they are thick. Place the dish under a hot broiler until the cheese is melted.

Scaloppine alla Buongustaia
VEAL CUTLETS WITH CHICKEN LIVERS
(Ristorante Gino Sabatini, Florence–Tuscany)

Use 6 or 8 thin veal slices weighing about 2 ounces each. Flatten the slices as much as possible with a rolling pin or cleaver. Flour them very lightly. Season the cutlets with salt and pepper and cook them in a heavy skillet over high heat in 1/4 cup hot olive oil with 1/2 teaspoon sage. When they are lightly browned on both sides add about 6 ounces of chicken livers cut in small pieces (one chicken liver per person). Brown these rather quickly, about 3 minutes, and add 3/4 cup canned Italian tomatoes with some of the juice drained off or an equal amount of ripe, fresh tomatoes that have been peeled, seeded, and coarsely chopped. Season well with salt and pepper and cook for about 3 minutes more. Serve the cutlets on a hot platter with the sauce and chicken livers poured over them, surrounded with a border of rice. Serves 4.

Costolette Milanese
VEAL CUTLETS MILANESE
(Lombardy)

Trim and flatten 4 very thinly sliced veal cutlets, or *scaloppine,* dip them in flour, shaking off all excess, and season them with salt and pepper. Dip them in beaten egg, then in fine bread crumbs. Melt 3 tablespoons butter in a frying pan and when it is hot put in

the veal, lower the heat and cook the cutlets slowly for 5 minutes on each side. Turn them once almost immediately so the butter will not all be absorbed on one side. Serve them on a hot platter with slices of lemon covered with finely chopped parsley. Serves 2.

Saltimbocca alla Romana
VEAL CUTLETS ROMAN STYLE
(Rome)

Flatten 8 small veal cutlets to a thickness of less than 1/4 inch. Season them with salt and pepper and on each one place a small leaf of fresh sage, then a thin slice of ham the same size as the slice of veal. Fasten veal and ham together with wooden toothpicks threaded through the meat and sauté the meat in 3 tablespoons hot butter, lightly on the ham side, more thoroughly on the veal side, about 10 minutes in all. Arrange the *saltimbocca* on a hot platter, deglaze the pan juices with a little white wine, and pour the sauce over the meat.

Another method is to roll the veal slices after placing the sage and ham on them, with the veal on the outside, and fasten the rolls with toothpicks or thread. Sauté the little rolls in butter until they are brown on all sides, add white wine to the pan to a depth of 1/2 inch, and simmer until the sauce is reduced. Remove the toothpicks or thread and serve the rolls on a hot platter with the sauce poured over them. Serves 4.

Olivette Tartufate
TRUFFLED VEAL OLIVES
(Ristorante Giannino, Milan–Lombardy)

Use 8 small slices of veal flattened as much as possible. Season the slices with salt and pepper.

Combine 1 cup minced ham with 2 tablespoons grated Parmesan cheese and 1 small minced truffle. Moisten the stuffing with a few drops of Marsala.

Lay about 2 tablespoons of stuffing on each slice of veal and roll up the slices. Thread the veal rolls on skewers, 2 to a skewer, and dust them with flour. Melt enough butter in a heavy skillet to cover the bottom to a depth of about 1/8 inch and brown the veal rolls on both sides. Add about 1/3 cup white wine to the pan and simmer the wine until it is almost evaporated. Arrange the skewers on a hot serving platter and pour the pan juices over them. Accompany the veal rolls with spring vegetables. Serves 4.

Cima di Vitello Genovese
VEAL GALANTINE GENOESE
(Liguria)

The *cima* is a sort of poor-man's galantine—all of its ingredients are inexpensive and readily available. It is not a highly seasoned dish and its flavor is bland and very delicate. The broth in which it has been cooked should by all means be saved for a *zuppa pavese* or another dish where stock is used.

Scrub a flat strip of flank or breast of veal, roughly 8 by 12 inches, clean it of skin and hard bits of cartilage, and pull it into a thin rectangle. Fold it in half and sew it up carefully and securely with kitchen thread, to form a bag.

Heat 2 tablespoons butter in a skillet and in it cook for 10 minutes 1/4 pound lean veal cut in small pieces and 1/4 pound sweetbreads soaked, cleaned, and cut in pieces. Put them through a meat grinder or chop them finely. Parboil for 4 or 5 minutes 1/4 pound calf's brains, soaked and cleaned. Combine the meats and add 1 raw artichoke base cut in small dice, 1/2 cup shelled raw peas, 4 tablespoons grated Parmesan, 1 teaspoon marjoram, 1/2 teaspoon salt, and pepper. Mix these ingredients together and add last of all 4 eggs, well beaten. Let this filling stand in the refrigerator for 1 hour.

Prop the veal bag upright in a deep container and fill it carefully with this semiliquid stuffing. Sew up the open side closely and securely. Wrap the veal in cheesecloth and tie the wrapped meat at each end and in two places around the center, like a large sausage. In a kettle or oval casserole large enough to hold the *cima* have boiling enough salted water to cover the meat. Place the *cima* carefully in the kettle and when the water comes to a boil again, cover the pot, lower the heat, and simmer the veal for about 1 3/4 hours. Cool it in the liquid. Remove it and chill it under slight pressure in the refrigerator. Remove the cheesecloth and the sewing thread, slice the *cima,* and serve it cold.

Fegato alla Veneziana
CALF'S LIVER VENETIAN
(Ristorante alla Colomba, Venice–Veneto)

Cut 1/2 pound calf's liver into very thin small cutlets about 1 inch by 1 1/2 inches. Slice thinly enough white onions to equal about half the quantity of liver. Heat olive oil about 1/8 inch in depth in a skillet and brown the onions in this briefly, then add the liver and turn or toss it over high heat to cook it on all sides. About 2 minutes should be sufficient, as the liver hardens if it is cooked too long. Add salt, pepper, 1 or 2 leaves of sage, and 2 teaspoons minced parsley for the last 30 seconds of cooking. Serve immediately. Serves 2.

Fegato di Vitello alla Toscana
CALF'S LIVER TUSCAN STYLE
(Tuscany)

Coat 6 thin slices of calf's liver lightly with flour and cook them 1 1/2 minutes on each side in 4 tablespoons hot oil. Season with salt and pepper and 1 tablespoon chopped fresh sage leaves and cook the slices another half minute on each side. Serve the liver with quarters of lemon.

Pork

Lombata di Maiale Ubriaca
ROAST PORK WITH WHITE WINE

Have the butcher saw through the rib bones of a loin of pork to partially separate the chops. Place the pork in a hot oven (425° F.) for 20 minutes to brown the surface. Skim the fat from the pan and add 1 clove of garlic, 3 cloves, 4 or 5 leaves of fresh sage, and salt and pepper. Add 1 cup white wine, lower the heat to slow (300° F.), and continue cooking the pork until the wine is reduced by half. Add 1 cup tomato sauce and stir it into the remaining juices. Cover the roast and cook it for about 2 hours, adding a little hot water if necessary. Remove the roast to a hot platter and carve it. Skim the fat from the sauce and pour the sauce over the meat.

Maiale Marinato
MARINATED FRESH HAM

Place a 2- to 3-pound piece of fresh ham in a bowl and add 1 small onion, chopped, 4 or 5 slices of carrot, 1 clove of garlic, chopped, 1 bay leaf, a pinch of thyme, 1 teaspoon chopped parsley, and salt and pepper. Pour 2 cups red wine over the meat and let it marinate 8 or 10 hours, turning it occasionally. Drain and dry the meat and brown it on all sides in 3 tablespoons butter heated in a heavy pot. Remove the meat and blend 2 teaspoons flour into the fat remaining in the pan. Stir in the strained marinade and 1 cup stock. Reheat the liquid, stirring, until it boils. Replace the meat, cover the pot, and simmer the meat over low heat for about 2 hours, adding a little hot water, if necessary. Remove the meat to a hot

serving dish. Skim the fat from the sauce and add 2 tablespoons capers. Reheat the sauce and pour it over the meat or pass it separately.

Costolette di Maiale Milanese
PORK CHOPS MILANESE

(Lombardy)

Trim all the fat from 4 pork chops, brush both sides with melted butter, season with salt and pepper, and dip in a mixture of fine bread crumbs and grated Parmesan cheese—about 3 tablespoons bread crumbs to 4 tablespoons Parmesan cheese. Heat 2 tablespoons olive oil and 2 tablespoons butter in a frying pan and brown the chops well on both sides over moderate heat. Add 1 young onion or 2 scallions, chopped, to the pan 1 or 2 minutes before completing the browning of the chops. Heat 2 tablespoons oil in a shallow baking dish and put in the chops. Add 4 or 5 tablespoons hot water to the frying pan, stir up the brown juices and onion, and pour this over the chops. Cook the chops in a moderate oven (350° F.), uncovered, for 15 minutes. Add 1 to 1 1/4 cups tomato sauce to the baking dish, cover it, and continue cooking the chops in the oven for about 1/2 hour, or until they are tender. Serves 4.

Costolette di Maiale Modenese
PORK CHOPS MODENA STYLE

(Emilia–Romagna)

Leave most of the fat on 4 pork chops and coat each side of them with the following mixture: 1 teaspoon dried sage, 2 teaspoons chopped fresh rosemary (less, if it is dried), 1 or 2 cloves of garlic, chopped, and salt and pepper.

Place the chops in a buttered frying pan and add enough hot water almost to cover them. Cover the pan and simmer the chops over low heat for 1 hour. Remove the cover, let the water evaporate, and allow the chops to brown on both sides. Add 1/3 to 1/2 cup white wine and simmer 2 or 3 minutes, or until there remains just enough sauce to serve with each chop. Serves 4.

Costolette di Maiale alla Toscana
PORK CHOPS TUSCAN STYLE
(Tuscany)

Cut the fat from 6 pork chops and rub salt and pepper and a few fennel seeds into each side. Heat 3 tablespoons olive oil in a heavy frying pan, add 1 chopped and mashed clove of garlic, and put in the chops. Brown them on both sides over fairly high heat. Then add a small amount of hot water, cover the pan, and complete the cooking over moderate heat. Serve with mashed potatoes.

Costolette di Maiale Marinate
MARINATED PORK CHOPS

Trim the fat from 6 pork chops and marinate them for 2 or 3 hours in a mixture of 1/3 cup olive oil, the juice of 1 lemon, half an onion, chopped, 1 teaspoon chopped parsley, and salt and pepper. Drain the chops, season them with salt and pepper, and broil them under moderate heat, turning them several times, until they are cooked through and browned. Serve with piquant sauce (see index).

Costolette di Maiale Panate
BREADED PORK CHOPS

Trim the fat from 4 loin pork chops and marinate them for an hour in 3/4 cup wine vinegar. Drain and dry the chops. Season them with salt and pepper and dip them first in flour, then in 1 egg beaten with 2 teaspoons water, and finally in 1 cup fine bread crumbs

combined with 1 tablespoon chopped parsley and 1 clove of garlic, chopped. Heat 3 tablespoons olive oil and 1 tablespoon butter in a skillet and brown the chops slowly for about 5 minutes on each side. Cover the skillet, place it in a slow oven (300° F.), and cook the chops for about 20 minutes, or until they are well done and tender. Serves 4.

Bracioline di Maiale al Pomodoro
PORK CHOPS WITH TOMATO SAUCE

Trim the fat from 6 pork chops and flatten them a little with a cleaver or wooden mallet. Season them with salt and pepper and brown them on both sides over high heat in 1 tablespoon butter and 2 tablespoons olive oil in a heavy skillet. Lower the heat to moderate, cover the skillet, and cook the chops 15 minutes or more on each side. Remove the excess fat from the pan, add 1/2 cup red wine and 1/4 cup Marsala, and reduce the liquid by one-third. Stir in 1 tablespoon tomato paste diluted with 1/4 cup water, add 1/2 clove of garlic and simmer for 5 minutes. You may add 1/2 teaspoon fennel seeds with the garlic, which gives a distinctive flavor to the sauce. Pour the sauce over the chops.

Filetto di Maiale alla Salvia
SKEWERED PORK TENDERLOIN

Cut a 1-pound tenderloin of pork in 1 1/2-inch slices. Thread them on 4 individual skewers with a slice of French bread, a slice of *prosciutto,* and a fresh leaf of sage between the slices of meat. Begin and end each skewer with a slice of bread. The slices of bread and *prosciutto* should be about the same in diameter as the slices of pork. Roll the filled skewers in olive oil, season them with salt and pepper, place them in a shallow baking dish, and cook them in a moderately hot oven (375° F.) for 45 minutes, turning them once. Remove the skewers before serving. Serves 4.

Lamb

Cervelli d'Agnello Napoletana
LAMB BRAINS NEAPOLITAN
(Campania)

Soak 4 lamb brains in cold water for 20 minutes, drain them, cover them again with cold water, and bring them to a boil. Drain them again, rinse them in cold water, and pat them dry. Coat the bottom of a shallow baking dish with olive oil and place the brains in the dish. Sprinkle them with 4 teaspoons wine vinegar, 1 teaspoon capers, 8 or 10 pitted sliced black Italian olives, and coat the surface with fine bread crumbs. Spoon 4 tablespoons melted butter over the bread crumbs and place the dish in a hot oven (450° F.) for about 10 minutes. Serves 4.

Agnello con Riso
LAMB STEW WITH RICE

Cut 2 pounds lamb leg or other lean lamb into cubes. Brown them on all sides in 4 tablespoons hot olive oil, add 1 onion, sliced, and cook until the onion is lightly browned. Season with salt and pepper and a pinch of orégano and add 3 tablespoons tomato paste blended with 1/2 cup white wine and 1/2 cup water. Cover the saucepan and simmer the lamb for about 1 hour, or until it is tender, adding a little hot water if needed. Cook 1/2 pound rice, mold it in a ring, and turn it out onto a round serving dish. Place the lamb with its sauce in the center.

Potacchio Marchigiana
LAMB STEW OF THE MARCHES
(The Marches)

Cut 1 1/2 pounds lamb from the leg into 3/4-inch cubes and brown the meat on all sides in 2 tablespoons olive oil with 1 clove of garlic, chopped, and 1/2 teaspoon fresh rosemary. Add salt and pepper and 1/2 cup white wine and simmer until the wine has almost evaporated. Now add 3/4 cup tomato sauce or 3 tablespoons tomato paste diluted with light stock. Add enough stock, or water, to cover the meat generously, cover the pan, and simmer the stew over low heat until the meat is tender.

Chicken may be prepared in the same way and takes less time to cook.

Agnello Saltato ai Piselli
SAUTÉED LAMB WITH PEAS

Cut 2 pounds shoulder or leg of lamb in cubes as for a stew. Brown them on all sides in 1 1/2 tablespoons butter. Add salt and pepper and blend in 1 tablespoon flour. Add 1 cup stock combined with 3 tablespoons tomato sauce and a dozen tiny white onions. Cover the pan and simmer the lamb for 1 hour or more, or until it is tender. Add 2 pounds peas that have been cooked separately. Reheat and serve with steamed potatoes or boiled rice.

Abbacchio alla Cacciatora
SPRING LAMB HUNTER STYLE
(Rome)

The true *abbacchio* is a baby milk-fed lamb seen in Rome in the spring and often roasted whole. But for this recipe one may use the spring lamb found in our markets, which is much larger. Though tender, it will not have the almost white meat of the true *abbacchio*.

Cut 2 pounds spring lamb—leg, loin, or saddle—into serving pieces as for a stew. Season the pieces with salt and pepper and rub them with garlic. Heat 2 tablespoons butter and 2 tablespoons olive oil in a heavy pan and brown the lamb on all sides. Sprinkle in 1 tablespoon flour, blend it with the fat, and add 1 clove of garlic, chopped, a good pinch each of rosemary and sage, 1 small green pepper, coarsely chopped, 1 cup white wine, and 1/2 cup wine vinegar. Cook over moderate heat until the sauce thickens slightly. Add 1 cup hot stock or water, cover the saucepan, lower the heat, and cook for about 30 minutes, or until the meat is tender. A few minutes before serving stir in 5 or 6 chopped anchovy filets.

Agnello al Vino Bianco
ROAST LAMB WITH WHITE WINE AND ANCHOVIES

Remove the fell and part of the fat from a leg of young lamb. Pierce the meat in 4 places with a pointed knife and insert sections of 1 clove of garlic cut in quarters. Place it in a roasting pan. Season it with salt and pepper, pour 3/4 cup white wine into the pan, and roast it 15 to 18 minutes per pound in a moderately slow oven (325° F.), basting it from time to time. Add a small amount of hot stock to the pan, if necessary. When the lamb is done, remove it to a hot platter. Skim the fat from the pan juices and add to the remaining sauce 4 chopped anchovy filets, 1 teaspoon finely grated lemon rind, and 2 teaspoons finely chopped parsley. Heat the sauce, stirring, to dissolve the anchovies. Pass it separately.

Agnello Arrosto all'Aretina
MARINATED ROAST LAMB

Remove the fell and as much fat as possible from a leg of young spring lamb. Rub it with salt and pepper and 1 teaspoon rosemary. Sprinkle it with 1/4 cup olive oil and 3 tablespoons wine vinegar. Pierce it here and there with a sharp knife to permit a little juice to run out. Let it marinate 6 hours, basting it from time to time with the juices collected in the bottom of the container. Roast it 15 to 18 minutes per pound in a moderately slow oven (325° F.), adding the juices of the marinade and basting it several times with the pan juices. It should remain pink in the center. The same method of cooking may be used for a shoulder or quarter or other cuts of lamb for roasting.

Spezzatini di Capretto alla Trentina
YOUNG KID OR LAMB TRIESTE STYLE
(Trentino–Alto Adige)

For this recipe you may use rabbit or young spring lamb, though the original calls for kid.

Cut the meat into serving pieces, season the pieces with salt and pepper, dip them in beaten egg, then in bread crumbs, and place them in hot oil or lard about 3/8 inch deep in a frying pan. Add the grated peel of 1 lemon and brown the pieces on all sides. Remove some of the fat, add 1/2 cup or more of hot milk, salt to taste, cover the pan, and simmer the meat until it is tender.

Miscellaneous Meats

Trippa all'Anconetana
TRIPE ANCONA STYLE
(The Marches)

Melt 3 tablespoons butter in a heavy pan and add 1/2 pound boiled tripe cut into small strips. Add salt and pepper and sauté the tripe for a few minutes over low heat, stirring occasionally. Beat 2 egg yolks with 3 or 4 tablespoons of the hot broth in which the tripe was boiled or of another light stock. Add 2 to 3 tablespoons grated Parmesan and add the mixture to the tripe. Heat, stirring, just until the eggs begin to thicken, add the juice of a lemon and 1 tablespoon minced parsley, and transfer the tripe immediately to a serving dish. Serves 2.

La Trippa alla Fiorentina
TRIPE FLORENTINE
(Trattoria Sostanza, Florence–Tuscany)

Cut 1 pound boiled tripe into 2-inch strips the width of a finger and put the strips in a saucepan with 1 cup strained meat sauce such as that from stewed beef Florentine (see index) and 1 teaspoon fresh marjoram. Cover the pan and simmer the tripe for an hour, or until it is well cooked but still firm. Sprinkle it with Parmesan before serving. Serves 4.

Trippa alla Triestina
BROILED TRIPE TRIESTE STYLE
(Friuli–Venezia Giulia)

Wash thoroughly under running water 1 pound tripe. Cover it with cold water, bring it to the boiling point, and drain it. Now cover it with boiling salted water and add 1 clove of garlic, 1 small onion, and 1 small stalk of celery, all cut in pieces. Simmer the tripe for 1 hour or more, until it is tender. Drain it, dry it thoroughly, place it in an earthen dish, and sprinkle it generously with olive oil and a little salt and pepper. Let it stand for an hour or two. Cut it into serving pieces and broil it 3 minutes on each side under a hot broiler. Serve it with a crisp green salad. Serves 4.

Animelle alla Ciociara
SWEETBREADS CIOCIARA
(Ristorante Passetto–Rome)

Soak 2 pairs of sweetbreads in cold water for 1 hour. Drain them and put them in a saucepan with enough salted water to cover. Bring the water to a boil and simmer the sweetbreads for 4 minutes. Drain and cool them and remove the skin and hard tubes, but leave the sweetbreads whole. Wipe them dry and brown them on all sides in 4 tablespoons olive oil heated in a sauté pan. Drain off any excess oil, add to the pan 4 tablespoons butter, 3/4 cup sliced mushrooms that have been cooked 3 minutes in a little water and lemon juice, 1/4 cup julienne of ham, and salt and pepper, and heat all together. Blend in 1 teaspoon flour and add 1 large ripe peeled tomato, seeded and diced, and 1/2 cup white wine. Reheat the mixture and, when it reaches the boiling point, allow it to simmer for 5 to 8 minutes. Serve immediately. Serves 4.

Lepre Dolce-Forte
SWEET AND SOUR WILD HARE
(Tuscany)

The following recipe may be used for rabbit as well as for wild hare.

Skin, clean, and cut a wild hare into serving pieces and put the pieces in an earthenware terrine or casserole. Bring 2 cups red wine almost to a boil with 1/2 onion, chopped, 2 cloves, 1 tablespoon chopped parsley, 1 bay leaf, a sprig of thyme, and a few peppercorns. Cool the marinade, pour it over the hare, and let the meat marinate for 6 hours.

In a saucepan sauté 1 onion and 4 slices of fat bacon, both chopped, until the onion is golden and the bacon is crisp. Remove the pieces of hare from the marinade, dry them, roll them in flour, and sauté them in the bacon fat until they are lightly browned on all sides. Strain the marinade over the hare, bring it to a boil, and cook it until it is reduced by half. Add about 2 cups hot chicken stock, or enough barely to cover the pieces of hare, cover the saucepan, and simmer the hare for 1 hour.

In a small heavy saucepan heat 2 tablespoons sugar with a few drops of water until it begins to caramelize. Stir in 1/2 cup vinegar and add this mixture to the sauce in which the hare has been cooking, with 1 tablespoon each of chopped candied fruits and grated bitter chocolate and 2 tablespoons each of raisins and pine nuts. Simmer for about 5 minutes longer.

Lepre alla Trentina
WILD HARE TRENTO
(Ristorante Forst, Trento–
Trentino-Alto Adige)

In a broad saucepan melt 1 tablespoon each of butter, oil, and lard. Add a wild hare, cleaned and cut into serving pieces, together with salt, pepper, 1/2 teaspoon rosemary, 2 bay leaves, and 1 teaspoon juniper berries. Brown the meat on all sides and sprinkle over it 1 tablespoon flour. Add 1 1/4 cup white wine, stir in the brown juices in the pan, and allow the liquid to simmer until the wine is reduced by three-

quarters. Add enough hot stock or water to half cover the meat, cover the pan, and continue cooking until the meat is tender. Remove the pieces of hare to a hot serving dish and strain the sauce over them. Serve with polenta.

Lepre in Salmi Excelsior
WILD HARE EXCELSIOR
(Savoy Excelsior Palace, Trieste–
Friuli-Venezia Giulia)

Have a wild hare cut into serving pieces—that is to say, separate the legs and shoulders and divide the breast in two. Put the meat in a bowl with 1 small carrot, 1 small stalk of celery, and 1 small onion, all sliced, 2 bay leaves, 1/4 teaspoon each of rosemary, thyme, and marjoram, 3 or 4 cloves, and freshly ground pepper and add enough red wine to cover the pieces. Add the liver and heart, finely chopped, and marinate the meat for 48 hours.

When you are ready to cook the hare, heat 2 tablespoons diced bacon in a heavy pot with 1 tablespoon butter. Drain the pieces of meat, reserving the marinade, pat them dry with absorbent paper, and brown them on all sides in the fat. When they have attained a fine golden color, strain the marinade and add the vegetables to the pot. When these in turn have browned a little, add the strained marinade, and allow it to reduce by half. Add 2 large ripe tomatoes that have been peeled, seeded, and coarsely chopped, about 1 cup stock, and salt to taste. When the meat is tender, remove it to a hot deep dish. Reduce the sauce should this be necessary, strain it through a sieve, and add 1/2 cup heavy cream. Reheat the sauce without boiling and pour it over the hare. Serve at once with polenta or with mashed potatoes.

Vegetables

Carciofi alla Fiorentina
ARTICHOKES FLORENTINE
(Tuscany)

Place 6 cooked or canned artichoke bases in a buttered shallow baking dish. On each, arrange a few diced mushrooms that have been sautéed in butter and a few small cooked cauliflower flowerets. Make 1 1/2 cups cream sauce by melting 1 1/2 tablespoons butter, blending in 1 1/2 tablespoons flour, and adding gradually 1 1/2 cups milk and thin cream combined. Add 3 tablespoons grated Parmesan. Mask the filled artichoke bases with this sauce and put them in a hot oven (400° F.) for about 10 minutes, or until the surface is lightly browned.

Carciofi alla Parmigiana
ARTICHOKES PARMESAN
(Emilia–Romagna)

Cut 1 box of frozen artichoke hearts into thin vertical slices. Thaw the slices on paper towels, which will absorb the water. Season them with salt and pepper, dip them lightly in flour, then in beaten egg, and brown them on both sides in a frying pan in 3/4 cup hot olive oil. Drain the slices on absorbent paper.

In a small pan brown 1 slice of bacon, cut in small dice, with 1 small chopped onion. Add 3 tablespoons tomato paste, salt and pepper, and 1 cup warm water. Simmer the sauce for 10 minutes.

In a buttered baking dish place a layer of the artichoke slices, cover them with half the sauce, and repeat this procedure with the remaining artichoke slices and sauce. Sprinkle grated Par-

mesan over the surface and bake in a moderately hot oven (375° F.) for 20 minutes. Serves 4.

Carciofi alla Milanese
ARTICHOKES MILANESE
(Lombardy)

Cut the stems from 6 artichokes and with scissors cut 1/2 inch from the tip of each leaf. Parboil the artichokes for 7 minutes in salted boiling water. Drain them, spread the center leaves apart slightly, and remove the chokes with a spoon or knife. (Frankly, this is not very easy.) In the center of each artichoke place a generous teaspoon of butter and about 2 teaspoons grated Parmesan or Romano cheese. Place the artichokes in a heavy buttered casserole, sprinkle 1 tablespoon water over each, cover the casserole closely, and steam over very low heat for about 50 minutes, or until a leaf pulls away with ease. Add a few drops of water should the artichokes become too dry.

Carciofi Ripieni alla Siciliana
STUFFED ARTICHOKES SICILIAN
(Sicily)

Cut the stems from 6 medium-sized artichokes and with scissors trim 1/2 inch from the tip of each leaf. Parboil the artichokes for 7 minutes in boiling salted water, drain them, and press the leaf ends down against a board to open them slightly. Remove the center chokes entirely with a pointed spoon. (As we've said, this is not easy.) Now in the center and between the leaves insert the following stuffing so that there is a little at the base of each leaf: Mix 1 1/2 cups fine bread crumbs, 1 1/2 cups grated

Parmesan, 3/4 cup finely chopped parsley, and salt and pepper.

Place a peeled clove of garlic in the center of each artichoke, put them in a heavy casserole, add water to a depth of about 1/2-inch, and pour 2 tablespoons olive oil over each artichoke. Cover the pot and steam over low heat or in a slow oven (300° F.) for about 45 minutes, or until a leaf pulls out easily and the artichoke bases are tender. Remove the garlic cloves before serving.

Sparagi Parmigiana
ASPARAGUS PARMESAN
(Emilia–Romagna)

Wash 2 1/2 pounds fresh asparagus, cut off the hard ends, and peel off some of the skin. Cook, or steam, the asparagus in salted boiling water for 15 minutes, or until it is almost done. Drain the stalks and spread them in a wide shallow baking dish. Pour over them 6 tablespoons melted butter, sprinkle 1/2 cup grated Parmesan over the tips, and place them in a hot oven (400° F.) for about 10 minutes, or until the cheese is lightly browned.

Fave Fresche Stufato
STEWED LIMA BEANS WITH HAM

Heat 2 tablespoons butter with 1 tablespoon olive oil and add 1/2 onion, finely chopped. When the onion is slightly brown add 1/2 cup finely diced *prosciutto* or baked ham. Stir and cook the mixture for 1 or 2 minutes. Add 1 small head of tender lettuce, coarsely sliced, 3 cups shelled fresh Lima beans, salt and pepper, and water or chicken stock to half cover the beans. Cover the pan and cook the beans slowly until they are tender and the liquid is evaporated. Serves 4 to 6.

Fagiolini al Prosciutto
GREEN BEANS WITH HAM

Wash 1 1/2 pounds fresh string beans and cook them in boiling salted water until they are tender but still firm. Drain the beans. Melt 2 1/2 tablespoons butter in a saucepan, add 1/2 cup finely diced ham, and sauté it briefly until it is slightly browned. Add the beans, season them with salt and pepper, and sauté them briefly over high heat, stirring carefully to blend all together. Sprinkle them with 1 tablespoon finely minced parsley combined with 1 finely minced clove of garlic.

Fagioli all' Uccelletto
BEANS TUSCAN STYLE
(Tuscany)

Soak 3/4 pound white beans overnight, drain them, and add 4 cups water, 2 tablespoons olive oil, 2 cloves of garlic, cut in pieces, 1 large peeled and seeded tomato, coarsely chopped, and a good pinch of sage. Cover the pan and simmer the beans slowly until they are tender, which may take 2 to 2 1/2 hours. At the end season them with salt and pepper and stir in another tablespoon of olive oil. Serves 4.

Carote Agrodolce
SWEET AND SOUR CARROTS

Scrape and slice thin 1 pound carrots and boil them in salted water barely to cover until they are tender. Drain the carrots and reserve the liquid. In a saucepan melt 2 tablespoons butter, blend in 2 teaspoons flour, and add gradually 1 cup of the reserved carrot stock. Add 1 tablespoon sugar, pepper and salt if needed, and 1 to 1 1/2 tablespoons vinegar, according to taste. Simmer the sauce, stirring, until it is thickened and smooth, add the carrots, and continue cooking until they are thoroughly heated.

Cavolfiore Piemontese
CAULIFLOWER PIEDMONTESE
(Piedmont)

In 1 1/2 tablespoons butter sauté 1 finely chopped onion until it is lightly browned. Add 2 chopped anchovy filets, 1/3 cup stock, 1 tablespoon wine vinegar, freshly ground pepper, and 1 teaspoon chopped parsley and basil combined. Simmer 1 minute, add 2 tablespoons butter, and let it just melt in, stirring. Pour this over a small, whole cauliflower that has been boiled and drained and placed in a heatproof dish. Sprinkle the cauliflower with grated Parmesan or Romano cheese and glaze it briefly under a hot broiler. Serves 4.

Sedani alla Parmigiana
CELERY PARMESAN
(Emilia–Romagna)

Wash a large bunch of celery, cut off the leaves, and cut the stalks into 4-inch pieces. Boil them for about 15 minutes, or until they are tender, in 6 cups water with 1 onion, cut in pieces, 2 slices of bacon, 2 or 3 cloves, and a little salt and pepper. Drain the celery and place half of it in a buttered shallow baking dish. Cover it with 3/4 cup tomato sauce and sprinkle it with 4 tablespoons grated Parmesan. Repeat this procedure with the rest of the celery and the same amount of tomato sauce and cheese. Bake the celery in a hot oven (400° F.) for 10 minutes. The tomato sauce may be canned or fresh, or made by combining 1/2 cup tomato paste with 1 cup of the strained stock in which the celery was cooked. Serves 4.

Melanzana alla Fiorentina
EGGPLANT FLORENTINE
(Tuscany)

Peel a large eggplant and slice it into rounds 1/4 inch thick. Put these in a baking dish well coated with olive oil. Cover the eggplant with round slices of peeled tomatoes, season with salt and pepper, and on the tomatoes place thin slices of *mozzarella* cheese. Repeat these layers until all the eggplant is used, topping the dish with slices of *mozzarella*. Sprinkle 1/2 cup olive oil over all and bake the eggplant in a moderately slow oven (325° F.) for an hour and a half.

Melanzana alla Parmigiana
EGGPLANT PARMESAN
(Emilia–Romagna)

Heat together a 16-ounce can (2 cups) of Italian tomatoes, 1/4 cup water, 2 tablespoons olive oil, and 2 tablespoons tomato paste. Simmer the mixture for 20 minutes, or until you have a tomato sauce the consistency of a thin purée. Or if you prefer, use 2 generous cups prepared tomato sauce.

Cut a large eggplant into slices less than 1/2 inch thick and cover the slices with boiling water. Let them stand for 5 minutes and drain them on absorbent paper. Sauté them in hot olive oil 1/8 inch deep until they are lightly browned on both sides. Place half the eggplant slices in the bottom of a shallow baking dish and season them with salt and pepper. Combine 1 1/2 cups fine bread crumbs, 2 cloves of garlic and 1 tablespoon parsley, both finely chopped, and 1/2 cup grated Parmesan. Scatter half this mixture over the eggplant slices and add half of the tomato sauce and a few thin slices of *mozzarella* cheese. Add, in order, the remaining eggplant slices, bread-crumb-and-cheese mixture, and tomato sauce, and more slices of *mozzarella*. Bake the eggplant in a hot oven (400° F.) for 15 minutes, or until the *mozzarella* is melted and all is bubbling hot.

Melanzana alla Romana
EGGPLANT ROMAN STYLE
(Rome)

Peel 2 small eggplants and slice them thin lengthwise. Brown the slices on both sides in hot olive oil 1/8 inch deep and drain them on absorbent paper. Melt 2 tablespoons butter in a baking dish and add a thin layer of meat sauce (see index) or the sauce from a beef stew *(stracotta)*. Arrange in the dish a layer of eggplant slices, sprinkle them lightly with salt, then add a layer of thinly sliced *mozzarella* cheese and a little grated Parmesan mixed with chopped fresh basil leaves. Now cover with meat sauce and add a few spoonfuls of tomato sauce. Add another layer of eggplant slices and repeat until all the eggplant is used. Moisten the last layer with meat sauce and some tomato sauce and bake the dish in a moderately hot oven (375° F.) for about 15 minutes, or until it is bubbling hot. Serves 4.

Funghi con Pignole
MUSHROOMS WITH PINE NUTS

Wash and slice 1 pound firm fresh mushrooms. Melt 2 tablespoons butter in a saucepan, add the mushrooms, and cook them about 3 minutes. Add salt and pepper, 1 small onion, finely chopped, and 1/2 cup pine nuts or blanched slivered almonds. Stir and cook the mushrooms for 5 minutes. Serves 4 to 6.

Funghi alla Genovese
MUSHROOMS GENOESE
(Liguria)

Wash and slice 1 pound firm fresh mushrooms. Melt 1 tablespoon butter with 2 tablespoons olive oil, add the mushrooms, and sauté them for 5 to 8 minutes, or until their liquid has evaporated. Add salt and pepper, 1 clove of garlic, minced, and 1 teaspoon fresh orégano or marjoram, finely chopped. Cook the mushrooms another minute, stirring. Serves 4 to 6.

Funghi in Umido
BRAISED MUSHROOMS
(Tuscany)

Clean 1 pound mushrooms and cut them in quarters. In 1/4 cup olive oil over low heat, brown 2 cloves of garlic, cut in quarters. Remove the garlic and add 6 or 8 fresh mint leaves. Add the mushrooms and a little salt and pepper, cover the pan, and simmer the mushrooms slowly for 2 or 3 minutes. Add 3 or 4 tablespoons tomato sauce (canned or fresh) and continue cooking for about 10 minutes, or until the mushrooms are done. Serves 4.

Funghi alla Parmigiana
MUSHROOMS PARMESAN
(Emilia–Romagna)

Wash, but do not peel, 1 pound large mushrooms. Remove the stems, peel them, and chop them. Mix the chopped stems with 2 cloves of garlic and 1 1/2 tablespoons parsley, both finely minced, 3 tablespoons grated Parmesan, 1/2 teaspoon orégano, 1/2 cup fine bread crumbs, and a pinch each of salt and pepper. Place the mushroom caps side by side in a shallow oiled baking dish, stem sides up. Fill them with the above mixture and pour about 1/3 cup water into the baking dish. Pour 1/2 cup olive oil over the mushrooms, distributing it evenly over the filling of each one. Bake the mushrooms 1/2 hour in a moderately hot oven (350° F.). Serves 4.

Cipolline Agrodolce
SWEET AND SOUR ONIONS

Peel 2 dozen very small white onions. Heat 3 tablespoons olive oil in a shallow heavy pan broad enough to hold the onions in one layer. Add the onions and 1 tablespoon finely diced bacon. Allow the onions to brown a little on all sides. Add 1/2 cup sherry, 1/2 cup wine vinegar, 2 tablespoons sugar, 2 tablespoons raisins, salt, and a pinch of dried red pepper flakes. Simmer the onions over low heat until they are soft and the sauce is reduced and thick. Serve cold. Serves 4.

Piselli al Finocchio
PEAS WITH FENNEL

Shell 2 pounds peas and cook them

in boiling salted water with half a head of fennel cut in 2 pieces. When they are tender, remove the fennel and mash it through a sieve. Drain the peas and put them in a saucepan with 2 tablespoons melted butter and salt and pepper. Sauté them briefly over low heat, add the mashed fennel, stir all together, and serve very hot.

Peperoni Fritti
FRIED SWEET PEPPER RINGS

Slice green peppers crosswise into rings, remove seeds and pulp, and dip the rings in olive oil, then in flour, then in beaten egg. Fry them in deep hot oil (380° F.) until they are golden brown. They are excellent with grilled meats.

Spinaci alla Romana
SPINACH ROMAN STYLE
(Rome)

Cook 2 pounds spinach in the usual way—that is, with no more water than remains on the leaves after washing— slowly and just until it is softened. Drain it thoroughly and chop it. In 3 tablespoons bacon fat sauté a small onion, chopped, until it is softened, add 2 or 3 tablespoons plumped seedless raisins and 2 tablespoons pine nuts and stir these together for a few seconds. Now stir in the chopped spinach, add salt and pepper and a good dash of grated nutmeg, and cook all together very slowly for 15 minutes, stirring from time to time. Serves 4.

Spinaci alla Borghese
SPINACH WITH ANCHOVIES

Wash 2 pounds spinach and cook it in a large covered saucepan over low heat, with only the water remaining on the leaves. When it is softened, drain it well, pressing out all the water. Melt 3 tablespoons butter slowly with 4 chopped anchovy filets and 1 cut clove of garlic. When the anchovies are dissolved add the spinach, a little salt if

needed, pepper and a dash of nutmeg. Stir and heat all well together. Remove the garlic (if you can find it!) and serve.

Frittelle di Patate
POTATO CAKES

Boil, peel, and mash 1 1/2 pounds potatoes. Add 1 tablespoon butter, 4 tablespoons flour, 1 small onion, finely chopped, 4 tablespoons grated Parmesan, 1 tablespoon parsley, finely chopped, 2 well-beaten eggs, and salt and pepper. Beat the mixture well, adding 2 to 3 tablespoons milk if it is very stiff. Form it into small cakes 1/2 inch thick, coat them with fine bread crumbs, and sauté them in hot oil 1/8 inch deep until they are golden on both sides.

Purè di Patate
PURÉE OF POTATOES

Boil, peel, and mash 2 pounds potatoes. Brown 3 tablespoons butter in a saucepan with a slice of onion. When the onion is brown remove it. Add the potatoes and stir and cook them a few minutes, adding gradually 1/2 cup milk, or more if you prefer a very soft purée. When the potatoes are thoroughly heated add salt, pepper, a good dash of nutmeg, and 3 tablespoons grated Parmesan.

Pomodori Ripieni alla Siciliana
STUFFED TOMATOES SICILIAN
(Sicily)

Cut a slice from the base, not the stem end, of 4 medium-sized tomatoes and hollow out the centers. In 3 tablespoons olive oil sauté 1 medium onion, chopped, until it is softened. Remove the pan from the heat and add 2 teaspoons parsley, finely chopped, 4 anchovy filets, cut in small bits, 3 tablespoons bread crumbs, 2 teaspoons drained capers, a very little salt, a dash of pepper, and a dash of nutmeg. Add 2 tablespoons of the firm parts of the flesh you removed from the tomatoes, but not seeds or juice. Mix all together and fill the tomatoes with this stuffing. Coat the tops well with bread crumbs. Place the tomatoes in an oiled shallow baking dish, moisten the tops with a little olive oil, replace lightly the slices you removed from the tomatoes to form little caps, and bake them for 30 minutes in a moderately hot oven (375° F.). Serves 4.

Zucchini Genovese
ZUCCHINI GENOA STYLE
(Liguria)

Scrub but do not peel 4 small zucchini, cut off the stem ends, and slice in long narrow strips. Heat 3 tablespoons olive oil in a broad frying pan and cook the zucchini for 5 to 8 minutes over fairly high heat, turning them as they brown. Add 1/2 teaspoon salt, freshly ground pepper, 1 small clove of garlic, chopped and mashed, 1 tablespoon parsley, chopped, and 1 teaspoon orégano. Lower the flame and cook the zucchini 3 or 4 minutes. Serves 4.

Zucchini Liguria
STUFFED ZUCCHINI LIGURIAN
(Liguria)

Boil 4 medium-sized zucchini in salted water for 5 minutes. Drain them, slit them lengthwise, and scoop out a hollow along the centers. Chop and reserve the pulp you have removed, to add to the stuffing. Make 1/3 cup heavy cream sauce with 1 tablespoon butter, 1 tablespoon flour, and 1/3 cup milk or cream and mix with it 1 slice of bread, crumbled, 1 slice of *prosciutto*, ham, or bacon, chopped, 3 or 4 mushrooms, chopped, 1/2 teaspoon orégano, 2 tablespoons grated Parmesan, and salt and pepper. Add the chopped centers of the zucchini and 1 small egg, beaten, and mix all together. Fill the zucchini with the stuffing, place them in a buttered baking dish, sprinkle them with a little olive oil, and bake 1/2 hour in a moderately hot oven (350° F.). Serves 4.

Zucchini alla Bella Napoli
ZUCCHINI NEAPOLITAN
(Campania)

Heat 3 tablespoons butter and 3 tablespoons olive oil in a saucepan and add 1 medium-sized onion, sliced. When the onion is softened add 4 ripe, peeled, seeded, and coarsely chopped tomatoes, several leaves of fresh basil, 1/2 teaspoon marjoram, and salt and pepper. Cover the pan and simmer the mixture over low heat until it is thickened, which may take about 3/4 of an hour. Force the sauce through a sieve.

Slice 6 zucchini into rounds and coat the rounds with flour, shaking them together in a large strainer to remove the excess flour. Fry them in half an inch of hot oil, turning each piece once, until they are lightly browned.

Place a layer of the browned zucchini in a shallow baking dish, cover it with thin slices of *mozzarella* cheese and then with some of the tomato sauce. Continue in the same way until all the pieces of zucchini are used, topping the dish with tomato sauce and *mozzarella*. Bake the dish in a moderately hot oven (375° F.) for about 20 minutes.

Zucchini in Salsa Piccante
ZUCCHINI IN PIQUANT SAUCE
(Tuscany)

Prepare a green sauce consisting of 2 tablespoons parsley, 1 clove of garlic, and 2 anchovy filets, all finely chopped, 2 tablespoons vinegar, 4 tablespoons olive oil, and salt and pepper. Slice thinly 4 or 5 small zucchini, dip the slices in flour, and shake them in a sieve to remove the excess. Fry them in deep hot oil (380° F.) until they are browned and drain them on absorbent paper. Combine them well with the sauce and let them stand an hour or more before serving. Serves 4.

Salads

Insalata Verde
MIXED GREEN SALAD

Italian dressing for green salads is practically identical with French dressing: 1 part wine vinegar or lemon juice, 3 to 4 parts olive oil, salt and pepper, and sometimes garlic. The following dressing is a variation often encountered, where anchovies replace the salt. Also this combination of fresh ingredients is a welcome change from the usual mixed greens.

Chop and mash 2 anchovy filets, combine them with 1/2 teaspoon prepared mustard, freshly ground pepper, 1 tablespoon wine vinegar and 4 tablespoons olive oil. In a salad bowl combine the following ingredients, well washed and cleaned: 1 head of endive with the leaves separated and cut lengthwise, the heart of a small head of escarole, cut rather fine, 1 small head of fennel cut in thin slices, and 2 sliced radishes. Pour the dressing over the salad and toss well.

Insalata Capricciosa I
SALAD CAPRICE I
(Birreria 'L Caval 'D Brôns,
Turin–Piedmont)

Mix together 3 cups celeriac, or celery root, cut in julienne strips (or finely sliced hearts of celery), 1/2 cup smoked tongue and 1 cup *prosciutto*, both cut in julienne strips, 1/2 cup cooked sliced mushrooms, and 2 cucumbers prepared as follows: Peel the cucumbers and cut them lengthwise into 8 strips. Remove the seeds and cut the strips into 1 1/2-inch lengths. Roll the pieces up in a clean cloth, and squeeze it firmly to remove as much water as possible.

Add salt and pepper and about 3/4 cup homemade mayonnaise, or enough to coat all the ingredients, and mix well. Serve surrounded by tender young salad greens.

Insalata Capricciosa II
SALAD CAPRICE II
(Gran Ristorante e Bar da Giacomino,
Naples–Campania)

Combine a bowl of small tender young salad greens with 1 or 2 sliced tomatoes, 6 black and 6 green Italian olives, pitted and quartered, 1/2 cup finely sliced celery, and 1/4 cup diced tuna fish. Dress the salad at the last minute with salt and pepper, 1 part lemon juice, and 3 parts olive oil, and toss it.

Insalata di Scampi
SHRIMP SALAD

Line a salad bowl with leaves of tender young lettuce and on these place 3 boiled potatoes, sliced. Distribute over the potatoes 1 1/2 tablespoons capers, 3 chopped anchovy filets, and 18 cooked shrimp, sliced in half lengthwise. Combine 1 tablespoon lemon juice, 3 tablespoons olive oil, and salt and pepper, and stir the mixture into 1/4 cup mayonnaise. Pour the dressing over the salad and serve. All ingredients should be chilled.

Insalata Siciliana
SICILIAN SALAD
(Sicily)

Here, we are sparing you the small octopuses called for in the original recipe and have replaced them with crab meat, which is equally good.

Place in a salad bowl 1 pound (about 2 1/2 cups) sliced, boiled potatoes, 1/2 cup boiled, fresh white shell beans (or dried ones, first soaked and boiled), 1/2 cup black Italian olives, pitted and cut in quarters, and 1 clove of garlic, 2 teaspoons parsley, and 2 teaspoons fresh basil, all finely chopped.

Warm 3/4 cup olive oil and add 4 anchovy filets cut in bits, mashing them with a fork until they are well blended. Add the juice of a lemon, a very small pinch of salt, pepper, and 1/2 tablespoon capers. Pour three-quarters of this dressing over the salad and toss it thoroughly. Make a well in the center and fill it with 4 ounces of diced tuna fish, drained of its oil. Surround it with a ring of 6 ounces of cooked crab meat. Spread the remainder of the dressing over the top. Serve this as a salad or as hors-d'oeuvre.

Antipasto di Cetrioli e Peperoni
CUCUMBER AND GREEN PEPPER SALAD

A delicious vegetable salad or hors-d'oeuvre is made as follows: Peel and slice thinly 2 cucumbers, sprinkle them with a little salt, and let them stand for an hour. Drain off the water, place the cucumbers in a salad bowl, and sprinkle them with 1 teaspoon vinegar and 3 teaspoons oil. Remove the seeds and pith from 1 small green pepper, slice it in julienne strips, and dress it with a small quantity of vinegar and oil, salt and pepper, stirring to coat the strips on all sides. Spread the green pepper on the cucumbers and over the green pepper spread 2 or 3 thinly sliced fresh firm mushrooms. Coat the surface of the salad with mayonnaise and on it arrange 2 hard-cooked eggs, each cut in 6 slices lengthwise.

Antipasto di Primavera
SPRING SALAD HORS-D'OEUVRE

Cook separately in salted boiling water 2 cups shelled spring peas, 1 cup diced young green beans, 4 or 5 very small new potatoes, and half a box frozen artichoke hearts. Drain the vegetables when they are tender but still firm. Cool them, peel and slice the potatoes, and cut the artichoke hearts into quarters. Dress all the vegetables together with 1 part lemon juice, 3 parts oil, salt and pepper. Allow the mixture to marinate in the refrigerator until ready to serve. Spread the salad on an oval dish, coat it with mayonnaise flavored with tarragon and mustard, and decorate it with slices of hard-cooked eggs and cucumbers, and a few capers.

Desserts

Banane alla Fiamma 'L Caval 'd Brôns
BANANAS FLAMBÉ OF THE BRONZE HORSE
(Birreria 'L Caval 'd Brôns, Turin–Piedmont)

This dish may be prepared in a broad chafing dish at the table. Melt 4 tablespoons butter over a high flame, add 1/2 cup sugar, 4 strips of lemon rind (only the yellow part, or "zest"), and 16 dates pitted and cut into quarters lengthwise. Let the mixture caramelize to a light brown color. Add 5 bananas cut into 3/4-inch pieces. Stir and turn the pieces until they are well heated, but do not allow them to soften too much. Flame the bananas with 1/2 cup warmed rum and serve at once.

Pesche alla Piemontese
PEACHES PIEDMONTESE
(Piedmont)

Peel and halve 4 large yellow peaches, remove the pits, and scoop out the hollows slightly with a spoon to enlarge them. Mash this extra pulp and reserve it. Combine 1/2 cup dried and crumbled macaroons, 1 1/2 tablespoons sugar, and 1 tablespoon softened butter. When these are well mixed, add 1 egg yolk and the reserved peach pulp. You may also add a few slivered almonds. Fill the hollow of each peach half with this mixture, place the halves in a buttered baking dish, and pour a few drops of Marsala over each one. Bake the peaches in a moderately hot oven (375° F.) for about 20 to 30 minutes, or until they are just tender. Add a little water to the baking dish, if necessary. Serve the peaches hot or cold.

Pere Ripiene alla Milanese
STUFFED PEARS MILANESE
(Lombardy)

Peel and cut in half lengthwise 4 firm pears. Remove the cores and fill each pear with some of the following mixture: 3 tablespoons sugar, 4 chopped maraschino cherries, 2 dozen chopped toasted blanched almonds, and 4 or 5 drops of almond extract. Place the pears in a shallow baking dish, pour 1 tablespoon sherry over each pear half, and bake in a moderately slow oven (325° F.) for 15 minutes, or until they are tender but not too soft. Serve them hot or cold.

Cassata alla Siciliana I
SICILIAN ICE CREAM
(Sicily)

For this dish use 1 pint rich vanilla ice cream and 3/4 pint chocolate ice cream. Make the special filling to go in the center as follows: Whip 1/2 cup heavy cream and stir in 1/4 cup powdered sugar and 1/2 cup mixed candied fruits cut in small dice. Beat the white of 1 egg until it is stiff and fold it thoroughly into the whipped cream mixture.

With a large spoon dipped in water, line the bottom and sides of a 1 1/2-quart circular mold with the vanilla ice cream to a depth of about 1/2 inch and smooth the surface. Now cover the vanilla ice cream with a layer of chocolate ice cream. (The ice cream will spread more easily if it is somewhat softened.) Fill the hollow in the center with the cream and egg-white mixture, smooth the top, and cover it with wax paper and the lid of the mold. Chill the mold in an electric freezing unit until the *cassata* is quite firm throughout. Unmold the *cassata* and slice it in wedges.

Cassata alla Siciliana II
SICILIAN CREAM CHEESE CAKE
(Sicily)

Combine 1 1/4 pounds *ricotta* cheese, 1 cup powdered sugar, 1 teaspoon vanilla extract, and 2 tablespoons *crème de cacao* and beat the mixture vigorously until it is smooth and fluffy. Add 2 tablespoons each of grated chocolate and chopped candied fruit and mix well.

Cut a moist spongecake into 1/2-inch slices, or use split ladyfingers, and line the bottom and sides of a circular mold with the slices. Turn the filling into the mold, cover it with more cake slices, and chill it in the refrigerator overnight. Turn the cake out onto a serving dish, sprinkle it with powdered sugar, and decorate it with candied fruit.

Plombières alla Torinese
FROZEN CHESTNUT PUDDING
(Piedmont)

Beat 3 eggs with 1/4 cup sugar in the top of a double boiler. Add 1 3/4 cups scalded milk, place the pan over hot water, which you keep just below the boiling point, and stir the mixture for 7 minutes. Add this custard, which should measure about 3 cups, to 1 1/2 cups *crème de marrons* mixed with 2 tablespoons maraschino liqueur. *Crème de marrons* is a sweetened vanilla-flavored chestnut purée that can be purchased in cans. If it is unobtainable, make your own by pressing cooked chestnuts through a potato masher, adding sugar syrup and a few drops of vanilla, and cooking these together briefly. The consistency should be that of a soft syrupy purée. The proportions for this pudding should be about 2 parts of custard to 1 of chestnut purée. Freeze

the pudding in a large ice tray and when it is almost hardened stir in, but not too thoroughly, 1/2 cup cream, whipped.

Serve the dessert heaped on a serving dish and surrounded by whole chestnuts in syrup.

Ponce alla Romana
ROMAN PUNCH
(Rome)

This is the famous Roman punch that was served in Edwardian days midway of the prodigious dinners then fashionable or, to translate one Italian writer, "served just before the roast because it aids digestion and prepares the stomach to receive without nausea the remaining food." In our (fortunately) simpler day, it may be served as a dessert.

Boil for 5 to 6 minutes 1 cup sugar with 1 3/4 cups water and the grated outer rind of 1 orange and 1 lemon. Allow the syrup to cool. Add the juice of 2 oranges and 2 lemons. Freeze it in an ice cream freezer or the freezing compartment of the refrigerator. In the second case, stir the sherbet occasionally as it hardens.

Combine 1/2 cup sugar with 1/4 cup water. Boil the syrup until it forms a long thread from a spoon. This stage registers 240° F. on a candy thermometer. Beat 1 egg white stiff. Gradually pour the hot syrup into the egg white, beating constantly until the mixture is cool and thick. Add this Italian meringue to the frozen sherbet and mix them together well. Stir in 1/2 cup rum and serve the sherbet in glass cups.

If you prefer the sherbet very firm, return it to the freezer again before serving.

Zabaione
HOT WINE CUSTARD

This delicious Italian sweet is not difficult to make, although care must be used to control the temperature and to serve it at the point of perfection. *Zabaione* is served, preferably, in stemmed glasses, with a spoon, and is accompanied by spongecake, ladyfingers, or simple biscuits.

For each egg yolk, use 1 tablespoon sugar and 2 tablespoons Marsala. To serve 6, beat in the top of a double boiler 8 egg yolks and 2 egg whites with 1/2 cup sugar. When the mixture is very thick and creamy add 1 cup Marsala, place the pan over simmering hot water, and heat the mixture gradually, never ceasing to beat it with a rotary or electric hand beater. When the *zabaione* is very thick and hot, but just before it reaches the boiling point, spoon it into glasses and serve it at once.

Zuppa Inglese
ITALIAN TIPSY CAKE

The name of this dish must be an Italian joke, we have always felt, for "English soup" is as distantly related to this showy, rich, and delicious dessert as a dish could possibly be. However, there is a family resemblance between *zuppa inglese* and the English trifle, a word undoubtedly impossible to translate into the Italian language.

You will need 3 layers of spongecake, each about 3/4 inch thick and 9 inches in diameter. Place one layer on a large serving plate, sprinkle it with 1/3 to 1/2 cup rum, spread it with about 1 cup jam or fruit preserves—strawberry, raspberry, or what you will—and pour over the jam 2 cups vanilla custard. On this, place the second layer of spongecake, spread it with the same amounts of jam and custard (no rum this time), and then add the third layer of cake. This you impregnate with 1/3 to 1/2 cup rum and cover with whipped cream, flavored with sugar and vanilla—about 1 1/2 cups cream, measured before whipping. Decorate the cake with candied fruits. Serves 12.

VANILLA CUSTARD

In the top of a double boiler beat 6 eggs, add 3/4 cup sugar and continue beating until thoroughly blended. Add gradually 4 cups hot milk or thin cream, stirring with a whisk. Place the pan over simmering, not boiling, water and cook the custard for 6 to 7 minutes, never ceasing to stir with a whisk. When the custard thickens remove the pan from the heat, stand it briefly in cold water, and stir in 3/4 teaspoon vanilla extract. Let the custard cool before using it. Makes about 6 cups.

Amaretti
ALMOND MACAROONS

Cut 1/2 pound almond paste into small pieces. Almond paste can be purchased in cans. Combine it with 1 cup plus 2 tablespoons very fine granulated sugar and 2 egg whites. Work the mixture well until it is free of all lumps. Force it through a pastry tube onto a baking sheet lined with oiled brown paper or shape it with a spoon into rounds about 1 inch wide. Leave spaces between the rounds for the paste to spread. Dot each macaroon with pine nuts. Bake the macaroons in a moderately slow oven (325° F.) for about 15 to 20 minutes. Remove them from the paper before they are completely cooled.

Certosina
ALMOND SPICE CAKE
(Emilia-Romagna)

In a saucepan heat 5/8 cup sugar, 1/2 cup honey, and 2/3 cup water. Stir the syrup continually over moderate heat until it boils up. Remove the pan from the heat and stir in thoroughly 1 cup flour that has been sifted with 1 teaspoon cinnamon, 1/2 teaspoon each of nutmeg and clove, 1/4 teaspoon salt, and 1/2 teaspoon baking soda. When all is thoroughly blended add 3/4 pound blanched, peeled, and lightly toasted almonds, broken in large pieces, and 3/4 cup citron cut in small dice. Mix all well together and pour the mixture into a well-buttered 9-inch pie pan. Decorate the top with a few whole almonds, candied cherries, and other candied fruits. Bake the cake for 40 minutes in a slow oven (300° F.). Cool the cake before taking it out of the pan. To serve, cut it into narrow strips with a sharp knife.

Ricciarelli di Siena
ALMOND CREAMS SIENA
(Tuscany)

Pound 6 ounces of ground blanched almonds in a mortar, adding 3/4 cup sugar little by little. Rub the paste through a fine sieve and work in 1/4 cup sifted confectioners' sugar and a few drops of vanilla. Or, instead of making this paste, use 1/2 pound almond paste, which can be purchased in cans. Crumble it and combine it with 1/4 cup confectioners' sugar. Beat 2 egg whites to a creamy froth with a whisk and add them gradually to the almond and sugar mixture, beating thoroughly after each addition.

Shape the paste into small ovals about 1/4 inch thick and place them on oiled brown paper on a baking sheet. Let the paste stand for several hours or overnight, then dry the *ricciarelli* in a very slow oven (275° F.) for 30 minutes, being very careful not to let them color. Remove the cakes from the paper with a spatula before they are cold. Cool them on a rack and sprinkle them generously with confectioners' sugar.

If you prefer, you may spread the paste out in a single layer and cut it into lozenge shapes after baking.

Cavallucci di Siena
ANISE CAKES
(Tuscany)

In a bowl combine 2 1/2 cups flour, 1/4 cup finely chopped candied orange peel, 1 tablespoon powdered anise seeds, 1/2 teaspoon cinnamon, and 1/2 cup chopped walnuts.

In a saucepan dissolve 1 1/2 cups sugar in 1 cup water, bring to a boil, and cook the syrup until it forms a thread from a spoon or a candy thermometer registers 230° F. Add the flour and nut mixture, remove the saucepan from the heat, and stir vigorously until all is well mixed. If necessary, add a little water to make the dough workable. Pour the thick paste onto a lightly floured board to cool a little. When the paste is cool enough to handle, knead it thoroughly and roll it out 1/4 inch thick. Cut the paste into round cakes about 2 inches in diameter and bake them on a buttered and floured baking sheet in a slow oven (275° F.) for about 30 minutes, so that the "little horses" can dry without becoming brown. They should be hard on the outside but still somewhat soft in the center.

Torta di Carote
CARROT TORTE
(Hotel Paradiso, Torbole del Garda– Trentino-Alto Adige)

Mix thoroughly 1/2 cup plus 1 tablespoon fine granulated sugar with 4 egg yolks. Beat the mixture until it is thick. Stir in 1/4 pound blanched, peeled, and finely grated almonds and 1/4 pound finely grated carrots. Fold in carefully but thoroughly 4 stiffly beaten egg whites. Put the mixture in a buttered shallow 9-inch tart tin or pie plate and bake it for 1 hour in a very slow oven (275° F.). This *Torte* is like a moist spongecake and is excellent served with custard sauce, whipped cream, or *zabaione* (see index).

Pitte con Niepita
EASTER TURNOVERS
(Calabria)

These small turnovers contain a filling of unusual flavor and they are a specialty at Eastertime in Calabria.

Make a pastry dough with 2 cups flour, a pinch of salt, 8 tablespoons butter (1/2 cup), and 4 tablespoons sugar. Add 1/3 cup ice water, or enough to make a manageable dough, and roll it out thin on a floured board. Or use your own favorite pastry recipe.

For the filling, mix 1 cup firm grape marmalade or jam, 1/4 cup sugar, 1/8 teaspoon cinnamon, 1/2 cup ground walnut meats, 6 tablespoons cocoa, and 1 tablespoon rum or brandy. If your grape marmalade is not truly firm, heat the mixture and thicken it with 1 tablespoon potato starch dissolved in a few drops of water. Cool before adding the rum.

Cut the dough into rounds 3 to 3 1/2 inches in diameter, place a spoonful of filling in the center of each, fold the rounds in half, moisten the edges, and press them firmly together. Prick the tops with a pointed knife, brush with egg yolk, and bake the turnovers on a floured baking sheet for 15 minutes in a hot oven (400° F.), or until they are golden. These are good either hot or cold.

Cuscinetti di Teramo
CUSHIONS OF TERAMO
(Abruzzi e Molise)

Combine 2 cups flour, 1/2 teaspoon salt, 2 teaspoons sugar, 3 tablespoons oil, and 1/2 to 3/4 cup white wine, to make a firm but tender dough. Knead the paste briefly and roll it out very thin, 1/8 inch or less. Cut it into rounds 3 1/4 inches in diameter. Place on each a spoonful of thick, firm marmalade or jam mixed with a few slivered almonds. The marmalade may be apricot, orange, cherry, or any other flavor desired. Fold the rounds over like turnovers, rolling up the edges and pressing them together. Spread the turnovers on a tray or board and let them stand several hours to dry the paste a little. Fry

them in deep hot oil (370° F.). When the "cushions" are golden, drain them on absorbent paper and serve them warm.

Panforte di Siena
SIENA NUT CAKE
(Tuscany)

Combine 3/4 cup (1/4 pound) almonds, blanched, 3/4 cup (1/4 pound) hazelnuts, lightly toasted, 3 tablespoons cocoa, 1 1/2 teaspoons cinnamon, 1/4 teaspoon allspice, 1/2 cup flour, and 1/2 cup each of finely cut candied orange peel, citron, and lemon peel. In a large saucepan combine 1/2 cup each of honey and sugar, bring them to a boil, and simmer the syrup just until a little of it dropped into cold water forms a soft ball or a candy thermometer registers 238° F. Remove at once from the heat and add the fruit and nut mixture. Mix well.

Turn the mixture into a 9-inch spring-form pan lined with buttered paper and bake the cake in a slow oven (300° F.) for 30 minutes. Cool the cake before removing the pan sides. Sprinkle with a thick coating of confectioners' sugar.

Panforte di Siena is a hard and flavorful sweet, which must be cut with a sharp, strong knife. It will keep for weeks.

Fashingkrapfen
VIENNESE FRIED CAKES
(Trentino-Alto Adige)

Dissolve half an envelope of dried yeast in 1/3 cup tepid water. Add 1/4 teaspoon salt, 1 1/2 teaspoons sugar, 1 cup warm cream, 3 1/2 tablespoons melted butter, 3 lightly beaten egg yolks, and 2 cups flour or more, enough to make a soft but manageable dough. Knead it briefly, put it in a floured bowl, cover it with a cloth, and leave it in a warm place to rise to double its bulk. Knead it down lightly and lay it on a floured board. Pull or roll it gently into a 1/4-inch layer and cut it into rounds with a 2-inch biscuit cutter. In the centers of half the disks place a maraschino cherry or a bit of apricot jam. Brush these disks of dough with milk and place another round on each one, pressing the edges together very lightly. Place these little sandwiches on a floured baking sheet or towel as you make them. Let them stand for half an hour in a warm place. Fry them a few at a time in clarified butter or butter and lard combined, 2 inches deep in a frying pan. Do not crowd them. After placing them in the hot fat, cover the pan for a minute or two. Then turn the cakes and, when they are golden, drain them on absorbent paper. Sprinkle with powdered sugar and serve.

Witwe Küsse
WIDOWS' KISSES
(Trentino-Alto Adige)

In the top of a double boiler over simmering water beat 4 egg whites with 1/2 cup plus 1 tablespoon fine granulated sugar. Use a rotary beater and work the mixture until it is fairly firm. Remove the top of the double boiler from the hot water and stir into the egg whites 1 cup chopped nut meats (walnuts or almonds) and 4 tablespoons finely diced citron. With a spoon, drop little heaps of the mixture on a greased baking sheet. Bake in a slow oven (300° F.) for 25 to 30 minutes.

Fondante Napoletana
NEAPOLITAN FONDANT ROLL
(Campania)

Sift 3 cups powdered sugar into a bowl. Beat the white of 1 large egg until it is fluffy and combine it thoroughly with the sugar. Add 1 teaspoon vanilla extract and mix all well together. Cream 4 tablespoons sweet butter until it is well softened and add it to the egg white and sugar, beating all together until the mixture is as fluffy as possible. Divide the cream into three equal parts and add 3 drops red vegetable coloring to one and 3 drops of green to another, leaving the third part white. Chill the cream in the refrigerator until it is firm enough to handle. With a spatula dipped in cold water, shape the green part into an oblong 1/2 inch thick, spread the white part on this, and the pink part on top. Form the gaily colored sandwich into a roll, coat it thickly with chopped toasted almonds or chopped walnut meats, wrap it in wax paper, and chill it in the refrigerator for 12 hours. To serve it, remove the paper and cut the roll into slices. This makes a gay-looking candy roll for special occasions.

Sauces

Salsa di Pomodoro
TOMATO SAUCE

Cook 2 medium onions, sliced, in 1 tablespoon butter and 3 tablespoons olive oil until they are soft and golden. Add 1 carrot, grated, 1 chopped clove of garlic, and 3 or 4 sprigs of chopped parsley and simmer for 3 minutes. Add 2 pounds fresh tomatoes, coarsely chopped, 1/3 teaspoon thyme, several leaves of fresh basil, 1/2 teaspoon salt, freshly ground pepper and celery salt to taste, and 1/2 cup meat stock. Cover the pan and simmer the sauce for 1 hour to 1 1/4 hours. When it is fairly thick, force it through a fine sieve. This recipe makes enough sauce for 2 dozen *cannelloni* or 1 pound spaghetti.

Ragù Bolognese I
BOLOGNESE MEAT SAUCE I
(Emilia–Romagna)

This meat *ragù*, which is more than a sauce, may be served with any pasta. In Bologna it is often used in baked green *lasagne*, combined with rich cream sauce and cheese.

In 1 tablespoon melted butter, brown slowly and lightly 1/2 cup bacon and 1/4 cup ham, both cut in small dice. Add 1 medium-sized onion, 1 carrot, and 1 stalk of celery, all finely chopped. When the vegetables have softened add 3/4 pound beef and 1/4 pound each of veal and fresh lean pork, all finely chopped. Stir and partially cook the meat. Add 3/4 cup stock and 1/2 cup white wine. Simmer the mixture until the liquid has almost evaporated. Add 2 tablespoons tomato paste, 1/2 teaspoon salt, freshly ground pepper to taste, 2 or 3 cloves, a dash of nutmeg,

and hot water almost to cover the mixture. Cover the saucepan and continue to simmer the sauce slowly for about 45 minutes. Add 1/4 pound sliced mushrooms and 2 diced chicken livers and cook 10 minutes longer. Stir in 1/2 cup cream before serving the *ragù*. It should be thick. Makes 3 1/2 to 4 cups.

Ragù Bolognese II
BOLOGNESE MEAT SAUCE II
(Al Pappagallo, Bologna–Emilia-Romagna)

This simpler version of Bologna meat sauce may be used with baked green *lasagne, cannelloni,* spaghetti, or any other dish requiring a meat sauce.

In 2 tablespoons butter, sauté over low heat 1 medium-sized onion, 1 small carrot, and 1 small stalk of celery, all finely chopped. When they are softened, add 3/4 pound beef and 1/4 pound lean pork, both ground. Cook the meat over low heat for 10 to 15 minutes. Add pepper to taste, 1/2 teaspoon salt, 1/4 cup fresh tomato sauce or tomato paste, 1/2 cup white wine, and 1/4 cup water or stock. Simmer the mixture slowly for about 1 1/4 hours, adding another 3/4 cup stock little by little. This sauce should be rather thick. Makes about 2 1/2 cups.

MEAT SAUCE FLORENTINE

You will find the recipe for this versatile sauce on page 534.

Salsa Marchigiana
MARCHES SAUCE FOR PASTA
(The Marches)

Chop finely 1 onion and cook it in 1 tablespoon each of lard and butter, until it is pale gold. Add 2 small stalks of celery, finely chopped, and 1 small carrot, grated. Cook the vegetables together for 6 to 8 minutes and when they are slightly browned add 1 tablespoon minced parsley and 1 generous tablespoon julienne of ham. Cook for 2 or 3 minutes more and add 2 tablespoons tomato paste blended with 3/4 cup dry white wine, a pinch each of marjoram and thyme, and salt and pepper. Cover the pan and simmer the sauce for about 30 minutes, or until it is fairly thick. Add a little hot water, if necessary.

This sauce may be used with macaroni, spaghetti, or other pasta.

Salsa Napoletana I
NEAPOLITAN SAUCE I
(Campania)

In 1 tablespoon melted butter, cook 1 chopped onion and 1 tablespoon minced ham until the onion is softened and pale gold. Add 1/2 cup Marsala, 1/2 cup light veal stock, a pinch of thyme, 1 bay leaf, pepper, 2 cloves, and 2 or 3 minced mushroom stems. Cover the saucepan and simmer the mixture until the liquid is reduced by half.

Meanwhile, in another saucepan combine 1 cup rich meat sauce (see Bolognese meat sauce or meat sauce Florentine) or beef gravy, 1 cup tomato sauce, and 1/2 cup stock made from venison or other game. Simmer this mixture until it is reduced by one-third, add the first mixture to it, simmer all together for 2 or 3 minutes, and force the sauce through a strainer.

Use with pasta or other dishes.

Salsa Napoletana II
NEAPOLITAN SAUCE II
(Campania)

Another version of Neapolitan sauce for spaghetti is prepared as follows:

In 4 tablespoons hot olive oil cook slowly 1 onion, minced, 1 carrot, grated,

5 tablespoons minced green pepper, and 1 clove of garlic, minced. After 10 minutes stir in 2 cans (4 cups) plain prepared tomato sauce, salt and pepper, and 1 teaspoon each of fresh thyme and marjoram or 1/2 teaspoon each if the herbs are dried. Simmer the sauce for 20 minutes.

Pesto
GARLIC AND BASIL SAUCE
(Liguria)

Pesto is considered by many the most delicious of all sauces for pasta.

In a mortar mix 3 cloves of garlic, chopped, 3 tablespoons minced sweet basil leaves, 3 tablespoons grated Italian cheese, 1 tablespoon chopped pine nuts or walnut meats, and 1/4 teaspoon salt. Pound the mixture with a pestle to a smooth paste. Still pounding, add very gradually about 4 to 6 tablespoons olive oil and work the mixture thoroughly to a smooth sauce. One tablespoon fresh parsley, chopped, added with the basil gives color.

Pesto may be stored in the refrigerator with a little oil on top. When serving this sauce with hot *trenette* or other pasta, add it to the hot pasta together with a lump of butter and mix well at the table. Serve grated cheese with the dish, if desired.

Stir a spoonful of *pesto* into hot *minestrone* for *minestrone genovese*.

Salsa Verde Piemontese
GREEN SAUCE PIEDMONTESE
(Birreria 'L Caval 'd Brôns, Turin–Piedmont)

Put into a mortar 3/4 cup parsley, 1 1/2 tablespoons capers, and 1 1/2 tablespoons sour cucumber pickle, all finely chopped. Add 1 slice of bread without the crust, crumbled, and work all together to a paste. Force it through a sieve. Blend in 3 tablespoons olive oil, 3/8 cup vinegar, 1/2 teaspoon sugar, and salt to taste. Serve this sauce with boiled meats, which the Italians call *bollito,* cold meats, or poached fish.

One clove of garlic, finely chopped, or 2 or 3 filets of anchovy, chopped, or both, may be worked in the mortar with the other ingredients.

Salsa Piccante
PIQUANT SAUCE

In a saucepan combine 1 small slice of ham, half a stalk of celery, half a small onion, 1 small clove of garlic, and 1 teaspoon parsley, all chopped, with salt and pepper, 1 bay leaf, and 1 cup wine vinegar. Cover the pan and simmer the mixture until it is reduced by about two-thirds. Blend 1 teaspoon potato starch with 1 cup stock and add it to the mixture. Simmer the sauce, stirring, until it is well blended and slightly thickened. Strain the sauce and add 2 tablespoons capers and 1 teaspoon prepared mustard. Reheat it and at the last minute stir in half a table-spoon sweet butter. Serve with broiled pork chops or other meats.

Salsa Bordelaise
BORDELAISE SAUCE

Simmer together 1/2 cup red wine, 1 shallot, chopped, 1/4 teaspoon salt, 2 pepper corns, crushed, half a bay leaf, and a pinch each of marjoram and thyme. When the wine is reduced by half, add 1/2 cup strong stock, or 1/2 teaspoon meat glaze dissolved in 1/2 cup water, and simmer the sauce for 10 minutes, or until it is again reduced by half. Strain the sauce and stir in 1 teaspoon minced parsley, 1 teaspoon butter, and 1/2 teaspoon lemon juice. Use with broiled beef.

MADEIRA SAUCE

Cook 2 cups brown sauce until it is reduced to about 1 cup. Add 1/3 cup Madeira. Bring the sauce again just to a boil.

Breads

Lyric Neapolitan Pizza
(Hotel Vesuvio, Naples–Campania)

Here is Signor Fiorentino's rhymed recipe, to put you in the mood for *pizza*.

500 grammi di farina
sopraffina
pocchissimo sale,
di lievito grammi 20,
2 bicchieri di latte e per il tutto
100 grammi di strutto.
Dal quantitativo su indicato
150 grammi di farina vien prelevato
e un sol bicchier di latte
nel quale è sciolto il lievito indicato.
Questa piccola dose sia impastata
lasciando in lungo tepido
acciocché addivenga lievitata;
ed è buon costume
che raggiunga il doppio
del suo volume.
Aggiungere il resto della farina,
lo strutto e il rimanente latte
e queste prime cose . . . sono fatte.
Rifare poi l'impasto,
di nuovo lasciar crescere
con attenzione e acume
per fare che raggiunga
due volte il suo volume.
Poi prendere la pasta,
stenderla sulla lamiera
mettendoci sopra
mozzarella e pomodoro a raggiera,
origano, un po di parmigiano
e con generosa mano
aggiungi olio d'olivo . . .
Indi . . .
cuoci, cuoci a fuoco vivo!

Pizza alla Royal
(Royal Hotel, San Remo–Liguria)

The bread dough for this *pizza* is a de luxe variety more like pastry than like the ordinary heavy type often used, which is a real test of ones digestion. The following quantity serves 4, assuming that these are American servings rather than the enormous slabs the Italian appetite seems to handle with ease.

Sift 2 cups flour with 3/4 tablespoon sugar and 1/2 teaspoon salt. Dissolve 1 1/2 teaspoons dry yeast (1/2 envelope) in 2 tablespoons tepid water. Make a well in the flour, put in the dissolved yeast, and mix together. Add 3 tablespoons mashed potato, 1/4 cup olive oil, and 1 small egg, beaten. Mix all well together and knead for 3 to 4 minutes, or until the dough is elastic and light. Place it in a floured bowl, cover it with a cloth, and let it rise for 1 1/2 hours. Roll the dough out very thin, between 1/8 inch and 1/4 inch thick, and fit the dough into a baking sheet which has previously been brushed with oil. Or, if you prefer, divide it into two parts and roll each to fit a flan ring placed on a baking sheet. Brush the dough with olive oil and cover it with a layer of peeled, seeded, coarsely chopped fresh tomatoes. Four large tomatoes will suffice. Sprinkle with salt and pepper and a good quantity of thyme and orégano. Over the tomatoes place thin slices of Fontina cheese and fill the spaces between the slices with anchovy filets forming squares or a lattice design. Sprinkle the *pizza* lavishly with grated Parmesan, let it stand half an hour, and bake it about 12 minutes in a hot oven (400° F.). Serve at once.

Pizza alla Napoletana
NEAPOLITAN PIZZA
(Grand Hotel Villa d'Este, Cernobbio–Lombardy)

Sift 4 cups flour with 1 teaspoon salt and 1 tablespoon sugar. Add 1 1/2 teaspoons dry yeast (1/2 envelope) dissolved in 1/4 cup tepid water, and 3 tablespoons oil and mix all into a dough, adding about 1/2 cup milk, more or less, or enough to make a manageable dough. Knead it until it is smooth and elastic and divide it into 6 equal parts. Form these into balls and allow them to rise in a warm place for about 2 hours.

Peel and cut up 2 pounds ripe tomatoes and cook them on a slow fire for half an hour with 3 tablespoons olive oil, 1/2 teaspoon salt, 1 teaspoon sugar, and 1 clove of garlic, minced.

Roll out the balls of dough to thin disks, about 1/8 to 1/4 inch thick, place them on baking sheets, and spread the tomatoes on them. Scatter finely diced Fontina cheese over each disk, place a few anchovy filets on each, and add a pinch of orégano and a teaspoon or more of oil. Place your individual *pizze* in a very hot oven (450° F.) and bake them for 10 minutes. Serve at once.

Pizza Calabrese
PIZZA CALABRIA
(Calabria)

It is not surprising that the Calabrians prefer this, their super-*pizza*, to all others.

To 4 cups flour sifted with 1 teaspoon salt, add 1 1/2 teaspoons dry yeast (1/2 envelope) dissolved in 1/2 cup tepid water. Add just enough more tepid water to make a soft dough. Knead the dough for several minutes, place it in a floured bowl, cover it with a towel, and let it rise to double its bulk. This may take an hour or more. Beat it down, add to it 6 tablespoons lard and 2 egg yolks, saving a fraction of egg yolk to glaze the pie. Knead the

dough well and then divide it into 2 pieces, one almost twice the size of the other. Roll out the larger piece and with it line the bottom and sides of a 12-inch pie tin. The other piece will serve as the top of your pie.

Peel 2 pounds ripe tomatoes, remove the seeds, and cut the tomatoes up coarsely. Put them in a saucepan with 1/2 cup olive oil and 1 clove of garlic and 1 teaspoon basil leaves, both chopped, and cook them slowly to a thick consistency. Allow the mixture to cool. Add 1 cup canned tuna fish, after draining off the oil, 3/4 cup halved and pitted black Italian olives, 2 tablespoons chopped anchovy filets, 1 tablespoon drained capers, and a good dash of pepper.

Pour this mixture into the dough shell in the pie tin. Roll the second piece of pastry out into a disk large enough to cover the pie, place it over the filling, roll the lower edges over the top, and form a ropelike edging. Glaze the surface with a little melted fat and then with egg yolk. Let the pie stand in a warm room for 20 minutes to rise. Bake it in a very hot oven (450° F.) for 25 to 30 minutes and serve it at once.

Grissini
BREAD STICKS
(Piedmont)

Thin crisp bread sticks are a specialty of Turin, though they are found all over Italy.

Dissolve 1 teaspoon dry yeast in 1/3 cup tepid water and mix it thoroughly into 1 cup sifted flour. Knead the mixture for 5 minutes and let this soft dough, or sponge, stand in a floured bowl covered with a damp cloth for about 2 hours.

Sift 1 cup flour with 1 teaspoon salt and 1 teaspoon sugar and add 1/4 cup tepid milk and 3 tablespoons melted butter. Mix well and add this dough to the sponge. Knead the dough for 7 minutes and let it stand in the floured bowl again for about 2 hours, or until it doubles in bulk. Knead it again for a few minutes and divide it into 24 pieces. Roll each piece between the palms of your hands and on a board into very thin long sticks. Place them side by side on baking sheets, leaving almost an inch between each stick and stretching them to elongate as much as possible. Press the ends with your thumb to anchor them lightly to the pan. Brush the bread sticks with milk and bake them in a hot oven (400° F.) for about 12 minutes, or until they are light brown and crisp. Cool them and store in a tin box.

Panettone
MILAN CHRISTMAS FRUIT BREAD
(Lombardy)

Dissolve 1 envelope of dry yeast in 1/4 cup tepid milk. Cream together 1/4 pound softened butter and 1/3 cup sugar. Add gradually 3 beaten eggs. Sift together 3 cups flour and 1/2 teaspoon salt. Into the flour mix the dissolved yeast and then the egg and butter mixture. Add 1/4 cup milk, if needed. The dough should be soft but firm enough to knead. Knead it on a floured board for 5 minutes, sprinkling on a little more flour, if necessary, to keep it from sticking. Put the dough in a floured bowl, cover it with a damp cloth, and let it stand in a warm place until it doubles in bulk, an hour or more. Knead it again for 5 minutes and let it stand until it doubles in bulk. Flatten it out on the board and over the surface sprinkle 4 tablespoons seed-less raisins, 4 tablespoons diced citron, and 1 tablespoon grated lemon rind. Fold the dough over and flatten it out with a rolling pin two times. Form it into ball and place it in a buttered deep round pan. It should half fill the pan. Let the *panettone* rise again for an hour, brush it with beaten egg yolk diluted with a little water, and bake it 30 to 40 minutes in a moderate oven (350° F.), or until it is puffy and brown.

Pizza Pasquale alla Triestina
TRIESTE EASTER BREAD
(Friuli–Venezia Giulia)

The following rich and delicious bread resembles brioche, and keeps better.

Make a sponge with 1 cup flour and 1 envelope of dry yeast dissolved in about 2/3 cup tepid water. Work it well with a wooden spoon and let it stand in a warm place to rise to double its bulk.

In a bowl put 3 cups flour sifted with 1 teaspoon salt and stir in 3 eggs and 1 egg white, 3/4 cup sugar dissolved in 2/3 cup warm milk, 1/4 pound melted butter, 1 teaspoon vanilla, and 2 tablespoons rum. Add the sponge. Mix all well together and let the dough rise again to double its bulk. Stir it down and put it in a round buttered and lightly floured baking pan or in 2 bread-loaf pans, half filling each pan. Let it rise again to double its bulk. Brush the cake with melted butter and bake it in a moderate oven (350° F.) for about 40 minutes, or until it is browned and firm.

Miscellany

Fritto Misto Fiorentina
FLORENTINE "MIXED FRY"
(Tuscany)

Any or all of the following ingredients may be used in a *fritto misto:* Tiny thin slices, or *scaloppine,* of veal, small filets of chicken breast, parboiled calf's brains and sweetbreads in small pieces, hearts of small young artichokes cut in thin slices, soaked in ice water and lemon juice, and dried, parboiled cauliflower flowerets, and thin slices of zucchini and eggplant. Each piece should make a small mouthful. The pieces are seasoned with salt and pepper, dipped in frying batter, and fried in deep hot oil (370° F.). The veal, chicken, and artichokes should go in first as they take longest to cook—about 5 minutes. Add the other ingredients and cook until all are golden brown. Drain the *fritto misto* and serve it immediately, heaped on a hot platter, with lemon sections.

BATTER FOR FRYING

Blend 1 cup flour with 3 tablespoons olive oil. Add a pinch of salt and gradually stir in 3/4 cup tepid water until the mixture is like smooth thin cream. Let it stand 1 to 2 hours. Just before using the batter, stir in the beaten white of 1 egg.

Fritto Misto alla Milanese
MILAN "MIXED FRY"
(Lombardy)

For each person use 1 small thin slice each of veal and of calf's brains, sweetbreads, kidneys, and liver. Use also a quarter of an artichoke heart as well as a thin slice or two of zucchini. The brains, sweetbreads, and artichoke should first be parboiled, cooled, and dried. Other ingredients are used raw. The small bits of veal should be pounded very thin.

Season each piece with salt and pepper, dip it in flour, shaking off all excess, then in beaten egg and fine bread crumbs. Fry the pieces in butter combined with a little olive oil to the depth of almost half an inch in the frying pan. First heat this fat until all bubbles disappear, but do not allow it to brown. Add the pieces, keep the heat moderately high, and cook them, turning them once, until they are golden brown. Sprinkle them with chopped parsley and serve with sections of lemon.

Season and dip the liver, kidneys, and veal last because their wet surfaces absorb the flour quickly. Put the artichoke pieces in the pan first as they take slightly longer to cook. This dish can be made with just the sweetbreads, liver, and artichoke hearts, or with any other combination of the above ingredients, if you cannot obtain them all.

Polenta Pasticciate
BAKED CORN MEAL WITH
MUSHROOM SAUCE
(Lombardy)

Boil 1/2 pound fine polenta, or yellow corn meal, in 1 1/2 cups of salted water combined with 1 1/2 cups stock reserved from the cooking of a vegetable—cauliflower or string beans, for instance. Stir the corn meal with a wooden spoon until all the lumps have disappeared and continue cooking slowly until the polenta comes away from the sides of the pan. This will take about 15 to 20 minutes. Stir in 2 tablespoons butter and 1/4 cup grated Parmesan and spread the polenta in a shallow buttered baking dish to cool.

Make a cream sauce with 2 tablespoons butter, 1 1/2 tablespoons flour, 2 cups milk, salt, pepper and a pinch of nutmeg. Cook the sauce 5 minutes and stir in 2 tablespoons grated Parmesan and 1/2 pound mushrooms that have been washed, sliced, and sautéed 2 to 3 minutes in a little butter.

Turn the polenta out onto a board and slice it sideways with a fine string into two thin layers. Put one layer in the buttered baking dish and cover it with half the cream sauce and mushrooms. Add the second layer and the rest of the sauce. Sprinkle the polenta with grated Parmesan, dot it with butter, and heat it in a moderately hot oven (375° F.) for 15 minutes, or until it is golden brown.

Pizzetta di Carne e Patate al Forno
POTATO AND MEATBALL CASSEROLE
(The Marches)

Make very small meatballs with 1 pound ground meat (lamb or beef), salt, pepper, a good dash of grated nutmeg, and 2 beaten eggs. Brown the meatballs in 2 tablespoons each of butter and oil without cooking them too much. In a buttered baking dish place a layer of sliced boiled potatoes, sprinkle them with grated Parmesan and dot them with butter. Place a layer of meat balls on the potatoes and continue filling the dish in the same way, making the top layer potatoes. Sprinkle with Parmesan, dot with butter and cook in a moderately hot oven (375° F.) until the surface is browned.

Doratini di Ricotta Romana
RICOTTA FRITTERS ROMAN STYLE
(Rome)

Mix well together 1/2 pound *ricotta* cheese, 1/2 cup flour, 2 whole eggs, 1 egg yolk, the grated zest of 1 lemon, a pinch of salt, and 1 teaspoon brandy or rum. Chill the mixture in the refrigerator for several hours.

Form the cheese mixture into balls the size of walnuts and drop them into deep hot fat (390° F.). As they brown, remove them and drain them on absorbent paper. Pile them in a pyramid on a warm plate, sprinkle them with powdered sugar, and serve. To serve the fritters with broiled meat or a *fritto misto,* omit the sugar.

Mozzarella in Carrozza
MOZZARELLA IN CRUSTS
(Campania)

Cut the crusts from slices of bread and, between each two, put slices of *mozzarella* cheese cut the same size as the bread. Dip the edges of these sandwiches in milk, then in bread crumbs. Dip the whole sandwich in beaten egg, then in fine bread crumbs. Fry the sandwiches in hot oil or fat 1/2 inch deep in the pan until they are golden brown.

To make small cocktail hors-d'oeuvre, cut the *mozzarella* in 3/4-inch cubes. Roll the cubes in flour and dip them in beaten egg, then in bread crumbs. Dip them again in egg and bread crumbs and fry them in hot oil.

Fonduta Piemontese
FONDUE PIEDMONTESE
(Ristorante Il Cucolo, Turin–Piedmont)

Cut 1/4 pound Fontina cheese into small dice. If Fontina is not obtainable, use 1/4 pound *mozzarella* and 3 tablespoons coarsely grated Swiss cheese. Put the cheese in the top of a double boiler with 1 tablespoon potato starch blended with 3/4 cup milk. Stir the mixture over hot water until it is well melted and smooth. Beat in quickly 1 egg yolk and pour the mixture onto a hot plate. Drop a few paper-thin slices of truffle on top, surround the fondue with slices of bread sautéed in butter, and serve at once.

Panzerotti
STUFFED CRÊPES WITH
TOMATO SAUCE
(Ristorante Giannino, Milan–Lombardy)

Prepare a thick cream sauce with 3 tablespoons butter, 4 tablespoons flour, and 1 cup milk. Allow it to cool. Add a generous 1/2 cup minced ham, 1/3 cup diced *mozzarella,* 4 tablespoons grated Parmesan, and 1 egg. Chill the mixture in the refrigerator.

Combine gradually 2/3 cup milk with 6 tablespoons flour and a pinch of salt. When the mixture is smooth, add 2 well-beaten eggs. Butter well a rectangular cake tin, 7 by 11 inches, for instance, and pour in just enough of the batter to make a 1/8-inch-thick layer. Bake the batter in a hot oven (400° F.) for 10 minutes, or until it is firm. Or cook it on top of the stove in a rectangular griddle. Turn out the pancake, which is a sort of square crêpe, onto a cloth or board, and repeat the operation. Let the two pancakes cool. Spread the chilled filling on the pancakes and roll them up like large sausages. Cut these diagonally into slices about 1 inch thick. Spread some tomato sauce over the bottom of a shallow baking dish, place the prepared slices on this, and on each slice put a slice of *mozzarella.* Spread a little more tomato sauce on top, sprinkle with grated Parmesan, and bake in a hot oven (400° F.) for 15 minutes.

Pizzetta alla Perugina
PERUGIA HAM AND CHEESE PIE
(Umbria)

Into 2 cups sifted flour mix 4 tablespoons butter, cut in small bits, 1/2 teaspoon salt, 2 eggs, and 3 tablespoons milk, or enough to make a soft dough. Knead the dough for a short time and divide it in two. Roll half of it out into a rectangle about 1/8 inch thick. With this dough, line an 8-inch-square shallow pan or a flan ring placed on a baking sheet. Spread over it 1 1/2 cups minced ham combined with 1 1/8 cup cheese, half of it grated Swiss cheese and half diced Bel Paese. Roll out the rest of the dough and cover the *pizzetta,* turning the edges of the dough and pressing them together with a fork. Prick holes here and there in the surface, brush it with egg yolk, and bake the pie in a hot oven (425° F.) for 10 minutes. Reduce the heat to moderate (350° F.) and bake 10 minutes more. Cut the *pizzetta* into rectangles or lozenge shapes and serve it warm.

Canederli
SOUP DUMPLINGS
(Trentino–Alto Adige)

Dice 1 strip of bacon and put it in a saucepan with 1 teaspoon butter, 1 onion, minced, and 1/2 cup peeled fresh Italian sausage cut in small pieces. Cook these together until the onion is somewhat softened and then mix in 2 1/2 cups coarsely crumbled stale bread or hard rolls. Cook the mixture briefly, remove it from the heat, and add 1 cup milk. Let the mixture stand an hour or more. Mix in, one by one, 3 eggs, add 1 tablespoon minced parsley, 2 tablespoons grated Parmesan, a little grated nutmeg, and salt and pepper, if necessary. Stir well with a wooden spoon and add, a little at a time, enough flour to make the mixture firm enough to hold together. Form it into balls smaller than walnuts and drop them, one by one, into 8 cups boiling consommé or chicken broth. Lower the heat and allow the dumplings to poach for 20 to 25 minutes. Serve broth and dumplings with grated Parmesan cheese. Or if you prefer, you may poach the *canederli* in salted water, drain them, and serve them with melted butter or meat sauce.

List of Illustrations

General Index

General references to important foods and specialties in this book are included in this index, but it does not list recipes. All recipes are listed in the recipe index.

Many entries are grouped in categories. Main headings include bars, cafés, cheeses, churches, hotels, museums, restaurants, and wines.

Recipe Index